Understanding

THE NEW

SQL:
A COMPLETE GUIDE

The Morgan Kaufmann Series in Data Management Systems
Series Editor, Jim Gray

Understanding THE NEW

SQL:
A COMPLETE GUIDE

JIM MELTON
Digital Equipment Corporation

ALAN R. SIMON

MORGAN KAUFMANN PUBLISHERS
San Mateo, California

Sponsoring Editor: Bruce M. Spatz
Production Manager: Yonie Overton
Production Editor: Carol Leyba
Cover & Text Design/Composition: Rebecca Evans & Associates
Cover Illustration: Telegraph Colour Library/F.P.G.
Proofreaders: Susan Festa & Fran Taylor
Printer: Port City Press

Morgan Kaufmann Publishers, Inc.
Editorial Office:
2929 Campus Drive, Suite 260
San Mateo, CA 94403

97 96 95 94 93   5 4 3 2 1

Library of Congress Cataloging-in-Publication Data

Melton, Jim.
    Understanding the new SQL: a complete guide / Jim Melton, Alan R. Simon.
        p.   cm. — (The Morgan Kaufmann series in data management systems)
    Includes index.
    ISBN 1–55860–245–3
    1. Data base management.   2. SQL (Computer program language
I. Simon, Alan R.   II. Title.   III. Series.
QA76.9.D3M445   1993
005.75′6—dc20   92–38385
                                                        CIP

*To Jim and Della, who wanted me to have more than they did;
to Merlin, who got me through the dark years; and most of all,
to Barbara, who is the best ever in my life.*

JIM

*I'd like to thank all those who have supported me throughout
both my professional career and my life, particularly my parents
and my brother Jordan.*

AL

JIM GRAY
Digital Equipment Corporation

The SQL database programming language is the standard way to represent and manipulate data in this decade. Because of its importance in commercial and governmental applications, it has been the subject of a major international standardization effort recently approved as SQL-92 (sometimes called SQL2). As a consequence, database vendors are busy enhancing their systems products to meet the standard. Conformance to SQL-92 by current and future vendors will be required by most government and commercial purchasing authorities. Knowing SQL and the SQL-92 standard will be a great advantage for programmers. Applications written in SQL-92 will be portable to all hardware platforms for many years to come.

SQL-92 is a major advance over the earlier standard and over most SQL implementations. It abstracts the underlying concepts of SQL and then expresses them in a more general way. For example, a *table expression* can be used anywhere a *table* could be used in earlier SQL designs. This property is called orthogonality. A lack of orthogonality is the bane of earlier SQL standards and of many "old" SQL products. Earlier SQL standards were first steps toward a complete language, but they lacked major features like schema evolution, client/server verbs, transaction isolation levels, dynamic SQL, embeddings in Ada, and C, foreign character support, and relational operators like outer join and union. SQL-92 corrects these shortcomings and presents a complete language.

Jim Melton was the editor of the SQL-92 standard, which is the basis for this book. The standard is an imposing document—over 500 pages of small type. While it defines the SQL-92 language, it gives no design rationale or examples. This book offers what most people need from the standard, plus much that is missing from the original document. *Understanding SQL* gives a narrative tour of the language from the basics of relational theory to exotic features like left-outer-join. The authors give the design rationale for each feature, show the syntax as railroad diagrams, and then provide examples using the features in a running application.

Melton and Simon do an admirable job of covering the basics, gracefully evolving from simple ideas to the most advanced concepts of the language. This evolutionary presentation is a tribute to the orthogonal design of the new SQL. It also reflects the authors' deep understanding of the issues and their talent for explaining them. Finally, the book provides a hint of the next SQL—SQL3—which Melton is also editing. Its main direction is to unify the object-oriented database and relational database paradigms. SQL3 will probably be approved late in this decade.

This book will be a valuable reference for the programmer who wants to understand the why and how of SQL-92. Each concept and feature is rationalized and explained by example. The database system implementor will also find much of value here. The book nicely complements the standard, explaining why the SQL-92 language designers made the choices they did and how they intended the language to be used. It is a welcome addition to the "Data Management Systems Series."

FOREWORD

. . . .

DONALD D. CHAMBERLIN
IBM Almaden Research Center

From its beginning as a 23-page research paper presented at an ACM conference in 1974, the SQL language has grown to become the most widely used relational database sublanguage, implemented by virtually all suppliers of relational systems and codified by national and international standards. Like any living language, SQL continues to evolve to meet the growing and changing needs of its users. This book deals with an important part of this evolution, the SQL-92 Standard recently adopted by the American National Standards Institute (ANSI Document No. X3.135-1992).

From the beginning, a major objective of the SQL language has been to exploit the potential of the relational model for data independence and nonprocedural access to data. By expressing data access in terms of "what" is needed rather than "how" to find it, SQL makes applications independent of access paths, permitting automatic query optimization and performance tuning of databases without affecting application code. Similarly, SQL's high level of abstraction improves programmer productivity by supporting set-oriented queries and updates and by providing multiple logical views of data. As relational systems are increasingly challenged by object-oriented database technology, these advantages remain as important as ever.

In addition to data independence, the original SQL specification attempted to unify what had traditionally been three separate processes: data manipulation, definition, and control. SQL provided, for the first time, a single syntax for data manipulation (both in ad-hoc queries and in programmed applications), data definition (*e.g.*, definition of logical views), and data control (*e.g.*, specification of assertions to protect the integrity of data). The SQL-92 standard adds significant new functions to each of these areas, while preserving the tradition of a unified syntax that encompasses all three areas. SQL-92 also improves the orthogonality of the language by removing some restrictions that originated with early SQL implementations. Finally, SQL-92 provides a formal specification for several features (*e.g.*,

PREPARE, EXECUTE, and ALTER TABLE) that are included in most SQL products but were omitted from previous versions of the standard.

To be successful, a language standard must meet the needs of real users, be implemented with reasonable cost and performance, and be simple enough to understand. In order to balance these requirements, the ANSI SQL committee includes representatives of both users and implementors of database systems. The committee members have worked hard to retain the original spirit of the language while adding the features needed by today's complex database applications. The result is a standard whose size can be intimidating at first. Experience will tell whether the committee has arrived at a successful balance of function, practicality, and usability.

As editor of the SQL-92 standard, Jim Melton is uniquely qualified to explain and motivate its various features. Alan Simon is a technical author and consultant who has written many books about computing and who has a good deal of experience with databases. The two authors present their material in a clear and straightforward way, illustrated with many examples. Their book should be a sufficient reference to SQL-92 for most programmers, making it necessary to resort to the formal standard only in unusual cases. This book is an important contribution to understanding the history of the SQL standard, its current status, and the ongoing work that will ultimately result in future versions of the standard.

CONTENTS

. . . .

Part V   **Appendices**

A   **Designing SQL-92 Databases**   **397**

B   **A Complete SQL-92 Example**   **413**

C   **The SQL-92 Annexes: Differences, Implementation-Defined and Implementation-Dependent Features, Deprecated Features, and Leveling**   **441**

D   **Relevant Standards Bodies**   **465**

A Word About SQL, Databases, and Programmers

SQL is undoubtedly the most accepted and implemented interface language for relational database systems. Michael Stonebraker has referred to SQL as "intergalactic dataspeak" (a fact which served as the inspiration for our cover). Indeed, like Fortran, C, and COBOL, SQL may be among the most widely used and understood computer languages around.

The third revision of the ANSI and ISO standard for SQL has now been published, and all programmers concerned with relational database applications will be affected by it. Because of the influence of the relational model of data, few programmers are unaware of relational database systems and many use them daily. Even programmers who use PC database systems like dBASE®, Paradox, and other "Xbase" systems will be affected by SQL—in their relationship to SQL-92 as well as through Xbase standardization efforts.

Why We Wrote This Book

Most of the books on SQL with which we are familiar are either oriented toward end users who might type queries into an interactive terminal or they are critiques of the language. Neither approach is really adequate for the broad variety of use that now characterizes SQL programming. Moreover, with the increasing use of SQL, many people are learning SQL without the benefit (or disadvantage) of knowing the earlier SQL-89. We believe that there is a need for a book that presents the entire SQL language from the novice level through the expert level. In taking such an approach, we wanted to focus not only on interactive SQL use, but also on the ways in which real applications will use the language.

■ Who Should Read It

Because of the orientation and style that we chose for the book, we believe that it will be useful to a broad range of readers. Application programmers were our primary audience, but we also kept in mind the needs of database administrators and designers as well as system analysts.

We hope that our book will be a helpful resource to programmers at every level. In addition, system designers and implementors can benefit from knowing the design rationale and choices represented in the standard. We have even included some fairly esoteric material from the SQL-92 standard with the intent to present it more clearly than the standard does. This may be of help to engineers building the SQL DBMS systems that implement SQL-92.

■ How We Organized The Book

SQL-92 is a large language and no linear treatment of it can ever succeed completely. Printed books, however, are inherently linear. We have tried to organize the book so that you can read it cover-to-cover if you are so inclined. However, we know that most readers don't approach technical books like this. Instead, you might prefer to skip around and first read the chapters or sections of particular interest to you, or that contain information required for your current projects. Both the amount of material in each chapter and the structure of the discussions are intended to facilitate this kind of "real-world" use.

We start off with basic concepts, move into foundation material, proceed through some rather complex areas related to all aspects of the language, and then spend quite a lot of the book presenting many different areas of SQL-92. In all cases, when a particularly important concept is used, we give you a cross-reference to the location where it is discussed in detail.

Conformance to the SQL-92 standard is based on three "levels" of the language, ranging from features used in older systems to those that won't be seen for some time. We have not been compulsive about specifying the level for every feature of SQL, but we have mentioned leveling when it seemed especially useful. The levels are also summarized in Appendix C for your consultation.

This book is meant to be used in place of the standard and is not merely a rehash of the standard. While the standard is designed to tell vendors how to write an SQL DBMS, this book is intended to tell application writers how to *use* such a DBMS. If you are interested in the details of the language specification, Appendix D tells you how to buy a copy of the standard for your own use.

However, this book is not a substitute for product documentation. It discusses the entire SQL-92 language, not only those parts implemented by a specific vendor or at any specific point in time. You will frequently need documentation for your specific products to write your applications. On the other hand, it may also give you some idea of what your system may be capable of in future incarnations.

Features

One thing that should distinguish this book from most others is the nature of our example. Almost all database books choose one of two example applications that they use to illustrate language features. These seem to be a payroll application and a parts database. We have long since tired of these applications, so we tried to find something that could be more fun. We selected a video and music store as our sample application. This example is based upon a real database developed by one of us (Simon) for a chain of retail stores in Arizona. Appendix B presents a fairly large selection of code and database definition for this application.

Anybody who has ever read a programming language manual or text knows that the authors always have to present the syntax of the language elements (the statements, for example). One of the most common techniques for this is the use of Backus-Naur Form (BNF), which we use extensively in this book. However, BNF is not the easiest thing to read, so we have augmented this in places with another style called "railroad diagrams." Many readers will already be familiar with this kind of illustration, but we believe that some readers might appreciate a quick explanation.

The notation uses lines and words that you can follow to determine valid SQL constructs—just like riding a train to a particular destination. They have straight lines through "stations" (*e.g.*, keywords and nonterminal symbols), they have switches that access different paths, and they have switches that take you back again (see page **???RR1???** for an example).

Conventions

A quick note on the typographical conventions we use:

- Type in this font (Stone Serif) is used for all ordinary text.
- *Type in this font (Stone Serif italic) is used for terms that we define or for emphasis.*
- **Type in this font (Stone Serif semibold) is used to represent host language identifiers when they appear in ordinary text.**
- Type in this font (Letter Gothic bold) is used for all our examples, syntax presentation, and SQL keywords that appear in ordinary text.
- *Type in this font (Letter Gothic bold italic) is used to distinguish C tokens in BNF presentations.*

Acknowledgements

Writing any book is a labor of love—with the emphasis all too often on "labor." It's hard, but rewarding. It's rare to do it alone—the assistance of others is invaluable: for reviews, for bouncing ideas off, and just for offering encouragement. We cannot go without acknowledging and thanking the wonderful and talented people who reviewed our book and offered help throughout the process. Joe Celko (DBMS magazine), Keith Hare (JCC, Inc.), Donald Slutz (Tandem), Garth Reid (Digital Equipment Corporation), and Bryan Higgs (Digital Equipment Corporation) were very helpful in their reviews of the original outline and of the book itself. Jim Gray (Digital Equipment Corporation) not only reviewed the book, but was very instrumental in getting the book published. We especially want to thank Phil Shaw (then of IBM Corporation, now with Oracle Corporation) and Bruce Horowitz (BellCore) for their extensive reviews—the depth and breadth of several chapters were inspired by their comments and suggestions.

We'd also like to thank Bruce Spatz, Yonie Overton, Carol Leyba, and others at Morgan Kaufmann Publishers for their outstanding support during the conception, writing, and production of this book. Bruce provided us with tremendously helpful feedback and suggestions about the content and style of the book, and Yonie truly worked miracles during the production process; to them and others, we are grateful.

And, of course, while writing a book, lots of other things in life go neglected. We are immensely grateful to our Significant Others—Barbara Edelberg and Ann Mergo—for picking up the slack and keeping our lives on track while the book was in progress. We don't know if it's true to say that we couldn't have done it without them, but we are positive that it would have been more difficult and not nearly as much fun. Thanks!

JIM MELTON
Digital Equipment Corporation

ALAN R. SIMON

PART I

SQL-92 Basics

CHAPTER 1

· · · · · · · · · · · · · · · · · · ·

Introduction to SQL-92

1.1 Introduction

Conceived in the mid-1970s as a database language for the then new relational model, SQL was first standardized in 1986 and was modestly enhanced in 1989. In 1992, work was completed on a significantly revised version of the SQL standard. SQL products and implementations are now so widespread that it would be extremely difficult for any active programmer or applications developer to do his or her work without familiarity with the current SQL standard. Even today's personal computer (PC) database products are heavily influenced by SQL as more and more of those products are integrated with software environments from midrange and mainframe computers.

This book will teach you what you need and want to know about the SQL language and about the 1992 standard. If you are already an SQL programmer who has used products based on, or conformant to, the SQL-89 standard, you will be able to learn the differences between SQL-89 and SQL-92. If you are new to SQL programming, you will be able to learn all of SQL-92, including those parts that were already standardized in SQL-89.

This book provides a reference for the entire SQL-92 language because it covers the full language, not just those portions already implemented by several products. Because of its comprehensive coverage, you can use this book as a primary reference for a number of years as conformant products are developed. In this sense, we provide a supplement to the documentation that accompanies the database management system products.

We introduce and explain all of the concepts that you need in order to work with products that implement SQL-92, and we demystify the jargon coined by users of those products. In addition, we cover the philosophies associated with relational database systems and with SQL in particular. We do not attempt to provide a complete course in database theory, relational theory, or computer programming.

3

Except for a brief review of some foundational topics in this chapter, we assume that you are already comfortable with these disciplines. Finally, although we stress the importance of good database design, we do not attempt to provide a textbook on database design theory or methodology. There are many excellent books on this subject[1] and we do not wish to dilute the subject of SQL-92 with what are related but distinct areas of study.

1.2   What is SQL?

SQL (correctly pronounced "ess cue ell," instead of the somewhat common "sequel") is a *data sublanguage* for access to relational databases that are managed by relational database management systems (RDBMS). Many books and articles "define" SQL by parenthetically claiming that the letters stand for Structured Query Language. While this was true for the original prototypes, it is not true of the standard. When the letters appear in product names, they have often been assigned this meaning by the product vendors, but we believe that users are ill-served by persuasions that the word "structured" accurately describes the language. The letters, by the way, don't stand for anything at all. They are not an abbreviation or an acronym, merely the result of the evolution of research projects.

1.2.1   Data Sublanguages Versus Applications Languages

As the name suggests, a data sublanguage is one that is used in association with another language for the specialized purpose of accessing data. The sort of programming languages with which most people are familiar include COBOL, Fortran, and C. These languages were designed to allow application programmers to express their computational requirements efficiently. Fortran was designed primarily to support application programmers interested in building numeric or engineering applications, while COBOL is generally felt to be more suitable for writing business-oriented applications, and C is often cited as being well-designed for systems programming applications.

Languages such as LISP and Prolog that may be less well known were designed for other classes of applications—primarily for building certain classes of artificial intelligence systems.

None of these languages was designed specifically for manipulating data stored under the control of database management systems. It has been found that specialized languages for this purpose are very useful because they permit application writers to accurately (and often concisely) express the data management requirements of the application and get the desired results.

However, a data language by itself is usually insufficient for writing real applications. In almost all cases, an application has a mixture of requirements: perform some calculations, manipulate some information, and manage some data. In this common sort of application, it is usually helpful if the application writer

---

[1]   Toby J. Teorey, *Database Modeling and Design: The Entity-Relationship Approach,* Morgan Kaufmann Publishers, San Mateo, CA, 1990.

can build the calculation or manipulate portions of the application by using a language well-suited for the purpose, reverting to a specialized data language only for those parts of the application that require it. In this way, the data language is often viewed as (and called) a *data sublanguage* with respect to the *primary programming language,* or *host language.*

There are many relational data sublanguages to choose from (*e.g.,* QUEL from Relational Technology, Inc—now ASK/Ingres, and RDML from Digital Equipment Corporation), but only one has been formally standardized for access to relational databases: SQL. It is undoubtedly true that other relational languages have similar expressive power and that at least some are more faithful to the relational model, but SQL has the distinct advantage of being widely implemented and used. This, more than anything else, is the reason SQL has been selected for standardization.

1.2.2 Procedural Versus Nonprocedural Languages

Another useful classification for computer programming languages is the degree of procedural support provided within the language's programming constructs, that is, within the basic building blocks inherent in most application programming languages. Constructs such as IF-THEN-ELSE, DO WHILE, DO UNTIL, CASE, and even the much maligned GO TO all deal primarily with *how* application functions should be performed. The order in which operations are to be performed is rigidly specified and created by the programmer.

Nonprocedural languages, on the other hand, are oriented more toward the results of certain operations, leaving the *how* aspects to the "black box"—the underlying software environment. The approach of nonprocedural languages tends to be more of a hands-off, goals-oriented boss approach, as contrasted with the former model which might represent the ultimate micromanager. Basically, the nonprocedural language says, "Look through this stuff, and get me something based on certain criteria; I don't care how you do it, just do it."

SQL is heavily oriented toward a nonprocedural model, whereas C, COBOL, Ada, and most languages with which you are familiar tend to be procedural in nature. In fact, most of the basic programming constructs don't even exist in SQL, which means your applications usually require a combination of SQL and some host language to perform your required functions.

1.3 Why Do You Want This Book?

Unlike most books that address the SQL language, this book takes the long view. It takes time for standard language features to be introduced into commercial products, and rather than concentrate on the features that products X and Y might include in their current versions, we focus on a *standards orientation* toward SQL.

Because of the apparent size of SQL-92, it is likely that products will require several years, and several release cycles, to implement the entire language. Although the standard itself provides a partial prioritization of the features to be implemented, experience suggests that not every product will implement the features in exactly the same order and at the same time. Therefore, we chose to document all of the SQL-92 capabilities so that the maximum coverage is given to you up front.

We also chose to document the entire SQL-92 standard, not just the new features that did not appear in SQL-89. We believe it's unfair to ask someone new to relational technology to use one book (and one style) to get started and then another to pursue more advanced topics. Instead, we believe that such readers are better served by having all of the material available in one volume, in one style, fully integrated.

How might this comprehensive presentation affect the reader who is already intimately familiar with SQL-89? We believe that the organizational techniques we employ in this book clearly separate those components of SQL-92 inherited from SQL-89 from those new to SQL-92. Accordingly, the experienced SQL programmer can easily skip over the material with which he or she is familiar and concentrate only on truly new information.

The expansion of SQL that we touched on earlier (into an increased number of PC products, for instance) will bring more and more of you into the world of SQL. Perhaps you have spent your entire database development career working with dBASE or a similar language, but now find yourself developing client/server database applications which require SOL interfaces to some other DBMS product. The widespread acceptance of SQL—an acceptance seconded by the expanding number of products based on or interfacing with the language—is likely to touch most developers' job responsibilities at some point.

Now that we've introduced SQL, let's turn our focus to the database foundation of the language: the relational model.

1.4 The Relational Model

1.4.1 History and Basics

In June 1970, the Association for Computing Machinery published a paper in their journal, *Communications of the ACM,* by Dr. E.F. Codd, then of the IBM Research Laboratory (IBM Corporation) in San Jose, California. This paper, entitled "A Relational Model of Data for Large Shared Data Banks" was the first hint that many people had of a new model for databases: the relational model.

As defined by Dr. Codd in this seminal paper, the relational model of data provided a number of important characteristics that made database management and use relatively easy, error-resistant, and predictable. Most important, the relational model:

- Describes data with its *natural* structure, without adding any additional structure for machine representation or implementation purposes.
- Provides a mathematical basis for the treatment of derivability, redundancy, and consistency of relations.
- Provides independence *of* the data from the physical representation of the data, *of* the relationships between the data, and *of* implementation considerations related to efficiency and like concerns.

The article contrasted this *relational view of data* with previous methods of data management, most notably the then popular CODASYL database methodology. (CODASYL, the Committee for Data System Languages, developed COBOL as well as a specification for the network database model.)

As a side point, note that we do not wish to imply that the CODASYL methodology has gone by the wayside; indeed, many popular CODASYL-based products are selling well today.

1.4.2 Mathematical Foundations

The mathematical foundations of the relational model provide an interesting and important characteristic: closure. The basic element in the relational model is the relation. All relational operations on relations produce relations! This closure makes it feasible to prove the correctness of many manipulation operations. The various operators that have been defined on relations have precise mathematical characteristics; for example, some are commutative, some are distributive, and some are associative. These characteristics can be used, by optimizers in production-quality products, for instance, to determine faster and more effective methods of data manipulation.

For most people, the usual visualization of a relation takes the form of a table. A table, as we are used to it in other contexts, has rows and columns. The columns of a relation correspond to the *data items* for each of the *records* that are represented by the rows of the relation. Table 1-1 illustrates this point.

TABLE 1-1
Movie Titles
(name of
relation)

Title	Type of Movie	Our Cost	Current Rental Price
Lethal Weapon	Action	$23.95	$2.99
Batman	Action	$25.95	$2.99
The Little Mermaid	Animated	$23.95	$1.99
. . . and so on.			

The simple tabular form of the data is easy for most people to grasp. The relational model represents all data (conceptually, of course) in this form. The relational model has many other important characteristics that we will discuss in detail in Chapter 2.

1.4.3 Other Database Models

There are many other data models that have been used for database management. We have already mentioned the CODASYL network data model. A network model database has several (often many) *record types* that contain data of some specific format. The relationships between records of different types are formed by means of explicit pointers that are stored in individual records of data. For example, a record representing a specific department in a company would contain a pointer to the record representing some employee who works for that department. The record for that employee, in turn, contains a pointer to the record for some other employee working for the same department. The remaining employees working for that department are similarly "linked" together. These pointers are often in the form of *disk addresses* or other similar physical pointers that must be maintained by the application program. The dependence of the data on the physical structure is easy to see. There have been countless (Dare we say arguments? We dare!) arguments on the topic of whether network database technology is more or less efficient than other models. We do not wish to revisit those discussions here; let's leave that to the academicians and theoreticians while we concentrate on practical aspects.

It is important to consider that the network model really involves two sorts of data: *records* and *pointers*. The records contain the users' data, while the pointers connect records together or "contain the structure." This fact requires that a data sublanguage for a network data model have two sets of statements: one set to manipulate the records and the other to do likewise for the pointers. As a result, the language is roughly twice as large as one that has only one sort of data and corresponding statements.

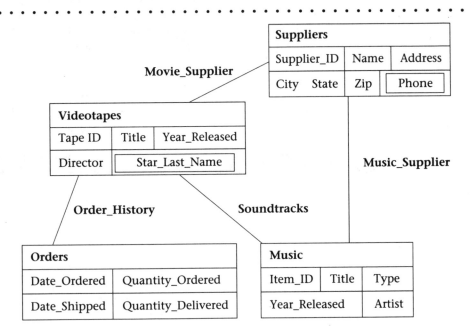

FIGURE 1-1
A Sample
CODASYL
Network
Database

Another model that has been widely used is the "hierarchical model." One of the most popular implementations of this model is IBM's IMS product, which uses a language called DL/I (Data Language/I). The distinguishing characteristic of the hierarchical model (vis-à-vis the network model) is that the parent-child record structure resembles an inverted tree—a hierarchy—rather than a multiple path network topology. Some critics consider this a limitation that makes the model unsuitable for many applications, but most implementations of the hierarchical model have introduced "work-arounds" that avoid the difficulties associated with the restriction. Considering the thousands of IMS applications residing on IBM mainframes around the world, it's obvious that IMS and the hierarchical model have their uses! One characteristic of the hierarchical model, as shown by Date's Universal Data Language (UDL)[2] is that the hierarchical addressing mechanism is generally much simpler than that of the network mechanism. This fact is probably responsible for the success of the hierarchical model.

Other models that have had at least some implementations include the entity-relationship model (popular in some repository, or data dictionary, products), the entity-attribute-relationship model (closely related to the previous one), and the binary-relation model. We do not discuss these models further because of the relative paucity of implementations of database management systems using them. Basically, most database textbooks refer to the "Big 3" models: hierarchical, network, and relational. However, more competition looms . . . .

A "new" model has surfaced in recent years, called the *object-oriented model*. The object-oriented, or *OO,* model can arguably be considered the fourth primary database model on which a multitude of successful commercial products will be based. This model deserves a book (and, indeed, has many books) devoted to it. In the simplest sense, this model allows each data element to be treated as a unique object with its own identification and characteristics. Information is located by means of the object identity, rather than by the values associated with the objects. It is claimed that this technique can reduce application programming, improve productivity, and reduce errors. Clearly, we shall hear more from this model in the future.

1.5 The History of the SQL Language

After Dr. Codd published his seminal paper on the relational model, research began at the IBM San Jose Research Laboratory on a language to implement that model; the language was called SEQUEL for Structured English Query Language. As part of a project called System R, IBM developed a research database system, also called System R. SEQUEL was the Application Program Interface (API) to System R. This language was first implemented in a prototype, again called SEQUEL, between 1974 and 1975. In the next couple of years, a revised version called SEQUEL/2 was defined; the name of this version was later changed to SQL. (No doubt, this is the source of the popular belief that SQL stands for Structured Query Language and is pronounced "sequel.") The System R project ran from 1971 to 1979 and eventually evolved into a distributed database project called System R* (pronounced "are star").

In the late 1970s, it became common knowledge that IBM was going to develop a relational database product based on the SQL language. Consequently, other vendors began to build and market their own products. At least one, from Relational Software, Inc. (the current Oracle Corporation), beat IBM's product to market. IBM's first product, introduced in 1981, was known as SQL/DS. In 1983, IBM released the first version of its DB2 product.

By 1992, there were certainly scores, and perhaps hundreds, of SQL implementations in the world. SQL had certainly become a *de facto* standard of the relational

---

2 C. J. Date, *An Introduction to Database Systems,* vol. 1, fifth edition, Addison-Wesley, Reading, MA, 1990.

database world by the mid-1980s. It also became a *de jure* standard in 1986 with the publication of an American National Standards Institute (ANSI) standard for that language (SQL-86). A follow-on standard was published in 1989 (SQL-89). We discuss the history of the SQL standardization process in detail in Appendix F.

Other relational languages have been defined and implemented. Some of these have been commercial successes, but none of them have had as wide a following as SQL. A company called Relational Technology, Incorporated (RTI), later called Ingres Corporation and currently ASK/Ingres, sold many copies of a database system called Ingres (initially developed at the University of California at Berkeley by Michael Stonebraker, Eugene Wong, and others). The data sublanguage of Ingres was QUEL, or Query Language. Digital Equipment Corporation's Rdb/VMS and Rdb/ELN relational database products provided a data sublanguage called RDML (called RDO by some). Both of these languages were quite popular with users of those vendors' products, but neither attracted a wide following among competing vendors (although each had other implementations from competitors).

Is the success and *de facto* standardization of SQL due to its excellence as a data sublanguage? Well, you will have to judge that for yourself as you go through this book and as you use SQL products. However, we can say that IBM's influence and marketing savvy certainly didn't hurt SQL's acceptance. The fact that SQL was the basis for early, not entirely successful, formal standardization also sent a signal to vendors that it would be relatively safe to bet on SQL. Like most languages, SQL has some very strong points and some very weak ones. SQL-92 has resolved many of the weak points found in earlier versions of the SQL standard, but it is far from perfect. We shall survey efforts to further improve the language in Chapter 20.

1.6 SQL-92, The New Revision

SQL-86 and SQL-89 were rightfully criticized for being incomplete. In fact, the language specified by those standards lacked many basic necessities for a commercial database system. For example, neither standard allowed an application (nor a user, nor an administrator, nor anybody else) to alter the definition of a database once it was defined. Users couldn't create new tables, add new user privileges, or delete columns from tables. Even though that capability was provided by all commercial SQL implementations, it was implemented in different ways by various vendors and thus failed to meet the least common denominator requirement of a standard.

Other features that were widely implemented but in varying ways, and thus were omitted from SQL-86 and SQL-89 include dynamic SQL, system tables, a variety of set operations, and extended error-handling facilities.

When work was completed on the specification that became SQL-89, the standards groups had already started working on further revisions that would make SQL a truly production-quality database language. In addition to adding features already widely implemented, the groups felt that it was important to get ahead of the curve by engineering into the next revision of the standard some new features that had not been as widely implemented. By doing this, they hoped to avoid future problems caused by divergent implementations (*i.e.,* they could avoid having to define a least common denominator again). This approach has been widely debated and even criticized, but it appears to have been a successful experiment; vendors are rapidly implementing many of these new features, and doing so in a standard-conforming way. The implementors are now free to work on efficient implementations instead of language design, at least where these new features are concerned.

1.6.1 New Features

What new features were added to SQL-92? Any list would have to include:

- Increased generality and orthogonality in the use of scalar-valued and table-valued query expressions
- Support for capabilities (especially DROP, ADD, and ALTER statements) to define and redefine tables
- Additional referential integrity facilities (including referential actions), subqueries in CHECK constraints, separate assertions, and user-controlled deferral of constraints
- Support for dynamic execution of SQL language
- Improved diagnostic capabilities, in particular, a new status parameter (SQLSTATE), a diagnostics area, and supporting statements
- Support for data type conversions (CAST expressions among data types)
- Additional data types (DATE, TIME, TIMESTAMP, BIT string, variable-length character and bit strings, and NATIONAL CHARACTER strings)
- Support for certain facilities required for Remote Database Access (RDA), notably connection management statements and qualified schema names
- Capability for domain definitions in the schema
- Definition of an *information schema*
- Support for additional scalar operations, such as string operations for concatenation and substring, date and time operations, and a form of conditional expressions
- Additional set and join operators (for example, union join, natural join, set difference, and set intersection)
- Support for scrolled cursors
- A requirement for a flagging capability to aid in portability of application programs
- Support for character sets beyond the one required to express SQL language itself; support for explicit collations
- Support for transaction consistency levels
- Support for temporary tables
- Additional security features

- Additional programming language support (MUMPS, Ada, and C; although the American National Standards Institute actually specified Ada and C support in an interim standard that the International Organization for Standardization didn't have)
- A better definition for direct invocation of SQL language (interactive SQL)

1.6.2   Size of SQL-92

The addition of all of these new features could be expected to make the resulting standard much larger. And, indeed, SQL-92 runs about 580 pages in length, while SQL-89 is *only* 115 pages. Before concluding that SQL-92 is 5 times as large as SQL-89, we examined the contents of the two documents very closely. A careful consideration of the actual content of the languages, adjusted to reflect the SQL-92 features that were already implemented by virtually every product and the rather more careful and complete specification of SQL-89 features in the SQL-92 document, suggests that the actual language is between 1.5 and 2 times as large as a realistic SQL-89.

1.6.3   Levels of SQL-92

Even a factor of 1.5 or 2 makes SQL-92 a substantial increase in size over SQL-89. It is completely unreasonable to expect vendors to implement the additional language features in only one or two releases. Beside the fact that many features are complex and will take some effort in and of themselves, vendors have competing requirements for their implementation resources. Users always need more performance, system management and other physical aspects of database systems not covered by the standard are constantly being improved, and integration of the database system with the vendors' other products is required by the marketplace.

As a result, SQL-92 is defined on three levels: Entry SQL, Intermediate SQL, and Full SQL. Entry SQL was designed to be almost identical to SQL-89. There are a few differences, though, and these fall into several categories.

1. *Features that replace deprecated SQL-89 features:* A deprecated feature is one that might be deleted from some future revision of the standard, although it remains in the current version, SQL-92. This category includes a more conventional format for parameter lists, the SQLSTATE status parameter, and the ability to rename columns in a select list. (Don't worry, all of these will be explained as we get to them.)

2. *Features that are incompatible with SQL-89:* These incompatibilities were introduced with the greatest reluctance, but they form a foundation for a more dependable implementation. This category includes a new requirement for colons preceding formal parameter names in SQL procedures and an enhanced definition of the WITH CHECK OPTION feature of views.

3. *Features specified to ease the transition from SQL-89 to SQL-92:* This category includes *delimited identifiers*, needed to help users avoid the conflicts that will be caused by the large number of new reserved keywords in SQL-92.

4. *Features that correct errors in SQL-89:* This category contains several items that were approved by the standards committees as corrections to the SQL-89 definition, but that were never published for the general public because SQL-92 overtook processing of the corrections. Included are changes to correct two minor errors dealing with the syntax and behavior of C programs that use SQL, removal of two syntax rules (one was unnecessary because of syntax changes to eliminate ambiguities; the other was incorrect because the syntax prohibited the situation covered by the rule), and addition of the ability to use PL/I and COBOL binary variables for access to SQL data.

To elaborate on item 4, SQL-92 addresses the following limitations found in SQL-89.

- Correct C binding definitions
- Allow implementor restrictions on valid authIDs
- Permit use of PL/I and COBOL binary types with SQL bindings
- Remove unnecessary rule to distinguish parameters and columns (replace by use of colons on parameter names)
- Remove incorrect rule to specify default when lengths are omitted in a C array specification (length is required, so no default is possible)
- Handle data in C given to database with no null-character terminator

Intermediate SQL is designed to encompass approximately half of the remaining new features of the language. These features were selected based on the standards committees' perceptions of market requirements, what vendors have already implemented, and the relative ease of implementation. Many vendors think that Intermediate SQL implementations will begin to appear within two or three years after publication of SQL-92.

Full SQL is (what a surprise!) the whole language. Features thought to be particularly difficult to implement or of relatively low utility to the marketplace were generally placed in the Full SQL level.

1.6.4 Conforming to SQL-92

SQL-92 specifies a much more comprehensive definition of what it means to conform to the standard. One important aspect is the requirement of a *flagger* for the Intermediate and Full levels. This flagger will tell you, the application programmer, if you use any features of SQL that are nonstandard (*i.e.,* vendor extensions or those that come from a level higher than the one to which the implementation claims conformance).

A quick diversion: In order to follow the next paragraph, you should know what some of the acronyms we use mean.

- ANSI   American National Standards Institute
- ISO   International Organization for Standardization

- NIST   National Institute for Standards and Technology
- FIPS   Federal Information Processing Standard

These are all discussed in detail in Appendix F. Now, back to the subject of conformance . . . .

Of course, conformance can be claimed to Entry SQL, Intermediate SQL, or Full SQL. Similarly, NIST's revised FIPS PUB 127-2 (see Appendix F for a complete discussion of NIST and FIPS) allows similar claim of conformance, although the FIPS also requires that the implementor adhere to a number of limits, such as the minimum number of tables supported, number of columns per table, and so forth. However, NIST's test facilities are designed specifically to test for conformance to the FIPS, not directly to the ANSI (or ISO) standard. Consequently, any difference would make it difficult for a vendor to prove direct conformance to the ANSI or ISO standard because there are no known test facilities for these standards. At this time, there are no incompatibilities (nor are any expected), so the concern is only hypothetical.

One aspect of conformance claims to the ANSI or ISO standards or to the FIPS is the specification of items that the standard says are "implementation-defined." The standard defines this phrase to mean, "possibly differing between SQL-implementations, but specified by the implementor for each particular SQL-implementation." This means that the implementation must define, in its documentation, each and every aspect of SQL-92 that is left implementation-defined by the standard. In many cases, this requires specifying only a simple numeric value (such as "the precision of INTEGER is 31 bits"), while in other cases it requires that the documentation describe how the implementation will implement a particular capability.

SQL-92 also uses another term, similar to but different from implementation-defined: *implementation-dependent*. This term is used to describe aspects of an SQL DBMS for which the standard does not specify particular behaviors and that the implementations need not document. (Indeed, the standard attempts to discourage vendors from documenting such aspects.) In particular, application programmers should avoid relying on any behavior that is implementation-dependent.

1.7 Chapter Summary

In this introductory chapter, we have told you the purpose of this book and how you will benefit from it. We have also told you what SQL is, how it relates to the relational model of data management, and how it came about. Finally, we explained the differences between SQL-89 and the new revision, SQL-92, as well as discussing conformance to SQL-92. You should now have an understanding of the origin and underlying principles of SQL, which will be helpful in understanding the more detailed discussions in Chapter 2.

Now, on to the really important material: getting started with SQL.

CHAPTER 2

. . . .

Getting Started with SQL-92

2.1 Introduction

In this chapter, we introduce some of the basic concepts and terminology that we will use in the remainder of the book. Much of the jargon that we define here may be, or at least seem, familiar to you. However, at least some of these terms have varying definitions depending on the context (or even the person talking). To avoid confusion, we define the terms here even though you may already know them.

In addition to defining terms and concepts, we introduce the database example employed in the remainder of the book. Throughout the book, particularly when discussing SQL concepts or features, we provide references to specific chapters in which a given topic is explored in greater detail. In sections 2.4 and 2.5, we delve a bit further into the relational model that we introduced in Chapter 1.

2.2 Database Management System Concepts

In this section, we briefly define the concepts of a database and of a database management system, often abbreviated as DBMS. Within the scope of interest of this book, we will discuss some of the principal characteristics of databases and DBMSs.

First of all, let's see just what a database is.

2.2.1 What is a Database?

In the most general sense, a database is a collection of data, usually pertaining to some reasonably well-defined purpose. One example of this broad definition might be the collection of data related to compact discs (CDs) and videotapes. Let's say a record and video store or a distributor somewhere collected such data and stored it in a computer in some form. If this data were transformed into a database, it would likely be of the type that we mean to discuss here.

When discussing databases stored on computer systems, we have to get a little more particular about how the data is stored, related, and so on. A computer file containing music and video data as in our example, can be said to loosely comprise a database, but most people would not think of it as such. Instead, data has to be stored in a way that lends it certain characteristics before most computer-literate people would say that it comprised a database.[1]

In order to say that data has been stored in a database (as opposed to just being stored), certain conditions must be satisfied.

- The data must have a known format (that is, the format of the data must be well-defined to the computer system, not just to application programs that use it). This format is defined by the *metadata*, or data about data.

- The data should be stored, retrieved, and modified only by a special type of computer program—the database management system.

- The data should be under transaction control. That is, a formal set of rules and guidelines must ensure that integrity is maintained during and after operations on data. This is especially important when multiple users and applications are simultaneously accessing the data.

If the music and video information in our example were stored in a manner consistent with these characteristics, then it would probably be recognized as having been stored in a database.

An important point to remember is that a database almost always comprises far more than simply a database management system (which is discussed in the next section) and its data. In real-world applications, there are a number of other subsystems that make up a database environment, as illustrated in Figure 2-1.

2.2.2 What is a Database Management System?

A database management system is a special computer program built to store data into, retrieve data from, and modify data stored in a database. In general, DBMSs require that the user (some user, at least) define the format of the data very specifically. At a minimum, this requires that the user define the number of data items, the data types of those items, and how the items are related to one another. The user may be required to specify how the data items are physically stored on the computer's disks or how the data can be located quickly.

One of the most significant advantages of a DBMS is that it protects the data from many sorts of ill-formed operations. Consider a sequence of operations that

[1] When large amounts of data were first being collected and made available for access, the term *data bank* was often used to refer to the data collection. The terms *database* and *data bank* were used more or less interchangeably in those early days. It was only later that formal characteristics were ascribed to databases, while data banks remained somewhat of a generic concept. In Chapter 1 we mentioned Dr. Codd's paper, which introduced the relational model; it was entitled "A Relational Model of Data for Large Shared Data Banks."

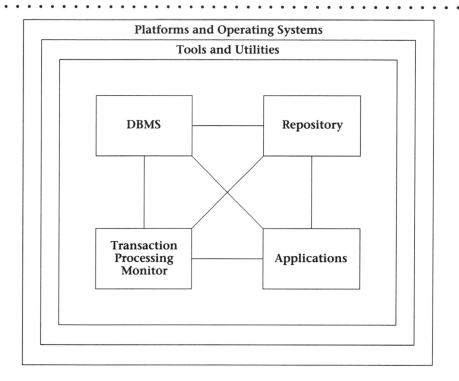

FIGURE 2-1
Database
Components

make changes to a database of bank accounts (to use an example so trite as to be a cliché): one common sequence is the transferal of money from one account to another. A typical sequence of operations is to subtract the transfer amount from one account and then add it to the other. If the operations were to be interrupted for any reason after the subtraction but before the addition, then the money would have simply disappeared! A DBMS cannot allow this to happen. To protect against this sort of problem, the DBMS applies transaction semantics to the operations.

2.3 Data and Metadata

Earlier, we told you that a DBMS keeps information pertaining to the format of the data it manages. This information is often called metadata, or data about data. In the context of an SQL database management system, which we will explore shortly, metadata looks a lot like data. The metadata of a database describes the data that the database contains. It is often also self-describing; that is, it describes the metadata itself as well as the user data.

Database systems have to maintain the metadata as well as the user data. There are often specific interfaces, such as special statements, used for metadata mainte-nance. SQL database systems have such special statements, usually called DDL (data definition language), though we shall see later that *definition* is only part of the function of these special statements.

2.4 Data Models

In Chapter 1, we briefly mentioned the relational model for data along with several other data models. There is much that could be said about database models, but our brevity is in keeping with the goals of this book. It is not our intent to cover comprehensively even the relational model (particularly from a theoretical viewpoint), much less the other data models. There are many important articles and research papers and any number of excellent reference books that cover the topics very well.

The short version, though, is that the relational model of data management has become extremely popular in the industry for several reasons. The relational model:

- Is conceptually simple; most application programmers can grasp the important concepts and apply them to their work regardless of their experience levels.

- Has a mathematical foundation; therefore, most of the important operational aspects of the model can be proved and many new propositions can be tested for soundness even before implementations are built.

- Has a largely nonprocedural nature, making it practical to build implementations that range from very low cost and low performance to those that have extremely high performance with proportionally higher cost.

Incidentally, we should tell you: SQL does not claim to be a faithful implementation of the relational model! Instead, SQL is *based* on the relational model. This important distinction is closely related to some of the theoretical foundations of the relational model.

One characteristic of the relational model is that no table is permitted to contain duplicate rows (that is, no two rows may have identical values in all columns when the columns are considered as a unit). SQL does not always enforce this restriction because user (read *customer*) input to the standards process repeatedly confirms that users sometimes need the ability to bypass that restriction. Dr. Codd has often proposed that SQL be modified to mandate that restriction, but the standard continues to make it optional instead of required.

Such flexibility has certain implications on both the SQL standard and on implementations of the language. One implication is that the mathematical foundation of the relational model does not always provide the same support for SQL. The semantics of some operations will differ because of this permissiveness. One can argue that, because SQL is not 100% faithful to the model, it is not relational at all; we believe that's going a bit far. SQL is strongly biased towards the relational model and virtually all users will perceive it as being relational; however, as we have shown, there are certain exceptions.

A brief note regarding SQL and nonrelational database implementations, particularly object-oriented databases: As object-oriented databases undergo various standardization efforts, parallel efforts will occur with respect to object-oriented languages. Research work in "Object-Oriented SQL" (OOSQL) may well result in SQL having applicability beyond relational databases.

Having said all that, let's spend a little time looking at the relational model itself and trying to understand some of its concepts.

2.5 The Relational Model

We already introduced, in Chapter 1, some of the more basic attributes of the relational model; let's take a longer look at them now.

2.5.1 Tables, Columns, and Rows (or Relations, Attributes, and Tuples)

The basic unit of data is the *relation* (the *table* in SQL, with the primary difference that a relation can never have duplicate rows, while a table can). A relation is made up of one or more *attributes* (*columns* in SQL). Each column (we will use the SQL terminology here to avoid confusion) has associated with it a data type. You already know what a data type is: It's the characteristic of a piece of data that says it is a character string, an integer, a floating-point number, or whatever. Data is stored in a table in *tuples* (*rows* in SQL). As a result, a table looks a bit like a matrix, with the columns identifying the individual data elements (by name, usually, as well as by data type) and the rows representing *records* of related data.

We've also heard an analogy drawn with a check register, with its Check Number, To, and Amount columns and the individual checks (too many, in our case!) acting like rows. Or, getting back to our example, a table might look like a CD distributor's account sheet, as in Table 2-1.

TABLE 2-1

Customer	CD	Cost	# Ordered
Zip's Records and Video	No Fences	5.99	25
Loco Records	No Fences	6.25	10
Best Video	Emotions	5.99	35

Here, we can see that this table has four columns and three rows. The first column is named **Customer** and appears to have a data type of *character string*. The second is named **CD** and also has a data type of character string. The third column is called **Cost** and has a data type of decimal. The fourth column is called **# Ordered** (although, as we shall see, that's not a proper SQL name) and is an integer.

The rows obviously relate to three different customers and specific CD orders. The entire contents of one row relate to one and only one customer order for a given CD. By contrast, the entire contents of one column—a vertical slice—deal with a single attribute or property (such as cost) for all rows in the table.

Something important to note is that even though the rows and columns of a table comprise a matrix on the horizontal and vertical axes, the rows and columns are not equivalent entities. That is, there are important differences between rows and columns with respect to

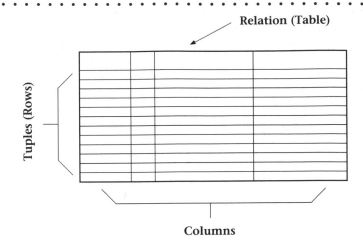

FIGURE 2-2
Relational Model Components

Relation (Table)

Tuples (Rows)

Columns

- *Volatility:* The number of rows in a table will typically change far more frequently than the number of columns. Rows are often added or deleted as, for example, new CDs come into stock or discontinued albums are omitted. In contrast, the number of columns will change only when we discover a need to record more (or less) information in every row.

- *Complexity of Change:* When rows are added or deleted or a data value is modified, no metadata change is necessary (although a specific DBMS implementation may contain *pseudo-metadata* with row counts within a table, *etc.*). When columns are added to, deleted from, or modified within a table, however, metadata change is necessary. Depending on the complexity of your specific database—the types of key and referential integrity constraints, the privilege model, and the like—this metadata change may be somewhat complex.

2.5.2 Primitive Data Types

In the relational model of data management, there is the concept of a primitive data type, but only because there are rules in the model that describe how to deal with data of different types. For example, some operations in the relational model (such as the comparison of two data items) require that the data types be the same for two or more items.

However, the model does not prescribe what these data types are. Of course, SQL does, as we shall see in the following sections.

Nevertheless, the relational model does tell us something about the characteristics of the data types. The most important of these characteristics is atomicity, which means that the individual data items of each data type are *indivisible* and must be treated as a unit.[2]

---

2   Later in this chapter, we'll talk about atomicity in the context of the transaction model and the ACID principles. For the sake of clarification, these two types of atomicity are not identical. Data item atomicity is of a spatial nature, whereas transaction atomicity is temporal in nature.

Most of us have no difficulty grasping this concept when we're talking about integers. Some of us might think that a floating point number can be broken into its mantissa and exponent, but it's really just a single number when the database is dealing with it. Many of us (Okay, C and Pascal programmers, raise your hands) often think of a character string as an array of characters, but the relational model encourages us to treat a character string as an atomic unit.

2.5.3 Relational Operations

The relational model also defines a number of specific operations that can be performed on tables, on rows, and on individual data elements. Let's explore these briefly.

The most important operation is *selection*, or identifying a specific row (or rows) in a table. Selection is normally done by specifying one or more predicates that are used to filter a table to identify the rows for which the predicate is true. (A predicate is really nothing more than a question asked about the truth of something, or a statement about that truth; the *value* of a predicate is normally either *true* or *false*, though it can sometimes be *unknown* because insufficient information is available to determine the answer reliably.)

Another operation in the relational model is the *union*. It often happens that two tables have the same structure. Consider a database with one table of VHS cassette tapes and another of laser disk movies. The chances are high that the structure of the two tables is the same. (Why, you ask, wouldn't we put them into the same table with an additional column to capture the format? Well, we might, but some people might not, and it's not our place to tell people how they have to write their applications!) If we needed to produce a report that combined information about the two tables at the same time, we could combine these tables into a single *virtual* table (one that doesn't physically exist, but is materialized only as required) containing the rows of both tables. Let's look at an example. Consider Tables 2-2 and 2-3.

TABLE 2-2
VHS Tapes

TITLE	COST	STOCK QTY
48 Hours	29.95	6
Pretty Woman	55.95	18
About Last Night	14.95	9
Rocky Horror Picture Show	99.99	1
A Night at the Opera	14.95	5

TABLE 2-3
Laser Disks

TITLE	COST	STOCK QTY
Pretty Woman	55.95	3
48 Hours	29.95	2
Beverly Hills Cop II	29.99	0

You might actually wish to find out the total number of copies of *Pretty Woman*, regardless of the format. The union of these two tables is the way to go; the tables have the same format, so they may be joined in union.

TABLE 2-4
Unnamed
Virtual Table

TITLE	COST	STOCK QTY
48 Hours	29.95	6
Pretty Woman	55.95	18
About Last Night	14.95	9
Rocky Horror Picture Show	99.99	1
A Night at the Opera	14.95	5
Pretty Woman	55.95	3
48 Hours	29.95	2
Beverly Hills Cop II	29.99	0

The order of the rows is not important in the relational model. In many situations, applications don't care about the order of rows; for example, if all you're doing is adding up a column of numbers, it doesn't matter in which order you see the numbers. In other situations, applications do care and they must instruct the database system to sort the rows.

In our example, the union operation causes no ordering to take place, so the fact that the rows appear in Table 2-4 in the order that they appeared in the two source tables is accidental (although rather probable in real implementations!).

Another operation is called the join. A join operation is a way of combining data from two tables based (usually, at least) on the relationships between the data in those tables. Let's look at another example. Consider Tables 2-5 and 2-6.

TABLE 2-5
VHS Tapes

NUMBER	TITLE	COST	STOCK QTY
285B	48 Hours	29.95	6
101J	Pretty Woman	55.95	18
092R	About Last Night	14.95	9
588M	Rocky Horror Picture Show	99.99	1
288C	A Night at the Opera	14.95	5

TABLE 2-6
Miscellaneous
Information

NUMBER	RATING	CATEGORY
588M	R	Cult
092R	PG-13	Romance
101J	R	Romance
288C	G	Comedy
285B	R	Adventure

If we wished to learn the rating of a film costing less than $15.00, we would have to combine information from these two tables, because the information cannot be obtained from either table alone. However, if we join the two tables based on the values of the NUMBER column (which the tables have in common), we can get a virtual table that looks like Table 2-7.

TABLE 2-7
Unnamed
Virtual Table

NUMBER	TITLE	COST	STOCK QTY	RATING	CATEGORY
101J	Pretty Woman	55.95	18	R	Romance
092R	About Last Night	14.95	9	PG-13	Romance
288C	A Night at the Opera	14.95	5	G	Comedy
285B	48 Hours	29.95	6	R	Adventure
588M	Rocky Horror Picture Show	99.99	1	R	Cult

From this virtual table, we can now get the information that we need.

2.5.4 Closure of the Relational Model

In Chapter 1, we discussed an important characteristic of the relational data model: its property of closure. The result of any operation on one or more relations is also a relation. The examples in Table 2-2 through 2-7 illustrate that the result of a union or a join is also a table. The property of closure is also true for SQL but, remember, SQL deals with tables, not relations.

Now that we've given you some background on the relational model, let's go on to visit SQL and discuss how SQL relates to relational databases.

2.6 SQL Concepts

As we've discussed, SQL is based on the relational model, but it is not a perfect implementation of that model. The most important difference, at least from the viewpoint of theory, is that SQL's basic data object is the table and not the relation.

If you've a mathematical leaning, this analogy will help. A relation is mathematically equivalent to a set. You'll recall that a set is a collection of unique objects—no duplicates. By contrast, a table is equivalent to a *multiset,* which is defined to be set-like, *but with duplicates permitted.* (A lot of recent literature has taken to using the unfortunate term *bag* for this concept, but we continue to prefer multiset as evoking more pleasant images.)

SQL has a number of other concepts; some of these have direct analogs in the relational model, while others do not. Some of these analogs are listed below; however, we don't attempt to distinguish among them because, after all, our intent is to learn SQL.

- views
- schemas
- catalogs

- users
- privileges
- domains

Basic SQL concepts are summarized in Figure 2-3. It is important that users and developers understand these concepts because, as we've said, there is much more to a database than just the data. You can most effectively utilize DBMS products when you thoroughly understand the underlying concepts.

FIGURE 2-3
Summary of
SQL Concepts

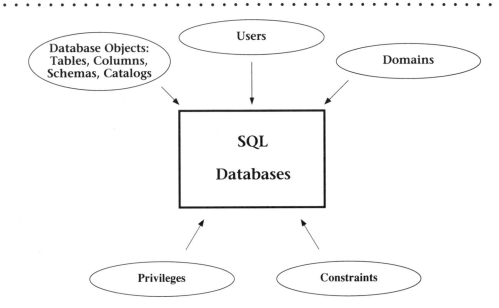

2.6.1 Views

One important capability that SQL provides is the ability to define a virtual table (well, "define the derivation of the virtual table" is probably more accurate) and save that definition in the database (as metadata, of course) with a user-defined name. The object formed by this operation is called a view.

A view is an example of a virtual table. That is, it is generally not physically materialized anywhere until it is needed—when some SQL statement references it, for instance. The metadata about the view (including the name of the view, the names and data types of each column, and the way in which the rows are to be derived) is stored persistently in the database's metadata, but the actual data that you will *see* in the view aren't physically stored anywhere in association with the derived table. Rather, the data are stored in base tables (*persistent base tables* in SQL) from which the view's rows are derived.

In general, operations can be performed against views just as they can be performed against persistent base tables. (Let's agree to use just *base tables* from here on, unless there's a reason to clarify.) The major exception to this rule is that some virtual tables, including views, cannot be updated directly. The reasons for this can be found in relational theory and in much of the relational literature, but let's summarize it here: If you cannot determine uniquely the row of the base table to update, then you cannot update the view.

Views are a very helpful mechanism for using a database. For example, you can define complex queries once and use them repeatedly without having to re-invent them over and over. Furthermore, views can be used to enhance the security of your database, as we shall see.

2.6.2 Users and Privileges

An important component of any computer system is the user. Okay, we're being a little tongue-in-cheek. But the point is important, especially when you are concerned about the security of your data. If you don't know who's there, you don't know who's reading—or changing—your data.

Let's consider our entertainment distributor from a few pages back. We doubt that he or she would want just anybody to be allowed to request a shipment of 10,000 CDs to a store. It's likely that there will be restrictions on such activity. For example, only sales personnel would be allowed to start such a transaction, while only shipping clerks could cause the shipping orders to be printed and deleted.

In SQL, the concept of a user is captured by an *authorization identifier*. Every operation in an SQL system is validated according to the authorization identifier that attempts to invoke the operation. Now, the details of authorization identifiers (authIDs for brevity) are strictly left up to implementations. After all, a PC implementation of SQL has different requirements than a mainframe implementation. In some systems (this seems to be most common on Unix® implementations), the user's logon ID is used for his SQL authID; in others, entire groups of users might be given the same authID.

As we shall see in detail later, SQL requires an appropriate privilege for every sort of operation that can be performed on the database. For example, the SELECT privilege is required for a user to retrieve information from a table. Some privileges are granted on an entire table, while others may be granted on the entire table or only on selected columns of the table. (More on this in Chapter 13.)

2.6.3 Schemas and Catalogs

As we have already seen in our examples, very few applications are likely to be satisfied with only one table. Most applications require multiple tables, and most implementations are probably going to support many applications, each with its own set of tables. What happens if two applications happen to choose the same name for one of their tables? Well, there are a couple of possible solutions: Either, absolutely prohibit the possibility (sometimes called the *single namespace solution*) or provide a way to qualify the names with some higher order name (often called the *partitioned namespace solution*).

SQL has always provided the partitioned namespace solution. Tables exist in the context of a higher level object called a *schema*. This use of the word may confuse you if you are a data modeling expert, because it doesn't mean quite the same thing in SQL as it does in that domain. In SQL, a schema is simply the collection of all objects (*e.g.*, tables and views) that share a namespace. Schemas have names and those names can be used to qualify the names of the objects contained within that schema. You might have movie titles that are members of the Warehouse schema; you can always refer to the table as Warehouse Movie Titles. (No, this isn't the right syntax; we'll get to that later. This section is called concepts, remember?)

During the infancy of SQL database systems, it was very common for an SQL DBMS to support only a very few schemas (some commercially important systems have sometimes supported only one schema for an entire installation), so the names of the schemas were rarely duplicated at any given installation. However, as widely distributed databases are supported by some products and required by some users, the probability that two users will select the same name for their schemas increases. To address this problem, SQL-92 has adopted a convention of collecting schemas together into a unit called a *catalog*. A catalog provides a mechanism for qualifying the schema names to avoid name conflicts; it is also the conceptual repository for the metadata of all schemas *in* that catalog. Many people envision a catalog as the unit of management of a DBMS installation, although the SQL standard doesn't make that restriction.

What's to prevent duplicate catalog names? Nothing, really. It's going to happen. However, SQL-92 defines catalog names in a way that encourages implementations of SQL DBMSs to use a very large name space (such as that provided by a network naming service like X.500) for catalog names. This reduces the probability of duplicate catalog names. Since no naming scheme can ever completely eliminate the possibility, SQL-92 stops there. If duplicate catalog names become a problem, the people administering the database system will simply have to resolve it themselves. We believe that many implementations will provide facilities to aid this administration problem, like the ability to use a sort of alias to substitute for one of the duplicate catalog names. This escape hatch is not part of the SQL-92 standard, though.

By the way, when we talk about *connections* later on, we'll see that there is generally a sort of boundary surrounding the set of all catalogs that you can access at any one instant. That set might be very large, but it's generally the set of catalogs on all computer systems that you can reach without extraordinary action (such as dialing up to a different network environment). That set of catalogs is called a cluster, but it doesn't provide any sort of name space partitioning. In fact, the cluster itself doesn't really have a name—it's just a convenient term for discussing the set of catalogs that you can reach *now*.

2.7 SQL Data Types

Earlier, we said that SQL had a set of atomic data types that it supports. In earlier versions of the standard (*e.g.*, SQL-89), the data types were limited to exact numerics, approximate numerics, and character strings. In SQL-92, these have been augmented with bit strings, datetimes, and intervals. Each of these have variations, so let's look at them in some detail.

2.7.1   Exact Numerics

The exact numeric data types in SQL are those that can represent a value exactly. One category of these is the *true* integers, which are represented in SQL by INTEGER (it is permitted to abbreviate this as INT) and SMALLINT. The other category is intended to permit fractional components, but still provide an exact representation. This latter category consists of the DECIMAL and NUMERIC data types. Each of these data types deserves a closer look.

- INTEGER: This data type represents an integer value (a *counting number,* like the number of pieces of something). Its precision (the number of decimal digits or bits that can be stored, with the implementation choosing whether the precision of INTEGER is in terms of digits or bits) is implementation-defined, if only because the standard must be implementable on many different hardware architectures. When you want to declare some column to use this data type, you simply specify INTEGER—there are no parameters.

- SMALLINT: This data type also represents an integer value. Its precision is also implementation-defined, but is no greater than the precision of INTEGER. This allows an implementation to provide a certain amount of storage optimization if the application knows that larger numbers are not required. The precision must be in the same terms (digits or bits) as for INTEGER. Just as with INTEGER, there are no optional parameters on this data type, so you simply specify SMALLINT.

- NUMERIC: This data type has both a precision and a scale (the number of digits of the fractional component). The scale cannot be negative or larger than the precision, and the implementation will give you exactly the precision and scale that you request. When you want to specify this data type for some SQL object, you may simply specify NUMERIC and accept the default precision and scale for the implementation. Alternatively, you can specify either NUMERIC(p), where p is a precision value within the range supported by the implementation, or NUMERIC(p,s), where s is a scale value within the implementation's range. This data type is used for numbers with fractional components but exact precision, like money.

- DECIMAL: This data type also has both a precision and a scale. In this case, though, the precision supplied by the implementation may be greater than the precision that you specify—larger precisions are acceptable, but smaller ones are not. The scale will always be exactly what you requested. As with NUMERIC, you can specify this data type as DECIMAL, DECIMAL(p), or DECIMAL(p,s).

2.7.2   Approximate Numerics

The approximate numeric data types in SQL also represent numbers, but only approximately! In most implementations, you can expect these to be provided by floating point numbers. While it's possible with the exact numeric types to specify precisely the data values that they support—that is, you can easily specify the exact largest and smallest values—it's not quite that easy with the approximate numerics.

Okay, it is that easy, because computer systems are finite state machines and there are a finite number of bits that can be supported. However, the way that floating point numbers are represented in most computer systems makes it rather awkward to say that exactly *this* list of values is representable. Instead, the nature of the floating point hardware makes the precision more or less variable, depending on the range being represented. We don't want to spend a lot of time on that—there are lots of good references about this elsewhere. Just remember that SQL supports approximate numeric data as having both a mantissa (the significant digits) and an exponent (to derive the actual size of the number), just like floating point numbers.

There are three variations of approximate numeric data in SQL. They are used for data whose values have an extremely wide range and whose precision need not be absolute. Let's examine each of these data types in turn.

- REAL: This data type allows you to request a single-precision floating point data item. The precision is chosen by the implementation, but it's normally the default single-precision data type on the hardware platform. There are no options, so you simply specify REAL.

- DOUBLE PRECISION: This data type also has an implementation-defined precision, but that precision must be greater than the precision of REAL. (Contrast this with INTEGER, which must have a precision no greater than SMALLINT.) This usually translates to a double-precision floating point data item on your hardware. With no options, you specify only DOUBLE PRECISION.

- FLOAT: This data type allows you to specify the precision that you want. The resulting precision must be at least as large as the precision you request. This could be used, for example, for a portable application; if you request a precision of some value *p*, it might be honored by a single-precision on one platform and a double-precision on another. Because there's an option, you can specify either FLOAT or FLOAT(p) when you want this data type.

2.7.3 Character Strings

There are, depending on how you want to count, either two or four character string data types in SQL-92 (SQL-89 had only one). The two that we prefer to count are CHARACTER (which you can abbreviate as CHAR) and CHARACTER VARYING (which can be abbreviated as either CHAR VARYING or VARCHAR). CHARACTER VARYING is new in SQL-92.

SQL-92 also provides NATIONAL CHARACTER and NATIONAL CHARACTER VARYING (which can be abbreviated as NCHAR, NATIONAL CHAR, and NATIONAL VARCHAR). However, they are defined as specific, implementation-defined, special variations of CHARACTER and CHARACTER VARYING; that is, they are defined as CHARACTER (or CHARACTER VARYING) with a specific character set. We will discuss the implications and semantics of NATIONAL CHARACTER and internationalization in general in Chapter 18.

Let's take a close look at the two basic character data types.

- CHARACTER: This data type contains character strings. The specific character sets that can be stored in one of these are defined by your implementation, but it's probably going to include something like ASCII or Latin-1 for compatibility with earlier implementations. You can specify this as either CHARACTER or CHARACTER(x), where *x* is the number of characters that you want to store. If you specify only CHARACTER, it's equivalent to specifying CHARACTER(1). If you try to store, say, 5 characters into a column specified as CHARACTER(10), then you will still have 10 characters stored—the last 5 will be blanks.

- CHARACTER VARYING: If you don't want to blank-pad your character strings (in some applications, blanks have significance, so you can't afford to just add them whether you need them or not), then you will want to use CHARACTER VARYING. This data type allows you to store exactly the number of characters that you have in your data. You must specify CHARACTER VARYING(x); there is no default of 1 (or anything else) as there is for CHARACTER.

In both cases, each implementation will have an upper limit on the maximum value of the length. In some implementations, the limit might be fairly small (we know of at least one implementation that limited character strings to 240 characters until quite recently), while in others the limits might be extremely large (we have heard of one implementation that supports character strings of over 4 billion characters!). You can probably count on most implementations supporting something like 32,000 or 64,000 characters.

2.7.4 Bit Strings

Characters have certain semantics associated with them, and those semantics are normally those associated with written, natural language or something similar. If your application requires the ability to store arbitrary bit (or byte) strings, then CHARACTER isn't the appropriate data type to use. Before SQL-92, SQL implementations had no other choice, so CHARACTER (or some variation, like VARCHAR or LARGE VARCHAR) was often used for this purpose. To resolve that misuse of CHARACTER, SQL-92 provides two additional data types. Let's look at them.

- BIT: This data type allows your application to store arbitrary bit strings, unconstrained by character semantics. If you need to store only a single bit (for example, if you use *flags* in your data), then you can specify only BIT; if you want more, then you must specify BIT(x), where *x* specifies how many bits (not bytes or anything else) you want. Fixed-length bit strings have a default length of 1, just like fixed-length character strings.

- BIT VARYING: If your application wants to store one number of bits on one occasion and a different number at other times, this data type should be considered. Specified only as BIT VARYING(x) (there aren't any abbreviations), this type will give you a bit string that allows you to store any number of bits up to *x*. Variable-length bit strings have no default number of bits, so you must specify the desired maximum length.

As with the CHARACTER and CHARACTER VARYING types, implementations will have limits on the size of *x*. Those limits will probably be fairly large—at least 32,000 bits and perhaps as many as 4 billion bits.

2.7.5   Datetimes

Since the very earliest days of computers, applications have had a need to represent dates and times in stored data and to manipulate that information. Many approaches have been taken, but one characteristic was shared by all of them: they weren't standardized. Instead, every computer system or software system invented its own conventions for handling this sort of data.

This variability was clearly unacceptable. One frequent request received by participants in the SQL standardization efforts was to add a datetime data type. The only problem was deciding how to add that support without locking implementations into a specific implementation technique. The chosen approach expresses the datetime data types in a canonical form and defines the operations supported by SQL.

SQL-92 times are specified with a relationship to UCT, or universal coordinated time (previously called GMT, or Greenwich mean time). Different places on the surface of the earth experience different sun times, or sidereal times, because of their relative positions to the sun. Until the middle 1800s, individual communities kept their own time based on solar measurements; this posed an intolerable burden to railroad timekeepers in the large North American continent, so a system of time zones was instituted to place entire *strips* of the earth into specific time zones, with every community in one strip keeping the same time. This system was very popular and was quickly endorsed by the rest of the world. However, as with all reforms, this one was subject to political manipulation.

Some changes were very sensible: It would have caused much hardship if a city that happened to straddle an arbitrary strip boundary were forced to keep two different times. Other changes were more political: Nepal keeps time that is 15 minutes different from India as an expression of independence.

Still other changes are almost arbitrary. Many locales in the world advance their clocks by one hour in the summer and turn them back in the winter. This summer time is perceived as beneficial because daylight lasts until later and more outdoors work can be done. However, there are few standards related to this and different countries change their clocks on different days. Therefore, the offset from UTC of a given community's time will vary during the year, but not all communities change and those that do may not change on the same day. This further complicates time processing in SQL. SQL-92 requires that every SQL session have associated with it a default offset from UTC that is used for the duration of the session.

As a result, the language defines three specific forms of date and time and two variations on these. Let's examine each of them.

- DATE: This variation stores the year, month, and day values of a date. The year value is exactly 4 digits and can represent the years 0001 through 9999 (that's C.E. 1, or A.D. 1).[3] The month value is exactly 2 digits and is limited to values 01 through 12. The day value is also exactly 2 digits and is limited to values 01 through 31, although the month value can apply additional restrictions to a maximum of 28, 29, or 30.

  The length of a DATE is said to be 10 *positions*; in this way, SQL-92 does not appear to prescribe that implementations use character strings, packed decimal, or any other form internally.

  You specify a date data type by simply using DATE.

- TIME: This variation stores the hour, minute, and second values of a time. The hour value is exactly 2 digits and can represent the hours 00 through 23. The minutes value is also exactly 2 digits and can represent 00 through 59. The seconds value is again 2 digits, but a fractional value is optional. The seconds value is restricted to 00 through 61.999. . . . . Why 61 instead of the expected 59? Simply because of the phenomenon known as *leap seconds*— occasionally, the earth's official timekeepers will add one or two seconds to a minute to keep clocks synchronized with sidereal time.

  The maximum number of fractional digits is defined by your implementation, but the standard requires that it support at least 6 digits. If you don't specify a number when you are defining your data types, you'll get no fractional digits. The length of a TIME value is 8 positions; if there are any fractional digits, then the length is 9 plus the number of fractional digits. (The extra position is to account for the period that separates the integer seconds value from the fractional digits.)

  You specify a time data type by either specifying TIME or by specifying TIME(p). The value of p must not be negative, of course, and the maximum value is determined by your implementation.

- TIMESTAMP: This variation stores the year, month, and day values of a date as well as the hour, minute, and second values of a time. The lengths and the restrictions on the values correspond to those in the DATE and TIME data types. The only real difference is the default number of fractional digits. In TIME, the default was 0, but in TIMESTAMP, the default is 6 digits.

  Therefore, the length of a TIMESTAMP is 19 positions. If any fractional digits are specified, then the length is 20 positions plus the number of fractional digits (again, the extra position is to account for that period).

---

3 Unfortunately, SQL-92's date capability cannot handle B.C.E. or B.C. (Before the Common Era or Before Christ) dates due to lack of general agreement over issues such as how to handle the year 0, how far back to go (the pyramids? dinosaurs? Big Bang?), and the like. We believe that many products will support such dates, but they may do so in a variety of ways.

You specify a timestamp data type by either specifying TIMESTAMP or by specifying TIMESTAMP(p). The value of p must not be negative, of course, and the maximum value is determined by your implementation.

- TIME WITH TIME ZONE: This data type is exactly like the TIME data type except that it also adds additional information about the offset from UTC of the time specified. This offset is represented as an INTERVAL HOUR TO MINUTE (see section 2.7.6) that is permitted to contain values ranging from –12:59 to +13:00. (You might expect the range to be from –11:59 to +12:00, but the summer time problem causes the wider range to be required.) This added information requires an additional 6 positions, so the length of a TIME WITH TIME ZONE is 14. If fractional digits are specified, then the length is 15 plus the number of fractional digits.

- TIMESTAMP WITH TIME ZONE: This data type is exactly like TIMESTAMP with the addition of the UTC offset information. The additional information means that the length of TIMESTAMP WITH TIME ZONE is 25. If fractional digits are specified, then the length is 26 plus the number of fractional digits.

2.7.6   Intervals

Closely tied to the issue of storing and processing dates and times is the question of intervals. An interval is broadly defined as the difference between two dates or times. SQL-92 defines two categories of interval: year-month intervals and day-time intervals. The two cannot be mixed in any expression.

The reason for this differentiation is subtle, but important. A year-month interval can only express an interval in terms of years and an integral number of months. We always know (in the Gregorian calendar, at least) that a year has exactly 12 months. A day-time interval can express an interval in terms of days, hours, minutes, and seconds, because we know exactly how many hours there are in a day, minutes in an hour, and (barring the anomaly of leap seconds) seconds in a minute. However, we do not know exactly how many days are in a month, unless we know the month we're talking about in advance.

Therefore, answers to a question like, "What is the result of 1 year, 3 months, 19 days divided by 3?" cannot be determined unless we know the dates spanned by that interval. To avoid the anomalies associated with these problems, SQL-92 simply makes the restriction that intervals come in two, unmixable classes.

Intervals in SQL-92 always have a *datetime qualifier* associated with them. This qualifier specifies the class of the interval and the exact precision of the interval. The precision has two components: the leading field can have 1 or more digits and the seconds value (if part of the interval) can have a fractional component.

- *Year-Month Intervals:* This class of intervals can contain only a year value, only a month value, or both. When you specify a year-month interval, the interval qualifier will specify the maximum number of digits in the *leading* or *only* field. Therefore, you can specify INTERVAL YEAR, INTERVAL YEAR(p), INTERVAL MONTH, INTERVAL MONTH(p), INTERVAL YEAR TO MONTH, or INTERVAL

YEAR(p) TO MONTH. In all cases, if you don't specify *p*, the leading field precision defaults to 2 digits.

The length of a year-month interval is either the length of the year field, the length of the month field, or three more than the length of the year field (year field plus one for the hyphen separator, plus two for the month field).

- *Day-Time Intervals:* This class of intervals can contain only a day value, an hour value, a minute value, and/or a second value. If it contains two or more of them, it must contain both the leading field, the trailing field, and all fields that are logically between them. For the leading field, you may specify the precision; if you don't, it defaults to 2 digits. If the trailing field is seconds, then you may specify a precision for that, too. If you don't, then 6 digits is the default, which means that your implementation must support at least 6 digits, but it might support more.

  Examples of specifying correct day-time interval: INTERVAL DAY TO HOUR, INTERVAL DAY(6) TO MINUTE, INTERVAL SECOND(7), INTERVAL DAY(5) TO SECOND(10), or INTERVAL MINUTE(3) TO SECOND(4).

  The length of a day-time interval is computed as the length of the leading field plus the lengths of each other field (if any), plus the number of other fields; if the trailing field is SECOND and there's a fractional second precision, then the length is increased by 1 to account for the period.

Intervals and datetimes can be manipulated together. In fact, it's hard to completely separate these two data types. Sure, you can store dates or times without worrying about intervals, but if you ever wanted to subtract two times, you've got to have intervals!

Basically, you can subtract two dates or times to get an interval; you can subtract an interval from a datetime to get a datetime; you can add an interval to a datetime (or add a datetime to an interval) to get a datetime; or you can multiply or divide an interval by a scalar numeric value (or multiply a scalar numeric value by an interval) to get a new interval.

Now that we've looked at the datatypes that SQL-92 provides, let's turn our attention to what must be done when we don't know a value and to how we examine values of database objects.

2.8 **Logic and Null Values**

In what usually passes for real life, we don't always know all the answers when we need to know them. In fact, we often encounter situations where we'd like to know certain information, but it's either not yet available or not applicable to the specific subject.

The same applies in business situations (which, after all, we should consider since few of us would ever have used a computer system otherwise, at least until quite recently). If we're capturing information about people, for instance, we might need to record the maiden names of married women who take their husbands' names, but this is not applicable to single women or to men.

For many years, computerized applications took care of this by trying to use a value of the appropriate type that normally wouldn't be a valid value. For example, they might use blanks or the phrase Not Applicable for the MAIDEN NAME field, or the value –1 for the SALARY field. But, in many cases, there are no invalid values, so applications were forced to use more awkward mechanisms. Furthermore, different application programmers found different mechanisms and invalid values. Some programmers would use blanks and others the phrase Not Applicable or Not Specified or a string of asterisks. When one program stored data and another program read it, the use of different conventions could have results ranging from interesting to costly. (Have you ever received mail addressed to Joe N/A Smith?)

To many people, the solution is obvious: Require the data manager to consistently apply some rule that allows a distinction between real values and other situations (such as Not Applicable, Not Given, or whatever). In SQL, the solution has been to store a sort of flag along with every data item (well, almost every data item; as we shall see later, some items can never be unspecified and therefore do not need this flag) to indicate whether or not the data item has a real value. When the flag is set to indicate that no real value is provided, we say that the data item has *the null value*. This phrase is probably a bit misleading, because *null* means that there is no value at all; nevertheless, it's a convenient shorthand that you will often find in use.

The existence of null values leads to a further complication: three-valued logic. You may recall from logic classes that there is a system of logic that assumes all questions can be answered as True or False. Consequently, you can combine questions with *and* or *or* to discover more complex information.

For example, you could ask, "Is Mr. Big's salary greater than one million dollars?" and expect to get an answer of "True, his salary is greater than one million dollars." Similarly, you could ask, "Is Mr. Big's title 'President'?" and expect an answer of "True, his title is 'President'." You can combine these into a single question in two ways: "Is Mr. Big's salary greater than one million dollars *and* his title 'President'?"; or "Is Mr. Big's salary greater than one million dollars *or* his title 'President'?". You can easily see that these two complex questions are very different. The first asks if *both* facts are true, while the second asks if *either* is true.

In *normal* two-valued logic (the two values being True and False), combining two questions with *and* means that both have to be true for the result to be true; if either is false, then the result is false. If you combine the questions with *or*, then the result is true if either is true; the result is false only if both are false. This is fairly obvious, because we deal with it in everyday life.

However, if we add a third possibility to the various questions, we get a more complex situation. If the answer to the salary question, the title question, or both can be I Don't Know or Unknown, we must define the logical results. SQL-92 uses two sorts of table, shown here as Tables 2-8 and 2-9 to express these rules.

TABLE 2-8
Truth Table for AND

AND	True	False	Unknown
True	True	False	Unknown
False	False	False	False
Unknown	Unknown	False	Unknown

TABLE 2-9	OR	True	False	Unknown
Truth Table for OR	True	True	True	True
	False	True	False	Unknown
	Unknown	True	Unknown	Unknown

Let's try this out with our Mr. Big example. Suppose the answer to the salary question is I Don't Know because the value of the SALARY field for Mr. Big is null. The result of the title question is True, because we know that his title is President. Therefore, the answer to the questions combined with *and* is Unknown AND True, which the table says is Unknown. That makes sense, because the combined question can be True only if the answer to each part is True, but a False result is possible only if the answer to either part is False. We know that one part is True, but we don't know whether the other part is True or False, so we don't know the answer of the result.

If we combine the questions with *or*, the result is True. Why? Well, because the result of an *or* combination is True if either one is True alone. In this case, Mr. Big does have the title President, so that part is True. Therefore, it doesn't matter whether the answer to his salary question is True or False—or Unknown—the answer to the combined question is always True.

Three-valued logic (True, False, and Unknown) is a very powerful tool for querying data. Like any tool, though, it can be misused. Some of SQL's predicates (a *predicate* is a clause that expresses a possible truth about something) use three-valued logic in ways that may not be intuitively obvious. Our advice is to take care that you use the SQL definition of a word rather than the standard English definition. We'll cover SQL predicates in detail in Chapter 7.

We note in passing almost that not everyone approves of three-valued logic. Some notable database personalities have strongly urged the SQL standards committees to abandon the notion of null values in favor of default values. The standards bodies have resisted such suggestions because of years (even decades) of experience with the problems of using only default values. By contrast, other database personalities have suggested that two null values are required and that a four-valued logic is "the answer." To complicate this issue, a group called the DataBase Systems Study Group, or DBSSG, produced a study a number of years ago that identified as many as *29* possible meanings for a null indicator.

We should note that a future revision of the SQL standard will probably have *multiple null values*. Rather than the standard making a (probably arbitrary) decision about whether 1, 2, or 29 null values are required, the groups are likely to allow applications to define the null or nulls required.

2.9 Data Conversions

SQL has long been thought to have *strong typing*. That is, you could mix only operands of the same type in expressions. Now, SQL was never as rigid about its typing as languages like Pascal and Ada, because you could, for example, add an

INTEGER to a SMALLINT. However, unlike languages like PL/I, you could not add an INTEGER to a CHARACTER string, even if the CHARACTER string contained only digits.

In real applications, however, situations often arise where you must somehow add an INTEGER value to an integer value of some digits stored in a CHARACTER value. Before SQL-92, you were required to retrieve the character string containing the digits into your application program, use some application-specific mechanism to convert those digits to an integer, and then feed that integer value back into the database to be added to the INTEGER value. In SQL-92, however, you can specify certain conversions right in your SQL statements.

SQL-92 defines two sorts of data conversions: *implicit* and *explicit*. Implicit conversions continue to be fairly restricted, although not quite as much as in earlier versions of the standard. For example, you can now add an INTEGER to a REAL if your application requires it. If you want something a little more exotic, you must use the CAST function (see Chapter 6) to explicitly convert one type to another type that is compatible with the operation you want to perform. For example, if you happened to have a CHARACTER string that you know (through some application knowledge) contains only digits that can represent an integer value, then you can CAST that CHARACTER string to INTEGER; this will provide you with an integer value that you can add to your existing INTEGER. Of course, if you were wrong—the string contained some characters other than digits, say the letter X—you will get an error.

As you'll see in Chapter 8, the UNION set operator requires two tables that are identical in structure. If you need to combine two tables that are not quite identical in structure in a union-type of operation, then you have to somehow force the structure of the two tables to be the same. Consider a table with columns TITLE, MOVIE TYPE, and OUR COST and a second table with columns TITLE, MOVIE TYPE, and RATING. To form a union of these two tables, we somehow have to accommodate the OUR COST and RATING columns. One way to do this is to force rows from each table to have four columns: TITLE, MOVIE TYPE, OUR COST, and RATING. Of course, OUR COST is meaningless to rows coming from the second table, just as RATING is meaningless to rows from the first table. As we just saw in the preceding section on null values, meaningless data can be represented by a null value. Consequently, we would like to "cast" the null value to be the appropriate data type for OUR COST for all rows coming from the second table. Similarly, we would like to "cast" the null value to be the appropriate data type for RATING for all rows coming from the first table. This is a sort of data conversion operation, even though the *data* involved is the null value; SQL-92 supports just this type of conversion.

Thus far, we've learned about SQL data types and how we can use them as well as how we deal with their absence. Next, we examine how SQL lets you access your database.

2.10 SQL Statements

SQL causes things to happen by the execution of SQL statements. You can embed SQL statements into conventional third-generation programming languages, you can write SQL-only modules containing procedures that you call from your 3GL programs, or you can invoke SQL statements directly. In each case, the actions of you or of your 3GL program cause SQL statements to be executed.

SQL statements come in several categories: data manipulation statements, data definition statements, and management statements. Data manipulation statements, like the ones we will illustrate in Chapter 3, retrieve, store, delete, or update data in the database. Data definition statements allow you to define your database or to modify the definition of your database. Management statements allow you to control the database aspects of your application, such as the termination of transactions or the establishment of certain parameters that affect other statements.

Some statements must execute in the context of a transaction; if no transaction is active, then executing such statements causes a transaction to be started. Other statements must have no transaction active. Some sessions require that a session be active; if you don't have a session going, they will cause a default session to be established. Other statements establish sessions. All this will be made clear as we discuss the individual statements throughout the rest of the book.

2.11 Static Versus Dynamic Execution

SQL statements that are known when you write your application can be embedded directly into your application programs or written directly as modules and procedures. If you do this, you would normally precompile those embedded programs, which, conceptually (implementations differ widely in detail), separates the programs into an SQL part and a 3GL part. The SQL part may be compiled, just as you'd compile a module in an implementation that provided this facility, or it may be handled directly by the precompiler. The 3GL part may be compiled with the compiler for that language, or the precompiler might take care of that, too.

Regardless of the details, the fact that you knew the exact text of your SQL statements at the time you wrote your application means you can direct the SQL implementation (including the precompilers, compilers, and database system) to process the statements long before you have to execute your application. This paradigm is often called *static SQL* because the source text of the statements does not change while your application is running.

However, in many situations, you do not know the precise text of the statements when you write your application. Many so-called 4GL (forth-generation language) products have this limitation. Those products generate the SQL statements while the application is running, as the end user performs various actions at his or her workstation. Because the text of the SQL statement is not known (or not fully known) at the time the application was written, the application programmer cannot direct the implementation to process the statements in advance. They must be processed (compiled or optimized, for example) during program execution. This paradigm is called *dynamic SQL*.

Dynamic SQL has many complicated implications for application programmers as well as for implementations. In many cases, the performance of dynamic SQL is lower than that of static SQL; you can see that doing all of the processing during the execution of your application is bound to use more system resources than merely executing statements, most of which were processed earlier. Furthermore, because you don't know the text of the statements in advance, you don't always know how much data the statements will require from the application program or how much they'll return. These issues are covered thoroughly in Chapter 16.

2.12 The Transaction Model

No one needs the power of a DBMS to manage small amounts of noncritical data. Your personal pasta recipes, for example, can probably be managed with index cards. On the other hand, there are many applications in which the data has significant financial (or other) value. For example, an entertainment distributor that ships compact discs and video tapes to retail outlets may be dealing with millions of dollars of inventory. If records of the inventory, shipments, payments owed, and so forth were lost or damaged, the distributor could very well be driven into bankruptcy. It is extremely important that the data be protected against a wide range of potential problems. Of course, some problems are beyond the scope of a DBMS—physical security of the computer systems or protection against natural disasters, for instance. But some problems are well within the DBMS' scope and these should be addressed.

One problem that plagued application writers for years prior to the development of the DBMS was that of interrupted operations: an application begins to update the data and fails before it makes a complete update. This can be catastrophic. Consider the following sequence of events.

1. The application is told to process an order for 10,000 CDs for a store.
2. The application looks up the information about all the CDs in the database and finds that they're all available.
3. The application then subtracts the quantity of each CD ordered from the inventory quantity.
4. The application generates a shipping order record in the database. (Later, when all outstanding shipping orders are printed, this will trigger the loading of the CDs onto a truck and delivery to the store.)
5. Meanwhile, before the application can generate a billing record that would later be printed and sent to the store, the system crashes!

At this point, the inventory shows that the CDs have been shipped, and the trucking foreman loads the CDs onto a truck and drives away . . . but the store is never billed for the CDs! The distributor now has a major problem—he has shipped 10,000 CDs and will never get paid for them. Of course, the store owner is probably honest and will eventually call the distributor to ask why he hasn't received a bill. But the distributor will encounter delays in getting his money and there will be the added expense of tracking the situation to determine what happened. Some people might consider the reverse situation even worse: If the bill were sent to the store, but the CDs were never shipped, the distributor might be accused of fraud. Situations like this make it clear that there is often no safe order in which to do the operations to ensure against system problems.

The solution lies in a DBMS feature called the *transaction*. A transaction is an *atomic* unit of work (indeed, some DBMS systems use the phrase *unit of work* instead of transaction), meaning it either completely succeeds or has no effect at all (more about this shortly). Returning to the previous example, we might want to redefine the sequence as a transaction.

1. Look up the information about the CDs in the database.
2. If they're all available, then subtract the quantity ordered from the inventory quantity.
3. Generate a shipping order record.
4. Generate a billing record.
5. Update the accounts receivable to reflect the billing record.
6. Generate a reorder record to be printed later, so that replacements can be reordered from the CD manufacturers.
7. Instruct the DBMS to make all actions final.

Presumably, at the end of the day or at various points during the day, all the shipping order records will be printed (and deleted) to trigger the loading of trucks; all the billing records will be printed (and deleted) to be sent to the stores; and so forth.

If at any point anything goes wrong, the entire transaction is *rolled back*, or aborted. This means that *all* actions performed on behalf of the transaction are undone in the database; specifically, the quantity isn't subtracted from the inventory, the shipping order record isn't preserved, the billing record isn't preserved, accounts receivable are not updated, and the reorder record isn't preserved. If nothing goes awry, the database remains updated and all the followup actions are performed at the appropriate time.

Given this model, you can see that both the store and the distributor are protected, because any one database update occurs only if they are all successfully executed; if anything prevents the transaction from completing normally, then it is as though the transaction had never been started.

In recent years, transaction theory has taken quite a few steps forward. Numerous papers and books have advanced the understanding of transactions and helped implementors of DBMSs to build reliable systems. Much recent literature describes transactions as having ACID properties. (No, this doesn't mean that the transaction eats the flesh off your database, nor that it's psychedelic!) The acronym ACID stands for

Atomic, Consistent, Isolated, and Durable

In the book *Transaction Processing: Concepts and Techniques* by Jim Gray and Andreas Reuter,[4] we learn the following about the ACID properties of transactions.

- *Atomicity:* The transaction consists of a collection of actions. The system provides the all-or-nothing illusion that either all these operations are performed or none of them are performed—the transaction either commits or aborts.

- *Consistency:* Transactions are assumed to perform correct transformations of the abstract system state. The transaction concept allows the programmer to declare such consistency points and allows the system to validate them by application-supplied checks.

- *Isolation:* While a transaction is updating shared data, that data may be temporarily inconsistent. Such inconsistent data must not be exposed to other transactions until the updater commits. [Authors' Note: This means until all modifications are officially completed.] The system must give each transaction the illusion that it is running in isolation; that is, it appears that all other transactions either ran previous to the start of this transaction or ran subsequent to its commit.

- *Durability:* Once a transaction commits, its updates must be durable. The new state of all objects it updated will be preserved, even in case of hardware or software failures.

By using a DBMS that implements the ACID properties of transactions, your database operations and the data stored in that database will be protected against the sort of situations that a DBMS can handle. Now all you have to worry about is getting your transactions right!

2.13 Our Example

We've established that for the most part the examples in this book will deal with running a retail video and music store. There will be the occasional need to provide rather dry examples to explain a given topic, but for the most part we offer examples that fall within our sample application environment.

We do need to provide one caution relative to our example. As we introduce new SQL principles and syntax, we occasionally modify one or more table definitions specified in a previous chapter, introduce new tables for the duration of a single example, or make some assumptions. Don't be concerned; even though our overall sample application will be consistent throughout the book, the many examples stand alone and do not rely on syntax, sample data, or other examples from previous chapters. We will explicitly give you all you need to understand each example, including table definitions and assumptions, sample data, or both.

---

4   Jim Gray and Andreas Reuter, *Transaction Processing: Concepts and Techniques,* Morgan Kaufmann Publishers, San Mateo, CA, 1993.

In addition to the SQL-92 syntax examples—and our consolidation of these examples in Appendix B—you may wish to review Appendix A, in which we *briefly* discuss the principles of data modeling and database design. You may wonder, for example, why we use multiple tables to store information about movies instead of consolidating the information into a single table. The answer—*normalization*—can be found in Appendix A. Many of you will be intimately familiar with database design principles, but those of you who haven't been exposed to this subject will find a concise discussion to help you decipher some of the *whys* behind our example.

2.14 Chapter Summary

In this chapter, we've presented a great deal of background information about database concepts, the relational model, and especially SQL.

Some of the more important points to remember include:

- A database is more than just an arbitrary collection of data; rather, a rigid set of rules and operations provides a great deal of added value to the data. Among these rules is the requirement of transaction control: permitting orderly simultaneous access to and modifications of the data by multiple users.

- The fundamentals of the relational database model are relatively simple. You don't need to worry about physical pointers or access methods, but rather simple tuples and attributes (in SQL, that's rows and columns). Furthermore, the relational model is grounded in mathematical principles.

- SQL is *based on* the relational model, but there are distinctions between pure relational databases and SQL databases.

- Many different data types exist within SQL-92. There is a wide variety of available data types on which you can base your data.

- Null values are somewhat more complex than "nothing's here."

You now have enough basic information about SQL to begin learning simple data definition and manipulation statements, which we visit in Chapter 3.

CHAPTER 3

· · · · · · · · · · · · · · · · · ·

Basic Table Creation and
Data Manipulation

3.1 Introduction

Like any language that interfaces with a database management system, SQL has many important and valuable features. The most basic facilities in any database system are the retrieval, manipulation, and modification of data. SQL accomplishes these functions with four basic data manipulation statements: SELECT, INSERT, DELETE, and UPDATE. In our first look at these statements, we explore only their most basic capabilities. In later chapters, we will investigate in detail the more advanced aspects of the statements as well as the other components of SQL that they require.

In this chapter we learn how to perform the following functions with SQL:

- Retrieve all the rows in a table
- Retrieve all nonduplicate rows in a table
- Retrieve rows based on simple criteria, such as the value within a particular column
- Retrieve only selected columns from a table (as compared to all columns)
- Updating some or all rows, such as multiplying a particular column's value by, say, 75% (perhaps to put all movies on sale, for example)
- Inserting new rows—and appropriate values—into a table
- Deleting some or all rows from a table

. . . and much more. Again, the statements we discuss in this chapter should be viewed for now as standalone. That is, the statements are issued and a certain set of actions occurs. In reality, your own applications will likely contain the mixture of some host language (as we discussed in Chapter 2) and the SQL may be static or dynamic, embedded or module-based. For now, though, we concentrate on the basic functions of the statements themselves, rather than on their role in an overall information system.

We also see how to create simple SQL tables as a way of helping you to understand the data objects on which the four basic statements, SELECT, INSERT, DELETE, and UPDATE, operate. In Chapter 4, Data Definition Language, we will discuss table creation in much more detail. Initially, however, we concentrate on basic table creation without all of the powerful features SQL provides.

By the way, in this chapter, you get your first real look at the details of our sample application: the music and video store introduced in Chapter 2 (section 2.13). Don't forget that we introduce this application incrementally—as we introduce a new concept, we show how it enhances the application.

3.2 Set Orientation

As we discussed in Chapter 1, SQL is a set-oriented language. This means that most of the SQL statements that operate on data don't do so one row at a time, but deal with entire groups of rows at once. Sometimes, these groups of rows are entire tables; in other cases, the group of rows is identified by the statement to be a part of a table or even rows from more than one table.

There are two primary models through which data is managed in database and file environments. The first, which many users of COBOL, Ada, and other third-generation programming languages (3GLs) will find familiar, is on a single-instance basis. That is, a particular record of a file or row of a relational database is accessed, examined, and manipulated according to some procedural logic, which is usually encoded in a programming language of some sort. SQL-92 contains facilities, called cursors, to manage single-instance processing requirements; cursors are discussed in subsequent chapters (primarily in Chapter 12).

The alternative processing model, and the one we explore through most of this chapter's statements, is set-oriented; that is (in the case of SQL databases), one or more tables are managed as a whole. Based on rules provided for the entire set of data being considered, data are retrieved from, updated within, or deleted from the specified table(s), without the need to process each row individually in the course of program logic. For those unfamiliar with set-oriented processing, the process will be second nature by the conclusion of this chapter.

3.3 Basic Table Creation

As we discussed in Chapter 2, relational databases are organized around tables, columns, and rows. (Quick quiz: SQL calls them tables, columns, and rows; what are the corresponding relational terms? If you don't remember, or if you skipped over Chapter 2 and don't know the answer, take a look at section 2.5.1.) All SQL-92 data manipulation statements must operate on tables that have been created by you or someone else at some prior time. (Technically, that's not quite accurate. Because of SQL-92's ability to represent tables as table value constructors—seen in

Chapter 9—many SQL-92 data manipulation statements can operate on tables in that form instead of on only those tables stored in the database.)

SQL-92 tables are created through the CREATE TABLE statement. The basic CREATE TABLE statement requires a list of the columns being created, the data types, and, if applicable, sizes of values within each column, in addition to other related aspects (such as whether or not null values are permitted). We'll explore the many alternatives of CREATE TABLE and other aspects of data definition in Chapter 4; our purpose here is to create several simple tables with which we can examine the effects of basic data manipulation statements.

A quick word on SQL-92 syntax: In general, SQL-92 is a free-format language. Statements may be divided among multiple lines for readability, spaces may be used liberally to offset words from one another; parentheses may often be used as well to improve understanding of the order in which portions of a statement are grouped and processed.

In our sample database application, there are several tables that deal with videotapes. For example, our main table that maintains inventory and revenue data might be created as follows:

```
CREATE TABLE MOVIE_TITLES (
        TITLE                        CHARACTER ( 30 ) NOT NULL,
        YEAR_RELEASED                DATE,
        OUR_COST                     DECIMAL ( 5,2 ),
        REGULAR_RENTAL_PRICE         DECIMAL ( 5,2 ),
        CURRENT_RENTAL_PRICE         DECIMAL ( 5,2 ),
        REGULAR_SALE_PRICE           DECIMAL ( 5,2 ),
        CURRENT_SALE_PRICE           DECIMAL ( 5,2 ),
        PART_OF_SERIES               CHARACTER ( 3 ),
        MOVIE_TYPE                   CHARACTER ( 10 ),
        VHS_OWNED                    INTEGER,
        BETA_OWNED                   INTEGER,
        VHS_IN_STOCK                 INTEGER,
        BETA_IN_STOCK                INTEGER,
        TOTAL_VHS_UNITS_RENTED       INTEGER,
        TOTAL_BETA_UNITS_RENTED      INTEGER,
        TOTAL_VHS_UNITS_SOLD         INTEGER,
        TOTAL_BETA_UNITS_SOLD        INTEGER,
        TOTAL_VHS_RENTAL_REVENUE     DECIMAL ( 9,2 ),
        TOTAL_BETA_RENTAL_REVENUE    DECIMAL ( 9,2 ),
        TOTAL_VHS_SALES_REVENUE      DECIMAL ( 9,2 ),
        TOTAL_BETA_SALES_REVENUE     DECIMAL ( 9,2 ) ) ;
```

The MOVIE_TITLES table contains a number of columns having different data types: INTEGER, DECIMAL, and CHARACTER. (Each of these data types and their variations was discussed in Chapter 2.)

A corresponding table can also be created as follows:

```
CREATE TABLE MOVIES_STARS (
            MOVIE_TITLE              CHARACTER ( 30) NOT NULL,
            YEAR_RELEASED           DATE,
            ACTOR_LAST_NAME         CHARACTER ( 35 ) NOT NULL,
            ACTOR_FIRST_NAME        CHARACTER ( 25 ) ) ;
```

In creating each of these tables, the NOT NULL clause is used to indicate that no row within that table is permitted to have a null value for that column's value. That is, the MOVIE_TITLES table must not have any rows with an empty TITLE; this makes a great deal of sense, since the rest of the columns are meaningless without a specific TITLE to which they relate. NOT NULL is a simple example of a *constraint*. We'll discuss other constraints in Chapter 10.

We should note that in our sample, we assume that the combination of a movie's title and the year it was released will be sufficient to uniquely identify a given movie. For example, movies such as *The Ten Commandments* and *A Star is Born* have been remade several times. For the purposes of our database, we'll assume that no two movies by the same title were released in the same year.

The ACTOR_FIRST_NAME column, however, is permitted to have null values to allow for one-name stars such as Cher and Sting, or for group stars such as The Marx Brothers or Monty Python.

Another brief syntactic note: At first, we will show all SQL statements ending with a semicolon (;). Later, when we discuss embedded SQL, we will show how some languages use a semicolon to terminate an SQL statement, while other languages use other conventions.

Let's look at how the rows of data might look in the MOVIES_STARS table, Table 3-1, (disregarding the year released for now).

In actuality, of course, any sizable video store would have a database of thousands of movie titles. For obvious reasons of space (and boredom), we need to present portions of tables rather than entire lists of thousands of movies. And remember, we are also dealing with a music store, so we have thousands of CD /album/tape titles as well. This restriction *does* present a problem in certain circumstances, such as when we introduce expressions like COUNT. In these instances, we will make the obviously faulty assumption that the respective segments we present for our examples represent the entire table. The important thing is that you understand the concepts presented in each example, and not whether your favorite Mickey Rourke title is included! Okay, back to SQL.

Because most of SQL's data manipulation statements are set-oriented, the order in which the rows are processed is not significant. There are, of course, situations in which the order of rows is important (such as retrieving rows to be displayed on a terminal or report); SQL's cursors provide an ordering facility for that requirement. Your implementation will likely have some hidden order to rows, such as the order in which they are physically stored in the database, but that is unimportant to SQL.

MOVIE_TITLE	ACTOR_LAST_NAME	ACTOR_FIRST_NAME
The Way We Were	Redford	Robert
The Way We Were	Streisand	Barbra
Prince of Tides	Nolte	Nick
Prince of Tides	Streisand	Barbra
Life of Brian	Monty Python	
48 Hours	Nolte	Nick
48 Hours	Murphy	Eddie
A Star is Born	Kristofferson	Kris
A Star is Born	Streisand	Barbra
Another 48 Hours	Murphy	Eddie
Another 48 Hours	Nolte	Nick
Beverly Hills Cop	Murphy	Eddie
Beverly Hills Cop	Reinhold	Judge
Beverly Hills Cop II	Murphy	Eddie
Beverly Hills Cop II	Reinhold	Judge
Pretty Woman	Roberts	Julia
Pretty Woman	Gere	Richard
Moonstruck	Cher	
Moonstruck	Cage	Nicholas
Raising Arizona	Cage	Nicholas
Raising Arizona	Hunter	Holly
The Outlaw Josey Wales	Eastwood	Clint
The Outlaw Josey Wales	Locke	Sondra
Duck Soup	Marx Brothers	
A Night at the Opera	Marx Brothers	

TABLE 3-1
MOVIES_STARS

3.4 Basic Data Manipulation

Given Table 3-1, let's look at some sample data manipulation statements. The basic retrieval method is through the SELECT statement. The basic syntax of the SELECT statement is

```
SELECT columns
   FROM tables
   WHERE predicates
```

The complete syntax for a SELECT statement is more complicated, but this is sufficient to introduce the statement for now. Diagram RR1 shows what the limited statement looks like in *railroad diagram* form.

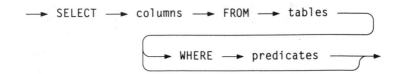

Depending on your predicates, or search criteria, the specified column(s) will be retrieved from some or all rows in the table. For example, to retrieve a list of the movie titles stored in the MOVIES_STARS table (of which Table 3-1 is a portion), you would issue the following statement (which contains no search criteria):

```
SELECT MOVIE_TITLE
   FROM MOVIES_STARS ;
```

which would yield the result shown in Table 3-2.

TABLE 3-2

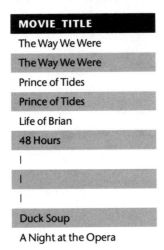

MOVIE_TITLE
The Way We Were
The Way We Were
Prince of Tides
Prince of Tides
Life of Brian
48 Hours
I
I
I
Duck Soup
A Night at the Opera

3.4.1   DISTINCT

Since most of the movie titles are stored more than once in the MOVIES_STARS table, based on the fact that there is usually more than one star in that movie, a great deal of redundant information is retrieved in the form of duplicate movie titles. To eliminate the duplicate titles, the DISTINCT clause may be used as part of the SELECT statement:

```
SELECT DISTINCT MOVIE_TITLE
   FROM MOVIES_STARS ;
```

which would yield the result shown in Table 3-3.

TABLE 3-3

MOVIE_TITLE
The Way We Were
Prince of Tides
48 Hours
A Star is Born
Another 48 Hours
Beverly Hills Cop
Beverly Hills Cop II

3.4.2 Inside the SELECT Statement

At this point, it's time for us to talk a little bit about what the term, SELECT *statement,* really means. SQL has two distinct uses of the word SELECT. One of these is, in fact, to initiate a SELECT statement. The other is to define a table-valued expression (often called a *query expression*), which can appear in many places in the language. In fact, almost anywhere that you can use a table, you can use one of these table-valued expressions.

In *direct invocation* of SQL (usually interpreted to mean *interactive* SQL), we can use a SELECT statement that retrieves multiple rows from a table. This is possible because the rows are merely displayed on your terminal or on your printer. However, if you write an application program using SQL statements that interact with a 3GL program, you cannot use a multiple-row SELECT statement, because it could retrieve an arbitrary number of rows and 3GLs cannot deal with that sort of uncertainty. In embedded SQL, the SELECT statement can return (at most) one row; if it attempts to return more than one row, you will get an error.

Although we often use the SELECT statement in this book to illustrate the contents of a table or to demonstrate the result of some feature, you must understand that the actual SELECT statement of embedded SQL does not have this behavior.

Similarly, the SELECT statement (or query expression) in SQL cannot use the ORDER BY clause except in direct invocation. Cursors can be defined with an ORDER BY clause, as we will see in Chapter 12.

3.4.3 ORDER BY

To receive the same result we saw with SELECT, but in alphabetical order, the ORDER BY clause may be added to the statement:

```
SELECT DISTINCT MOVIE_TITLE
  FROM MOVIES_STARS
  ORDER BY MOVIE_TITLE ASC ;
```

In this example, only one column is used for the ordering. ASC indicates ascending order, as opposed to DESC for descending order. The statement yields the result shown in Table 3-4. (Remember, our example is predicated on a working database that contains thousands of movie titles, all of which cannot be shown in any given table segment used in this book. Accordingly, some titles are seen here that did not appear in the earlier *unordered* segment, Table 3-1.)

TABLE 3-4

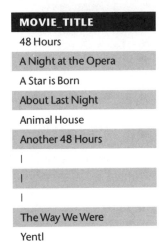

MOVIE_TITLE
48 Hours
A Night at the Opera
A Star is Born
About Last Night
Animal House
Another 48 Hours
The Way We Were
Yentl

3.4.4 WHERE and *

The WHERE clause is the primary vehicle by which retrieval of certain rows that meet a particular set of conditions is accomplished. For example, to answer the question "What movies do we carry that star Eddie Murphy?" you might issue the following statement:

```
SELECT *
  FROM MOVIES_STARS
  WHERE ACTOR_LAST_NAME = 'Murphy' ;
```

The WHERE clause requires a search condition (one or more predicates combined with AND, OR, and NOT) to specify the conditions under which you want rows to be chosen for inclusion in your set of data. We'll learn more about the WHERE clause in Chapter 9.

The asterisk (*) means "give me all columns" (unlike our previous examples, where only one column, MOVIE_TITLE, was specified). Table 3-5 shows the answer SQL-92 will yield for our SELECT * statement with WHERE clause. However—a *big* caution here—the use of the asterisk is not necessarily a good idea. You should be extremely careful when you choose to write SELECT *. In earlier versions of the SQL standard, like SQL-89, the structure of a database couldn't be changed by an application, so the meaning of SELECT * never varied. However, in SQL-92, you can add columns to or drop columns from your tables (as you have been able to with real products in use for many years now). That makes the meaning of SELECT * variable; at one point, it might mean "get me columns A,B, and C from Table X," while after a structural change, it might mean "get me columns A, B, D, and F from Table X."

TABLE 3-5

MOVIE_TITLE	ACTOR_LAST_NAME	ACTOR_FIRST_NAME
48 Hours	Murphy	Eddie
Another 48 Hours	Murphy	Eddie
Beverly Hills Cop	Murphy	Eddie
Beverly Hills Cop II	Murphy	Eddie
Coming to America	Murphy	Eddie
I		
I		
Raw	Murphy	Eddie

If you are using direct invocation of SQL at your terminal, the effect is merely more or fewer columns being displayed on the screen (and, of course, it is a tremendous shortcut compared with having to explicitly and repeatedly type in a long list of column names). However, if you are writing an embedded SQL program, the entire program can start returning errors related to an improper number of columns. Therefore, excepting direct invocation, we recommend that you avoid using SELECT * in favor of explicitly coding the exact list of columns that you want to retrieve. It takes a bit more typing when you are developing your programs, but the good programming concept of avoiding system-provided default values and actions directly applies to this recommended explicitness. At some points in this book we will use an asterisk as a space saver in our examples; in practice, we would explicitly list the column names.

Speaking of explicitly stating the actions you wish to occur; the same generalization can be applied to selection parameters. Let's see how predicates sometimes (often, actually) have to be coupled together in order to achieve the desired results.

3.4.5 Search Conditions Using AND

Note the result (Table 3-6) yielded by the following SELECT statement. To receive a list of movies that star Demi Moore, the following statement does *not* yield the correct result.

```
SELECT MOVIE_TITLE, ACTOR_LAST_NAME, ACTOR_FIRST_NAME
   FROM MOVIES_STARS
   WHERE ACTOR_LAST_NAME = 'Moore' ;
```

TABLE 3-6

MOVIE_TITLE	ACTOR_LAST_NAME	ACTOR_FIRST_NAME
About Last Night	Moore	Demi
Ten	Moore	Dudley
Ordinary People	Moore	Mary

In this case, our request must be more specific. Use of the AND operator will satisfy our needs (see Table 3-7).

```
SELECT MOVIE_TITLE, ACTOR_LAST_NAME, ACTOR_FIRST_NAME
  FROM MOVIES_STARS
  WHERE ACTOR_LAST_NAME = 'Moore'
    AND ACTOR_FIRST_NAME = 'Demi' ;
```

TABLE 3-7

MOVIE_TITLE	ACTOR_LAST_NAME	ACTOR_FIRST_NAME
About Last Night	Moore	Demi
Mortal Thoughts	Moore	Demi

In Chapter 5, we'll discuss the use of AND, OR, and other search condition operators in more detail.

3.4.6 More SELECT Statements

Let's look at our MOVIE_TITLES table (Table 3-8, again, just a small portion of the database) to examine some other forms of the SELECT statement.

TABLE 3-8

TITLE	OUR_COST	REGULAR_RENTAL_PRICE	CURRENT_RENTAL_PRICE	REGULAR_SALE_PRICE	CURRENT_SALE_PRICE
The Way We Were	14.95	1.99	1.99	19.95	19.95
Prince of Tides	55.95	3.99	3.99	65.95	65.95
48 Hours	29.95	2.99	1.99	34.95	31.95
A Star is Born	24.95	1.99	1.99	29.95	29.95
Another 48 Hours	29.95	2.99	1.99	34.95	34.95
Beverly Hills Cop	29.95	2.99	1.99	34.95	34.95
Beverly Hills Cop II	29.95	2.99	1.99	34.95	34.95
Pretty Woman	55.95	3.99	3.99	65.95	65.95
Silverado	24.95	1.99	1.99	29.95	29.95
Moonstruck	35.95	2.99	2.99	39.95	39.95
Raising Arizona	24.95	1.99	1.99	29.95	29.95
Animal House	14.95	1.99	1.99	19.95	19.95
Ten	14.95	1.99	1.99	19.95	12.95

Perhaps we are interested in listing all movies that are on sale, either as rentals or with a special sale price. We can find these by comparing the current rental and sale prices with their respective regular prices (see Table 3-9). If either is less than the regular price, the movie is on sale. To accomplish this, we introduce two new aspects to the SELECT statement: the OR operator (as compared with the AND operator just covered) and the use of a comparison operator; in this case, the less than (<) sign.

To avoid any possibility of misunderstanding between you and your DBMS (or, for that matter, between you and the people who will maintain your programs years from now), you might want to use parentheses whenever you combine multiple predicates to ensure that the intended results are obtained.

```
SELECT TITLE, REGULAR_RENTAL_PRICE,
       CURRENT_RENTAL_PRICE, REGULAR_SALE_PRICE,
       CURRENT_SALE_PRICE
  FROM MOVIE_TITLES
  WHERE
    (CURRENT_SALE_PRICE < REGULAR_SALE_PRICE) OR
    (CURRENT_RENTAL_PRICE < REGULAR_RENTAL_PRICE) ;
```

TABLE 3-9

TITLE	OUR_ COST	REGULAR_ RENTAL_ PRICE	CURRENT_ RENTAL_ PRICE	REGULAR_ SALE_ PRICE	CURRENT_ SALE_ PRICE
48 Hours	29.95	2.99	1.99	34.95	31.95
Another 48 Hours	29.95	2.99	1.99	34.95	34.95
Beverly Hills Cop	29.95	2.99	1.99	34.95	34.95
Beverly Hills Cop II	29.95	2.99	1.99	34.95	34.95
Ten	4.95	1.99	1.99	19.95	12.95

Suppose you want to see the total amount of units, both VHS and Beta, rented for each movie in stock. We might use the table shown in Table 3-10 to start.

TABLE 3-10

TITLE	TOTAL_VHS_ UNITS_RENTED	TOTAL_BETA_ UNITS_RENTED	TOTAL_VHS_ UNITS_SOLD	TOTAL_BETA_ UNITS_SOLD
The Way We Were	321	89	23	8
Prince of Tides	875	132	98	21
The Seven Samurai	562	76	24	12
48 Hours	1234	234	456	98
Casablanca	987	143	134	32
Ishtar	2450	346	234	210
North Dallas Forty	890	123	122	18

Then we could use the query:

```
SELECT TITLE, TOTAL_VHS_UNITS_RENTED,
    TOTAL_BETA_UNITS_RENTED,
    TOTAL_VHS_UNITS_RENTED + TOTAL_BETA_UNITS_RENTED
  FROM MOVIE_TITLES;
```

which yields the following result:

TABLE 3-11

TITLE	TOTAL_VHS UNITS_RENTED	TOTAL_BETA UNITS_RENTED	
The Way We Were	321	89	410
Prince of Tides	875	132	1007
The Seven Samurai	562	76	638
48 Hours	1234	234	1468
Casablanca	987	143	1130
Ishtar	2450	1346	3796
North Dallas Forty	890	123	1013

In later chapters, we'll discuss additional forms of data manipulation as well as advanced forms of the SELECT statement.

3.5 Updating Information

It's not sufficient just to be able to retrieve information from your database; data modifications are required as part of most applications. The SQL UPDATE statement is used to modify the values of one or more columns in one or more rows, according to the search conditions you specify. The format of the UPDATE statement is shown in Diagram RR2.

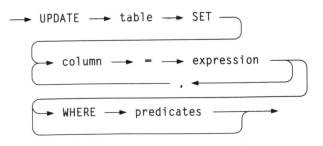

Suppose that the store is running a special weekend promotion to celebrate the grand opening of another branch, and all movies will be on sale for 99 cents. The following statement can be used to adjust all current rental prices to the new sale price.

```
UPDATE MOVIE_TITLES
   SET CURRENT_RENTAL_PRICE = 0.99 ;
```

Suppose we want to reduce the current rental price of all tapes by $1.00 except for those tapes that currently rent for $1.99. The following statement would accomplish this change.

```
UPDATE MOVIE_TITLES
   SET CURRENT_RENTAL_PRICE =
       (CURRENT_RENTAL_PRICE - 1.00)
   WHERE CURRENT_RENTAL_PRICE < > 1.99 ;
```

The <> operator signifies *not equal to*. Table 3-12 results.

TABLE 3-12

TITLE	OUR_COST	REGULAR_RENTAL_PRICE	CURRENT_RENTAL_PRICE	REGULAR_SALE_PRICE	CURRENT_SALE_PRICE
I					
I					
I					
Another 48 Hours	29.95	2.99	1.99	34.95	34.95
Beverly Hills Cop	29.95	2.99	1.99	34.95	34.95
Beverly Hills Cop II	29.95	2.99	1.99	34.95	34.95
Pretty Woman	55.95	3.99	2.99	65.95	65.95
Silverado	24.95	1.99	1.99	29.95	29.95
Moonstruck	35.95	2.99	1.99	39.95	39.95
Raising Arizona	24.95	1.99	1.99	29.95	29.95
I					
I					
I					

Let's go back to our earlier example of listing movies currently on sale, either on a rental or for-sale basis (see Table 3-9). Suppose the store institutes a policy that all movies currently on sale as rentals (current rental price is less than the regular rental price) but that don't have a purchase price that is on sale (current sale price less than the regular sale price) will have a current sale price that is $5.00 less than the regular sale price. We can accomplish this by issuing:

```
UPDATE MOVIE_TITLES
    SET CURRENT_SALE_PRICE = (REGULAR_SALE_PRICE - 5.00)
  WHERE
    (CURRENT_RENTAL_PRICE < REGULAR_RENTAL_PRICE)
    AND
    (CURRENT_SALE_PRICE = REGULAR_SALE_PRICE) ;
```

which yields Table 3-13.

TABLE 3-13

TITLE	OUR COST	REGULAR RENTAL PRICE	CURRENT RENTAL PRICE	REGULAR SALE PRICE	CURRENT SALE PRICE
The Way We Were	14.95	1.99	1.99	19.95	19.95
Prince of Tides	55.95	3.99	3.99	65.95	65.95
Yentl	24.95	1.99	1.99	29.95	24.95
48 Hours	29.95	2.99	1.99	34.95	29.95
A Star is Born	24.95	1.99	1.99	29.95	29.95
Another 48 Hours	29.95	2.99	1.99	34.95	29.95
Beverly Hills Cop	29.95	2.99	1.99	34.95	34.95
Beverly Hills Cop II	29.95	2.99	1.99	34.95	29.95
Pretty Woman	55.95	3.99	3.99	65.95	65.95
Silverado	24.95	1.99	1.99	29.95	29.95
Moonstruck	35.95	2.99	2.99	39.95	39.95
Raising Arizona	24.95	1.99	1.99	29.95	29.95
The Outlaw Josey Wales	24.95	1.99	1.99	29.95	29.95
Duck Soup	14.95	1.99	1.99	19.95	19.95
A Night at the Opera	14.95	1.99	1.99	19.95	19.95
About Last Night	14.95	1.99	1.99	19.95	19.95
Animal House	14.95	1.99	1.99	19.95	19.95
Ten	14.95	1.99	1.99	19.95	12.95

Let's look at the statement used to yield Table 3-13. It is not sufficient to simply reduce (via the SET) the current sale price by $5.00 for each rental movie on sale (as denoted by the price comparison in that area), because there may be movies already on sale both in the rental and for-sale areas. An additional comparison must be done as part of the predicate to ensure that only those movies not currently on sale (as determined by current and regular sale prices being equal) are updated.

You can change multiple column values in the same UPDATE statement. Assume that our sole distributor reduces our cost on every movie by $1.00 and, correspondingly, we want to reduce the regular sale price by $1.00. (We'll be nice and pass our savings on to the customer; in fact, let's put that in our advertising strategy.) You could utilize:

```
UPDATE MOVIE_TITLES
    SET OUR_COST = ( OUR_COST - 1.00 ),
        REGULAR_SALE_PRICE = (REGULAR_SALE_PRICE - 1.00 ) ;
```

To take this example a bit further, let's do the price reduction for all movies except for the movie *Reds*.

```
UPDATE MOVIE_TITLES
    SET OUR_COST = ( OUR_COST - 1.00 ),
        REGULAR_SALE_PRICE = (REGULAR_SALE_PRICE - 1.00 )
    WHERE TITLE <> 'Reds' ;
```

3.6 Inserting Information

The way that data is put into a table for retrieval or modification is with an INSERT statement. There are several variations of the SQL-92 INSERT statement. In the simplest instance, a list of values is provided (as part of the statement) that provides each column of the new row in the order specified at the time the table was defined (or subsequently altered).

```
INSERT INTO table
    VALUES (value-1, value-2,..., value-n) ;
```

For example, the following statements add new rows to the MOVIES_STARS table.

```
INSERT INTO MOVIES_STARS
    VALUES (
      'Rocky Horror Picture Show',
      1977,
      'Curry',
      'Tim' ) ;

INSERT INTO MOVIES_STARS
    VALUES (
      'Rocky Horror Picture Show',
      1977,
      'Bostwick',
      'Barry' ) ;
```

```
INSERT INTO MOVIES_STARS
    VALUES (
    'Rocky Horror Picture Show',
    1977,
    'Loaf',
    'Meat' ) ;
```

(Okay, so the last one might be a bit inaccurate . . .)

The alternative form of the INSERT statement is useful for large tables (in terms of number of defined columns), particularly when only some columns will have data entered initially. In fact, this form is preferable to the one we just saw because of the self-documenting nature of the format:

```
INSERT INTO table (column-1, column-2,..., column-n)
    VALUES (value-1, value-2,..., value-n) ;
```

The columns specified as part of the INSERT statement needn't be in any specific order as long as the orders of the column and value lists match with one another. For example, the following statement will add a new row to the MOVIE_TITLES table with partially complete information.

```
INSERT INTO MOVIE_TITLES
        ( TITLE, YEAR_PRODUCED, OUR_COST,
          REGULAR_RENTAL_PRICE, CURRENT_RENTAL_PRICE,
          REGULAR_SALE_PRICE, CURRENT_SALE_PRICE   )
    VALUES (
        'Rocky Horror Picture Show', 1977, 19.95,
        2.99, 2.99, 24.95, 24.95 ) ;
```

The resulting table *may* look like Table 3-14.

TABLE 3-14

TITLE	OUR_ COST	REGULAR_ RENTAL_ PRICE	CURRENT_ RENTAL_ PRICE	REGULAR_ SALE_ PRICE	CURRENT_ SALE_ PRICE
The Way We Were	14.95	1.99	1.99	19.95	19.95
I					
I					
I					
I					
Animal House	14.95	1.99	1.99	19.95	19.95
Ten	14.95	1.99	1.99	19.95	12.95
Rocky Horror Picture Show	19.95	2.99	2.99	24.95	24.95

Why do we say that the table *may* look like that above? In the above case, the new row is inserted at the end of the table. Placement of new rows is an implementation-specific issue. Since any order-specific processing is handled through the ORDER BY clause or through the use of implementation techniques like indices, physical placement is not an issue for most casual users.

In fact, the SQL language provides no mechanism at all for users to control the physical placement of a row in a table. If your implementation uses the value of some column or the sequence in which rows were added as a physical placement criterion, then the behavior may be predictable. However, the standard leaves such behavior strictly to the implementor's decision.

In general, we recommend that column names be specified even if every column in the new row will be assigned a value. Diagram RR3 illustrates this point. This protects against subsequent reordering of the table's columns or other unforeseen problems.

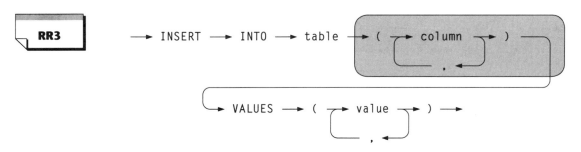

3.7 Deleting Information

The DELETE statement operates in much the same way as the SELECT statement, with the primary distinction that rows meeting specified criteria are deleted rather than retrieved. Diagram RR4 illustrates the syntax of the DELETE statement.

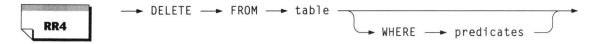

For example, the following statements will delete all rows for the movie *Raising Arizona* if our store decides to remove that movie from its inventory.

```
DELETE FROM MOVIE_TITLES
  WHERE TITLE = 'Raising Arizona' ;

DELETE FROM MOVIES_STARS
  WHERE TITLE = 'Raising Arizona' ;
```

In Chapter 10, we'll discuss how the concept of referential integrity can be applied to ensure that rows from multiple tables that are "related" to one another can be protected from deletion of information from one table but not another. With the previous deletion statement sequence, you are forced to remember all of the tables in which relevant data might appear.

To delete all records from a given table, the following statement would be used.

```
DELETE FROM MOVIES_STARS ;
```

Note that, in all forms of the delete statement, no column names are specified; entire rows are deleted rather than individual columns. To "delete" information from a specific column in one or more rows—while still maintaining the rows' existence in the database—the UPDATE statement would be used to set the value of the column to null. (As we will see in Chapter 4, it is also possible to completely eliminate all data and metadata for a column from a table.)

3.8 Chapter Summary

In this chapter, we looked at basic SQL-92 operations: creating simple tables, retrieving information, and updating tables through update, deletion, and insertion operations. We discussed how you can retrieve one or more rows and/or retrieve one or more columns from a single table. We also saw how you can "blindly" retrieve all rows regardless of their contents.

We discussed how you can use WHERE to specify many different varieties of selection criteria: equality to a specific value, having a value greater than or less than some other value, and combining selection criteria by using AND and OR.

Further, we saw that information access is not limited to retrieval. Data may be inserted into, updated within, or deleted from any given table through statements analogous to the basic SELECT statement.

Those readers unfamiliar with previous versions of SQL now have a basic understanding of the types of functionality supported by the language and are ready to move ahead to the more advanced facilities of SQL-92.

CHAPTER 4

· · · · · · · · · · · · · · · · · ·

Basic Data Definition Language (DDL)

4.1 Introduction

In the previous chapter, we briefly looked at how tables and columns were created in SQL. You will recall that the CREATE TABLE statement is used to . . . well, create tables. Along with a table, one or more columns are created at that time. And, as you might also recall, the properties of those columns—in a most elementary sense, the data types and (if applicable) sizes—are also defined.

In Chapter 2, we talked about a number of other database objects: schemas, catalogs, views, and others. As we learn in this chapter, SQL's Data Definition Language (DDL) has facilities through which you can define not only tables and columns but also other database objects. Additionally, we discuss how you can modify and delete these objects through DDL (although many SQL experts refer to this function as Schema Manipulation Language, or SML).

There are several advanced DDL facets that we don't discuss in this chapter, deferring them for consideration until Chapter 10. These facets include:

- UNIQUE and PRIMARY KEY: These are the uniqueness constraints.
- CHECK: Among other things, this is used to enforce ranges and lists of values for specific columns.
- FOREIGN KEY, REFERENCES, and the other aspects of referential integrity: These specific kinds of multitable integrity constraints ensure that referential integrity is maintained.

Keep in mind, then, as we go through this chapter that we are discussing *basic* DDL. The advanced concepts we discuss in Chapter 10 will round out your repertoire of DDL skills.

4.2   Data Definition Fundamentals

As we have said before, the basic unit of data on which SQL operates is the table. Because SQL operations are based on this explicit structure, tables are the basic unit of data management you will encounter. Before we can make much progress in our investigation of tables and how they are created and destroyed, we need to understand the matrix in which tables are embedded. Tables are embedded in a matrix structure of increasing abstractions (remember that tables themselves are composed of rows and columns). Figure 4-1 illustrates the relationship between the data objects we discuss in this chapter; specifically, it shows how collections of columns (tables) are contained within collections of tables (schemas), which are further contained within collections of schemas (catalogs).

Finally, an SQL-92 database consists of all data described by schemas under the control of a given DBMS at any one time. It corresponds directly to a cluster of catalogs. (In point of fact, the SQL standard shrinks from actually using or defining the word *database,* presumably because the word already carries a variety of meanings among different vendors and users. Instead, it uses the term *SQL-data* to refer to the data and *schema* to refer to metadata.)

FIGURE 4-1
Abstraction in
the SQL
Database
Environment

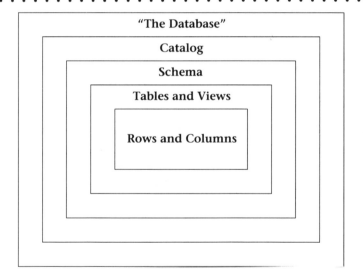

Let's look a little more closely at some of the data objects summarized in Figure 4-1. We introduced many of them in Chapter 2; in the sections that follow, we give an SQL *spin* to the generic concepts.

4.2.1   Schema Concepts

We can think of tables as being *contained* in a higher level construct called a *schema.* We use the idea of containment in many places in this book when discussing relationships between database objects. This usage doesn't imply any sort of physical storage containment or proximity. Instead, it simply means that the containing object has a hierarchical relationship to the contained object; for example, for each schema, there are zero or more tables, and for each table, there is exactly one schema to which it belongs.

We can think of a schema as a place where tables and related objects can be collected together under one qualifying name. SQL provides statements for creating and destroying schemas, too, as we shall see later in this chapter. Perhaps an analogy would be helpful: The relationship between a schema and its tables is similar to that of an operating system file directory and the files contained within that directory.

Schemas were originally designed (in SQL-86, for instance) as *containers* for tables that allowed a specific user, identified by an authorization identifier, to be able to create his or her own tables without the concern of choosing the same table name as some other user. In SQL-86 and SQL-89, the name of a schema was identical to the authorization identifier of the user who created—and owned—the schema. In SQL-92, however, this tight coupling between schemas and users was eliminated in recognition of the user's need to create multiple schemas.

As long as schema names and authorization identifiers had a one-to-one correspondence, there was no problem with having duplicate schema names. After all, a given authorization identifier was unique within the system. However, with the freedom of a single user to create and own multiple schemas comes the possibility that two or more users would want to use the same name for their schemas. The fact that DBMSs are moving rapidly toward distributed database support poses a further complication, since management problems (including naming problems) are magnified significantly in a distributed environment. To reduce the probability as well as the impact of schema name duplication, SQL-92 provides a container for schemas, called a *catalog,* which we discuss next.

All of the objects contained in a schema are owned by the same authorization identifier that owns the schema itself. A schema is initially created with a CREATE SCHEMA statement; its initial definition can be modified after the fact by using the statements presented in this chapter.

The full names of schema objects have three components: the catalog name, the schema name, and the object name. Using table as the object, the three components would be specified in the order:

catalog name . schema name . table name

Components are separated by periods when more than one is used. For example, if you have a catalog named CAT1 and it contains a schema named STORE, which in turn contains a table named MOVIE_TITLES, then you can refer to that table as MOVIE_TITLES, as STORE.MOVIE_TITLES, or as CAT1.STORE.MOVIE_TITLES. If there is any chance of ambiguity (for example, if you are trying to define a view in schema BUSINESS that references a table in schema STORE), you must *qualify* the table name (that is, explicitly state the name of the schema to which you are referring). If you write your table names without specifying a schema name (or with a schema name but not a catalog name), a default schema name (and catalog name) is supplied by the system for you. This default depends on several factors, but you can sometimes govern the default by the way in which you write your programs (Chapter 11 provides more information on customizing your programs).

4.2.2 Catalog Concepts

Catalogs are named collections of schemas in an SQL environment. An SQL environment contains zero or more catalogs and a catalog contains one or more schemas. Every catalog contains a schema named INFORMATION_SCHEMA that contains the views of the information schema, or *system tables*. (See Chapter 19 for further details on the information schema.) The creation and destruction of catalogs is implementation-defined; that is, SQL provides no facilities for this. The set of catalogs that can be referenced in any SQL statement, during any particular transaction or during the course of an SQL session, is also implementation-defined.

We like to think of a catalog as a unit of management for a DBMS environment. At any instant in time, a DBMS can access only a finite number of catalogs (perhaps only one). This finite number is called a *cluster*; the names of catalogs must be unique within a cluster. (Note that in the SQL standard, a cluster has no name of its own.)

A cluster contains all of the catalogs that an SQL DBMS can access in a single connection (see Chapter 15 for a discussion of connections and remote access). Therefore, the name of a connection provides a sort of a name for a cluster, although it cannot be used to qualify the name of catalogs in the cluster.

4.2.3 Tables

Let's discuss tables themselves a bit further now. SQL provides several types of tables, most of which are new to SQL-92. SQL-89 provided three types of tables.

- Persistent base tables (usually shorted to base tables)
- Viewed tables (or views)
- Derived tables

For many applications, these three types are perfectly adequate; however, other applications, such as those that successively refine their information, demand additional types of tables. We'll take a brief look at these three basic table types, after looking more closely at the concept of a table.

A table is a *multiset* of rows. (In Chapter 2, we discussed the concept of a multiset.) A row is a nonempty sequence of values. This means that a row has to have at least one column, and the order among columns is the same for all rows within a table; you would never find TITLE before OUR_COST in one row but following it in another. Every row of the same table has the same number of columns and contains a value for every column of that table. The ith value in every row of a table is a value of the ith column of that table. The row is the smallest unit of data that can be inserted into a table and deleted from a table.

The *degree* of a table is the number of columns of that table. At any instant in time, the degree of a table is the same as the cardinality of each of its rows and the cardinality of a table is the same as the cardinality of each of its columns. A table whose cardinality is 0 is said to be empty.

A table is either a *base table*, a *viewed table*, or a *derived table*. Further, a base table is either a *persistent base table*, a *global temporary table*, a *created local temporary table*, or a *declared local temporary table*. A base table is a table whose data is actually stored somewhere—either on disk or in memory. Contrast this with a virtual table, whose data is *derived* as it is requested by an application. Of course, the data "visible" in a virtual table must have originated in one or more base tables, but it may have been transformed in the process. Some virtual tables exist only for the duration of an SQL statement (see Chapter 9 for information on query expressions), whereas others are specified in the metadata of your database and have some degree of persistence to them.

Virtual tables with persistent metadata are known as *views* or *viewed tables*. (There isn't a special name for the other sort of virtual table, so most people refer to these by the generic, virtual tables.)

Base Tables

Let's look at the types of base tables.

- *Persistent Base Table:* A named table defined by a CREATE TABLE statement that does *not* specify TEMPORARY.
- *Global Temporary Table:* A named table defined by a CREATE TABLE statement that specifies GLOBAL TEMPORARY.
- *Created Local Temporary Table:* A named table defined by CREATE TABLE statement that specifies LOCAL TEMPORARY.
- *Declared Local Temporary Table:* A named table that is declared as a component of a module.

Temporary Table Rules and Characteristics

Global temporary tables and created local temporary tables are a bit like persistent base tables because their definitions are in a schema and stay there until explicitly removed. However, they differ from persistent base tables because their physical existence (their *extension* if you prefer that terminology) is effectively materialized *only* when they are referenced in an SQL session.

Every module or embedded SQL program in every SQL session that references a created local temporary table causes a distinct instance of that created local temporary table to be materialized. That is, the contents of a *global* temporary table or a created local temporary table *cannot* be shared between SQL sessions like the contents of a persistent base table (Figure 4-2). In addition, the contents of a created *local* temporary table cannot be shared between modules or embedded SQL programs in a single SQL session.

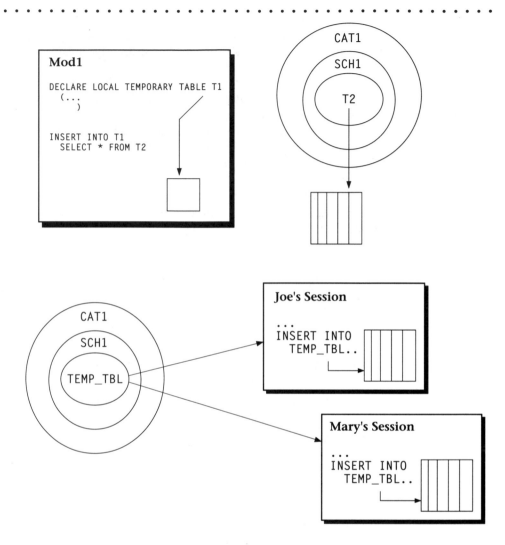

FIGURE 4-2
Temporary
Tables and
Sessions

In SQL language, the name and the scope of the name of a global temporary table or of a created local temporary table are indistinguishable from those of a persistent base table. The contents of these table types vary in their distinction.

- Global temporary table contents are distinct within SQL sessions.
- Created local temporary tables are distinct within modules and embedded SQL programs within SQL sessions.

A declared local temporary table manifests itself the first time any procedure is executed in the module (or embedded SQL program) that contains the temporary table declaration. To put this another way, a declared local temporary table is accessible only by the execution of procedures within the module (or SQL statements in the embedded SQL program) that contains the temporary table declaration. All references to a declared local temporary table are prefixed by MODULE.

Let's look at a few examples of temporary tables. If you create a temporary table with

```
CREATE GLOBAL TEMPORARY TABLE GTT (....)
```

then you can insert rows in it and share the data among all your modules or embedded SQL programs (in the same session!) as follows.

```
INSERT INTO MYSCHEMA.GTT VALUES (....)

SELECT * FROM GTT....
```

The same is true for local temporary tables except that you cannot share data between modules or embedded programs in your session.

Declared local temporary tables are declared with

```
DECLARE LOCAL TEMPORARY TABLE MODULE.DLTT (....)
```

This declaration allows you to access the table from the same module or embedded program in which it was declared.

```
INSERT INTO MODULE.DLTT VALUES (....)

SELECT * FROM MODULE.DLTT WHERE....
```

The materialization of a temporary table does not persist beyond the end of the SQL session in which the table was materialized. Temporary tables are effectively empty at the start of an SQL session. Depending on how they were defined, their contents may be cleared whenever a transaction is committed or rolled back, or the contents may be carried forward into the next transaction.

If you define your temporary tables (any type) using the clause ON COMMIT PRESERVE ROWS, then the rows are kept there until (1) you delete them with a DELETE statement, (2) you DROP the entire table, or (3) your session ends. If you define it using ON COMMIT DELETE ROWS, all rows in the table are automatically deleted at the end of every transaction that's terminated with a COMMIT statement (or committed by an external agent, as discussed in Chapter 14).

So what use are temporary tables? There may be occasions when you wish to store some temporary results within the course of your application, and—depending on some condition, possibly external to your database—take a given course of action with your temporary results. Temporary tables are a means to accomplish this without having to explicitly destroy (DROP) tables after each usage. You can draw an analogy between temporary tables and the local variables in your favorite programming language: they're great for intermediate results and working storage, but they don't allow you to save their data until some future execution of your application.

The use of temporary tables offers a few additional advantages worth mentioning. Since the data in temporary tables are private to an SQL session (perhaps even to a module), there are no problems of interaction with other users. This means that no locking is required and performance may improve over that of persistent tables, which are open to shared access. Furthermore, if you specify ON COMMIT DELETE ROWS, the DBMS needn't log your updates to the table, because they aren't intended to survive transactions—even in the result of a crash. Again, better performance results.

Derived and Viewed Tables

A *derived* table is one obtained directly or indirectly from one or more other tables through the evaluation of a query expression. The values of a derived table are derived from the values of the underlying tables when the query expression is evaluated.

A viewed table is a named derived table defined by a CREATE VIEW statement. A viewed table is called a *view*.

While all base tables are automatically updatable, you may define derived tables that are either updatable or read-only. The operations INSERT, UPDATE, and DELETE are permitted for updatable tables, subject to the appropriate privileges. The operations INSERT, UPDATE, and DELETE are not allowed for read-only tables.

4.2.4 Columns

Every column has a column name. A value of a column is the smallest unit of data that can be selected from a table and the smallest unit of data that can be updated. Additionally, all values of a column in a table have the same data type.

Every column also has a nullability characteristic of *known not nullable* or *possibly nullable*. A column that is possibly nullable has the potential to be set to the null value by an SQL statement. Even if it is possibly nullable, however, other factors may prevent it from taking the null value at any given time. Only if the DBMS can determine for certain (according to SQL-92 rules) that a column can never become null is the column said to be known not nullable.

Every column also has a default value. The default value of a column is the value that is stored into that column in a row when the row is inserted into the table without specifying a value for the column. If a column doesn't have an explicit default value, then the default value will be the null value. If the column also specifies NOT NULL, then you *must* specify a value for the column whenever you INSERT a row into the table; otherwise, the NOT NULL constraint will be violated.

4.3 Basic DDL Statements

In Chapter 3, we discussed a trio of data manipulation statements that can modify the given state of data in one or more tables: INSERT, UPDATE, and DELETE. However, when manipulating the tables themselves—as well as columns, schemas, and the other data definition components discussed herein—these three statements are not used. That is, in order to end the existence of a table itself, not just the rows within it, you do not DELETE the table, you DROP it. Similarly, to modify the definition of a table by adding, changing, or deleting one or more columns, you ALTER the table definition rather than UPDATE it. Therefore, the CREATE, ALTER, and DROP statements are DDL analogs of the manipulation statements INSERT, UPDATE, and DELETE. Table 4-1 summarizes this correspondence.

TABLE 4-1

Function	Data Manipulation	Data Definition
Bringing something into existence	INSERT	CREATE
Modifying something	UPDATE	ALTER
Getting rid of something	DELETE	DROP

Note that the metadata for SQL tables, columns, and the rest of the objects is not directly modifiable through these statements; the DBMS itself handles this function within the information schema (see Chapter 19) as a result of your statements. You could say that your data definition statements effect "behind-the-scenes" data manipulation actions on the metadata. We'll look more closely at examples of these statements throughout this chapter.

4.3.1 SQL Syntax for Tables and Columns

In Chapter 3, we discussed a simple version of the CREATE TABLE statement. This statement, as should be obvious, causes the creation of a table and column structure that matches that specified in the particular case. Columns can be specified to take on several properties, including data types and collations (and, in most cases, sizes), default values, permissibility of null values (nullability), and specific character sets.

Data Types

In Chapter 2, we discussed the data types supported by SQL-92. Table 4-2 summarizes these data types.

Default Value

When you create a column in a table, you can specify what the default value for the column is (in inserted rows when you don't specify a real value for the column). You can specify that the default value is a literal value (of the appropriate data type, of course), one of the datetime value functions (CURRENT_DATE, CURRENT_TIME, or CURRENT_TIMESTAMP), a user value (CURRENT_USER, SESSION_USER, or SYSTEM_USER), or NULL. The datetime and user values are evaluated when the default value is put into the row in the database.

SQL-92 Data Type	Usage Example(s)	
CHARACTER/CHAR	ALBUM_TITLE	CHAR (25)
CHARACTER VARYING/ VARCHAR/CHAR VARYING	ARTIST_NAME	VARCHAR (20)
NATIONAL CHARACTER/NCHAR/ NATIONAL CHAR	CITY_RELEASED_IN	NCHAR (15)

NATIONAL CHARACTER VARYING/
   NCHAR VARYING/
   NATIONAL CHAR VARYING
	NEXT_TOUR_CITY	NCHAR VARYING (20)

INTEGER/INT	VHS_ON_HAND	INTEGER
SMALLINT	NUMBER_EMPLOYEES	SMALLINT
NUMERIC	OUR_COST	NUMERIC (7,2)
	VHS_REVENUE	NUMERIC (9)
DECIMAL/DEC	CURRENT_PRICE	DECIMAL (6,2)
	BONUS	DECIMAL (7,2)
FLOAT	RADIUS	FLOAT (23)
	DISTANCE	FLOAT
REAL	WIDTH	REAL
DOUBLE PRECISION	VOLUME	DOUBLE PRECISION
BIT	FLAG_FIELD	BIT
	FLAG_FIELD2	BIT (100)
BIT VARYING	FLAG_FIELD_3	BIT VARYING (125)
DATE	DATE_RELEASED	DATE
TIME	TIME_RENTED	TIME
TIMESTAMP	TIME_ROW_ACCESSED	TIMESTAMP
TIME WITH TIME ZONE	INTERNATIONAL_CHAIN_TIME TIME WITH TIME ZONE	
TIMESTAMP WITH TIME ZONE	WORLDWIDE_RECORD_ACCESS_TIME TIMESTAMP WITH TIME ZONE	
INTERVAL	HOW_LONG_AN_EMPLOYEE INTERVAL YEAR TO MONTH	
	HOW_LONG_IN_STORE INTERVAL HOUR TO SECOND	

Null Values

As we discussed in Chapter 2, SQL-92 null values are used to represent information that is essentially out of bounds; that is, not part of a legitimate range or set of values. The use of null values alleviates the need to use blanks, 0, -1, or some other flag to indicate *not available, not applicable,* or *unknown.*[1] Most SQL-92 data elements (such as columns, host variables, value expressions) are permitted a value of NULL.

---

[1]   Refer back to Chapter 2 for a complete discussion of null values.

It is sometimes desirable to prevent the setting of a column or variable to a value of NULL. For example, the following statement must be prevented.

```
INSERT INTO MOVIE_TITLES
   (OUR_COST, CURRENT_RENTAL_PRICE,
      REGULAR_RENTAL_PRICE)
   VALUES (10.99, 3.99. 3.99) ;
```

Following execution of this statement, a row will exist in the MOVIE_TITLES table with some values for the columns specified, but without a movie title; that is, the absence of an explicit value for the TITLE column will insert a null value into that column in the new row. We now have a meaningless row in our table; if we were to do this repeatedly, we would eventually compromise the integrity of the data within that table.

This type of problem can be prevented by specifying—at creation time— that a particular column cannot take on a value of NULL. This is done by using the NOT NULL clause, as in

```
CREATE TABLE MOVIE_TITLES
    (TITLE CHAR (30) NOT NULL,
     |
     |  )
```

It is important to remember that a null value is different from any valid value for a data type. That is, null is not the same as zero, nor blanks, nor any other user-chosen designator.

It is important to be careful about using (and overusing) NOT NULL. It might be tempting to define most or all columns as NOT NULL—say, for price and quantity information (we have to have that information, do we not?)—but at points in your applications this information may simply be temporarily unknown. NOT NULL forces a non-null value to be always present, and overusing this can cause unnecessary headaches.

By the way, the NOT NULL clause is really something called a *column constraint*. A constraint is an application rule that the DBMS enforces for you. You would specify constraints (and there are three types: column constraints, table constraints, and assertions) in your database definitions to express rules that must always be enforced in your business. The DBMS will ensure that they are never violated, and you cannot commit a transaction if any constraints are violated.

In Chapter 10, we will discuss the CHECK constraint, a multipurpose clause through which many different types of constraints can be expressed. As a preview, we will tell you that the NOT NULL constraint is equivalent to the following CHECK constraint.

```
CHECK (column-name IS NOT NULL)
```

Now that we've seen the various components of a column definition, let's put it together with the aid of Diagram RR5.

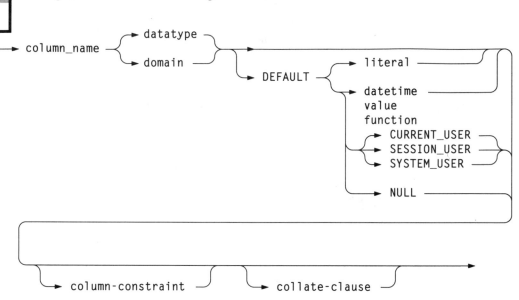

4.3.2 Character Sets

A quick note: Throughout most of this book, we will stick to familiar Latin characters, the only type of characters supported by most computer systems until very recently. Later, in Chapter 18, Internationalization, we'll show you how to use character sets other than Latin (to write applications that will support users in Japan or Israel, for example).

4.3.3 Domains

A domain is a sort of *macro* that you can define to pull together a specific data type (and, if applicable, size), as well as some characteristics we'll discuss later in the book: defaults, constraints, and collations. You can then use the name of the domain to define columns that inherit the data type (and other characteristics) of the domain.

For example, you might want to ensure that all columns that deal with some form of titles (movie, CD, or tape titles) have a data type of CHARACTER VARYING, are no more than 35 characters in length, and do not permit insertion of null values. The CREATE DOMAIN statement can be used to create a specific domain that is used subsequently in CREATE TABLE statements.

```
CREATE DOMAIN TITLE_TYPE VARCHAR (35)
    CHECK (VALUE IS NOT NULL);
```

```
|
|
CREATE TABLE MOVIE_TITLES
  (TITLE TITLE_TYPE,
    |
    |  )  ;
```

The column TITLE inherits the data type and size specification, as well as the specification that null values are not permissible.

When you create a domain, you specify the data type; you can also specify a default value, CHECK constraints, and so forth. These characteristics are all given to any column based on the domain. However, columns can override the default value and (if applicable) the collation of the domain. Also, the columns can add constraints in addition to those of the domain. In a domain constraint (which can only be a CHECK constraint), the key word VALUE is used to represent the value of the column defined on the domain.

4.3.4 Temporary Tables

As we discussed earlier in this chapter, there may be cases where you only want a table to exist only during a specific period of time. One way to accomplish this is to CREATE a table and subsequently DROP it. Alternatively, SQL-92 permits tables to be created on a temporary basis.Assume that you wish to create a table into which you can group and organize video and music sales information for end-of-month processing, but that the table's data is meaningless after reports are printed and mailed—the data doesn't need to be preserved. You might issue the following DDL statement.

```
CREATE LOCAL TEMPORARY TABLE SALES_SUMMARY_INFO (
    column 1,
    column 2, ... ) ;
```

The expanded syntax of the CREATE TABLE statement permits the creation of temporary tables (as designated by the word TEMPORARY) whose data are either LOCAL (as in the previous case) or GLOBAL in scope.

Additionally, the syntax permits you to specify whether you want the contents of these temporary tables to be preserved for the duration of your entire session or to be deleted at the end of every transaction during your session. Note that the contents of a temporary table can never be preserved between sessions except by copying them into a persistent base table.

The definition of a created local temporary table looks like this:

```
CREATE LOCAL TEMPORARY TABLE MOVIES_ON_SPECIAL (
    TITLE CHARACTER(30),
    {{{other columns}}}
  )
```

When this definition is executed, the metadata for the temporary table is put into your schema (most likely—your mileage may vary), but no space is allocated to hold data.

When you execute the first SQL statement in your session that references this table (for example SELECT title FROM MOVIES_ON_SPECIAL or, more useful, INSERT INTO MOVIES_ON_SPECIAL...), the table "automatically" comes into being. That is, the database system allocates space to hold the table's data *for your session*. If some other user (in another session, of course) executes the same statement, the DBMS allocates *more* space to hold the table's data for *that* user's session. When you have finished executing all of your SQL statements and have completed your session, the DBMS deallocates all of the space for the table (possibly deleting any data still in the table).

Now, recall that a *local* temporary table cannot be shared between different modules (or compilation units) in your session. Therefore, if you are running two compiled pieces of embedded SQL, they will each get their own allocated space for the local temporary table, and they cannot share the data in that table.

If your application is written using modular programming techniques and you want to share temporary table data between various modules, you will have to create a *global* temporary table:

```
CREATE GLOBAL TEMPORARY TABLE MOVIES_ON_SPECIAL (
    TITLE CHARACTER(30),
    {{{other columns}}}
)
```

When that definition is executed, the metadata for the temporary table is put into your schema (most likely—your mileage may vary), but no space is allocated to hold data. In this respect, the global temporary table is just like the local temporary table.

The difference is that multiple modules (or compilation units of embedded SQL) can share the data in a global temporary table; however, other users simultaneously using a temporary table with the identical name actually get their own, personalized copies of it. This permits applications to share definitions (metadata) for tables without the worry of interfering with data contributed by fellow users.

In both cases, you can specify ON COMMMIT DELETE ROWS or ON COMMIT PRESERVE ROWS. If you specify ON COMMIT DELETE ROWS in a temporary table definition, the contents of the table will be deleted every time you commit your transaction. (You don't have to worry about this when you abort your transaction with a ROLLBACK statement—see Chapter 14—because any data you put into the table will be removed automatically as the effects of all statements in the transaction are undone.) If you specify ON COMMIT PRESERVE ROWS, the data will not be deleted at the end of the transaction; this permits you to commit your work without having to recreate the contents of the temporary tables. Of course, the data will be deleted at the end of your session in any case.

4.3.5 Modification of Table Structures: The ALTER and DROP Statements

Tables can be removed from your database via the DROP TABLE statement. For example:

```
DROP TABLE MOVIES_STARS ;
```

will remove from your database all data within the MOVIES_STARS table, as well as the structure itself. Note that the actions of this statement are *not* the same as

```
DELETE FROM MOVIES_STARS ;
```

The DELETE statement removes all data, but leaves the table structure and associated metadata intact. The DROP statement likewise removes all data, but also removes the table structure and associated metadata; it's as if the table never existed.

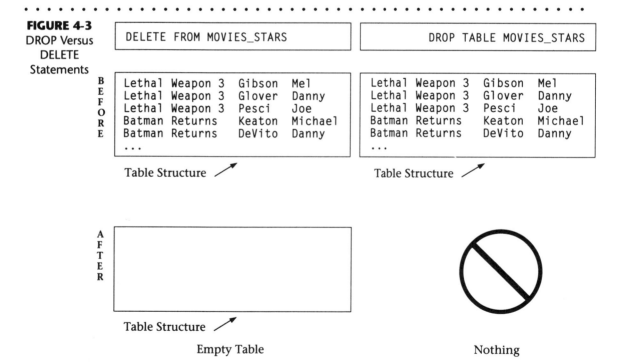

FIGURE 4-3
DROP Versus
DELETE
Statements

The structure of a table may be modified through the ALTER TABLE statement. Within the context of this statement, columns may be added, modified, or removed. For example, assume that Beta videotape sales are abysmal, and you decide to rent and sell only VHS format tapes. You can remove the columns related to Beta tapes from your MOVIE_TITLES table through the following statements.

```
ALTER TABLE MOVIE_TITLES
  DROP COLUMN BETA_OWNED ;

ALTER TABLE MOVIE_TITLES
  DROP COLUMN BETA_IN_STOCK ;

ALTER TABLE MOVIE_TITLES
  DROP COLUMN TOTAL_BETA_UNITS_RENTED ;
  |
  |
  |
```

Note that in the above course of actions, the structures for the specified columns as well as the data contained within those columns are removed from the database. If you wish to preserve any of this information—specifically, historical revenue data—you might perform actions such as the following (Advance warning: There is a caveat, which we discuss immediately after the example).

```
UPDATE MOVIE_TITLES
  SET TOTAL_VHS_RENTAL_REVENUE =
      TOTAL_VHS_RENTAL_REVENUE +
      TOTAL_BETA_RENTAL_REVENUE,
      TOTAL_VHS_SALES_REVENUE =
      TOTAL_VHS_SALES_REVENUE +
      TOTAL_BETA_SALES_REVENUE ;

ALTER TABLE MOVIE_TITLES
  DROP COLUMN BETA_RENTAL_REVENUE ;

ALTER TABLE MOVIE_TITLES
  DROP COLUMN BETA_SALES_REVENUE ;
```

However—and this is *very* important—SQL-92 does not *require* that an implementation permit both data manipulation statements and data definition statements to be executed in the same transaction. If your implementation permits this, you can probably execute the preceding sequence of statements; if not, the first ALTER TABLE statement in this sequence will get an error. Even if your implementation does support the mixing of DML and DDL statements in a transaction, SQL-92 doesn't specify the semantics of that mixture—your implementator is required to tell you (in the product documentation, for example) what the behavior is. Therefore, something as intuitively obvious as our sample sequence of statements may not be possible within given implementations. If that's the case, you need to divide the data manipulation and data definition statements among multiple transactions. (Transaction management syntax, including invocation and termination, is discussed in Chapter 14.)

Columns can be added to tables; this is also accomplished through the ALTER TABLE statement. Table 4-3 summarizes this and the other ALTER and DROP statements we've discussed in this section.

```
ALTER TABLE MOVIE_TITLES
   ADD COLUMN DIRECTED_BY VARCHAR (20) ;
```

As an alternative to our earlier example, you can create new, more generically named columns and store the accumulated revenue figures in the new columns through the following sequence.

```
ALTER TABLE MOVIE_TITLES
   ADD COLUMN TOTAL_SALES_REVENUE DECIMAL (9,2) ;

ALTER TABLE MOVIE_TITLES
   ADD COLUMN TOTAL_RENTAL_REVENUE DECIMAL (9,2) ;

UPDATE MOVIE_TITLES
   SET TOTAL_SALES_REVENUE = TOTAL_VHS_SALES_REVENUE,
      TOTAL_RENTAL_REVENUE =
      TOTAL_VHS_RENTAL_REVENUE ;

ALTER TABLE MOVIE_TITLES
   DROP COLUMN TOTAL_VHS_SALES_REVENUE;

ALTER TABLE MOVIE_TITLES
   DROP COLUMN TOTAL_VHS_RENTAL_REVENUE;
```

Of course, the same caveat about mixing DML and DDL in a transaction applies.

TABLE 4-3
Column Management Within Existing SQL-92 Tables

DESIRED ACTION	STATEMENT
Add a new column to a table	ALTER TABLE table_name ADD COLUMN column-definition ;
Modify a column within a table	ALTER TABLE table_name ALTER COLUMN column_name ;
Remove a column from a table	ALTER TABLE table_name DROP COLUMN column_name ;

4.3.6 Schemas

As we mentioned earlier in this chapter, a schema consists of the collection of objects associated with a particular schema name that is known to the system at a particular instant in time. Schemas are created using the CREATE SCHEMA statement, followed by the creation of objects—primarily tables, domains, and views— within that schema.

```
CREATE SCHEMA MOVIE_INFORMATION ....

CREATE TABLE MOVIE_TITLES ....

CREATE TABLE MOVIES_STARS ....
```

In Chapter 13, we'll discuss SQL-92 security and permission issues. When a schema is created, an AUTHORIZATION clause can be specified to identify the owner of the schema and of the objects in the schema. Among other things, this clause specifies who can determine access privileges for objects in the schema.

Schemas can be removed via the DROP SCHEMA statement. Issuers are permitted to state whether the removal of the schema CASCADEs, or ripples, to contents of the schema. Alternatively, the RESTRICT clause specifies, "If there are still any schema contents remaining, don't execute the DROP command." The DROP SCHEMA statement,

```
DROP SCHEMA MOVIE_INFORMATION CASCADE ;
```

will remove the schema, all associated tables and columns, as well as the data contained in those tables. If objects in *other* schemas reference an object in the schema being dropped, they will automatically be resolved by dropping those referencing objects or updating them to eliminate the reference. Alternatively,

```
DROP SCHEMA MOVIE_INFORMATION RESTRICT ;
```

will be successfully executed *only* if all tables (and other objects) were DROPped prior to the execution of the statement.

4.3.7 Views

An SQL-92 view can be viewed as a virtual table; that is, a table that doesn't physically exist, but rather is formed by a query expression against one or more tables. In this chapter, we discuss views derived from single tables. In Chapter 9, we'll introduce multiple-table views.

Assume that you would like to perform a number of operations against your MOVIE_TITLES, but including only titles that are on sale. You can always issue a number of SELECT, UPDATE, INSERT, and DELETE statements against the MOVIE_ TITLES table, always including:

```
... FROM MOVIE_TITLES
    WHERE
      (CURRENT_SALE_PRICE < REGULAR_SALE_PRICE) OR
      (CURRENT_RENTAL_PRICE <
        REGULAR_RENTAL_PRICE) ;
```

along with other parts of query expressions.

An easier way—one which requires far less typing overall—is to create a view against which your operations can be run.

```
CREATE VIEW MOVIES_ON_SALE AS
    SELECT * FROM MOVIE_TITLES
      WHERE
        (CURRENT_SALE_PRICE < REGULAR_SALE_PRICE)
         OR
        (CURRENT_RENTAL_PRICE <
              REGULAR_RENTAL_PRICE) ;
```

Following creation of the preceding view, you can then issue your data manipulation statements against MOVIES_ON_SALE and be guaranteed that only the movies that meet the on sale constraint are included. To see which movies on sale have fewer than 10 VHS copies in the store, you would issue the following SELECT * statement. (Don't forget our cautionary remark about SELECT *: It's just as important in view definitions.)

```
SELECT * FROM MOVIES_ON_SALE
  WHERE VHS_IN_STOCK < 10 ;
```

Views can also include a subset of all the columns of a particular table. Assume that you wish to create a view that contains only the historical volume and revenue amounts for each movie. You might use the following statement.

```
CREATE VIEW MOVIE_HISTORY_INFO (
  TITLE, TOTAL_VHS_UNITS_RENTED,
  TOTAL_BETA_UNITS_RENTED,
  TOTAL_VHS_UNITS_SOLD,
  TOTAL_BETA_UNITS_SOLD,
  TOTAL_VHS_RENTAL_REVENUE,
  TOTAL_BETA_RENTAL_REVENUE,
  TOTAL_VHS_SALES_REVENUE,
  TOTAL_BETA_SALES_REVENUE)
AS SELECT TITLE, TOTAL_VHS_UNITS_RENTED,
  TOTAL_BETA_UNITS_RENTED,
  TOTAL_VHS_UNITS_SOLD,
  TOTAL_BETA_UNITS_SOLD,
  TOTAL_VHS_RENTAL_REVENUE,
  TOTAL_BETA_RENTAL_REVENUE,
  TOTAL_VHS_SALES_REVENUE,
  TOTAL_BETA_SALES_REVENUE
  FROM MOVIE_TITLES ;
```

Here's a recommended shortcut for the preceding view definition: You can exclude the column names from the CREATE VIEW part of the statement and automatically create your view with the columns and names specified after the SELECT portion of the statement. You would write instead:

```
CREATE VIEW MOVIE_HISTORY_INFO
  AS SELECT TITLE, TOTAL_VHS_UNITS_RENTED,
      TOTAL_BETA_UNITS_RENTED,
      TOTAL_VHS_UNITS_SOLD,
      TOTAL_BETA_UNITS_SOLD,
      TOTAL_VHS_RENTAL_REVENUE,
      TOTAL_BETA_RENTAL_REVENUE,
      TOTAL_VHS_SALES_REVENUE,
      TOTAL_BETA_SALES_REVENUE
      FROM MOVIE_TITLES ;
```

You can then issue SELECT * FROM MOVIE_HISTORY_INFO and receive a complete list of only the specified columns. You could, for example, issue:

```
SELECT *
 FROM MOVIE_HISTORY
 WHERE TOTAL_BETA_SALES_REVENUE > 1000 ;
```

and receive a list of movies—with the specified historical data columns—which have sold in excess of $1,000 in Beta format.

Why would you want to specify column names in the first part of your view definition? One reason is to create virtual columns whose values are derivations of the values of other columns. For example, you might want to create a view UNITS_RENTED as follows.

```
CREATE VIEW UNITS_RENTED (
      TITLE,
      TOTAL_VHS_UNITS_RENTED,
      TOTAL_BETA_UNITS_RENTED,
      TOTAL_UNITS_RENTED,
   AS SELECT TITLE,
      TOTAL_VHS_UNITS_RENTED,
      TOTAL_BETA_UNITS_RENTED,
      TOTAL_VHS_UNITS_RENTED +
            TOTAL_BETA_UNITS_RENTED
      FROM MOVIE_TITLES ;
```

In the preceding example, the column TOTAL_UNITS_RENTED doesn't really exist. If you issue a SELECT * FROM UNITS_RENTED, the VHS and Beta rental unit values for each title will be added together and appear as a column along with the real columns' values.

Views that are updatable result in UPDATE, INSERT, and DELETE operations being applied against the underlying base table(s). For example,

```
UPDATE MOVIES_ON_SALE
  SET CURRENT_RENTAL_PRICE = .99
  WHERE TITLE = "Lethal Weapon 3" ;
```

will update the current rental price for this movie both in the view and in the MOVIE_TITLES base table. Therefore, queries issued against MOVIE_TITLES as well as MOVIES_ON_SALE will reflect the correct rental price for the movie *Lethal Weapon 3*.

Views cannot be ALTERed. A view definition really consists of its name, the names of its columns, and the query expression used to derive its rows; none of these is an obvious candidate to modify, so SQL-92 prohibits it. In a future version . . . perhaps.

View definitions can, however, be DROPped, as in

```
DROP VIEW MOVIES_ON_SALE ;
```

Dropping a view doesn't make any changes to any data in your database. The only effect it has is to remove from the schema the metadata describing the view. Obviously, you won't be able to use that view any more, but the data in the underlying base table remains unchanged.

Views are also widely used to assist with security and permission/accessibility issues. We will discuss these uses further in Chapter 13.

4.4 Chapter Summary

In this chapter we discussed a number of SQL-92 objects, as well as their creation, modification where applicable, and deletion. From the basic concept of tables and columns to the use of views and domains, SQL-92 database environments can be tailored to your individual application and system needs.

So far, we have concentrated on simple object creation and manipulation. Many simple applications can be built around the statements we have discussed to this point. In the upcoming chapters, we'll discuss further query expression characteristics, as well as the use of multiple tables within query expressions.

CHAPTER 5

. . . .

Values, Basic Functions, and Expressions

5.1 Introduction

Thus far, we have taken a somewhat cavalier approach to describing SQL-92 values and related concepts such as value functions and value expressions. That is, our examples have presumed the placement of some type of values into the database and the corresponding retrieval of those values from appropriate tables, as well as the use of values in our statements. Now, we discuss these concepts more formally and explain how they apply to SQL-92.

We discuss basic SQL functions and expressions, deferring discussion of some of the more advanced topics (such as CASE, NULLIF, COALESCE, and CAST) until Chapter 6. Many of the functions and expressions that we discuss—such as string concatenation, substring extraction, date-related functions, and others—will look conceptually familiar to users of commercial DBMS packages. In this chapter, you learn how these facilities are supported in SQL-92.

5.2 Types of SQL Values

Intuitively, we all know what a value is. However, in the context of SQL, the word has a fairly precise meaning. The SQL meaning is, in fact, consistent with the meaning that we intuit, but let's have a look at it anyway. There are several types of values in SQL, and each has important characteristics that we should understand.

One type of value in SQL is the value stored in some row of a table. That value is the value of the row (called a *row value,* cleverly enough) and it usually has more than one component (one for each column of the table). Each of the components is also a value—a scalar, or atomic, value. Therefore, every row of a table has one value for each column of the table. Of course, some of these values may be null, but this is merely a special case of value.

A literal value is another type of SQL value. A literal represents a value that you can "see" just by looking at it. Still another type of SQL value is the information that is passed between the SQL statement and the 3GL program that invokes the statement. These values are passed in *parameters* and *host variables*. We learn more about these two types of SQL values later in this chapter.

Finally, SQL has a type of value that is computed by the DBMS, either as an expression of some sort that is based on the other types of values or as a function that operates on other types of values, producing a new value.

5.3 Literals

In Chapter 2, we discussed the many data types supported by SQL-92. Each corresponding data type can have literals associated with it. The formal definition of a literal is a non-null value, but for our purposes a literal may be viewed as a constant: a specific unchangeable value that complies with the constraints of its data type. Literals can be further decomposed into several categories, which in turn are further decomposed, as illustrated in Figure 5-1.

FIGURE 5-1
SQL Literals

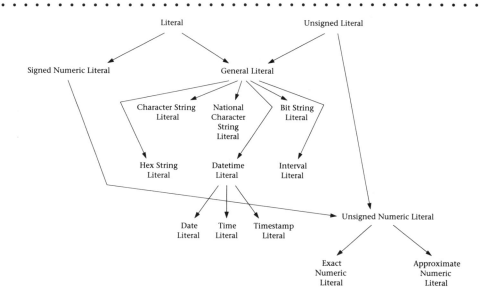

In Table 5-1, we take a look at some examples of literals for the various SQL data types.

SQL-92 Data Type	Literal Example(s)
CHARACTER	'Lethal Weapon 3'
CHARACTER VARYING	'48 Hours'
NATIONAL CHARACTER	乱[1]
NATIONAL CHARACTER VARYING	タンポポ[2]
INTEGER	258734
SMALLINT	98
NUMERIC	2.99
	3
DECIMAL	1.99
	5
FLOAT	1.56E-4
	200E10
REAL	1.56E-4
DOUBLE PRECISION	3.1415929265432E00
BIT	B'01111110'
	X'7E'
BIT VARYING	B'01111110011111'
	X'1F3A2'
DATE	DATE '1929-10-29'
TIME	TIME '09:00:05.01'
TIMESTAMP	TIMESTAMP '1987-10-19 16:00:00.00'
TIME WITH TIME ZONE	TIME '10:45-07:00'
TIMESTAMP WITH TIME ZONE	TIMESTAMP '1933-04-05 03:00:00+01:00'
INTERVAL	INTERVAL '10:30' MINUTE TO SECOND

TABLE 5-1
Literals for SQL
Data Types

Note: The "data types" in the left column of the preceding table are only the names of the data type, exclusive of any lengths, precisions, or scales. Take a moment to derive the complete datatype for some of the literals. It is also possible, as we shall see in Chapter 6, to write a literal for an entire row or a table.

Literals, like all values in SQL, can only be used in specific places in the language. Generally, you can use an SQL literal anywhere that you can supply a value to the database system. You can also use literals in value expressions. Because literals have a data type, you can only use them in places where data of that type are permitted.

Just above, we showed you some sample literals for each SQL data type. However, what the DBMS must know is what data type a given literal is. Now, let's look at the *exact* data type of several literals in Table 5-2.

[1] This is the film title, *Ran*, in Japanese (Kanji character set).

[2] This is *Tampopo* in Kanji.

TABLE 5-2

Literal	SQL-92 Data Type
`'This is a literal'`	`CHARACTER(17)`
`N'Σπø'`	`NATIONAL CHARACTER(4)`
`135`	Exact numeric data type (`INTEGER` or `SMALLINT`). The precise data type is implementation-defined, but `SMALLINT` is a reasonable choice.
`64591.645`	Exact numeric data type (`DECIMAL` or `NUMERIC`). The precise data type is implementation-defined, but `DECIMAL` `(8,3)` might be chosen.
`12E-5`	Approximate numeric data type (`REAL`, `FLOAT`, or `DOUBLE PRECISION`). The exact data type is implementation-defined, but `REAL` is possible.
`B'10101'`	`BIT(5)`
`X'1F30'`	`BIT(16)`
`DATE '12-10-1980'`	`DATE`
`TIME '14:35:10.55'`	`TIME(2)`
`TIME '12:20:00.000+05:50'`	`TIME(3) WITH TIME ZONE`
`TIMESTAMP '12-10-1980 08:00:00'`	`TIMESTAMP(0)`
`INTERVAL '3' DAY`	`INTERVAL DAY`

You will notice immediately that SQL uses the apostrophe (') to enclose character string literals (as well as some other types of literals). However, the apostrophe is a character that you might wish to put into a character string literal. SQL allows you to do this by using two consecutive apostrophes in the literal to represent one apostrophe:

```
'John''s house'
```

The two consecutive apostrophes cannot be separated by any white space, comments, or a newline.

Unlike the C programming language, SQL does not provide any sort of escape character for character string literals that might give, for example, the ability to encode arbitrary values as though they were characters.

Occasionally, you will find that your application requires you to provide a very lengthy literal, perhaps longer than the width of your terminal (or, heaven help you, your punch cards). SQL-92 provides for this problem by permitting character string literals and bit string literals to cross line boundaries. The syntax is really pretty simple. For example, you could write:

```
'This is a very long character string literal that will not fit'
'on a single line, so we can continue it across multiple lines if'
'that''s the best way to represent our data.'
```

As we said earlier, SQL is generally a free-format language without any reliance on line boundaries. However, there are two instances in SQL where line boundaries make a difference, as we shall see later in Chapter 11 in our discussion of language embeddings. One of these instances stems from the fact that all implementations of any computer language, including SQL, have physical limits on the number of source characters that can be coded between line boundaries (represented in SQL by the concept *newline*). To get around this limitation, SQL-92 gives you the ability to write literals that cross line boundaries. Actually, you can put any number of *separators* (white space, newline indicators, and SQL comments) between the parts of a literal; the only requirement is that at least one newline be included between each part. Therefore, you can write literals like this:

```
B'101010111000011010100'    -- This example illustrates
 '1100111000101011100'      -- multiple separators, including
 '11'                       -- comments, white space, and newlines
```

Of course, the actual value of that literal is

```
B'1010101110000011010100110011100010101110011'
```

The separators are completely ignored, as long as at least one newline is included. The following example would *not* be valid, since no newline is included.

```
B'10101' '1011101'
```

Sometimes, you may need to specify a character string literal with no characters in it (not even a blank). SQL-92 permits this: You just use two consecutive apostrophes (`''`) and the character string literal's data type is CHARACTER, but with length 0 (which is not a permitted data type for a column definition).

5.4 Parameters

When you write SQL statements to accomplish the purposes of your application, you can occasionally code the entire context of the statement as a simple character string. For example, you might know that your application will always give all video employees a 10% raise, perhaps because you intend to execute the application only once. In that case, you can write:

```
UPDATE EMPLOYEES
  SET SALARY = SALARY * 1.1
  WHERE DEPT = 'Video'
```

In most cases, however, you have other criteria for your SQL statements and those criteria will change from execution to execution. For example, you might give your video employees a 10% raise, but your music employees a 20% raise. Of course, you could write two statements:

```
UPDATE EMPLOYEES
   SET SALARY = SALARY * 1.1
   WHERE DEPT = 'Video'

UPDATE EMPLOYEES
   SET SALARY = SALARY * 1.2
   WHERE DEPT = 'Music'
```

But that doesn't really solve the problem; it merely puts it off. Suppose those values are correct this year, but next year the values are different, you add new departments, or you get rid of one department. You would have to rewrite your application if you used this technique and that's not a good thing to have to do!

Instead, SQL permits you to write your SQL statement so that it requires values to be passed to the statement from the application. This technique requires a special type of SQL value called a *parameter* or *host variable*. If you write your application using SQL module language, then parameter is the appropriate word; if you use embedded SQL, then host variable is the right phrase. (See Chapter 11 for more information on module language and embedded SQL in the discussion on language bindings.) In SQL-92, both parameters and host variables are signaled by a colon (:). For example, the following statement uses two parameters. (We will use this term because it's more generic. In almost every situation, you can substitute the phrase host variable and still be correct. When there's a need to distinguish, we'll make it clear.)

```
UPDATE EMPLOYEES
   SET SALARY = SALARY * :raise
   WHERE DEPT = :department ;
```

By the way, the use of lower-case letters for the parameter names has no significance; we use that convention for illustration purposes only.

When our host program invokes that SQL statement, it has to supply two values: an exact numeric value (not an INTEGER, but a DECIMAL or NUMERIC) and a character string. (Earlier versions of SQL didn't require the colon before a module language parameter, but the colon before an embedded SQL host variable has always been required.)

5.4.1 Types of Parameters

SQL distinguishes three categories of parameters: *status parameters*, *data parameters*, and *indicator parameters*. The distinction between data parameters and indicator parameters is based on use, as we shall see in a moment. But let's see what we mean by these three categories first.

A status parameter is used to return (to the application) status information about the execution of an SQL statement. SQL-92 defines two status parameters: SQLCODE and SQLSTATE; earlier versions of SQL defined only the SQLCODE status parameter. Chapter 17, which covers diagnostic and error management, contains more information about these parameters. For now, we will simply note that SQLCODE is an exact numeric data type and SQLSTATE is a character string with 5 characters. (You should plan to use SQLSTATE most of the time; SQLCODE is supported for compatibility with existing applications, but it is deprecated—meaning that it might not be supported in future versions of the standard.)

A data parameter is used to pass data from an application to the DBMS or from the DBMS to an application. Data parameters can be any data type, but your choice of application programming language will make restrictions on the data types that you can use in any given application. When you retrieve data from your database, you will use a data parameter to tell the DBMS where to put the data, as follows.

```
SELECT DISTRIBUTOR INTO :dist
  FROM MOVIE_TITLES
  WHERE TITLE = 'Terminator' ;
```

As we saw in the previous example, you also use a data parameter to supply information to your SQL statements. This can also be data that will be put into the database. For example,

```
INSERT INTO MOVIES_STARS
  VALUES ('Hamlet', 1990, 'Gibson', 'Mel') ;
```

will do just fine when you know the information in advance, but the general case would be

```
INSERT INTO MOVIES_STARS
  VALUES (:title, :year, :last_name, :first_name) ;
```

An indicator parameter has two purposes. The first (indeed, the primary) purpose is to allow the DBMS and the host program to exchange information about whether the data parameter is meaningful or whether the data exchanged is null. Let us explain the convention that SQL uses. If you specified the use of an indicator parameter to accompany a data parameter and the data returned from the DBMS to the host program in that data parameter is not null (that is, it's a real value), then the DBMS will set the indicator parameter to 0. If the data that the DBMS would like to pass to the host program is null, then the DBMS will set the indicator parameter to -1 and won't touch the data parameter.

Yes, that seems a little complicated. It is, but it's caused by the fact that conventional 3GLs don't support the concept of nulls. The only way that the DBMS can indicate the "nullness" of a data item is to pass the flag back to the host program separately. By the way, if you try to retrieve data that is null and you don't specify an indicator parameter, the DBMS will give you an error; therefore, unless you're sure you won't encounter any null values, it's probably a good idea to use indicator parameters.

If the host program wishes to *send* a null value to the database, it sets the indicator parameter to some negative value (although we strongly recommend the use of -1 for compatibility with expected future enhancements to SQL). If the DBMS sees the negative value in an indicator parameter, it won't even look at the associated data parameter; if the indicator parameter is 0, the DBMS will retrieve that value stored in the data parameter.

The secondary purpose of indicator parameters is to let you know whether the DBMS had to truncate (chop off) characters in a character string when you retrieved it. Suppose you are retrieving a column from the database that is defined as NAME CHARACTER(50) but you had decided to allocate only 30 characters in your host program (Okay, maybe that wasn't too smart, but you probably had a really good reason at the time). If you happen to retrieve a row where the value in the NAME column is longer than 30 characters, SQL will put the first 30 characters of the data into your host program buffer and will set the indicator parameter—assuming you specified one, that is—to 50, telling you how much room you should have allowed. This use of the indicator parameter applies only to retrieval of data from the DBMS and not to sending data to the DBMS. By the way, if you didn't specify an indicator parameter, you would get a warning to let you know about the truncation. Diagram RR6 demonstrates the format of the indicator parameter in railroad diagram form.

You will have noticed by now that we keep using the word *associated*. We do this because indicator parameters aren't distinguishable by the way in which they're declared. You can determine that a parameter is an indicator parameter only by the way in which it's used. In particular, you would write something like

```
:dist INDICATOR :dist_ind
```

to specify that the data parameter :DIST has an associated indicator parameter named :DIST_IND. The keyword INDICATOR is optional, too, so you could have written:

```
:dist :dist_ind
```

However, we prefer to always use the keyword INDICATOR to avoid confusion about whether or not we forgot a comma. Let's see what it looks like in a statement.

```
SELECT DISTRIBUTOR
  INTO :dist :dist_ind
  FROM MOVIE_TITLES
  WHERE TITLE = 'Terminator' ;
```

Similarly, you might write:

```
INSERT INTO MOVIE_STARS
  VALUES (:title, :year, :last_name, :first_name
      INDICATOR :first_ind) ;
```

in the (likely!) case that not all movie stars have two names (Cher, Sting, and Madonna, to name a few).

5.5 Special Values

SQL-92 supports special values that can be important to your applications. The value specified by SESSION_USER is equal to the value of the user authorization identifier of the current SQL-session (sessions were briefly mentioned in Chapter 2 and are discussed in Chapter 15). In this way, your programs can access SESSION_USER to determine the authID of the user executing SQL statements.

SQL-92 allows SQL statements to execute under the authorization identifier of the session or under a user-specified authorization identifier associated with the module containing the SQL statements. (See Chapter 11 for more information on this topic.) If your module doesn't specify an authorization identifier, then the session authorization identifier is used. In any case, the authorization identifier associated with the module is specified by CURRENT_USER. If the module has no authID, then CURRENT_USER and SESSION_USER are the same.

For example, suppose you have logged into your computer system using the login ID of 'JOE_USER', but you identified yourself to your SQL database as 'PAYROLL_CLERK'. In this case, the value returned by SESSION_USER will be 'PAYROLL_CLERK'. If you're executing an SQL statement in a module that does not have an explicit module authorization identifier and that statement uses the special value CURRENT_USER, then it will also return the value 'PAYROLL_CLERK'.

Similarly, SYSTEM_USER is another special value that contains an implementation-defined string. This string identifies the operating system user who has executed an SQL-92 module. In our example in the previous paragraph, SYSTEM_USER would return 'JOE_USER'.

SESSION_USER, CURRENT_USER, and SYSTEM_USER have a character string data type. An individual SQL-92 implementation can specify the length of the strings and whether fixed or variable length character strings are used. For compatibility with applications written to use earlier versions of SQL, you can simply code USER when you mean CURRENT_USER.

Note that all of these values have been folded to upper case. Remember the discussion about identifiers in Chapter 2? Because these identifiers are regular identifiers (as opposed to delimited identifiers), the database system will fold them to upper case for all operations. If you prefer to use delimited identifiers, then you would have identified yourself to the SQL database as '"Payroll_clerk"' and SESSION_USER will return the value 'Payroll_clerk' to you.

One important use of these special values is recording the identity of a user (for example, in a table designed to capture information about who is executing certain applications). An application might invoke the following SQL statement.

```
INSERT INTO LOG (INFORMATION)
  VALUES ('User ' || SYSTEM_USER ||
      ',
      using authID ' || SESSION_USER
  || ' executed at ' || CURRENT_TIMESTAMP) ;
```

(The two vertical bars, ||, mean "concatenate" as we shall see shortly.)

5.6 Column References

In SQL, you can reference a column in many of the same places you can use any other value. Obviously, there are situations where it's not meaningful to reference a column—the restriction being that you must have created a context for the column reference.

A column reference can be as little as the name of a column, but the full form is a qualifier, a period, and a column name. For example:

```
MOVIE_TITLES.TITLE
```

The table name (MOVIE_TITLES, in this case) gives us the required context. That qualifier has to identify a table that is being *processed* by the SQL statement. Consider the following example:

```
SELECT MOVIE_TITLES.TITLE
  FROM MUSIC_SUPPLY_COST
  WHERE MUSIC_SUPPLY_COST.SUPPLIER =
    'Random Distributors'
```

In this case, even though MOVIE_TITLES is a valid table name (that is, it is the name of a table that we know about), it has no meaning in this SQL statement. This statement deals only with the table named MUSIC_SUPPLY_COST, so we can reference only columns that are in that table. The statement,

```
SELECT MUSIC_SUPPLY_COST.MUSIC_TITLE
  FROM MUSIC_SUPPLY_COST
  WHERE SUPPLIER = 'Random Distributors'
```

is valid. It is equivalent to

```
SELECT MUSIC_TITLE
  FROM MUSIC_SUPPLY_COST
  WHERE SUPPLIER = 'Random Distributors'
```

because the column has an *implicit* qualifier equal to the name of the (only) table.

The rule is that the column reference has to be in the *scope* of a table reference. In Chapter 3, we discussed table references, including the possibility of providing a correlation name. Now, we'll see one reason why correlation names can be useful.

There will be situations where there are two (or more) tables involved (see Chapter 8). When you find yourself in this situation, there are two possibilities:

1. The name of each column that you reference is unique in all of the tables that you're using; or
2. The names of one or more columns that you reference exist in two or more of the tables that you're using.

In the first case, you can simply use the column name when you want to reference the column. In the second case, you must qualify the column name to tell the database system *which* column you mean. For example, suppose you have a column called NAME in two tables (EMPLOYEE and CUSTOMER, perhaps). If you wanted to retrieve the name of an employee who sold some goods to a particular customer, you would have to specify EMPLOYEE.NAME in your select list.

Sometimes, it is inconvenient to use the actual name of the table to qualify a column name, perhaps because the table name is rather long or difficult to type. In that case, SQL allows you to define a correlation name for the table that you can use as a qualifier. (Note: There are other reasons why you might—or must—use a correlation name. You'll read about this in Chapter 8.) For example, you might code a query as

```
SELECT MSC.MUSIC_TITLE
  FROM MUSIC_SUPPLY_COST AS MSC
  WHERE SUPPLIER = 'Random Distributors'
```

In this example, MSC is a correlation name for the table MUSIC_SUPPLY_COST. The keyword AS is optional and may be omitted, although we always prefer to include it for clarity. (If you like, you can think of correlation names as a sort of *alias* for tables, but SQL doesn't use that term.)

Correlation names are actually a lot more interesting than they would seem from the preceding discussion. Let's take a slightly longer look at them to better understand their usefulness and the rules associated with them.

First, it's important to remember that a correlation name always hides the name of the table. Therefore, if you write:

```
SELECT * FROM MOVIE_TITLES AS MT
   WHERE MOVIE_TITLES.OUR_COST > 10.95
```

you will get an error; in the context of this SELECT statement, the table name MOVIE_TITLES simply doesn't exist once the correlation name has been defined. Instead, you'll have to write:

```
SELECT * FROM MOVIE_TITLES AS MT
   WHERE MT.OUR_COST > 10.95
```

(or let the column name remain unqualified, since there are no ambiguities in this example).

Second, although you can often use the table name as a sort of implicit correlation name (as though you specified MOVIE_TITLES AS MOVIE_TITLES), they're *not* really the same thing. The following statement is *valid* SQL:

```
SELECT * FROM CATALOG1.MYSCHEMA.MOVIE_TITLES
   WHERE CATALOG1.MYSCHEMA.MOVIE_TITLES.OUR_COST > 10.95
```

but this one is *invalid* and will give you an error:

```
SELECT * FROM CATALOG1.MYSCHEMA.MOVIE_TITLES AS MT
   WHERE CATALOG1.MYSCHEMA.MT.OUR_COST > 10.95
```

Why? Simply because the correlation name acts as a replacement for the *entire* qualified table name, not just the identifier alone! Therefore, don't think of FROM MOVIE_TITLES as a shorthand for FROM MOVIE_TITLES AS MOVIE_TITLES—they're different in that very important way.

We just told you that you could use a column reference only in the scope of a table reference. Let's try to define this scope a little more carefully.

If the column reference contains an explicit qualifier, then it must be in the scope of a table name or a correlation name that is the same as that qualifier. Furthermore, there can be only one such table name or correlation name. Actually, scopes can be nested, and in the innermost such scope, there can only be one such name. The table identified by the qualifier must contain a column with the name you use in the column reference. Therefore,

```
SELECT MSC.MUSIC_TITLE FROM MOVIE_TITLES AS MSC
```

isn't valid, even though MSC is a valid correlation name. The table associated with MSC doesn't have a column named MUSIC_TITLE.

If the column reference doesn't have an explicit qualifier, then it has an *implicit* qualifier. The database system decides what that qualifier is. In this case, the column reference has to appear in the scope of one or more table names or correlation names that identify a table containing a column with the name you gave in the column reference. If there's exactly one such table name or correlation name, then that name is the implicit qualifier for the table reference. If it turns out that there are two or more such table names or correlation names in the innermost scope, then you'll get an error—*unless* they both (all) identify tables that are part of a joined table (discussed in Chapter 8); in this case, the column name must identify a column in every one of those tables and the column reference identifies any and all of the columns at the same time! If this occurs, the implicit qualifier is chosen by your implementation, but you never see it (or need to see it).

And, it's almost too obvious to say, but . . . the data type of a column reference is the same as the data type of the column that it references (bet you were surprised by that!).

5.7 Some Terminology

SQL-92 uses a few special terms to distinguish among various sets of values.

- *Value Specification:* This is a value specified by itself without any operators (not an expression). It can be a literal, a parameter, or host variable (including an indicator), a dynamic parameter, or one of the special values CURRENT_USER, SESSION_USER, or SYSTEM_USER. In a domain definition, the special value VALUE is included (meaning the value of the column in the row).
- *Simple Value Specification:* This is a more limited set of values; it can only be a parameter or host variable (without an indicator) or a literal.
- *Target Specification:* This isn't always a value but is often a way to specify the place (target) to put output from an SQL statement; it is either a parameter or host variable (with indicators allowed).
- *Simple Target Specification:* This simplest form is only a parameter or host variable without an indicator.

5.8 Set Functions

Since SQL-92 supports management of database data as a set, a number of special set-oriented functions are provided. Set functions can best be viewed as a collection of functions that search a table and perform behind-the-scenes calculations that you would otherwise have to do yourself in your programs. Set functions include facilities to count the number of rows in a table, return the maximum and minimum values within specific columns, and calculate averages and sums (many people call these *aggregate functions*).

5.8.1 COUNT

The COUNT(*) set function returns the number of rows in the specified table. For example, let's go back to our MOVIE_TITLES table. The complete syntax of COUNT is shown in Diagram RR7.

Assume that we have an *extremely* small video store, only a few movies in stock, and therefore small database tables (see Table 5-3).

TABLE 5-3

TITLE	OUR_COST	REGULAR_RENTAL_PRICE	CURRENT_RENTAL_PRICE
The Way We Were	14.95	1.99	1.99
Prince of Tides	55.95	3.99	3.99
Yentl	24.95	1.99	1.99
48 Hours	29.95	2.99	1.99
A Star is Born	24.95	1.99	1.99
Another 48 Hours	29.95	2.99	1.99
Beverly Hills Cop	29.95	2.99	1.99
Beverly Hills Cop II	29.95	2.99	1.99
Pretty Woman	55.95	3.99	3.99
Silverado	24.95	1.99	1.99
Moonstruck	35.95	2.99	2.99
Raising Arizona	24.95	1.99	1.99
The Outlaw Josey Wales	24.95	1.99	1.99
Duck Soup	14.95	1.99	1.99
A Night at the Opera	14.95	1.99	1.99
About Last Night	14.95	1.99	1.99
Animal House	14.95	1.99	1.99
Ten	14.95	1.99	1.99

The statement,

```
SELECT COUNT (*)
  FROM MOVIE_TITLES ;
```

will yield the result of 18, indicating that 18 rows are in the table. Of course, in real life, our database tables would contain more rows than that and would therefore yield a larger number as a result.

Let's go back to our MOVIES_STARS table (see Table 5-4).

TABLE 5-4

MOVIE TITLE	ACTOR_LAST_NAME	ACTOR_FIRST_NAME
The Way We Were	Redford	Robert
The Way We Were	Streisand	Barbra
Prince of Tides	Nolte	Nick
Prince of Tides	Streisand	Barbra
Yentl	Streisand	Barbra
48 Hours	Nolte	Nick
48 Hours	Murphy	Eddie
A Star is Born	Kristofferson	Kris
A Star is Born	Streisand	Barbra
Another 48 Hours	Murphy	Eddie
Another 48 Hours	Nolte	Nick
Beverly Hills Cop	Murphy	Eddie
Beverly Hills Cop	Reinhold	Judge
Beverly Hills Cop II	Murphy	Eddie
Beverly Hills Cop II	Reinhold	Judge
Pretty Woman	Roberts	Julia
Pretty Woman	Gere	Richard
Silverado	Kostner	Kevin
Silverado	Kline	Kevin
Silverado	Glover	Danny
Silverado	Denehy	Brian
Moonstruck	Cher	
Moonstruck	Cage	Nicholas
Raising Arizona	Cage	Nicholas
Raising Arizona	Hunter	Holly
The Outlaw Josey Wales	Eastwood	Clint
The Outlaw Josey Wales	Locke	Sondra
Duck Soup	Marx Brothers	
A Night at the Opera	Marx Brothers	
About Last Night	Belushi	James
About Last Night	Lowe	Rob
About Last Night	Moore	Demi
Animal House	Belushi	John
Animal House	Matheson	Tim
Ten	Derek	Bo
Ten	Moore	Dudley

The COUNT(*) set function will yield a result of 36. Just as we discussed in Chapter 3, there may be times when you wish to eliminate duplicate rows from your specific query. The DISTINCT set quantifier can be used to specify a column from which duplicates will be eliminated from consideration. The statement,

```
SELECT COUNT (DISTINCT MOVIE_TITLE)
  FROM MOVIES_STARS ;
```

will result in an answer of 18 (the same as the COUNT(*) from the MOVIE_TITLES table).

You can also make additional restrictions on the table that you are counting. That is, you don't have to retrieve the count of rows in a physical base table, but from a virtual table that is generated by the statement that contains the COUNT expression. For example, you could say:

```
SELECT COUNT(*)
  FROM MOVIES_STARS
  WHERE ACTOR_LAST_NAME = 'Moore'
```

which would return the value of the number of movies starring Dudley Moore, Demi Moore, Mary Tyler Moore, and others with the same last name.

5.8.2 MAX

The MAX function is used to return the maximum value within a specified column. Assume that you wish to learn the most expensive movie sale price that you have in stock (see Table 5-5).

The statement,

```
SELECT MAX(CURRENT_SALE_PRICE)
  FROM MOVIE_TITLES ;
```

will yield an answer of 65.95. Behind the scenes, only one of the rows that meet the MAX (CURRENT_SALE_PRICE) restriction (two do so in our example, but it doesn't matter how many) will be retained; it doesn't matter which one.

Now, let's see why it's important to understand the behavior of SQL. Suppose you wanted, for some reason, to expand the preceding query to get the titles of all movies priced at the maximum and to get that maximum price. If you quickly sounded out the query, you'd probably say:

select the title, and the maximum prices, from the MOVIE_TITLES table

and you might be tempted to write:

```
SELECT TITLE, MAX (CURRENT_SALE_PRICE)
  FROM MOVIE_TITLES ;
```

TABLE 5-5

TITLE	OUR COST	REGULAR RENTAL_PRICE	CURRENT RENTAL_PRICE
The Way We Were	14.95	19.95	19.95
Prince of Tides	55.95	65.95	65.95
Yentl	24.95	29.95	24.95
48 Hours	29.95	34.95	34.95
A Star is Born	24.95	29.95	29.95
Another 48 Hours	29.95	34.95	34.95
Beverly Hills Cop	29.95	34.95	34.95
Beverly Hills Cop II	29.95	34.95	34.95
Pretty Woman	55.95	65.95	65.95
Silverado	24.95	29.95	29.95
Moonstruck	35.95	39.95	39.95
Raising Arizona	24.95	29.95	29.95
The Outlaw Josey Wales	24.95	29.95	29.95
Duck Soup	14.95	19.95	19.95
A Night at the Opera	14.95	19.95	19.95
About Last Night	14.95	19.95	19.95
I			
I			
I			
I			
Animal House	14.95	19.95	19.95
Ten	14.95	19.95	12.95

but that is *not* valid SQL syntax. SQL has a rule that says if any column of the select list is (or uses) a set function, then all of them have to be (or use) set functions! You could write:

```
SELECT TITLE, (SELECT MAX (CURRENT_SALE_PRICE
              FROM MOVIE_TITLES)
    FROM MOVIE_TITLES
```

to this rule, but that would give you the names of *all* movies (Table 5-6), no matter what their price!

TABLE 5-6

The Way We Were	65.95
Prince of Tides	65.95
Yentl	65.95
48 Hours	65.95
A Star is Born	65.95
Another 48 Hours	65.95
I	
I	
I	

Instead, you need to use a *subquery.* We cover subqueries briefly in Chapter 7 and discuss them further in Chapter 9. For now, look at subqueries as a query within another query that yields some type of intermediate result.

For example, let's take our request again, and do a better job of sounding it out. In fact, let's do that in two parts:

- *Part 1:* What is the maximum current sales price within the MOVIE_TITLES table?
- *Part 2:* What movies sell at that price (from Part 1)?

The SQL manner of doing this is

```
SELECT TITLE, CURRENT_SALE_PRICE
  FROM MOVIE_TITLES
  WHERE CURRENT_SALE_PRICE =
      (SELECT MAX(CURRENT_SALE_PRICE)
         FROM MOVIE_TITLES)
```

Our Part 1 query is this subquery: SELECT MAX (CURRENT_SALES_PRICE).... The subquery will yield the result of 65.95, which then becomes the comparison value for the main query: SELECT TITLE,...WHERE CURRENT_SALE_PRICE = 65.95. This then will yield the correct result of

Prince of Tides	65.95
Pretty Woman	65.95

Note that the MAX function is not restricted to numeric data types (INTEGER, REAL, and the like). CHARACTER, DATE, and other data types can have the MAX function used for columns of that type. The statement:

```
SELECT MAX (ACTOR_LAST_NAME)
  FROM MOVIE_TITLES ;
```

would probably give an answer of 'ZZ Top' (from the movie *Back to the Future 3*).

5.8.3 MIN

Assume you have that portion of the MOVIE_TITLES table shown in Table 5-7.

TABLE 5-7

TITLE	TOTAL VHS UNITS RENTED	TOTAL BETA UNITS RENTED	TOTAL VHS UNITS SOLD	TOTAL BETA UNITS SOLD
The Way We Were	321	89	23	8
Prince of Tides	875	132	98	21
Yentl	562	76	24	12
48 Hours	1234	234	456	98
A Star is Born	987	143	134	32
Another 48 Hours	987	145	143	43
Beverly Hills Cop	453	78	78	12
Beverly Hills Cop II	542	98	67	11
Pretty Woman	1702	265	205	41
Silverado	432	87	131	15
Moonstruck	321	92	98	16
Raising Arizona	765	134	123	64
The Outlaw Josey Wales	234	45	98	11
Duck Soup	132	32	19	9
A Night at the Opera	131	29	18	8
About Last Night	214	89	23	4
Animal House	2450	346	234	210
Ten	890	123	122	18

The MIN function can be used in a manner similar to that of MAX, except in finding the smallest value in a given column. The statement:

```
SELECT MIN (TOTAL_VHS_UNITS_RENTED)
  FROM MOVIE_TITLES ;
```

will yield a result of 131.

The MAX and MIN functions can be combined into a single statement, if desired.

```
SELECT MAX (TOTAL_VHS_UNITS_RENTED),
  MIN (TOTAL_VHS_UNITS_RENTED)
  FROM MOVIE_TITLES ;
```

which provides a result of 2450 and 131. As with the MAX function, MIN is not restricted to numeric data types.

5.8.4 SUM

The SUM set function allows you to sum the values in a specified column. Only numeric data types are acceptable as input, though integer-based data types (INTEGER and SMALLINT) and other numeric data types (REAL, DECIMAL, FLOAT, and the like) can be used. An additional constraint is that the result of the SUM function must be within the range of the source data type. If, for example, you were SUMming a column of type SMALLINT and your particular SQL-92 implementation designates 2047 as the largest number acceptable for SMALLINT data, then the SUM of each row's value must be less than or equal to 2047 even though each row's value is already within range.

Given Table 5-7, the statement:

```
SELECT SUM(TOTAL_BETA_UNITS_SOLD)
  FROM MOVIE_TITLES ;
```

will yield the result of 633.

5.8.5 AVG

The AVG set function returns the average of the values in the specified column. As with the SUM function, only numeric data types are permitted. The statement:

```
SELECT AVG (CURRENT_SALE_PRICE)
  FROM MOVIE_TITLES ;
```

will yield the answer that the average current sale price of all movies is 29.788 . . . , or $29.79.

We've now looked at the SQL-92 set functions. Together, the complete syntax for these set functions can be written as shown in Diagram RR8.

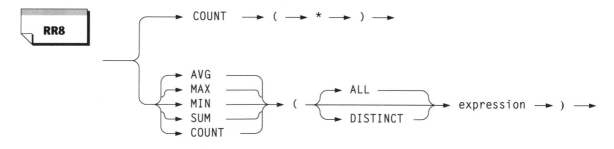

We now look at some other useful functions of SQL-92, starting with value functions.

5.9 Value Functions

Those readers familiar with commercial database management software, particularly those packages used on personal computers, are used to a wide variety of functions used for string manipulation, date-related tasks, and other such facilities. SQL-92 contains three types of value functions, designed to help you perform these necessary chores within your programs. These three categories are

- Numeric Value Functions
- String Value Functions
- Datetime Value Functions

5.9.1 Numeric Value Functions

Numeric value functions always return a numeric value, though they may "operate" on other types of data. The five numeric value functions are POSITION, CHARACTER_LENGTH, OCTET_LENGTH, BIT_LENGTH, and EXTRACT. The complete syntax for SQL-92's numeric value functions is shown in Diagram RR9.

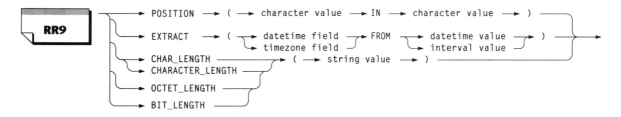

POSITION searches for the presence of a particular string in another string. If the search string is located, the POSITION function returns a numeric value that indicates the position in the source string where the search string was found. If the search string is not found, the function returns a 0 value.

The syntax of the POSITION function is

```
POSITION (string IN source )
```

Some examples follow:

```
POSITION ('4' IN '48 Hours')            -- returns a value of 1
POSITION ('48' IN '48 Hours')           -- returns a value of 1
POSITION ('48' IN 'Another 48 Hours')   -- returns a value of 9
POSITION ('Ugly' IN 'Pretty Woman')     -- returns a value of 0,
                                        -- indicating search string
                                        -- wasn't found
```

```
POSITION ('' IN 'The Way We Were')     -- returns a value of 1;
                                       -- a search string with a
                                       -- length of 0 (a null string)
                                       -- always returns a value of 1
POSITION ('101' IN '000101001001010') -- returns a value of 4
```

CHARACTER_LENGTH, or CHAR_LENGTH, returns the length in characters of a character string. Some examples follow:

```
CHARACTER_LENGTH ('Duck Soup')        -- returns a value of 9
CHAR_LENGTH ('Terminator 2')          -- returns a value of 12
```

Two numeric value functions can be used for system programming tasks that you might need to do. OCTET_LENGTH returns the length in octets of a character or string, while BIT_LENGTH returns the length in bits.

If you use BIT_LENGTH on a character string, it returns the value of OCTET_LENGTH times 8. If you use CHARACTER_LENGTH on a bit string, it will try to interpret the bit string as a character string and return the (apparent) number of characters.

Examples:

```
OCTET_LENGTH ('Annie Hall')   -- returns a value of 10,
                                 assuming one octet per
                                 character; for multi-
                                 octet implementations,
                                 the returned value would
                                 be different
OCTET_LENGTH ('1011100001')   -- returns a value of 2, because
                                 10 bits require at least 2
                                 octets for representation
BIT_LENGTH ('01111110')       -- returns a value of 8
```

The final SQL-92 numeric value function is the EXTRACT function, which isolates a single field of a datetime or an interval (see Chapter 4) and converts it to a number.

Example:

```
EXTRACT (YEAR FROM DATE '1992-06-01') -- returns a numeric
                                      -- value of 1,992
```

5.9.2 String Value Functions

String value functions are perhaps the most familiar SQL-92 functions to longtime DBMS users. The complete syntax of SQL-92's string value expression is shown in Diagram RR10. Let's look at each individually.

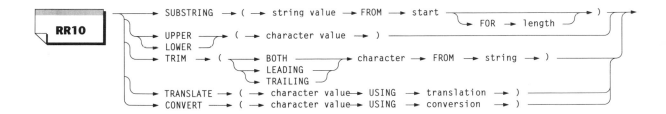

SUBSTRING

The SUBSTRING function is used to extract a substring—either bit or character—from a source bit string or character string.

Example:

```
SUBSTRING ('Another 48 Hours' FROM 1 FOR 9)
```

returns Another 4.

As this example shows, the SUBSTRING value function takes three operands. The first is the string from which a substring is to be taken, the second is the starting point for the substring, and the last (which is optional and has a default value of 'the rest of the string') specifies the length of the substring to be taken.

SUBSTRING has a couple of interesting behaviors that make it a little easier to use. If the start is after the string (for example, SUBSTRING('abc' FROM 10)), then the result of the substring is an empty string (''). If the start is "before" the string and the length is enough to take the substring into the string (for example, SUBSTRING('abc' FROM -2 FOR 4)), then the SUBSTRING acts like the source string has a bunch of noncharacters preceding it. The result of the last example would be 'ab'. If any of the three operands is null, then the result is also null.

The operands can be literals, as in our examples so far, but they can also be any sort of value expression (as long as the first one is a character string and the other two are exact numerics, that is).

More Examples:

```
SUBSTRING ('abcdef' FROM -8 FOR 2)
        has the value ''
SUBSTRING ('abcdef' FROM -2 FOR 6)
        has the value 'abcd'
SUBSTRING ('abcdef' FROM 2 FOR 3)
        has the value 'bcd'
SUBSTRING ('abcdef' FROM 3 FOR -2)
        returns an error, because the "end" of the
        substring preceded the "beginning"
```

```
SUBSTRING ('abcdef' FROM 7 FOR 3)
        has the value ''
SUBSTRING ('abcdef' FROM 3)
        has the value 'def'
SUBSTRING (B'101101' FROM 3 FOR 2)
        has the value B'11'
```

Of course, these examples all use a character string literal as the source of the substring, but you can use any meaningful character value, including expressions, columns, parameters, and so forth.

UPPER and LOWER

The UPPER and LOWER value functions convert (or fold) a particular string to all upper or lower case characters, respectively.

Examples:

```
UPPER ('Batman')      -- returns 'BATMAN'
LOWER ('SUPERMAN')    -- returns 'superman'
```

A couple of quick notes regarding UPPER and LOWER: if you use either of these functions on an accented character (example: the German ö), the case conversion would be applied (UPPER ('ö') would become an 'Ö'). Other character sets with no concept of upper and lower case—Hebrew, for example—would not be affected by usage of these functions.

TRIM

The TRIM function allows you to strip leading blanks, trailing blanks, or both from a character string. In fact, SQL allows you to strip off any character, such as leading and trailing zeros, asterisks, or whatever you (don't) want. For example:

```
TRIM (LEADING ' ' FROM ' TEST ')     has the value  'Test '
TRIM (TRAILING ' ' FROM ' TEST ')    has the value  ' Test'
TRIM (BOTH ' ' FROM ' TEST ')        has the value  'Test'
TRIM (BOTH 'T' FROM 'TEST')          has the value  'ES'
```

If you write TRIM (LEADING FROM ' TEST '), this is the equivalent to the first example, where you specified a blank character; that is, blanks are the default to the TRIM function.

TRANSLATE and CONVERT

Several other string functions belong to the area of internationalization, a subject we discuss in Chapter 18. We'll briefly introduce them for the sake of continuity with the other string functions. The TRANSLATE function translates a source string from its character set to the same or a different character set, using the rules specified in a particular translation.

The CONVERT function converts a source string from its form-of-use to another form-of-use, using rules specified in a conversion.

5.9.3 Datetime Value Functions

Three "current" functions are used in SQL-92 to get the current date, time, or timestamp. CURRENT_DATE is fairly straightforward, and takes no arguments. CURRENT_TIME and CURRENT_TIMESTAMP have one argument—precision—which specifies the fractional seconds precision to be returned with the time. CURRENT_TIME returns a time, while CURRENT_TIMESTAMP returns a timestamp (date + time, as we mentioned in Chapter 4). The complete format for SQL-92's datetime value function is given in Diagram RR11.

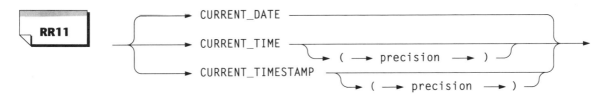

Examples:

```
CURRENT_DATE            -- returns whatever the current
                           date is, such as
                           1992-06-01; note that the
                           returned value is of type
                           DATE, and not a string value
CURRENT_TIME (2)        -- returns the current time
                           to 2 decimal places of
                           precision, such as 12:00:05.54
CURRENT_TIMESTAMP (1)   -- returns a timestamp, such as
                           1980-05-17:09:00:05.2
```

Note that the value returned is correct for the timezone of your session.

5.10 Value Expressions

There are five categories of SQL-92 value expressions.

1. Numeric value expressions
2. String value expressions

3. Datetime value expressions

4. Interval value expressions

5. Conditional value expressions

We'll discuss the first four types, deferring discussion of CASE, NULLIF, and COALESCE—the conditional value expressions—until Chapter 6.

5.10.1 Numeric Value Expressions

Numeric value expressions allow an application to compute numeric values using addition, subtraction, multiplication, and division. Any numeric data types can participate in these data types and they can be mixed. SQL defines rules for the data type of the result of an arithmetic expression based on the data types of the operands. In general, if any approximate numeric type participates in a numeric value expression, the result will have some approximate numeric type; and, if the operation is division, the result will have some approximate numeric type regardless of the data types of the operands. The specific data type of the result will be defined by your implementation; the standard doesn't define it because of the widely-differing platforms on which SQL systems are implemented.

Let's take a look at the complete syntax of the numeric value expression, as shown in Diagram RR12.

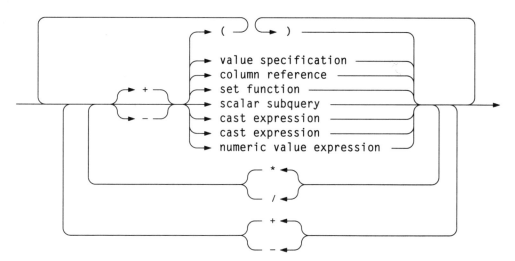

Some examples of numeric value expressions are

- –3

- 5+1

- 8/3–15

- 16*(5–4)

All of the preceding examples show the use of numeric literals in numeric value expressions, but you can use column names, parameters and host variables, and subqueries (see Chapter 9, Query Expressions), like the following.

- +ESTIMATE
- SAL * 1.15
- :velocity / 2.0E3
- 18 + (COST – (PRICE/6.5 + 2 * :adjust))

5.10.2 String Value Expressions

Concatenation is the only operator allowed in string value expressions in the SQL-92 standard, but it is possible that implementations might provide other operators as an extension. Concatenation is denoted by two vertical bars (||). Two or more input values are concatenated together to form a new string value.

Examples:

```
'Star ' || 'Wars'         -- results in 'Star Wars'
'Rocky' || ' ' || 'V'     -- results in 'Rocky V'
CUST_NAME || ' ' || CUST_ADDRESS
                          -- results in a single string
                          -- with a customer name
                          -- and address
|| B'0001'                -- results in B'1010110001'
```

The corresponding railroad diagram is shown in Diagram RR13.

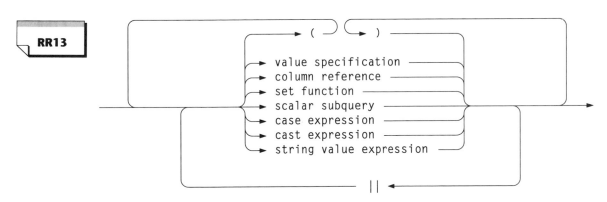

5.10.3 Datetime Value Expressions

Now let's take a look at the datetime value expression. The syntax is shown in Diagram RR14.

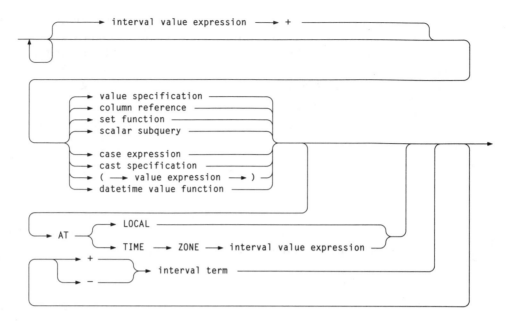

Datetime value expressions operate on date-oriented data types, including DATE, TIME, TIMESTAMP, and INTERVAL. (We will use the word *datetime* to express dates and times in general when we don't need to distinguish between the two.)

The result of a datetime value expression is always another datetime. For example, if you subtract an interval from a datetime, or add an interval to a datetime, the result is another datetime. The expression:

```
CURRENT_DATE + INTERVAL '1' DAY
```

has the same value that CURRENT_DATE would give you tomorrow. (Recall that addition is commutative; therefore, you can add a datetime to an interval or an interval to a datetime and get the same result—the same isn't true for subtraction, though!)

SQL also manages time zone information along with datetimes (except the data type DATE, which has no time zone information associated with it). Times are handled by the database system in UCT (universal coordinated time), which we all used to call GMT (Greenwich mean time). Time zones are really nothing more than offsets from UCT. (We addressed this in Chapter 2, so we won't repeat it here.)

You can tell SQL that a datetime is expressed as a local time (in the time zone associated with your SQL session) or you can give it an explicit time zone. For example, a valid datetime value expression is

```
TIME '10:45:00' AT LOCAL
```

This tells the database system that I want it to represent (or store, perhaps) the time of 10:45 A.M. in my local time zone. On the other hand, I could have said:

```
TIME '10:45:00' AT TIME ZONE INTERVAL '+09:00' HOUR TO MINUTE
```

and it would tell the database system that I want to represent the time in Tokyo. The "stuff" that follows the words TIME ZONE represents an interval (with only hours and minutes fields, of course); it can be a literal, a host variable or parameter, a database column, or any other value. Its value has to be between +13:00 and –12:59, though.

5.10.4 Interval Value Expressions

If you subtract one datetime from another, you will get an interval as the result.

Example:

```
CURRENT_DATE - DATE_RELEASED -- results in the time a
                             -- movie or CD has been
                             -- available
```

The correct syntax for this expression is a little different than the example, though. You must express that concept as follows.

```
(CURRENT_DATE - DATE_RELEASED) YEAR TO MONTH
```

Authors' note: Although the format of the interval value expression isn't all that complicated, inspection of the format will show you that there is a lot of recursion (that is, use of the item being defined in its own definition). Recursion is especially difficult to represent in railroad diagrams, so we won't even attempt it here. The syntax of the interval value expression, as described here and shown in Appendix G, will give you enough information to write such expressions.

The reason that the previous expression is required arises from the fact that the subtraction of two datetimes *could* (and does, in this case) result in an invalid interval (that is, an interval that is neither a year-month interval nor a day-time interval). Therefore, you must tell SQL what sort of interval you wish to get from the subtraction. We chose a year-month interval for this example, but you could also choose a day-time interval if that serves your needs better.

In addition, you can add two intervals together or subtract two intervals to get another interval.

```
INTERVAL '6' DAY - INTERVAL '1' DAY -- results in an interval
                                    -- of 5 days
INTERVAL '6' DAY + INTERVAL '1' DAY -- results in an interval
                                    -- of 7 days
```

You cannot mix year-month and day-time intervals in a single interval value expression because the result would not meet the condition of being either a year-month interval or a day-time interval.

You can also multiply or divide an interval by a numeric constant to get another interval.

```
INTERVAL '6' DAY * 3 -- results in an interval of 18 days
3 * INTERVAL '6' DAY -- results in an interval of 18 days
INTERVAL '6' DAY / 2 -- results in an interval of 3 days
```

And, of course, intervals can be negative or positive, so you can also write things like

```
INTERVAL -'6' DAY -- results in an interval of -6 days
```

which is equivalent to

```
- INTERVAL '6' DAY
```

As always, although we have used literals in our examples, you can use any appropriate value expression throughout.

5.11 Chapter Summary

There are some functions and expressions with which you may be familiar that aren't supported by SQL-92. For example, some string operations, such as "stuffing" a substring into another string at a particular starting point, aren't included among the formal SQL-92 functions. Some SQL-92 implementations may include extensions to support these operations; product reference manuals often provide details and, if supported, applicable syntax. SQL-92 does, however, support a far richer set of functions than do previous versions, bringing SQL standard capabilities more in line with those many readers are accustomed to in personal computer and other database environments.

The subjects discussed in this chapter will help you round out the basic operations discussed in Chapter 3, especially in terms of expanding your repertoire of manipulation tasks with respect to obtaining summary information using set functions. In Chapter 6, we'll discuss how to perform explicit data conversions using the CAST specification, as well as conditional value expressions using CASE, NULLIF, and COALESCE.

Advanced Features
of SQL-92

Advanced Value Expressions: CASE, CAST, and Row Value Expressions

6.1 Introduction

In Chapter 5, we covered the basic set functions, value functions, and value expressions incorporated into SQL. To write complex applications, however, you will often need more power than is available through these basic facilities. Data sublanguages have often been criticized for their lack of rich programming constructs, forcing users and developers to rely on the facilities of host languages or external environments. SQL-92 introduces some of these facilities to the SQL world, including :

- A conditional expression (CASE)
- A data conversion expression (CAST)
- A way to deal with an entire row of data at one time (row value constructor)

Also, we'll introduce a slight style change for the rest of the book's examples: Our SQL keywords will be in capital letters, while identifiers will be in lower case letters.

Technically, you were not permitted to use lower case letters for any identifiers in SQL-89, nor are you for Entry SQL-92. However, many (even most) implementations permit it, so we will use this convention because the statements are easier to read.

6.2 The CASE Expression

There are many application situations where you might find it necessary to change the representation of the data. Applications developers often strive to find a balance among storage requirements (limiting the amount of storage needed), understandability, and other factors. For example, you might code Marital Status as 1, 2, 3, 4, meaning single, married, divorced, or widowed. It is often more efficient to store the short code than the long one, but human readers of reports will prefer the longer words. This conversion shouldn't require host program intervention, but should be manageable in the DBMS.

Additionally, applications sometimes need to generate null values based on information derived from the database and should be able to do so without involving the host programs. Conversely, you may wish to convert a null into some more concrete value, like a zero (0).

The SQL-92 solution to these problems is a CASE expression. This is similar in concept to the CASE statement of some programming languages, but is a conditional *expression,* not statement. Therefore, it can be used (almost) everywhere a value expression can be used.

6.2.1 CASE and Search Conditions

The syntax of the CASE looks like:

```
CASE
   WHEN search-condition₁ THEN result₁
   WHEN search-condition₂ THEN result₂
   ...
   WHEN search-conditionₙ THEN resultₙ
   ELSE resultₓ
END
```

If search-condition$_1$ is true, then the value of the CASE is result$_1$. If not, then if search-condition$_2$ is true, then the value is result$_2$. If none of the search-conditions$_i$ are true, then the value of the CASE is result$_x$. All of the value$_i$ and result$_i$ must have *comparable* data types. The data type of the CASE (again!) is the data type determined by the union-datatype rules.

The ELSE result$_x$ is optional. If it's not specified, then ELSE NULL is implicit. At least one of the result$_i$ has to be something besides the keyword NULL.

As an example, say that we need to make some type of calculation based on the NUMBER_OF_PROBLEMS column in the CUSTOMERS table (see Chapter 22); let's say we assign some type of weighting that will be used for problem resolution priorities. We can use the CASE expression with predicates, such as

```
SELECT cust_name,
    CASE
       WHEN number_of_problems = 0
          THEN 100,
       WHEN number_of_problems > 0
         AND number_of_problems < 4
          THEN number_of_problems * 500
       WHEN number_of_problems >= 4
```

```
              AND number_of_problems <= 9
                THEN number_of_problems * 400
            ELSE (number_of_problems * 300) + 250
          END,
        cust_address
  FROM customers
```

Let's take a look at another example using CASE.

```
UPDATE employees
  SET salary = CASE
                  WHEN dept = 'Video'
                    THEN salary * 1.1
                  WHEN dept = 'Music'
                    THEN salary * 1.2
                  ELSE 0
                END
```

Still another example—which can help avoid getting certain types of errors with which most programmers are familiar—is

```
...
CASE
  WHEN n < > 0 THEN x/n
  ELSE 0
END
```

6.2.2   CASE and Values

You can use a shorthand version of the CASE statement for value comparisons. If $value_t = value_1$, then the value of the CASE is $result_1$. If not, then if $value_t = value_2$, then the result is $result_2$. If none of $value_1 \ldots value_n$ are equal to the desired $value_t$, then the value of the CASE is $result_x$. All of the $result_i$ can be either a value expression or the keyword NULL. All of the $value_i$ must be *comparable*, and all of the results must have *comparable* data types. The data type of the CASE is the data type determined by the union-datatype rules.

The syntax is

```
CASE value_t
  WHEN value_1 THEN result_1
  WHEN value_2 THEN result_2
  ...
  WHEN value_n THEN result_n
  ELSE result_x
END
```

In fact, this is really just a shorthand for the CASE expression:

```
CASE
  WHEN value_t = value_1 THEN result_1
  WHEN value_t = value_2 THEN result_2
  ...
  WHEN value_t = value_n THEN result_n
  ELSE result_x
END
```

The ELSE $result_x$ again is optional. If it's not specified, then ELSE NULL is implicit. At least one of the $result_i$ has to be something besides the keyword NULL. This last form can be transformed to the previous form by deleting the $value_t$ and replacing every $result_i$ with $value_t = result_i$.

Assume that in our MOVIE_TITLES table we decided to encode the column MOVIE_TYPE with an integer rather than the CHARACTER(10) needed to spell out Horror, Comedy, Romance, and our other movie types. We can still return a text string to applications through the use of the CASE expression, as in

```
SELECT title,
  CASE movie_type
    WHEN 1 THEN 'Horror'
    WHEN 2 THEN 'Comedy'
    WHEN 3 THEN 'Romance'
    WHEN 4 THEN 'Western'
    WHEN.....
    ELSE NULL
  END,
    our_cost
FROM movie_titles ;
```

6.2.3 NULLIF

SQL provides null values and defines the behavior of the various arithmetic and other operators when applied to null values. Sometimes, however, people choose to represent missing or unknown or inapplicable information in other ways, either for historical reasons or general preference. For example, missing OUR_COST values might be represented by a -1 value. And, it is sometimes useful to convert such missing information flags to null values, in order to get the null behavior defined by SQL. This can be done with a CASE expression, as follows:

```
...WHERE vhs_sales_revenue / CASE
                    WHEN our_cost=-1
                      THEN NULL
                      ELSE our_cost
                    END
```

> 52

Such a CASE expression is expected to be relatively common, so a special syntax shorthand is provided for it. The expression

```
...WHERE vhs_sales_revenue / NULLIF(our_cost, -1) > 52
```

namely, the expression NULLIF(our_cost, -1), is simply a shorthand for

```
CASE WHEN our_cost=-1 THEN NULL ELSE our_cost END
```

6.2.4 COALESCE

The final form of the CASE expression is the COALESCE expression, which has the syntax:

```
COALESCE (value1, value2,... valuen)
```

If $value_1$ is not null, then the value of the COALESCE is $value_1$. If $value_1$ is null, then $value_2$ is checked. This continues until either a non-null value $value_j$) is found—in which case, the value of the COALESCE is $value_j$—or every value, including $value_n$, is found to be null—in which case, the value of the COALESCE is NULL. The data types of all the $value_1 \ldots value_n$ must be *comparable*; the data type of the COALESCE is the data type determined by the same union-datatype rules applicable to the NULLIF expression.

COALESCE is also just a shorthand (as is NULLIF) for a variation of CASE that is used quite often. Therefore,

```
COALESCE (1, value2,value3)
```

is equivalent to

```
CASE
  WHEN value1 IS NOT NULL
    THEN value1
  WHEN value2 IS NOT NULL
    THEN value2
  ELSE value3
END
```

Example:

```
COALESCE (salary, commission, subsistence)
```

In the context of a query expression, you might issue:

```
SELECT name, job_title,
    COALESCE (salary, commission, subsistence)
  FROM job_assignments
```

This expression would first attempt to return a person's salary. In the absence of a regular salary (that is, the stored value is null), a commission is sought. Subsequently, in the absence of a commission, a subsistence (allowance) is checked. If none of the columns has a non-null value, then null is returned.

Actually, there are other, more important uses for COALESCE, which we will discuss in Chapter 8 in the context of the OUTER JOIN.

Diagram RR15 summarizes the syntax of the case expression.

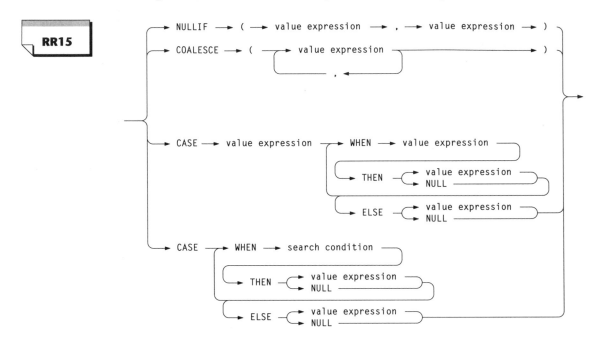

6.3 The CAST Expression

SQL has always been considered a *strongly-typed* language. This means that you cannot have expressions that contain arbitrary data types. Some languages, like PL/I, allow almost arbitrary mixing of data types in expressions; for example, you can add an integer and a character string together (as long as the character string looks like an integer) or you can concatenate an integer and a character string. Other languages, like Pascal, don't allow mixing of *any* sort; you cannot even add short integer with a long integer in a language as strongly typed as Pascal.

SQL falls somewhere in between these extremes, but is closer to Pascal than to PL/I. In SQL-86 and SQL-89, you could compare or add an INTEGER with a SMALLINT, but not with a CHARACTER. In SQL-92, you can mix exact numerics and characters in a single expression by CASTing to appropriate data types.

There are many times, however, when your application knows that the contents of a character string are only digits that look like an integer. You would like to be able to add the integer value corresponding to that character string to an actual INTEGER, but SQL-86/SQL-89 wouldn't let you. Well, SQL-92 doesn't let you do it indiscriminately—that is, without expressing it precisely. However, if you express it appropriately, you can do it in SQL-92 and needn't escape to your host program to perform the necessary type mixing and conversion functions.

The appropriate way to express this is to explicitly do a data conversion using the CAST expression. CAST allows you to convert data of one type to a different type, subject to a few restrictions.

1. You can convert any exact or approximate numeric value to any other numeric data type. If the value being converted doesn't fit in the new data type, then you get an error. If you try to convert a value with a fractional component to a type with less fractional precision, then the system will round or truncate (implementation-defined) for you.

2. You can convert any exact or approximate numeric value to any character string type.

3. You can convert any exact numeric value to a single-component interval, such as INTERVAL MINUTE or INTERVAL YEAR.

4. You can convert any character string to any other data type, with a few restrictions. First, if you are converting to another character string type, then they must have the same character set (see Chapter 18). Second, the contents of the character string must make sense for the target data type; for example, if the new type is DATE, then the character string must contain 4 digits, a hyphen, 2 digits, another hyphen, and 2 more digits. In fact, the character string must exactly mimic a valid literal of the data type to which you are CASTing. When converting character strings to numeric, datetime, or interval types, leading and/or trailing spaces are ignored. When converting a character string to a bit string, the bit representation of the characters are placed into the bit string.

5. You can convert a DATE to a character string or to a TIMESTAMP (filling in the TIME part of the TIMESTAMP with 00:00:00. You can convert a TIME to a character string, a TIME with different fractional seconds precision, or a TIMESTAMP (filling in the DATE part of the TIMESTAMP with values for today). You can convert a TIMESTAMP to a character string, a DATE, a TIME, or another TIMESTAMP with different fractional seconds precision.

6. You can convert a year-month INTERVAL to a character string, to an exact numeric, or to another year-month INTERVAL with different leading field precision. You can convert a day-time INTERVAL to a character string, to an exact numeric, or to another day-time INTERVAL with different leading field precision.

7. You can convert a bit string to a character string or to a bit string. When converting a bit string to a character string, the bits are placed into the character string as though they were the bits of characters.

The entire syntax for CAST is summarized in Diagram RR16.

One use for CAST is to make two tables that are not quite the same structure look alike. For example, if you have one table of EMPLOYEES that has HIRE_DATE defined as a DATE and a second table of INTERVIEWEES that has INTERVIEW_DATE defined as a CHARACTER, you could CAST one of these two columns to be the same data type as the other; this would make the columns into the same data type and would contribute to making it possible to union the two tables, an operation that requires identical column properties (see Chapter 8).

Another use is to make it possible to compare two tables. In the previous example, if you wanted to JOIN the tables (also discussed in Chapter 8) based on certain column values in two tables being equal to one another, you could have a WHERE clause like

```
WHERE employees.hire_date =
    CAST (interviewees.interview_date AS DATE)
```

For making two tables look like one another, the ability to CAST (NULL AS datatype) is invaluable. It allows you to fill in the column that has no correspondence in one table with NULLs of the proper data type.

A very important use for CAST is to allow you to access database data that your host language can't handle (for example, DATE data from any host language). By using CAST, you can retrieve and store such data easily. (For the datetime types, you would CAST to and from CHARACTER, for example.)

6.4 Row Value Constructors

In SQL-86 and SQL-89, virtually all data operations were on single values or single columns. For example, if you needed to compare all columns of a row in one table with all columns in a row of another table, you would have to write a fairly complicated expression.

In SQL-92, however, you can do it very simply. For example, you might write:

```
WHERE (C1, C2, C3) = (CA, CB, CC)
```

whereas, in SQL-89, you would need to have written:

```
WHERE C1 = CA AND C2 = CB AND C3 = CC
```

A row value constructor is basically a parenthesized list of values. It can be used in many places where a value is permitted (but, unfortunately, not in every place) as long as the degree is appropriate. The syntax for a row value syntax is given in Diagram RR17.

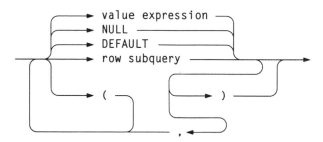

If the row value constructor is used as the insert-values of an INSERT statement, then any value can be NULL or DEFAULT. NULL obviously makes the inserted value for the corresponding column in the table null, while DEFAULT makes the inserted value the default value for the column.

The values (other than NULL and DEFAULT) can be simple values or value expressions. In cases where the row value constructor can be only a single value (degree equal to one), the parentheses may be left off.

A row value constructor can be thought of as a literal for an entire row or even for a one-row table (although this is probably carrying the analogy too far—the individual values don't have to be literals, but can be parameters, host variables, or even subqueries). A row value constructor can also be a *subquery* (a concept introduced in Chapter 7 and explored in detail in Chapter 9). In this case, if the cardinality of the subquery is 0, then the row value constructor is a row of null values; if it's 1, then the row value constructor is the row returned by the subquery; if it's greater than 1, then you get an error.

Let's look at another example, one somewhat more complicated. If you were to write:

```
WHERE ( c1, c2, c3 ) < ( ca, cb, cc)
```

you would get exactly the same effect as

```
WHERE ( c1 < ca ) OR
      ( c1 = ca AND c2 < cb ) OR
      ( c1 = ca AND c2 = cb AND c3 < cc )
```

The less-than operation is evaluated left to right on the row values and stops whenever it finds a pair that satisfies the comparison. Note that this is the same result that ORDER BY (see Chapter 12) would give if the two expressions were rows in a table.

6.5 Chapter Summary

In this chapter, we discussed how to use SQL's more advanced value expressions. The CASE expression allows you to return values that are computed from database values (or, for that matter, to store values that are computed from input values). The CAST expression allows you to perform explicit data conversions in your SQL application. The row value constructor allows you to manipulate rows of data at one time instead of one value at a time.

The advanced value expressions are among the major enhancements to SQL-92 (as compared with previous versions of the standard). For example, the CAST data conversions are far easier to use than the old way of required host program intervention. Similarly, the CASE expression brings host language programming constructs (somewhat) into the data sublanguage world, permitting multiple choice operations within the context of your SQL statements. Finally, row value constructors provide an alternative, easier to use method of multiple column value comparisons and other operations than previous SQL syntax permitted.

In this chapter and in Chapter 5, we've taken our first steps beyond basic SQL syntax. You already knew, for example, how to create simple tables (introduced in Chapter 3) as well as other data objects such as schemas, views, domains, and the like (discussed in Chapter 4). The basic data manipulation statements discussed in Chapter 3 have been enhanced with simple value expressions and value specifications, special values, and now *advanced* value expressions.

In Chapter 7, we turn our attention to the subject of *predicates,* features that allow you to perform wildcard pattern matching, range of value and list of value searching, and other functions that will further add to your SQL repertoire.

CHAPTER 7

. . . .

Predicates

7.1 Introduction

In Chapter 3, we discussed basic SQL-92 data manipulation statements. We illustrated that the power of SQL-92 is unleashed when you can specify criteria for your data retrieval and modification operations. For example, `SELECT * FROM MOVIE_TITLES` is a valid data retrieval statement, but the `SELECT` statement becomes far more useful when you specify search parameters through the use of facilities such as the `WHERE` clause.

Even though we didn't explicitly state it in Chapter 3, we looked at some basic predicates in that chapter. More specifically, we illustrated how simple comparison predicates, using familiar symbols such as =, <, and >, can be used to restrict your data manipulation statements to operations on certain data.

In this chapter, we take a more extensive look at the different types of SQL-92 predicates, including other comparison predicates. We discuss `IN`, `LIKE`, `NULL`, `EXISTS`, and others. We also introduce the concept of a subquery in the context of certain predicates.

7.2 What is a Predicate?

A predicate is really an expression that asserts a fact about values. The expression can be True, meaning that the fact is correct; it can be False, meaning that the fact is incorrect; or it can (often) be Unknown, meaning that the DBMS is unable to determine whether the fact is correct or incorrect. (Unknown can occur if some of the values are null, for example.)

7.3   Subqueries

In order to understand how some of the SQL-92 predicates function, we need to briefly explain the concept of a subquery. We introduced an example of a subquery in Chapter 5, and we discuss them in more detail in Chapter 9.

A subquery is a query expression that appears in the body of another expression, such as a SELECT statement, an UPDATE, or a DELETE statement. For example,

```
SELECT title, vhs_in_stock
  FROM movie_titles
  WHERE title IN
    ( SELECT movie_title
        FROM movies_stars
        WHERE
          actor_last_name = 'Gibson' AND
          actor_first_name = 'Mel' )  ;
```

Subqueries are one method by which information from multiple tables can be related to one another. In the above example, the subquery—the SELECT of movie titles in which Mel Gibson stars—is evaluated (handled) first by SQL-92, and a list of movie titles (as we have requested) is produced, internal to the system. Then, the main query—matching the TITLE column from MOVIE_TITLES with the produced list of Mel Gibson films—produces the list of titles from the number of VHS titles we have in stock. (Incidentally, there is at least one more way to handle this request, by joining the two tables and filtering the result with a WHERE clause—we leave that solution as an exercise for the reader. We will discuss the various types of JOIN operations in the next chapter)

Note the use of the keyword IN, which we discuss later in this chapter as one of our predicates. The IN predicate is used to perform subquery searching and matching, as we shall see.

Again, we'll discuss subqueries in more detail in Chapter 9, specifically in the context of multiple nestings. For the purposes of this chapter, we discuss several predicates—IN, EXISTS, UNIQUE, and MATCH—that utilize subqueries in their operations. We point out that most predicates can be true, false, or unknown, but a few (*e.g.*, NULL) can only be true or false.

7.4   Comparison Predicate

The comparison predicate uses the so-called Big Six comparison types (see Table 7-1), which are common to most programming languages.

The usage of these comparison predicates is fairly self-explanatory for those used to programming or even basic mathematics. However, let's briefly look at some, using Table 7-2 in our examples.

TABLE 7-1

Comparison	SQL-92 Symbol
1. equal	=
2. not equal	<>
3. less than	<
4. greater than	>
5. less than or equal	<=
6. greater than or equal	>=

TABLE 7-2
MOVIE_TITLES

TITLE	OUR_ COST	REGULAR_ RENTAL_ PRICE	CURRENT_ RENTAL_ PRICE	REGULAR_ SALE_ PRICE	CURRENT_ SALE_ PRICE
The Way We Were	14.95	1.99	1.99	19.95	19.95
Prince of Tides	55.95	3.99	3.99	65.95	65.95
Yentl	24.95	1.99	1.99	29.95	24.95
48 Hours	29.95	2.99	1.99	34.95	34.95
A Star is Born	24.95	1.99	1.99	29.95	29.95
Another 48 Hours	29.95	2.99	1.99	34.95	34.95
Beverly Hills Cop	29.95	2.99	1.99	34.95	34.95
Beverly Hills Cop II	29.95	2.99	1.99	34.95	34.95
Pretty Woman	55.95	3.99	3.99	65.95	65.95
Silverado	24.95	1.99	1.99	29.95	29.95
Moonstruck	35.95	2.99	2.99	39.95	39.95
Raising Arizona	24.95	1.99	1.99	29.95	29.95
The Outlaw Josey Wales	24.95	1.99	1.99	29.95	29.95
Duck Soup	14.95	1.99	1.99	19.95	19.95
A Night at the Opera	14.95	1.99	1.99	19.95	19.95
About Last Night	14.95	1.99	1.99	19.95	19.95
Animal House	14.95	1.99	1.99	19.95	19.95
Ten	14.95	1.99	1.99	19.95	12.95

Example 1. This predicate produces Table 7-3.

```
SELECT *
  FROM movie_titles
  WHERE our_cost = 24.95 ;
```

TABLE 7-3

TITLE	OUR COST	REGULAR RENTAL PRICE	CURRENT RENTAL PRICE	REGULAR SALE PRICE	CURRENT SALE PRICE
Yentl	24.95	1.99	1.99	29.95	24.95
A Star is Born	24.95	1.99	1.99	29.95	29.95
Silverado	24.95	1.99	1.99	29.95	29.95
Raising Arizona	24.95	1.99	1.99	29.95	29.95
The Outlaw Josey Wales	24.95	1.99	1.99	29.95	29.95

Example 2. Here we get Table 7-4.

```
SELECT title, our_cost
  FROM movie_titles
  WHERE our_cost < 24.95 ;
```

TABLE 7-4

TITLE	OUR COST
The Way We Were	14.95
Duck Soup	14.95
A Night at the Opera	14.95
About Last Night	14.95
Animal House	14.95
Ten	14.95

Example 3. Comparisons don't have to be against numeric data types; character, date, and other types can be used as well. Note that the specific collating sequence will determine whether, say, a *4* is greater than or less than a *Q* in terms of value. The preceding query will return all rows where the TITLE *begins* with a character greater than a capital *Q:* the letters *R* through *Z* and anything else of a greater value in that collating sequence, as shown in Table 7-5.

```
SELECT title
  FROM movie_titles
  WHERE title > 'Q' ;
```

TABLE 7-5

TITLE
The Way We Were
Yentl
Silverado
Raising Arizona
The Outlaw Josey Wales
Ten

Example 4. In example 4, the entire table (Table 7-2) will be returned, since all titles have a sales price greater than or equal to our cost, or at least that's what we hope!

```
SELECT *
  FROM movie_titles
  WHERE regular_sale_price >= our_cost ;
```

Example 5. This query will give us a list (Table 7-6) of all movies that don't rent at our bargain price.

```
SELECT title, current_rental_price
  FROM movie_titles
  WHERE current_rental_price <> 1.99 ;
```

TABLE 7-6

TITLE	CURRENT_RENTAL_PRICE
Prince of Tides	3.99
Pretty Woman	3.99
Moonstruck	2.99
	)

Example 6. A query designed to see how many expensive movies we carry, as shown in Table 7-7.

```
SELECT *
  FROM movie_titles
  WHERE our_cost >= 35.95 ;
```

TABLE 7-7

TITLE	OUR COST	REGULAR RENTAL PRICE	CURRENT RENTAL PRICE	REGULAR SALE PRICE	CURRENT SALE PRICE
Prince of Tides	55.95	3.99	3.99	65.95	65.95
Pretty Woman	55.95	3.99	3.99	65.95	65.95
Moonstruck	35.95	2.99	2.99	39.95	39.95
)					

7.4.1 BETWEEN

A special variant of the comparison predicate is the BETWEEN predicate, which has the form

```
value1 BETWEEN value2 AND value3
```

This is equivalent to

```
value1 >= value2  AND  value1 <= value3
```

Example (Table 7-8 is returned):

```
SELECT *
  FROM movie_titles
  WHERE our_cost BETWEEN 11.00 AND 27.50 ;
```

You should take note of the details of the equivalent expression of this predicate. The order of the operands has some unexpected implications that can catch you off guard if you don't pay close attention:

```
10 BETWEEN 5 AND 15
```

is true, but

```
10 BETWEEN 15 AND 5
```

is false! That's because the equivalent way of expressing BETWEEN (using AND) has a specific order to it. This obviously doesn't matter much when you're using literals, as our example does, but if might matter a lot if you provide value2 and value3 by using host variables, parameters, or even subqueries.

TABLE 7-8

TITLE	OUR_ COST	REGULAR_ RENTAL_ PRICE	CURRENT_ RENTAL_ PRICE	REGULAR_ SALE_ PRICE	CURRENT_ SALE_ PRICE
The Way We Were	14.95	1.99	1.99	19.95	19.95
Yentl	24.95	1.99	1.99	29.95	24.95
A Star is Born	24.95	1.99	1.99	29.95	29.95
Silverado	24.95	1.99	1.99	29.95	29.95
Raising Arizona	24.95	1.99	1.99	29.95	29.95
The Outlaw Josey Wales	24.95	1.99	1.99	29.95	29.95
Duck Soup	14.95	1.99	1.99	19.95	19.95
A Night at the Opera	14.95	1.99	1.99	19.95	19.95
About Last Night	14.95	1.99	1.99	19.95	19.95
Animal House	14.95	1.99	1.99	19.95	19.95
Ten	14.95	1.99	1.99	19.95	12.95

7.4.2 NOT BETWEEN

Still another variant of the comparison predicate is the use of NOT BETWEEN, as in

    value1 NOT BETWEEN value2 AND value3

This predicate is equivalent to

    NOT (value1 BETWEEN value2 AND value3)

or, in other words, value1 is outside the range between value2 and value3. (The same one-way attribute applies to NOT BETWEEN, too.)

Example (returning Table 7-9):

```
SELECT title, our_cost
  FROM movie_titles
  WHERE our_cost NOT BETWEEN
    29.95 AND 35.95 ;
```

TABLE 7-9

TITLE	OUR COST	REGULAR RENTAL PRICE	CURRENT RENTAL PRICE	REGULAR SALE PRICE	CURRENT SALE PRICE
The Way We Were	14.95	1.99	1.99	19.95	19.95
Prince of Tides	55.95	3.99	3.99	65.95	65.95
Yentl	24.95	1.99	1.99	29.95	24.95
A Star is Born	24.95	1.99	1.99	29.95	29.95
Pretty Woman	55.95	3.99	3.99	65.95	65.95
Silverado	24.95	1.99	1.99	29.95	29.95
Raising Arizona	24.95	1.99	1.99	29.95	29.95
The Outlaw Josey Wales	24.95	1.99	1.99	29.95	29.95
Duck Soup	14.95	1.99	1.99	19.95	19.95
A Night at the Opera	14.95	1.99	1.99	19.95	19.95
About Last Night	14.95	1.99	1.99	19.95	19.95
I					
I					
I					
I					
Animal House	14.95	1.99	1.99	19.95	19.95
Ten	14.95	1.99	1.99	19.95	12.95

BETWEEN is also used with the various character, bit and datetime data types as well.

7.5 NULL Predicate

The NULL predicate is used to determine if a column in a selected row has a null value. The syntax is

```
column name IS NULL
```

Example (returning Table 7-10): For purposes of this example, assume that any empty value in ACTOR_FIRST_NAME is a null value, not one or more blanks.

```
SELECT movie_title, actor_last_name,
       actor_first_name
  FROM movies_stars
  WHERE actor_first_name IS NULL ;
```

TABLE 7-10

MOVIE_TITLE	ACTOR_LAST_NAME	ACTOR_FIRST_NAME
I		
I		
I		
Silverado	Kostner	Kevin
Silverado	Kline	Kevin
Silverado	Glover	Danny
Silverado	Denehy	Brian
Moonstruck	Cher	
Moonstruck	Cage	Nicholas
Raising Arizona	Cage	Nicholas
Raising Arizona	Hunter	Holly
The Outlaw Josey Wales	Eastwood	Clint
The Outlaw Josey Wales	Locke	Sondra
Duck Soup	Marx Brothers	
A Night at the Opera	Marx Brothers	
About Last Night	Belushi	James
About Last Night	Lowe	Rob
About Last Night	Moore	Demi
Animal House	Belushi	John

TABLE 7-11

MOVIE_TITLE	ACTOR_LAST_NAME	ACTOR_FIRST_NAME
Moonstruck	Cher	
Duck Soup	Marx Brothers	
A Night at the Opera	Marx Brothers	

You won't be surprised to learn that you can combine the NOT operator with the NULL predicate. The format is

```
value IS NOT NULL
```

and the predicate is true if and only if the provided value is not null. If the value is null, then the predicate is false.

One place where the IS NULL predicate might not behave exactly as you expect it to is when it operates on a row with more than one column:

```
WHERE (actor_last_name, actor_first_name)
  IS NULL
```

will be true only if *both* values are null. However, with

```
WHERE (actor_last_name, actor_first_name)
   IS NOT NULL
```

also will be true only if *both* values are not null!

There are two more possible variations:

```
WHERE NOT (actor_last_name, actor_first_name) IS NULL
```

will be false if both are null, and true if either are null, and (one more here) true if neither is null. Similarly,

```
WHERE NOT (actor_last_name, actor_first_name)
   IS NOT NULL
```

is true if either or both is null and false only if neither is null.

Confused? This is why you were told in elementary school not to use double negatives! Table 7-12 captures and makes some sense out of the preceding examples.

TABLE 7-12
Null Predicate
Semantics

EXPRESSION	R IS NULL	R IS NOT NULL	NOT R IS NULL	NOT R IS NOT NULL
degree 1: null	True	False	False	True
degree 1: not null	False	True	True	False
degree >1: all null	True	False	False	True
degree >1: some null	False	False	True	True
degree >1: none null	False	True	True	False

7.6 IN Predicate

We introduced the IN predicate earlier, while introducing subqueries. The format of the IN predicate is either:

```
value_t IN (value_1, value_2, . . . . .)
```

OR

```
value_t IN subquery
```

The first form of the IN predicate permits the usage of a list of values in place of a subquery. Assume that we want to examine our current rental prices for selected movie costs (that is, our costs), the goal being searching for inconsistencies. We could issue the following statement:

```
SELECT title, current_rental_price
  FROM movie_titles
 WHERE our_cost IN
         (14.95, 24.95, 29.95 ) ;
```

All movies that cost us either $14.95, $24.95, or $29.95 will evaluate True to the IN predicate, and in turn produce a list of titles and accompanying current rental prices for those movies.

In the second form, the subquery is evaluated to produce an intermediate result, against which further processing can be performed. We've already looked at a brief example of a subquery within a SELECT statement. As we mentioned earlier, subqueries can also be contained within statements that modify data, such as UPDATE statements. For example, to promote our *Animal House* store-wide promotion, we decide to put all movies in which John Belushi starred on sale with a 10% rental discount. Note that as a result of our normalized database design (normalization is discussed in Appendix A, but you don't have to worry about that for now), the various columns required to do this are contained in two different tables: REGULAR_RENTAL_PRICE and CURRENT_RENTAL_PRICE are contained within MOVIE_TITLES, while ACTOR_FIRST_NAME and ACTOR_FIRST_NAME reside in MOVIES_STARS. By using a subquery—accompanied by the IN predicate—we can accomplish our goal.

```
UPDATE movie_titles
   SET current_rental_price =
      (regular_rental_price * .9)
 WHERE title IN
    ( SELECT movie_title FROM movies_stars
        WHERE
           actor_last_name = 'Belushi' AND
           actor_first_name = 'John' )  ;
```

Once the subquery produces its list of selected movie titles, that list is processed against the MOVIE_TITLES table and the appropriate rental prices are discounted for *Animal House, Blues Brothers, Neighbors,* and others.

As you must surely expect by now, the IN predicate has a negative companion, NOT IN. The format of this is exactly the same as the IN predicate, but you substitute NOT IN for IN. And, as you guessed, NOT IN is true only if the provided value is not found in the values returned by the subquery or in the parenthesized list of values.

7.7 LIKE Predicate

Users of commercial database products are familiar with wildcards or special characters used to perform partial matches. SQL-92 features the LIKE predicate, together with the % and _ special characters, to do pattern matching among character string data.

The percent sign (%) is used to stand for zero or more characters in the search pattern, while the underscore (_) stands for exactly one character in the column's value. More than one of either special character may be used, [depending on the specific search criteria you have in mind (see Table 7-13)].

TABLE 7-13

Pattern	Explanation	Would Match
'ABC%'	Match any character string value beginning with 'ABC'	'ABCDEF' 'ABC'
'%ABC'	Match any character string value ending with 'ABC'	'XYZABC' 'ABC'
'%ABC%'	Match any character string value which contains 'ABC' anywhere in the string	'ABC' 'ABCDEF' 'XYZABC' 'XYZABCDEF'
'ABC_'	Match any character string value that begins with 'ABC' and is followed by a single character	'ABCD'
'_ABC'	Match any character string value that is four characters in length and ends with 'ABC'	'XABC'
'_ABC%'	Match any character string value that begins with any character, has 'ABC' as the second, third, and fourth characters, respectively, and ends with any number of other characters	'XABCDEFG' 'XABC'

There might be occasions where you want to include either '%' or '_' in your search string (see Table 7-14). To do this, you can use the keyword ESCAPE to designate another character as the *escape* character, which in turn designates a *real* percent sign or underscore immediately following the escape character. Your escape character must be one which is not used explicitly elsewhere in your search string.

TABLE 7-14

Desired Match Value	SQL-92 Predicate	Would Match
'10%'	LIKE '%10$%%' ESCAPE '$'	'10%' '810%' 'A10%'
	LIKE '%10$%%' ESCAPE '$'	'10%' '10% DISCOUNT' 'A 10% DISCOUNT'

By the way, the LIKE predicate can't deal with row values, so you can only test one character string at a time.

Before we leave our discussion of the LIKE predicate, let's look at some examples from our MOVIE_TITLES table. Note that some of the retrieved titles don't appear in the abbreviated master table (Table 7-2) earlier in this chapter, but are included in the results to illustrate the respective query.

```
SELECT title
  FROM movie_titles
  WHERE title LIKE 'Bev%' ;
```

TITLE
Beverly Hills Cop
Beverly Hills Cop II

```
SELECT title
  FROM movie_titles
  WHERE title LIKE '%Bev%' ;
```

TITLE
Beverly Hills Cop
Beverly Hills Cop II
Down and Out in Beverly Hills
Troop Beverly Hills

```
SELECT title
  FROM movie_titles
  WHERE title LIKE '%#%%'
    ESCAPE '#' ;
```

TITLE
The Ten % Solution

```
SELECT title
  FROM movie_titles
  WHERE title LIKE
    '_*_*_*%' ESCAPE '#' ;
```

TITLE	
M*A*S*H	In the preceding LIKE predicate, the first underscore in the
F*I*S*T	string designates a single character 'wildcard' match; the next character (*) signifies that a specific asterisk is desired; this is repeated two more times, and then the % is used for a multiple character (or none) match. In this case, the ESCAPE serves no function (but does no harm).

Unlike comparison predicates (= and <> in particular), blanks are significant in the LIKE predicate. Therefore, although

```
'Rocky' = 'Rocky  '
```

is usually true, and

```
'Rocky' LIKE 'Rocky'
```

is true, you'll find that

```
'Rocky' LIKE 'Rocky  '
```

is always false!

7.8 EXISTS and UNIQUE Predicates

The EXISTS predicate is somewhat similar in function to the IN predicate. It is true if and only if the cardinality of the subquery is greater than 0 and is false otherwise. The format of the EXISTS predicate is

```
EXISTS subquery
```

Our first example in the chapter—producing an in stock list of Mel Gibson movies (see section 7.3)—can be expressed using the EXISTS predicate in place of IN:

```
SELECT title, vhs_in_stock
  FROM movie_titles m
  WHERE EXISTS
    ( SELECT *
        FROM movies_stars
        WHERE
          movie_title = m.title AND
          actor_last_name = 'Gibson' AND
          actor_first_name = 'Mel' )  ;
```

Note that this predicate tests to see whether the subquery is empty or not, not whether some value appears in the values returned by the subquery. However, the analog with the IN predicate is real.

The EXISTS predicate has been criticized because it is true only when there is *definitely* at least one row that meets the criteria of the subquery. If you apply the meaning "maybe" to a predicate that is neither false or true, but is unknown, then you might get unexpected results. For example, in the example above, you may have rows for some actor whose last name is 'Gibson', but whose first name is null for some reason. Those rows will not meet the criteria for the subquery and will therefore not satisfy the EXISTS criteria, either. However, it may be that those rows *should* satisfy the criteria because you know that you're going to put Mel's first name into those rows later on. All we can offer you here is: Be very careful that you know the semantics of your data and that you write the intended query; and, if you think that you might have the problem we've suggested, consider coding your query a little differently.

The UNIQUE predicate is used to determine if duplicate rows exist in a virtual table (one returned from a subquery). The format is

```
UNIQUE subquery
```

If any two rows in the subquery are equal to one another, the UNIQUE predicate evaluates to False.

Suppose we've decided that it's confusing to stock movies and CDs with the same title (there go all the soundtrack sales . . .). We could check to see if we've violated this rule by using a UNIQUE predicate:

```
UNIQUE (SELECT name FROM
            (SELECT title as name FROM movie_titles)
        UNION
        (SELECT title as name FROM music_titles) )
```

7.9 OVERLAPS Predicate

The OVERLAPS predicate has a very specific purpose: to determine whether two intervals of time overlap with one another. Suppose your database includes a schedule of meetings at your company and you'd like to ensure that any new meetings that you want to schedule don't conflict with any other meetings already scheduled. You might express your meeting as starting at 1:00 P.M. on the first of June, 1995 and lasting for 2 hours, while somebody else listed their meeting as starting at 12:30 P.M. on the same day and lasting until 1:30 P.M. Do those meetings overlap? Yes, we can see that they do. The challenge is to allow SQL to make the determination.

The format of the OVERLAPS predicate is

```
event-information OVERLAPS event-information
```

Either event-information can be of the form:

```
( start-time, duration )
```

or

```
( start-time, end-time )
```

but they don't have to have the same form.

Both start-time and end-time have to be the same variety of datetime (that is, either DATE, TIME, or TIMESTAMP). If the first form is used, then the duration has to be an interval that can be added to the datetime form used by start-time. Those rules were discussed in Chapter 2.

If the starting time of either event or the ending time of either event (remember that the ending time can be computed as the starting time plus the duration) lies between the starting and ending times of the other event, then the events overlap. Sometimes, even when the starting time or the ending time is null, we can tell that there is an overlap, but other times it's not clear.

For example:

```
( TIME '10:45:00', INTERVAL '1' HOUR )
    OVERLAPS
( TIME '10:00:00', TIME '10:30:00')
```

is false. But

```
( TIME '10:45:00', INTERVAL '1' HOUR )
    OVERLAPS
( TIME '10:00:00', TIME '11:30:00')
```

is true. And

```
( TIME '10:45:00', INTERVAL '1' HOUR )
    OVERLAPS
( TIME '11:00:00', NULL)
```

is true, because the length of the interval is unimportant since 11:00 is always going to be during the period 10:45 to 11:45. Incidentally, the intervals can also be negative, so that the start-time is really the end of the event. SQL even allows you to reverse the start and end times. That makes the OVERLAPS predicate symmetrical, unlike the BETWEEN predicate.

If two intervals touch without crossing, then the OVERLAPS predicate will report false.

```
(TIME '10:00:00' , TIME '11:00:00' )
    OVERLAPS (TIME '11:00:00' , TIME '12:00:00' )
```

is false—the two intervals don't overlap.

7.10 SOME, ANY, and ALL

SQL also provides a type of predicate called a *quantified comparison predicate*. This sort of predicate allows the application of an existential quantifier or a universal quantifier to a comparison operator. The *existential quantifier* asks, Is there any value at all in the stuff we're searching that meets our requirements? Whereas, a *universal quantifier* asks, Does every value in the stuff we're looking at meet the requirements? Let's look at some examples to clarify this admittedly murky subject. Consider the question, Are there any movies whose titles are the same as the last name of a movie star in that movie? There are a couple of ways that we could ask the question, but let's use the IN predicate that we just learned:

```
SELECT COUNT(*)
  FROM movie_titles AS m
  WHERE title IN
    (SELECT movie_title
       FROM movies_stars AS s
       WHERE s.movie_title = m.title AND
         s.actor_last_name = s.title)
```

However, that returns to *us* (or to our application) the number of such movies and we have to use that number to make a decision—zero or non-zero. If we want to actually use that information as part of another query, then we could use something really awkward like (let's just look at segments of the code, following WHERE):

```
SELECT....
  WHERE
    (SELECT COUNT(*)
       FROM movie_titles AS m
       WHERE title IN
         (SELECT movie_title
            FROM movies_stars AS s
            WHERE s.movie_title = m.title AND
              s.actor_last_name = m.title)) > 0
```

but that's unnatural and probably not *very* efficient in most DBMS implementations. It is also possible to simply use the IN predicate directly, which is certainly more natural:

```
SELECT....
  WHERE title IN
    (SELECT movie_title
       FROM movies_stars AS s
       WHERE s.movie_title = m.title AND
         s.actor_last_name = m.title)
```

This is better, but not always what we want to ask, as we shall shortly see. Instead, SQL allows us to use something like

```
SELECT...
  WHERE title = SOME
    (SELECT movie_title
      FROM movies_stars
      WHERE s.movie_title = m.title AND
          s.actor_last_name = m.title)
```

Now, this WHERE clause will return all rows whose title appears anywhere in the titles returned from the subquery. That's exactly what the IN variant just preceding does (and, in fact, the SQL standard actually defines the IN predicate to be equivalent to a quantified comparison predicate, using equality for the operator and SOME to signal the existential quantifier. However, there are variations available using the quantified comparison predicate that the IN predicate can't hope to match.

For example, if we needed to use a greater-than relationship instead of equality, we can use the quantified comparison predicate, but couldn't use the IN predicate. Furthermore, if we wanted to find out if *every* row in the subquery—instead of at least one row—met the criteria, then a quantified comparison predicate is required and the IN predicate doesn't help at all.

We might want to know whether some actor happens to star in *every* movie whose title is the same as his last name. That query might look like

```
...
  WHERE actor_last_name = ALL
    (SELECT title
      FROM movie_titles m movies_stars s
      WHERE s.movie_title = m.title AND
          s.actor_last_name = m.title)
```

The format of the quantified comparison predicate is shown in Diagram RR18.

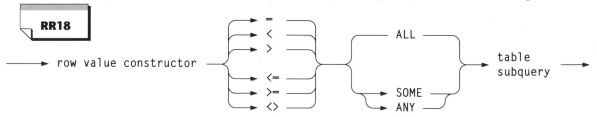

RR18

The usage comp refers to the Big 6 comparison operators that we discussed in section 7.4, under comparison predicates. The usage quantifier refers to the keyword ALL, for the universal quantifier, or one of the keywords SOME or ANY, for the existential quantifier (SOME and ANY produce the same result, but sometimes one "sounds better" than the other). And, of course, value and subquery are the value being checked and the subquery against which it's to be checked.

As you might expect, if either the supplied value is null or if the subquery returns no rows at all, then the result cannot be evaluated and the result of the predicate is unknown.

There isn't a negative version of this subquery—at least, there's not one that uses the NOT keyword. If you want to ask:

```
value = NOT SOME subquery
```

which is not valid SQL, then you simply rephrase it to read:

```
value <> SOME subquery
```

If the value is really a row value, then the degree of the table produced by the subquery has to be the same as the degree of the row value; otherwise, the subquery must be degree 1.

7.11 MATCH Predicate

SQL-92 provides a MATCH predicate that corresponds to the referential integrity restrictions that you can place on your tables (discussed in Chapter 10). To give you a brief introduction to referential integrity for purposes of this discussion, a table may have a FOREIGN KEY through which its rows correspond (by values in one or more columns) to rows in some other table. FOREIGN KEYs usually—but don't have to—relate to some PRIMARY KEY in the other table.

By using this query, you can test rows before attempting to insert them into a table to ensure that they won't violate a referential integrity constraint. This advance check might help you avoid getting certain errors and might therefore make your application logic simpler.

The syntax for the MATCH predicate is shown in Diagram RR19.

In this predicate, row-value is the value of the candidate row that you are considering inserting into your table. UNIQUE is used to simulate a PRIMARY KEY constraint on the target table. The subquery is normally one that selects every row from the target table (but, because the predicate is available for more general use, you're not restricted to that convention). criterion is either nothing at all or the keyword PARTIAL or FULL.

If you provide no criterion, then the predicate is true if:

- Any value in row-value is null; or
- No value in row-value is null and every value in row-value is equal to the corresponding value in some row of the subquery (exactly one row if UNIQUE is specified).

Otherwise, the predicate is false.

If you specify FULL, then the predicate is true if:

- Every value in row-value is null, or
- No value in row-value is null and every value in row-value is equal to the corresponding value in some row of the subquery (exactly one row if UNIQUE is specified).

Otherwise (including the case where *any* value in row-value is null), the predicate is false.

If you specify PARTIAL, then the predicate is true if:

- Every value in row-value is null; or
- Every non-null value in row-value is equal to the corresponding value in some row of the subquery (exactly one row if UNIQUE is specified).

Otherwise, the predicate is false.

How would this work for you? In our sample database, we have a rule that says every row in the MOVIES_STARS table must have a corresponding row in the MOVIE_TITLES table (identified by the title columns in the tables having the same value). We use both the TITLE and the YEAR_PRODUCED columns for the PRIMARY KEY of the MOVIE_TITLES table and for the FOREIGN KEY of the MOVIES_STARS table (MOVIE_TITLE and YEAR_PRODUCED are the column names in the latter table).

Now, we could define the rule to say that if either FOREIGN KEY field is null in MOVIES_STARS, then the row is alright, because we're not going to be compulsive. That means that we could store a row in the MOVIES_STARS table that claimed that Mel Gibson starred in *The Year of Living Foolishly* simply by leaving the YEAR_PRO-DUCED field null—that is, the movie title doesn't even have to correspond to a real movie. Okay, that's probably not a reasonable thing to do in *this* application, but it could be done. This corresponds to the option of not specifying a criterion.

Alternatively, we could allow storage of Mel's row only if the values for the FOREIGN KEY were all filled in correctly, or of they were all null. This obviously corresponds to our FULL option.

Finally, we could allow insertion of rows for Mel as long as any values that were filled in actually corresponded to meaningful movies or actual years of production of *some* movie. It still might not be a movie that has Mel in it, but that's a problem of external accuracy (valid data) and not one of database integrity.

Those three situations would correspond to

```
...
WHERE ('The Year of Living Foolishly', NULL)
MATCH
  (SELECT title, year_released
    FROM movie_titles)
```

and

```
      ...
   WHERE ('The Year of Living Foolishly', NULL)
   MATCH FULL
      (SELECT title, year_released
         FROM movie_titles)
```

and

```
      ...
   WHERE ('The Year of Living Foolishly', NULL)
   MATCH PARTIAL
      (SELECT title, year_released
         FROM movie_titles)
```

respectively. In this case, the second (MATCH FULL) example would always be false because of the NULL.

7.12 Search Conditions

SQL uses the phrase search-condition to indicate any combination of predicates that are used together to make a combined test. The syntax for a search condition is given in Diagram RR20.

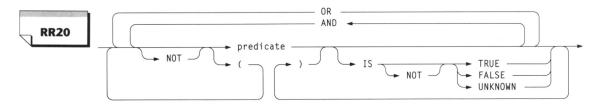

In some of our examples, we've used two predicates hooked together with the keyword AND to ensure that *both* predicates are true in order for a row to meet our criteria. Similarly, we've sometimes used OR to permit a row to meet the criteria if *either* predicate is true. And, as we mentioned above, SQL allows you to precede any predicate with NOT to invert the meaning of the predicate. The combination of predicates with AND, OR, and NOT comprises a search-condition.

Because SQL supports nulls and predicates that are unknown, we say that the language uses three-valued logic (True, False, and Unknown—we discussed these in Chapter 2). You will recall that Boolean logic tells us that the result of an AND is true if and only if *both* of the operands are true. Therefore, True AND True is true, but True AND False is false. How about True AND Unknown, though? If the unknown were replaced by true, then the predicate would be true, but if it were replaced by false, then the predicate would be false. To resolve the dilemma, we say that True AND

Unknown is unknown. Similar rules apply for OR: True OR True is true, as is True OR False, but False OR False is always false. How about False OR Unknown? In this case, if the unknown were replaced by false, then the result would be false, but a replacement with true would make the result true. As a result, we make the result of False OR Unknown also unknown. (By the way, the AND and OR operations are *reflexive,* which means that the operands can be in either order with the same result.) Finally, NOT True is false, NOT False is true, and NOT Unknown is (although it sounds funny to say it!) still unknown.

Sometimes, predicates combined into search conditions "sound funny" when you read them aloud. It might "sound better" if you could say "this test is false" or "this one is true". To support this occasional need, SQL-92 search conditions allow you to use the keywords TRUE, FALSE, and UNKNOWN to expand the evaluation of predicates. These Boolean search conditions are an alternative means to express the basic search conditions we've been exploring so far. For example, an alternative manner to express the query "list all movies that don't have a current rental price of $1.99" would be

```
SELECT title
  FROM movie_titles
  WHERE current_rental_price = 1.99 IS FALSE ;
```

Now, this one doesn't "sound better" than (in our opinion, it doesn't even sound as good as) the same query without the IS FALSE. However, others might think it does.

Similarly, a list of all movies starring Eddie Murphy can be found using:

```
SELECT movie_title
  FROM movies_stars
  WHERE
      (actor_last_name = 'Murphy' AND
      actor_first_name = 'Eddie) IS TRUE ;
```

A guideline: The more complex a search condition is, the more likely you will want to at least consider using the IS TRUE, IS FALSE, or IS UNKNOWN variations. For instance, if you wanted to retrieve all movies where the actors' first names, last names, or both are null, you could write:

```
SELECT movie_title
  FROM movies_stars
  WHERE
      (actor_last_name = 'X' AND
      actor_first_name = 'X') IS UNKNOWN
```

Note that we don't have to ask for a real name, just any non-null value. Yes, there are other ways to ask the same query, but this one might "sound" better to some application programmers.

What exactly does IS UNKNOWN mean? First, IS UNKNOWN is not the same as IS NULL. Remember that null is a characteristic of an SQL data item. Unknown, in contrast, is a characteristic of a predicate. The differences may appear to be subtle between the two concepts and the corresponding syntactical expressions, but they must be used correctly in order to develop SQL applications.

7.13 Chapter Summary

Predicates, as we have seen, are a valuable facility to assist your database searches. Rather than having to manually sift through voluminous amounts of data, comparison operators, LIKE, subqueries and IN, and so forth can help you expand or limit your searches to the most appropriate degree of precision. In Chapter 8, we'll discuss the relational operators and how they are represented and utilized in SQL-92. Together with the material we've discussed so far, particularly predicates, you can start to build real-life systems to handle your information processing requirements.

Working with Multiple Tables:
The Relational Operators

8.1 Introduction

So far—except for a brief discussion of subqueries—we have discussed SQL-92 statements that deal with single tables. Since one of the primary purposes of relational databases is to relate information among tables in a database, we now examine the major SQL-92 facilities that help you do this. In this chapter, we discuss the many different types of join operations, concentrating on the formats just introduced with this latest version of SQL. We also discuss the UNION, INTER-SECT, and EXCEPT operators and how they are used for multiple table management. In addition, we explore a number of relational operators and learn how they behave in a fairly informal way. In Chapter 9, we'll cover the material in a more substantial manner.

8.2 Join Operations: An Overview

In Chapter 7, we briefly examined how SQL-92 subqueries can be used to relate one table to another to retrieve cross-referenced data. Information may be *joined* among tables even without using subqueries. Previous versions of SQL (SQL-86 and SQL-89) supported the relational join operation through the basic SELECT...WHERE statement. SQL-92 greatly expands the toolbox of statements you can use to join information across tables.

To assist with our examples in this chapter, let's introduce a new table into our sample database. Since our store handles both videos and music (CDs and tapes), we need a table similar to our MOVIE_TITLES table, but for our music inventory management. We can create such a table with the following:

```
CREATE TABLE music_titles (
    title                      CHAR (30) NOT NULL,
    artist                     CHAR (30),
    artist_more                CHAR (30),
    distributor                CHAR (25),
    record_label               CHAR (20),
    type                       CHAR (10),
    greatest_hits_collection   CHAR(15),
    category                   CHAR (10),
    date_released              DATE,
    our_cost                   DECIMAL (9,2),
    list_price                 DECIMAL (9,2),
    current_price              DECIMAL (9,2),
    still_available            CHAR (1),
    cd_in_stock                INTEGER,
    cassette_in_stock          INTEGER,
    8-track_in_stock           INTEGER,
    lp_in_stock                INTEGER
    total_cd_sold              INTEGER,
    total_cassette_sold        INTEGER,
    total_8-track_sold         INTEGER,
    total_lp_sold              INTEGER,
    total_cd_returned          INTEGER,
    total_cassette_returned    INTEGER,
    total_8-track_returned     INTEGER,
    total_lp_returned          INTEGER) ;
```

Note that the column ARTIST_MORE is used primarily for an artist's first name if the artist is a person and not a group (excepting, as in our video movie examples earlier, people like Cher and Sting). Alternatively, it might be used to distinguish between two artists of the same name, such as when the original Jefferson Airplane had become the Jefferson Starship but there was a new Jefferson Airplane with some of the original members of the band . . . never mind. Anyway, some sort of designator as to which artist it is could go into this column.

8.3 Types of Join Operations

In this chapter, we discuss several different types of join operations. These include:

- Old style joins
- Cross joins
- Natural joins
- Condition joins
- Column name joins
- Inner joins
- Outer joins (left, right, or full)

TABLE 8-1
Portion of
Populated Table

TITLE	ARTIST . . .	RECORD_ LABEL	GREATEST_ HITS_ COLLECTION	CATEGORY . . .
Ropin' the Wind	Brooks	Liberty	No	Country
Wayne's World	*null*	Reprise	No	Soundtrack
Dangerous	Jackson	Epic	No	Rock
Luck of the Draw	Raitt	Capitol	No	Rock
Juice	*null*	MCA	No	Soundtrack
Nick of Time	Raitt	Capitol	No	Rock
No Fences	Brooks	Liberty	No	Country
Eagle When She Flies	Parton	Columbia	No	Country
Alabama Greatest Hits Vol. 2	Alabama	RCA	Yes	Country
The Way We Were	Streisand	Columbia	No	Soundtrack
Funny Girl	Streisand	Columbia	No	Soundtrack
MacArthur Park	Harris	Columbia	No	Easy
Camelot	Harris	Columbia	No	Soundtrack

There is also another type of join operation, the union join, which we discuss following our coverage of union operations in general. The complete syntax for all the ways of joining tables is demonstrated in Diagram RR21.

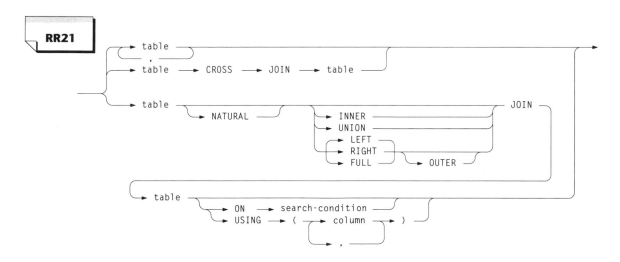

Let's now take a look at each of these join operations, in turn.

8.3.1 Old-Style Joins

So far, the SELECT statements we have examined have always included a single table name following the keyword FROM, as in

```
SELECT column-list
  FROM  single-table-name
```

You can, however, specify multiple table names after the FROM, which causes SQL to perform a relational join operation, as in

```
SELECT table1.*, table2.*
  FROM table1, table2  ;
```

The above statement causes a virtual table to be produced that includes the Cartesian product of the source tables.

TABLE 8-2
The Two
Source Tables

	Table1		Table2	
Name	**Address**	**Phone**	**Name**	**Salary**
Jones	111 Maple	555-1111	Jones	30000
Smith	222 Elm	555-2222	Smith	20000
Walters	333 Birch	555-3333	Walters	40000

TABLE 8-3
Joined Table

Name	**Address**	**Phone**	**Name**	**Salary**
Jones	111 Maple	555-1111	Jones	30000
Jones	111 Maple	555-1111	Smith	20000
Jones	111 Maple	555-1111	Walters	40000
Smith	222 Elm	555-2222	Jones	30000
Smith	222 Elm	555-2222	Smith	20000
Smith	222 Elm	555-2222	Walters	40000
Walters	333 Birch	555-3333	Jones	30000
Walters	333 Birch	555-3333	Smith	20000
Walters	333 Birch	555-3333	Walters	40000

The resulting virtual table (Table 8-3) is basically meaningless, since the cross-product of the join causes each row from the first table to be matched with each possible row from the second table. A more meaningful result can be obtained by using the WHERE clause in the SELECT statement to create an *equi-join*. For example, the following statement yields Table 8-4.

```
SELECT table1.*, table2.*
  FROM table1, table2
  WHERE table1.name = table2.name ;
```

	Name	Address	Phone	Name	Salary
TABLE 8-4 Joined Table	Jones	111 Maple	555-1111	Jones	30000
	Smith	222 Elm	555-2222	Smith	20000
	Walters	333 Birch	555-3333	Walters	40000

Note that the "Name" column appears twice, since we specified all columns (via the *) in each table to be included in the newly created table. We can further refine our join to produce Table 8-5.

```
SELECT TABLE1.*, TABLE2.SALARY
   FROM TABLE1, TABLE2
   WHERE TABLE1.NAME = TABLE2.NAME ;
```

	Name	Address	Phone	Salary
TABLE 8-5 Joined Table	Jones	111 Maple	555-1111	30000
	Smith	222 Elm	555-2222	20000
	Walters	333 Birch	555-3333	40000

By eliminating the duplicate column from the resulting table, we not only make the result a bit more intuitive, but we are actually improving performance by reducing the amount of data to be transferred.

The simplest way to view this form of SQL-92 join processing is that the first example—the cross-product table—is always internally created (logically, anyway; optimizers will certainly take shortcuts) and any WHERE conditions, such as those that specify an equijoin, are subsequently processed against the complete virtual table in much the same way as WHERE conditions are processed against any individual table. That is, in our simple example above, the nine-row table is created and the condition of TABLE1.NAME = TABLE2.NAME is checked against each of the nine rows; only three pass the test, and they become the final result.

Let's look at our example database. Suppose we want to produce a list of all actor-singers for whom we currently have both a CD (or tape) and a movie in stock. We can issue the following statement:

```
SELECT m.actor_last_name, m.actor_first_name
   FROM movies_stars AS m, music_titles AS t
   WHERE m.actor_last_name = t.artist
       AND m.actor_first_name = t.artist_more ;
```

Recall that we now must use M and T as correlation names (aliases) for MOVIES_STARS and MUSIC_TITLES, respectively. The above statement creates a virtual table that initially matches each row from MOVIES_STARS with each row from MUSIC_TITLES. Following the initial table creation, the last and first names of the actors are compared with those of the music artists. Matches are reflected in the final result table, Table 8-6.

TABLE 8-6

ACTOR_LAST_NAME	ACTOR_FIRST_NAME
Streisand	Barbra
Streisand	Barbra
|	
|	
|	
Harris	Richard
Harris	Richard
|	
|	
|	

Note that duplicate data occurs as a result of multiple matches for Barbra Streisand, Richard Harris, and others due to multiple entries in each of our two source tables. Use of DISTINCT will eliminate duplicate data results to give us Table 8-7.

```
SELECT DISTINCT
      m.actor_last_name, m.actor_first_name
    FROM movies_stars m, music_titles t
    WHERE m.actor_last_name = t.artist
        AND m.actor_first_name = t.artist_more ;
```

TABLE 8-7

ACTOR_LAST_NAME	ACTOR_FIRST_NAME
Streisand	Barbra
Harris	Richard
|	
|	
|	

Note that tables can be joined against themselves. Assume that we have two tables, one for employees and one for departments. Tables 8-8 and 8-9 are perhaps overly complex for the small amount of data involved, but should illustrate how join operations work.

	EMP_NUM	EMP_NAME	SALARY	STORE
TABLE 8-8 EMPLOYEES	2	Jones	25000	KOLB
	3	Smith	30000	PARK
	5	Rubins	20000	KOLB
	8	Jordan	22000	PARK
	12	Sanders	40000	KOLB
	15	Michaels	35000	PARK

	STORE_CODE	STORE_NAME	MANAGER
TABLE 8-9 STORES	KOLB	Kolb Road, East	12
	PARK	Park Heights Mall	15

Suppose that for all employees earning $25,000 or more, we wish to see the stores at which they work and the name of the stores' managers. The following statement will do this.

```
SELECT e.name, s.store_name, m.name
  FROM employees AS e, stores AS s,
       employees m
 WHERE salary >= 25000
       AND e.store = s.store_code
       AND s.manager = m.emp_num ;
```

Okay, let's try to see what's going on here. First, the join above is among *three* tables, two of which are actually the same. Unlike our previous examples, which utilized two source tables, there is no restriction in SQL-92 that limits you to two source tables. Second, the EMPLOYEES table is used twice, once each under two different correlation names (E and M, which we choose because E is mnemonic for EMPLOYEES and M for Managers).

The first thing that happens is that a single virtual table is created from the cross-product of the three-way join, as shown in Table 8-10.

TABLE 8-10
Virtual Table

	E				S				M		
EMP_NUM	EMP_NAME	SALARY	STORE	STORE_CODE	STORE_NAME	MANAGER	EMP_NUM	EMP_NAME	SALARY	STORE	
2	Jones	25000	KOLB	KOLB	Kolb Road, East	12	2	Jones	25000	KOLB	
2	Jones	25000	KOLB	KOLB	Kolb Road, East	12	3	Jones	30000	PARK	
2	Jones	25000	KOLB	KOLB	Kolb Road, East	12	5	Jones	20000	KOLB	

Basically, each possible combination among the source tables is created. Following this, the parameters from the WHERE clause are applied to do two things: First, find the rows where SALARY is greater than or equal to $25,000. Then, eliminate nonsense rows from the join cross-product by the use of equality qualifications. The store codes must match and the employee number of the employee's manager must also match. The result is shown in Table 8-11.

TABLE 8-11

NAME	STORE_NAME	NAME
Jones	Kolb Road, East	Sanders
Smith	Park Heights Mall	Michaels
Sanders	Kolb Road, East	Sanders
Michaels	Park Heights Mall	Michaels

To exclude store managers from the list, an additional condition can be added to the end of the preceding SELECT statement:

```
SELECT e.name, s.store_name, m.name
  FROM employees AS e, stores AS s,
       employees m
  WHERE salary >= 25000
       AND e.store = s.store_code
       AND s.manager = m.emp_num ;
       AND e.name < > m.name  ;
```

which will give you the result table shown as Table 8-12.

TABLE 8-12

NAME	STORE_NAME	NAME
Jones	Kolb Road, East	Sanders
Smith	Park Heights Mall	Michaels

Now, let's turn our attention to the newly added join operations of SQL-92.

8.3.2 The CROSS JOIN

The CROSS JOIN produces the same cross-product (see Tables 8-13 and 8-14) that we saw above when no conditions are expressed via a WHERE clause.

```
SELECT *
  FROM table1  CROSS JOIN table2  ;
```

TABLE 8-13

	Table1		Table2	
Name	**Address**	**Phone**	**Name**	**Salary**
Jones	111 Maple	555-1111	Jones	30000
Smith	222 Elm	555-2222	Smith	20000
Walters	333 Birch	555-3333	Walters	40000

TABLE 8-14
Joined Table

Name	**Address**	**Phone**	**Name**	**Salary**
Jones	111 Maple	555-1111	Jones	30000
Jones	111 Maple	555-1111	Smith	20000
Jones	111 Maple	555-1111	Walters	40000
Smith	222 Elm	555-2222	Jones	30000
Smith	222 Elm	555-2222	Smith	20000
Smith	222 Elm	555-2222	Walters	40000
Walters	333 Birch	555-3333	Jones	30000
Walters	333 Birch	555-3333	Smith	20000
Walters	333 Birch	555-3333	Walters	40000

Therefore, it is equivalent to the basic old-style join without a WHERE clause.

8.3.3 The NATURAL JOIN

A natural join (more properly known as a natural equi-join, because it selects rows from the two tables that have equal values in the relevant columns) is based on all columns in the two tables that share the same name. Note that in our sample database, related columns don't necessarily share the same name (for example, MOVIE_TITLES.TITLE and MOVIES_STARS.MOVIE_TITLE). To use the natural join, the column names must be the same.

```
SELECT *
  FROM t1 NATURAL JOIN t2 ;
```

T1		T2	
C1	**C2**	**C3**	**C4**
10	15	10	BB
20	25	15	DD

Joined Table		
C1	**C2**	**C4**
10	15	BB

NATURAL can also be used to qualify some of the join types we investigate in the coming sections: inner, outer, and union.

8.3.4 Condition JOIN

Any columns may be used to match rows from one table against those from another. Note the use of the keyword ON, as opposed to WHERE.

```
SELECT *
  FROM t1 JOIN t2
  ON t1.c1 = t2.c3  ;
```

T1		T2	
C1	**C2**	**C3**	**C4**
10	15	10	BB
20	25	15	DD

Joined Table			
C1	**C2**	**C3**	**C4**
10	15	10	BB

In our sample database, we could join information from tables MOVIE_TITLES and MOVIES_STARS by using a condition join as follows:

```
SELECT t.title, .....
  FROM movie_titles AS t JOIN movies_stars AS S
  ON (t.title = s.movie_title) AND
     (t.year_released = s.year_released) ;
```

This sort of JOIN has an interesting—perhaps even surprising—side-effect on the *scope* of qualifiers (correlation names and exposed table names) that is worth spending a few moments discussing. Let's consider an example of a three-way join (we could use inner or outer joins):

```
SELECT select-list
  FROM movie_titles AS t JOIN movies_stars as S
                         ON join-condition-1
                    JOIN some_other_table AS X
                         ON join-condition-2
    WHERE search-condition
```

Because JOINs are effectively performed from left to right, the first join to be performed is

```
movie_titles AS t JOIN movies_stars as S
```

That JOIN has an ON clause with a search condition (the join-condition-1). The search-condition can reference columns in MOVIE_TITLES and in MOVIES_STARS, but *cannot* reference any columns in SOME_OTHER_TABLE. That's because the *scope* of the search-condition of the ON clause is only that first JOIN.

The second JOIN, is of course:

```
(result of first JOIN) JOIN some_other_table
```

which also has an ON clause with a search-condition (join-condition-2). That search-condition can reference columns in SOME_OTHER_TABLE and can also reference columns in the result of the first JOIN. Because the first JOIN doesn't obscure its source tables, the second search-condition can reference columns in MOVIE_TITLES and MOVIES_STARS as well as SOME_OTHER_TABLE!

You will want to use your knowledge of this scoping characteristic to help you decide how to code your ON clauses—sometimes you'll put a particular predicate in one ON clause and sometimes in another. Of course, the search-condition in the WHERE clause and the select-list can both reference columns from all three tables.

8.3.5 Column Name JOIN

Natural JOINs use all columns with the same names to manage the matching process. If we only want to use some of those columns, we can explicitly specify those column names:

```
SELECT *
  FROM t1 JOIN t2
  USING (c1, c2)  ;
```

| T1 | | | T2 | | |
C1	C2	C3	C1	C2	C4
10	15	XX	10	15	XX
20	25	YY	15	25	YY

| Virtual Table | | | |
C1	C2	C3	C4
10	15	XX	XX

There is a surprise waiting for you when you use JOIN with a USING clause: The columns referenced in the USING clause have no qualifier! Let's see an example to illustrate this. (Assume for the moment that the MOVIE_TITLE column in the MOVIES_STARS table was really named TITLE.)

```
SELECT select-list
  FROM movie_titles JOIN movies_stars
       USING (title)
  WHERE search-condition
```

In this example, the select-list can contain references to MOVIE_TITLES. OUR_COST and MOVIES_STARS.ACTOR_LAST_NAME; so can the search-condition in the WHERE clause. However, *neither* one of them can reference MOVIE_TITLES.TITLE or MOVIES_STARS.TITLE! Instead, if they reference the column on which the JOIN is performed at all, it can only be with the simple identifier TITLE. Therefore:

```
SELECT movie_titles.our_cost, title
  FROM movie_titles JOIN movies_stars
      USING (title)
  WHERE title LIKE 'Ten%'
```

is valid, but:

```
SELECT movie_titles.our_cost, movie_titles.title
  FROM movie_titles JOIN movies_stars
      USING (title)
  WHERE movie_titles.title LIKE 'Ten%'
```

is *invalid* .

The same restriction exists in the NATURAL join:

```
SELECT title, t.our_cost, s.actor_last_name
  FROM movie_titles AS t NATURAL JOIN movies_stars AS s
```

is valid, but substituting T.TITLE or S.TITLE would be invalid.

8.3.6 Joins So Far

So far, we've discussed several styles of JOIN. The old-style JOIN and the CROSS JOIN are essentially the same. The NATURAL JOIN uses any columns with the same name in the two source tables for an implicit equijoin (JOIN where the values in those columns are equal), while the column name JOIN allows you to specify a USING clause so that you can further restrict the columns used to a subset of those with the same name.

By contrast, the *condition* JOIN lets you specify an arbitrary search condition to determine how the rows of the two tables will be joined. In many ways, the ON clause is redundant with the WHERE clause; however, we like to use the ON clause to specify conditions specifically related to the JOIN and use the WHERE clause for additional filtering of the result of the join.

8.3.7 The INNER JOIN

The types of JOIN operations we've discussed thus far are known in SQL-92 terminology as *inner joins*. For the sake of clarity, you can explicitly specify that a particular statement represents an INNER JOIN:

```
SELECT *
  FROM t1 INNER JOIN t2
  USING (c1, c2)  ;
```

The use of INNER has no additional effects, but helps your statement to be completely self-documenting.

8.3.8 The OUTER JOIN

As opposed to INNER JOINs, the OUTER JOIN operations preserves unmatched rows from one or both tables, depending on the keyword used: LEFT, RIGHT, or FULL. That is, INNER JOINs disregard any rows where the specific search condition isn't met, while OUTER JOINs maintain some or all of the unmatched data. Let's look at some examples.

LEFT OUTER JOIN

The LEFT OUTER JOIN preserves unmatched rows from the *left table,* the one that precedes the keyword JOIN. Let's look at our condition JOIN example earlier, where we use values in differently named columns as our matching criteria.

```
SELECT *
  FROM t1 LEFT OUTER JOIN t2
  ON t1.c1 = t2.c3  ;
```

T1		T2	
C1	C2	C3	C4
10	15	10	BB
20	25	15	DD

Joined Table			
C1	C2	C3	C4
10	15	10	BB
20	25	*null*	*null*

Our INNER JOIN produced only one row in the joined table. Our OUTER JOIN, however, by virtue of the keyword LEFT, produces two rows.

By definition, each row in the first table in a LEFT OUTER JOIN must be included in the result table. The first row, where C1 = 10, had a match found in the right table (T2), and the join operation is completed to produce a new row. The second row, however, has no corresponding row in T2 where C3 = 20. Therefore, the values from T1 (C1 = 10, C2 = 25) are added to a new row in the resulting virtual table, accompanied by *null* values for columns C3 and C4 of that new row.

RIGHT OUTER JOIN

The RIGHT OUTER JOIN operates similar to a LEFT OUTER JOIN, except the RIGHT, or second-named, table has its rows preserved.

```
SELECT *
  FROM t1 RIGHT OUTER JOIN t2
  ON t1.c1 = t2.c3  ;
```

T1		T2	
C1	C2	C3	C4
10	15	10	BB
20	25	15	DD

Joined Table			
C1	C2	C3	C4
10	15	10	BB
null	*null*	15	DD

FULL OUTER JOIN

The FULL OUTER JOIN acts as a combination of LEFT and RIGHT OUTER JOINs.

```
SELECT *
  FROM t1 FULL OUTER JOIN t2
  ON t1.c1 = t2.c3  ;
```

T1		T2	
C1	C2	C3	C2
10	15	10	BB
20	25	15	DD

Joined Table			
C1		C3	
10	15	10	BB
20	25	*null*	*null*
null	*null*	15	DD

In Chapter 6, we promised that we'd show you a more interesting use of COALESCE—well, here it is. We're going to show a four-way OUTER JOIN (without a net, no less) to illustrate that your joins won't always be simple two-way A JOIN B operations; among other things, we'll try to show you that OUTER JOINs are not associative (even though INNER JOINs are) and we'll show how COALESCE is really helpful.

Suppose we have tables Q1, Q2, Q3, and Q4 to hold quarterly video and music sales results; each table has an ID and a TOTAL column (ID is the account number and TOTAL is the sales total for that account for the appropriate quarter). Any account can have one record for the quarter, or no entry at all. To select sales by quarter, you'd write:

```
SELECT *
  FROM q1 FULL JOIN q2 ON (on-clause-1-2)
          FULL JOIN q3 ON (on-clause-12-3)
          FULL JOIN q4 ON (on-clause-123-4)
```

Now, on-clause-1-2 is obviously Q1.ID = Q2.ID. We might initially write on-clause-12-3 as Q1.ID=Q3.ID. But, then we would only match Q3 rows with the Q1-Q2 result rows that have non-null values for Q1.ID; otherwise, we would miss Q1-Q2 result rows that are null for Q1.ID but have a value for Q2.ID. Thus, on-clause-12-3 must be one of the following:

```
ON( q1.id=q3.id  OR  q2.id=q3.id )

ON(COALESCE( q1.id , q2.id ) = q3.id )
```

Then we need a similar analysis for on-clause-123-4. We might initially write it as ON(Q1.ID=Q4.ID), but then we would match only Q1-Q2-Q3 result rows with values for Q1.ID. So, our on-clause-123-4 must be one of the following:

```
ON(q1.id=q4.id  OR  q2.id=q4.id OR q3.id=q4.id)

ON( COALESCE(q1.id, q2.id, q3.id) = q4.id)
```

The previous example demonstrates how COALESCE can really make multi-way OUTER JOINs possible. Now, let's quickly explore associativity of OUTER JOINs.

If you did a three-way inner join, like

```
SELECT * FROM t1, t2, t3
```

the result would be exactly the same (except for the order of the columns) as:

```
SELECT * FROM t2, t3, t1
```

This is called *associative* behavior—meaning that you can associate (join, in this case) T1 with T2 first, then that result with T3; or you can associate T2 with T3 first, then that result with T1. However, OUTER JOINs are less friendly in this way. Specifically,

```
SELECT * FROM t1 LEFT OUTER JOIN t3
                 LEFT OUTER JOIN t3
```

will give you very different results than

```
SELECT * FROM t2 LEFT OUTER JOIN t3
                LEFT OUTER JOIN t1
```

We'll let you work out the differences yourself—an exercise for the reader. The message is that you need to be *very* careful how you write your outer joins or you'll get some really unexpected results.

8.4 The UNION Operator

Before we discuss our next type of JOIN operator, we need to examine the UNION operator and how it works. UNION is used to combine two tables whose respective column data types are *union compatible* (that is, comparable). The data type of each column of the result is determined from the data types of the columns in the source tables; see *union datatype*). With SQL-86 and SQL-89, UNION was limited to cursor operations (we discuss cursors in Chapter 12). SQL-92 permits UNION operations to be performed within query expressions.

Assume that we create two tables, usisng the following:

```
CREATE TABLE music_titles (
     title                    CHAR (30) NOT NULL,
     artist                   CHAR (30),
     artist_more              CHAR (30),
     distributor              CHAR (25),
     record_label             CHAR (20),
     greatest_hits_collection CHAR(15),
     category                 CHAR (10),

     |
     |
       ) ;

CREATE TABLE discontinued_albums
     title                    CHAR (30) NOT NULL,
     artist                   CHAR (30),
     artist_more              CHAR (30),
     distributor              CHAR (25),
     record_label             CHAR (20),
     greatest_hits_collection CHAR(15),
     category                 CHAR (10),
     |
     |
       ) ;
```

If the column names, data types, and other properties of these two tables are identical, we can specify:

```
SELECT *
  FROM music_titles
UNION
SELECT *
  FROM discontinued_albums ;
```

The preceding statement will produce a resulting virtual table (Table 8-15) with all rows from the first table *plus* all rows from the second table (again, be careful about the use of SELECT * as compared with specifying all columns; care should be taken as to which form you use in various circumstances).

TABLE 8-15
MUSIC_TITLES

TITLE	ARTIST . . .	RECORD_ LABEL	GREATEST_ HITS_ COLLECTION	CATEGORY . . .
Ropin' the Wind	Brooks	Liberty	No	Country
Wayne's World	*null*	Reprise	No	Soundtrack
Dangerous	Jackson	Epic	No	Rock
Luck of the Draw	Raitt	Capitol	No	Rock
Juice	*null*	MCA	No	Soundtrack

TABLE 8-16
DISCONTINUED
ALBUMS

TITLE	ARTIST . . .	RECORD_ LABEL	GREATEST_ HITS_ COLLECTION	CATEGORY . . .
Disco Lives Forever	Various	Duck Records	No	Disco
The Punks	The Punks	Punk Records	Of course not	Punk Rock

The resulting UNION table is given as Table 8-17.

TABLE 8-17
UNION Table

TITLE	ARTIST ...	RECORD LABEL	GREATEST HITS COLLECTION	CATEGORY ...
Ropin' the Wind	Brooks	Liberty	No	Country
Wayne's World	*null*	Reprise	No	Soundtrack
Dangerous	Jackson	Epic	No	Rock
Luck of the Draw	Raitt	Capitol	No	Rock
Juice	*null*	MCA	No	Soundtrack
I				
I				
I				
Disco Lives Forever	Various	Duck Records	No	Disco
The Punks	The Punks	Punk Records	Of course not	Punk Rock
I				
I				

Several items must be noted. First, the virtual tables are a very important consideration in UNION operations. Therefore, the following statement is *incorrect*:

```
SELECT title, artist
  FROM music_titles
UNION
SELECT record_label, category
  FROM discontinued_albums ;
```

Even though the source tables are union-compatible in their entirety, the different column projections within each query expression above make the statement invalid (because the *virtual tables* that are being UNIONed don't have union-compatible columns).

UNION normally eliminates duplicate rows. If MUSIC_TITLES was somehow to have a row entry that was identical to one found in DISCONTINUED_ALBUMS, only one copy of that row will find its way into the resulting virtual table.

You can, if desired, preserve duplicate rows in the virtual table through the use of ALL. Suppose we have a table for inventory at each of our two stores. The result might not be meaningful without identification by store, but we could produce a comprehensive inventory list with each row preserved as follows:

```
SELECT title, artist, ...
  FROM music_titles_kolb
UNION ALL
SELECT title, artist,...
  FROM music_titles_mall ;
```

If our tables look like those shown as Tables 8-18 and 8-19, the resulting table would look like Table 8-20 (remember, ordering is not defined by the standard).

TABLE 8-18
MUSIC_TITLES_
KOLB

TITLE	ARTIST . . .	RECORD_LABEL	CD_IN_STOCK	CASSETTE_IN_STOCK
Ropin' the Wind	Brooks	Liberty	35	12
Wayne's World	null	Reprise	2	11
Dangerous	Jackson	Epic	88	10
Luck of the Draw	Raitt	Capitol	32	14
Juice	null	MCA	18	17

TABLE 8-19
MUSIC_TITLES_
MALL

TITLE	ARTIST . . .	RECORD_LABEL	CD_IN_STOCK	CASSETTE_IN_STOCK
Ropin' the Wind	Brooks	Liberty	35	12
Wayne's World	null	Reprise	2	11
Dangerous	Jackson	Epic	77	20
No Fences	Brooks	Liberty	11	11
Juice	null	MCA	10	27

TABLE 8-20

TITLE	ARTIST . . .	RECORD_LABEL	CD_IN_STOCK	CASSETTE_IN_STOCK
Ropin' the Wind	Brooks	Liberty	35	12
Wayne's World	null	Reprise	2	11
Dangerous	Jackson	Epic	88	10
Luck of the Draw	Raitt	Capitol	32	14
Juice	null	MCA	18	17
Ropin' the Wind	Brooks	Liberty	35	12
Wayne's World	null	Reprise	2	11
Dangerous	Jackson	Epic	77	20
No Fences	Brooks	Liberty	11	11
Juice	null	MCA	10	27

Note that for "Ropin' The Wind" and "Wayne's World" the same rows (assuming for our example that the values in all of the other columns of the two tables are identical to one another) are preserved in the result.

The use of CORRESPONDING will sometimes make it possible to form the UNION, INTERSECTion, or difference (EXCEPT) of two tables that have common columns but that aren't actually union-compatible. CORRESPONDING without a column list will form virtual tables that have only the common columns (columns with the same name) from the two source tables and then UNION (or INTERSECT or EXCEPT) them. Specifying the column list further restricts the columns in the source virtual tables (and the result) to the common columns in the list.

In our above example, it would be unlikely that each album's inventory data at each store would be identical, but we use ALL to be sure that each row is preserved. Suppose we just want to produce a comprehensive list of titles and artists that we have in the two stores. Some albums are in both stores, some only in the Kolb store, and some only in the mall store. We could use:

```
SELECT * FROM music_titles_kolb
UNION CORRESPONDING (title, artist, artist_more)
SELECT * FROM music_titles_mall  ;
```

This example selects the three *interesting* columns from each store's table and produces a result that has all the rows from both stores. Even though we used SELECT *, the additional use of CORRESPONDING (...) reduced the columns from each store—and in the result—to just the three in the column list. If we issue the above statement against our two table segments above, our result is Table 8-21.

TABLE 8-21

TITLE	ARTIST	ARTIST_MORE
Luck of the Draw	Raitt	Bonnie
No Fences	Brooks	Garth

(Note: The ARTIST_MORE column wasn't included in the above original segments because of space limitations.)

Now, something about this SELECT...UNION CORRESPONDING statement and the result must be understood. We asked for a SELECT * for each source table, which—as we discussed in Chapter 3—translates to a column select list of all of the columns in the table(s): TITLE, ARTIST, ARTIST_MORE, RECORD_LABEL, CD_IN_STOCK, and so on. Our result, however, only has three columns—the same three we specified after the UNION CORRESPONDING. What happened? The following logical sequence of actions takes place as the statement is processed and executed.

1. The asterisks (*) are translated into the complete column list as part of the SELECTs.

2. Those new column lists from step 1 above are then *further reduced* by the CORRESPONDING specification; in effect, the columns whose names do not

appear in the CORRESPONDING list (whether explicit or implicit) are thrown away, as if they were never specified at all.

3. The UNION CORRESPONDING processing will eliminate duplicates and produce the query result, with only three columns.

Therefore, even though you may specify SELECT *..., your result will only contain the specific columns you specify as part of UNION CORRESPONDING, regardless of whether your source tables have 10 or 1000 columns. If you do not specify an explicit CORRESPONDING column list, then all columns with the same name in both tables form an implicit list.

The syntax of CORRESPONDING is shown in Diagram RR22.

8.4.1 Alternative Syntax

It is inconvenient, as well as non-intuitive, to keep repeating the SELECT * FROM... phrase in UNION queries, but the potential syntax ambiguities make it *impossible* to specify something like

```
SELECT *
  FROM t1 UNION t2  ;
```

There is, however, a parentheses-assisted shortcut that can be used:

```
SELECT *
  FROM (TABLE t1 UNION TABLE t2 ) ;
```

This is equivalent to specifying:

```
SELECT *
  FROM
    (SELECT *
       FROM t1)
    UNION
    (SELECT *
       FROM t2)
```

8.5 UNION JOIN

Earlier, we mentioned that there was a final type of join operation, one we would discuss after introducing UNION. The SQL-92 UNION JOIN works in a manner similar to that of the FULL OUTER JOIN, with one major difference. Recall that with the FULL OUTER JOIN, column matches may be specified that result in a single consolidated row. The UNION JOIN has no provisions for column matching, but rather:

1. Creates a new virtual table with the union of all columns from the source tables.
2. Creates a row in the new table with the values from the respective columns from each source table, with null values assigned to columns within each row from the other table.

For example, let's look at our FULL OUTER JOIN example from earlier:

C1	C2	C3	C2
10	15	10	BB
20	25	15	DD

The UNION JOIN results in

Joined Table			
C1		C3	
10	15	null	null
20	25	null	null
null	null	10	BB
null	null	15	DD

Unlike the FULL OUTER JOIN, *no attempt* is made to match rows by column name or in any other manner.

It is also interesting to note these equivalencies:

    a CROSS JOIN b

is equivalent to any of the following:

    a INNER JOIN b ON 2=2
    a LEFT OUTER JOIN b ON 2=2
    a RIGHT OUTER JOIN b ON 2=2
    a FULL OUTER JOIN b ON 2=2

(where "2 = 2" is any predicate that is *always* true).

Similarly,

    a UNION JOIN b

is equivalent to,

```
a FULL OUTER JOIN b ON 2=3
```

(where "2 = 3" is any predicate that is *always* false).

You can consider the joins to have a sort of ordering to them, too:

- FULL OUTER JOIN contains both LEFT OUTER JOIN and RIGHT OUTER JOIN
- Both LEFT OUTER JOIN and RIGHT OUTER JOIN contain INNER JOIN
- CROSS JOIN contains INNER JOIN
- LEFT OUTER JOIN INTERSECT RIGHT OUTER JOIN is the same as INNER JOIN

As you can see, SQL-92 could have provided fewer ways to express these concepts, but the existence of the various options makes it easier and more direct to write many queries.

8.6 The INTERSECT and EXCEPT Operators

There may be occasions when working with two tables that you would like to easily determine which rows exist in both of those tables or, alternatively, which rows exist in one table but not in another. The SQL-92 INTERSECT and EXCEPT set operators are used in these cases.

INTERSECT returns all rows that exist in the intersection of two tables; that is, in both tables.

```
SELECT *
  FROM music_titles
INTERSECT
SELECT *
  FROM discontinued_albums ;
```

The preceding query will return, for example, all discontinued albums that have been re-released.

ALL and CORRESPONDING function with INTERSECT in the same manner as with UNION. To perform the preceding query, but eliminate from "sameness" consideration all information about numbers in stock, pricing, and the like, you can

```
SELECT *
  FROM music_titles
INTERSECT CORRESPONDING
    (title, artist, artist_more, distributor,
        record_label)
SELECT *
  FROM discontinued_albums ;
```

EXCEPT is used to return all rows that are in the first table *except* those that also appear in the second table. To obtain a list of all albums in current release that have never been discontinued, you could issue:

```
SELECT *
  FROM music_titles
EXCEPT CORRESPONDING
    (title, artist, artist_more, distributor,
          record_label)
SELECT *
  FROM discontinued_albums ;
```

8.7 Another Example

Let's look at one more example from our video and music store database that utilizes one of the operators we've discussed in this chapter; we'll also see some more examples in Appendix B.

Suppose we want to produce a comprehensive list of all videos we have in stock, along with the soundtrack album information, if indeed there is a soundtrack for that movie. That is, we want all of our movies to be included and some of our CDs or tapes. We can use the LEFT OUTER JOIN, which you'll recall preserves all rows from the *left* table regardless of whether there is a match with a row in the *right* table. Assume that we have no non-soundtrack albums that have the same title as that of a movie, and that the year a movie was released is the same as the year the soundtrack was released.

```
SELECT movie_titles.title, movie_titles.year_released,
    music_titles.record_label,...{rest of select list}
  FROM movie_titles LEFT OUTER JOIN music_titles
  ON movie_titles.title = music_titles.title AND
    movie_titles.year_released = music_titles.date_released
```

TABLE 8-22
MOVIE_TITLES

TITLE	YEAR_RELEASED
Lethal Weapon 3	1992
Batman Returns	1992
A Star is Born	1977
Unforgiven	1992
Saturday Night Fever	1978
Grease	1977

TABLE 8-23
MUSIC_TITLES

TITLE	YEAR_RELEASED	RECORD_LABEL
Grease	1977	xyz
Saturday Night Fever	1978	abc
Eagles' Greatest Hits	1976	Elektra
A Star is Born	1977	def
Flat as a Pancake	1979	xxx

TABLE 8-24
Result Table

TITLE	YEAR_RELEASED	RECORD_LABEL
Lethal Weapon 3	1992	*null*
Batman Returns	1992	*null*
A Star is Born	1977	def
Unforgiven	1992	*null*
Saturday Night Fever	1978	abc
Grease	1977	xyz

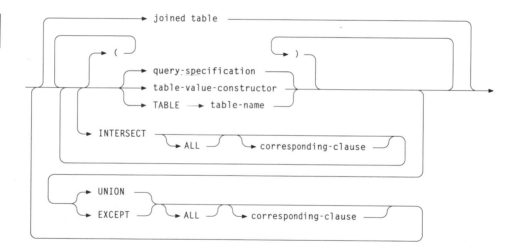

8.8 Chapter Summary

As we've seen in this chapter, there are many ways in which tables can be combined with one another to provide consolidated information (as summarized in Diagram RR23). SQL-92 has introduced a far richer set of these operators than had been available in earlier versions of SQL. Depending on the needs of your applications, you now have access to a robust set of operators, from which you can likely choose exactly the statement that meets your specific needs of the moment. You can

- Find all rows that appear in one table but not another.
- Find all rows that appear in more than one table.

- Explicitly eliminate certain columns from consideration when performing JOIN and UNION operations.

and many of the other types of functions we discussed.

In the next couple of chapters, we'll look at some more advanced DML operations and, in the spirit of working with multiple tables, the means through which integrity of data may be maintained among those tables.

CHAPTER 9

· · · · · · · · · · · · · · · · · ·

Advanced SQL Query Expressions

9.1 Introduction

To this point, we've discussed the basic SQL statements that you will use to write your applications, and we've talked about the kinds of values and basic relational operators that you can use in those statements. Now, it's time to delve a bit deeper and clarify the more complex query expression facilities of SQL.

In this chapter, we dissect SQL's query expression and study each of its components; then we see how they build on one another. After that, we look more closely at the relational operators to understand their precise syntax and semantics. We also tackle the concept of grouped tables that causes so much confusion; during that discussion, we'll have to re-examine the set functions to see how their behavior is affected by grouping operations. Many of the statements we've discussed in the preceding chapters are revisited, this time from a more formal orientation.

We also introduce the *table value* concept and show where it can help you write your applications. Finally, we take a very close look at subqueries and discuss their uses and restrictions, a subject we briefly introduced earlier. Initially, we diverge from our music and video examples to concentrate on theoretical examples which may be easier to follow as we explore statement internals.

This chapter tells you the inside story about the most important elements of SQL: the query expression and the query specification. The two phrases sound awfully similar, don't they? Well, there's an easy way to remember the difference: use an analogy with value specifications and value expressions (we discussed them in Chapter 5). You may recall that a value specification is a simple value, like a literal, whose value is provided by a host variable or a parameter, or by the value given by a special value function like CURRENT_TIME. A value expression is a way to combine value specifications with appropriate operators to produce a new value; the simplest value expression is just a value specification.

Using this analogy, we can see that a query specification is a way to produce a virtual table in SQL that can be used in a query expression to combine with other query specifications to produce a new virtual table. And the simplest form of query expression should be just a query specification. Actually, that's not quite right. There are three "simplest forms" of query expression, and we cover them all in this chapter.

9.2 Query Specifications

The query specification of SQL is what many people call the SELECT statement because it starts off with the keyword SELECT. As we have seen before, the SELECT statement is really a different beast—subtly different, but different in important ways. You will recall that the SELECT statement is really a statement that can be executed by itself and that it must return no more than one row. By contrast, a query specification is an expression that starts with the keyword SELECT and has other syntactic similarities with the SELECT statement. However, a query specification cannot be used by itself, and it is allowed to return more than one row. The syntax for a query specification is shown in Diagram RR24.

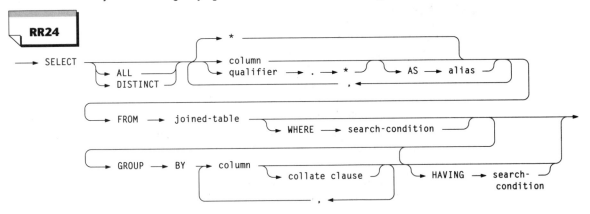

The query specification is the most basic operation that deals with tables in SQL. It is the building block on which other virtual tables are built. A table specification is not used *directly* in many other places in SQL, because it is part of another important building block, the query expression, which we'll discuss shortly.

Like several other SQL components, the query specification creates a virtual table. (We say *virtual* table because the table is not normally materialized. Instead, the rows of the table are produced, even computed, as they are required.) Like any other tables, these virtual tables have columns and rows. The columns of these tables have data types, names (but see below for more information about names of the columns), and all the other attributes of columns. The table has a degree (number of columns) and cardinality (number of rows).

Let's take a very close look at the query specification. Because it's so important to our understanding of SQL, we're going to take it slow and work through all of the details. The basic form of a query specification is:

```
SELECT select-list table-expression
```

(There is another form that you can use, too:

```
SELECT quantifier select-list table-expression
```

where quantifier is either DISTINCT or ALL. If you don't specify a quantifier, then ALL is the default and means "don't eliminate any duplicates from the resulting table." DISTINCT, on the other hand, means "if the table that results from the query specification has any duplicate rows, eliminate all redundant duplicates—all of them except one.")

The select-list comes in two forms. You can either use just an asterisk:

```
*
```

meaning "all columns that are part of the table corresponding to the table-expression," or you can use:

```
select-sublist [ , select-sublist ]...
```

In this case, a select-sublist is either a derived-column or a qualifier (remember from Chapter 5, that a qualifier is either a table name or a correlation name that identifies a table in a particular scope) followed by a period and an asterisk:

```
t.*
```

A derived-column is a value expression (which may be as simple as a column name, possibly with a qualifier) optionally followed by the keyword AS and a derived-column-name:

```
  value-expression
| value-expression AS derived-column-name
```

The derived-column-name gives the derived-column a name. Now, if your value-expression is:

```
movie_titles.title
```

then the column already has a name: TITLE. However, if your value-expression was:

```
movie_titles.current_rental_price/2
```

the column doesn't have a name! In many situations, you must know the names of all of your columns (actually, some of the rules of SQL simply don't work correctly if columns don't have names). As a result, the SQL standard says that an implementation must *assign* a name to any columns that do not have names. If you anticipate using such columns, we strongly recommend that you use the AS clause to give those columns names that are meaningful to you:

```
movie_titles.current_rental_price/2 AS discounted_price
```

Let's look at some examples of query specifications with what we know now (we haven't looked at the table-expression yet, so we'll leave that placeholder there).

```
SELECT DISTINCT current_rental_price table-expression
```

This example will return a set (not a multiset, because we used DISTINCT) of the CURRENT_RENTAL_PRICEs in our table-expression. This will allow us, for example, to determine the unique, different prices of all our movies. Let's see another one.

```
SELECT movie_titles.*, music_titles.* table-expression
```

This example will select *all* columns from the MOVIE_TITLES table and all columns from the MUSIC_TITLES table as they appear in the table-expression.

```
SELECT * table-expression
```

This last example will select all columns from the table-expression. When you use the standalone asterisk, or the select-sublist of qualifier.*, you are telling the DBMS that you want all the columns from the table-expression (or all available with the specified qualifier). However, because you can add columns to or drop columns from base tables (see Chapter 4), the *meaning* of "all columns" might change. Because of this, your programs might quit working or start working incorrectly. *We strongly recommend that you avoid the use of the asterisk as a select-list or as a select-sublist.* In interactive SQL, the asterisk is extremely useful (it beats the heck out of repeatedly entering a long list of column names), but it can cause very surprising results in embedded SQL programs or in module language.

9.2.1   Table Expressions

Okay, now it's time to see what a table-expression is. You probably won't be surprised to learn that it is an expression involving tables and that it produces a virtual table. A table-expression is:

```
from-clause
[ where-clause ]
[ group-by-clause ]
[ having-clause ]
```

The `from-clause` is always required. As you see from the format, the other clauses are all optional. If you specify them, they must be in the given order, but you can skip any or all of them.

Think of these clauses as operators that take input and produce output. Each clause in a `table-expression` produces a virtual table. In fact, the input to the `from-clause` is one or more tables (base tables or views). The input to the `where-clause` is the virtual table produced by the `from-clause`. The input to the `group-by-clause` is the virtual table produced by the `where-clause`; if there is no `where-clause`, then it is the virtual table produce by the `from-clause`. Finally, the input to the `having-clause` is the table produced by the `group-by-clause`, `where-clause`, or `from-clause`.

The format of the `from-clause` is:

```
FROM table-reference [ , table-reference ]...
```

(`table-reference`s were covered in Chapter 8). Therefore, a `from-clause` might look like:

```
FROM t1, t2
```

or

```
FROM movie_titles, distributors
```

If there is only one `table-reference` in the `from-clause`, the resulting virtual table has exactly the same number of columns (with the same names, data types, and other attributes) as the table identified by the `table-reference`. If there are two or more `table-reference`s, then the columns of the resulting virtual table are the same as the columns of each of the input tables in the order that those tables are listed in the `from-clause`. Therefore, if the table MOVIE_TITLES has columns TITLE, OUR_COST, and CURRENT_RENTAL_PRICE; and DISTRIBUTORS has columns DIST_NAME, and DIST_PHONE; then the resulting virtual table of our example would have columns TITLE, OUR_COST, CURRENT_RENTAL_PRICE, DIST_NAME, and DIST_PHONE. Therefore, the resulting virtual table's *degree* is the *sum* of the degrees of each participating input table.

If there is only one `table-reference` in the `from-clause`, the resulting virtual table has exactly the same number of rows as the table identified by the `table-reference`, and the rows are identical to the rows of that table (except, of course, for the order of rows, since order is irrelevant in tables). If there is more than one `table-reference`, the rows of the resulting virtual table are determined by joining each row of each input table with each row of each other input table. So, the first row retrieved from MOVIE_TITLES would be combined with the first row retrieved from DISTRIBUTORS; next, the first row retrieved from MOVIE_TITLES would be combined with the second row retrieved from DISTRIBUTORS; and so forth until the first row retrieved from MOVIE_TITLES is combined with the last row retrieved from DISTRIBUTORS. Then the second row retrieved from MOVIE_TITLES is combined with the first row retrieved from DISTRIBUTORS. You can probably guess the rest. This is the *Cartesian product* of the input tables. The resulting virtual table's *cardinality* is therefore the *product* of the cardinalities of each participating input table.

Let's make this a bit more precise by looking at Tables 9-1 and 9-2, MOVIE_TITLES and DISTRIBUTORS. The resulting virtual table of

```
FROM movie_titles, distributors
```

is shown in Table 9.3.

TABLE 9-1
MOVIE_TITLES

TITLE	OUR_COST	CURRENT_RENTAL_PRICE
Unforgiven	34.95	3.99
Batman Returns	33.95	3.99
Lethal Weapon 3	23.95	2.99
Young Frankenstein	21.95	1.99

TABLE 9-2
DISTRIBUTORS

DIST_NAME	DIST_PHONE
Cheaper Distributors	555-9999
Eastern Movies, Inc.	555-8888
Western Films, Inc.	555-4444

TABLE 9-3

TITLE	OUR_COST	CURRENT_RENTAL_PRICE	DIST_NAME	DIST_PHONE
Unforgiven	34.95	3.99	Cheaper Distributors	555-9999
Unforgiven	34.95	3.99	Eastern Movies, Inc.	555-8888
Unforgiven	34.95	3.99	Western Films, Inc.	555-4444
Batman Returns	33.95	3.99	Cheaper Distributors	555-9999
Batman Returns	33.95	3.99	Eastern Movies, Inc.	555-8888
Batman Returns	33.95	3.99	Western Films, Inc.	555-4444
Lethal Weapon 3	23.95	2.99	Cheaper Distributors	555-9999
Lethal Weapon 3	23.95	2.99	Eastern Movies, Inc.	555-8888
Lethal Weapon 3	23.95	2.99	Western Films, Inc.	555-4444
Young Frankenstein	21.95	1.99	Cheaper Distributors	555-9999
Young Frankenstein	21.95	1.99	Eastern Movies, Inc.	555-8888
Young Frankenstein	21.95	1.99	Western Films, Inc.	555-4444

The degrees of the input tables were 3 and 2, respectively, so the degree of the resulting table is 3 + 2, or 5. The cardinalities of the input tables were 4 and 3, respectively, so the cardinality of the resulting virtual table is 4*3, or 12. Also, note that the names of the columns of the resulting virtual table are taken from the input tables.

The from-clause creates a virtual table that may (if there is more than one input table) have a different shape than its input table. (The word *shape* is occasionally used to express the degree of a table, and the names, data types, and other attributes of its columns.) By contrast, the where-clause produces an output table with exactly the same shape as its input table.

The format of the where-clause is:

```
WHERE search-condition
```

(search-condition was defined in Chapter 7.) Think of the where-clause as a sort of filter that examines each row in the input table and decides whether to pass it on or toss it out. It passes on any row that matches the search-condition (that is, for which the search-condition is true) and throws out any row for which the search-condition is either false or unknown. For example, if we apply the where-clause:

```
WHERE movie_titles.title <> 'Young Frankenstein'
    AND (distributors.dist_name NOT LIKE 'Eastern%')
```

to our example above, the resulting virtual table would be as shown in Table 9-4.

TABLE 9-4

TITLE	OUR COST	CURRENT RENTAL PRICE	DIST_NAME	DIST PHONE
Unforgiven	34.95	3.99	Cheaper Distributors	555-9999
Unforgiven	34.95	3.99	Western Films, Inc.	555-4444
Batman Returns	33.95	3.99	Cheaper Distributors	555-9999
Batman Returns	33.95	3.99	Western Films, Inc.	555-4444
Lethal Weapon 3	23.95	2.99	Cheaper Distributors	555-9999
Lethal Weapon 3	23.95	2.99	Western Films, Inc.	555-4444

Note that the shape of the table hasn't changed, but there are fewer rows in the result—all rows that didn't satisfy the search-condition have been eliminated.

9.2.2 GROUP BY

The format of the group-by-clause is:

```
GROUP BY grouping-column [ , grouping-column ]...
```

and grouping-column is a column-reference optionally followed by a collate-clause (but only if the column-reference identifies a column whose data type is character string). The collate-clause identifies the collation used for comparing the columns (see Chapter 18).

The result of a group-by-clause is a virtual table, as we've already said, but that result is called a *grouped table*. The input table is partitioned into one or more groups; the number of groups is the minimum such that, for each grouping-column, no two rows of any group have different values for that grouping-column. That is, for any group in the resulting grouped table, every row in the group has the same value for the grouping-column. Otherwise, the group-by-clause produces an output table that is identical to the input table. The example below and in Table 9-5 show what a group-by-clause might look like.

```
SELECT movie_type, AVG (current_rental_price)
    FROM movie_titles
    GROUP BY movie_type
```

TABLE 9-5
MOVIE_TITLES

TITLE	MOVIE_TYPE	CURRENT_RENTAL_PRICE
Lethal Weapon 3	Action	2.99
Unforgiven	Western	3.99
The Outlaw Josey Wales	Western	2.99
Kelly's Heroes	War	2.99
Shaft	Action	2.99
Shaft's Big Score	Action	1.99

The resulting table would look like Table 9-6.

TABLE 9-6

MOVIE_TYPE	AVG(CURRENT_RENTAL_PRICE)
Action	2.66
Western	3.49
War	2.99

Note that the virtual table (the grouped table) has the same number of columns and (presumably, although we haven't shown this explicitly) the same data types and other attributes. However, we've used the notation of another horizontal line to indicate that the table has been divided into two groups based on the values in column MOVIE_TYPE. MOVIE_TYPE is the grouping-column for this group-by-clause.

Now, the having-clause is another filter. This time, though, the filtering operation is applied to the grouped table resulting from the preceding clause. If there is a group-by-clause, the grouped table resulting from it is the input to the having-clause. On the other hand, if there is no group-by-clause, the entire table resulting from the where-clause (or from-clause if there is no where-clause) is treated as a grouped table with exactly one group. In this case, there is no grouping-column. The format of the having-clause is:

```
HAVING search-condition
```

The search-condition is applied to each *group* of the grouped table, although not really to the *rows* of the groups. That's because the only columns of the input table that the having-clause can reference are the grouping columns, unless the columns are used in a set function. Therefore, the following is a valid having-clause for our example:

```
HAVING movie_type = 'Western'
    OR movie_type = 'War'
```

The result of applying this having-clause to our example is shown in Table 9-7.

TABLE 9-7

MOVIE_TYPE	AVG(CURRENT_RENTAL_PRICE)
Western	3.49
War	2.99

This is *not* a valid having-clause:

```
HAVING our_cost = 2.99
```

because OUR_COST is not a grouping column. In our example, all columns appear to be character strings, so there are no set functions available to allow us to reference any columns other than MOVIE_TYPE. Therefore, if we had omitted the group-by-clause and thus had no grouping column, we could not have had a having-clause, either. Why? Because the only columns of the input table that you can reference in a having-clause are grouping columns or they must be referenced in a set function.

If MOVIE_TYPE had been an integer column with values like 1, 2, or 3 (say, we have some type of enumerated encoding that is processed by host applications) instead of a character string column, then a valid having clause would be:

```
HAVING AVG (MOVIE_TYPE) = 2
```

and we could have used this having-clause with or without a group-by-clause (though we can't say what an "average movie type" really tells you!).

On the other hand, you might *really* be interested only in movies whose rental cost is greater than $1.99 and only want to compute the average rental of those. You can use SQL-92's *nested table* facility for that.

```
SELECT movie_type, AVG (current_rental_price)
  FROM ( SELECT *
           FROM movie_titles
           WHERE current_rental_price > 1.99 )
  GROUP BY movie_type
```

The nested SELECT * FROM... isn't a subquery in SQL's definition of the term, but it is a nested table expression. Therefore, the GROUP BY (and the select-list) only operates on a virtual table of movies (unnamed, by the way!) whose CURRENT_RENTAL_PRICE is more than $1.99.

The search-condition of a having-clause can also contain subqueries, which we'll cover later in this chapter. It's worth mentioning here, however, that the subquery is evaluated once for each *group* in the input grouped table and the value of the subquery is used in the application of the search-condition to the group.

Like the where-clause and group-by-clause, the having-clause produces a resulting table with the same shape as its input table.

Okay, let's see what the entire table-expression looks like at one shot:

```
FROM t1, t2
  WHERE t1.c11 <> 'W' AND
    (t2.c21 = 'R' OR t2.c21 = 'T')
  GROUP BY t1.c13
  HAVING t1.c13 = 'XYZ'
```

9.2.3 Updatable Query Specifications

Query specifications are not only applicable when retrieving information, but also when you need to update data. A query specification is *updatable* only if:

- You don't use DISTINCT as a quantifier
- The value-expressions in the select-list are all column-references, and none of them appear more than once
- The from-clause has only one table-reference, and it identifies either a base table or an updatable derived table
- The base table ultimately identified by the table-reference isn't referenced (directly or indirectly) anywhere in the where-clause
- You don't use a group-by-clause or a having-clause.

If you violate any of these, then the query specification is read-only. If you use it in a view definition or a cursor specification, you cannot execute UPDATE, DELETE, or INSERT (for a view) on it.

9.3 Query Expressions

You've already had an introduction to query expressions in Chapter 4 (and other places). In fact, we used the concept a lot in Chapter 8, without really calling it by name. However, in this chapter, we are going to examine thoroughly this important element of the SQL language.

In its simplest form, a query expression is merely a query specification. There are two other "simplest forms" of query expressions that we also cover later in this chapter (TABLE table-name and VALUES row-value), but just now, we're going to explore the more complex forms of the query expression. First, let's review what we learned in Chapter 8.

There are many different forms of a query expression; that is, the format is very flexible and you can write a wide variety of query expressions. A query expression can be either a joined-table (more on that later, too) or a non-join-query-expression, which is either a non-join-query-term or a query expression and a query-term separated by some operators. The operators are UNION or EXCEPT, and they can optionally be followed by ALL and/or a corresponding-specification.

As you recall, UNION specifies that the table indicated by the query expression and the table indicated by the query-term are to be combined with a union operation. If ALL is specified, then redundant duplicate rows are retained; otherwise, they are eliminated. EXCEPT specifies that the resulting virtual table is to contain all rows from the table indicated by the query expression *except* those that also appear in the table indicated by the query-term. Again, if ALL is specified, then the number of copies of any specific row value in the result is equal to the number of such copies in the table indicated by the query expression, less the number in the table indicated by the query-term.

A query-term is either a non-join-query-term or a joined-table, and a non-join-query-term is either a non-join-query-primary or a query-term and a query-primary separated by the operator INTERSECT, optionally followed by ALL and/or a corresponding-specification.

If INTERSECT is specified, the resulting virtual table contains rows that appear in both the query-term and the query-primary. If ALL is specified, then the number of copies of any specific row value in the result is equal to the lesser number of such copies in the table indicated by the query-term and the number in the table indicated by the query-primary.

(Incidentally, the particular arrangement of INTERSECT versus UNION and EXCEPT gives INTERSECT a higher precedence than the other two. This means that, in a statement that doesn't use parentheses to resolve precedence relationships, INTERSECT operations will be performed before UNION and EXCEPT operations. For example:

```
t1 UNION t2 INTERSECT t3 EXCEPT t4
```

will be done in this order:

```
t2 INTERSECT t3 (call the result TX)
t1 UNION TX     (call the result TY)
TY EXCEPT t4
```

Note that operators of the same precedence are effectively executed left to right.

A query-primary is either a non-join-query-primary or a joined-table. A non-join-query-primary is either a simple-table or a non-join-query-expression enclosed in parentheses.

And a simple-table is either a query specification, a table-value, or an explicit-table. An explicit-table is the keyword TABLE followed by a table-name; it is just a shorthand for SELECT * FROM table-name, so you must be careful to use it only when the shape of the table is appropriate.

9.3.1 CORRESPONDING

So far, we've left out the definition of a corresponding-specification, but now it's time to include it. The format is:

```
CORRESPONDING [ BY ( column-name [ , column-name ]... ) ]
```

so that you can specify just CORRESPONDING, or you can specify CORRESPONDING BY followed by a parenthesized list of column names. If you leave off the optional BY clause, the DBMS will make up a BY clause for you that includes every column-name that appears in both of the tables. If you include the BY clause, every column-name that you include must be the name of a column in both of the tables. In railroad diagram form, it looks like RR22 (see Chapter 8, section 8.4).

9.3.2 Results of Query Expressions

Like everything else we've discussed in this chapter, the result of a query expression—and of each of its component expressions, terms, and primaries—is a virtual table. The rules are fairly simple, too: The tables have to have the same number of columns, and the data types of the "corresponding columns" (by which we do *not* mean the columns of the corresponding-specification, but the first column of each of the two tables followed by the second column of each of the two tables, and so forth) need not be identical, but need only be comparable (that is, they can be compared). The names of the corresponding columns need not be identical. If they are, the name of the resulting column is the same name; otherwise, the name of the resulting column is assigned by the DBMS. The data type and other attributes of the result columns are the same as the data types of the input columns, with suitable rules to resolve differences caused by the comparable requirement. For example, if one input column were CHARACTER(5) and the other CHARACTER(10), the output column would be CHARACTER(10). We call such tables *union-compatible tables*.

9.3.3 Examples of Query Expressions

Okay, now that we've presented a rather complicated picture of query expressions, let's look at a few examples. The first example:

```
SELECT c1 FROM t1
```

is a query expression because it's a query specification. The next example:

```
(SELECT c1 FROM t1)
```

is also a query expression because it's a query expression in parentheses. The third example:

```
SELECT * FROM t1
UNION
SELECT * FROM t2
```

is a query expression that is valid only if T1 and T2 have (almost) identical definitions. The last example:

```
SELECT c1, c2, c3
  FROM t1
INTERSECT ALL CORRESPONDING BY ( c2, c3 )
SELECT c4, c2, c3
  FROM t2
```

is also a query expression using several options.

9.4 Joined Table

Now, let's add joined-table to our list. You will recall the discussion earlier in this chapter that specified the results of the from-clause; that clause produced a resulting virtual table that was the Cartesian product of its input tables (if there were more than one, at least); the number of columns of the result was the sum of the numbers of columns of the input tables, and the number of rows in the result was the product of the number of rows of the input tables. Well, one alternative of a joined-table is a cross-join:

```
table-reference CROSS JOIN table-reference
```

The resulting virtual table of T1 CROSS JOIN T2 is exactly the same as FROM T1, T2.
    Another alternative of joined-table is a qualified-join, which is:

```
table-reference [ NATURAL ] [ join-type ]
    JOIN table-reference [ join-spec ]
```

The join-type is either INNER, UNION, LEFT OUTER, RIGHT OUTER, or FULL OUTER (the keyword OUTER is optional in all three cases, but we recommend that you use it to make your programs more readable) and indicates the type of join that you want. If you don't use join-type at all, the result is the same as if you had used INNER.

An INNER JOIN is one where the rows in the result table are the rows from the first table that meet the specified criteria, combined with the corresponding rows from the second table that meet the specified criteria.

An OUTER JOIN, by contrast, is one where the rows in the result table are the rows that would have resulted from an INNER JOIN *and* the rows from the first table (LEFT OUTER JOIN), the second table (RIGHT OUTER JOIN) or both tables (FULL OUTER JOIN) that had no matches in the other table.

A UNION JOIN (sometimes called OUTER UNION in the relational literature) produces only those rows in the first and second tables that had *no* matches in the other table. The behavior of

```
t1 UNION JOIN t2
```

is a bit like that of

```
(t1 FULL OUTER JOIN t2) EXCEPT (t1 INNER JOIN t2)
```

The join-spec gives the criteria for the join. A join-spec is either the keyword ON followed by a search-condition:

```
ON search-condition
```

or the keyword USING followed by a parenthesized list of column names:

```
USING ( column-name [ , column-name ]... )
```

If the ON variant is used, the result of the join contains every row of the Cartesian product of the two tables that satisfies the search-condition. For example:

```
ON t1.c1 = t2.c2 * 2 AND t1.c3 <> t2.c4
```

The most common case in real applications, though, is commonly known as an *equi-join*. In an equi-join, the criteria is for one or more columns of rows in one table to be equal to one or more columns of rows in the other table:

```
ON t1.c1 = t2.c1 AND t1.c2 = t2.c2
```

Because this practice is so common, SQL-92 provides the following alternative:

```
USING (c1, c2)
```

This is useful (and valid) only if the columns to be used for the join have the same names in both tables (and have comparable data types), because it is identical to the ON variant just above. In the USING variant, you select the columns that you wish to use to determine the result of the join. If you want to use *every* column with the same name in both tables for the join, you can use the NATURAL variation. A natural join is an equi-join based on the equality of every column with the same name in the two tables. The join

```
t1 NATURAL JOIN t2
```

is equivalent to:

```
t1 JOIN t2 USING (Cx, Cy, ...)
```

where Cx, Cy, etc. are the columns with the same name in both tables. That, in turn, is equivalent to:

```
t1 JOIN t2 ON t1.Cx = t2.Cx AND t1.Cy = t2.Cy AND...
```

or:

```
t1 INNER JOIN t2 ON t1.Cx = t2.Cx AND t1.Cy = t2.Cy AND...
```

Now that we've gone through all of the various types of JOINs in SQL-92 (both the old-style join and all of the new JOIN types) and the various set operators (UNION, EXCEPT, and INTERSECT) in some detail, we think it would be useful to look at the *formal* definitions of these operators from SQL-92. We'll do these in list form so you can easily follow the steps and corresponding logic.

We'll start with the JOIN definitions. SQL-92 approaches the specification of *joined-table* (the way that JOINs are expressed) by decomposing the functions into basic components and the putting them together in ways that produce the desired result. Let's do the same here. First we'll see what restrictions there are on the syntax and what the shape of the result is (that is, the number of columns and the names and data types of the columns).

1. Since a JOIN always has two source tables, let's call them T1 and T2. Let's also call the *table references* TR1 and TR2 (to clarify: the *tables* themselves are T1 and T2; the possibly qualified names of the tables are TR1 and TR2). Since table references always have a correlation name (even if the system assigns one without telling you about it), let's call the correlation names CN1 and CN2.
2. Let's use the symbol CP to mean:
   ```
   SELECT * FROM tr1, tr2
   ```
   or, equivalently,
   ```
   SELECT * FROM tr1 CROSS JOIN tr2
   ```
3. If you specify NATURAL JOIN, you cannot specify UNION, ON, or USING.
4. If you specify UNION JOIN, you cannot specify ON or USING.

5. If you don't specify NATURAL or UNION, you have to specify either ON or USING.

6. If you specify JOIN without any other join type, then INNER JOIN is implicit.

7. If you specify ON, all of the column references in the search condition have to reference a column of T1 or of T2 (they can also be an "outer reference" to a column in a query expression that contains the joined-table). If any value expression in the search condition is a set function, the joined-table has to be contained in the select-list or HAVING clause of some outer query expression *and* the set function must reference a column of that outer query expression.

8. If you specify any JOIN with an ON clause, the shape of the resulting table is the same as the shape of CP.

9. If you specify any JOIN with NATURAL or USING, the shape of the resulting table is determined this way:

   • If you specified NATURAL, let's use the phrase *corresponding join columns* to mean all columns that have the same name in both T1 and T2 (and have no duplicate names in either T1 or T2).

   • If you specified USING, we'll use the phrase *corresponding join columns* to mean all columns whose name appears in the column name list (they must all have the same name in both T1 and T2, and they cannot have duplicate names in either T1 or T2).

   • Each pair of corresponding join columns has to be comparable, of course.

   • Let's use the term *SLCC* to mean "a select-list of corresponding join columns," each of which is of the form:

     COALESCE (ta.c, tb.c) AS c

   • (where C is the name of the corresponding join column), with the COALESCE clauses in the same order as the corresponding join columns appeared in T1 (this was chosen arbitrarily—it could have been T2, but the standards committees chose T1).

   • Let's use the term *SLT1* to mean "a select-list of column names in T1 that are *not* corresponding join columns, in the order they appear in T1." Let's also use the term *SLT2* to mean "a select-list of column names in T2 that are *not* corresponding join columns, in the order they appear in T2."

   • The shape of the result is the same as the shape of:

     SELECT slcc, slt1, slt2 FROM tr1, tr2

   Therefore, the common columns appear first in the result table, followed by the noncommon columns from T1, and ending with the noncommon columns from T2.

Next, let's see what rows are actually returned in the result.

1. First, let's define the symbol T to mean one of 5 things:
   - If you specified UNION JOIN, then T is empty (has no rows).
   - If you specified CROSS JOIN, then T has all the rows that CP has.
   - If you specified ON, then T has all the rows of CP that satisfy the search-condition.
   - If you specified NATURAL or USING, and there are some corresponding join columns, then T has all the rows of CP for which the values in the corresponding join columns are equal.
   - If you specified NATURAL or USING, and there were no corresponding join columns, then T has all the rows that CP has.

2. Let's use the symbol P1 to mean "all rows of T1 that appear as a partial row in T" (recall that the rows in T are rows from T1 combined with rows from T2). Similarly, let's use P2 to mean "all rows of T2 that appear as a partial row in T."

3. Let's use the symbol U1 to mean "all rows of T1 that do not appear as a partial row in T" and U2 to mean "all rows of T2 that do not appear as a partial row in T."

4. Now, let's use X1 to be the same rows as U1 except we'll append some null values on the *right* (as many null values as T2 has columns). We'll also use X2 to be the same rows as U2 except we'll append some null values on the *left* (as many null values as T1 has columns).

5. Let's invent two distinct names, N1 and N2, to reference the virtual tables X1 and X2. (Remember, X1 and X2 are sets, or multisets, of rows, not the names of those sets or multisets.) And let's use the name TN to reference the virtual table T.

6. If you specified INNER JOIN or CROSS JOIN, we'll use the symbol S to identify the same rows as T.

7. If you specified LEFT OUTER JOIN, we'll use the symbol S to identify the rows that result from:
   ```
   SELECT * FROM tn
   UNION ALL
   SELECT * FROM n1
   ```

8. If you specified RIGHT OUTER JOIN, we'll use the symbol S to identify the rows that result from:
   ```
   SELECT * FROM tn
   UNION ALL
   SELECT * FROM n2
   ```

9. If you specified `FULL OUTER JOIN`, we'll use the symbol S to identify the rows that result from:

```
SELECT * FROM tn
UNION ALL
SELECT * FROM n1
UNION ALL
SELECT * FROM n2
```

10. If you specified `UNION JOIN`, we'll use the symbol S to identify the rows that result from:

```
SELECT * FROM n1
UNION ALL
SELECT * FROM n2
```

11. Now, let's use SN as a name for the virtual table S.

12. If you specified `NATURAL` or `USING`, the result of the `JOIN` is the same rows that would result from:

```
SELECT slcc, slt1, slt2 FROM sn
```

13. If you didn't specify `NATURAL` or `USING`, the result of the `JOIN` is the same rows that are in S.

We agree that this seems really confusing when you first read it. However, we encourage you to take the time to read it through carefully. You'll find that it's extremely logical and can help you to understand exactly how the various types of `JOIN` work.

Now, let's take the same kind of look at the `INTERSECT`, `EXCEPT`, and `UNION` operators that can participate in query expressions. We'll start off with determining the shape of the result.

1. All query expressions use one or more simple tables that may or may not be combined with these set operators. You'll recall from earlier in this chapter that a simple table can be either a `query-specification`, a `table value constructor`, or `TABLE table-name`.

   - If the simple table is a `query-specification`, the shape of the simple table is the same as the shape of the `query-specification`.

   - If the simple table is `TABLE table-name`, the shape of the simple table is the same as the shape of that table.

   - If the simple table is a `table value constructor`, the shape of the simple table is the same as the shape of the `table value constructor` except that all the column names are provided by the DBMS (uniquely in the SQL statement).

2. If the query expression doesn't have any `UNION`, `INTERSECT`, or `EXCEPT` operators, then the shape of the query expression is the same as the shape of the simple table. Otherwise, it's more interesting . . . .

3. Let's use the symbol T1 to represent the table on the left of the set operator and TN1 to be its name. Similarly, let's use T2 to represent the table on the right and TN2 to be its name. We'll use the symbol TR to be the result of the operation (not its name, though). Finally, let's use the symbol OP to be the set operator (UNION, *etc.*)

4. If you do not specify CORRESPONDING, then T1 and T2 must be of the same degree (have the same number of columns). For all respective columns (columns in the same position in the table) in T1 and T2 that happen to have the same name, the respective result column in TR has that name. All other columns of TR have a DBMS-provided name (unique in the SQL statement).

5. If you do specify CORRESPONDING, there has to be at least one column in T1 and in T2 with the same name (and no columns of either T1 or T2 can be duplicates).

   - If you specify a column-list with CORRESPONDING, let's use the symbol SL to mean "a select-list identical to that column-list"; of course, every column in the select-list has to be a column in both T1 and T2.

   - If you don't specify a column-list, let's define SL to mean "a select-list of every column that has the same name in both T1 and T2, in the order they appear in T1."

6. If you specify CORRESPONDING, the expression TN1 OP TN2 is effectively replaced by:

   ```
   (SELECT sl FROM tn1) OP (SELECT sl FROM tn2)
   ```

   This has the effect of eliminating all the columns of T1 and T2 that are not corresponding columns. Because all the respective columns of the two new source tables have the same name, the name of the respective result column in TR has the same name, too.

7. Whether or not you specify CORRESPONDING, the data type of a result column is determined by the data types of the two source columns. (We've already said that the data types of the source columns have to be comparable.) The result column's data type is determined by the union data type rules that we gave you in Chapter 3.

Okay, now we know the shape of the result table. Let's see how to determine the actual rows of that result.

1. Obviously, if there is no set operator, the result has exactly the same rows as the simple table.

2. If there is a set operator, let's examine the contents of the two source tables. First, we'll define the symbol R as "a copy of any row that is a row of T1, a row of T2, or a row that is in both T1 and T2." We decided to say "a copy" because we're later going to talk about how many copies of R there might be in the result table, and it can get too confusing if we defined R to be a row *in* T1 or T2.

3. Now, tables in SQL are multisets, so R may have one or more copies in T1 or in T2 (or both). Let's let the symbol M mean "the number of copies of R in T1" and let N be "the number of copies of R in T2." (Of course, both M and N are greater than or equal to zero since, for example, T1 might not have *any* copies of R if it is a copy of a row that exists only in T2.)

4. If you didn't specify ALL, we have to take care of duplicate elimination.

   - If you specified UNION and either M or N is greater than zero, then the result has exactly one copy of R; otherwise, the result has no copies of R. This means, of course, that R doesn't exist, since it was required to be a copy of a row in either T1 or T2.

   - If you specified EXCEPT and M is greater than zero but N is equal to zero, then the result has exactly one copy of R; otherwise, the result has no copies of R.

   - If you specified INTERSECT and both M and N are greater than zero, the result contains exactly one copy of R; otherwise, the result has no copies of R.

5. If you did specify ALL, we don't eliminate duplicates from the result and the results look like this:

   - If you specified UNION, the number of copies of R in the result is M + N.

   - If you specified EXCEPT, the number of copies of R in the result is M – N, except that it obviously cannot be negative, so the number is zero if N is greater than M.

   - If you specified INTERSECT, the number of copies of R in the result is the smaller of M and N.

Again, we recognize that it can be pretty intimidating to read these rules for the first time. However, if you take the time to really understand them, you'll have a much better grasp of the actions that the DBMS must (effectively!) take when processing the set operators.

9.5 Grouped Tables

Earlier in this chapter, we mentioned the notion of a grouped table. Put simply, a grouped table is the table that results from the use of a GROUP BY and/or a HAVING clause. You can think of a grouped table as a *table of tables* or a *table of groups*. Each group has the same value for the grouping column or columns, unless there aren't any grouping columns, in which case there's only one group anyway. Set functions operate on the individual groups in the grouped table, as we illustrated earlier.

In Chapter 5, we examined set functions and we learned that the set functions operated on the table that was provided to produce a result. Therefore, if you wrote:

```
SELECT SUM(salary)
  FROM employees
```

you would get back a single row (with a single column) that contained the total of the salaries for employees. However, the set functions can also be applied in grouped-table situations. Assume that our EMPLOYEES table looks like Table 9-8.

TABLE 9-8

DEPT_NO	LAST_NAME	FIRST_NAME	SALARY
12	Mitchell	Andrea	20000
15	Walters	Marvin	20000
12	Richards	Martha	30000
15	Young	Gail	40000

Consider the following:

```
SELECT dept_no, SUM(salary), AVG(salary),
        MAX(salary), MIN(salary)
    FROM employees GROUP BY dept_no
```

That query will return as many rows as there are departments that have employees assigned to them; each row will have five columns containing (1) the number of the department, (2) the total of its salaries, (3) the average salary, and (4) the highest and (5) the lowest salary in the group. Our result is shown in Table 9-9.

TABLE 9-9

DEPT_NO	SUM(SALARY)	AVG(SALARY)	MAX(SALARY)	MIN(SALARY)
12	50000	25000	30000	20000
15	60000	30000	40000	20000

You can also use the COUNT functions:

```
SELECT COUNT(*)
    FROM employees
    GROUP BY dept_no
```

which will return the number of employees *in each group* (in our brief example, two for each group). Contrast this with:

```
SELECT COUNT(*)
    FROM employees
```

This query will return one row with a value of 4, the total number of employees in the entire EMPLOYEES table. The difference is the absence of the GROUP BY clause, of course. Without that clause, you don't have a grouped table, and the COUNT function counts the entire table instead of the rows in the groups.

When you write a `query-specification` that contains a GROUP BY clause or a HAVING clause, the resulting virtual table is a grouped table (as we said above). In this case, no select-list column in the query-specification can reference a column of the table-expression in the query-specification unless that column is a grouping column or the reference is in the form of a set function invocation that has the column as a parameter.

9.5.1 Grouped Views

Views that are defined using query expressions that define grouped tables are called *grouped views*. There's not really anything special about a grouped view other than the characteristics of grouped tables. However, SQL-92 does place some leveling restrictions on the uses of grouped views. In particular, Entry SQL programs cannot make grouped tables out of grouped views (that is, you can't write a `table-expression` with a GROUP BY or HAVING clause if the FROM clause identifies a grouped view), and they cannot join grouped views with other tables, even other grouped views. Furthermore, Entry SQL programs cannot use set functions on grouped views or use a subquery on a grouped view in a comparison predicate. Finally, you cannot execute a single-row SELECT statement on a grouped view in Entry SQL.

9.6 Table Value Constructor

We mentioned earlier in this chapter that there were three "simplest" forms of a query specification. The third of those simplest forms is called a *table value constructor*. Think of it as a table literal, if you must. Although not quite accurate, as we'll see, it's close enough to give you a fairly decent mental picture of what's intended.

Earlier, in Chapter 6, we discussed the row value constructor as a way of representing an entire tuple, or row, of data at one time. The table value constructor is analogous to that, except that it (of course) is used to represent an entire table of data (that is, the cardinality can be greater than one).

The syntax of the table value constructor is shown in Diagram RR25. You'll recall that a `row-value-constructor` is a parenthesized list of value expressions, separated by commas.

The most common place to find a table value constructor is in the INSERT statement, which we've seen already. However, the ability to use a table value constructor in the INSERT statement is hidden in the details. Recall that the format of the INSERT statement uses a query expression.

```
INSERT INTO table-name
  [ ( column-name [ , column-name ]... ) ]
  query expression
```

Well, one alternative of that query expression is a table value constructor. Using this alternative, the syntax looks like the following:

```
INSERT INTO table-name
  [ ( column-name [ , column-name ]... ) ]
    VALUES row-value-constructor
         [ , row-value-constructor ]...
```

Of course, the degree of each `row-value-constructor` has to be the same as the number of (explicit or implicit) `column-name`s, which means that they all have to have the same degree, too. The rows inserted are represented by the `row-value-constructors` (one each).

Similarly, anywhere that you can use a query expression, you can also use a `table-value-constructor` of the same degree. Consider the `table-subquery` (more about this below): as we shall see, a subquery (including a `table-subquery`) is really a query expression enclosed in parentheses. That query expression can be a `table-value-constructor`, so you can code an `IN` predicate as follows:

```
IN ( VALUES (5), (10), (15) )
```

To be honest, we don't know why you'd want to do this, since the same effect could be had with:

```
IN ( 5, 10, 15 )
```

but there are other cases where it could be more interesting. For example, as we showed you in Chapter 7, the first operand of the `IN` predicate can be a `row-value-constructor`. Thus, you could code something like:

```
( title, actor_first_name, actor_last_name )
IN VALUES ( '10', 'Bo', 'Derek'),
        ('M*A*S*H*', 'Donald', 'Sutherland'),
        ('Unforgiven', 'Clint', 'Eastwood')
```

which couldn't be coded without the `table-value-constructor`.

9.7 Subqueries

We introduced subqueries in Chapter 5; now let's discuss them further. A subquery is just what it sounds like: a query that is a part of another query. Yet, that's an oversimplification. A subquery is (syntactically the same format as) a query expression in parentheses. Subqueries can return atomic values (degree and cardinality both equal to 1), row values (degree greater than or equal to 1, but cardinality equal to 1), or table values (degree and cardinality both greater than or equal to 1), depending on the situation in which they are used. Actually, in all cases, it's possible for the subquery that you write to have a cardinality of 0 or greater than 1, and the rules of SQL-92 specify what result you'll get in either case.

In general, most situations where you can use a subquery will treat the value of the subquery as the null value if the cardinality is 0. Similarly, when the cardinality is required to be no greater than 1, you'll get an error if the subquery identifies more than one row.

By contrast, when a scalar subquery is required (degree and cardinality = 1), SQL-92 simply doesn't permit you to specify a subquery that returns more than a single column: any attempt to do so will give you syntax errors. Similarly, for a row subquery or a table subquery, the number of columns returned (the degree of the subquery) must be appropriate for the use of the subquery.

In SQL-89, the use of subqueries was severely restricted. They could appear only in a very limited number of places in the languages. This was widely viewed as undesirable under the principle of maximum orthogonality (separation of unrelated concepts). Because subqueries are nothing more than a way to produce values, and because there are many places in SQL where values can be used, it was widely believed that SQL should allow the use of subqueries in any place where another kind of value could be used.

SQL-92 goes a very long way toward satisfying that requirement, although arguably it doesn't go all the way. While we believe that SQL-92 represents a substantial improvement in orthogonality over SQL-89, we also hope that future versions will be yet more thorough.

The format of a subquery (though we just told you what it looks like) is:

```
( query-expression )
```

9.8 Chapter Summary

In this chapter, we've taken a more formal approach to SQL query expressions. That is, rather than presenting language facets with "to do this, you enter this" or "if you do this, this is what you'll get," we've presented the inside story behind query expressions.

We discussed query specifications and the subtle differences from routine SELECT statements. We looked at table expressions and the GROUP BY and HAVING clauses. Finally, we discussed subqueries in the context of permissible usage within SQL-92.

In the next chapter, we'll turn our attention away from the data manipulation orientation of the last four chapters. We'll now look at how SQL handles constraints and referential integrity aspects, and how you can use these facilities to enhance the integrity of your databases.

CHAPTER 10

· · · · · · · · · · · · · · · · · · ·

Constraints, Assertions, and Referential Integrity

10.1 Introduction

Your organization's database is only as good as the integrity of the data contained within its tables or records. That is, the reliability of the data is critical to your applications, decision support and query tools, and other aspects of your information systems environment that utilize your database. Outright errors in the data are an obvious problem, although not the only one. Missing information, lost linkages among data elements, and other problems can result in incorrect reports and can lead the database users to lose confidence in the overall database environment.

The integrity of the data can be ensured by applying *constraints,* or rules, to the structure of the database and its contents. There are two primary methods by which these constraints can be specified, applied, and enforced:

- Through the applications programs and software systems that utilize the database.
- Alternatively, through the database management system itself.

Traditionally, application programs have been the medium through which such constraints have been applied. Examples include:

- Verifying that an input value for a particular data item is within the correct range of values (*e.g.,* a new employee's age must be between 16 and 90, and hourly wage must be greater than the minimum wage rate), or is from the correct list of values (*e.g.,* a new movie's type can only be CHILDREN, HORROR, COMEDY, OTHER).

- Verifying that the relationship between two or more values is correct (*e.g.,* the sale price of a movie is never less than that which we paid).

The growing use of relational database management systems, particularly in personal computer environments, introduced the concept of *database-enforced constraints* to many information systems users. That is, instead of having to write COBOL, C, or some 4GL code to specify and enforce constraints, the data definition language provides facilities to perform these functions. There are several major advantages to database-enforced constraints as compared with those managed through procedural applications code.

1. Since the tables in a relational database are used by many different applications, each and every constraint must be specified—and modified, whenever necessary—in each applicable program when the application-enforced model is used. In contrast, database-enforced constraints can usually be designated in a single location (typically in the data definition language) and still apply to all necessary applications.

2. Application-enforced constraints are usually more complex to code and manage than are database-enforced constraints. For example, to validate a list-of-values constraint in procedural code, program constructs such as loop control and if-then-else statements are necessary, as illustrated in the following pseudocode:

do until all input is correct:
>*get movie title*
>*get movie cost*
>. . .
>*get movie type*
>. . .
>*if movie type = 'Children'*
>>*or if movie type = 'Horror'*
>>*or if . . .*
>*then movie type is correct*
>>*else*
>>>*repeat loop*
>>*end if*
end do loop

A corresponding database-enforced constraint, however, is usually specified through one or two clauses.

The very nature of the relational model—the division of a database's data among logically related tables, together with logical relationships among those tables—introduces an additional consideration with respect to database constraints, namely, that of keeping update anomalies, redundant data, and similar problems to a minimum. This is done through *normalization*. (See Appendix A for a discussion of this concept in the relational model.) Data normalization typically requires several physical SQL tables to make up the instantiation of some logical object or entity. For example, a MOVIE is represented by several different SQL tables: MOVIE_TITLES and MOVIES_STARS. In a more comprehensive database environment, perhaps ten or more SQL tables would be used to describe various aspects of our movies.

Because of this split among multiple tables, it is highly desirable that constraints be utilized to ensure that the following types of situations do *not* occur.

- While the following rows exist in the MOVIES_STARS table:

Wall Street	Douglas	Michael
Wall Street	Sheen	Charlie
Wall Street	Sheen	Martin

  there is no row in our "main movie table" (MOVIE_TITLES) for the movie *Wall Street*. Therefore, we have a lost data problem.

- We received prerelease information about a movie called *The Certifier* and we enter preliminary information in our MOVIE_TITLES and MOVIES_STARS tables. Several months later when the movie is released on videocassette, the title has been changed to *The Last Certifier*. We issue an UPDATE MOVIE_TITLES SET... statement to correct the title in one table but forget to do so in the MOVIES_STARS table. Until we remember that we forgot (?!), we have a problem of a lost relationship between these two tables; simple join operations, for example, will not make the association between applicable rows because of the difference in the titles.

In this chapter we look at the facilities provided by SQL-92 to handle different types of constraint specification and enforcement. First we look at some basic constraints, then turn our attention to those dealing with referential integrity.

10.2 Column Constraints and Table Constraints

Let's expand on our basic table definitions of Chapter 4 by adding constraints to the DDL. Let's look at some of the basic constraints you can specify on columns and in tables. Diagram RR26 shows what these constraints look like in railroad diagram form.

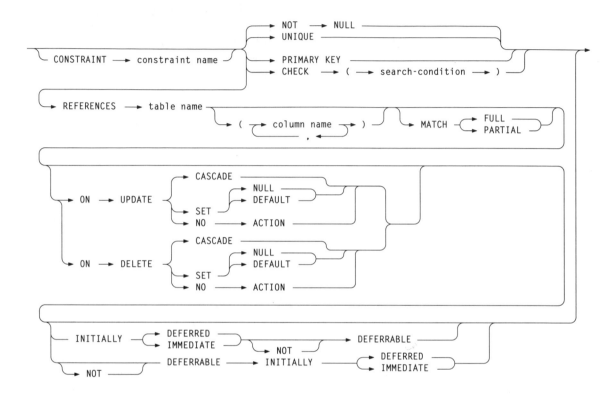

10.2.1 NOT NULL

In Chapter 4, we briefly mentioned the NOT NULL constraint while discussing basic Data Definition Language syntax. Since NOT NULL is an example of an SQL-92 constraint (and, arguably, the simplest to specify and understand), we will quickly repeat our discussion.

NOT NULL indicates that null values are not permissible in any row of the table for the specified column(s). That is,

```
CREATE TABLE movie_titles
    (title CHARACTER (30) NOT NULL,
    |
    |
    )
```

will ensure that no row in the MOVIE_TITLES table will have a null value in the TITLE column. As we previewed in Chapter 4, and mention later in this chapter, this constraint can also be specified using the multipurpose CHECK constraint.

10.2.2 UNIQUE

In many situations, we want to ensure that a specific row or group of rows designates some type of unique identifier for a table. For example, we may have a table of music distributors from which we order CDs and tapes. Since each distributor has a different company name, we can specify:

```
CREATE TABLE distributors
    (dist_name CHARACTER VARYING (30) UNIQUE,
    |
    |
    |
    ...)
```

Alternatively, we can specify the uniqueness constraint in a slightly different way:

```
CREATE TABLE distributors
    (dist_name CHARACTER VARYING (30),
    |       -- {rest of column definitions}
    |
    |
        UNIQUE (dist_name),
    ...)
```

SQL-89 required you to specify NOT NULL UNIQUE in your constraint definition; you were not permitted to say UNIQUE without also saying NOT NULL. Additionally, the ordering of the two constraints was restrictive; you could not say UNIQUE NOT NULL, but rather had to place the NOT NULL constraint first. SQL-92 relaxes that requirement and allows UNIQUE on its own; that is, SQL-92 (at least in the Intermediate and Full levels) allows *one* row with a null value in it for a single-column UNIQUE constraint. Still, specifying UNIQUE without NOT NULL is considered a dangerous practice by leading relational database proponents and is not recommended. For syntactical completeness, however, we'll show you what happens if you were to use only the UNIQUE constraint.

SQL-92 also defines a UNIQUE column constraint to be exactly the same as a CHECK constraint on the table, as we will see later.

Let's look at our DISTRIBUTORS example again. With the above constraint definition, the following table contents would be legal within SQL-92.

DIST_NAME ...
Princess Music
Ron's CDs
null
Warbuck Direct

The following table contents would *not* be legal with our definition.

DIST_NAME ...
Princess Music
null
Ron's CDs
null
Warbuck Direct

In SQL-92 terminology, the concept of UNIQUE may be defined as meaning "neither equal nor both null." In our example, no two DISTRIBUTORS rows may have DIST_NAMES that are equal, nor may any two rows both have null values.

10.2.3 CHECK

One of the most flexible, and therefore useful, constraints within SQL-92 is the CHECK constraint. This allows you to specify a wide range of rules for your tables, such as range of values, list of values, and others.

The syntax of the CHECK constraint is:

```
CHECK (search-condition)
```

As we shall see, the *search-condition* can be any sort of search condition that we've learned to use. However, there is one unusual aspect to them. Let's say that you're defining a CHECK constraint on table MOVIE_TITLES. In this search condition, you refer to any column of that table (*e.g.,* OUR_COST) just by its name—the context is always the current row of that table. By contrast, if you need to access a column in another table, you have to use a subquery.

As with UNIQUE (discussed above), there are several alternate syntax specifications for CHECK. Assume that we want to ensure that OUR_COST for all movies is less than $100.00.

```
CREATE TABLE movie_titles
    (.....
     our_cost DECIMAL (9,2)
         CHECK (our_cost < 100.00),
     |
     |
     )
```

Alternatively, the constraint could be specified as follows:

```
CREATE TABLE movie_titles
    (.....
     our_cost DECIMAL (9,2),
```

```
    |  -- {rest of column definitions}
    |
    CHECK (our_cost < 100.00) ,
    |
    |
    )
```

It is important to note the rule that applies to the search condition of the CHECK constraint. Specifically, the search condition must not be false for any row in the table (as opposed to having to be true). This means that the table can be *empty* and the CHECK constraint will be satisfied (that is, no row violates the search condition because there are no rows!). This is somewhat subtle but is important to understand, especially when analyzing and debugging your applications. That is, the search condition can evaluate to Unknown and the CHECK constraint is satisfied.

Perhaps you also want to be sure that OUR_COST is positive. You could specify this with an additional CHECK clause.

```
....CHECK(our_cost < 100),
    CHECK(our_cost > 0) .....
```

Or, you could specify the two conditions in a single constraint.

```
...CHECK(our_cost < 100 AND our_cost > 0)
```

In this case, all of the CHECK clauses in a table are effectively ANDed together. This is true even if the CHECK clauses reference different columns. For example:

```
...CHECK(our_cost < 100),
   CHECK (emp_hourly_rate > 0)
```

is equivalent to

```
...CHECK (our_cost < 100 AND emp_hourly_rate > 0)
```

Let's look at some of the typical business rules you are likely to want to specify through your database and how they might be coded using the CHECK constraint.

Minimum or Maximum Values

We already saw how a maximum value (OUR_COST < 100.00) can be specified. Similarly, a minimum value constraint can be designated. To ensure that all employees earn at least the current minimum wage rate, you might specify:

```
CREATE TABLE employees (
        emp_last_name        VARCHAR (30) NOT NULL,
        emp_first_name       VARCHAR (15) NOT NULL,
        emp_address          VARCHAR (30),
        emp_city             VARCHAR (15),
        emp_state            CHAR(2),
```

```
            emp_zip                  VARCHAR(9),
            emp_phone                CHAR(8),
            emp_start_date           DATE,
            emp_hourly_rate          DECIMAL (7,2)
            |
            |
            |
            CHECK (emp_hourly_rate >= 4.25),
            |
            |
            |
            )
```

On occasion, you might wish to designate a minimum or maximum value check against some dynamic value rather than a hard-coded one as in the examples above. Assume that some table COMPETITION_PRICES contains information collected about your competitors, and you wish to ensure that no movie title is sale-priced higher than the maximum price charged by any competitor for any movie.

```
CREATE TABLE competition_prices
    (
    |
    |
    |
    max_price DECIMAL (8,2),
    |
    |
    | )

CREATE TABLE movie_titles
    (
    |
    |
    |
    current_sale_price DECIMAL(9,2),
    |
    |
    CHECK (current_sale_price <=
        (SELECT MAX (max_price)
            FROM competition_prices ) )
    |
    )
```

You should be aware that any constraint that references data in more than one table is checked after a change to any of those tables (both COMPETITION_PRICES and MOVIE_TITLES, in this case).

We can also specify constraints for a column's values against other values in the same table. Assume that we want to ensure that no movie has a current sales price that is lower than our lowest cost for *any* movie. We can code the following in our database definition.

```
CREATE TABLE movie_titles
    (
    |
    |
    |
     our_cost DECIMAL (9,2),
     current_sale_price DECIMAL(9,2),
    |
    |
    CHECK (current_sale_price >=
        (SELECT MIN (our_cost)
            FROM movie_titles) )
    |
    )
```

Range of Values

It's often desirable to place both minimum and maximum permissible values on one or more columns. Many DBMS products allow you to specify a parameter such as *RANGE,* in which the boundary values are designated. SQL-92 allows you to use a combination of CHECK and BETWEEN. Assume that we wish to place "reasonable-ness" boundaries on our numeric columns within MOVIE_TITLES. We can do so as follows:

```
CREATE TABLE movie_titles (
    title                CHAR (30) NOT NULL,
    year_released        DATE,
    our_cost             DECIMAL(9,2),
    regular_rental_price DECIMAL(9,2),
    current_rental_price DECIMAL(9,2),
    regular_sale_price   DECIMAL(9,2),
    current_sale_price   DECIMAL(9,2),
    part_of_series       CHAR(3),
    movie_type           CHAR(10),
    vhs_owned            INTEGER,
    beta_owned           INTEGER,
    vhs_in_stock         INTEGER,
    beta_in_stock        INTEGER,
    |
    |
    |
```

```
                        CHECK (
                             (our_cost BETWEEN .99 AND 100.00)
                             AND
                             (regular_rental_price BETWEEN .25 AND 100.00)
                             AND
                             (current_rental_price BETWEEN .25 AND 100.00)
                             AND
                             (vhs_owned BETWEEN 0 AND 1000)
                             AND
                             (beta_owned BETWEEN 0 AND 1000)
                             AND ... )
                             |
                             |
                             |

                        )
```

Several points are worth noting about the first example. Note the use of AND as part of the above constraint. If applicable, OR may also be used as part of a CHECK constraint, as well as NOT or any Boolean expression (including any predicate).

Additionally, the sign (positive or negative) of a particular column's permissible values can be designated through the CHECK constraint. By specifying that a value is (BETWEEN 0 and {some value}) or (BETWEEN ({some negative value} and 0), positive and negative values, respectively, can be enforced. An important point to remember is that the ordering of the values within the BETWEEN clause is *very* important. Remember the meaning of BETWEEN: allowable values are (1) greater than or equal to the first value, and (2) less than or equal to the second value (see Chapter 7). Therefore, the following syntax is *not* correct:

```
CHECK (some_negative_number BETWEEN 0 AND -10000)
```

In fact, that CHECK constraint can *never* be satisfied (except by an empty table).

List of Values

It's often desirable to specify that a specific list of values—and no others—are permissible values for a given column. For example, we may wish to specify that each and every row in the MOVIE_TITLES table must have one of a given set of values for the MOVIE_TYPE column. We can do so as follows:

```
CREATE TABLE movie_titles (
        title           CHAR (30) NOT NULL,
        |
        |
        |
        part_of_series  CHAR(3),
        movie_type      CHAR(10),
```

```
  |
  |
  |
CHECK (movie_type IN
    ('Horror', 'Children', 'Comedy', 'Musical',
     'Romance', 'Western', 'Adventure', 'Other' ) ) )
```

Additionally, "pseudo-Boolean" values (Boolean values aren't supported in SQL-92) can be designated in the same manner.

```
CHECK (part_of_series IN
    ('Yes', 'No' ) )
```

Alternatively, True or False could be used as the pseudo-Boolean values (with appropriate lengths specified for the appropriate columns, of course), as could the numeric values 1 and 0.

Given pairs of values (or any number of values) can also be specified through the use of CHECK. Assume that the following rules must be specified between two columns in a given table SAMPLE_TABLE.

- COLUMN1 can have a value of either NO or YES.
- If COLUMN1 has a value of NO, COLUMN2 must have a value of NO.
- If COLUMN1 has a value of YES, COLUMN2 may have a value of either YES or NO.

These rules can be specified as follows:

```
CREATE TABLE sample_table
    (column1 CHARACTER (3) NOT NULL,
     column2 CHARACTER (3) NOT NULL,
     CHECK ( ( column1, column2) IN
       ( VALUES (   'NO',   'NO' ),
               (   'YES',  'NO' ),
               (   'YES',  'YES' ) )   )
    )
```

The combination of IN and VALUES permits the required pairings to be designated.

Exclusion from Another Table

On occasion, you might wish to make certain that values in some column in a table are different from those of some other table. For example, we may have some table DISCONTINUED_ALBUMS in which we store rows for each music album (or CD) that has been discontinued. We can ensure that (for unique album titles) no discontinued album appears in our MUSIC_TITLES table.

```
CREATE TABLE music_titles
    (title CHARACTER (30) NOT NULL,
    artist CHARACTER (30) NOT NULL,
    |
    |
    |
    )

CREATE TABLE discontinued_albums
    (title CHARACTER (30) NOT NULL,
    |
    |
    |
    CHECK ( title <> ANY
        ( SELECT title FROM music_titles ) )
    |
    |
    |
    )
```

This sort of constraint allows you to effectively form a unique constraint across more than one table! Another way to achieve the same effect is:

```
CHECK ( UNIQUE ( SELECT DISTINCT title
                 FROM music_titles
               UNION
                 SELECT DISTINCT title
                 FROM discontinued_albums ) )
```

10.2.4 Constraint Names

Each of the above constraints may, optionally, have a name assigned to it. In reality, all constraints have a name, though not necessarily one assigned by the user. For example, our list-of-values constraint above may have been written:

```
CREATE TABLE movie_titles (
    title               CHARACTER (30)
                        CONSTRAINT title_not_null NOT NULL,
    |
    |
    |
    part_of_series      CHARACTER(3),
    movie_type          CHARACTER(10),
    |
    |
    |
```

```
CONSTRAINT check_movie_type
CHECK (movie_type IN
     ('Horror', 'Children', 'Comedy', 'Musical',
      'Romance', 'Western', 'Adventure', 'Other' ) )
```

We strongly recommend that constraint names always be used, even though they are optional. Applications can then report more complete information when constraint violations occur, because they can get the name of the violated constraint out of the diagnostics area, thereby helping with the problem analysis process. Constraint names are new to SQL-92. If you don't give names to your constraints, the DBMS will assign them for you—but they will probably be less meaningful and less mnemonic than those you have chosen yourself.

Whether you or the DBMS assigns the constraint name, it will be reported with any error caused by violating the constraint (see Chapter 17), and you can use the name to SET the constraint to DEFERRED or IMMEDIATE (see Chapter 14) or to DROP the constraint (see Chapter 4).

Note also that constraint names may be assigned as well to the two constraints that don't directly utilize CHECK: NOT NULL and UNIQUE. Additionally, these two constraints could, if desired, be expressed using CHECK, as:

```
CHECK (columnname IS NOT NULL)

CHECK (UNIQUE (SELECT columnname FROM table) )
```

Column and table constraints can be specified as DEFERRABLE or NOT DEFERRABLE. If you don't use either clause, the default is NOT DEFERRABLE. DEFERRABLE means that you can instruct the DBMS to *defer* checking the constraint until you commit your transaction or until you give further instructions. NOT DEFERRABLE, of course, means that the constraint is to be checked at the end of every SQL statement. If you specify that a constraint is DEFERRABLE, you can also specify its initial state at the beginning of each transaction (INITIALLY IMMEDIATE or INITIALLY DEFERRED). If you specify NOT DEFERRABLE, you can also specify INITIALLY IMMEDIATE.

10.3 Assertions

As we have seen, SQL has several types of constraints. Of those that we've examined so far, all have been "attached" to tables or to columns in tables. However, SQL-92 also provides you with a new kind of constraint that isn't attached to a particular table. This constraint, called an *assertion,* is a standalone constraint in a schema and is normally used to specify a restriction that affects more than one table.

A table (or column) constraint is normally used to make a restriction on the data that is stored in the table (or column) to which the constraint is attached. It is possible (given some awkwardness) to express restrictions involving multiple tables with regular table CHECK constraints, but this is not really recommended. Instead, you should use assertions for that purpose.

Let's suppose that you want to ensure that the total dollar value of movies in stock plus the total dollar value of music (CDs, tapes, albums) in stock is never greater than some limit imposed by your insurance company or banker, say $500,000. To express this restriction as a table constraint would be awkward at best. First, you'd have to decide whether to put the constraint on the MOVIE_TITLES table or on the MUSIC_TITLES table. Then you'd have to write something like this:

```
CREATE TABLE movie_titles (
    title...
    ...
    CONSTRAINT maximum_inventory
      CHECK ( SUM (our_cost) +
        ( SELECT SUM (our_cost)
            FROM music_titles )
        < 500000 ),
    ...
    )
```

which is actually equivalent to the slightly longer:

```
CREATE TABLE movie_titles (
    title...
    ...
    CONSTRAINT maximum_inventory
      CHECK ( ( SELECT SUM (our_cost)
                  FROM movie_titles )
              + ( SELECT SUM (our_cost)
                    FROM music_titles )
          < 500000 ),
    ...
    )
```

In the first example, the expression SUM(OUR_COST) is equivalent to the sub-query (SELECT SUM(OUR_COST) FROM MOVIE_TITLES) because it's in the context of the table itself. That, of course, will work—most of the time—but it sure doesn't feel natural to put it here. After all, the constraint really doesn't say anything about the rows of MOVIE_TITLES directly, as this constraint does:

```
CREATE TABLE movie_titles (
    title...
    ...
    CONSTRAINT maximum_inventory
      CHECK ( ( SELECT SUM(our_cost)
                  FROM movies ) < 500000 ),
    ...
    )
```

or as does the equivalent (and both easier and more appropriate):

```
CREATE TABLE movie_titles (
   title...
   ...
   CONSTRAINT maximum_inventory
     CHECK ( SUM(our_cost) < 500000 ),
   ...
   )
```

These two are equivalent, but the latter is more appropriate as a table constraint since it doesn't need a subquery to calculate the sum.

The two pairs of examples are essentially the same except that the first contains the sum of two subqueries and the second contains only a single subquery. We don't really recommend that you do either sort of restriction with a table constraint like this, but at least the second pair is more natural (in that it deals only with the table to which it is attached).

A more natural way to express the same restriction is to state it as a *standalone* constraint—that is, as an assertion.

```
CREATE ASSERTION maximum_inventory
    CHECK ( ( SELECT SUM (our_cost)
                  FROM movies )
            + ( SELECT SUM (our_cost)
                    FROM music_titles )
          < 500000 )
```

Note that the syntax of the CHECK portion of the assertion is identical to the CHECK constraint and that we even named the constraint the same as in the previous examples. However, as an assertion, this CHECK is not attached to any particular table. This has two advantages. We've already stated the first: It is more natural to express restrictions not specific to one table as standalone constraints instead of as table constraints.

The other advantage is due to a subtle characteristic of table constraints: Because table constraints are intended to govern the restrictions on data stored in that table, they are required to be true if *and only if* there is some data stored in the table to which they are attached! This means that the constraint in our first example would *always* be satisfied if the MOVIE_TITLES table were empty. Therefore, if we happened to close out the movie section, we could stock as many CDs as we'd like without violating the constraint—and our banker might not be happy to learn that we've now stocked $2,000,000 worth of CDs in a down economy! By contrast, an assertion expresses a restriction that must always be obeyed (or satisfied) in the database, regardless of whether any particular table has data stored in it or not. (Of course, some assertions might require that a table have data stored in it, but we think you know what we mean.)

Note that some table constraints can never be violated.

```
CREATE TABLE sample (
    col1...
    ...
    CONSTRAINT table_never_empty
      CHECK ( ( SELECT COUNT(*)
                 FROM sample ) > 0 ),
    ...
    )
```

This constraint can never be violated because it's satisfied when the table is empty and it's true when the table is not empty. If we were to express this as an assertion, though, the assertion would, indeed, guarantee that the table always had at least one row stored in it.

```
CREATE ASSERTION sample_table_never_empty
  CHECK ( ( SELECT COUNT(*) FROM sample ) > 0 )
```

The format of the statement to create an assertion is:

```
CREATE ASSERTION constraint-name
  CHECK ( search-condition ) [ attributes ]
```

The constraint name is always required for assertions. We've already mentioned that all constraints have names, but the system will assign a name for table or column constraints that you don't name yourself (mainly to be compatible with programs written before SQL-92 was implemented). However, assertions are standalone objects in the schema, so they must have a name, and SQL-92 requires you to give them a name of your choosing. (Being new, they don't have to worry about pre-SQL-92 programs.)

The search-condition is described in Chapter 7; basically, it consists of one or more predicates (multiple predicates are connected with ANDs, ORs, and NOTs) which express the condition that must be satisfied (alternately, that must not be violated) in the database. It may reference one or more tables, but it has no inherent table context, so you'll have to provide the context by using a query expression (actually, you have to use a subquery; see discussion in Chapter 9).

The attributes are the same as for any other constraint. You can specify that the assertion is to be DEFERRABLE or NOT DEFERRABLE; if it is DEFERRABLE, you may choose to SET CONSTRAINT constraint-name DEFERRED at some time in your application and later SET CONSTRAINT constraint-name IMMEDIATE to cause it to be checked.

If the constraint is DEFERRABLE, you can also say that it is INITIALLY DEFERRED, meaning that every transaction will start off with the assertion in the deferred mode, as though you had issued a SET CONSTRAINT constraint-name DEFERRED statement. Of course, you can specify INITIALLY IMMEDIATE whether the assertion is DEFERRABLE or NOT DEFERRABLE, just as with other constraints.

Assertions, like other constraints, have some restrictions. For example, all of the values used have to be literals or database values; you can't reference host variables or parameters, datetime functions, CURRENT_USER, SESSION_USER, or SYSTEM_USER. Assertion names, like any constraint names, can be qualified with a schema name. If you choose to do this and your CREATE ASSERTION statement is part of a CREATE SCHEMA, then the schema names have to match. Most assertions will reference one or more database columns; you must have REFERENCES privileges on each column that your assertions reference. If your assertion doesn't reference a particular column, but does reference a table (*e.g.,* using COUNT(*)), then you have to have REFERENCES privileges on at least one column of the table.

10.4 PRIMARY KEY

The relational database model contains the concept of a *key,* that is, one or more columns within a table that have some unique value by which individual rows can be identified. In some cases, a single column (such as a social security number or employee ID number) is enough to uniquely identify given rows. In other cases, a combination of columns (as in the example below) is required.

Let's look at our MOVIES_STARS table. For purposes of the following example (to make the explanation easier to understand), let's disregard the YEAR_RELEASED and assume that all movie titles are unique. Therefore, we initially have the following table definition (we will need to modify this, as we will see).

```
CREATE TABLE movies_stars
    (movie_title      CHARACTER (30) NOT NULL,
    actor_last_name   CHARACTER (35) NOT NULL,
    actor_first_name  CHARACTER (25));
```

TABLE 10-1

MOVIE_TITLE	ACTOR_LAST_NAME	ACTOR_FIRST_NAME
The Way We Were	Redford	Robert
The Way We Were	Streisand	Barbra
Prince of Tides	Nolte	Nick
Prince of Tides	Streisand	Barbra
⏐		
⏐		
⏐		

In Table 10-1, no single column is sufficient to uniquely identify given rows. Since any movie may have (and usually does have) more than one star, there will be multiple rows in which the same movie title appears. Similarly, the combination of ACTOR_LAST_NAME and ACTOR_FIRST_NAME is also not enough to constitute a key, since actors (especially the stars, who appear in our database table) appear in many movies over the course of their careers. Only the combination of three columns—in this case, all of the columns of the table—is sufficient to constitute a key.

In some tables, there are multiple *candidate keys*. That is, there are several different options from which you can choose a column or combination of columns for the unique identification process. Assume for a moment that our MOVIE_TITLES table has a column MOVIE_NUMBER, a column which has a unique value in each row. MOVIE_NUMBER is a candidate key, as is TITLE (or in our original example, the combination of TITLE and YEAR_RELEASED).

Whichever candidate key you choose becomes your *primary key*. The primary key is the concept, and related syntax, with which we are concerned in SQL-92. Since movie titles are unique for the purposes of this example, we can designate that column as a primary key:

```
CREATE TABLE movie_titles
    (title CHARACTER (30) PRIMARY KEY,
    |
    |
    |
    )
```

SQL-89 required you to say NOT NULL PRIMARY KEY. SQL-92 (in the Intermediate and Full levels) permits you to state only PRIMARY KEY, though this means the same thing; primary keys have the inherent property that no row can have a null value for the primary key columns.

Additionally, this means that *no* column that forms part of a multiple column primary key may have a null value. This restriction presents somewhat of a problem for our application as currently defined. Recall from Table 10-1 that the column ACTOR_FIRST_NAME does *not* have a NOT NULL constraint applied, in order to allow for single-name actors and actresses (Sting, Cher) or for groups (the Marx Brothers). However, as we also said above, we need all three columns in the MOVIES_STARS table to uniquely identify any given row. Therefore, we have a perplexing problem: how to resolve these two conflicting problems.

Our view is that primary keys (and foreign keys; see section 10.5.1) are important characteristics of your database and should be implemented and maintained through your SQL syntax whenever possible. Therefore, we will add a NOT NULL constraint to the ACTOR_FIRST_NAME column definition in order to be able to create key definitions. Single-name actors and groups will then have one or more blanks in the ACTOR_FIRST_NAME column, likely placed there by some host application program. This is representative of the types of tradeoff decisions you must often make when designing and implementing your SQL databases. When facets such as those discussed above conflict, you must decide which to implement and which to work around.

Primary keys may also be designated through table constraints (discussed earlier in this chapter in conjunction with CHECK). Let's look at our alternative primary key definition.

```
CREATE TABLE movies_stars
    (movie_title        CHARACTER (30) NOT NULL,
    actor_last_name     CHARACTER (35) NOT NULL,
    actor_first_name    CHARACTER (25) NOT NULL,
```

```
CONSTRAINT stars_pk PRIMARY KEY
   ( movie_title, actor_last_name, actor_first_name ),
)
```

Many implementations use the idea of an *index* (as in the typical CREATE INDEX . . . statement) to enforce uniqueness in a table. However, we feel that because uniqueness is an inherent property of data, it should not be relegated to being an implementation issue but should be designated in the standard. Therefore, whether or not a specific SQL-92 implementation supports indices (indices also have additional uses, such as performance enhancement), the PRIMARY KEY does designate support for key fields.

Now that we've seen how to define primary keys, let's turn our attentions to FOREIGN KEYs and the concept of referential integrity.

10.5 Referential Integrity

The SQL-92 syntax for the constraints dealing with referential integrity can be seen in Diagram RR27.

RR27

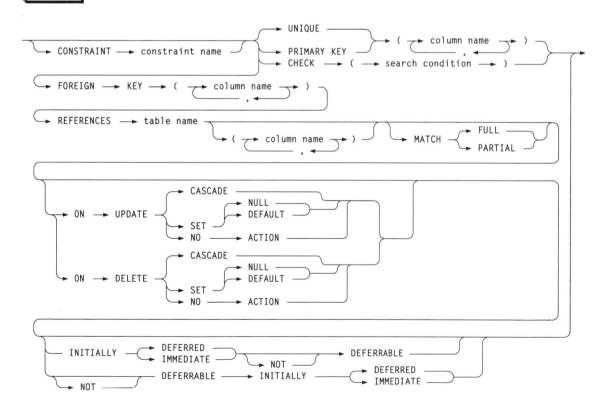

10.5.1 FOREIGN KEY

A *foreign key* is a column or group of columns within a table that references, or relates to, some other table through its values (see Figure 10-1). The foreign key must always include enough columns in its definition to uniquely identify a row in the referenced table.

. . . .

FIGURE 10-1
Foreign Key
Usage in SQL-92

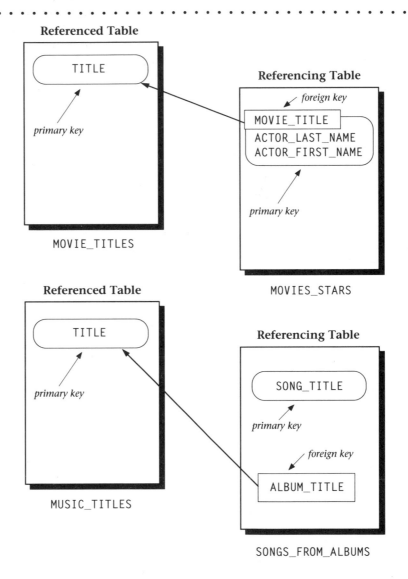

The primary reason for defining foreign keys within the data definition language is to ensure that rows in one table always have corresponding rows in another table; that is, to ensure that integrity of data is maintained. Recall, for example, the potential data integrity problem at the beginning of this chapter:

several rows exist in the MOVIES_STARS table for the movie *Wall Street* but there is no corresponding row for that movie in the MOVIE_TITLES table. In this situation, there is a problem with lost linkages between data elements of one table and those of another.

To ensure that such a problem does not occur, we can define a foreign key in the MOVIES_STARS table that corresponds to our earlier defined primary key of the MOVIE_TITLES table. The syntax to accomplish this is as follows:

```
CREATE TABLE movies_stars
    (
     |
     |
     |
    CONSTRAINT titles_fk FOREIGN KEY ( movie_title )
      REFERENCES movie_titles (title)
    )
```

In the above code segment, the key words FOREIGN KEY flag the designated column (MOVIE_TITLE) as the foreign key through which the table MOVIE_TITLES is referenced (through the latter table's primary key column TITLE). Note that you can use both PRIMARY KEY and FOREIGN KEY definitions within any table; the primary key of a given table (in our current example, MOVIES_STARS) has no bearing on the definition of a foreign key through which another table is referenced.

```
CREATE TABLE movies_stars
    (movie_title        CHARACTER (30) NOT NULL,
     actor_last_name    CHARACTER (35) NOT NULL,
     actor_first_name   CHARACTER NOT NULL(25),

    CONSTRAINT stars_pk PRIMARY KEY
      ( movie_title, actor_last_name, actor_first_name ),
    CONSTRAINT titles_fk FOREIGN KEY ( movie_title )
      REFERENCES movie_titles ,
     |
     |
     |
    )
```

As with primary keys, there are several different syntactical ways in which you can define foreign keys. You could, for example, state:

```
CREATE TABLE movies_stars
    (movie_title CHARACTER (30)
            CONSTRAINT title_not_null NOT NULL
            CONSTRAINT titles_fk
              REFERENCES movie_titles (title),
```

```
                    |
                    |
                    |
                    )
```

If your foreign key references the primary key of the referenced table (as opposed to some candidate key that wasn't selected as the primary key; refer to our discussion earlier in this chapter), you can omit the column reference.

```
CREATE TABLE movies_stars
 (movie_title CHARACTER (30) NOT NULL
     REFERENCES movie_titles,
  |
  |
  |
  )
```

You can also omit the primary key reference for foreign key definitions coded as table constraints, as in our first foreign key example.

```
CREATE TABLE movies_stars
   (
     |
     |
     |
   CONSTRAINT titles_fk FOREIGN KEY
      ( movie_title ) REFERENCES movie_titles
   )
```

Finally, the constraint name for the foreign key *may* be omitted though, as we stated earlier in this chapter, we strongly recommend naming all of your constraints for diagnostic purposes.

```
CREATE TABLE movies_stars
    (
      |
      |
      |
    FOREIGN KEY ( movie_title )
      REFERENCES movie_titles (title)
    )
```

In the above example, TITLE could be omitted since the primary key is being referenced rather than a nonprimary candidate key.

One more rule: If your foreign and primary or candidate keys are one-column keys, you can use the earlier "short" form (with the column definition). If they are multicolumn, you must use the later form (separate constraint).

10.5.2 Referential Constraint Actions

When you specify a FOREIGN KEY, you may only wish to prohibit the execution of any SQL statement that might violate the referential integrity tables. This was the only referential integrity capability defined by SQL-89. However, you might prefer that the DBMS update other tables to keep them in sync with the changes you make. The feature that does this is called *referential actions*.

To this point, we've essentially explained SQL-89-style referential integrity. Now, let's look at the features provided by SQL-92.

Setting a Default

Suppose that you have a business rule that requires that whenever you drop a distributor, you automatically switch the distributor for those movies to some specific other distributor—that is, to your default distributor. To specify a restriction rule in your database that prohibits dropping a distributor as long as you stock movies distributed by that company, you would write something like this:

```
CREATE TABLE movie_titles
    (title               CHARACTER (30) NOT NULL,
     |
     |
     |

     distributor         CHARACTER VARYING(25)
             REFERENCES distributors,
     |
     |
     |
    )
```

However, to tell the database system to automatically set the distributor to the default, you would code something like this:

```
CREATE TABLE movie_titles
    (title               CHARACTER (30) NOT NULL,
     |
     |
     |

     distributor         CHARACTER VARYING(25)
                                 DEFAULT 'Big East, Inc.'
        REFERENCES distributors
          ON DELETE SET DEFAULT,
     |
     |
     |
    )
```

SET NULL

You may want to establish a business rule that if a distributor goes out of business, all of the movies available from that company have the DISTRIBUTOR column set to null, indicating "no distributor currently available (until we get another one)." You can specify this automatic action as follows:

```
CREATE TABLE movie_titles
     (title               CHARACTER (30) NOT NULL,
      |
      |
      |

      distributor         CHARACTER VARYING(25)
              REFERENCES distributors
                   ON DELETE SET NULL,
      |
      |
      |
      )
```

CASCADE

Suppose you receive prerelease information about a movie entitled *The Certifier*, an epic starring Arnold Schwarzenegger as a postal worker. You enter information about this movie in your database, including tables MOVIE_TITLES and MOVIES_STARS. Before you actually receive the tapes and begin renting this blockbuster, the title is changed to *The Last Certifier*. The name change can be automatically handled in any tables (such as MOVIES_STARS), through the use of CASCADE.

```
CREATE TABLE movies_stars
    (
      |
      |
      |
    CONSTRAINT titles_fk FOREIGN KEY
       ( movie_title ) REFERENCES movie_titles
                 ON UPDATE CASCADE,

    )
```

Likewise, in our earlier example with distributors and the tapes, we can ensure that any company name changes among the distributors cascade through to the MOVIE_TITLES table by the following:

```
CREATE TABLE movie_titles
     (title              CHARACTER (30) NOT NULL,
      |
      |
      |

      distributor      CHARACTER VARYING(25)
              REFERENCES distributors
                 ON UPDATE CASCADE,
      |
      |
      |
      )
```

NO ACTION

You can set any of three referential actions (CASCADE, SET NULL, or SET DEFAULT) on each of the two activities DELETE and UPDATE (see Table 10-2).

Table 10-2
Referential
Actions in SQL-92

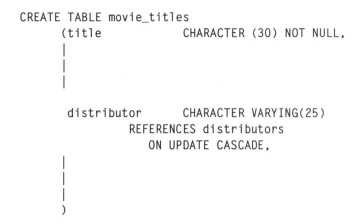

	ACTION			
ACTIVITY	CASCADE	SET NULL	DELETE	NO ACTION
DELETE	✓	✓	✓	✓
UPDATE	✓	✓	✓	✓

The default for either activity is NO ACTION, so you can also code the defaults to say that you want the database system to ensure that you have a valid state at the end of your statement.

```
CREATE TABLE movie_titles
     (title              CHARACTER (30) NOT NULL,
      |
      |
      |

      distributor      CHARACTER VARYING(25)
         REFERENCES distributors
         ON UPDATE NO ACTION
         ON DELETE NO ACTION,
      |
      |
      |
      )
```

NO ACTION means just what it says: If the referential constraint remains unsatisfied at the end of the SQL statement, then no actions are performed. Actually, the phrase was chosen to indicate that no *referential* actions were performed; however, the effect is that the SQL statement making the changes is "undone" and therefore effectively performs "no action" either. Instead, the DBMS will give you an error.

Let's consider some examples. Suppose we have our MOVIE_TITLES with the PRIMARY KEY constraint on TITLE and the MOVIES_STARS table with a FOREIGN KEY constraint on its column MOVIE_TITLE that specifies ON UPDATE NO ACTION. If we try to execute:

```
UPDATE movie_titles
    SET title = 'One Extremely Strange Movie'
WHERE title = 'Rocky Horror Picture Show'
```

then the presence of rows in MOVIES_STARS listing Tim Curry, Susan Sarandon, and others will cause the UPDATE statement to fail. If that FOREIGN KEY had said ON UPDATE CASCADE, then Tim, Susan, *et al.* would now be shown as starring in *One Extremely Strange Movie*.

On the other hand, ON UPDATE SET NULL would attempt to have them starring in no movie at all—which would violate the PRIMARY KEY of MOVIES_STARS and would thus cause the UPDATE statement to fail, too.

The action (or lack of it) doesn't have to be the same for the two activities. You can choose to SET NULL for DELETE and have NO ACTION for UPDATE if you wish:

```
CREATE TABLE movie_titles
    (title              CHARACTER (30) NOT NULL,
     |
     |
     |

     distributor        CHARACTER VARYING(25)
                 REFERENCES distributors
                     ON UPDATE CASCADE
                     ON DELETE SET NULL,
     |
     |
     |
     )
```

10.6 Multiple Cascades

So far, we have dealt with referential integrity between two tables. There are probably occasions when you would want multiple levels of cascades specified in your referential integrity constraints. Let's take our MOVIE_TITLES and MOVIES_STARS example (the key data definition segments are reproduced below) and add a new table. Suppose we have a customer-help function through which customers (and employees) can browse to find out information about various awards won by movies we have in stock. On Academy Awards weekend, we may want to put on sale all tapes we have in stock that have won the Best Picture award. We can access our system and produce a quick list of Best Picture winners. To accomplish this, we first add a new table to our other two.

```
CREATE TABLE movie_titles
    (title CHARACTER (30) PRIMARY KEY,
    |
    |
    |
    )


CREATE TABLE movies_stars
    (movie_title          CHARACTER (30) NOT NULL,
    actor_last_name       CHARACTER (35) NOT NULL,
    actor_first_name      CHARACTER (25) NOT NULL,

    CONSTRAINT stars_pk PRIMARY KEY
      ( movie_title, actor_last_name, actor_first_name ),
    CONSTRAINT titles_fk FOREIGN KEY ( movie_title )
      REFERENCES movie_titles
        ON DELETE CASCADE
        ON UPDATE CASCADE,
    |
    |
    |
    )


CREATE TABLE movie_awards (
    movie_title      CHARACTER (30),
    first_name       CHARACTER (35),
    last_name        CHARACTER (25),
    award            CHARACTER VARYING(10),

FOREIGN_KEY (movie_title, first_name, last_name)
  REFERENCES movies_stars
    ON UPDATE CASCADE
    ON DELETE CASCADE,
    |
    |
    | )
```

With a structure like this, when you change the name (or just the spelling of the name) of a movie, that change is cascaded to the MOVIE_STARS table, changing the spelling of the movie's name in every row associated with that movie in the other table, too. Those changes will, in turn, be cascaded to the MOVIE_AWARDS table, changing the name in that table. Also, if you change the spelling of a movie star's name, that change will also be reflected in the MOVIE_AWARDS table. Similarly, if you delete a movie (because you no longer carry it in stock), that deletion will cause the MOVIE_STARS entries to be deleted along with the MOVIE_AWARDS that those stars won. Figure 10-2 illustrates the three-level cascade.

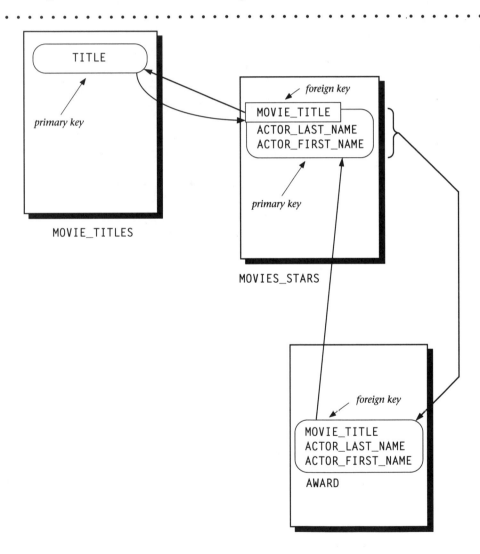

FIGURE 10-2
Cascading Among Multiple SQL-92 Tables

FOREIGN KEYs can even reference the table in which they're defined. For example, an EMPLOYEES table may have a column EMP_ID and another column

MGR_ID. Of course, you'd want all store managers to also be employees, so you could ensure that by specifying:

```
|
|
|
emp_id                    INTEGER PRIMARY KEY,
mgr_id                    INTEGER REFERENCES employees,
|
|
|
```

10.7 More About Referential Integrity Constraints

To better understand how referential integrity works, we have to know a little bit more about how SQL-92 expects statements to behave. Realize that various DBMS products might implement this in a different way, but the end result will be the same. Think of every SQL statement as having three phases: a *setup* phase, an *execution* phase, and a *cleanup* phase. During the setup phase, the DBMS first identifies every row that will be directly affected by the statement and then identifies every *matching* row for every directly affected row. (A matching row is a row in a referencing table whose foreign key values identify some directly affected row in the referenced table.)

During the execution phase, the DBMS performs the action of the statement on the directly affected rows (if the statement is a DELETE statement, then the row isn't actually deleted, but is "marked for deletion"). No new matching rows are ever added to the list of matching rows as a result of any direct actions.

During the cleanup phase, the referential actions are performed. In general, when a directly affected row causes some referential action, that action is performed and any referential actions caused by *that* action are then performed. Although this may sound like a depth-first tree walk, for those of you who stayed awake during graph theory, referential integrity actions have been very carefully designed to allow them to be performed in any order at all to arrive at a correct, consistent state of the database. (If any of those referential actions involve a row deletion, then those rows are also merely marked for deletion. The reason for this is to avoid certain anomalies that could result from actually deleting the rows before the referential actions have "died down.") At the end of the cleanup phase, any rows that are marked for deletion are actually deleted.

10.8 More About Constraints and Assertions

Let's spend just a little more time on the subject of constraints and assertions to really grasp some of the subtle issues. For example, we told you that constraint checking was done only at the end of statements and not during processing of individual rows, but we didn't tell you why it's that way. Consider a table that has unique ID numbers for each movie:

```
CREATE TABLE movie_titles (
  id        INTEGER constraint movie_titles_pk PRIMARY KEY,
  title     CHARACTER (30),
  |
  |
  |
  )
```

After populating the table with thousands of movies and giving them ID values of 0, 1, 2, . . . , we learn that we'd really rather use 1, 2, 3, . . . , instead. An obvious UPDATE statement would be:

```
UPDATE movie_titles
    SET id = id + 1 ;
```

If the constraint were checked during the update of each row, then the very first row that got updated (unless it happened to be the one with the highest ID value) would cause the constraint to be violated, and the statement would fail with an error. However, by waiting until the end of the UPDATE statement, after all rows have been processed, the constraint is not violated and the statement succeeds.

There are many examples of the usefulness of this characteristic. We leave as an exercise for the reader the reason why end-of-statement checking is necessary for a FOREIGN KEY constraint with ON DELETE CASCADE when the FOREIGN KEY points to the same table where it is defined.

```
CREATE TABLE employees (
  emp_id              INTEGER PRIMARY KEY,
  mgr_id              INTEGER REFERENCES employees
                                ON DELETE CASCADE )
```

10.9 Chapter Summary

The material covered in this chapter should help you to further specify your SQL data definitions so that a great deal of the tedious processing inherent in information systems applications will be automatically handled by your underlying database management system. Each and every column may have a range of values, a list of values, a maximum or minimum value, or some other constraint designated at definition time. Further, each table may have a primary key designated through which the data from other tables may be related to the data of that table.

Through the use of foreign keys—which typically are used in conjunction with primary keys but may also be coordinated with nonprimary candidate keys if so desired—several different types of referential integrity constraints may also be specified at data definition time. These include cascading of data value modifications to related tables, automatically deleting certain logically linked rows, and setting various default or null values upon certain actions.

P A R T   I I I

SQL and Applications

CHAPTER 11

. . . .

Accessing SQL from the Real World

11.1 Introduction

There are several primary models under which information "subsystems" (or logically grouped components of an organization's overall information system) operate. In one model, around which we have oriented our examples and discussion so far, the bulk of the operations are ad hoc queries, most of which can't be foreseen. ("Hey, Marty, how many of that new 'Partridge Family Reunion' CD do we have on back order?" or "Mike, check and see if we have any movies with both Stallone and Schwarzenneger.") In these circumstances, an interactive query might be the logical process through which the desired information is obtained. It is unlikely, however, that your customers or even your clerks would be interested in forming SQL queries on their own; some sort of veneer is usually required.

An alternative model is built around operations that regularly follow one another with predictable logic, branching instructions, and object (tables, views, *etc.*) usage. For example, your CD and movie automatic reordering systems, payroll, end-of-month reporting, and other regular functions may fall into this category. Your business operations may require more facilities than those provided solely by SQL. For these reasons, a typical environment will contain a mixture of SQL facilities (data definitions, data manipulation statements, transaction control, and others) and features from some type of host language: a third-generation language (3GL) or fourth-generation language (4GL). In this chapter, we explore several ways in which your SQL environments are incorporated into your overall information systems. We discuss data access methods (introduced earlier in Chapter 2) as well as embedded SQL and module SQL. We also briefly introduce the topic of cursors, which are discussed in detail in the next chapter.

11.2   Data Access Methods and Data Types

There are differences in the ways that conventional programming languages and SQL process data. SQL, as we have said earlier, is a set-at-a-time language. Most SQL statements operate on an arbitrary number of rows of data at one time. For example, the statement:

```
UPDATE movie_titles
    SET current_rental_price =
        regular_rental_price * 0.5
```

will halve the rental cost for every movie (as compared with its regular rental price), regardless of whether there are only two or three or literally hundreds of thousands of titles in our table.

Languages such as C, Fortran, COBOL, and Pascal cannot deal with such sets of data. They can only handle a finite, known number of items at a time; thus they require *loop control* logic during file processing. It is possible to store rows of data into arrays of data structures in some languages, but the maximum size of those arrays is severely limited and must usually be known in advance. This creates a sort of mismatch between how SQL is used and how those other languages are used. This mismatch has sometimes been called an *impedance mismatch,* using a term from electronics. In many cases, that mismatch doesn't really matter very much, because you can decide whether you want to perform a particular operation in SQL or in your host program. In other cases, though, it may matter very much.

For example, suppose that your application is required to scan through many rows in some table and make decisions about what to do based on the contents of the rows. Perhaps you want to consider all CDs that are classified as classical music, display the title, artist, and price on a screen, and cut the price by 10% or by 20% as determined by a (human) operator's input. It would be difficult to accomplish this purely in SQL because SQL has no conditional statement execution capabilities[1] (but see Chapter 20, Future Directions). It would also be difficult to accomplish it purely in, say, COBOL (minimally, it would require cumbersome ways of retrieving one row at a time and then processing those rows in the COBOL program as if they were records within a file). What this application requires is a mixture of SQL and a conventional programming language. However, the impedance mismatch between SQL and COBOL makes this mixture a bit awkward.

Another kind of mismatch (also sometimes called an *impedance mismatch,* but don't worry about the dual use of the term) occurs in the data types supported by SQL and by the various programming languages that interface with SQL. As we discussed in Chapter 2, SQL supports several data types. You know that other programming languages also support specific data types. However, what you may not have thought about is this: it is very rare for the data types supported by two different programming languages to be the same. For example, Fortran has integer

---

[1]   There is, as we discussed in Chapter 6, the CASE expression, but that expression and its forms (CASE, NULLIF, and COALESCE) have limited capability with respect to the conditional execution as compared with a full-featured conditional processing programming construct.

and floating point data types but doesn't have a decimal data type; COBOL, on the other hand, has integer and decimal types but doesn't have a floating point type.

This mismatch makes it very difficult to write an SQL statement that can be invoked from just any language. You must know what language you plan to use when you write your SQL statements. In fact, you should have some idea of what language you plan to use when you design your database. Put another way, the kinds of data stored in your database may determine what programming languages you can use to manipulate your database. If you have floating point data (*i.e.,* REAL, FLOAT, or DOUBLE), you shouldn't count on using COBOL to manipulate it. If you have decimal data (*e.g.,* NUMERIC, DECIMAL), you may not want to write your applications in Fortran or C.

In fairness, we want to point out that the situations discussed in the preceding paragraph were absolutely true in SQL-89; however, SQL-92 provides the CAST facility (see Chapter 6) that you can use specifically to avoid this type of impedance mismatch (think of CAST as an impedance-matching transformer—if you must).

11.3 Applications Interface Mechanisms for SQL

There are (at least in the SQL standard) three different ways of writing your application when you want to use SQL. You can directly invoke SQL statements, you can embed SQL statements directly in your host language programs, or you can write SQL statements separately in a module and call them from your host language programs. The first technique is known as *direct invocation;* the second method is called *embedded SQL;* the third is called *module language.*

Direct invocation is most similar to the *ad hoc* model we presented at the beginning of the chapter. That is, no formal program structure in the form of a host language environment is needed for the statements. There are, however, limitations on what types of SQL statements may be directly invoked. Perhaps more importantly, there is the requirement that everything be handled exclusively through a set model. We'll discuss these details in the next section.

Of the other two forms, most vendors (today) provide only embedded SQL implementations, while a few (*e.g.,* Digital Equipment Corporation) provide both embedded SQL and module language. There are advantages and disadvantages to both approaches.

In embedded and module SQL, the SQL standard defines rules for how the SQL data types match the host language data types. Some of them are pretty obvious: for example, the SQL INTEGER data type maps pretty cleanly to a Fortran INTEGER or a C **int**. Other matches are not quite as obvious. For instance, SQL has a TIMESTAMP data type, but no programming language contains an analogous type (at least not in the standard for those languages). As a result, SQL cannot map the TIMESTAMP type directly to any host language type. Instead, SQL requires you to use a CAST function (see Chapter 6) to convert the TIMESTAMP data in the data base to character data in the host program (and vice versa).

11.4 Direct Invocation

While direct invocation is relatively straightforward, there are some complicating factors that must be considered. First, the details of directly invoking SQL statements are not covered very thoroughly by the SQL-92 standard (though it's covered better there than in earlier versions of the standard). There are some rules that state which types of SQL statements are supported. These include:

- SQL schema statements
- SQL transaction statements
- SQL connection statements
- SQL session statements
- searched DELETE statements (DELETE FROM MOVIE_TITLES WHERE...)
- multiple-row SELECT statements (SELECT * FROM MOVIES_STARS WHERE...)
- INSERT statements (INSERT INTO MUSIC_TITLES...)
- searched UPDATE statements (UPDATE MOVIE_TITLES SET... WHERE...)
- temporary table declarations

There are many other details that aren't covered, though, and implementations vary greatly with respect to direct invocation environments. This isn't, however, a major problem, since your mainstay applications will rarely be based on interactive SQL.

The impedance mismatches we discussed earlier are minimized in an interactive SQL environment. First, the output destination for your queries (a terminal or PC screen, a file, or whatever) can accept an arbitrary number of rows for output. Second, cursors and all of the related syntax (see the next chapter) aren't used. Finally, the data being returned don't have to be matched with any host language variables, so the data type impedance mismatch is likewise minimized.

11.5 Embedded SQL

11.5.1 Introduction

One of the means by which SQL facilities and host language programs can interact is through the use of embedded SQL. As noted by the term, SQL statements and declarations are embedded, or directly included, in another, more traditional programming language.

Virtually all vendors of SQL database systems implement embedded SQL using a preprocessor technique (in fact, we don't know of any exceptions to this statement, although it is certainly possible to design systems in other ways). Using this technique, you write your embedded SQL programs containing a mixture of SQL statements and "native" statements (statements that conform to the standard or implementor's rules for the 3GL in which you're embedding the SQL statements). You then use a preprocessor provided by the DBMS vendor to analyze the embedded SQL source code and "split" it between the SQL and the 3GL statements. The 3GL code then is compiled in the normal way with the appropriate compiler, while the SQL code is given to the DBMS in some implementation-defined way for analyzing and converting into a form that the DBMS can execute.

The SQL standard specifies the *effective* algorithm that accomplishes this split; this algorithm effectively produces an SQL *module*. (We say *effective* and *effectively* because no vendor is required to implement the processing in exactly that fashion, but they must all end up with a result that behaves the same as one that the algorithm would have produced.) The rules are really not too complicated (although we note that the SQL standard sometimes makes the rules appear more complicated than they really are). For instance, all OPEN statements for a specific cursor (see Chapter 12) are *effectively* converted into a single SQL procedure that contains an OPEN statement; the OPEN statement is *effectively* replaced in the resulting 3GL code by a CALL statement that calls that procedure.

Even though few vendors actually implement SQL's module language or follow that exact algorithm to preprocess embedded SQL programs, we find that we can better understand the behavior of the preprocessors if we keep this model in mind (Figure 11-1).

. . . .

FIGURE 11-1
Embedded SQL
Language
Structure

host language statement
host language statement
host language statement

```
        embedded SQL statement
```

host language statement
host language statement

```
        embedded SQL statement
```

host language statement
host language statement

```
        embedded SQL statement
```

Any SQL statements so embedded begin with the words EXEC SQL (except in MUMPS, as we'll see later) and are followed by the SQL statement, such as:

```
EXEC SQL SELECT movie_title,....
```

As we mentioned above, the preprocessor will *effectively* replace each of those embedded statements with a call to the *effective* procedure in the *effective* SQL module that corresponds to the embedded program.

Correspondingly, any SQL declarations, such as those in which variables are defined, begin and end, respectively, with

```
EXEC SQL BEGIN DECLARE SECTION...
```

and

```
EXEC SQL END DECLARE SECTION...
```

Depending on particular language syntax among the specified host languages, there may or may not be a terminator—END-EXEC, a semicolon, or a close parenthesis—following the above statements.

There are rules about where the SQL declarations can appear. Those rules are partly dependent on the language, but the general rule is: anywhere you can put a normal host language declaration, you can also put an SQL declaration. SQL declarations, by the way, are used to declare host language variables, that the SQL statements will use (for example, to transfer data to or from the host program).

The preprocessor doesn't actually replace the embedded SQL declarations with any reference to the *effective* SQL module, but it uses the information associated with those declarations (like the variable names and data types) to do syntax checking on the other embedded SQL statements and to properly translate the other embedded SQL statements, generating the appropriate data conversions, actual parameters and formal parameters for the effective procedures, and so forth.

11.5.2 Embedded Exception Declarations

When embedded SQL is being used, we can provide exception statements for the application to use to handle program exceptions. The WHENEVER declarative statement allows you to designate what actions you would like to follow when certain situations occur. This means that you don't have to write code following every SQL statement that checks the values of the status variables and jumps to the appropriate place; you can instruct the SQL preprocessor to do it for you.

The syntax for the WHENEVER declaration is:

```
WHENEVER condition condition-action
```

Further, condition takes one of two forms:

```
SQLERROR
```

or

```
NOT FOUND
```

and condition-action is either:

```
CONTINUE
```

or

GOTO (which may also be written as GO TO)

When you specify SQLERROR as your condition, you are telling the system to take the specified action when the value of SQLSTATE (see Chapter 17) has a value that indicates an exception or when the value of SQLCODE (see Chapter 17) is negative (a value that indicates an exception). Correspondingly, NOT FOUND means to take the specified action when the value of SQLSTATE is 02000 or the value of SQLCODE is equal to 100 (a value that means "no data").

With respect to the condition-actions, CONTINUE implies "if the specified condition occurs, then take no special action, but continue with the next statement." By contrast, GOTO (or GO TO) implies that if the specified condition occurs, then control should be transferred to the statement identified by the target specified. Depending on the host language, the target may be an integer (as in Fortran labels) or a label identifier (COBOL paragraph name, *etc.*) as required by the specific rules of that language.

The presence of a WHENEVER statement sets appropriate actions for all embedded SQL statements that physically follow it in the embedded SQL program. To choose a new course of actions, you simply code a new WHENEVER statement, which will then set the exception/not found actions for subsequent embedded SQL statements.

Some examples of the WHENEVER statement and various actions are:

WHENEVER SQLERROR GO TO 100

If the above statement were to appear in a Fortran PROGRAM, it would have the effect of placing a statement such as:

IF SQLCODE .LT. 0 GO TO 100

following every embedded SQL statement. Since WHENEVER is actually a declarative statement (rather than a procedural one), a single WHENEVER statement like that demonstrated above may apply to a number of embedded SQL statements. (In fact, many preprocessors will insert a statement exactly like our example after every embedded SQL statement affected by the WHENEVER statement.)

Correspondingly, you might have a statement like:

WHENEVER NOT FOUND CONTINUE

The effect of the above statement would be as if you had written a source language statement checking for a SQLCODE of 100 and executed what we might call a no operation (or do nothing) statement, like a Fortran CONTINUE statement (or even no statement at all).

To illustrate what we mean by "all embedded SQL statements that physically follow," consider this example:

```
EXEC SQL statement1;
EXEC SQL WHENEVER SQLERROR GO TO x;
EXEC SQL statement2;
EXEC SQL WHENEVER NOT FOUND GO TO y;
EXEC SQL statement3;
EXEC SQL WHENEVER SQLERROR CONTINUE;
EXEC SQL statement4;
```

In this example, the behavior is as follows:

- If statement1 had either an error or a no data condition, no special action is taken and execution continues with statement2.
- If statement2 encountered an error, the flow of control of the program continues at label x (not shown in the example). If statement2 encountered no data, execution still continues with statement3.
- If statement3 caused an error, control continues at label x; if it got the no data condition, then control continues at label y.
- If statement4 got a no data condition, then control goes to label y, but if it gets an error, then control continues with the statement that follows statement4.

One last caveat: This is called an *embedded exception declaration* because you can use it only in embedded SQL. If you choose to use module language, then you must explicitly check the value of SQLSTATE (or SQLCODE or both) after invocations of module procedures.

11.5.3 Embedded SQL Declarations

Earlier in this chapter (in section 11.5.1), we said that an embedded SQL declaration was used to declare any host program variables used by the embedded SQL statements. For example, in the statement:

```
INSERT INTO movies_stars VALUES (:hv1, :hv2, :hv3)
```

we see that the statement will insert a single row into the MOVIES_STARS table and that values for the three columns of that row come from three host variables (named **hv1**, **hv2**, and **hv3**). In order for the preprocessor to have any chance at all of ensuring that the host variables have the correct data type for the three columns of the MOVIES_STARS table, it has to have some access to the definitions of those host variables.

Of course, it would be *possible* for the preprocessor to simply parse the entire host program and build a symbol table (including any "include" files, should they be specified). However, that's tantamount to rebuilding the first few phases of the host language compiler! DBMS vendors are rightfully reluctant to bite that much off for a couple of reasons: first, it's redundant work, since there is already a compiler with that responsibility; second, it would consume resources that could be better applied to implementing new features or to improving performance; and third, there are better ways to resolve the problem.

The better way that SQL uses is to require that all host variable declarations (well, at least those that declare host variables that are used in embedded SQL statements) be contained between the aforementioned EXEC SQL BEGIN DECLARE SECTION and EXEC SQL END DECLARE SECTION statements (which delimit what the standard calls an "embedded SQL declare section" and which have to be completely contained on one source line with nothing except white space between the keywords). Therefore, the SQL preprocessor need only parse the host language statements that appear between those two statements. (By the way, "EXEC SQL" applies to all languages except MUMPS, which requires "&SQL(" instead.)

Because the syntax of various host languages varies so much, SQL has different rules regarding the permitted syntax of the variable declarations for each language. We note here that the SQL standard considers the statements in the embedded SQL declare section to belong to SQL and not to the host program. This distinction was unimportant in SQL-86 and SQL-89, since the contents always obeyed host language rules; however, in SQL-92, additional syntax has been added that violates the host language rules and must therefore be handled by the preprocessor.

For every language except MUMPS, you can optionally include a single *embedded character set declaration* in your embedded SQL declare section. This declaration tells the preprocessor what character set is most likely going to be used for the variable names and character set literals in the embedded SQL program (see Chapter 18, Internationalization, for information on this aspect of SQL-92). The embedded character set declaration is SQL NAMES ARE character-set-name.

Here's an important consideration: If you explicitly define (in your embedded SQL declare section) either SQLCODE or SQLSTATE with the proper data type, then that is the one that will be used for reporting the status of SQL statements. If you explicitly define *both* of them with the proper data type, then they'll both be used to report status. If you fail to define either one (or define them with the wrong data type such that the preprocessor guesses that you meant something else), then the preprocessor will assume that you only want to use SQLCODE (this is for compatibility with SQL-86 rules) and that you defined SQLCODE somewhere outside of your embedded SQL declare section. (If you failed to define it at all, you will probably get a host language compilation error later on!)

We should point out that the designers of the language embeddings went to great lengths to make the embedded SQL declare sections feel as close as possible to the host language variable conventions. In spite of a few omissions and a few extensions, we believe that they succeeded fairly well.

Let's look at the embedded SQL declare section rules for each of the languages supported in the SQL-92 standard.

Ada

An Ada variable definition is permitted to be a normal Ada host identifier (or several of them, separated by commas), followed by a colon, followed by an Ada type specification. This can optionally be followed by an Ada expression to initialize the variable (or variables) to some user-defined value. The valid Ada types specifications are:

```
SQL_STANDARD.CHAR
SQL_STANDARD.BIT
SQL_STANDARD.SMALLINT
SQL_STANDARD.INT
SQL_STANDARD.REAL
SQL_STANDARD.DOUBLE_PRECISION
SQL_STANDARD.SQLCODE_TYPE
SQL_STANDARD.SQLSTATE_TYPE
SQL_STANDARD.INDICATOR_TYPE
```

and

```
CHAR
BIT
SMALLINT
INT
REAL
DOUBLE_PRECISION
SQLCODE_TYPE
SQLSTATE_TYPE
INDICATOR_TYPE
```

In both cases, CHAR can optionally be followed by CHARACTER SET IS character-set-name (and the IS is also optional).

SQL_STANDARD is an Ada package that is specified in the SQL-92 standard. We've included the full text of the package later in this chapter (section 11.8). The package defines each of the data types as well as a number of other symbolic values. The embedded SQL declare section has to be specified within the Ada scope of Ada **with** and **use** clauses that effectively specify:

```
with SQL_STANDARD;
use SQL_STANDARD;
use SQL_STANDARD.CHARACTER_SET;
```

As you would expect, each declaration must be separated from the others with a semicolon.

Therefore, whether you specify (for example) SQL_STANDARD.REAL or simply REAL, you'll get the same effect. Each of the data types specifies an *Ada* data type (as provided in the package). Of course, they must correspond to a valid SQL data type. These correspondences are shown in Table 11-1.

TABLE 11-1

ADA Package Type	Equivalent SQL Data Type
CHAR	CHARACTER with the same length and character set
BIT	BIT with the same length
SMALLINT	SMALLINT
INT	INTEGER
REAL	REAL
DOUBLE_PRECISION	DOUBLE PRECISION
SQLCODE_TYPE	exact numeric, with implementor-defined precision
SQLSTATE_TYPE	CHARACTER(5)
INDICATOR_TYPE	any exact numeric with scale zero

Of course, the appropriate data types for SQLCODE and SQLSTATE definitions are SQLCODE_TYPE and SQLSTATE_TYPE, respectively (see Diagram RR28).

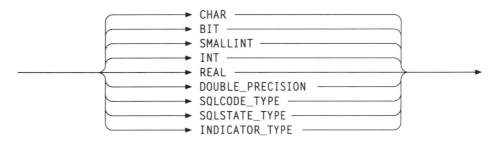

C

A C variable definition is permitted to be a normal C variable declaration, such as **long**, **short**, **float**, **double**, or **char** followed by the C identifier (or a sequence of C identifiers separated by commas). This may optionally be preceded by a C indication of storage class: **auto**, **extern**, or **static**. It may also be optionally preceded by a C class modifier: **const** or **volatile**. If **char** is specified, then you must follow the C identifier with an array specification to give the size of the char array; you can also optionally follow it with CHARACTER SET IS character-set-name (the IS is optional). You can also optionally follow any of the variable definitions with an initial value specification.

In addition to the normal C types, you can specify VARCHAR or BIT (where VARCHAR has the same format requirements and options as **char** and where BIT also requires the array specification and permits the initial value).

Of course, every declaration must be terminated with a semicolon.

Each of the data types that you provide specifies a *C* data type, which must correspond to a valid SQL data type. These correspondences are shown in Table 11-2.

C Declared Type	Equivalent SQL Data Type
char	CHARACTER with the same length and character set
VARCHAR	CHARACTER VARYING with the same length and character set
short	SMALLINT
long	INTEGER
float	REAL
double	DOUBLE PRECISION
BIT	BIT with the same length (in C, it is a **char** with the length divided by the number of bits in a **char,** usually 8)

TABLE 11-2

The appropriate data type for SQLCODE is **long,** and for SQLSTATE, it's **char[6]** (see Diagram RR29).

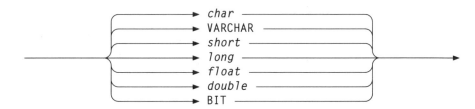

COBOL

A COBOL variable definition is permitted to be a normal COBOL identifier (always at level 01 or 77!) followed by a type specification, optionally followed by other COBOL syntax to specify the initial value, a picture clause, and so forth. (Of course, like any other COBOL declaration, this must be followed by a period.)

In this case, the type specification can be one of the following:

- PICTURE IS X(...) (where PIC and PICTURE can be used interchangeably); the (...) is optional and 1 is the default value. This may be optionally preceded by CHARACTER SET IS character-set-name. Both instances of IS are optional.

- PICTURE IS B(...) (where PIC and PICTURE can be used interchangeably); the (...) is optional and 1 is the default value. The B(...) is replaced by X(...) where the new value is the old value divided by the number of bits in a COBOL X picture (usually 8). Both instances of IS are optional.

- PICTURE IS S9(...) (where PIC and PICTURE can be used interchangeably); the (...) is optional and 1 is the default value. This can optionally be followed by V9(...) to indicate the position of the decimal point and the precision following it. Again, the (...) is optional and defaults to 1. This can optionally be followed by USAGE IS DISPLAY SIGN LEADING SEPARATE. Both instances of IS are optional. Alternately, the first 9(...) can be eliminated and only the V9(...) be used instead.

- PICTURE IS S9(...) (where PIC and PICTURE can be used interchangeably); the (...) is optional and 1 is the default value. This can optionally be followed by USAGE IS COMPUTATIONAL (where COMP and COMPUTATIONAL can be used interchangeably). Both instances of IS are optional.
- PICTURE IS S9(...) (where PIC and PICTURE can be used interchangeably); the (...) is optional and 1 is the default value. This can optionally be followed by USAGE IS BINARY. Both instances of IS are optional.

As with the other languages, each COBOL data type declaration has a corresponding SQL data type. They are are shown in Table 11-3.

TABLE 11-3

COBOL Declared Type	Equivalent SQL Data Type
PICTURE X	CHARACTER with a length equal to the number in parentheses
PICTURE B	BIT with a length equal to the number in parentheses; of course, this corresponds to a COBOL character type (X) with a number equal to the given number divided by the number of bits in an X (usually 8)
PICTURE 9 DISPLAY	NUMERIC with the same precision and scale
PICTURE 9 COMPUTATIONAL	Some exact numeric type
PICTURE 9 BINARY	SMALLINT or INTEGER

The appropriate data type for SQLCODE is PICTURE S9(pc) USAGE COMPUTATIONAL (where *pc* is an implementation-defined precision) and for SQLSTATE, it's PICTURE X(5) (see Diagram RR30).

RR30

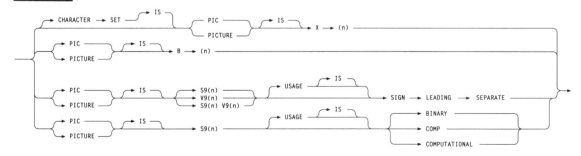

Fortran

A Fortran variable definition is a type specification followed by a normal Fortran identifier (or multiple identifiers separated by commas). The type specification is one of the following:

- CHARACTER optionally followed by an asterisk and an integer giving the length in characters. This can optionally be followed by CHARACTER SET IS character-set-name (the IS is optional).

- BIT optionally followed by an asterisk and an integer giving the length in bits.

- INTEGER (note that the optional asterisk and length in bytes permitted by the Fortran standard is not permitted here).

- REAL (note that the optional asterisk and length in bytes permitted by the Fortran standard is not permitted here).

- DOUBLE PRECISION

As with the other languages, each Fortran declaration has a corresponding SQL data type. These are shown in Table 11-4.

TABLE 11-4

Fortran Declared Type	Equivalent SQL Data Type
CHARACTER	CHARACTER with the same length
BIT	BIT with the same length (but the Fortran equivalent is really CHARACTER with the length divided by the number of bits in a CHARACTER, usually 8
INTEGER	INTEGER
REAL	REAL
DOUBLE PRECISION	DOUBLE PRECISION

The appropriate data type for SQLCODE is INTEGER, and for SQLSTATE, it's CHARACTER*5. By the way, for use with earlier Fortran (FORTRAN) standards, you are permitted to abbreviate these two status variable names to 6 characters (SQLCOD and SQLSTA); however, we recommend that you use the full names if your compiler permits (see Diagram RR31).

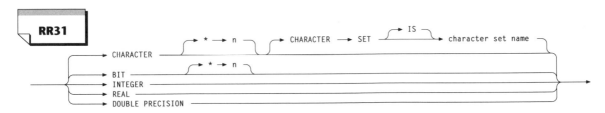

MUMPS

A MUMPS variable definition is a type specification followed by a MUMPS identifier (or multiple identifiers separated by commas). If the type specification VARCHAR is used, then each MUMPS identifier must be followed by an integer in parentheses giving the maximum length. For numeric variables, you can use INT, REAL, or DEC optionally followed by a parenthesized integer giving the precision (the integer may optionally be followed by a comma and another integer giving the scale). Each such declaration is terminated with a semicolon.

Readers who know the MUMPS language will immediately realize that this is a sham—MUMPS has no declarations, as all variables are automatically allocated and contain only variable-length character strings. However, to satisfy the conventions and requirements of SQL, the standard provides a way to declare variables to ensure that the preprocessor doesn't get confused. To be fair, the real reason for including the MUMPS variable declarations is so that the preprocessor can determine the proper SQL data types. Table 11-5 shows the corresponding types.

TABLE 11-5

MUMPS Declared Type	Equivalent SQL Data Type
VARCHAR	CHARACTER VARYING with the same length
INT	INTEGER
DEC	DECIMAL with the same precision and scale
REAL	REAL

The appropriate data type for SQLCODE is INT, and for SQLCODE, it's VARCHAR(5) (see Diagram RR32).

Pascal

A Pascal variable definition is permitted to be a normal Pascal identifier (or more than one separated by commas) followed by a colon, followed in turn by a type specification and a semicolon. The type specification can be one of the following:

- PACKED ARRAY (1..x) OF CHAR (where *x* is the length of the Pascal array of characters), optionally followed by CHARACTER SET IS character-set-name (the IS is optional).
- CHAR, optionally followed by CHARACTER SET IS character-set-name (the IS is optional).
- PACKED ARRAY (1..x) OF BIT (where *x* is the length of the Pascal array of bits)
- BIT
- INTEGER
- REAL

Pascal, like the other languages, has an equivalent SQL data type for each of these (see Table 11-6).

TABLE 11-6

Pascal Declared Type	Equivalent SQL Data Type
PACKED ARRAY [1..N] OF CHAR	CHARACTER with the same length
CHAR	CHARACTER(1)
PACKED ARRAY [1..N] OF BIT	BIT with the same length (but the Pascal equivalent is either CHAR or PACKED ARRAY OF CHAR with a length equal to the specified length divided by the number of bits in a CHAR, usually 8)
BIT	BIT(1) (but the Pascal equivalent is CHAR)
INTEGER	INTEGER
REAL	REAL

The appropriate data type for SQLCODE is INTEGER, and for SQLSTATE, it's PACKED ARRAY [1..5] OF CHAR (see Diagram RR33).

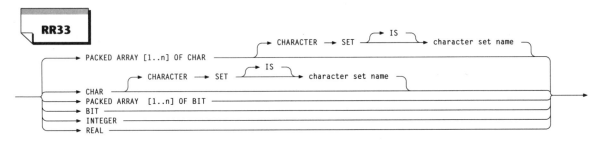

PL/I

In PL/I, each PL/I variable declaration starts off with DCL or DECLARE (which are equivalent). There is then either a normal PL/I identifier, or a list of such identifiers in parentheses and separated by commas. This is followed by a type specification and a semicolon.

A type specification is one of the following:

- CHARACTER (...) (CHAR and CHARACTER are synonymous); the (...) contains the length in characters. You can optionally specify VARYING after the keyword CHARACTER, and you can also optionally specify CHARACTER SET IS character-set-name just before the semicolon (the IS is optional).

- BIT (...); the (...) contains the length in characters. You can optionally specify VARYING after the keyword CHARACTER.

- DECIMAL FIXED or FIXED DECIMAL, either one followed by an integer in parentheses giving the precision; the integer may optionally be followed by a comma and another integer giving the scale (DECIMAL and DEC are equivalent)

- BINARY FIXED or FIXED BINARY, either one optionally followed by an integer in parentheses giving the precision (BINARY and BIN are equivalent)
- BINARY FLOAT or FLOAT BINARY, either one followed by an integer in parentheses giving the precision (BINARY and BIN are equivalent)

Just as with all other languages, there are SQL equivalents for each of these (see Table 11-7).

TABLE 11-7

Pascal Declared Type	Equivalent SQL Data Type
CHARACTER	CHARACTER with the same length and character set
BIT	BIT with the same length
DECIMAL FIXED	DECIMAL with the same precision and scale
BINARY FIXED	SMALLINT or INTEGER (depending on the precision)
BINARY FLOAT	FLOAT with the same precision

The appropriate data type for SQLCODE is FIXED BINARY (p) where *p* is an implementation-defined precision, and for SQLSTATE, it's CHARACTER(5) (see Diagram RR34).

RR34

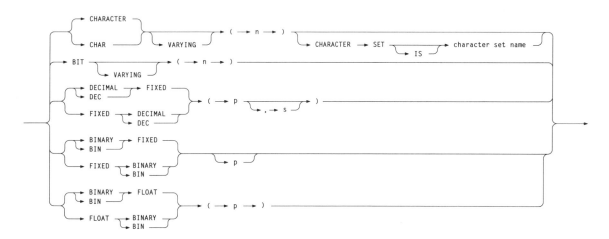

By the way, your implementation may very well provide an embedded SQL capability for languages other than those we've discussed. Many vendors discover that their customers want to use other languages. The standard may only provide a binding with seven languages, but that certainly doesn't prohibit a vendor from providing others. Other languages for which we've seen bindings include BASIC, LISP, Modula-2, and even assembly languages.

11.5.4 Embedded SQL statements

Now that we've taken a long, lingering look at the way that you define your host variables for use in embedded SQL, let's take a much briefer look at the way that you actually embed your SQL statements.

The rules for embedding the actual SQL statements are really rather simple. First, every embedded statement has to be preceded by EXEC SQL, and the EXEC SQL has to appear on a single line with nothing except white space between the keywords (except in MUMPS, where you start the embedded statement with "&SQL("—with no white space at all—instead of EXEC SQL). Second, if you need to continue the embedded SQL statement across source line boundaries, you must use the conventions of the host language for such continuations; similarly, if you want to use host language comments, you must use the rules of the host language for determining where you can place those comments. Third, depending on the language into which you're embedding, you may have to end the embedded SQL statement with some sort of terminator. In Ada, C, Pascal, and PL/I, the terminator is a semicolon; in COBOL, it's END-EXEC; in Fortran, there's no terminator at all; and in MUMPS, it's a close parenthesis.

If you declare any temporary tables or cursors (including dynamic cursors; see Chapter 16) in your embedded SQL program, the declaration has to physically precede any references to the temporary table or the cursor. If your host language supports scoping rules (as C or Pascal does), then you can redefine variables in *nested scopes* and the embedded SQL statements in that nested scope will use the most local definition. (However, this does not apply for Entry SQL conformance.)

The SQL standard has always defined the SQL language as though it were to be written as SQL alone, not embedded in another language. The technique for writing "pure" SQL is called *module language,* which we discuss next. We'd like to point out that SQL defines embedded SQL processing as a syntax transformation that takes an embedded program and extracts the SQL into an SQL module, replacing all SQL statements (except declarations) with a CALL of the corresponding procedure in that module, and leaving a pure 3GL program. Although this technique is not widely implemented (Digital Equipment Corporation's Rdb/VMS SQL product is the best known), it still serves as an excellent mental model even if your implementation deals directly with embedded SQL alone.

11.6 Module Language

So far, most of the examples in this book have been presented as though we were using a form of interactive SQL—a convenient way to present new material and show immediate results. However, as we cautioned early, the standard's definition of *direct invocation of SQL* is rather loose and allows vendors to implement lots of variations. In this chapter, we've talked mostly about combining SQL with other programming languages to implement your applications; to this point, we've discussed embedded SQL, which virtually all SQL DBMS vendors provide and which is quite popular with application writers.

However, there is another paradigm for binding your SQL statements to the 3GL statements of your application, called *module language.* Module language allows you to write your SQL statements separately from your 3GL statements and combine them into an application with your linker. This has several advantages and some disadvantages.

First, you can hire SQL specialists to write the SQL code for your application without worrying about what 3GL they're trained to use; similarly, you can hire the best 3GL programmers without worrying about training them in the finer points of SQL coding. Second, you can utilize the concepts of modular programming to cleanly separate the set-at-a-time operations from the traditional data processing and similar aspects of your applications. Third, you can write the SQL in a way that permits you to choose or rechoose your 3GL at a later point in development with minimal changes to the SQL code. Finally, you can almost certainly use your favorite debuggers with full source-code facilities, at least on the 3GL parts of your application; if you use embedded SQL, you will often find that your debuggers are nearly useless on the source code.

On the other side of the coin, embedded SQL is more widely implemented than module language, which may be an important factor, especially if you want the freedom to use different DBMSs for your application. Furthermore, many people find it easier to understand and maintain an application when they can read both the 3GL and the SQL code together in a smooth flow, instead of having to look at two pieces of code simultaneously.

We should point out that the SQL standards have always used module language as the definitional technique for all of SQL. In fact, in SQL-86 and SQL-89, the definition of embedded SQL was in an appendix to the standard (which caused NIST to initiate an effort to publish a new standard, X3.168, which formalized embedded SQL definitions; see Appendix F).

Okay, now that we've told you why you might want to use module language, or why you might not want to, let's have a look at what it *is.* In short, a module consists of a module header followed by a mixture of procedures and declarations. The procedures contain the actual SQL statements, and the declarations allow you to declare your cursors and temporary tables. The syntax for a module is shown below and in Diagram RR35.

```
MODULE [ module-name ] [ NAMES ARE character-set-name ]
    LANGUAGE { ADA | C | COBOL | FORTRAN | MUMPS | PASCAL | PLI }
        [ SCHEMA schema-name ] [ AUTHORIZATION authID ]
        [ temporary-table-declarations... ]
        { cursor-declaration | dynamic-cursor-declaration | procedure }...
```

If you don't specify a module-name, then the module is unnamed (which isn't usually a problem, but if you have multiple modules and none of them have names, it might make it harder to debug your application). The NAMES ARE clause tells the module language compiler that the identifiers in the module are going to be expressed either in the specified character set or in the basic set of SQL characters

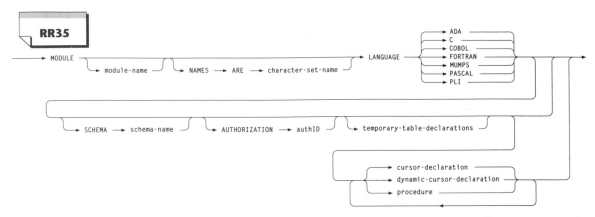

only. The LANGUAGE clause tells the compiler how to build the calling sequences for the procedures in the module, because that can vary from language to language.

You must have either a SCHEMA clause, an AUTHORIZATION clause, or both. SQL-86 and SQL-89 only permitted the AUTHORIZATION clause, and it specified both the name of the schema that would be used as a default qualifier for table names (and view names) in SQL statements in the module *and* the authorization identifier to be used for privilege checking while executing statements in the module. SQL-92 divides these two concepts so that you can specify the default schema and the authorization identifier separately.

You can declare as many temporary tables as you need in the module (even none at all). Note that all of the temporary table declarations have to appear before any cursors or procedures but that you can mix cursor declarations and procedures in any order as long as you declare a cursor before any procedures that reference it. We'll see what cursor declarations look like in Chapter 12, and we'll find out about dynamic cursors in Chapter 16; for now, let's look at procedures.

A procedure is, as the name suggests, a programming element that can be called from another programming element. In fact, SQL procedures are like procedures in other languages in many ways: they have parameters, they have a name, and they contain executable statements. They differ from procedures in some languages by having only a single executable SQL statement and by requiring a minimum of one parameter. The syntax for a procedure is shown below and in Diagram RR36.

```
PROCEDURE proc-name
    ( parameter-declaration [ , parameter-declaration ]... )
        SQL-statement ;
```

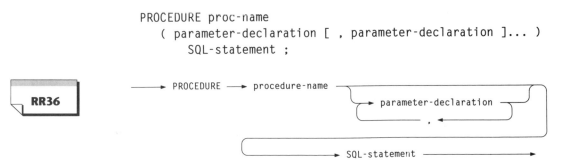

Optionally, you can replace the parenthesizes list of comma-separated parameter declarations with:

```
parameter-declaration...
```

but we strongly recommend the use of the more conventional notation with parentheses and commas (the other form will probably be omitted from a future version of the standard in any case). You should note that at least one `parameter-declaration` is required in any case. The minimum requirement for a procedure is to have at least one status parameter, either SQLSTATE or SQLCODE (see Chapter 17 for more details); you can choose to use both of them if you prefer, though we strongly recommend using SQLSTATE and note that SQLCODE may be omitted from a future version of the standard. If you want to pass other data into the SQL statement or if you want to have the SQL statement return data to your application, you will have to declare additional parameters. A `parameter-declaration` looks like this:

```
parameter-name data-type
```

or

```
SQLCODE
```

or

```
SQLSTATE
```

Obviously, a `parameter-name` cannot be a reserved word (especially not SQLCODE or SQLSTATE!); in addition, SQL requires that `parameter-names` (except the status parameters) always be preceded by a colon. Therefore, here are some valid parameter names.

```
:SERIAL_NUMBER
:"TABLE"
:PARAM1
```

You have to use the colon both when you declare the parameter and when you use it in an SQL statement. Parameters come in four "flavors": they can be *input parameters, output parameters, input and output parameters,* or *neither input nor output parameters.* You will have already guessed that *input parameters* are those that pass data from the host program into the procedure and that *output parameters* are those that pass data back to the host program from the procedure; we're sure that you've also figured out that *input and output parameters* are parameters that serve both functions. But what about *neither input nor output parameters*? Well, SQL can tell by how a parameter is used in the SQL statement of a procedure whether it is for input, for output, or for both. If you happen to code a parameter declaration that you don't actually use in the statement, then SQL doesn't know whether you might later modify the procedure to use it for input, output, or both, so SQL declares it to be "none of the above."

Let's see some examples of procedures.

```
PROCEDURE discount_movies
  ( SQLSTATE, :title CHARACTER VARYING(25), :discount DECIMAL(3,2) )
      UPDATE movie_titles
        SET current_purchase_price = current_purchase_price - discount
      WHERE movie_title = :title;

PROCEDURE drop_titles
  ( :star CHARACTER VARYING(25),
    SQLCODE,
    :reason CHARACTER(2)
    SQLSTATE )
      DELETE FROM movie_titles
        WHERE title IN (SELECT movie_title
                        FROM movies_stars
                        WHERE :star = actor_last_name );

PROCEDURE star_name
    ( :star_last CHARACTER VARYING(25),
      :star_first CHARACTER VARYING(25),
      :title CHARACTER VARYING(25),
      SQLSTATE )
  SELECT "Starring: " || actor_last_name
    INTO :star_last
    FROM movies_stars
    WHERE actor_last_name = :star_last AND
          actor_first_name = :star_first AND
          movie_title = :title;
```

In the first example, we provide the title of a movie and the amount by which its price is to be discounted and specify that the status is to be returned in SQLSTATE. In the second example, we provide for getting information back from both SQLCODE and SQLSTATE; we also provide a parameter that isn't used at all. In the third example, we use one parameter for both input and output: to retrieve a variation of the star's last name into the same parameter that we use to provide the name to the database. Useless? Probably, except that it won't perform the concatenation if SQLSTATE indicates "no data."

Let's see now what an entire module might look like using those three sample procedures.

```
MODULE demo_module NAMES ARE ascii
  LANGUAGE FORTRAN
  SCHEMA test_schema AUTHORIZATION book_authors

PROCEDURE discount_movies
  ( SQLSTATE, :title CHARACTER VARYING(25), :discount DECIMAL(3,2) )
      UPDATE movie_titles
```

```
            SET current_purchase_price = current_purchase_price - discount
          WHERE movie_title = :title;

PROCEDURE drop_titles
  ( :star CHARACTER VARYING(25),
    SQLCODE,
    :reason CHARACTER(2)
    SQLSTATE )
       DELETE FROM movie_titles
         WHERE title IN (SELECT movie_title
                            FROM movies_stars
                           WHERE :star = actor_last_name );

PROCEDURE star_name
    ( :star_last CHARACTER VARYING(25),
      :star_first CHARACTER VARYING(25),
      :title CHARACTER VARYING(25),
      SQLSTATE )
  SELECT "Starring: " || actor_last_name
    INTO :star_last
    FROM movies_stars
    WHERE actor_last_name = :star_last AND
          actor_first_name = :star_first AND
          movie_title = :title;
```

It really is as simple as that. Of course, what we have not shown here is the (Fortran, in this case) code that we'd write to actually *use* the procedures in this module. You can see examples of that in Appendix B.

11.6.1 Some Additional Information About Privileges

You have seen that SQL modules optionally allow you to specify AUTHORIZATION authID. We hinted that specifying the clause told the DBMS to use that authID for checking whether the SQL statements in the procedures of the module have the appropriate privileges to see and update the data they reference. However, what if you do *not* specify that clause? In this case, the DBMS will use the authID associated with your session for privilege checking.

We have heard the phrase *definer's rights* used to describe modules that do contain the AUTHORIZATION clause, because it's the privileges of the *defined* authID that determine the actions of the statements in the module. Of course, most implementations will have some sort of restrictions on what modules you can use, so you don't get super-user privileges by simply ferreting out a module with such an authID.

We've also heard the term *invoker's rights* used to refer to modules that don't have an AUTHORIZATION clause. This means that the privileges of the user that invokes procedures in the module are used to determine the actions.

You should also note that there is no way in embedded SQL to specify an explicit authID, so embedded SQL always acts like an invoker's rights module (unless a vendor extension provides a definer's rights capability).

11.6.2 An Implementation Note

When an SQL DBMS processes a module (whether it's an actual SQL module or merely the implied module associated with an embedded program), the results of that processing aren't really specified by the SQL standard. In some implementations, the module is compiled and converted to machine-language code that is linked with the 3GL portion of the program to be invoked at run-time. In others, the result might somehow be saved in the actual database, either in machine language for easy and fast execution or in an intermediate form that is later interpreted or even compiled into machine code at runtime. In still others, the SQL statements may simply be interpreted at runtime. All these implementation techniques are valid, even desirable, based on criteria such as implementation cost, storage facilities, and performance requirements.

11.7 Other Binding Styles

In this chapter, we've talked mostly about embedded SQL and module language programming. However, there are other ways of binding SQL statements to your application. We've already talked about one: direct invocation of, or interactive, SQL. Another, dynamic SQL, is a sort of binding style, but not quite. Although dynamic SQL is invoked via *normal, static* statements (that is, those statements bound "normally" in module language or embedded SQL), the actual statements that are to be executed are neither module nor embedded, but dynamic. See Chapter 16 for a full explanation of dynamic SQL.

A call-level interface (CLI) is another kind of binding, forming a cross between dynamic and static SQL. In general with CLI, SQL statements are passed as source text (parameters) to subroutines where they are dealt with. This means that they are given to the DBMS itself for execution, which sort of implies dynamic SQL, but without the static statements that are normally used for dynamic SQL. A future version of the SQL standard will probably have a definition of CLI.

Another binding is called *remote database access*. In fact, there is another standard called RDA or Remote Database Access (ISO/IEC 9579-1 and 9579-2) that specifies an RDA facility for accessing SQL databases remotely. Of course, an application that wishes to remotely access an SQL DBMS using RDA still has to bind its 3GL statements to its SQL statements in one of the bindings we've described already; nonetheless, there are some differences in the behavior of programs using RDA. It is beyond the scope of this book to discuss RDA and remote access in general; we will say that the RDA standard has gone to great lengths to be as transparent as possible, but it does include minor issues that strictly local access does not encounter.

11.8 Package SQL_STANDARD

The Ada package SQL_STANDARD that we mentioned in section 11.5.3 is listed below, where csp is an implementation-defined package and cst is an implementation-defined character type such that within the scope of an Ada **use** clause for SQL_STANDARD.CHARACTER_SET, string literals can be of type SQL_STANDARD. CHAR. bs, ts, bi, ti, dr, dd, bsc, and tsc are implementation-defined integer values. t is INT or SMALLINT, corresponding with an implementation-defined exact numeric type of indicator parameters.

```
package SQL_STANDARD is
   package CHARACTER_SET renames csp;
   subtype CHARACTER_TYPE is CHARACTER_SET.cst;
   type CHAR is array (POSITIVE range <>) of CHARACTER)_TYPE;
   type BIT is array (NATURAL range <>) of BOOLEAN;
   type SMALLINT is range bs..ts;
   type INT is range bi..ti;
   type REAL is digits dr;
   type DOUBLE_PRECISION is digits dd;
   subtype INDICATOR_TYPE is t;
   type SQLCODE_TYPE is range bsc..tsc;
   subtype SQL_ERROR is SQLCODE_TYPE range SQL_TYPE'FIRST..-1;
   subtype NOT_FOUND is SQLCODE_TYPE range 100..100;
   type SQLSTATE_TYPE is new CHAR (1..5);
   package SQLSTATE_CODES is
       AMBIGUOUS_CURSOR_NAME_NO_SUBCLASS:
               constant SQLSTATE_TYPE := "3C000";
       CARDINALITY_VIOLATION_NO_SUBCLASS:
               constant SQLSTATE_TYPE :="21000";
       CONNECTION_EXCEPTION_NO_SUBCLASS:
               constant SQLSTATE_TYPE :="08000";
       CONNECTION_EXCEPTION_CONNECTION_DOES_NOT_EXIST:
               constant SQLSTATE_TYPE :="08003";
       CONNECTION_EXCEPTION_CONNECTION_FAILURE:
               constant SQLSTATE_TYPE :="08006";
       CONNECTION_EXCEPTION_CONNECTION_NAME_IN_USE:
               constant SQLSTATE_TYPE :="08002";
       CONNECTION_EXCEPTION_SQLCLIENT_UNABLE_TO_ESTABLISH_SQLCONNECTION:
               constant SQLSTATE_TYPE :="08001";
       CONNECTION_EXCEPTION_SQLSERVER_REJECTED_ESTABLISHMENT_OF_SQLCONNECTION:
               constant SQLSTATE_TYPE :="08004";
       CONNECTION_EXCEPTION_TRANSACTION_RESOLUTION_UNKNOWN:
               constant SQLSTATE_TYPE :="08007";
       DATA_EXCEPTION_NO_SUBCLASS:
               constant SQLSTATE_TYPE :="22000";
       DATA_EXCEPTION_CHARACTER_NOT_IN_REPERTOIRE:
               constant SQLSTATE_TYPE :="22021";
       DATA_EXCEPTION_DATETIME_FIELD_OVERFLOW:
               constant SQLSTATE_TYPE :="22008";
       DATA_EXCEPTION_DIVISION_BY_ZERO:
               constant SQLSTATE_TYPE :="22012";
       DATA_EXCEPTION_ERROR_IN_ASSIGNMENT:
               constant SQLSTATE_TYPE :="22005";
```

```
DATA_EXCEPTION_INDICATOR_OVERFLOW:
        constant SQLSTATE_TYPE :="22022";
DATA_EXCEPTION_INTERVAL_FIELD_OVERFLOW:
        constant SQLSTATE_TYPE :="22015";
DATA_EXCEPTION_INVALID_CHARACTER_VALUE_FOR_CAST:
        constant SQLSTATE_TYPE :="22018";
DATA_EXCEPTION_INVALID_DATETIME_FORMAT:
        constant SQLSTATE_TYPE :="22007";
DATA_EXCEPTION_INVALID_ESCAPE_CHARACTER:
        constant SQLSTATE_TYPE :="22019";
DATA_EXCEPTION_INVALID_ESCAPE_SEQUENCE:
        constant SQLSTATE_TYPE :="22025";
DATA_EXCEPTION_INVALID_PARAMETER_VALUE:
        constant SQLSTATE_TYPE :="22023";
DATA_EXCEPTION_INVALID_TIME_ZONE_DISPLACEMENT_VALUE:
        constant SQLSTATE_TYPE :="22009";
DATA_EXCEPTION_NULL_VALUE_NO_INDICATOR_PARAMETER:
        constant SQLSTATE_TYPE :="22002";
DATA_EXCEPTION_NUMERIC_VALUE_OUT_OF_RANGE:
        constant SQLSTATE_TYPE :="22003";
DATA_EXCEPTION_STRING_DATA_LENGTH_MISMATCH:
        constant SQLSTATE_TYPE :="22026";
DATA_EXCEPTION_STRING_DATA_RIGHT_TRUNCATION:
        constant SQLSTATE_TYPE :="22001";
DATA_EXCEPTION_SUBSTRING_ERROR:
        constant SQLSTATE_TYPE :="22011";
DATA_EXCEPTION_TRIM_ERROR:
        constant SQLSTATE_TYPE :="22027";
DATA_EXCEPTION_UNTERMINATED_C_STRING:
        constant SQLSTATE_TYPE :="22024";
DEPENDENT_PRIVILEGE_DESCRIPTORS_STILL_EXIST_NO_SUBCLASS:
        constant SQLSTATE_TYPE :="2B000";
DYNAMIC_SQL_ERROR_NO_SUBCLASS:
        constant SQLSTATE_TYPE :="07000";
DYNAMIC_SQL_ERROR_CURSOR_SPECIFICATION_CANNOT_BE_EXECUTED:
        constant SQLSTATE_TYPE :="07003";
DYNAMIC_SQL_ERROR_INVALID_DESCRIPTOR_COUNT:
        constant SQLSTATE_TYPE :="07008";
DYNAMIC_SQL_ERROR_INVALID_DESCRIPTOR_INDEX:
        constant SQLSTATE_TYPE :="07009";
DYNAMIC_SQL_ERROR_PREPARED_STATEMENT_NOT_A_CURSOR_SPECIFICATION:
        constant SQLSTATE_TYPE :="07005";
DYNAMIC_SQL_ERROR_RESTRICTED_DATA_TYPE_ATTRIBUTE_VIOLATION:
        constant SQLSTATE_TYPE :="07006";
DYNAMIC_SQL_ERROR_USING_CLAUSE_DOES_NOT_MATCH_DYNAMIC_PARAMETER_SPEC:
        constant SQLSTATE_TYPE :="07001";
DYNAMIC_SQL_ERROR_USING_CLAUSE_DOES_NOT_MATCH_TARGET_SPEC:
        constant SQLSTATE_TYPE :="07002";
DYNAMIC_SQL_ERROR_USING_CLAUSE_REQUIRED_FOR_DYNAMIC_PARAMETERS:
        constant SQLSTATE_TYPE :="07004";
DYNAMIC_SQL_ERROR_USING_CLAUSE_REQUIRED_FOR_RESULT_FIELDS:
        constant SQLSTATE_TYPE :="07007";
FEATURE_NOT_SUPPORTED_NO_SUBCLASS:
        constant SQLSTATE_TYPE :="0A000";
```

```
FEATURE_NOT_SUPPORTED_MULTIPLE_ENVIRONMENT_TRANSACTIONS:
        constant SQLSTATE_TYPE :="0A001";
INTEGRITY_CONSTRAINT_VIOLATION_NO_SUBCLASS:
        constant SQLSTATE_TYPE :="23000";
INVALID_AUTHORIZATION_SPECIFICATION_NO_SUBCLASS:
        constant SQLSTATE_TYPE :="28000";
INVALID_CATALOG_NAME_NO_SUBCLASS:
        constant SQLSTATE_TYPE :="3D000";
INVALID_CHARACTER_SET_NAME_NO_SUBCLASS:
        constant SQLSTATE_TYPE :="2C000";
INVALID_CONDITION_NUMBER_NO_SUBCLASS:
        constant SQLSTATE_TYPE :="35000";
INVALID_CONNECTION_NAME_NO_SUBCLASS:
        constant SQLSTATE_TYPE :="2E000";
INVALID_CURSOR_NAME_NO_SUBCLASS:
        constant SQLSTATE_TYPE :="34000";
INVALID_CURSOR_STATE_NO_SUBCLASS:
        constant SQLSTATE_TYPE :="24000";
INVALID_SCHEMA_NAME_NO_SUBCLASS:
        constant SQLSTATE_TYPE :="3F000";
INVALID_SQL_DESCRIPTOR_NAME_NO_SUBCLASS:
        constant SQLSTATE_TYPE :="33000";
INVALID_SQL_STATEMENT_NAME_NO_SUBCLASS:
        constant SQLSTATE_TYPE :="26000";
INVALID_TRANSACTION_STATE_NO_SUBCLASS:
        constant SQLSTATE_TYPE :="25000";
INVALID_TRANSACTION_TERMINATION_NO_SUBCLASS:
        constant SQLSTATE_TYPE :="2D000";
NO_DATA_NO_SUBCLASS:
        constant SQLSTATE_TYPE :="02000";
REMOTE_DATABASE_ACCESS_NO_SUBCLASS:
        constant SQLSTATE_TYPE :="HZ000";
SUCCESSFUL_COMPLETION_NO_SUBCLASS:
        constant SQLSTATE_TYPE :="00000";
SYNTAX_ERROR_OR_ACCESS_RULE_VIOLATION_NO_SUBCLASS:
        constant SQLSTATE_TYPE :="42000";
SYNTAX_ERROR_OR_ACCESS_RULE_VIOLATION_IN_DIRECT_STATEMENT_NO_SUBCLASS:
        constant SQLSTATE_TYPE :="2A000";
SYNTAX_ERROR_OR_ACCESS_RULE_VIOLATION_IN_DYNAMIC_STATEMENT_NO_SUBCLASS:
        constant SQLSTATE_TYPE :="37000";
TRANSACTION_ROLLBACK_NO_SUBCLASS:
        constant SQLSTATE_TYPE :="40000";
TRANSACTION_ROLLBACK_INTEGRITY_CONSTRAINT_VIOLATION:
        constant SQLSTATE_TYPE :="40002";
TRANSACTION_ROLLBACK_SERIALIZATION_FAILURE:
        constant SQLSTATE_TYPE :="40001";
TRANSACTION_ROLLBACK_STATEMENT_COMPLETION_UNKNOWN:
        constant SQLSTATE_TYPE :="40003";
TRIGGERED_DATA_CHANGE_VIOLATION_NO_SUBCLASS:
        constant SQLSTATE_TYPE :="27000";
WARNING_NO_SUBCLASS:
        constant SQLSTATE_TYPE :="01000";
WARNING_CURSOR_OPERATION_CONFLICT:
        constant SQLSTATE_TYPE :="01001";
```

```
                    WARNING_DISCONNECT_ERROR:
                          constant SQLSTATE_TYPE :="01002";
                    WARNING_IMPLICIT_ZERO_BIT_PADDING:
                          constant SQLSTATE_TYPE :="01008";
                    WARNING_INSUFFICIENT_ITEM_DESCRIPTOR_AREAS:
                          constant SQLSTATE_TYPE :="01005";
                    WARNING_NULL_VALUE_ELIMINATED_IN_SET_FUNCTION:
                          constant SQLSTATE_TYPE :="01003";
                    WARNING_PRIVILEGE_NOT_GRANTED:
                          constant SQLSTATE_TYPE :="01007";
                    WARNING_PRIVILEGE_NOT_REVOKED:
                          constant SQLSTATE_TYPE :="01006";
                    WARNING_QUERY_EXPRESSION_TOO_LONG_FOR_INFORMATION_SCHEMA:
                          constant SQLSTATE_TYPE :="0100A";
                    WARNING_SEARCH_CONDITION_TOO_LONG_FOR_INFORMATION_SCHEMA:
                          constant SQLSTATE_TYPE :="01009";
                    WARNING_STRING_DATA_RIGHT_TRUNCATION_WARNING:
                          constant SQLSTATE_TYPE :="01004";
                    WITH_CHECK_OPTION_VIOLATION_NO_SUBCLASS:
                          constant SQLSTATE_TYPE :="44000";
             end SQLSTATE_CODES;
      end SQL_STANDARD;
```

11.9 Chapter Summary

In this chapter, we've taken you beyond the basic—and advanced—facilities of the SQL statements themselves that we discussed in the earlier chapters. You now know about the different binding styles supported by SQL and, depending on the support of your particular implementation(s) and on what is most appropriate for your applications, can choose the module and embedded forms of SQL. The language-specific material included in this chapter should give you a thorough understanding of how SQL can be used together with the languages specified by the standard.

In the next chapter, we'll turn our attention to the subject of cursors, an important part in making embedded and module SQL work.

CHAPTER 12

. . . .

Cursors

12.1 Introduction

We've mentioned several times that SQL processes data by sets. The primary mechanism used to permit SQL to do row-by-row access—an important facility when SQL is combined with C, COBOL, Ada, or another language—is the cursor. In this chapter, we explore cursors and how they are used within SQL.

12.2 Cursors: The Basics

Assume that you need to compute the standard deviation of the rental cost of movies. Since there is no function to do that in SQL, you must retrieve that data into your application program and compute that value there. In other situations, your application may require the ability to display rows of data (formatted in some special way, perhaps) on a screen and allow a user to identify rows for deletion or modification by using a pointer of some sort, like a cursor.

The languages in which you write your applications (that is, the languages that invoke the SQL code: C, COBOL, Ada, and the others we discussed in the previous chapters) do not support sets or multisets of data. They are capable of dealing with only one or a few pieces of data at a time. This particular difference between SQL and the host languages is what we call an *impedance mismatch*. SQL has facilities to help resolve this mismatch.

The technique involves an object called a *cursor*. A cursor is something like a pointer that traverses a collection of rows. If your application has to traverse many rows of data, you cannot retrieve them all at once because your host language can't deal with an arbitrary number of rows. However, you can retrieve them one at a time by using a cursor.

Suppose you want to compute the standard deviation of the movie rental prices of all movies whose current sales price is greater than $39.95. A SELECT statement would look something like this:

```
SELECT current_rental_price FROM movie_titles
  WHERE current_sales_price > 39.95;
```

However, as we said in Chapter 11, this statement cannot be executed as part of an application program because it may (and probably will) retrieve many rows of data. (It can be executed in interactive SQL because that merely displays the result on your terminal.) The way this must be handled is to declare a cursor for that expression and then use the cursor to retrieve the data. The SQL statements would look something like the statements below. Now, this doesn't show the flow of control that your application program would have to provide. We won't show that in detail here; you can deduce that yourself from your knowledge of Chapter 11. However, let's sketch the whole thing just to show how you would use the cursor. (Note that we're using a pseudocode here instead of one of the several languages that the SQL standard specifies.)

The FETCH statement (discussed in detail later in this chapter; see section 12.4) is the SQL equivalent of a READ or GET statement.

```
DECLARE std_dev CURSOR FOR
SELECT current_rental_price FROM movie_titles
  WHERE current_sales_price < 39.95;
OPEN std_dev;
```

loop:

```
FETCH std_dev INTO :price;
```

if no-data return, then go to finished;

accumulate information required for standard deviation computation;

go to loop;

finished:

```
CLOSE std_dev;
```

compute the standard deviation;

You will note that this logic permits your application to deal with only one row of data at a time but also permits it to handle all the rows, no matter how many there are. If you have written programs in COBOL, Pascal, or some other language in which you use loop control to cycle through one or more records in a file you are already familiar with the fundamentals of cursor usage.

In this loop of FETCH statements, you can also perform database operations on the rows that you fetched. For example, you can update or delete the fetched rows.

```
DECLARE std_dev CURSOR FOR
    SELECT current_rental_price FROM movie_titles;

OPEN std_dev;
```

loop:

```
FETCH std_dev INTO :price;
```

if no-data return, then go to finished;

if :price is greater than 99.99, then
```
    DELETE FROM movie_titles WHERE CURRENT OF std_dev;
```

if :price is greater than 39.95, but less than or
    equal to 99.99, then
    get user to enter new price from terminal;
```
    UPDATE movie_titles
        SET current_rental_price = :newprice
      WHERE CURRENT OF std_dev;
```

if :price is less than or equal to 39.95, then
    accumulate information required for standard deviation
computation;

```
go to loop;
```

finished:

```
CLOSE std_dev;
```

```
compute the standard deviation;
```

In this example, the application was able to do some maintenance on the MOVIE_TITLES table while it was accumulating the information required for the computation. The new form of the UPDATE statement shown here specifies the row to be updated by specifying WHERE CURRENT OF STD_DEV instead of WHERE search-condition. We call this a *positioned* UPDATE statement.

12.2.1 Syntax

Let's take a closer look at all of these new statements. There are actually only six new statements, and two of these are merely variations on old familiar set-oriented *searched* statements.

First, there is the cursor declaration. This is not an executable statement but a declaration. In it, you specify the name of the cursor (whose only use is in other cursor-related statements). The scope of the cursor name is the module or compilation unit in which it was declared; therefore, you cannot use modular programming techniques to split operations on one cursor among several compilation units or modules.

The format of a cursor declaration is shown below and in Diagram RR37.

```
DECLARE cursor-name [ INSENSITIVE ] [ SCROLL ] CURSOR FOR
        query-expression [ order-by ] [ updatability ]
```

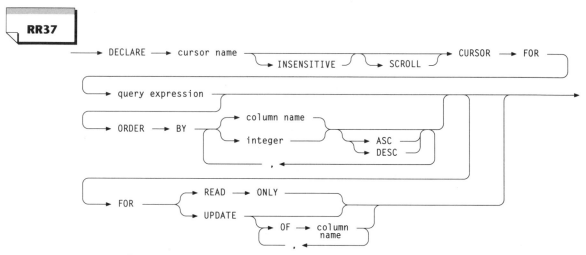

The cursor-name is just a normal SQL identifier. You have to be sure that the cursor-name is different from any other cursor-name in the same module or compilation unit. The query-expression is SQL's normal query expression that we saw in Chapters 3 and 9.

If we leave off all of the optional parts, then we are left with:

```
DECLARE cursor-name CURSOR FOR query-expression
```

which is the most basic form of a cursor declaration. Even this limited form allows us to perform many powerful operations on our data one row at a time. The query-expression identifies the rows that we wish to retrieve (and possibly update or delete), and other statements actually manipulate that set of rows for us.

However, there are situations in which we need a bit more control over the rows we have identified. One of the most basic forms of control that we often need is to sort the rows according to some criteria. The optional order-by clause is used for this purpose.

12.2.2 Ordering and Column Naming

The order-by is defined as:

```
ORDER BY sort-specification [ , sort-specification ]...
```

The syntax of `sort-specification` is defined to be:

```
{ column-name | unsigned-integer }
   [ COLLATE BY collation-name ] [ ASC | DESC ]
```

If you use a `column-name`, it has to be the name of a column that is in the select list of the `query-expression`. SQL doesn't allow you to order by columns that you don't select into the cursor. There are times, however, when your select list has columns that don't have names. For example, you might declare a cursor like this:

```
DECLARE cursor1 CURSOR FOR
 SELECT current_sales_price, our_cost,
        current_sales_price - our_cost
   FROM movie_titles
```

The first column of the cursor is named CURRENT_SALES_PRICE and the second is named OUR_COST. However, the third column has no name! As we saw in Chapter 9, you could (and probably should) have declared your cursor like this:

```
DECLARE cursor1 CURSOR FOR
 SELECT current_sales_price, our_cost,
        current_sales_price - our_cost AS markup
   FROM movie_titles
```

which would have given the third column the name MARKUP. However, for whatever reason, let's assume that you failed to do that. In that case, you can identify the column using the number 3 (indicating the third column). To order by the third column and the first column of that cursor, you could use:

```
ORDER BY 3, CURRENT_SALES_PRICE
```

IMPORTANT: The ability to use a position number for ordering has been deprecated in SQL-92, meaning that some future version of SQL might prohibit it entirely. We recommend that you always use the AS clause to give a name to columns that otherwise wouldn't have a name.

Of course, the keyword ASC means "sort in ascending order" and DESC means "sort in descending order." Therefore, if you want to sort in ascending order by the markup value and in descending order by the current sales price, you would declare your cursor to look like this:

```
DECLARE cursor1 CURSOR FOR
 SELECT current_sales_price, our_cost,
        current_sales_price - our_cost AS markup
   FROM movie_titles
     ORDER BY markup, current_sales_price DESC
```

One tricky thing about ASC and DESC: They are "sticky" when you specify them, but the initial default is ASC. That is, whenever you specify either ASC or DESC on some column in an ORDER BY clause, all columns specified after that will have the same sort order until you use the other one. Therefore, if you specify:

```
ORDER BY markup DESC, current_sales_price
```

you will get *both* columns sorted in descending order. If you want the third column to be descending and the first to be ascending, you have to specify:

```
ORDER BY markup DESC, current_sales_price ASC
```

12.2.3 Updatability

Once in a while, you may encounter a situation that requires you to make sure your cursor is not updated, even if somebody else comes along to "maintain" your application and (perhaps without fully understanding the application) adds an UPDATE or DELETE statement. You'd like to be able to define the cursor as read-only, even though it could theoretically be updated. (Another reason for defining a cursor as read-only is to permit your DBMS implementation to perform certain performance optimizations that cannot be used for updatable cursors.) In other situations, you might want to ensure that only some columns of the cursor can be updated while some are guaranteed to be unchanged. SQL-92 provides you with an updatability clause on your DECLARE CURSOR to allow you to control this.

The updatability is either FOR READ ONLY or FOR UPDATE. If you specify FOR READ ONLY, then you cannot execute UPDATE or DELETE statements on that cursor. If you specify FOR UPDATE, you can also specify a list of column names.

```
FOR UPDATE OF column-name [ , column-name ]...
```

If you leave off the list of column-names (or if you don't even specify FOR UPDATE), the default is an implicit list of all the column names in the underlying table of the cursor. FOR UPDATE means that you can execute UPDATE or DELETE statements on the cursor, but you cannot update any column that was not listed. Therefore, if you define the following cursor:

```
DECLARE cursor1 CURSOR FOR
 SELECT current_sales_price, our_cost
   FROM movie_titles
     FOR READ ONLY
```

any UPDATE WHERE CURRENT or DELETE WHERE CURRENT statements that identify that cursor will get an error. If you defined the cursor as:

```
DECLARE cursor1 CURSOR FOR
 SELECT current_sales_price, our_cost
   FROM movie_titles
     FOR UPDATE OF current_sales_price
```

then a statement that said:

```
UPDATE movie_titles
    SET current_sales_price = current_sales_price / 2
  WHERE CURRENT OF cursor1
```

would work just fine, but:

```
UPDATE movie_titles
    SET our_cost = our_cost / 2
  WHERE CURRENT OF cursor1
```

would get an error.

12.2.4 Sensitivity

Cursors as defined in SQL-86 and SQL-89 had a significant problem: The standard simply didn't tell DBMS implementors enough about cursor characteristics. One of the characteristics that was left unspecified turns out to be pretty important for some applications. We've already briefly discussed transaction semantics in Chapter 2 (and will do so in more detail in Chapter 14), so you know that changes that your application makes in a transaction cannot be affected by other transactions that may be concurrently accessing the database. However, what if your *own* application executes statements that overlap with one another?

Consider the situation where you open a cursor of, say, all rows that identify movies costing more than $89.00, and you are merrily fetching and updating rows but (for reasons known to yourself) you insert a searched update statement that lowers the price of all movies costing over $79.00 by $20.00. What (we ask with a straight face) happens to the rows in your cursor that you haven't processed yet? Do some of those rows disappear because they no longer cost more than $89.00, or do they remain in the cursor for you to process. If they remain in the cursor, does their price get lowered by $20.00 or not? Here's how the code might look.

```
DECLARE cursor1 CURSOR FOR
    SELECT current_rental_price
      FROM movie_titles
      WHERE current_sales_price > 89.95;

OPEN cursor1;
```

loop:

```
FETCH cursor1 INTO :price;
```

if no-data return, then go to finished;

perform whatever action is appropriate;

if you got interrupted by a phone call from the boss, then

```
UPDATE movie_titles
   SET current_rental_price = current_rental_price - 20.00
WHERE current_rental_price > 79.95;
```

go to loop;

finished:

```
CLOSE cursor1;
```

Okay, so perhaps this isn't the most realistic situation, but you can picture what we're trying to evoke here: a cursor is opened using certain criteria and, while it's still open, another SQL statement that affects (some of) the same rows of the underlying table is executed.

Well, SQL-92 allows you to protect yourself against just this sort of problem. You can declare a cursor to be *insensitive,* meaning that it will not see the effects of other statements *in the same transaction* while it's open. Of course, if you close the cursor and then reopen it, you will see the effects of those other statements. Let's look at this in a little more detail.

Using the keyword INSENSITIVE declares the cursor to be an insensitive cursor as described above. (The absence of INSENSITIVE doesn't mean that cursor is *sensitive;* there are really three possible types of cursors: sensitive, insensitive, and indeterminant. However, SQL-92 defines only insensitive and indeterminant cursors. A future version of the SQL standard may define sensitive cursors, too.)

An insensitive cursor is one that is implemented in a way that guarantees that the rows seen by the cursor will not be affected by other statements executed as part of the same transaction. Consider this second example.

```
DECLARE std_dev CURSOR FOR
   SELECT current_rental_price FROM movie_titles
   WHERE current_sales_price < 39.95;
```

```
OPEN std_dev;
```

loop:

```
FETCH std_dev INTO :price;
```

if no-data return, then go to finished;

accumulate information required for standard deviation computation;

```
DELETE FROM movie_titles WHERE
   current_sales_price < 39.95;
```

go to loop;

finished:

```
CLOSE std_dev;
```

compute the standard deviation;

After the DELETE statement (which you will notice deletes exactly the same set of rows that the cursor identified!), what will happen on the next FETCH? Now, you can well argue that any application that does anything this dumb gets whatever happens, but there are more complex examples that you may find compelling. Let's go ahead and answer the question anyway.

In an indeterminant cursor (like that which SQL-89 provided), the answer to the question is "I don't know." The DBMS was free to do whatever was convenient. In some implementations, the cursor would happily keep on retrieving all the rows it had identified, while in others, it would immediately see the no-data situation. In still others, the result would depend on many other factors, such as the presence of indices or the READ ONLY option, or even on the timing between the DELETE WHERE and the next FETCH!

However, in an INSENSITIVE cursor (new to SQL-92), the cursor will not be affected by the DELETE . . . WHERE statement. As we've already said, if you close the cursor and then reopen it, the results of the DELETE . . . WHERE will be seen. By the way, in SQL-92, you cannot specify FOR UPDATE and INSENSITIVE on the same cursor; INSENSITIVE forces the cursor to be read-only.

To get the full meaning of INSENSITIVE, it may help to imagine that opening an INSENSITIVE cursor causes the DBMS to immediately locate every row that the cursor identifies, copy them into some temporary table, and then make the cursor operate on the rows of that temporary table. (In fact, we suspect that many implementations will do exactly this.)

SQL-92 provides one more feature to help you avoid problems that might be caused by the interaction between an open cursor and other statements in the same transaction in your application. If you attempt to delete or update a row of an indeterminant cursor (see section 12.5.1, Positioned Delete and Update Statements) that has been updated or deleted by a statement other than a statement associated with the same cursor (a searched statement or a statement associated with a different cursor), then you'll get a warning to notify you of the conflict. (Similarly, if you execute a searched update or delete statement that updates or deletes a row of an open cursor, you'll get the same warning.)

12.2.5 Scrollable Cursors

There are occasional applications where you are not able to process your cursor's rows in the default fashion, that is, fetching the next row, processing it, and then repeating. Instead, you may need to back up and revisit a row you've already processed or skipped over. You may need to start at the end of the cursor and work backward for some reason. You may need to skip some rows or go directly to a specific row. SQL-92 permits you to do this with *scrollable* cursors.

If you specify SCROLL, you can use additional syntax on your FETCH statements that allow you to do more than fetch the next row. In SQL-89, the only move that you could make when retrieving rows through a cursor was to retrieve the very next row. Even if you knew that the next row wasn't "interesting," but the one after it was, you still had to retrieve the "uninteresting" row in order to get to the interesting one. However, with SQL-92's SCROLL cursors, you can skip around as you see fit. We'll talk more about that along with the FETCH statement below. In SQL-92, you cannot specify SCROLL and FOR UPDATE on the same cursor; SCROLL forces the cursor to be read-only.

You might object to INSENSITIVE and SCROLL cursors being read-only (we do), because there are applications in which you'd like to have those characteristics and still be able to update the cursor. However, there are many difficult DBMS implementation issues that have to be resolved to give you those combinations. Perhaps a future version of the SQL standard will provide them.

12.3 OPEN and CLOSE

As we've hinted already in our examples, the first thing that you have to do to use a cursor (after declaring it, of course!) is to open it. The OPEN statement is quite straightforward. It is an executable statement and its format is:

```
OPEN cursor-name;
```

If the cursor is already open, then you'll (obviously) get an error.

Note that the OPEN statement doesn't have any parameters or host variables associated with it. All data that must be supplied by the host program is specified in the cursor declaration, but it is actually obtained when the OPEN is executed. The cursor declaration:

```
DECLARE cursor2 CURSOR FOR
  SELECT current_rental_price
    FROM movie_titles
    WHERE current_sales_price > :minprice;
```

tells the DBMS that you want to handle only those movies whose price is greater than some threshold that you will specify in a host variable or parameter. However, recall that the cursor declaration is a declaration that is processed by the compiler, not an executable statement. Therefore, when you execute:

```
OPEN cursor2;
```

the DBMS has to obtain the value from the host variable or parameter :MINPRICE at that time and then evaluate the cursor to see what rows belong to it. If your cursor declaration has any special values like CURRENT_USER or CURRENT_TIME, they will be evaluated during the OPEN execution, too.

When you're finished with your cursors, you'll want to close them. This may free up system resources (which always seem to be scarce!) and is just generally good practice; it might protect you against an accidental operation on the cursor that could inadvertently ruin your data.

The CLOSE statement merely closes the cursor. Of course, if the cursor isn't open, then you'll get an error. (A quick note on terminology: Even though we said that you'd get an error, we note that you might simply CLOSE all your cursors at the end of your work without regard to whether or not you'd opened them. In that case, the "error" wouldn't indicate a program bug at all, but would simply be an informational signal. That's why SQL-92 calls these notification *exception conditions* instead of *errors*.) You cannot use the cursor again until you reopen it, at which time new values for host variables or parameters and for special values will be derived. For example:

```
CLOSE cursor2;
```

12.4 FETCH

The FETCH statement allows your application to retrieve data into your program space, one row at a time. The syntax of FETCH is shown below and in Diagram RR38.

```
FETCH [ [ orientation ] FROM ] cursor-name INTO targets
```

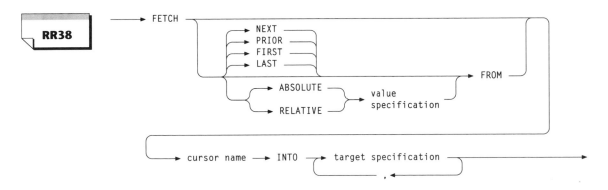

The cursor-name is obvious; it is the name of an open cursor that was declared in the same module or compilation unit that contains the FETCH statement. targets is also pretty obvious: it is a comma-separated list of host variables or parameters that will associate the data with the row that the FETCH retrieves. The number of entries in the list must correspond exactly to the number of columns in the cursor. Of course, you can have data parameters and indicator parameters (or data host variables and indicator host variables) for each column.

The orientation is associated with SCROLL cursors. The "normal" orientation is NEXT, which means "retrieve the next row associated with the cursor." This is the default behavior if you don't specify an orientation. PRIOR means "retrieve the previous row associated with the cursor." If you've done several NEXTs, then a PRIOR will retrieve a row that you've previously seen. FIRST means "retrieve the first row associated with the cursor" and LAST means . . . (anybody? Speak up!) "retrieve the last row associated with the cursor." Finally, you can specify ABSOLUTE value or RELATIVE value (*value* is a literal or a host variable or parameter; it must be exact numeric with scale 0). ABSOLUTE says "retrieve the row in the position specified by *value*" and RELATIVE means "skip forward (or backward) the number of rows specified by *value*." FETCH RELATIVE 0 means "retrieve the row I just retrieved." If the row identified by RELATIVE or ABSOLUTE doesn't exist (that is, the value would require retrieving a row before the first row or after the last row in the cursor), you'll get the no-data condition and the cursor will be positioned before the first row or after the last row of the cursor.

Actually, some applications will benefit from a clever little trick put into the SQL standard. If you use the orientation ABSOLUTE 1, you will of course get the first row of the cursor; however, if you specify ABSOLUTE -1, you'll get the last row! In fact, if you have *n* rows in a cursor and specify ABSOLUTE -*n*, you'll get the first row. That makes ABSOLUTE orientation similar to RELATIVE orientation. Of course, if you only have, say, 15 rows in your cursor and you specify ABSOLUTE 18 or ABSOLUTE -29, you can expect to get an error. (Actually, you'll get the no-data condition.) The same is true if you specify ABSOLUTE 0 or if you specify NEXT or PRIOR and you're at the end or the beginning of the cursor.

By the way, SCROLL cursors are one way that you can see the effects of specifying, or not specifying, INSENSITIVE on your cursor declarations. If you FETCH some row, then FETCH the NEXT row, and then FETCH the PRIOR row of a cursor that specified INSENSITIVE, you'd get the same row that you first FETCHed. However, if the cursor didn't specify INSENSITIVE and some DELETE statement (other than WHERE CURRENT OF that cursor) had deleted the row, it would depend on the details (and even the timing!) of your implementation.

12.5 Cursor Positioning

This is a good time to talk about the position of a cursor. Open cursors always have a position. That position can be before some row of the table, on some row of the table, or after the last row of the table. These are the only possibilities. If the cursor is before some row, then a FETCH NEXT will get that row and a FETCH PRIOR will get the row before that row (and FETCH RELATIVE 0 will get a no-data condition). If the cursor is on some row, then a FETCH NEXT will get the row that follows, a FETCH PRIOR will get the row preceding it, and a FETCH RELATIVE 0 will get the same row again. If the cursor is positioned after the last row, then FETCH NEXT will get the no-data condition and FETCH PRIOR will get the last row of the table. By the way, FETCH NEXT and FETCH RELATIVE 1 have the same effect; the same is true for FETCH PRIOR and FETCH RELATIVE -1.

12.5.1 Positioned DELETE and UPDATE Statements

The positioned DELETE statement deletes the current row of the cursor. Its format is:

```
DELETE FROM table-name WHERE CURRENT OF cursor-name
```

You will recall from Chapter 9 that query expressions that identify more than one table are never updatable (this goes for cursors as well as for views). Therefore, there's only one table-name from which the rows of this cursor are derived or this statement would be invalid (since the cursor would be read-only). If the cursor is on some row of the table, that row is deleted. If the cursor is not on some row of the table, you'll get an error. Of course, the cursor has to be declared in the same module or compilation unit that contains the positioned DELETE statement.

The positioned UPDATE statement updates the current row of the cursor. Its format is:

```
UPDATE table-name SET set-list
  WHERE CURRENT OF cursor-name
```

Like the positioned DELETE, this statement requires that the cursor have an updatable query expression, which means that there's only one table. The set-list is a comma-separated list of:

```
column-name = source
```

and source is either a value expression, the keyword NULL, or the keyword DEFAULT. Each column identified in the set-list must be part of the FOR UPDATE column-list (implicit or explicit) or the statement is invalid. If the cursor has an ORDER BY, you cannot update any column used in the ordering. You cannot update the same column more than once in a single positioned UPDATE statement. If the cursor is not positioned on a row, you'll get an error. If any error is raised during the update, the row isn't updated and the cursor remains positioned on that row.

12.6 Chapter Summary

Remember that cursors are your primary tool in using SQL data in a row-at-a-time manner. You can retrieve, delete, insert, and update into tables. There are some restrictions having to do with the updatability of cursors, but those should have little effect on your applications as long as you aware of them.

Now that we've discussed the basic subjects of program structure and data positioning in this chapter (and the previous one), let's turn our attention to the SQL facilities through which you can protect your information. In the next chapter, we'll discuss privileges and security and how these apply to users.

CHAPTER 13

. . . .

Privileges, Users, and Security

13.1 Introduction

The very nature of databases—consolidating data into a logically cohesive group that many different applications and users can access—gives rise to the potential for security problems. Although the physical capability may exist, for example, for all end users throughout an organization to access all forms of organizational data through the DBMS, there are likely many cases where certain users should not have one or more types of access privileges. For example:

- Only certain employees should be able to change movie and CD prices.
- Customers using the customer assistance subsystem should never have access to our business functions (sales, payroll, *etc.*).
- Only managerial personnel should be able to access employee information, and only corporate management should be able to update that information.
- Customers may browse movie titles and corresponding sales and rental prices, but should not be able to see our purchase prices.

SQL provides you with the capability to *protect,* or control access to, various types of database objects, including:

- Tables
- Columns
- Views
- Domains
- Character sets
- Collations
- Translations

The first three types of objects had security attributes in SQL-89, while domains, character sets, collations, and translations have security properties new to SQL-92.

Security properties have evolved greatly since SQL-86. There are six kinds of protection in SQL-92: *seeing, creating, modifying, deleting* (these correspond, respectively, to SELECT, INSERT, UPDATE, and DELETE operations), *referencing* (this was new to SQL-89, and corresponds to referential integrity REFERENCES use as well as to other constraints), and *using* (this is new to SQL-92, and corresponds to using domains, character sets, collations, and translations). In SQL-86, you could protect tables against seeing rows, creating new rows, modifying rows, and deleting rows; in addition, you could protect against modifying columns of a row. In SQL-89, you could also protect against referencing columns of a table in a FOREIGN KEY referential integrity constraint. In SQL-92, you can protect against inserting data into individual columns; you can also protect against using domains, character sets, collations, and translations.

The general philosophy in SQL is to hide information about schema objects from users who don't have any privileges to use those objects. For example, if there were a table named EMPS_TO_BE_FIRED, knowledge of its existence would probably upset current employees. Therefore, you want the same error to be returned from SELECT * FROM EMPOLYEES (if that table doesn't exist) as from SELECT * FROM EMPS_TO_BE_FIRED when you don't have any privileges on EMPS_TO_BE_FIRED. If you returned "No such table" from one and "No privileges on table" from the other, you will have admitted that such a table exists, which raises a security issue. Consequently, SQL-92 says, "Either no such table or no privilege on table" (or words to that effect).

In Chapter 5, we introduced the idea of users and authorization identifiers. Recall that the authIDs are a sort of surrogate for the users: it's the only way that a user is known to an SQL database system. Privileges are granted to users in the form of authIDs. Privileges, once granted, could never be revoked in SQL-89; in SQL-92, they can be revoked. There's also the concept of PUBLIC, which is a sort of pseudo-authID that identifies every authID that is now known to the DBMS or ever will become known to the DBMS. You can grant privileges to PUBLIC just as to an individual user. In our earlier example, if you wanted to allow everyone interested in accessing a terminal in your video store to browse the list of movies in stock, you would probably grant the seeing privilege to PUBLIC on the appropriate table or tables.

In the SQL model, the creator of an object is always the owner of that object. The owner has every possible privilege on the object with one exception that we'll discuss later in this chapter. (Briefly, the owner of a view has privileges that are limited by the privileges he/she has on the table(s) that underlie the view.) The owner of an object can grant some (or all) privileges on that object to other users. If the owner wishes to relinquish a certain level of control, he can grant the privilege in a way that permits his grantee to grant the privilege to still other users, either with or without the ability for *them* to pass the privilege on. The ability to pass a privilege onto others is called the *with grant option,* which we will discuss fully later in this chapter.

You may be wondering about privileges with respect to the DDL operations we discussed in Chapter 4 (CREATE, ALTER, and DROP). The rules in SQL-92 with respect to these are as follows:

1. You can perform any DDL operations in a schema that *you own*.
2. You cannot perform any DDL operations in a schema that you don't own.
3. No one else can perform any DDL operations in any schema that you own (just clarifying the point directly above).
4. And finally, you *cannot* override these rules.

Most SQL products do, however, provide some sort of facility by which you can override these restrictions, by giving others permission to perform DDL operations within schemas you own; but the capabilities and syntax among these products vary widely. For purposes of the standard, however, the rules stated above apply.

13.2 GRANT

In order to give a privilege on some object that you own (or for which you have a privilege) to some other authID, you use the GRANT statement. The format of the GRANT statement is:

```
GRANT privilege-list
  ON object
  TO user-list [ WITH GRANT OPTION ]
```

The SQL-92 privilege-list is defined as:

```
  privilege [ , privilege ]...
| ALL PRIVILEGES
```

where privilege is:

```
  SELECT
| DELETE
| INSERT [ ( column-name [ , column-name ]... ) ]
| UPDATE [ ( column-name [ , column-name ]... ) ]
| REFERENCES [ ( column-name [ , column-name ]... ) ]
| USAGE
```

and object is defined as:

```
  [ TABLE ] table-name
| DOMAIN domain-name
| CHARACTER SET character-set-name
| COLLATION collation-name
| TRANSLATION translation-name
```

and user-list is:

```
    authID [ , authID ]...
  | PUBLIC
```

Diagram RR39 illustrates the GRANT statement in railroad diagram form.

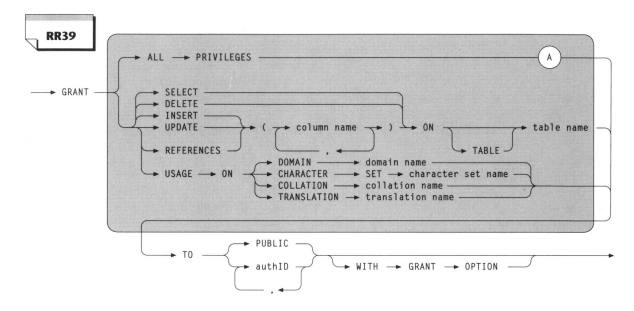

Several rules apply to the usage of the privileges. You can only use INSERT, UPDATE, SELECT, DELETE, and REFERENCES if the object is a table (if TABLE is not specified, then a table-name is assumed). Correspondingly, you can only use USAGE if the object is a domain, character set, collation, or translation. If you list more than one privilege, all of the privileges that you specify are granted to the user or users—but *only* if you have the privilege. If you don't actually have one or more of the privileges specified, you'll get an error on the GRANT statement.

In a single GRANT statement, you can only grant privileges on a single object, but (if the object is a table) you can grant different privileges on the same or different columns of the table. For INSERT, UPDATE, and REFERENCES, the statement will grant the privilege to every column in the table if you don't specify a column-name.

If you don't specify WITH GRANT OPTION, then the privilege cannot be passed on to other users by the user(s) to whom you are granting the privilege. If you do use the optional WITH GRANT OPTION, you have given permission for the user(s) to whom you are granting the privilege to pass it on to other users.

There's also something unique about granting privileges in SQL at the table level (as opposed to the column level). Granting a privilege (INSERT, UPDATE, or REFERENCES) on the table not only means "grant it on every column currently defined in the table," but it also means "grant it on every column added to the table in the future." This way, DDL modifications in the future that may add columns to a table definition don't require any overt action on your part to maintain your defined security model.

Let's take a look at some examples of the various SQL-92 privileges.

13.2.1 Basic Viewing Privileges

To GRANT viewing privileges for a table to a selected user or group of users, you would code:

```
GRANT SELECT
  ON employees
  TO STORE_MGR;
```

This GRANT statement will grant the SELECT privilege on the EMPLOYEES table to the user who has the authID STORE_MGR.

13.2.2 Deletion Privileges with Further GRANT Permission

To GRANT deletion privileges on another table to another user or user group, you could issue:

```
GRANT DELETE
  ON transactions
  TO AUDIT_MGR
  WITH GRANT OPTION;
```

This statement will allow the user AUDIT_MGR to delete rows from the TRANSACTIONS table; it will also allow that user to grant the same privilege to other users (by virtue of WITH GRANT OPTION).

13.2.3 Update Privileges on a Specific Column

```
GRANT UPDATE ( current_rental_price )
  ON movie_titles
  TO STORE_MGR;
```

The above allows STORE_MGR to update the CURRENT_PRICE column of the MOVIES table but no other columns within that table.

13.2.4 Insertion Privileges

```
GRANT INSERT
  ON movie_titles
  TO BUYER;
```

This statement gives BUYER the ability to insert new rows into the MOVIES table and to specify values for every column of that table. If the statement had been written as:

```
GRANT INSERT ( title, current_rental_price )
    ON movie_titles
    TO ASST_MGR;
```

then the user known as ASST_MGR would be allowed to insert new rows into the MOVIE_TITLES table but would be permitted only to specify a value for the TITLE and CURRENT_RENTAL_PRICE columns; all other columns would be set to their default values (if they have one) or to null (if they have no default and are nullable).

13.2.5 PUBLIC Access and Privileges on VIEWS

Suppose you issue the following statement:

```
GRANT SELECT
    ON movie_titles
    TO PUBLIC;
```

This statement will permit *anyone* to look at the MOVIES table, including customers using in-store Help/Browse terminals. However, the MOVIE_TITLES table probably has sensitive information that you don't want the public to see. Therefore, you'd normally define a view (called, say MOVIE_INFORMATION) that selects the relevant information (perhaps the title, rating, current rental and sale prices, and a line of summary), then grant the SELECT privilege on that view rather than on the base table, as follows:

```
GRANT SELECT
    ON movie_information
    TO PUBLIC;
```

13.2.6 REFERENCES

Remember that our MOVIES_STARS table contains the names of movies as well as other price and accounting-related information. Of course, we want the movies mentioned in that table to be coordinated with data from the MOVIE_TITLES table, too, so we defined a FOREIGN KEY on the MOVIE_TITLE column (of MOVIES_STARS) to point to the MOVIE_TITLES table (see Chapter 10 for a review of FOREIGN KEYS). To control access by the definers of tables that have FOREIGN KEYs to your table, you will want to allow only authorized users that privilege:

```
GRANT REFERENCES (title)
    ON movie_titles
    TO REVIEWER;
```

This statement will permit REVIEWER to define another table (or tables) that have FOREIGN KEY references to the MOVIES table.

Let's look at a slightly different example. Suppose your distributor provides you with advanced information about movies coming out on video over the next few months, but only on the condition that you not release the information to anyone. You honor that agreement by storing all the information about those movies in another table named UPCOMING_MOVIES and granting no privileges to anyone. You certainly wouldn't want one of your clerks, or customers, writing a table like this:

```
CREATE TABLE what_movies (
  title CHARACTER (30) REFERENCES upcoming_movies
);
```

All that clerk would then have to do have to do is INSERT a bunch of rows into his table and wait to see which ones succeeded and which ones failed. That way, he or she would have gotten the title information just as surely as if he'd had SELECT privilege on the UPCOMING_MOVIES table. However, if a special privilege is required to define the REFERENCES (foreign key) attribute, then your clerk would be unable to ferret out that particular information.

(Another reason for requiring some privileges for the definition of a FOREIGN KEY on your table is that the existence of that reference can prevent you from making changes to your own table, especially if the FOREIGN KEY were defined with NO ACTION.)

13.2.7 Constraints and Privileges

Similarly, you have to have SELECT privilege to define a constraint that is based on information stored in a table. Suppose you defined a table using this CREATE TABLE statement:

```
CREATE TABLE dummy (
  dummy_col INTEGER,
    CHECK ((SELECT salary FROM employees
          WHERE title = 'President')
            BETWEEN :x AND :y)
  )
```

By repeatedly executing this statement with different values for the host variables (or parameters) :x and :y, someone could determine the salary of the company's president! A similar invasive query could determine salaries of co-workers, a supervisor, or others. To prevent this type of situation, SQL-92 requires that you have the SELECT privilege on the EMPLOYEES table (and, therefore, on the SALARY column of that table) in order to define such a constraint.

13.2.8 USAGE

For other reasons, a user has to have the USAGE privilege to use a domain to define a column. There aren't any security implications in using domains, but rather there are implications related to DROPping the domain. Remember (from Chapter 4) that you could either say:

```
DROP DOMAIN domain-name CASCADE
```

or

```
DROP DOMAIN domain-name RESTRICT
```

The RESTRICT option, as you recall, means "if there are any columns that are based on this domain, give me an error and do not actually drop the domain." Unlike other objects, however, the CASCADE option on DROP DOMAIN means that the attributes of the domain (data type, default value, constraints, and collation) are transferred to the column directly. If the column already had a default value, however, the column default supersedes the domain's default value and is thus not transferred to the column.

This process will not drop columns or destroy data, but it could cause views to be dropped if the view definition contains a CAST that references the domain being dropped; similarly a constraint or assertion with such a CAST would be dropped. By selectively granting USAGE privilege on your domains, you can control who is allowed to use (or even see) them and therefore limit the inconvenience (to you and to others) that dropping your domain might cause. In organizations (unlike our simple video and music chain) where you have hundreds of applications developers using your SQL-92 environment and corresponding DBMS products, such control can be invaluable during the software development and maintenance phases.

The situation is exactly the same for character sets, collations, and translations. Only those users to whom you grant USAGE privilege on those objects can see them and use them in their data definitions or in their SQL programs.

13.2.9 ALL PRIVILEGES

The special syntax ALL PRIVILEGES is used as a sort of shorthand. It translates to:

- A list of privileges that includes
- Every privilege on the specified object
- On which the user executing the GRANT has a grantable privilege.

For example, suppose you have SELECT privilege on MOVIE_TITLES WITH GRANT OPTION and DELETE privilege on MOVIE_TITLES, but without GRANT OPTION. If you execute the statement:

```
GRANT ALL PRIVILEGES
    ON movie_titles TO USER2
```

then USER2 will end up with SELECT privilege on MOVIE_TITLES but will not get the DELETE privilege.

13.3 Other Rules

If you grant a privilege to a user and then, inadvertently or on purpose, grant the identical privilege to the same user, you have defined what we call a *redundant duplicate privilege*. There is no additional effect because the redundant grant is ignored. That way, you don't have to worry about revoking several times just in case you accidentally granted several times. If you grant the privilege once with GRANT OPTION and once without (in either order but without an intervening REVOKE), the actual privilege that the user has includes the GRANT OPTION.

If you execute a GRANT statement with one or more privileges and you don't have any of those privileges (or you don't have any of them WITH GRANT OPTION), then you'll get an error. If you try to grant more than one privilege and you have at least one of them WITH GRANT OPTION but you don't have some of them (or you don't have them WITH GRANT OPTION), you'll get a warning and the privileges that you do have WITH GRANT OPTION are granted.

When you create a view (via the CREATE VIEW statement), special rules take care of the privileges you get on that view. For most schema objects (like tables or domains), when you create the object, you *automatically* get every possible privilege on that object, and you get the privileges WITH GRANT OPTION. Views, however, are different. Because you may have created your view to correspond to rows in someone else's base tables (or even other views), the privileges you get on the view have to be based on the privileges that you have on those base tables or views.

For example, you will get the SELECT privilege on your view, but it will be WITH GRANT OPTION *only* if you have the SELECT privilege WITH GRANT OPTION on *each and every* table (base tables and views) that underlies the view. If you don't have the SELECT privilege on every underlying table, you can't even create the view. Similarly, you can get the INSERT, UPDATE, DELETE, and REFERENCES privileges on the view (and the columns of the view) only if you have those privileges on the underlying tables (and the corresponding underlying columns). Again, those privileges will be given to you WITH GRANT OPTION only if you hold them WITH GRANT OPTION on the underlying tables and columns.

Now, we have to consider what happens if you have created some view *V* that depends on some table *T* on which you have only some privileges but on which you are subsequently granted additional privileges. SQL-92 carefully defines how additional privileges are granted to you on your view *V* to properly reflect your augmented privileges on the underlying table *T*. That is, the privileges are adjusted so that they are just as they would have been if you had created your view after you were granted the additional privileges (see Figure 13-1).

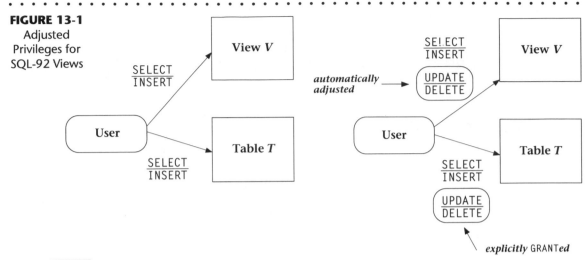

FIGURE 13-1
Adjusted
Privileges for
SQL-92 Views

13.4 Revoking Privileges

After granting privileges, you sometimes have to consider revoking those privileges. For example, some user may no longer need to access data in one of your tables, so you will wish to withdraw the privilege that user had to access that table. Or perhaps some user leaves the company and must not be allowed any access at all. The REVOKE statement is used to take privileges away from users. The format of the REVOKE statement is very similar to the GRANT statement, which is shown below and in Diagram RR40.[1]

```
REVOKE [ GRANT OPTION FOR ] privilege-list
  ON object
  FROM user-list [ RESTRICT | CASCADE ]
```

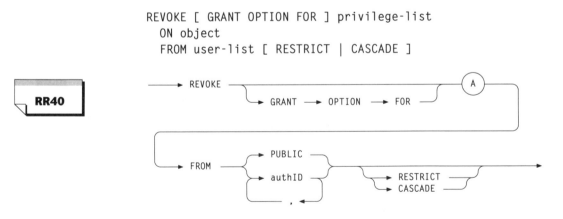

RR40

The major difference is the additional RESTRICT or CASCADE keyword. If you use RESTRICT, the system will check to see if the privilege that you granted was passed on to other users (obviously, this is possible only if you granted the privilege

---

1 The (A) in Diagram RR40 references Diagram RR39 in section 13.2.

WITH GRANT OPTION). If so, you will get an error message and the privilege will not be revoked; if not, the privilege will be revoked. If you use CASCADE, the privilege will be revoked, as will any *dependent* privileges that were granted as a result of your grant. A dependent privilege is one that could not exist if the privilege that you're trying to revoke was never granted, which is the state of events you are trying to achieve as a result of your REVOKE statement.

The other significant difference is the optional GRANT OPTION FOR clause. If you specify that clause, the actual privilege itself is not revoked but the GRANT OPTION is revoked. Of course, if the GRANT OPTION is taken away, you want the grant situation to be set to a state as though the GRANT OPTION never existed. Therefore, if you specify both GRANT OPTION FOR and CASCADE, then all grants that depend on that GRANT OPTION are revoked implicitly. If you specify GRANT OPTION FOR and RESTRICT and there are dependent privileges, you'll get an error.

If none of the privileges that you are trying to revoke actually exists, you'll get an error; if some of them exist, but not all of them, then you'll get a warning instead. There may be situations in which you revoke a privilege from a user only to find out later that the privilege is still held by that user. This can happen when something like the following has been done:

```
(you)    GRANT SELECT ON movie_titles TO USER1 WITH GRANT OPTION;
(USER1)  GRANT SELECT ON movie_titles TO USER2;
(you)    GRANT SELECT ON movie_titles TO USER2;
```

At this point, USER2 has the SELECT privilege from two sources, you and USER1. If you then execute:

```
REVOKE SELECT
  ON movie_titles FROM USER2;
```

you'll find that USER2 still is able to SELECT data from MOVIE_TITLES. Why? Simply because USER1 also granted the privilege. On the other hand, if you had executed:

```
REVOKE SELECT
  ON movie_titles
  FROM USER1 CASCADE;
```

then both USER1 and USER2 would lose their SELECT privilege on MOVIE_TITLES. This example shows that privileges can get rather complicated. In fact, graph theory (which, alas, has nothing to do with computer graphics) is used in the SQL-92 standard to describe the effects of GRANT and REVOKE statements.

Recall that we said earlier that granting a privilege on a table implicitly grants the same privilege on every column of the table, as well as on every column that would ever be added to the table in the future. An interesting side effect of this is that you can grant some privilege, say UPDATE, on a table (thereby granting that privilege on every column of the table) and then revoke that privilege from one or more columns of the table—without inhibiting the granting of that privilege to any new columns later added to the table!

However, this analogy does not apply to granting privileges to PUBLIC. While the failure to specify a column-list in a GRANT (or REVOKE) statement is, in one way, the same as specifying a column-list that contains every column of the table (and, though it's clearly impossible without a better crystal ball than we have at home, every column ever to be added to the table), a grant to PUBLIC is *not* the same as granting individually to every user and every user that will ever be known to the system. The difference is that a sequence like:

```
GRANT SELECT
  ON movie_titles
  TO PUBLIC;

REVOKE SELECT
  ON movie_titles
  FROM USER1;
```

will get an error (unless, of course, you have also explicitly granted SELECT on MOVIE_TITLES to USER1 in another statement). That's because USER1 does not have the SELECT privilege—PUBLIC does. USER1 is a member of PUBLIC, of course, and therefore can issue SELECT statements that select from the MOVIE_TITLES table, but USER1 does not have the privilege himself or herself, and you cannot therefore take it away without taking it away from PUBLIC.

13.5 Additional Details of REVOKE

At first glance, the REVOKE statement really seems pretty straightforward. After all, it is only supposed to eliminate privileges that already exist and leave the privilege structure of the database just as it would have been if the privileges had never been granted. Unfortunately, doing that is a bit more complicated than you might think. The complications are due largely, although not wholly, to the existence of WITH GRANT OPTION.

Let's have a look at an example to understand what goes on. Suppose that we have only two tables in our schema: MOVIE_TITLES and MOVIES_STARS. Both of these tables are in a schema named PRODUCTION, which is owned by the authID SCREEN_TUNES. By the very act of having created these two tables, we have created the many privileges shown in Table 13-1.

Now, to allow our employees the ability to execute SQL statements necessary to do their jobs, we give each of them the privileges required. Let's assume that we (under the authID SCREEN_TUNES) have granted the following privileges:

TABLE 13-1

Grantor	Grantee	Privilege	With Grant Option?
(the system)	SCREEN_TUNES	SELECT ON movie_titles	Yes
(the system)	SCREEN_TUNES	INSERT ON movie_titles	Yes
(the system)	SCREEN_TUNES	INSERT ON movie_titles (title)	Yes
(the system)	SCREEN_TUNES	INSERT ON movie_titles (our_cost)	Yes
(the system)	SCREEN_TUNES	INSERT ON movie_titles (...)	Yes
(the system)	SCREEN_TUNES	INSERT ON movie_titles (current_rental_price)	Yes
(the system)	SCREEN_TUNES	UPDATE ON movie_titles	Yes
(the system)	SCREEN_TUNES	UPDATE ON movie_titles (title)	Yes
(the system)	SCREEN_TUNES	UPDATE ON movie_titles (our_cost)	Yes
(the system)	SCREEN_TUNES	UPDATE ON movie_titles (...)	Yes
(the system)	SCREEN_TUNES	UPDATE ON movie_titles (current_rental_price)	Yes
(the system)	SCREEN_TUNES	DELETE ON movie_titles	Yes
(the system)	SCREEN_TUNES	REFERENCES ON movie_titles	Yes
(the system)	SCREEN_TUNES	REFERENCES ON movie_titles (title)	Yes
(the system)	SCREEN_TUNES	REFERENCES ON movie_titles (our_cost)	Yes
(the system)	SCREEN_TUNES	REFERENCES ON movie_titles (...)	Yes
(the system)	SCREEN_TUNES	REFERENCES ON movie_titles (current_rental_price)	Yes
(the system)	SCREEN_TUNES	SELECT ON movies_stars	Yes
(the system)	SCREEN_TUNES	INSERT ON movies_stars	Yes
(the system)	SCREEN_TUNES	INSERT ON movies_stars (movie_title)	Yes
(the system)	SCREEN_TUNES	INSERT ON movies_stars (actor_first_name)	Yes
(the system)	SCREEN_TUNES	INSERT ON movies_stars (actor_last_name)	Yes
(the system)	SCREEN_TUNES	UPDATE ON movies_stars	Yes
(the system)	SCREEN_TUNES	UPDATE ON movies_stars (movie_title)	Yes
(the system)	SCREEN_TUNES	UPDATE ON movies_stars (actor_first_name)	Yes
(the system)	SCREEN_TUNES	UPDATE ON movies_stars (actor_last_name)	Yes
(the system)	SCREEN_TUNES	DELETE ON movies_stars	Yes
(the system)	SCREEN_TUNES	REFERENCES ON movies_stars	Yes
(the system)	SCREEN_TUNES	REFERENCES ON movies_stars (movie_title)	Yes
(the system)	SCREEN_TUNES	REFERENCES ON movies_stars (actor_first_name)	Yes
(the system)	SCREEN_TUNES	REFERENCES ON movies_stars (actor_last_name)	Yes

```
GRANT SELECT ON movie_titles TO manager WITH GRANT OPTION ;
GRANT SELECT ON movies_stars TO manager WITH GRANT OPTION ;
GRANT UPDATE ON movie_titles TO manager ;
GRANT UPDATE ON movies_stars TO manager ;
GRANT UPDATE (current_rental_price) ON movie_titles
  TO asst_manager ;
GRANT DELETE ON movie_titles to manager ;
GRANT DELETE ON movies_stars to manager ;
```

Table 13-2 illustrates what the privilege list looks like after these GRANTs.

TABLE 13-2

Grantor	Grantee	Privilege	With Grant Option?
(the system)	SCREEN_TUNES	SELECT ON movie_titles	Yes
(the system)	SCREEN_TUNES	INSERT ON movie_titles	Yes
(the system)	SCREEN_TUNES	INSERT ON movie_titles (title)	Yes
(the system)	SCREEN_TUNES	INSERT ON movie_titles (our_cost)	Yes
(the system)	SCREEN_TUNES	INSERT ON movie_titles (...)	Yes
(the system)	SCREEN_TUNES	INSERT ON movie_titles (current_rental_price)	Yes
(the system)	SCREEN_TUNES	UPDATE ON movie_titles	Yes
(the system)	SCREEN_TUNES	UPDATE ON movie_titles (title)	Yes
(the system)	SCREEN_TUNES	UPDATE ON movie_titles (our_cost)	Yes
(the system)	SCREEN_TUNES	UPDATE ON movie_titles (...)	Yes
(the system)	SCREEN_TUNES	UPDATE ON movie_titles (current_rental_price)	Yes
(the system)	SCREEN_TUNES	DELETE ON movie_titles	Yes
(the system)	SCREEN_TUNES	REFERENCES ON movie_titles	Yes
(the system)	SCREEN_TUNES	REFERENCES ON movie_titles (title)	Yes
(the system)	SCREEN_TUNES	REFERENCES ON movie_titles (our_cost)	Yes
(the system)	SCREEN_TUNES	REFERENCES ON movie_titles (...)	Yes
(the system)	SCREEN_TUNES	REFERENCES ON movie_titles (current_rental_price)	Yes
(the system)	SCREEN_TUNES	SELECT ON movies_stars	Yes
(the system)	SCREEN_TUNES	INSERT ON movies_stars	Yes
(the system)	SCREEN_TUNES	INSERT ON movies_stars (movie_title)	Yes
(the system)	SCREEN_TUNES	INSERT ON movies_stars (actor_first_name)	Yes
(the system)	SCREEN_TUNES	INSERT ON movies_stars (actor_last_name)	Yes
(the system)	SCREEN_TUNES	UPDATE ON movies_stars	Yes
(the system)	SCREEN_TUNES	UPDATE ON movies_stars (movie_title)	Yes
(the system)	SCREEN_TUNES	UPDATE ON movies_stars (actor_first_name)	Yes
(the system)	SCREEN_TUNES	UPDATE ON movies_stars (actor_last_name)	Yes
(the system)	SCREEN_TUNES	DELETE ON movies_stars	Yes
(the system)	SCREEN_TUNES	REFERENCES ON movies_stars	Yes
(the system)	SCREEN_TUNES	REFERENCES ON movies_stars (movie_title)	Yes
(the system)	SCREEN_TUNES	REFERENCES ON movies_stars (actor_first_name)	Yes
(the system)	SCREEN_TUNES	REFERENCES ON movies_stars (actor_last_name)	Yes
SCREEN_TUNES	manager	SELECT ON movie_titles	Yes
SCREEN_TUNES	manager	SELECT ON movies_stars	Yes
SCREEN_TUNES	manager	UPDATE ON movie_titles	No
SCREEN_TUNES	manager	UPDATE ON movie_titles (title)	No
SCREEN_TUNES	manager	UPDATE ON movie_titles (our_cost)	No
SCREEN_TUNES	manager	UPDATE ON movie_titles (...)	No
SCREEN_TUNES	manager	UPDATE ON movie_titles (current_rental_price)	No
SCREEN_TUNES	manager	UPDATE ON movies_stars	No
SCREEN_TUNES	manager	UPDATE ON movies_stars (movie_title)	No
SCREEN_TUNES	manager	UPDATE ON movies_stars (actor_first_name)	No
SCREEN_TUNES	manager	UPDATE ON movies_stars (actor_last_name)	No
SCREEN_TUNES	asst_manager	UPDATE ON movie_titles (current_rental_price)	No
SCREEN_TUNES	manager	DELETE ON movie_titles	No
SCREEN_TUNES	manager	DELETE ON movies_stars	No

About now, our store manager discovers that she'd like to allow customers to browse the MOVIE_TITLES table, but only to see the titles, the current rental price, and the current sales price. To do this, she creates a view in the MANAGER schema:

```
CREATE VIEW customer_movies AS
  SELECT title, current_rental_price, current_sales_price
    FROM movie_titles
```

and then grants a privilege that makes this view usable by the general public:

```
GRANT SELECT ON customer_movies TO PUBLIC ;
```

Let's further assume that our manager decides to pass on the ability to SELECT from the MOVIE_TITLES table to the assistant manager and to the sales clerks.

```
GRANT SELECT ON movie_titles TO asst_manager, sales_clerk ;
```

At this point, the privilege graph (remember, we warned you that this involved graph theory!) has expanded to look like Table 13-3.

You'll admit that this is a startlingly large number of privileges for such a small database environment (2 tables, 1 view, 3 users, plus PUBLIC). Anyway, the arrows that are drawn between some of the privileges indicate *dependencies* in the privilege graph. Many of the privileges don't connect to any others, so they form isolated nodes in the graph; others form chains of privileges, as you see.

Now, let's see what happens when we issue the statement, using the authID SCREEN_TUNES.

```
REVOKE SELECT ON movie_titles FROM manager ;
```

We first determine a set of *identified* privileges. These will be those SELECT privileges granted by SCREEN_TUNES to MANAGER on MOVIE_TITLES (see Table 13-4). If the privilege were INSERT, UPDATE, or REFERENCES, we would include any privileges on the columns of MOVIE_TITLES as well. Clearly, this process identifies only the privilege shown in Table 13-4.

Next, we identify all privileges that were allowed to be created as a result of the identified privilege (or privileges). This means that the identified privilege had to have been granted WITH GRANT OPTION. It also means that we're looking for privileges whose grantor is the same as the grantee of any privilege in our identified list; furthermore, the privileges for which we're looking will be on the same object (the MOVIE_TITLES table in this case; it could also be on some column of the table) and will be for the same action (SELECT, in this case). This set of rules locates the two rows shown in Table 13-5.

TABLE 13-3

Grantor	Grantee	Privilege	With Grant Option?
(the system)	SCREEN_TUNES	SELECT ON movie_titles	Yes
(the system)	SCREEN_TUNES	INSERT ON movie_titles	Yes
(the system)	SCREEN_TUNES	INSERT ON movie_titles (title)	Yes
(the system)	SCREEN_TUNES	INSERT ON movie_titles (our_cost)	Yes
(the system)	SCREEN_TUNES	INSERT ON movie_titles (…)	Yes
(the system)	SCREEN_TUNES	INSERT ON movie_titles (current_rental_price)	Yes
(the system)	SCREEN_TUNES	UPDATE ON movie_titles	Yes
(the system)	SCREEN_TUNES	UPDATE ON movie_titles (title)	Yes
(the system)	SCREEN_TUNES	UPDATE ON movie_titles (our_cost)	Yes
(the system)	SCREEN_TUNES	UPDATE ON movie_titles (…)	Yes
(the system)	SCREEN_TUNES	UPDATE ON movie_titles (current_rental_price)	Yes
(the system)	SCREEN_TUNES	DELETE ON movie_titles	Yes
(the system)	SCREEN_TUNES	REFERENCES ON movie_titles	Yes
(the system)	SCREEN_TUNES	REFERENCES ON movie_titles (title)	Yes
(the system)	SCREEN_TUNES	REFERENCES ON movie_titles (our_cost)	Yes
(the system)	SCREEN_TUNES	REFERENCES ON movie_titles (…)	Yes
(the system)	SCREEN_TUNES	REFERENCES ON movie_titles (current_rental_price)	Yes
(the system)	SCREEN_TUNES	SELECT ON movies_stars	Yes
(the system)	SCREEN_TUNES	INSERT ON movies_stars	Yes
(the system)	SCREEN_TUNES	INSERT ON movies_stars (movie_title)	Yes
(the system)	SCREEN_TUNES	INSERT ON movies_stars (actor_first_name)	Yes
(the system)	SCREEN_TUNES	INSERT ON movies_stars (actor_last_name)	Yes
(the system)	SCREEN_TUNES	UPDATE ON movies_stars	Yes
(the system)	SCREEN_TUNES	UPDATE ON movies_stars (movie_title)	Yes
(the system)	SCREEN_TUNES	UPDATE ON movies_stars (actor_first_name)	Yes
(the system)	SCREEN_TUNES	UPDATE ON movies_stars (actor_last_name)	Yes
(the system)	SCREEN_TUNES	DELETE ON movies_stars	Yes
(the system)	SCREEN_TUNES	REFERENCES ON movies_stars	Yes
(the system)	SCREEN_TUNES	REFERENCES ON movies_stars (movie_title)	Yes
(the system)	SCREEN_TUNES	REFERENCES ON movies_stars (actor_first_name)	Yes
(the system)	SCREEN_TUNES	REFERENCES ON movies_stars (actor_last_name)	Yes
SCREEN_TUNES	manager	SELECT ON movie_titles	Yes
SCREEN_TUNES	manager	SELECT ON movies_stars	Yes

Continued

SCREEN_TUNES	manager	SELECT ON movies_stars	Yes
SCREEN_TUNES	manager	UPDATE ON movie_titles	No
SCREEN_TUNES	manager	UPDATE ON movie_titles (title)	No
SCREEN_TUNES	manager	UPDATE ON movie_titles (out_cost)	No
SCREEN_TUNES	manager	UPDATE ON movie_titles (...)	No
SCREEN_TUNES	manager	UPDATE ON movie_titles (current_rental_price)	No
SCREEN_TUNES	manager	UPDATE ON movies_stars	No
SCREEN_TUNES	manager	UPDATE ON movies_stars (movie_title)	No
SCREEN_TUNES	manager	UPDATE ON movies_stars (actor_first_name)	No
SCREEN_TUNES	asst_manager	UPDATE ON movies_stars (actor_last_name)	No
SCREEN_TUNES	manager	UPDATE ON movie_titles (current_rental_price)	No
SCREEN_TUNES	manager	DELETE ON movie_titles	No
SCREEN_TUNES	manager	DELETE ON movies_stars	No
(the system)	manager	SELECT ON customer_movies	No
(the system)	manager	UPDATE ON customer_movies	No
(the system)	manager	UPDATE ON customer_movies (title)	No
(the system)	manager	UPDATE ON customer_movies (our_cost)	No
(the system)	manager	UPDATE ON customer_movies (...)	No
(the system)	manager	UPDATE ON customer_movies (current_rental_price)	No
manager	manager	DELETE ON customer_movies	No
manager	PUBLIC	SELECT ON customer_movies	No
manager	asst_manager	SELECT ON movie_titles	No
manager	sales_clerk	SELECT ON movie_titles	No

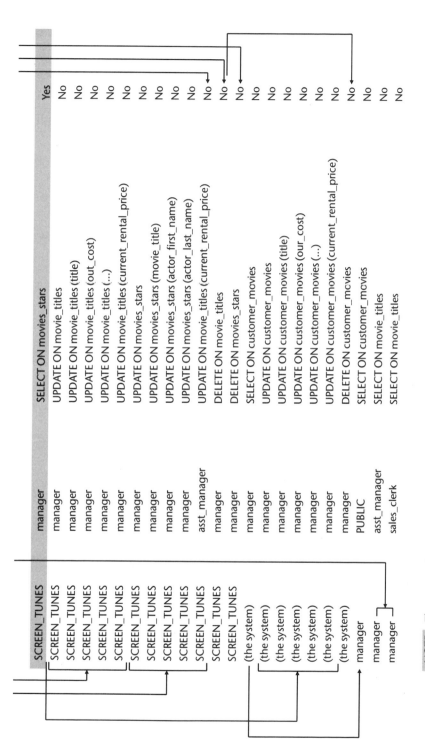

NOTE   The screened row is repeated from page 288.

TABLE 13-4

Grantor	Grantee	Privilege	With Grant Option?
SCREEN_TUNES	manager	SELECT ON movie_titles	Yes

TABLE 13-5

Grantor	Grantee	Privilege	With Grant Option?
manager	asst_manager	SELECT ON movie_titles	No
manager	sales_clerk	SELECT ON movie_titles	No

But this represents only *some* of the privileges that were allowed to be created by the identified descriptor. The others are view privileges (granted by the system to the owner of the view) that couldn't exist if we hadn't granted privileges to the view's owner. These privileges will have the system as a grantor and the same grantee as the identified privilege (MANAGER, in this case); they will also have the same action (SELECT) on some view (or a column of a view) owned by that grantor. These privileges are shown in Table 13-6.

Now, we further identify any privileges that were allowed to be created by the existence of *this* privilege, which turns up the one shown in Table 13-7.

Next we find all privileges that were allowed to be created by this last one. In our case, there are none, so we can move on to the next step.

We say that all of those privileges that were allowed to be created by an identified privilege are *directly dependent on* the identified privilege. At this point, we can construct a *privilege dependency graph* where we draw arrows from any privilege that allows another privilege to exist (that is, to any directly dependent privileges.) We don't care about any nodes (privileges) that aren't connected to anything else, unless they're one of our identified privileges. Such unconnected and unidentified privileges (call them *independent nodes*) will be unaffected by the statement, so we can ignore them (but not delete them from the privileges graph, because we're not revoking them!). Table 13-8 shows the results.

Now, we finally have to check if any of those privileges were created in more than one way, that is, if they were granted once as a result of the privilege being revoked and another time by some other privilege still in effect. This is done by examining each node of the graph and seeing if it has two or more incoming arrows (*arcs* in graph theory). In our case, none of them does, so they're all okay. If any did, we'd drop them (and *their* dependent privileges) from our area of concern. In addition, we check to see if there are any privileges that are not independent nodes and that cannot be reached from any independent node except through one of the identified privilege descriptors or descriptors allowed to be created by them. If we had any of these (we don't), we'd call them *abandoned* descriptors.

Now that we've collected all this data, we can start getting rid of the privileges. We get rid of all abandoned privileges, all identified privileges, and all views that are named in an abandoned privilege.

TABLE 13-6

Grantor	Grantee	Privilege	With Grant Option?
(the system)	manager	SELECT ON customer_movies	Yes

TABLE 13-7

Grantor	Grantee	Privilege	With Grant Option?
manager	PUBLIC	SELECT ON customer_movies	No

TABLE 13-8

Grantor	Grantee	Privilege	With GranT Option?
SCREEN_TUNES	manager	SELECT ON movie_titles	Yes
manager	asst_manager	SELECT ON movie_titles	No
manager	sales_clerk	SELECT ON movie_titles	No
(the system)	manager	SELECT ON customer_movies	Yes
manager	PUBLIC	SELECT ON customer_movies	No

Unfortunately, as complicated as this description is, it's not the whole story. In the interest of not terminally boring you, we've omitted details related to revoking only the GRANT OPTION FOR capability (as opposed to the actual privilege) and revocations that affect constraints, assertions, and domains. If you really want to know how revocation of privileges works in all its gory detail, we urge you to review the SQL-92 standard itself (see Appendix D for information about ordering standards).

13.6 Chapter Summary

On the surface, the SQL-92 privilege model appears somewhat simplistic, with two basic statements (GRANT and REVOKE) and a minimal list of privileges. In reality, the combination of these facets with the WITH GRANT OPTION clause and other aspects gives you a fair degree of power with respect to specifying and controlling access to your tables and their data. There are some limitations we mentioned with respect to DDL operations, but most SQL products feature extensions to overcome these restrictions.

Another consideration is that in real-life, complex information systems, there are other aspects of security and privileges that must be coordinated with those of your database. These include network security (distributed access control, authentication, *etc.*), operating system security, and the various permissions that deal with your CASE environments, along with other areas of your information systems. As you design and implement the security model for your SQL databases, you should also keep in mind how these facets relate to the similar security models elsewhere in your environment.

CHAPTER 14

· · · · · · · · · · · · · · · · · ·

Transaction Management

14.1　Introduction

We first discussed the concept of transactions in Chapter 2. In that chapter, we discovered what a transaction was and learned about some of the characteristics of transactions, such as the ACID properties:

- *Atomicity:* The "all-or-nothing" illusion that all operations within a transaction are performed, or none takes place

- *Consistency:* The transaction concept that permits programmers to declare consistency points and validate the correctness of incorporated transformations through application-supplied checks

- *Isolation:* The regulation that concurrent transactions have no effect on one another (except in some implementations, where some of the concurrent transactions may be "blocked" and therefore delayed or even forced to abort and restart)

- *Durability:* The condition that all updates of a transaction—that is, the new states of all objects—must be preserved, even in case of hardware or software failures

In this chapter, we discuss how transactions are constructed and managed within SQL. We look at applicable statements, as well as at various phenomena and respective SQL-92 isolation levels under which your database transactions may be managed.

14.2 SQL-92 Transaction Syntax

In SQL, there is no explicit statement that starts a transaction as there is in some systems. In SQL, you *explicitly* end a transaction by executing a COMMIT or ROLLBACK statement (SQL-89 required you to write COMMIT WORK and ROLLBACK WORK, but SQL-92 makes the keyword WORK optional). However, transactions are started *implicitly* whenever you execute a statement that needs the context of a transaction and no transaction is active. For example, a SELECT statement, an UPDATE statement, and a CREATE TABLE statement all require the context of a transaction. However, a CONNECT statement (see Chapter 15) doesn't require that context and therefore doesn't implicitly start a transaction.

If you don't tell SQL anything different, a *default transaction* will be started. That default transaction has several important characteristics (see Figure 14-1). First, it will permit both read and update (including insert and delete) operations. Second, it will have the maximum possible isolation from other concurrent transactions. Finally, it will set up a diagnostics area (see Chapter 17) with a default size.

FIGURE 14-1
SQL Transaction
Characteristics

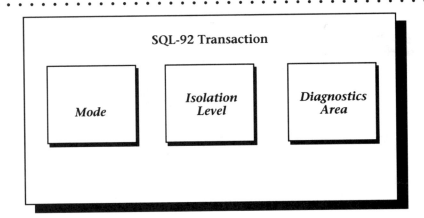

If you don't like the defaults, or if you just want to use good programming practice and write your applications to be self-documenting so there are no questions later, you can use the SET TRANSACTION statement before you execute a transaction-initiating statement. This statement allows you to set attributes to different settings.

The syntax for the SET TRANSACTION statement is shown below and in Diagram RR41.

```
SET TRANSACTION
q mode [ , mode ]...
```

where mode is either isolation-level, access-mode, or diag-size. The access-mode is either READ ONLY or READ WRITE. If you set READ ONLY, then you cannot execute any statements that will change the database (this includes UPDATE, INSERT, DELETE,

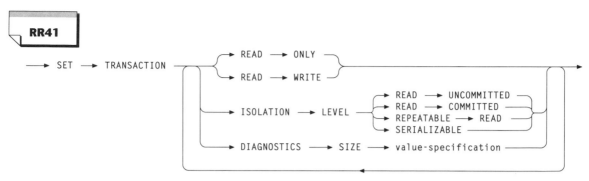

and the schema definition and manipulation statements). diag-size is the key-words DIAGNOSTICS SIZE followed by an integer (either a literal or a host variable or parameter) that specifies the size of the diagnostics area that you want (the number indicates the number of conditions that the diagnostics area can store for each SQL statement that you execute). isolation-level is the keywords ISOLATION LEVEL followed by either READ UNCOMMITTED, READ COMMITTED, REPEATABLE READ, or SERIALIZABLE. We'll discuss isolation levels in the next section.

For example, we may issue the following statement:

```
SET TRANSACTION
    READ ONLY,
    ISOLATION LEVEL READ UNCOMMITTED,
    DIAGNOSTICS SIZE 4
```

This statement indicates that no updates will be permitted during the course of the transaction, that the lowest level of isolation, READ UNCOMMITTED, will be present in the transaction, and the diagnostics area will be of size 4.

Alternatively, you my issue:

```
SET TRANSACTION
    READ WRITE,
    ISOLATION LEVEL SERIALIZABLE,
    DIAGNOSTICS SIZE 10
```

This statement will permit updates during the transaction as well as inquiries, the highest level of isolation under SQL-92, and a diagnostics area of size 10.

14.3 SQL-92 Isolation Levels

In SQL-92, transaction isolation levels are defined in terms of several possible phenomena, or weird, hard-to-explain occurrences (as in Bermuda Triangle events or Elvis sightings). The first is called the *dirty read* phenomenon. A transaction exhibiting this phenomenon has a very minimal isolation from concurrent trans-actions; in fact, it will be able to see changes made by those concurrent transactions even before they commit.

For example, let's say we have two transactions running in our system at the same time:

- T1, the video checkout/point of sale transaction
- T2, the inventory management transaction

If the checkout transaction (T1) modifies a row in the MOVIE_TITLES table—say a customer is buying a VHS copy of the *Gilligan's Island Anthology*—the number of VHS tapes on hand is decremented by one (from three to two). While that transaction is performing the credit card authorization operation (remember that transactions can comprise many different operations), the back office manager starts running the inventory management transaction (T2), a function that will produce an inventory report and initiate automatic economic order quantity (EOQ) inventory reordering functions. When dirty reads are permitted, transaction T2 will read the newly decremented quantity on hand column for *Gilligan's Island Anthology* and determine that we now have two copies on hand, the point at which four more copies of the tape are ordered.

Meanwhile, at the checkout counter, transaction T1 determines that the customer's credit limit on his or her charge card has been exceeded. The customer decides to postpone the purchase, and transaction T1 is rolled back; that is, all objects (including data values) are restored to the appropriate state as if the transaction had never begun in the first place. We now, once again, have three copies of *Gilligan's Island Anthology* in stock, and the database correctly reflects this.

However, transaction T2 has already accomplished the reordering, and we will *incorrectly* order four more copies of the tape, giving us seven in stock (Oh, boy, Mr. Howell!). The permissibility of the dirty read phenomenon has caused this situation to occur (see Figure 14-2).

Because of the possibility of making incorrect decisions based on uncommitted changes to the database, we recommend that you use this minimal isolation level only for transactions that do statistical functions, such as computing the average cost of movies sold in a month, where small imperfections won't have serious consequences.

The second phenomenon is called the *non-repeatable read*. If a transaction exhibits this phenomenon, it is possible that it may read a row once and, if it attempts to read that row again later in the course of the same transaction, the row might have been changed or even deleted by another concurrent transaction; therefore, the read is not (necessarily) repeatable. Let's go back to our checkout/inventory clashing transactions.

Let's say that the university store manager calls us and says, "We had a tremendous rental run on *Earth Girls Are Easy;* how many do you have, and how many can you spare?" Our back office manager starts the interstore transfer transaction (T1) , the first operation of which is to determine how many copies of a specific tape are currently in stock and what the recent activity has been. She discovers that we have four copies in stock and that the tape hasn't been rented in our store in two years. Figuring that we should keep one copy around, the back office manager replies that we have four, and can spare three.

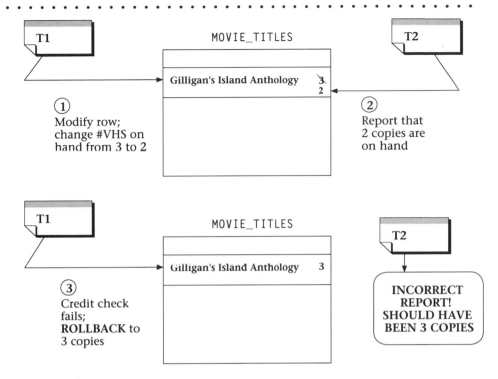

FIGURE 14-2
Dirty Read
Phenomenon

In the course of this transaction, while the university store manager puts our store on hold while he takes care of some pressing business, the checkout transaction (now T2) swings into action. Representatives from four different fraternities come into the store, each one checking out, yup, *Earth Girls Are Easy.*

The university store manager comes back on the phone and tells us that sure, he'll take three copies. Transaction T1 then attempts to reread the row for the tape, but *the value has been modified*. That is, the initial read during the transaction is nonrepeatable. Figure 14-3 illustrates this phenomenon.

Finally, there is the *phantom* phenomenon. When a transaction exhibits this phenomenon, a set of rows that it reads once might be a different set of rows if the transaction attempts to read them again. It's now Sunday night, a time when we run a number of weekly reports and database maintenance functions. Clerk number 1 is running the statistical transaction (T1), one in which a number of operations are used to provide a large number of reports based on movie prices and/or quantities. One of the operations is to calculate some quantity averages based on a given price range (minimum and maximum sales prices), while another operation performs some other calculations for the same price range.

Clerk number 2 is running the price modification transaction, in which sales prices are modified based on special sales and other factors. Assume transaction T1 performs the first operation mentioned above (price averages) in which some search condition (probably SELECT... WHERE... BETWEEN...) is used. Following completion of this operation—remember that the transaction T1 is still alive—transaction T2 causes some price changes to movies which (1) cause some movies

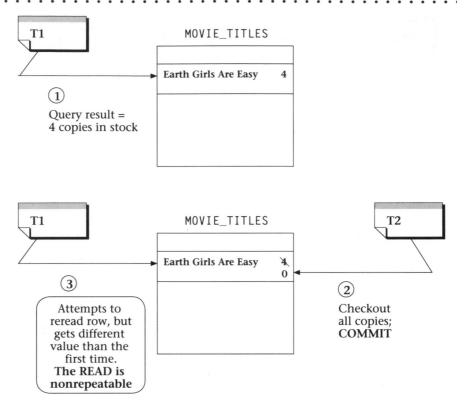

FIGURE 14-3
Nonrepeatable
Read
Phenomenon

that hadn't met the original search condition to now meet the BETWEEN clause, and (2) cause some movies that were in the original result to now be out of the desired range. However, transaction T1 then issues the same statement for its second operation, with *a different set of rows* satisfying the search conditions. Figure 14-4 illustrates how this phenomenon occurs.

A transaction with an isolation level of READ UNCOMMITTED means that your transaction may exhibit all of these phenomenon. This is normally very undesirable, and SQL prohibits you from performing any database updates of your own in this sort of transaction (that is, your implicit access-mode is READ ONLY, and you aren't even allowed to specify an access-mode of READ WRITE if you specify ISOLATION LEVEL READ UNCOMMITTED).

An isolation level of READ COMMITTED means that your transaction will not exhibit the dirty read phenomenon, but may exhibit the other two.

A transaction level specified as REPEATABLE READ guarantees that your transaction will not exhibit either the dirty read or the nonrepeatable read phenomena, but may exhibit the phantom phenomenon.

Finally, SERIALIZABLE means that your transaction will exhibit none of these three phenomena and also means that your transaction is *serializable;* that is, it and all concurrent transactions interact only in ways that guarantee there is some serial ordering of the transactions that will return the same result. Figure 14-5 lists all SQL isolation levels and phenomena.

FIGURE 14-4
Phantom Read
Phenomenon

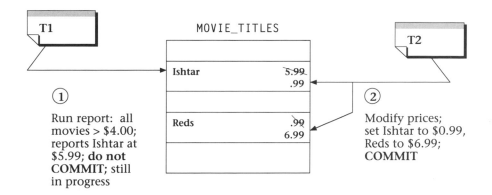

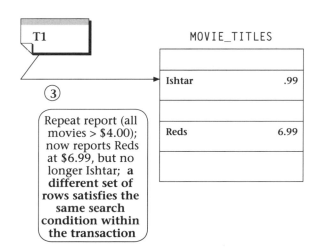

	Dirty Read	Nonrepeatable Read	
Level			**Phantom**
READ UNCOMMITTED	Possible	Possible	Possible
READ COMMITTED	Not Possible	Possible	Possible
REPEATABLE READ	Not Possible	Not Possible	Possible
SERIALIZABLE	Not Possible	Not Possible	Not Possible

TABLE 14-1
SQL-Transaction
Isolation Levels
and Phenomena[1]

Not all SQL DBMS products will necessarily provide all four levels of isolation. However, your SQL DBMS is required to provide you with an isolation level that is *at least* as secure as the one you request (that is, it cannot exhibit any phenomena prohibited by the level you specified), but it is free to set a higher degree of isolation

---

[1] ANS (American National Standard) Database Language SQL, ANSI X3.135-1992, Section 4.28, page 55.)

if it needs to do so. For example, some DBMSs don't implement all four levels of isolation, but might implement only READ COMMITTED and SERIALIZABLE. In that case, when you request REPEATABLE READ, the implementation must give you SERIALIZABLE rather than READ COMMITTED because the latter isolation level exhibits more phenomena than the level you requested.

14.4 Mixed DML and DDL

Some SQL implementations (but not all) allow your application to execute both DML and DDL statements during the course of a single transaction. On the surface, this appears to be a relatively trivial task, such as having several UPDATE statements intertwined with some CREATE TABLE and ALTER TABLE statements. In reality, the interactions between DML and DDL statements within a DBMS can be very complicated, so it is left up to the implementation as to whether mixed DDL and DML support within a single transaction is provided. If your implementation prohibits that mixing, any attempt to execute a DDL statement in a transaction whose first (transaction-initiating) statement is a DML statement, or *vice versa*, will give you an error.

14.5 Transaction Termination

When you have executed all of the statements required to make a logical, consistent set of changes to your database, you must terminate the transaction. If you want the changes that you made to become permanent in the database, you terminate the transaction with a COMMIT statement (or COMMIT WORK, if you prefer to use the optional keyword WORK). If you want to undo all of your changes—if you made an error somewhere or simply changed your mind—then you terminate the transaction with a ROLLBACK (ROLLBACK WORK) statement, which aborts the transaction.

In some environments (for example, if your system runs under the control of a transaction monitor), transactions my be started and/or terminated by agents other than your actual application program. In this case, if the transaction was started via this external mechanism (that is, other than because you executed a transaction-initiating SQL statement), then the transaction must *not* be terminated with a COMMIT or ROLLBACK statement. Instead, it must be terminated by that same external agent. If the transaction was started implicitly by an SQL statement, it must be terminated by a COMMIT or ROLLBACK statement. Any other combination will give you an error.

Keep in mind that it is possible for a ROLLBACK to be interrupted by a system crash, but the ROLLBACK *can never* fail. That is, it must always be possible to abort a transaction. Contrast this with COMMIT, which can fail for several reasons (system crash, *etc.*). A ROLLBACK can be interrupted by a crash or a downed communications line, but the transaction *will* be aborted by those factors—you just won't get control back from the statement. The *only* exception is if you start the transaction from the external agent and try to ROLLBACK in SQL, or *vice versa*.

14.6 **Transactions and Constraints**

In Chapter 10, we described constraints and assertions. One of the things that we talked about was the fact that specific constraints have a couple of constraint attributes. Let's quickly refresh our memories: A given constraint is either DEFERRABLE or NOT DEFERRABLE. If it is DEFERRABLE, then it is either INITIALLY DEFERRED or INITIALLY IMMEDIATE. In either case, the constraint is, at any given time, set to *deferred* or *immediate*. If a constraint is INITIALLY DEFERRED, then (surprise) its initial mode at the start of a transaction is *deferred*. Likewise, INITIALLY IMMEDIATE is as stated.

A constraint that is NOT DEFERRABLE is always checked at the end of every SQL statement (well, it is "effectively checked," which means that a smart implementation can often tell whether a check actually needs to be made or not). A constraint that is DEFERRABLE and is set to *immediate* mode is also checked at the end of every SQL statement. However, a constraint that is DEFERRABLE and is set to *deferred* mode is not checked at the end of every SQL statement; instead, it is checked only when its mode is set back to *immediate*, either implicitly by a COMMIT statement or explicitly by execution of a SET CONSTRAINTS statement.

The SET CONSTRAINTS statement is shown below and in Diagram RR42.

```
SET CONSTRAINTS constraint-list
    { DEFERRED | IMMEDIATE }
```

RR42

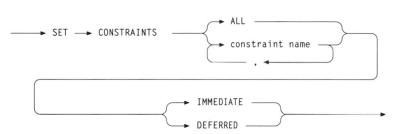

where constraint-list is either a list of constraint names or the keyword ALL. Only DEFERRABLE constraints can be named in the constraint-list; ALL implies only those constraints that are DEFERRABLE.

If you attempt to commit a transaction while you have one or more constraints in *deferred* mode, the DBMS will set the mode of those constraints to *immediate* and check them. (Put more bluntly, you can set constraints DEFERRED as much as you'd like, but they will *always* be set IMMEDIATE *and checked* before each transaction commits.) If any of them are violated, the DBMS automatically rolls back your transaction and gives you an error to tell you that's what it did. To avoid this inconvenient situation, we recommend that you explicitly execute a SET CON-STRAINTS ALL IMMEDIATE statement before you commit any transaction that has DEFERRABLE constraints that have been in *deferred* mode. (To help you out a little, NOT DEFERRABLE is the default for all constraints; if you specify a constraint as DEFERRABLE, but don't specify an initial mode, then INITIALLY IMMEDIATE is the default. This will minimize the surprises, because you have to explicitly set your constraint(s) to *deferred* for this to be a problem.)

14.7 Additional Transaction Termination Actions

When you terminate a transaction, any open cursors (see Chapter 12) are automatically closed. If you have any prepared dynamic statements (see Chapter 16), these statements may or may not be destroyed, depending on the implementation. Finally, while COMMIT statements may fail owing to any one of a number of causes, a ROLLBACK statement can never fail unless your transaction was started by that mysterious external agent.

With this understanding, let's look at an example that illustrates why you need this capability. Consider two tables:

```
CREATE TABLE employees (
    emp_id    INTEGER  PRIMARY KEY,
    emp_name  CHARACTER VARYING (30),
    dept      INTEGER NOT NULL REFERENCES department ) ;

CREATE TABLE department (
    dept_id   INTEGER PRIMARY KEY,
    dept_name CHARACTER (10),
    manager   INTEGER NOT NULL REFERENCES employees ;
```

With this arrangement, you cannot create a new DEPARTMENT unless it's managed by an existing employee, but you can't hire a new employee unless he or she is assigned to work for an existing department. How do you start populating the tables? The only way is to *defer* either or both of the NOT NULL constraints! As long as you've got the appropriate combinations of DEPARTMENTs and EMPLOYEEs in place before you COMMIT (or SET CONSTRAINTS ALL IMMEDIATE), this will allow you to populate the tables.

14.8 Chapter Summary

Transactions can be very complex, particularly those that are distributed. A number of issues must be addressed: commit protocols (such as two-phase commit, local commitment, nonblocking), specific product interactions (such as with transaction processing monitors and repositories), and others. It is beyond the scope of this book to delve too deeply into transaction theory, although a number of reference sources[2] are available. SQL-92 transaction management facilities aren't overly complex, but care should be taken when designating isolation levels, constraint handling, and other aspects of this subject. It's sometimes tempting, for example, to define the highest level of isolation (SERIALIZABLE) for each and every transaction specification, but this may be inefficient based on the characteristics of *your specific environment*.

---

[2] Jim Gray and Andreas Reuter, *Transaction Processing: Concepts and Techniques,* Morgan Kaufmann Publishers, San Mateo, CA, 1993.

CHAPTER 15

. . . .

Connections and Remote Database Access

15.1 Introduction

In this chapter, we discuss the relationship of *sessions* and *connections* to your applications. SQL-86 and SQL-89 did not have an explicit notion of a session in which your application ran, nor did they have the notion of a connection from your application to a session. However, modern database technology requires recognition of certain concepts that lead to these terms. In particular, a number of commercial SQL products are based on an architecture called *client/server*. In the client/server environment, one program (your application, perhaps) is a *client* for a service provided by another program (the database system, in our case), called the *server*. More detailed discussion is beyond the scope of this book, but we will acknowledge that different contexts might draw the boundaries differently; for example, in some situations, your application program might invoke or call the *client software*, which communicates with the *server software*, which then invokes or calls the database system (see Figure 15-1).

15.2 Establishing Connections

In SQL-89, when your program attempted to execute the first SQL statement, the DBMS was expected simply to accept the statement and start executing it. However, SQL-92 recognizes that other actions may have to take place before the DBMS can even be aware that it has been given a task to do. For example, a *context* for database execution has to be established. In some implementations, the context exists because the DBMS runtime code was linked with your application. In others, the context is established by execution of implementation-defined statements to connect the application program with the DBMS. In still others, system variables set up the context. SQL-92 resolves this issue by defining several statements that

FIGURE 15-1
Client/Server
Database
Environment

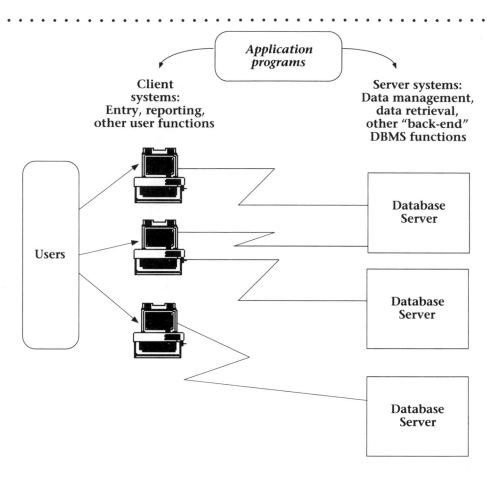

application programs use to control connections to DBMSs and by specifying the default behavior much more thoroughly than SQL-89 did.

First, for compatibility with pre-SQL-92 programs, there is always a default behavior. Second, for newer programs, SQL-92 allows complete control over the association between your application and the DBMS or DBMSs that it uses. Here is an outline of the behavior.

- Almost all SQL statements (there are a *few* exceptions, which we'll get to shortly) can execute only when there is a *connection* between the application program (client) and the DBMS (server).

- When your application tries to execute one of these statements and a connection has been established, the DBMS to which your application is connected executes the statement.

- When your application tries to execute one of these statements and a connection has not been established, the first thing that must happen is that a connection must be established. SQL-92 specifies that this connection is to a default server (or environment, or DBMS). How that default is determined remains implementation-defined, but it may involve environment variables or something similar. After the connection is established, the DBMS to which you are now connected executes the statement.

- If your first statement is a CONNECT statement (this is one of the exceptions), no default is established, but the requested server is contacted and a current connection is established to it (subject to normal security and so forth).

- You can execute a CONNECT statement to establish a connection to a second (or third . . .) server without disconnecting the earlier connection (or connections). The earlier connections are called *dormant connections* and the new one is called the *current connection.*

- Every connection has a session associated with it. The session associated with the current connection is the *current session,* and sessions associated with any dormant connections are *dormant sessions* (see Figure 15-2).

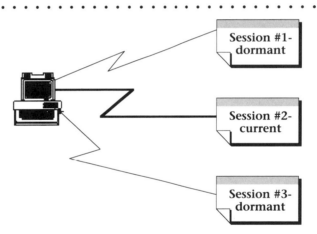

FIGURE 15-2
Multiple SQL
Connections
and Sessions

- If you have more than one connection in existence, then you can switch among them by using the SET CONNECTION statement.

- Because connections often occupy system resources, you may sometimes wish to explicitly get rid of connections; you can do this by using the DISCONNECT statement. If you fail to disconnect any (or all) of your sessions before your program terminates, then it will be done for you. If you try to disconnect *explicitly* while you have a transaction in progress, you'll get an error.

- Your implementation may either permit or prohibit changing connections while transactions are active. If yours prohibits that behavior, you'll get an error if you try. Otherwise, all statements executed during the transaction through all connections (on all sessions) are part of the same transaction.

15.3 Connection Statements

Let's take a closer look at these three statements: CONNECT, SET CONNECTION, and DISCONNECT.

15.3.1 CONNECT

The format of the CONNECT statement is demonstrated below and in Diagram RR43.

```
CONNECT TO target
    [ AS connect-name ]
    [ USER user-name ]
```

or, alternatively

```
CONNECT TO DEFAULT
```

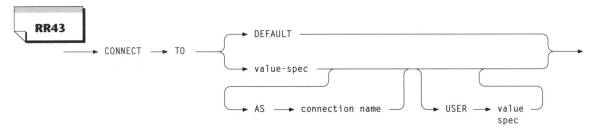

The target is a value specification (character string literal or a host variable or parameter) that identifies the server to which you wish to connect. The meaning of the contents of target is implementation-defined.

The connect-name is an identifier that you can use as a sort of alias for the connection. This can be used in the SET CONNECTION and DISCONNECT statements; it is also reported along with any errors at that connection. If you don't specify AS connect-name, then the default is to give you a connect-name identical to target.

The user-name is a value specification that you can use to identify yourself to the server. If you don't specify it, the default for user-name is your current authID. Your implementation may require that user-name be equal to your current authID, or it may restrict the values that you can use for user-name in other ways. If you violate these restrictions, you will get an error. If you specify a user-name, any leading or trailing blanks will be stripped off before it is used.

If you try to connect to a server and specify a connect-name that's already in use by your application, you'll get an error. If you try to CONNECT TO DEFAULT and your application already has a default connection established, you'll get that same error.

If you use CONNECT TO DEFAULT, the effect is almost the same as not issuing a CONNECT at all. (That is, when you execute the next SQL statement that requires a connection, it will execute on the default connection.) However, we do recommend that you use CONNECT TO DEFAULT in this case so that your programs will be self-documenting and thus easier to maintain! There is one difference, however: If your application never issues a CONNECT statement, but always uses the (implicit) default connection, any error that breaks the connection will be essentially transparent to you: the very next statement that you execute will go to the same default connection (although there are problems with maintaining your transaction, so you will have to re-execute all of the statements in that transaction).

Once you use a CONNECT statement, you will never be implicitly connected to the default connection in that application run. If your connection is broken, the next statement that you try to execute will get an error instead of making a default connection for you.

If the CONNECT statement cannot reach the server, you'll get an error. If it reaches the server, but the server refuses the connection (because, for example, it has insufficient resources or it doesn't accept your user-name, or perhaps it's the deodorant you wore this morning), then you'll get a different error. Once connected, though, your authID will be set to the user-name you specified (or implied).

15.3.2   SET CONNECTION

The SET CONNECTION statement is demonstrated below and in Diagram RR44.

        SET CONNECTION connect-name

or

        SET CONNECTION DEFAULT

Of course, there has to be a dormant connection named connect-name or a dormant default connection; otherwise, you'll get an error. If there is an dormant connection, your current connection is made dormant and the new connection becomes the current connection. If the new connection cannot become current for any reason, you'll get an error to signal this (for example, a network link may have gone down).

15.3.3   DISCONNECT

The DISCONNECT statement looks like the following and its syntax is shown in Diagram RR45.

        DISCONNECT connect-name

or

        DISCONNECT CURRENT

or

```
DISCONNECT ALL
```

If you use connect-name, there has to be a connection (current or dormant) by that name; if you use CURRENT, there has to be a current connection (that is, you cannot execute DISCONNECT CURRENT immediately followed by DISCONNECT CURRENT). If your current connection is identified by connect-name or if you use CURRENT, your current connection is destroyed and you have no current connection; you must use a CONNECT or SET CONNECTION statement to establish a new current connection if you want to continue executing SQL statements.

If you execute DISCONNECT ALL, your current connection is destroyed, as are all other connections.

If you have a transaction active on a connection that you are disconnecting, you'll get an error and the disconnect will fail. If any other sort of error is encountered during a DISCONNECT, the disconnect will succeed, but you'll get a warning message.

What are the practical implications of all this? Well, the notions of connections and sessions were created to support remote database access and client/server environments. In spite of that, they work perfectly well in "one box" situations, too. It's just that the number of meaningful connections is probably more limited (perhaps just to DEFAULT . . . but perhaps not).

15.4 RDA (Remote Database Access)

There is a related standard, called *Remote Database Access* (RDA for short). This standard defines protocols and services for accessing databases over network connections (actually, over Open Systems Interconnect, or OSI, connections, although the technology is not practically limited to OSI and can be implemented atop other protocol stacks such as TCP/IP). It is beyond the scope of this book to delve into RDA, but we do want to chat about it a little bit.

RDA allows you to execute a significant fraction of the available SQL statements, but not all of them. Actually, the limitation is caused by the fact that the existing RDA standard is oriented toward the Entry SQL level of SQL-92; future versions of that standard will address higher conformance levels of SQL-92.

When you use RDA to access an SQL DBMS, the RDA client software (okay, so we can't ignore the separation all the time) intercepts the SQL statements that your application is executing and decides how they should be handled. Most of the SQL statements are sent to the server for execution and the behavior is otherwise normal. The CONNECT, SET CONNECTION, and DISCONNECT statements are not sent to a server, but they're executed by the client software—that's how this whole thing works in the first place! The GET DIAGNOSTICS statement (see Chapter 17) is also executed by the client software so that information about all statements, including the CONNECT statements, can be captured.

The RDA standard is based strictly on the OSI protocol stack developed by the International Organization for Standardization (ISO), but work on the standard as well as on products to implement the standard has been undertaken by many groups. One notable group is a consortium called the SQL Access Group (SAG). This group was formed to prototype the RDA protocols and services and to feed back their results into the standards activities. In 1991, SAG members demonstrated software that implemented a large fraction of the RDA standard running on OSI network protocols; commercial products began to appear in mid-1992. In addition to implementing "pure" RDA, SAG also defined a way to provide RDA services on top of the popular TCP/IP network protocols, and 1993 marks the appearance of commercial implementations of that variation.

Another consortium, X/Open Company Ltd., was formed to publish Portability Guides (XPG) to guide application writers in creating applications that could run on many platforms (see Chapter 26). X/Open, among other SQL-related activities, publishes SAG specifications under the X/Open banner.

15.5 Termination Statements and Connections

Finally, your COMMIT and ROLLBACK statements are intercepted and handled differently than by pure SQL. In fact, they are dealt with by other network (*e.g.,* OSI) services that handle commitment of transactions. Now, these services will notify the server to commit or rollback the transaction, but it's not done with a COMMIT or ROLLBACK statement. These services are designed to handle both single-server (single connection) transactions, using a one-phase commit protocol, and multi-server (multiple connection) transactions, using a two-phase commit protocol.

15.6 Chapter Summary

As distributed database environments become increasingly prominent among information systems, connections will become more and more important to your SQL applications. The SQL-92 connection facilities, combined with standards such as RDA, will give your applications a great deal of flexibility with respect to distribution of data among resources. Keep in mind, however, that there is far more to truly distributed database environments, particularly heterogeneous (*e.g.,* running under multiple DBMS products), than simple connections. When coupled with distribution frameworks or front-end tools, though, the basic facilities of SQL-92 will help you avoid the patchworked workaround environments that were formerly necessary to achieve most database distribution.

CHAPTER 16

· · · · · · · · · · · · · · · · · · ·

Dynamic SQL

16.1 Introduction

Dynamic SQL is the name that is usually applied to the facility that allows you to execute SQL statements whose complete text you don't know until you're ready to execute them. This has a number of different aspects, and we cover all of them (well, at least all of the important ones) in this chapter.

16.2 What is Dynamic SQL?

Under many (perhaps even most) circumstances, you know in complete detail all of the SQL statements that you need to execute during your application, and you know them well in advance (when you are writing your application, normally). This knowledge allows you to write SQL modules or embedded SQL programs that contain those SQL statements and to write application program code to invoke those SQL statements in the sequence that they are needed. Whether you are writing an SQL module to do your store payroll, or whether you are writing C language programs with embedded SQL to do movie title lookups, you usually have a pretty good idea in advance of the SQL statements you'll need.

However, you will occasionally encounter situations in which the full text of the SQL statements aren't fully known while you are writing your application. It's even possible that you won't know *any* of the text of the statements. For example, you may sometimes allow an end user (the person sitting at the terminal running your application) to enter an SQL statement, or part of one. Of course, that user may use interactive SQL sometimes, but let's consider the case where he or she is really running your application and you only want him or her to enter a single SQL statement just for the purposes of your application. Well, you couldn't have coded that statement in advance, because you hadn't a clue about what the user might choose to enter. SQL-92 (and almost all SQL products of any level) allows you to use dynamic SQL facilities to execute that statement.

Another example involves a spreadsheet package that stores all of its data in an SQL database. As the user enters formulae into the cells of the spreadsheet, the package can convert those formulae into SQL statements that retrieve the appropriate data and compute the desired results. These SQL statements are generated in real-time and therefore couldn't possibly be coded in advance. However, dynamic SQL comes to the rescue again, allowing the spreadsheet package to "invent" statements as it requires them.

When you code your statements in an SQL module or in an embedded SQL program, you will process those statements through some sort of compiler—possibly a precompiler and then one or more compilers (see Chapter 11 for more information). That process gives the DBMS the opportunity to process the SQL statements and perhaps to optimize them. The compilers perform the required lexical and syntactic analysis on the SQL statements and then convert them to a form that the DBMS can use to further process them. Your DBMS then determines the most efficient ways to execute the statement in the context of the database (including use of indices, sequential scans, join algorithms, and so forth) and somehow saves the result of that analysis. As we saw in Chapter 11, this can take many forms, ranging from storing actual machine code somewhere in the database itself to building in-memory structures that are released as soon as the application has finished running one time. In any case, use of *static SQL* (a useful term for SQL coded into modules or embedded SQL programs) often has much or most of its processing overhead done long before application execution time.

By contrast, when you use dynamic SQL, none of that processing can be done in advance; it must all be done at application execution time. This often (but not always) results in reduced execution performance. As a consequence, you have to make careful decisions about when to use static SQL and when to use dynamic SQL. Normally, we believe that the appropriate choice is to use static whenever you know the whole text of your statements in advance and dynamic only when that's not the case. The decision can sometimes be slightly more complex, though. Often, the text of the SQL statements isn't completely known, but there are only a few choices. In such a case, you might choose to code each alternative into a module or embedded SQL program and then select which alternative to execute based on user input. This may be more effective than using dynamic SQL, but not if there are hundreds of alternatives.

SQL-92 does not allow you to execute *every* possible SQL statement dynamically. For some statements, it makes no sense at all to execute them dynamically. Other statements are used only to set up conditions for dynamic statements, so they must be handled as static SQL statements. In still other cases, static statements are provided explicitly to support dynamic SQL and are used in lieu of (potential, but nonexistent) dynamic alternatives. We cover all of this later in this chapter.

The philosophy of dynamic SQL is fairly simple; the realities are a bit more complicated. Let's look at it in this order: the overall philosophy first, followed by an outline of how it works, finishing up with the details.

16.3 The Philosophy of Dynamic SQL

SQL statements can be executed in dynamic SQL in two ways. They can be prepared for execution and then executed as often and as many times as required by the application. Alternatively, they can be prepared and executed in one step (called *execute immediate*). If you PREPARE an SQL statement for execution, the results of that preparation are preserved for the remainder of your session; you can execute the statement as many times as required by your application during that session without incurring the overhead of the preparation. (Think of the PREPARE step as doing the same work that would be done by the compiler/DBMS combination for static SQL.) If you use EXECUTE IMMEDIATE to execute an SQL statement, the results of the preparation are not preserved. If you want to execute the same statement again, you must incur the preparation overhead another time. Consequently, you will normally choose to use the separate PREPARE and EXECUTE steps for statements that will be executed more than once, and the EXECUTE IMMEDIATE statement for statements that will be executed only a single time. Why wouldn't you want to *always* use PREPARE/EXECUTE just in case? Simply because preserving the results of the preparation occupies system resources (*e.g.*, dynamic memory) and you could overload a small system if you did that for all transient statements. And just to make things balance out, if you know you're done with an SQL statement that you PREPAREd, you can DEALLOCATE PREPARE to get rid of it and release those scarce resources.

Now, when you use static SQL, you (typically) write both the SQL statements and the host language statements (if you don't actually write them both yourself, you probably have a good design document that is used by writers of both types of statements—don't you?). That allows you to write your host language statements and SQL statements to mesh seamlessly (or as seamlessly as the impedance mismatches allow!). You use the proper number of parameters or host variables for every SQL statement and always know whether you're FETCHing, UPDATEing, or DELETEing.

However, when you're using dynamic SQL, you sometimes don't know these details, which makes it pretty difficult to write the host language statements to support those SQL statements. You may not even know whether the dynamic SQL statement will retrieve data from the database or store data into it. Worse, you may not have a clue about the numbers and types of parameters or host variables to use!

SQL-92 solves this problem by allowing you to request the DBMS to describe the dynamic SQL statements. This description will tell you in great detail all of the information about the parameters used by the dynamic SQL statement. SQL-92 even allows you to describe the dynamic SQL statement once to get information about the *input parameters* (those that give data from the host program to the SQL statement) and again to get information about the *output parameters* (those that return data retrieved by the SQL statement to the host program). When you DESCRIBE a dynamic SQL statement, the results are put into an *SQL item descriptor area* (we'll just call them *descriptor areas* from now on). These descriptor areas are defined in detail later in this chapter.

Unfortunately, SQL-92 does not provide a facility that tells you what sort of SQL statement you're dealing with. If your dynamic statements come from outside your application, your application will have to scan the statement text to tell whether you're processing a SELECT or a CREATE TABLE. Of course, if your application is generating the dynamic SQL statements, then you won't have to scan at all—you'll already know what the statement is. Actually, you can tell whether you're dealing with a SELECT statement (or a dynamic cursor declaration) or any other statement: SELECT and cursors *always* have at least one returned value, while no other statement does (in SQL-92, at least). Of course, you still have to parse to tell the difference between SELECT and a cursor . . . .

16.3.1 Parameters

This talk of parameters brings us to look at the way information is passed to and from dynamic SQL statements. In static SQL statements, of course, you use a parameter or host variable (of the form :*name*). However, in dynamic SQL, there are no procedures to give meaning to parameters, and there's no host language context to give meaning to host variables. Consequently, dynamic SQL uses a convention known as a *dynamic parameter specification* (or *dynamic parameter* for short, although they are often called *parameter markers* as well), which is manifested by a question mark. Therefore, you will see dynamic SQL statements like this:

```
UPDATE MOVIE_TITLES
   SET CURRENT_RENTAL_PRICE = ? WHERE TITLE = ?
```

This statement has two dynamic parameters, both of them used to transmit data from the application program to the SQL statement. In static SQL, the data types of the host variables or parameters are declared and are available to the application program. In dynamic SQL, the data types of dynamic parameters must be inferred from the context. As a result, there are some limitations (covered later in this chapter) on exactly where you can use dynamic parameters.

When you have a dynamic SQL statement that contains names that aren't fully qualified (as in the preceding example, where the table name isn't qualified with a catalog and schema name), the system has to apply some default qualifications (just like the compilers do for static SQL). It's pretty simple to do that for static SQL, because you have the context of a module or an embedded program to use. For dynamic, there's not as much context, so SQL-92 provides several statements to set the appropriate defaults for dynamic SQL statements.

16.3.2 Normal and Extended Dynamic

Some dynamic SQL objects (dynamic SQL statement names and dynamic SQL cursor names) come in two "flavors." One flavor may be thought of as normal dynamic statement names and cursor names. The other is called extended dynamic statement names and cursor names. The primary difference is the *time* at which the name is known. Normal dynamic names are actual identifiers that you code in the statements that provide the dynamic SQL facilities. Extended dynamic names are represented in the dynamic-providing statements by parameters or host identifiers (:*name*); the *real* name of the dynamic name is provided at runtime by the application.

Normal dynamic names have the advantages of being self-documenting (that is, you or someone else can read your program and have a ghost of a chance of figuring out what's going on) and of allowing the DBMS to preallocate all resources necessary to operate on them. On the other hand, they also require that you know, *when you write your application,* the exact number (or at least the maximum number) of concurrently prepared statements and concurrently open cursors that your application will use.

By contrast, extended dynamic names allow your application to decide at runtime that it needs another prepared statement (without deallocating any existing prepared statements) or another dynamic cursor (without closing any existing open dynamic cursor) and to create one by assigning a new name to it. The disadvantage is that the DBMS must do additional work to deal with objects whose names or even whose existence aren't known until runtime. Because of these complications, SQL-92 doesn't prescribe extended dynamic names until the Full SQL level (see Appendix D for a discussion of leveling).

16.4 Outline of Dynamic SQL Processing

When you want to process a dynamic SQL statement, you store the text of that statement into a character string host variable and execute either a PREPARE statement or an EXECUTE IMMEDIATE statement. (Equivalently, you call the module procedure that contains the PREPARE or EXECUTE IMMEDIATE statement and pass the dynamic SQL statement as a character string parameter.) Let's look at the normal path of PREPARE/EXECUTE first; then we'll have a look at the EXECUTE IMMEDIATE alternative.

The PREPARE statement analyzes the dynamic SQL statement for appropriate syntax, to determine the data types of the dynamic parameters (if any) and to optimize the execution of the statement. The results of the preparation are associated with a statement name that you'll use in later statements when you want to identify that prepared statement.

If you need to, you can DESCRIBE the dynamic SQL statement, using the statement name associated with it. If you choose to DESCRIBE, then you must also ALLOCATE a descriptor area. Based on the information put into the descriptor area by DESCRIBE, you can then EXECUTE the statement (again, using the associated statement name). You can EXECUTE the statement using two alternatives: retrieve and store information into the descriptor area, or retrieve and store information directly from and into the host program (using host variables or parameters). If you don't DESCRIBE, you can still ALLOCATE a descriptor area and EXECUTE using that descriptor area, or you can bypass the descriptor area and EXECUTE using host variables or parameters.

As an alternative to all that, you can simply execute the dynamic SQL statement using EXECUTE IMMEDIATE. However, because EXECUTE IMMEDIATE does not allow the use of either descriptor areas or host variables or parameters, the dynamic SQL statement cannot contain any dynamic parameters.

Different actions are taken when you need to deal with cursors dynamically. These will be covered in the following detailed sections.

16.4.1 Parameters and Codes

In virtually all SQL DBMS products, you can use dynamic SQL. Until SQL-92, these products have used a data structure called an *SQL Descriptor Area,* or SQLDA, to deal with the information that must be exchanged in the use of dynamic SQL. The SQLDA was a data structure allocated in the 3GL program and its details (structure, codes, *etc.*) varied widely from product to product, making it exceedingly difficult to write a portable application. To make matters worse, the SQLDA included fields that were *pointers* (*i.e.,* memory addresses) of other data! Of course, this caused problems in several languages (such as COBOL and Fortran) that have no support for pointers or for dynamic storage allocation.

SQL-92 resolved this problem in a rather elegant way: by giving the DBMS the responsibility of allocating and managing the data necessary for dynamic SQL operation. This technique encapsulates the structure so that the implementation details are hidden from, and irrelevant to, the application program; it also lets the DBMS worry about storage allocation and deallocation and about handling pointer problems. Not only does this solve the problems that 3GLs like COBOL and Fortran had with the SQLDA, but it also solves the portability problem (without requiring any existing DBMS or application program to change the existing SQLDA mechanisms—the products can simply *add* the new technique and allow both to coexist).

An SQL *item descriptor* area (or *descriptor area*) is an area that an SQL DBMS can use to store information about dynamic parameters in your dynamic SQL statements. A descriptor area must have enough room to store information about as many parameters as you have in your dynamic SQL statement. Each dynamic parameter is represented in the descriptor area after execution of a DESCRIBE statement. The information recorded for each parameter is shown in Table 16-1.

Some of the fields in the descriptor area contain codes instead of real values. (Of course, these are only the codes seen by the application program; an implementation may use different codes internally, or in the SQLDA!) One of those fields, TYPE, contains a code that indicates the data type of the dynamic parameter or the database column being described. These values are shown in Table 16-2.

	NAME OF THE FIELD IN THE DESCRIPTOR AREA	DATA TYPE OF THE FIELD IN THE DESCRIPTOR AREA	MEANING OF THE FIELD IN THE DESCRIPTOR AREA
TABLE 16-1 Recorded Parameter Information	TYPE	Exact numeric, scale 0	Code for the data type
	LENGTH	Exact numeric, scale 0	Length (in characters or bits) for string types
	OCTET_LENGTH	Exact numeric, scale 0	Length (in octets) for strings
	RETURNED_LENGTH	Exact numeric, scale 0	Length (in characters or bits) returned from DBMS for strings
	RETURNED_OCTET_ LENGTH	Exact numeric, scale 0	Length (in octets) returned from DBMS for strings
	PRECISION	Exact numeric, scale 0	Precision for numeric types
	SCALE	Exact numeric, scale 0	Scale for exact numeric types
	DATETIME_INTERVAL_ CODE	Exact numeric, scale 0	Code for datetime/interval subtype
	DATETIME_INTERVAL_ PRECISION	Exact numeric, scale 0	Precision of interval's leading field
	NULLABLE	Exact numeric, scale 0	Whether associated database column is nullable or not
	NAME	Character string, length >=128	Name of associated database column
	UNNAMED	Exact numeric, scale 0	Whether associated column has "real name" or DBMS supplied
	COLLATION_CATALOG	Character string, length >=128	Catalog name for column's collation
	COLLATION_SCHEMA	Character string, length >=128	Schema name for column's collation
	COLLATION_NAME	Character string, length >=128	Collation name for column's collation
	CHARACTER_SET_ CATALOG	Character string, length >=128	Catalog name for column's character set
	CHARACTER_SET_ SCHEMA	Character string, length >=128	Schema name for column's character set
	CHARACTER_SET_ NAME	Character string, length >=128	Collation name for column's character set
	DATA	As specified by other fields	Actual data associated with dynamic parameter
	INDICATOR	Exact numeric, scale 0	Value for indicator parameter

TABLE 16-2
TYPE Information

Value	Data Type
Less than zero	Implementor-defined data types
1	CHARACTER
2	NUMERIC
3	DECIMAL
4	INTEGER
5	SMALLINT
6	FLOAT
7	REAL
8	DOUBLE PRECISION
9	DATE, TIME, or TIMESTAMP
10	INTERVAL
11	Reserved for future use by the standard
12	CHARACTER VARYING
13	Reserved for future use by the standard
14	BIT
15	BIT VARYING
Greater than 15	Reserved for future use by the standard

Another code field is DATETIME_INTERVAL_CODE. Table 16-3 shows what the DATETIME_INTERVAL_CODE will be if TYPE contains 9 (DATE, TIME, or TIMESTAMP), and Table 16-4 shows the codes for cases where TYPE contains 10 (INTERVAL).

TABLE 16-3
DATETIME_
INTERVAL_CODE
Information for
DATE, TIME, or
TIMESTAMP

Value	Data Type
1	DATE
2	TIME
3	TIMESTAMP
4	TIME WITH TIME ZONE
5	TIMESTAMP WITH TIME ZONE

Value	Data Type
TABLE 16-4 DATETIME_ INTERVAL_CODE Information for INTERVALs	
1	YEAR
2	MONTH
3	DAY
4	HOUR
5	MINUTE
6	SECOND
7	YEAR TO MONTH
8	DAY TO HOUR
9	DAY TO MINUTE
10	DAY TO SECOND
11	HOUR TO MINUTE
12	HOUR TO SECOND
13	MINUTE TO SECOND

When you DESCRIBE (for input) a dynamic SQL statement that contains a dynamic parameter, the information about that parameter is put into a descriptor area (which you specify). The DBMS will infer the data type information about the dynamic parameter from its context and fill in the relevant fields. (Other fields are ignored.) When you DESCRIBE (for output) a dynamic SQL statement that contains references to database columns, the information about those columns will be put into an item descriptor area.

Let's look at an example of how these are used. First, let's assume that we have a table defined as follows:

```
CREATE TABLE movie_title (
    title                   CHARACTER (30),
                            --Assume implementor-defined charset
    current_rental_price    DECIMAL (7,2) NOT NULL,
    duration                INTERVAL HOUR(1) TO MINUTE,
    PRIMARY KEY (title)
)
```

Let's describe the following dynamic SQL statement:

```
SELECT title, current_rental_price, duration
  FROM movie_titles INTO ?, ?, ?
```

to get the information about the database columns. First, we have to PREPARE the statement. (Assume that the host variable :stmt contains a character string representing the statement.)

```
PREPAPRE dynstmt FROM :stmt
```

This step causes the name DYNSTMT to be associated with the prepared (compiled) statement. Next, let's DESCRIBE the statement we've just prepared.

```
DESCRIBE OUTPUT dynstmt
  INTO SQL DESCRIPTOR 'my_descr' ;
```

The information we get from this is shown in Tables 16-5 through 16-7.

Now, recall that we said earlier that you have to allocate the descriptor areas. You can also deallocate them when you no longer need them (to recapture system resources), but they will automatically be deallocated for you when your session ends.

To allocate a descriptor area, you use the ALLOCATE DESCRIPTOR statement (bet you saw that coming, didn't you?):

```
ALLOCATE DESCRIPTOR desc-name
  [ WITH MAX occurrences ]
```

The desc-name is either a literal or a host variable or parameter (remember we called this category of things *simple value specifications*); obviously, it has to be a character string that follows the rules of an identifier. Actually, you can precede the simple value specification with the keyword LOCAL or the keyword GLOBAL (if you don't specify either one, then GLOBAL is assumed). LOCAL means that the descriptor is available only to the module or compilation unit in which you allocated it, while GLOBAL means that all of your modules or compilation units can share it during your session. occurrences is an integer simple value specification that tells the DBMS how many descriptor area items to make room for. If you leave it off, then you'll get whatever your vendor wants to give you. All values in all items of the descriptor area are initially undefined, so you either have to use a DESCRIBE to get the DBMS to fill them in, or you have to do it yourself with a SET DESCRIPTOR statement (coming right up).

When you're finished using a descriptor area and want to recover those scarce system resources, you can deallocate it:

```
DEALLOCATE DESCRIPTOR desc-name
```

Of course, if you give an incorrect name, you'll get an error. If you give a correct name (that is, the name of a descriptor that you've allocated with the same GLOBAL or LOCAL scope during the session), it will be deallocated, and everything currently stored in it will be lost forever!

TABLE 16-5
Descriptor
Area #1

Field	Value
TYPE	1
LENGTH	30
OCTET_LENGTH	30, assuming normal ASCII is implementor-default
RETURNED_LENGTH	30
RETURNED_OCTET_LENGTH	30
PRECISION	Doesn't matter
SCALE	Doesn't matter
DATETIME_INTERVAL_CODE	Doesn't matter
DATETIME_INTERVAL_PRECISION	Doesn't matter
NULLABLE	0
NAME	TITLE
UNNAMED	0
COLLATION_CATALOG	Implementation-defined
COLLATION_SCHEMA	Implementation-defined
COLLATION_NAME	Implementation-defined
CHARACTER_SET_CATALOG	Implementation-defined
CHARACTER_SET_SCHEMA	Implementation-defined
CHARACTER_SET_NAME	Implementation-defined
DATA	Set only when data is retrieved into descriptor area
INDICATOR	Set only when data is retrieved into descriptor area

TABLE 16-6
Descriptor
Area #2

Field	Value
TYPE	3
LENGTH	Doesn't matter
OCTET_LENGTH	Doesn't matter
RETURNED_LENGTH	Doesn't matter
RETURNED_OCTET_LENGTH	Doesn't matter
PRECISION	7
SCALE	2
DATETIME_INTERVAL_CODE	Doesn't matter
DATETIME_INTERVAL_PRECISION	Doesn't matter
NULLABLE	0
NAME	CURRENT_RENTAL_PRICE
UNNAMED	0

TABLE 16-6
(*continued*)

Field	Value
COLLATION_CATALOG	Doesn't matter
COLLATION_SCHEMA	Doesn't matter
COLLATION_NAME	Doesn't matter
CHARACTER_SET_CATALOG	Doesn't matter
CHARACTER_SET_SCHEMA	Doesn't matter
CHARACTER_SET_NAME	Doesn't matter
DATA	Set only when data is retrieved into descriptor area
INDICATOR	Set only when data is retrieved into descriptor area

TABLE 16-7
Descriptor
Area #3

Field	Value
TYPE	10
LENGTH	Doesn't matter
OCTET_LENGTH	Doesn't matter
RETURNED_LENGTH	Doesn't matter
RETURNED_OCTET_LENGTH	Doesn't matter
PRECISION	Doesn't matter
SCALE	Doesn't matter
DATETIME_INTERVAL_CODE	11
DATETIME_INTERVAL_PRECISION	1
NULLABLE	1
NAME	DURATION
UNNAMED	0
COLLATION_CATALOG	Doesn't matter
COLLATION_SCHEMA	Doesn't matter
COLLATION_NAME	Doesn't matter
CHARACTER_SET_CATALOG	Doesn't matter
CHARACTER_SET_SCHEMA	Doesn't matter
CHARACTER_SET_NAME	Doesn't matter
DATA	Set only when data is retrieved into descriptor area
INDICATOR	Set only when data is retrieved into descriptor area

If you want to retrieve information from a descriptor area, you use the GET DESCRIPTOR statement. This statement has two variations, one to get the number of filled-in items, and the other to get information from a specific item.

To get the number of filled-in items, the format is:

```
GET DESCRIPTOR desc-name
  target = COUNT
```

The desc-name is the name of a descriptor area that you have allocated with the same GLOBAL or LOCAL scope during the session. (We're getting tired of writing that phrase, and you're probably tired of reading it. How about if we just say *valid descriptor area* from now on, and you'll understand that we mean all that other stuff? okay?) target is a host variable or a parameter that you specify to receive the integer that tells you the number of items that are in use in this descriptor area.

To get information from a specific item, the format is:

```
GET DESCRIPTOR desc-name
  VALUE item-number
  target = item-name [ , target = item-name ]...
```

As before, desc-name is the name of a valid descriptor area. item-number is an integer simple value specification that identifies the specific item in the descriptor area; it should be less than the value you got (or could have gotten) from COUNT, or you'll get a no-data return; if it's greater than the number of occurrences allocated for the descriptor area, you'll get an error. target is a parameter or host variable of the appropriate data type to get the value stored in the item field identified by item-name (actually, these are *simple targets* because they can never be null; therefore, no indicator parameter or variable is needed or permitted). And item-name is one of the names in that table earlier in this chapter.

If the value of the INDICATOR field is negative (meaning that the item describes a null value) and you use GET DESCRIPTOR to get a value for DATA without also GETting a value for INDICATOR, you'll get an error. To be safe, you might test NULLABLE to see if the item can ever have a null value before attempting to retrieve DATA. Alternatively, you can always retrieve INDICATOR every time you retrieve DATA.

To put all of this in context, let's look at an example.

```
ALLOCATE DESCRIPTOR 'MYDESCRIPTOR' WITH MAX 20;

DESCRIBE...

GET DESCRIPTOR 'MYDESCRIPTOR' :number = COUNT;

GET DESCRIPTOR 'MYDESCRIPTOR' VALUE 1
  :datatype = TYPE,
  :length = LENGTH,
  :name = NAME;
  :nullable = NULLABLE
```

```
      if nullable = 0 then
         GET DESCRIPTOR 'MYDESCRIPTOR' VALUE 1
            :data = DATA ;

      else
         GET DESCRIPTOR 'MYDESCRIPTOR' VALUE 1
            :data = DATA ,
            :ind  = INDICATOR ;


   DEALLOCATE DESCRIPTOR 'MYDESCRIPTOR';
```

Occasionally, you may find yourself wanting to change the values of certain fields in some items of a descriptor area. One reason that you may want to do this is to specify that your host language variable or your parameter has a slightly different data type than the DBMS hoped you'd use. Consider this example: If you're writing your application in the C programming language, but the database that you're using contains DECIMAL data, you will often find yourself in the position of needing to access data that your programming language doesn't support. SQL-92 comes to the rescue again! In this case, if you DESCRIBE a statement and learn that one of the columns is DECIMAL with scale 0, then you can simply set the TYPE for that item to 4 (for INTEGER) and let the database system do automatic data type conversions for you. We'll cover this a bit more later on.

The format of the SET DESCRIPTOR statement is very close to that for GET DESCRIPTOR and has the same two variations:

```
   SET DESCRIPTOR desc-name
      COUNT = value
```

where desc-name is the name of a valid descriptor area and value is an integer simple value specification. This variation allows you to set the total number of items that you plan to use; if value is greater than the number of occurrences in the descriptor area, you'll get an error.

Your other alternative is:

```
   SET DESCRIPTOR desc-name
      VALUE item-number
      item-name = value [ , item-name = value ]...
```

Of course, desc-name is the name of a valid descriptor area and item-number is the number of the item that you're setting or changing. item-name is the name of one of the fields of an item as shown in the table earlier in this chapter. value is a simple value specification of the appropriate data type.

When you set fields in an item of a descriptor area, they are effectively set in the following order: TYPE, DATETIME_INTERVAL_CODE, DATETIME_INTERVAL_PRECISION,

PRECISION, SCALE, CHARACTER_SET_CATALOG, CHARACTER_SET_SCHEMA, CHARACTER_
SET_NAME, LENGTH, INDICATOR, and DATA, regardless of the order that you wrote them
in the SET DESCRIPTOR statement. (Of course, this applies only for a single SET
DESCRIPTOR statement; if you had two or more, the second one might foul up the
results of the first.) If you specify fields that are meaningless for the TYPE value, then
your instructions will be ignored for those fields and they'll be set to whatever your
implementor wants.

Well, that covers the statements that deal directly with the descriptor areas. As
we shall see, other statements use them in various ways. But before we get into the
more complicated statements, let's have a look at the simplest way to dynamically
execute SQL statements.

16.5   The EXECUTE IMMEDIATE Statement

The format of the EXECUTE IMMEDIATE statement is:

```
EXECUTE IMMEDIATE statement-variable
```

The statement-variable is a simple target (a parameter or host variable
without an indicator) that contains a character string that is the dynamic statement
that you want to execute. As we said earlier, a dynamic SQL statement that you're
going to execute using EXECUTE IMMEDIATE can't have any dynamic parameters in
it. Also, remember that the statement is executed on a one-shot basis; if you want
to execute it again, you'll have to go through all the overhead again. Therefore, if
you think you'll want to execute the statement more than once, consider the
PREPARE/EXECUTE alternative.

The effect of EXECUTE IMMEDIATE is the same as PREPARE, EXECUTE, and DEALLOC-
ATE PREPARE sequence. Here's a typical example.

```
EXECUTE IMMEDIATE 'UPDATE movie_titles SET
    current_rental_price = current_rental_price * 1.1'
```

As you'd expect, this example raises the rental price of every movie by 10%. Of
course, if you knew when you were writing your application that you'd want to do
that, you'd be better off coding the statement into your module or embedded SQL
program. But if you don't know that you're going to have to execute this statement,
then this is one way to do it dynamically. If the contents of the statement-variable don't follow the proper syntax of a valid preparable SQL statement, or if you
don't have the proper privileges to execute the statement, you'll get the appropriate
error. You'll also get an error if you try to execute a statement that has an SQL
comment or that has any dynamic parameters.

As long as the statement is properly constructed and you have the required
privileges to execute it, the effect is the same as if you had written the statement
into a module and executed it—except, of course, for performance.

16.6   PREPARE and EXECUTE Statements

If you find yourself with the need to execute an SQL statement dynamically and you expect to have to execute the statement more than once, or if the statement needs to use dynamic parameters, you will use the PREPARE statement to prepare the dynamic statement for execution and then use the EXECUTE statement to execute it as the need arises (that is, within the same session at most; many implementations only permit you to execute the dynamic statement in the same *transaction* in which it was prepared).

The format of the PREPARE statement is:

```
PREPARE statement-name
  FROM statement-variable
```

The statement-name is either an identifier that you use to identify the prepared statement in other statements (like the EXECUTE statement), or it's a simple value specification that you can optionally precede with GLOBAL or LOCAL (GLOBAL is the default). Of course, the identifier option is a normal dynamic statement name, while the simple value specification alternative is an extended dynamic statement name.

Let's look at a couple of examples.

```
PREPARE DYN1 FROM 'DELETE FROM MOVIE_TITLES
        WHERE TITLE LIKE ''%Dead%'''
```

Note the doubled apostrophes that stand for a single apostrophe within the character string literal. Another way to do this same statement might look something like this in C:

```
temp = "DELETE FROM MOVIE_TITLES WHERE TITLE LIKE '%Dead%'";
EXEC SQL PREPARE DYN1 FROM :temp;
```

If you didn't want to use a preknown statement name for this statement, but to invent one on the fly, you could use something like this:

```
dynstmt = "DYN1";
temp = "DELETE FROM MOVIE_TITLES WHERE TITLE LIKE '%Dead%'";
EXEC SQL PREPARE :dynstmt FROM :temp;
```

This last example illustrates the ability of the host program to provide both the name of a dynamic prepared statement and the text of the statement itself from host variables. In module language, this would look like:

```
dynstmt = "DYN1";
temp = "DELETE FROM MOVIE_TITLES WHERE TITLE LIKE '%Dead%'";
PREPSTMT (status, dynstmt, temp);
```

and the procedure (in the module) would be something like:

```
PROCEDURE PREPSTMT (SQLSTATE, :DYN_NAME CHARACTER(128), :STATEMENT CHARACTER(128))

    PREPARE :DYN_NAME FROM :STATEMENT;
```

Once you have prepared a dynamic SQL statement, you can use it repeatedly during the same transaction. Your implementation may allow you to use the same prepared statement in other transactions in the same SQL session.

The statements that you can prepare and execute dynamically (including EXECUTE IMMEDIATE) are: any schema definition or modification statement; any transaction statement (COMMIT, ROLLBACK, SET TRANSACTION, SET CONSTRAINTS); any session statement (SET CATALOG, SET SCHEMA, SET NAMES, SET SESSION AUTHORIZA-TION, and SET TIME ZONE); and several data manipulation statements (searched DELETE, searched UPDATE, single row SELECT, INSERT, and special versions of positioned DELETE and positioned UPDATE). You can also prepare a dynamic cursor specification, as we'll see a bit later in this chapter (section 16.10).

Once you have prepared a dynamic SQL statement, you're probably going to want to execute it. The format of the EXECUTE statement is:

```
EXECUTE statement-name
  [ result-using ] [ parameter-using ]
```

As before, statement-name is either an identifier you use to identify the prepared statement in other statements (like the EXECUTE statement), or it's a simple value specification that you can optionally precede with GLOBAL or LOCAL (GLOBAL is the default). Also as before, the identifier option is a normal dynamic statement name, while the simple value specification alternative is an extended dynamic statement name.

The result-using is an optional USING clause that specifies where the results of the dynamically executed statement (for example, the results of a FETCH statement) are supposed to go. If the statement doesn't return any results (for example, a DELETE statement), then you don't use a result-using. The parameter-using is also an optional USING clause; it specifies where the dynamically executed statement gets the values for the dynamic parameters in the statement. If the statement doesn't have any dynamic parameters, you don't use a parameter-using. Each of them can be either a using-arguments or a using-descriptor. A using-arguments specifies host variables or values that will be the target for results or the source for dynamic parameters. A using descriptor specifies a descriptor area that will be used as the target for results or as the source for dynamic parameters.

When a result-using or a parameter-using is a using-arguments, the format is:

```
USING arg [ , arg ]...
```

or

```
INTO arg [ , arg ]...
```

You use the USING alternative for a parameter-using and the INTO alternative for a result-using. (The way to remember this is that results go *into* the targets and the dynamic parameters *use* the source.) Actually, you can use USING in either place (for backwards compatibility with many existing products), but you cannot use INTO except in a result-using; in spite of that, we recommend using USING only for a parameter-using. The number of args must be equal to the number of results returned by the dynamic statement or the number of dynamic parameters in the dynamic statement.

When you execute the dynamic statement, if there are any dynamic parameters, the DBMS will retrieve the values to be associated with those dynamic parameters from the locations specified in the appropriate arg. These arg values can have indicators as well. Therefore, you can have something like this:

```
EXECUTE DYN1
  USING :arg1, :arg2 INDICATOR :argind2, :arg3
```

or

```
EXECUTE DYN1
  INTO :arg1, :arg2 INDICATOR :argind2, :arg3
```

or even

```
EXECUTE DYN1
  USING :arg1, :arg2 INDICATOR :argind2, :arg3
  INTO  :arg4, :arg5 INDICATOR :argind6, :arg6
```

Incidentally, the same arg name can be used in both the USING and the INTO clauses. The value is retrieved at the beginning of the statement (for USING), and a new value is set at the end of the statement (for INTO).

When a result-using or parameter-using is a using-descriptor, the format is:

```
USING SQL DESCRIPTOR descriptor-name
```

or

```
INTO SQL DESCRIPTOR descriptor-name
```

As with the using-arguments, you use USING for a parameter-using and INTO for a result-using (but see the discussion for using-arguments). And the descriptor-name is, of course, the name of a descriptor area that has enough items to account for all of the results or dynamic parameters (as appropriate) in the dynamic statement.

In this case, when you execute the dynamic SQL statement, the DBMS doesn't go to host variables or parameters to get the dynamic parameter values, and it doesn't try to store the results into host variables or parameters. Instead, it gets values from and stores results into a descriptor area.

Of course, the descriptor area has to have appropriate descriptions (data type, *etc.*) for the appropriate columns, so you must either initialize all of the items and fields or use DESCRIBE to let the DBMS do the initialization for you.

Let's next take a look at the DESCRIBE statement, and then we'll examine some more details about the USING (and INTO) clause.

16.7   The DESCRIBE Statement

As we've already mentioned, the purpose of the DESCRIBE statement is to provide you with information about the columns that you're retrieving with a dynamic SQL statement or about the dynamic parameters in your dynamic SQL statement. It comes in two forms, a *describe input statement* and a *describe output statement*. The format of the describe output statement is:

DESCRIBE [OUTPUT] statement-name using-descriptor

The keyword OUTPUT is optional, but the statement means the same thing with or without it. The statement-name is still either an identifier that you use to identify the prepared statement in other statements (like the EXECUTE statement), or it's a simple value specification that you can optionally precede with GLOBAL or LOCAL (GLOBAL is the default). Also as before, the identifier option is a normal dynamic statement name, while the simple value specification alternative is an extended dynamic statement name. As before, using-descriptor is:

USING SQL DESCRIPTOR descriptor-name

Similarly, a describe input statement has the format:

DESCRIBE INPUT statement-name using-descriptor

and statement-name and using-descriptor are as for a describe output statement.

When you execute a DESCRIBE statement (either variety) and the statement-name doesn't identify a dynamic SQL statement that has been PREPARED (and not deallocated) in the scope of the statement-name (including in the same session or transaction), you'll get an error.

When you execute a describe output statement, it stores into the descriptor area a description of the columns that make up the select list of the prepared statement. One implication of this is that the statement has an effect only when there is a select list in the prepared statement, and it must therefore be a dynamic single-row SELECT statement or a dynamic cursor. Actually, you can execute a describe output statement on any prepared statement without getting an error, but it will affect the descriptor area only if it is a dynamic single-row SELECT statement or a dynamic cursor. Here is how the descriptor area is set:

- If the prepared statement is a dynamic single-row SELECT statement or a dynamic cursor, then COUNT is set to the number of select-list columns in the statement; otherwise, COUNT is set to 0.

- If COUNT is greater than the number of occurrences specified when the descriptor area was allocated, you get a warning condition and no items in the descriptor area are set. (Obviously, if COUNT is 0, no items are set then, either.)

- Only the NULLABLE, NAME, UNNAMED, TYPE, and fields related to TYPE are set. In particular, the DATA and INDICATOR fields are not relevant to DESCRIBE, so they are not set.

- If the column being described is possibly nullable, the NULLABLE field is set to 1; otherwise, NULLABLE is set to 0.

- If the column has a user-defined name, NAME is set to that name and UNNAMED is set to 0. If the column has an implementation-defined name, UNNAMED is set to 1, and NAME is set to the implementation- defined name of the column.

- If the column is a character string column, TYPE is set to 1 or 12 (CHARACTER or CHARACTER VARYING, respectively), LENGTH is set to the length (or maximum length) in characters of the column, OCTET_LENGTH is set to the maximum possible length (in octets) of the column, CHARACTER_SET_CATALOG, CHARACTER_SET_SCHEMA, and CHARACTER_SET_NAME are set to the components of the fully qualified name of the character set associated with the column, and COLLATION_CATALOG, COLLATION_SCHEMA, and COLLATION_NAME are set to the components of the fully qualified name of the collation for the column.

- If the column is a bit string column, TYPE is set to 14 or 15 (BIT or BIT VARYING, respectively), LENGTH is set to the length (or maximum length) in bits of the column, and OCTET_LENGTH is set to the maximum possible length in octets of the column.

- If the column is an exact numeric column, TYPE is set to 2, 3, 4, or 5 (NUMERIC, DECIMAL, INTEGER, or SMALLINT, respectively), PRECISION is set to the precision of the column, and SCALE is set to the scale of the column.

- If the column is an approximate numeric column, TYPE is set to 6, 7, or 8 (FLOAT, REAL, or DOUBLE PRECISION, respectively) and PRECISION is set to the precision of the column.

- If the column is a datetime column, TYPE is set to 9, LENGTH is set to the length in positions of the column, DATETIME_INTERVAL_CODE is set to 1, 2, 3, 4, or 5 (for DATE, TIME, TIMESTAMP, TIME WITH TIME ZONE, or TIMESTAMP WITH TIME ZONE, respectively), and PRECISION is set to the fractional seconds precision of the column.

- If the column is an interval column, TYPE is set to 10, DATETIME_INTERVAL_CODE is set to a number between 1 and 13 (see the earlier table) to indicate the interval qualifier of the column, DATETIME_INTERVAL_PRECISION is set to the precision of the column's leading field precision, and PRECISION is set to the column's trailing field precision.

When all of the columns have been described, the DESCRIBE statement is finished and a description of every column in the dynamic SQL statement's select-list can be found in the descriptor area.

At this time, your application can use the GET DESCRIPTOR statement to inquire about the column descriptions and to take appropriate action based on that information. We'll illustrate this a little later in this chapter. Your application can also use SET DESCRIPTOR to change the values of items in the descriptor area, but we'll cover how and why later on.

When you execute a describe input statement, it stores into the descriptor area a description of the dynamic parameters that are in the prepared statement. One implication of this is that the statement has an effect only when there are dynamic parameters in the prepared statement. Actually, you can execute a describe input statement on any prepared statement without getting an error, but it will affect the descriptor area only if there are dynamic parameters. Here is how the descriptor area is set:

- If the prepared statement has at least one dynamic parameter, COUNT is set to the number of dynamic parameters in the statement; otherwise, COUNT is set to 0.

- If COUNT is greater than the number of occurrences specified when the descriptor area was allocated, you get a warning condition and no items in the descriptor area are set. (Obviously, if COUNT is 0, no items are set then, either.)

- Only the NULLABLE, NAME, UNNAMED, TYPE, and fields related to TYPE are set. In particular, the DATA and INDICATOR fields are not relevant to DESCRIBE, so they are not set.

- The NULLABLE field is set to 1 (all dynamic parameters are potentially nullable).

- NAME and UNNAMED are both set to implementation-defined values. That is, the dynamic parameters don't have column names, so these fields are irrelevant.

- The other fields are set just like those in the describe output statement above (except you should read *dynamic parameter* wherever the earlier list contains *column*).

When all of the dynamic parameters have been described, the DESCRIBE statement is finished and a description of every dynamic parameter in the dynamic SQL statement is stored in the descriptor area.

At this time, your application can use the GET DESCRIPTOR statement to inquire about the dynamic parameter descriptions and to take appropriate action based on that information. We'll illustrate this a little later in this chapter. Your application can also use SET DESCRIPTOR to change the values of items in the descriptor area, but we'll cover how and why later on.

16.8 The EXECUTE Statement Revisited

Now that we've got the DESCRIBE statement under our belts, let's reconsider the EXECUTE statement in light of DESCRIBE's behavior.

Suppose that you've prepared a dynamic SQL statement that has some dynamic parameters. Recall that the data types of the dynamic parameters are determined by their context, so the only way you can determine the appropriate data types to provide when the statement is executed is to describe the prepared statement with a describe input statement (unless, of course, you have intimate knowledge about the statement even before you've prepared it—for example, if you created the statement in your application program using knowledge about the data types to write the statement). Having described the statement, the information about the dynamic parameters is stored in the descriptor area that you specified.

At this point, you can execute the prepared statement (using EXECUTE, of course). You must provide input values for each of the dynamic parameters, and you can choose to provide them directly from your host variables or parameters, or you can provide them in the descriptor area itself. If you knew little enough about the statement to have to describe it, then you probably have not written your application in a way that would make it easy to provide input values in host variables or parameters, so you will probably choose to provide input values in the descriptor areas.

If you *do* choose to provide the dynamic parameter input values from host variables or parameters, the format of the EXECUTE statement will be:

```
EXECUTE statement-name USING arg [ , arg ]...
```

In this case, the number of args provided to the EXECUTE statement must *exactly* match the number of dynamic parameters in the prepared statement; otherwise, you'll get an error.

If you choose to go the descriptor area route, the format of the EXECUTE statement will be:

```
EXECUTE statement-name
  USING SQL DESCRIPTOR descriptor-name
```

Of course, the description of and restrictions on statement-name and descriptor-name are still as specified above in the earlier discussion of EXECUTE. But let's talk about the restrictions on the *contents* of the descriptor.

Recall that this option is meaningful *only* if the descriptor area has been appropriately set up for the prepared statement. The most direct way to do this is to DESCRIBE the prepared statement into the descriptor area. An alternative is to manually set up the fields of each required item in the descriptor area (using SET DESCRIPTOR). Let's assume that you decided to use DESCRIBE to do it, although it doesn't really matter for the purposes of this discussion.

When you execute the EXECUTE statement with USING SQL DESCRIPTOR, if the value of COUNT is greater than the number of occurrences in the descriptor, you'll get an error. Similarly, if the value of COUNT is not equal to the number of dynamic parameters in the prepared statement, you'll get a different error. If items 1 through COUNT are not valid (that is, all relevant fields having appropriate values corresponding to the TYPE field), you'll get yet a different error. If the value of INDICATOR for any item is not negative and the value for DATA isn't a valid value for the data type indicated by TYPE (and the other fields), you'll get an error for that, too. (If INDICATOR is negative, it means that you want the dynamic parameter to have the null value, so the value of DATA is irrelevant and isn't even verified.)

At this point, we could simply say that the value of DATA in each item of the descriptor is assigned to the corresponding dynamic parameter and the dynamic statement can be executed. We could say that, but it wouldn't be quite accurate. There's really a little more to it. (You were beginning to suspect that it wasn't quite that simple, weren't you?)

What really happens is that the DBMS first determines the data type of each dynamic parameter, by its context; this is the data type that would be represented by the information that a DESCRIBE INPUT statement would have put into the appropriate item in the descriptor area. Then the DBMS determines the data type specified by the actual information in the appropriate item in the descriptor area. Most of the time, these will be identical and our simple scenario in the preceding paragraph will be correct. However, you may have chosen to use a SET DESCRIPTOR to change the information in one or more items in the descriptor area to something different than the information that DESCRIBE put (or would have put) in there. In that case, the DBMS does a CAST from the DATA field (using the information actually in the item) to the data type of the dynamic parameter. Of course, this means that the information actually in the descriptor area has to specify a data type for which there is a valid CAST to the data type of the dynamic parameter; otherwise, you'll get an error of one sort or another (depending on whether the data type itself is improper for such a CAST, or whether the data type is alright but the actual data in DATA is inappropriate).

The last couple of paragraphs assume that you used the using-descriptor alternative. What if you used the using-arguments alternative? The same rules apply, including the implicit CAST. However, in this case, the data type of the arg is the relevant data type, and the value stored in the arg is CAST from the arg's data type to the data type of the dynamic parameter. Everything else behaves as described.

Now, we need to consider the other direction: data returned by the dynamic SQL statement. In this case, we can describe the prepared statement using a DESCRIBE OUTPUT statement, which will load up the descriptor area with a description of each select-list column in the statement. Our EXECUTE statement will look like this:

```
EXECUTE statement-name INTO arg [ , arg ]...
```

or

```
EXECUTE statement-name INTO SQL DESCRIPTOR descriptor-name
```

You can guess (and you'd be right) that the rules for statement-name and descriptor-name are the same as before. You'd also be right to guess that the rule requiring, for the using-arguments variant, the number of args to be identical to the number of select-list columns is also present (otherwise, you'll get an error). If you use the SQL DESCRIPTOR alternative, the value of COUNT must (you guessed it!) be equal to the number of select-list columns and must not be greater than the number of item occurrences created when the descriptor area was allocated. Also, items 1 through COUNT must be valid for the data type indicated by TYPE.

The same sort of CAST is done here as was done for the input case above. This time, the data from the select-list columns is CAST (from the actual data type of the select-list columns) to the data type indicated by the contents of the corresponding item in the descriptor area (or, for the using-arguments variant, to the data type of the corresponding arg). If that CAST is invalid, either because of an improper data type or because of data problems, you'll get an appropriate error.

If you choose the using-descriptor variant and the select-column has the null value, INDICATOR is set to –1 and DATA isn't set at all. If the select-list column is not null, INDICATOR is set to 0 and DATA is set to the value of the column. If the data is CAST to a character or bit string (or is already a character or bit string), RETURNED_LENGTH and RETURNED_OCTET_LENGTH are set to the length in characters or bits and the length in octets, respectively, of the value stored in DATA (or the actual select-list column).

In summary, if you know a lot about the dynamic parameters and select-list columns for your prepared statement, you are safe using the using-arguments forms of the USING (or INTO) clauses. However, if you don't know all the important aspects of the dynamic parameters or select-list columns, you'd probably be better off using the using-descriptor variants.

Now, we promised that we'd explain why you might want to use SET DESCRIPTOR after you've done a DESCRIBE. Okay, it's time.

Suppose you're writing your application in C (which, you will recall, has no decimal data type) and the prepared statement that you describe turns out, upon executing DESCRIBE, to have a select-list column (or dynamic parameter, or both) whose data type is DECIMAL. It would be most unfortunate if SQL simply said "Sorry, people, but you can't write this application in C." Well, the standards committees thought of that problem. That's why the CAST rules were put in for the EXECUTE statement. In this case, you can simply use SET DESCRIPTOR to change the TYPE (and PRECISION and SCALE, if required) columns of the appropriate item in the descriptor area to represent INTEGER or SMALLINT, or even REAL, FLOAT, or DOUBLE PRECISION, and force the DBMS to CAST the DECIMAL data into a data type that you can handle in your application program!

Of course, you could also explicitly code the CASTs into the SQL statement being executed dynamically, but sometimes that means that your end user has to code more than he or she really needs to. By using SET DESCRIPTOR to do the CASTs for you, the end user (who may be composing partial SQL statements) can focus on the job at hand and not on grubby details of data conversion.

16.9 Dynamic SQL and Cursors

So far, we've talked only about using dynamic SQL to deal with *set-oriented* statements. But real applications need to use cursors to deal with that annoying impedance mismatch between SQL and the conventional programming languages. That fact remains true whether you're using static SQL or dynamic SQL. So, SQL-92 has defined statements that will let you use cursors in dynamic SQL.

Logically enough, the most central statement here is the dynamic declare cursor. It is a very close analog to the DECLARE CURSOR for static SQL but has a somewhat different syntax, for reasons that will become immediately obvious when we show you:

```
DECLARE cursor-name [ INSENSITIVE ] [ SCROLL ] CURSOR
   FOR statement-name
```

Recall that the static DECLARE CURSOR ended up with a cursor-specification, which was a query-expression and a few other things (see Chapter 12 for a review of these terms).

However, in dynamic SQL, you simply don't know the query-expression (or the "few other things") in advance—that's why you're using dynamic SQL. Therefore, you declare a dynamic cursor that identifies a simple value specification (literal, host variable, or parameter) instead of a cursor-specification. Then, at runtime, the simple value specification is set up to be a character string representation of a cursor-specification! (Of course, if you choose to use a literal, then you still have to know the details when you write the application, but the more general case will allow you to plug the values in at runtime.)

The dynamic DECLARE CURSOR is a declarative statement, just like the static one. This means that the scope of the cursor name is the same as the scope of the cursor name of static cursors; you can't have a static cursor and a dynamic cursor with the same name in the same module or compilation unit. There's also a requirement that the module or compilation unit must have a PREPARE statement that references the same statement-name as the one in the dynamic DECLARE CURSOR.

There's a variation on dynamic cursors that we mentioned briefly earlier: *extended* dynamic cursors. An extended dynamic cursor is one whose *name* isn't known until runtime. This allows you to invent new cursors as you need them instead of limiting yourself to the dynamic cursors that you code in your application programs. Instead of declaring an extended dynamic cursor, you *allocate* it. The format of the ALLOCATE CURSOR statement is:

```
ALLOCATE ext-cursor-name
   [ INSENSITIVE ] [ SCROLL ] CURSOR
   FOR ext-stmt-name
```

In this case, both ext-cursor-name and ext-stmt-name are host variables or parameters and can be optionally preceded by GLOBAL or LOCAL (the default is still

GLOBAL). You cannot have more than one cursor concurrently allocated with the same actual name. However, ext-cursor-name isn't the name of the cursor. Rather, it is the *contents* of ext-cursor-name when you execute the ALLOCATE CURSOR statement that gives the name of the cursor. Therefore, these statements are valid:

```
ext1 = "CURS1";
EXEC SQL ALLOCATE :ext1 CURSOR FOR :stmt;
ext1 = "CURS2";
EXEC SQL ALLOCATE :ext1 CURSOR FOR :stmt;
```

These statements allocate two extended dynamic cursors, named CURS1 and CURS2. By contrast, these statements are *invalid:*

```
ext1 = "CURS1";
EXEC SQL ALLOCATE :ext1 CURSOR FOR :stmt;
ext2 = "CURS1";
EXEC SQL ALLOCATE :ext2 CURSOR FOR :stmt;
```

The last statement attempts to allocate a second cursor named CURS1, which is invalid and will get an error.

Before you can open the cursor, the statement-name for a normal dynamic cursor must identify a prepared statement, and that prepared statement must be a cursor-specification (see below).

An extended dynamic cursor is even more restrictive. You must have prepared a statement (again, a cursor-specification) and associated it with the ext-stmt-name *before* you execute the ALLOCATE CURSOR statement, or you'll get an error. If the ALLOCATE CURSOR statement succeeds, the extended cursor name is associated with the prepared cursor-specification.

Once you have a dynamic cursor name (regular or extended) and have a valid prepared cursor-specification associated with it, then you can use the cursor. As with static cursors, you must open the cursor before you do anything else. The format of a dynamic OPEN statement is very similar to the format of the static OPEN, but with one important difference:

```
OPEN cursor-name [ using-clause ]
```

The cursor-name is, of course, either a regular cursor-name, or an ext-cursor-name. If the cursor-name isn't associated with a prepared cursor-specification, you'll get an error. If it is an ext-cursor-name and it doesn't properly identify an allocated cursor in the appropriate scope, you'll get another error.

Note the using-clause. Obviously, this is either a using-arguments or a using-descriptor. If the cursor-specification associated with the cursor-name doesn't have any dynamic parameters in it, it doesn't matter whether or not you specify the using-clause (if you do, it won't be used). On the other hand, if the cursor-specification does have dynamic parameters, you must specify a using-clause; otherwise, you'll get an error. If you properly specify the using-clause, the effects are exactly the same as described earlier for the EXECUTE statement when you have dynamic parameters in the prepared statement and you specify a using-clause to provide the values to be given to those dynamic parameters. Note that you do not specify an INTO clause; that comes later, with the dynamic FETCH statement.

When you're finished using your dynamic cursor, you will normally close it (although, as with static cursors, terminating the transaction will tell the DBMS to close any open dynamic cursors for you). The format of the dynamic CLOSE statement is almost identical to the static version:

```
CLOSE cursor-name
```

The only difference is that cursor-name can be either a normal dynamic cursor name or an ext-cursor-name. The usual and expected restrictions apply, and the usual and expected errors will result from violations of those restrictions.

While the cursor is open, you will normally want to FETCH data through the cursor. The format of the dynamic FETCH statement is close to that for the static version:

```
FETCH [ [ orientation ] FROM ] cursor-name
   using-clause
```

The rules for the orientation and FROM are the same as for the static FETCH. The cursor-name can, of course, be either a normal dynamic cursor name or an ext-cursor-name, with the usual restrictions and errors. The using-clause is required here, though (not optional as in the dynamic OPEN statement). A valid cursor-specification will always have at least one select-list column, which means that every dynamic FETCH will retrieve at least one value. The using-clause tells the DBMS where to put those results.

Of course, the using-clause can be either a using-arguments or a using-descriptor, and the behavior is exactly as specified earlier for the EXECUTE statement when specifying the behavior for select-list column retrievals. As in that case, you may specify either USING or INTO, and we recommend INTO in this case, because you're FETCHing INTO the arguments or descriptor area.

Note that the dynamic OPEN, dynamic FETCH, and dynamic CLOSE statements are *not* preparable statements. They are static statements because you code them into your application program. However, they *operate* on dynamic cursors, so the only details that you have to know when you're writing your application is whether you want to declare (or allocate) the cursor to be INSENSITIVE or SCROLL. All other attributes are determined strictly at runtime based on the cursor-specification that you PREPARE.

16.9.1 Dynamic Positioned Statements

Similarly, there are static statements for deleting from and updating through a dynamic cursor. These statements are generally called the *dynamic positioned* DELETE and UPDATE statements. The format for the dynamic positioned DELETE statement is:

```
DELETE FROM table-name
   WHERE CURRENT OF cursor-name
```

This is identical to the static positioned DELETE statement except that the cursor-name can be either a normal cursor name or an ext-cursor-name. The behavior of the statement is precisely the same as the static positioned DELETE statement.

By the same token, the format for the dynamic positioned UPDATE statement is:

```
UPDATE table-name
   SET column-name = value [ , column-name = value ]...
   WHERE CURRENT OF cursor-name
```

and the only difference is the cursor-name can be a normal cursor name or an ext-cursor-name. The behavior here is also identical to the static positioned UPDATE statement.

However, life isn't always this simple. The problem with the dynamic positioned UPDATE statement is that you must know the column names when you write your application! This is sometimes practical but frequently impossible. Therefore, you really need to be able to PREPARE a positioned DELETE statement so that you can include different set-clauses (column-name = value) based on the actual cursor that you're dealing with.

The format of the *preparable* positioned UPDATE statement is:

```
UPDATE [ table-name ]
   SET column-name = value [ , column-name = value ]...
   WHERE CURRENT OF cursor-name
```

The table-name is optional here because it's not really needed. Updatable cursors in SQL-92 can have only one table anyway. The other reason is that it may sometimes be difficult to determine the table name without a detailed analysis of the cursor-specification. Except for that fact, the behavior is identical to the dynamic positioned UPDATE statement that we just discussed.

For symmetry, SQL-92 also includes a preparable positioned DELETE statement, whose format is:

```
DELETE [ FROM table-name ]
   WHERE CURRENT OF cursor-name
```

Technically, this statement isn't actually required, though the optionality of the table-name means that you may not have to analyze your cursor-specification just to delete a row via the cursor. The main reason this statement was included in SQL-92 was for symmetry with the preparable positioned UPDATE statement.

The more astute readers will have noticed that SQL-92 has an ALLOCATE CURSOR statement, but no DEALLOCATE CURSOR statement. It's not clear why this wasn't included, since such a statement would serve to free up those scarce system resources that statements like DEALLOCATE PREPARE and DEALLOCATE DESCRIPTOR are supposed to free up. Still, it's not there. Perhaps it will be in a future version of the standard.

16.10 A Dynamic SQL Example

Let's take a look at an example of a Dynamic SQL program:[1]

```
MODULE sql92_dyn
LANGUAGE C
AUTHORIZATION bryan

    DECLARE mycursor CURSOR FOR stmt_id

    PROCEDURE allocate_desc(SQLCODE,
                            :desc_name  CHAR(255));
       ALLOCATE DESCRIPTOR :desc_name;

    PROCEDURE deallocate_desc(SQLCODE,
                              :desc_name  CHAR(255));
       DEALLOCATE DESCRIPTOR :desc_name;

    PROCEDURE prepare_statement(SQLCODE,
                                :stmt_string  CHAR(255));
       PREPARE stmt_id FROM :stmt_string;

    PROCEDURE describe_input(SQLCODE,
                             :desc_name  CHAR(255));
       DESCRIBE INPUT stmt_id USING SQL DESCRIPTOR :desc_name;

    PROCEDURE describe_output(SQLCODE,
                              :desc_name  CHAR(255));
       DESCRIBE OUTPUT stmt_id USING SQL DESCRIPTOR :desc_name;

    PROCEDURE execute_statement(SQLCODE,
                                :in_desc_name CHAR(255));
       EXECUTE stmt_id USING SQL DESCRIPTOR :in_desc_name;

    PROCEDURE open_cursor(SQLCODE,
                          :in_desc_name  CHAR(255));
       OPEN mycursor USING SQL DESCRIPTOR :in_desc_name;
```

---

[1] Adapted from Jim Melton and Bryan Higgs, Details of SQL-92: Towards a Portable Dynamic JQL, *DB Programming and Design,* Nov. and Dec., 1992.

```
PROCEDURE fetch_cursor(SQLCODE,
                       :out_desc_name  CHAR(255));
  FETCH mycursor USING SQL DESCRIPTOR :out_desc_name;

PROCEDURE close_cursor(SQLCODE);
  CLOSE mycursor;

PROCEDURE deprepare_statement(SQLCODE);
  DEALLOCATE PREPARE stmt_id;

PROCEDURE get_count(SQLCODE,
                    :desc_name   CHAR(255),
                    :item_count  INTEGER);
  GET DESCRIPTOR :desc_name :item_count = COUNT;

PROCEDURE get_item_info(SQLCODE,
                        :desc_name CHAR(255),
                        :item_no   INTEGER,
                        :name      CHAR(128),
                        :type      INTEGER,
                        :len       INTEGER,
                        :data      CHAR(4000),
                        :indicator INTEGER);
  GET DESCRIPTOR :desc_name VALUE :item_no
      :name = NAME, :type = TYPE, :len = LENGTH,
      :data = DATA, :indicator = INDICATOR;

PROCEDURE set_count(SQLCODE,
                    :desc_name   CHAR(255),
                    :item_count  INTEGER);
  SET DESCRIPTOR :desc_name COUNT = :item_count;

PROCEDURE set_item_info(SQLCODE,
                        :desc_name CHAR(255),
                        :item_no   INTEGER,
                        :type      INTEGER,
                        :len       INTEGER,
                        :data      CHAR(4000),
                        :indicator INTEGER);
  SET DESCRIPTOR :desc_name VALUE :item_no
      TYPE = :type, LENGTH = :len,
      DATA = :data, INDICATOR = :indicator;
```

And here is the equivalent C code that uses it:

```
/*━━━━━━━━━━━━━━━━━━━━━━━━━━━━━━━━━━━━━━━━━━
 *  Simple interactive SQL program using SQL-92 style dynamic SQL.
 */
#include <stdio.h>
#include <stdlib.h>
#include "sql92_dyn.h"          /* Interface to SQL92_DYN SQL module procedures */

/* extern function declarations */
extern int get_command(char *command_buffer, size_t command_buffer_size);
extern int prompt_for_data(char *markers_desc_name);
extern void display_heading(char *select_list_desc_name);
extern void display_row(char *select_list_desc_name);

/* static, module-level data */
static long sqlcode;
#define SQL_UNSUCCESSFUL    (sqlcode < 0)
#define SQL_END_OF_DATA     (sqlcode == 100)

static char select_list_desc_name[256] = "SELECT_LIST_DESCRIPTOR";
static char markers_desc_name[256]      = "PARAMETERS_DESCRIPTOR";

#define MAX_CMD_LENGTH  4095
static char command_buffer[MAX_CMD_LENGTH + 1];

/**********************************************************
   *  Function to allocate the system SQL descriptor areas.
   */
static int allocate_sqldas(void)
{
/* Allocate the two system SQL descriptor areas */
ALLOCATE_DESC(&sqlcode, select_list_desc_name);
if (SQL_UNSUCCESSFUL)
    return 0;
ALLOCATE_DESC(&sqlcode, markers_desc_name);
if (SQL_UNSUCCESSFUL)
    {
    DEALLOCATE_DESC(&sqlcode, select_list_desc_name);
    return 0;
    }
/* Succeeded in allocating both system SQL descriptor areas */
return 1;
}
```

```
/**********************************************************
 *  Function to report an error.
 **********************************************************/
static void report_error(char *message)
{
fprintf(stderr, "\n%s\nSQLCODE = %ld\n\n", message, sqlcode);
}


/**************************************************************
 *  Function to prepare the command entered by the user,
 *  and then to describe the select list for the prepared command.
 *
 *  Any command entered by the user that is to be executed by SQL
 *  must first be PREPAREd. This function calls the SQL PREPARE
 *  function, and checks for success or failure.
 **************************************************************/
static int prepare_command(void)
{
PREPARE_STATEMENT(&sqlcode, command_buffer);
if (SQL_UNSUCCESSFUL)
    {
    report_error("Failed to prepare statement");
    return 0;
    }
DESCRIBE_OUTPUT(&sqlcode, select_list_desc_name);
if (SQL_UNSUCCESSFUL)
    {
    report_error("Failed to describe output");
    return 0;
    }
return 1;
}


/**************************************************************
 *  Function to execute a select statement entered by the user
 *  and display the resulting row data on the screen.
 **************************************************************/
static int execute_select(void)
{
unsigned int count;

/* Open the cursor */
OPEN_CURSOR(&sqlcode, markers_desc_name);
```

```
if (SQL_UNSUCCESSFUL)
    {
    report_error("Failed to open cursor");
    return 0;
    }
display_heading(select_list_desc_name);

/* Then, loop, fetching the data */
count = 0;
while (1)
    {
    FETCH_CURSOR(&sqlcode, select_list_desc_name);
    if (SQL_END_OF_DATA)
        break;              /* End of data */
    if (SQL_UNSUCCESSFUL)
        {
        report_error("Failed to fetch from cursor");
        break;
        }
    /* If we get here, we have a real row */
    count++;
    display_row(select_list_desc_name);
    }
printf("%u rows retrieved\n", count);

/* Finally, close the cursor */
CLOSE_CURSOR(&sqlcode);
if (SQL_UNSUCCESSFUL)
    {
    report_error("Failed to close cursor");
    return 0;
    }
return 1;
}


/*******************************************************************
 *  Function to execute a nonselect statement entered by the user
 *******************************************************************/
static int execute(void)
{
EXECUTE_STATEMENT(&sqlcode, markers_desc_name);
if (SQL_UNSUCCESSFUL)
    report_error("Failed to execute statement");
}
```

```
/*****************************************************************
 *  Function to execute the command entered by the user
 *****************************************************************/
static int execute_command(void)
{
long count;

/* Get information about markers */
DESCRIBE_INPUT(&sqlcode, markers_desc_name);
if (SQL_UNSUCCESSFUL)
    {
    report_error("Failed to describe statement");
    return 0;
    }
/* If there are any markers, we need the data placed */
/* into the SQL descriptor area. */
if (prompt_for_data(markers_desc_name))
    {
    GET_COUNT(&sqlcode, select_list_desc_name, &count);
    if (count > 0)
        execute_select();
    else
        execute();
    }
return 1;
}


/*****************************************************************
 *  Function to clean up the space allocated by the prepare
 *****************************************************************/
static int release_command(void)
{
DEPREPARE_STATEMENT(&sqlcode);
if (SQL_UNSUCCESSFUL)
    report_error("Failed to release statement");
}


/*****************************************************************
 *  Main entry point for program.
 *****************************************************************/
main()
{
printf("Welcome to the dynamic SQL executor...\n");
/* Allocate and initialize the two system SQL descriptor areas */
if (allocate_sqldas() != 0)
    {
```

```
    /* Loop, getting commands and executing them */
    while (1)
        {
        if (get_command(command_buffer, sizeof(command_buffer)) == 0)
            break;
        if (prepare_command())
            {
            execute_command();
            release_command();
            }
        }
    }
printf("Bye!\n");
}
```

16.11 Chapter Summary

As you can tell from this chapter, there is a great deal more to *knowing* SQL than just a cursory familiarity with the various data definition and data manipulation statements. Intelligent use of SQL facilities requires you to know, for example, when to use dynamic SQL and when to use a static model. Those of you who develop applications that utilize database-stored data in conjunction with other software systems—such as spreadsheets and decision support packages—are likely to find yourselves making heavy use of dynamic SQL.

The Finishing Touches

CHAPTER 17

· · · · · · · · · · · · · · · · ·

Diagnostics and Error Management

17.1 Introduction

Throughout this book so far, we've been telling you things like "you'll get an error" or "you'll get a warning" as we've described the requirements and actions of SQL statements. Now it's time to clarify what we mean by those phrases. We'll discuss SQLCODE and SQLSTATE, and what errors and conditions get reported to each of these, respectively.

17.2 SQLCODE and SQLSTATE

SQL-89 was a bit casual about the idea of errors, but it did distinguish among three situations: genuine errors, the no-data condition, and successful completion. SQL-92 enhances that taxonomy somewhat by distinguishing among those three and describing warnings.

In SQL-89 and most SQL products available today, the primary way of reporting errors is a status parameter (or host variable) called SQLCODE. The earlier standard (SQL-86 and SQL-89) really defined only two values for SQLCODE plus one range of values. The value 0 was returned by the DBMS to indicate *successful completion*, meaning that your statement executed completely successfully and actually did something. The value 100 was defined to indicate *no-data*, which meant that the statement didn't incur any errors, but found no rows on which to operate (for example, if the statement that you executed was a FETCH statement, but there were no more rows in the cursor). Finally, *all negative values* were defined to mean *error,* but the specific negative values associated with any specific error were left up to the implementations. As a result, implementations have differed wildly in the values returned for a given situation. If your applications were to be portable across SQL

DBMS products, the error handling by specific values had to be recoded for each target product.

SQL-92 was intended to fix problems like this, but the need not to obsolete many existing applications made it impossible to simply start defining values for SQLCODE. Instead, SQL-92 has added a second status parameter, called SQLSTATE, which has many predefined values and still leaves lots of room for implementor-defined values where needed. SQLCODE was defined to be an integer parameter and SQLSTATE is defined to be a 5-character string (using only the uppercase letters *A* through *Z* and the digits 0 through 9). This 5-character string is divided into two components. The first two characters are called the *class code,* and the last three characters are called the *subclass code.* Any class code that begins with the characters *A* through *H* or 0 through 4 indicates an SQLSTATE value that is defined by the SQL standard (or by another standard related to SQL, like RDA). For those class codes, any subclass code starting with the same character is also defined by the standard. Any class code starting with the characters *I* through *Z* or 5 through 9 is implementor-defined, and *all* subclass codes (with one exception) are also implementor-defined. The exception is subclass code 000, which *always* means *no subclass code defined.*

Because the SQL standard specifies so little about SQLCODE, it has been *deprecated,* meaning that it is still supported by the standard and by SQL products, but it may be deleted from some future version of the standard and will not be required in order for products to claim conformance to the standard. Actually, we believe that products will continue to implement it for years to come simply because of customers' requirements for support of existing applications. However, SQLSTATE is definitely the recommended way to go, especially if you're concerned with issues like portability of your applications.

Let's see how you would use SQLSTATE (and even SQLCODE) in your applications. First, let's look at an example using module language. A procedure in a module must include either a parameter that specifies SQLSTATE, one that specifies SQLCODE, or both, so you might write:

```
PROCEDURE MYPROC
  (SQLSTATE, :param1 DECIMAL (5,2), :param2 SMALLINT, :param3 CHARACTER (50))

UPDATE movie_titles
  SET current_rental_price =
      :param1 INDICATOR :param2
  WHERE title = :param3;
```

Then, to invoke that procedure from C, you would write something like:

```
        title = "Gone With The Wind";
        price = 1.95;
        notnull = 0;
        MYPROC (state, price, notnull, title);
```

To check on the result, you have to examine the returned value of SQLSTATE, as found in the state variable. You can check for successful completion, which has the code '00000,' like this:

```
if (strcmp (state, "00000"))
    whatever-you-do-in-C;
```

If you're writing in embedded SQL, the actions aren't all that different. Your program might look like:

```
title = "Gone With The Wind";
price = 1.95;
notnull = 0;
EXEC SQL UPDATE movie_titles
    SET current_rental_price =
 :price INDICATOR :notnull WHERE title = :title;
if (strcmp (SQLSTATE, "00000"))
    whatever-you-do-in-C;
```

Note that we used the host variable names directly in the SQL statement instead of parameter names (there aren't any parameters, after all), but we had to use the status parameter name (SQLSTATE) in the **if** statement, because there must be a host variable named SQLSTATE (or SQLCODE, or both). Note, too, that the SQL statement didn't actually use SQLSTATE or SQLCODE. The DBMS automatically set the status return value into the status parameter.

Recall from Chapter 11 that SQL provides a DECLARE SECTION where you declare all host variables that you plan to use in your embedded programs. The rules for the status parameters are:

- If you have explicitly declared a host variable named SQLSTATE as a 5-character string, then that will be used *automatically* for all of your embedded SQL statements.

- If you have explicitly declared a host variable named SQLCODE as an integer, then that will be used *automatically* for all of your embedded SQL statements.

- If you explicitly declared *both* of the above, then both will be used *automatically* for all of your embedded SQL statements.

- If you did *neither,* then the DBMS assumes that you declared SQLCODE only but did it somewhere other than in the BEGIN DECLARE SECTION and the preprocessor couldn't find it. This is really only for backward compatibility with SQL-89. We strongly recommend that you always explicitly declare your status parameters within the BEGIN DECLARE SECTION. (Also, we note that many implementations allowed you to INCLUDE a definition file, usually called INCLUDE SQLCA, that contained the SQLCODE declaration.

Again, we do not recommend this approach, but your implementation may require it until it conforms to SQL-92.)

People who write embedded SQL programs are usually far more interested in writing the *real* semantics of their applications than in the details of SQL error handling. In Chapter 11, we told you about the WHENEVER declarative statement that allows you to instruct your precompiler to do most of the work for you. What we didn't talk about in Chapter 11 is what sort of code you have to write to handle errors once the WHENEVER statement has caused a GOTO to be invoked.

Recall that you can write either:

```
WHENEVER error-type CONTINUE
```

which says that you are willing to ignore that error category and just continue executing the next statement in your program, or

```
WHENEVER error-type GOTO target-label
```

If you choose the GOTO alternative, any errors of the specified type (SQLERROR or NOT FOUND, as you will recall) will cause the flow of control for your program to change to the specified target-label. Now you have to worry about what to do once this happens.

In general, you will either terminate processing of your application and record some sort of error (for example, printing an error message on a terminal or console, recording an entry in a log somewhere, or setting off an alarm), or you will take action to correct the problem in the application and continue processing after that. Knowing which decision to take, knowing how to correct the problem, and knowing what sort of error to record usually requires that you know more about the situation than merely the overall nature of the problem. The rest of this chapter tells you how to get more information about the errors that you encounter. With this knowledge, your error processing can be more intelligent and discriminating, and your applications can be more useful to your clients.

Once you start using an SQL product, it won't take you long to figure out that SQLSTATE or SQLCODE don't often give you enough information about the results of your statements. There are several reasons for this:

- There may actually be several errors that occur during the execution of a single SQL statement. For example, the statement:

```
SELECT C1/C2, C3
  INTO :param1, :param2
  FROM TA
```

could get one error because of a division by zero (if C2 has the value 0) and a second error because C3 is null and no indicator parameter was specified; it could also get a third error if the cardinality of TA is greater than 1. Which error gets reported in SQLSTATE or SQLCODE?

- A complex application may have hundreds of SQL statements in it. When the application suddenly announces that it's encountered an error, locating the specific statement may be tedious and uncertain.

- Applications that operate concurrently on many databases may actually reuse the same SQL statements over and over at multiple databases. When an error occurs, it may be difficult to determine the specific context of the error.

SQL-92 comes to the rescue with the *diagnostics area* and the accompanying GET DIAGNOSTICS statement. The diagnostics area is a DBMS-managed data structure (but more on that shortly) that captures specific information about the results of each SQL statement (except one—be patient!). The GET DIAGNOSTICS statement (that's the one) is then used to extract the information from the diagnostics area. To protect you against the loss of the diagnostics area contents because of errors in the GET DIAGNOSTICS statement itself, SQL-92 prescribes that the GET DIAGNOSTICS statement status is reported only in SQLSTATE and SQLCODE but that the statement never changes the contents of the diagnostics area.

The diagnostics area actually has two components. One component is the *header* and contains information about the last SQL statement as a whole. The other area is like a *detail* area that contains information about each error, warning, or success code that resulted from the statement. Conceptually, it looks like the diagram in Figure 17-1.

FIGURE 17-1
Diagnostics Area

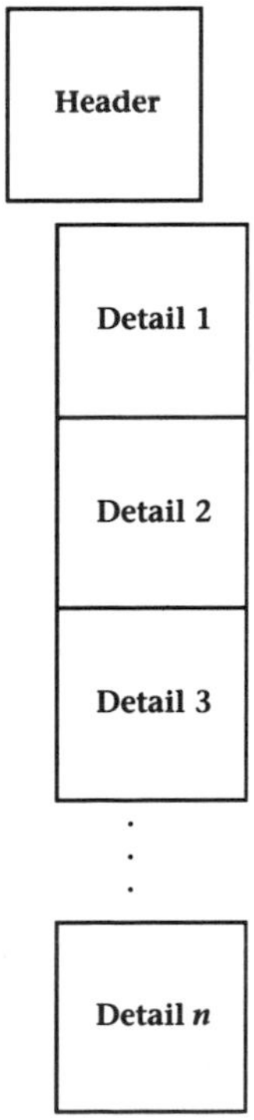

Header

Detail 1

Detail 2

Detail 3

Detail *n*

When each transaction starts, the diagnostics area is set up to contain the number of detail records that is the default for the implementation or that you specified in the SET TRANSACTION statement (see Chapter 14 for a review of these terms). A DBMS is *required* to put information corresponding to the status reported in SQLCODE or SQLSTATE into Detail 1. The DBMS *may* put additional information into subsequent Detail i areas, but there is no presumption of precedence or importance. In general, if the SQL standard specifies a particular error for a given situation and the implementation has another error for precisely the same problem, then the error defined by the standard must be reported in SQLSTATE and SQLCODE and also recorded in Detail 1. However, the DBMS may detect a more serious error (like a disk head crash) and choose to report *that* error in preference to, say, a divide by zero error.

A DBMS is also free to put information only into Detail 1 and not into any other detail area, even if there are potentially many more errors resulting from the SQL statement. Although this may superficially sound irresponsible, consider a DBMS that is designed to be extremely fast and efficient. As soon as it detects one error while executing an SQL statement, it reports the results and returns control to the application program, thus freeing up system resources for other users. Imagine, then, a different implementation that has been designed to have outstanding support for debugging, so it exhaustively pursues the entire statement to detect as many errors as possible. Both alternatives (and many in between) are valid, so you can expect to find them on the market. Read your product's documentation to see how it behaves.

The contents of the header area are shown in Table 17-1.

TABLE 17-1
Contents of Diagnostics Header Area

Contents	Data Type
NUMBER	Exact numeric, scale 0
MORE	Character string, length 1
COMMAND_FUNCTION	Character varying, length ≥ 128
DYNAMIC_FUNCTION	Character varying, length ≥ 128
ROW_COUNT	Exact numeric, scale 0

By using this information, you can identify the specific type of SQL statement that encountered the error, warning, or success condition. The value of NUMBER is the number of detail entries filled in as a result of the SQL statement. MORE will contain the character 'Y' if all conditions detected by the DBMS were recorded in the diagnostics area, and 'N' if additional conditions were detected but not recorded (for example, if there were too many conditions for the size of the diagnostics area created). If the statement being reported is a static SQL statement, COMMAND_ FUNCTION will contain a character string that represents the SQL statement. See section 17.3 for a list of the codes that represent each SQL statement. If the problem occurred during a dynamic SQL statement, COMMAND_FUNCTION will have 'EXECUTE' or 'EXECUTE IMMEDIATE' in it, and DYNAMIC_FUNCTION will have the code for the dynamic SQL statement itself.

ROW_COUNT contains the number of rows that were affected by the SQL statement. In some SQL implementations, another host language data structure, called the SQLCA, is used to capture this information. However, the same sort of problems applied to use of SQLCA (*e.g.,* too much variance between implementations), so it was replaced by other facilities, including the ROW_COUNT field in the diagnostics area header.

The detail areas are a bit longer, as you can see in Table 17-2. There is, as we've said, one detail area for each error, warning, or success condition the DBMS reports, with a minimum of one that corresponds to the condition reported in SQLSTATE or SQLCODE. In each filled-in detail area, the value of CONDITION_NUMBER is the sequence number of the detail area. This value ranges from 1 to NUMBER and corresponds to the value that you use in the GET DIAGNOSTICS statement to retrieve the information from the detail areas.

TABLE 17-2
Contents of
Diagnostics
Detail Area

Contents	Data Type
CONDITION_NUMBER	Exact numeric, scale 0
RETURNED_SQLSTATE	Character string, length 5
CLASS_ORIGIN	Character varying, length ≥max. length of an identifier
SUBCLASS_ORIGIN	Character varying, length ≥max. length of an identifier
CONSTRAINT_CATALOG	Character varying, length ≥max. length of an identifier
CONSTRAINT_SCHEMA	Character varying, length ≥max. length of an identifier
CONSTRAINT_NAME	Character varying, length ≥max. length of an identifier
CONNECTION_NAME	Character varying, length ≥max. length of an identifier
ENVIRONMENT_NAME	Character varying, length ≥max. length of an identifier
CATALOG_NAME	Character varying, length ≥max. length of an identifier
SCHEMA_NAME	Character varying, length ≥max. length of an identifier
TABLE_NAME	Character varying, length ≥max. length of an identifier
COLUMN_NAME	Character varying, length ≥max. length of an identifier
MESSAGE_TEXT	Character varying, length ≥max. length of an identifier
MESSAGE_LENGTH	Exact numeric, scale 0
MESSAGE_OCTET_LENGTH	Exact numeric, scale 0

RETURNED_SQLSTATE contains the SQLSTATE value that corresponds to the condition reported in the detail area. Because SQLSTATE values have both a class code and a subclass code, either of which can be defined by the standard or by an implementation, the diagnostics area separately tells you the source of the value returned. CLASS_ORIGIN will be 'ISO 9075' if the class code value is defined in the SQL standard; otherwise, it will depend on your implementation (for example, a Digital Equipment Corporation implementation might return 'Rdb/VMS' in this field for an implementor-defined class code). Similarly, SUBCLASS_ORIGIN will be

'ISO 9075' if the subclass code value is defined in SQL standard and will otherwise depend on the implementation.

If the detail area reports a constraint violation, the fields CONSTRANT_CATALOG, CONSTRAINT_SCHEMA, and CONSTRAINT_NAME will contain the fully qualified name of the constraint that was violated.

The CONNECTION_NAME and ENVIRONMENT_NAME fields contain the name of the connection and the environment to which you are connected when you executed the SQL statement that is being reported.

If the reported situation involves a table, CATALOG_NAME, SCHEMA_NAME, and TABLE_NAME will contain the fully qualified name of the table. If the situation involves a column, the table information will be completed and COLUMN_NAME will contain the name of the column.

If the situation involves a cursor, CURSOR_NAME will contain the name of the cursor.

The implementation may also record a character string that contains natural-language error text (or anything else the implementation chooses to record). The standard does not prescribe the contents of this string, partly because the standard couldn't possibly specify the contents in every natural language that people may use. Therefore, the implementation can choose whether or not to record anything in the MESSAGE_TEXT field; if it records something, the details are left to the implementor. However, we expect that most implementors will record a printable text string that describes the error in the user's selected natural language. The length, in characters, of this message is recorded in MESSAGE_LENGTH and the octet length in MESSAGE_OCTET_LENGTH.

After each SQL statement has been executed (except, as we noted, the GET DIAGNOSTICS statement itself), information is recorded in the diagnostics area. To avoid confusion between multiple statements, the diagnostics area is emptied (erased, if you prefer) at the beginning of each SQL statement (except GET DIAGNOSTICS). You can then use GET DIAGNOSTICS to retrieve any information available in it. If your statement completes with SQLSTATE '00000' (SQLCODE 0), meaning "successful completion," you would normally expect only a single detail area to be filled in. However, your implementation may report all sorts of other information at the same time, taking up other detail areas.

The format of the GET DIAGNOSTICS statement is:

```
GET DIAGNOSTICS target = item [ , target = item ]...
```

or

```
GET DIAGNOSTICS EXCEPTION number target =
    item [ , target = item ]...
```

If you use the first alternative, you will get information about the header of the diagnostics area. In that case, item can be one of these keywords: NUMBER, MORE, COMMAND_FUNCTION, DYNAMIC_FUNCTION, or ROW_COUNT. Anything else will cause an error. target is a host variable or a parameter; no indicator is needed or permitted.

If you use the second alternative, you'll get information from the detail areas of the diagnostics area. Here, number cannot be greater than the value you'd get from NUMBER in the header. number will always be the same value that is returned in CONDITION_NUMBER for the detail area. target is as before, and item must be one of:

- CONDITION_NUMBER
- RETURNED_SQLSTATE
- CLASS_ORIGIN
- SUBCLASS_ORIGIN
- ENVIRONMENT_NAME
- CONNECTION_NAME
- CONSTRAINT_CATALOG
- CONSTRAINT_SCHEMA
- CONSTRAINT_NAME
- CATALOG_NAME
- SCHEMA_NAME
- TABLE_NAME
- COLUMN_NAME
- CURSOR_NAME
- MESSAGE_TEXT
- MESSAGE_LENGTH
- MESSAGE_OCTET_LENGTH

Of course you can request any number of these items in a single GET DIAGNOSTICS statement. Also, because GET DIAGNOSTICS does not affect the contents of the diagnostics area, you can execute it multiple times to get different information, even about the same detail area. Therefore, you might do something like this in Fortran:

```
EXEC SQL BEGIN DECLARE
CHARACTER*128 CMDFNC, CONTMP, CURTMP
CHARACTER*128 CONNAM(10), CURNAM(10)
CHARACTER*5 SQLSTA
INTEGER NUM
EXEC SQL END DECLARE
EXEC SQL DECLARE CUR1 CURSOR FOR some-expression
EXEC SQL ON SQLERROR GOTO 1000
EXEC SQL OPEN CUR1
    .
    .
    .
```

```
1000   CONTINUE
       PRINT (5.1010) SQLSTATE
1010   FORMAT (' SQLSTATE was ', A)

       EXEC SQL GET DIAGNOSTICS :NUM = NUMBER, :CMDFNC =
    x               COMMAND_FUNCTION

       IF (NUM .GT. 10) NUM = 10

       DO 1100 I = 1, NUM
       EXEC SQL GET DIAGNOSTICS EXCEPTION :NUM
    x    :CONTMP = CONNECTION_NAME, :CURTMP = CURSOR_NAME
       CONNAM(NUM) = CONTMP
       CURNAM(NUM) = CURTMP
1100   CONTINUE
```

This example uses an embedded exception declaration to cause the flow of control to pass to the error-handling code whenever an SQL error is encountered. That code gets some header information and then gets up to 10 detail information items. We don't know what they did with it afterward, but you can be sure that . . . it was no picnic.

17.3 SQL Statement Codes

Table 17-3 contains the SQL statement character codes that are used in the diagnostics area.

TABLE 17-3
SQL Statement
Codes for
Diagnostics Area

SQL Statement	Identifier
<allocate cursor statement>	ALLOCATE CURSOR
<allocate descriptor statement>	ALLOCATE DESCRIPTOR
<alter domain statement>	ALTER DOMAIN
<alter table statement>	ALTER TABLE
<assertion definition>	CREATE ASSERTION
<character set definition>	CREATE CHARACTER SET
<close statement>	CLOSE CURSOR
<collation definition>	CREATE COLLATION
<commit statement>	COMMIT WORK
<connect statement>	CONNECT
<deallocate descriptor statement>	DEALLOCATE DESCRIPTOR
<deallocate prepared statement>	DEALLOCATE PREPARE

TABLE 17-3
(*continued*)

SQL Statement	Identifier
<delete statement: positioned>	DELETE CURSOR
<delete statement: searched>	DELETE WHERE
<describe statement>	DESCRIBE
<direct select statement: multiple rows>	SELECT
<disconnect statement>	DISCONNECT
<domain definition>	CREATE DOMAIN
<drop assertion statement>	DROP ASSERTION
<drop character set statement>	DROP CHARACTER SET
<drop collation statement>	DROP COLLATION
<drop domain statement>	DROP DOMAIN
<drop schema statement>	DROP SCHEMA
<drop table statement>	DROP TABLE
<drop translation statement>	DROP TRANSLATION
<drop view statement>	DROP VIEW
<dynamic close statement>	DYNAMIC CLOSE
<dynamic delete statement>	DYNAMIC DELETE CURSOR
<dynamic fetch statement>	DYNAMIC FETCH
<dynamic open statement>	DYNAMIC OPEN
<dynamic single row select statement>	SELECT
<dynamic update statement: positioned>	DYNAMIC UPDATE CURSOR
<execute immediate statement>	EXECUTE IMMEDIATE
<execute statement>	EXECUTE
<fetch statement>	FETCH
<get descriptor statement>	GET DESCRIPTOR
<get diagnostics statement>	GET DIAGNOSTICS
<grant statement>	GRANT
<insert statement>	INSERT
<open statement>	OPEN
<preparable dynamic delete statement: positioned>	DYNAMIC DELETE CURSOR
<preparable dynamic update statement: positioned>	DYNAMIC UPDATE CURSOR
<prepare statement>	PREPARE
<revoke statement>	REVOKE
<rollback statement>	ROLLBACK WORK

TABLE 17-3
(*continued*)

SQL Statement	Identifier
<schema definition>	CREATE SCHEMA
<select statement: single row>	SELECT
<set catalog statement>	SET CATALOG
<set connection statement>	SET CONNECTION
<set constraints mode statement>	SET CONSTRAINT
<set descriptor statement>	SET DESCRIPTOR
<set local time zone statement>	SET TIME ZONE
<set names statement>	SET NAMES
<set schema statement>	SET SCHEMA
<set transaction statement>	SET TRANSACTION
<set session authorization identifier statement>	SET SESSION AUTHORIZATION
<table definition>	CREATE TABLE
<translation definition>	CREATE TRANSLATION
<update statement: positioned>	UPDATE CURSOR
<update statement: searched>	UPDATE WHERE
<view definition>	CREATE VIEW

17.4 Chapter Summary

In this chapter, we've discussed SQLCODE, SQLSTATE, and the various aspects of SQL exception handling. With the facilities presented, you should be able to include robust exception handling in all of your SQL applications.

Remember that we discussed the program structure relative to exception handling in Chapter 11. In Appendix E, we provide the complete list of SQLCODE and SQLSTATE values.

CHAPTER 18

. . . .

Internationalization Aspects of SQL-92

18.1 Introduction

Until SQL-92, programming and database language standards simply did not provide any reasonable support for languages other than English. In fact, most programming language and database *products* provided no such support. Everybody "knew" that 7-bit or 8-bit characters were all that were supported, and there was an implicit assertion that these were all that were needed. As a result, most systems support ASCII (or its IBM analog, EBCDIC) or, occasionally, an 8-bit extension of ASCII (perhaps the ISO Latin-1 set).

Unfortunately, an 8-bit character set can support a maximum of 256 characters. Because of the way character sets are set up, such sets actually support about 192 characters. Similarly, a 7-bit set usually supports either 95 or 96 characters. It is quite possible to use such a set to support English, French, German, Arabic, Hebrew, or even Hindi. However, it is *not* possible to support all of these at the same time because the total number of characters far exceeds the number that an 8-bit character set can support.

Worse, it is impossible to support Japanese, Chinese, or Korean with an 8-bit character set. These languages routinely use thousands of characters, which require more bits per character for encoding. Several database system vendors have produced localized versions of their products that support a 16-bit character set for use in countries like Japan, China, or Korea, but it has not been until very recently that any DBMS vendor supplied an internationalized product that could simultaneously support multiple languages.

As SQL-92 was being developed, it became obvious, largely because of the international participation, that an important factor would be support of other character sets (that is, character sets other than that required for English or Western European languages). Several facilities are provided by SQL-92 that support character set internationalization requirements. (By the way, we say *character set interna-*

tionalization because it really is the character facilities that are affected and not such things as datetime formats, decimal points, or currency formats. Instead, SQL operates using canonical forms for all that and depends on user interface tools to generate localized forms for such data.)

18.2   Character Sets and Collations

In any computer language, whether it is a conventional programming language or a database language, every character string has a character set associated with it. Most languages do not allow the user to control the character set that is used for any given character string. (Some implementations of some languages permit the user to specify the character set to be used for *all* character strings in a specific program, but even this is uncommon.) As a result, the character set associated with a character string is whatever the vendor chose when the product you're using was designed. Because of the history of the development of computer systems, the most likely choice is an 8-bit character set like 8-bit ASCII or 8-bit EBCDIC, or their 7-bit predecessors. Many computer users, implementors, designers, and vendors have thus come to accept implicitly the false premise that one byte equals one character. In fact, most computer hardware makes the same assumption (look at the IBM 370 MVCL and DEC VAX MOVC5 instructions for examples).

However, a *character* is really a text element that is used to write a natural language (or perhaps an artificial display element used in writing, such as punctuation marks, bullet characters, and logos). Therefore, we have to accept that the one-character-equals-one-byte premise is artificial and undependable. Some character sets require two (or more) bytes per character; others have been designed to use one byte for some characters and two bytes for others. The specific mechanism used to encode characters for a computer is called an *encoding*, and a character set so encoded is called a *coded character set*. The way that character *strings* are represented (*e.g.*, one byte per character, two bytes per character, or even variable number of bytes per character) is called the *form-of-use* of the character set. The actual collection of characters that can be represented is called the *repertoire* of the character set. Finally, character strings expressed in a character set must have rules that control how those strings compare with one another; such a set of rules is called a *collation*. Every character set has a default collation (there may be many possible collations for a character set).

Therefore, a character set has three attributes that we will discuss here.

- The repertoire of characters
- The form-of-use
- The default collation

Each of these attributes has an important effect on character strings that have a specific character set. The repertoire determines the characters that can be expressed. In a purist sense, character sets that have only 96 characters should never permit a character string with a 97th encoding to be expressed, and some implementations provide this integrity service to applications. However, many implementations allow any encoding of the appropriate number of bits to be expressed (effectively defining a full 256 characters, even though many of them have no printed representation). There are positive aspects to both choices: the *laissez-faire* approach may provide higher performance, while the more restrictive approach may help applications avoid problems associated with uncontrolled input.

Two character strings can be compared to each other only if they have the same character repertoire (more properly, if their character sets have the same character repertoire). If you think about this for a few moments, the reason becomes obvious: If one string's character set contains, say, the character "double dagger" and the other string's character set doesn't, how can you compare a double dagger in the first string with any other character in the other string? Sure, we can determine that the double dagger is not equal to, say, the letter A, but is it less than or greater than the *A?*

The form-of-use determines how character strings are represented to the hardware and software. It has nothing to do with high-level issues like comparisons, but it has a great deal to do with how data is stored and manipulated by the underlying computer system. In an ideal world, we'd never have to worry about the form-of-use of a character string. But this isn't an ideal world. Although SQL-92 doesn't care about the form-of-use in its operations, when your SQL code exchanges data with your host language code, your host language program must know (or be able to find out) the form-of-use of character data so that it can invoke the appropriate routines to process that data.

Each character string has a collation associated with it; normally, it's the default collation of the character set, but it is possible to override the default and assign a specific collation to a specific string. However, collations affect *operations* and are really relevant only when you are comparing (or sorting, which is really nothing but a form of comparison) strings. Therefore, certain operations in SQL can be given specific collations, too.

Let's take a look at where all this is actually used in SQL-92. In Chapter 2, we told you that one of the data types supported by SQL-92 is CHARACTER and that another is NATIONAL CHARACTER. As we said then, NATIONAL CHARACTER is exactly the same as CHARACTER except that an implementation-defined character set is implied. Well, the full syntax to specify the data type CHARACTER is:

```
CHARACTER [ VARYING ] [ length ]
  [ CHARACTER SET charset-name ]
```

The list of charset-names that your implementation supports is specified in the documentation. For purposes of discussion, let's assume that we have access to an implementation that supports ASCII, LATIN1, KANJI, and SQL_TEXT. Therefore, we could write the following table definition:

```
CREATE TABLE t1 (
  col1   CHARACTER (10),
  col2   CHARACTER VARYING (50) CHARACTER SET KANJI,
  col3   CHARACTER (25)         CHARACTER SET LATIN1,
  col4   CHARACTER              CHARACTER SET ASCII,
  col5   NATIONAL               CHARACTER (30)
    )
```

In this example, the character set of COL1 is whatever the implementation has defined as the default for CHARACTER without a character set. The character set of COL2 is KANJI; COL3 has LATIN1, COL4 has ASCII, and COL5 has whatever the implementation has defined as the character set for NATIONAL CHARACTER. In all cases, the collation of the columns is the default collation for the character set.

If we want something different, we may write:

```
CREATE TABLE t2 (
  cola CHARACTER (10)           COLLATE FRENCH,
  colb CHARACTER VARYING (50)   CHARACTER SET KANJI
                                COLLATE JIS_X0212,
  colc CHARACTER (25)           CHARACTER SET LATIN1
                                COLLATE ISO8859_1,
  cold CHARACTER                CHARACTER SET ASCII
                                COLLATE EBCDIC,
  cole NATIONAL CHARACTER (30)  COLLATE RUSSIAN_GEORGIAN
    )
```

In these column definitions, the collations specified also have to be supported by the implementation, and your product's documentation will tell you which collations it supports.

You can make the same sort of character string specifications when you define parameters for your SQL procedures (in SQL modules). There are similar facilities provided in SQL-92 for host variable declarations. However, you must recall that host languages do not currently provide any support for internationalized character strings but support only that old, incorrect, assumption of one byte equals one character. As a result, the specification of character set for SQL parameters or for host variables merely allows you to assist in providing the appropriate interface between your SQL code and your host language code.

18.2.1 Coercibility

SQL-92 has defined a set of rules that determines the collation of the result of a character string operation (like concatenation or substring) based on the collations of the participating character strings. To cover all possible cases, SQL-92 has also defined another attribute of character strings (but this attribute is associated with specific strings and their specific appearance in an SQL expression; it is not associated with the character set at all). The attribute is called the *coercibility* of the character string, and it determines whether a specific character string has a rigid collation, whether it can be *coerced* to have a collation from another source, or whether it automatically picks up a collation from another source. The rules are defined for monadic operators (that is, operations that have only one character string operand, like SUBSTRING), dyadic operators (operations with two character string operands, like concatenation), and comparisons (see Tables 18-1, 18-2, and 18-3).

TABLE 18-1
Collating Coercibility Rules for Monadic Operators

Operand Coercibility and Collating Sequence		Result Coercibility and Collating Sequence	
Coercibility	Collating Sequence	Coercibility	Collating Sequence
Coercible	default	Coercible	default
Implicit	X	Implicit	X
Explicit	X	Explicit	X
No collating sequence		No collating sequence	

TABLE 18-2
Collating Coercibility Rules for Dyadic Operators

Operand 1 Coercibility and Collating Sequence		Operand 2 Coercibility and Collating Sequence		Result Coercibility and Collating Sequence	
Coercibility	Collating Sequence	Coercibility	Collating Sequence	Coercibility	Collating Sequence
Coercible	default	Coercible	default	Coercible	default
Coercible	default	Implicit	Y	Implicit	Y
Coercible	default	No collating sequence		No collating sequence	
Coercible	default	Explicit	Y	Explicit	Y
Implicit	X	Coercible	default	Implicit	X
Implicit	X	Implicit	X	Implicit	X
Implicit	X	Implicit	$Y \neq X$	No collating sequence	
Implicit	X	No collating sequence		No collating sequence	
Implicit	X	Explicit	Y	Explicit	Y
No collating sequence		Any, except Explicit	Any	No collating sequence	
No collating sequence		Explicit	X	Explicit	X
Explicit	X	Coercible	default	Explicit	X
Explicit	X	Implicit	Y	Explicit	X
Explicit	X	No collating sequence		Explicit	X
Explicit	X	Explicit	X	Explicit	X
Explicit	X	Explicit	$Y \neq X$	Not permitted: *invalid syntax*	

	Comperand 1 Coercibility and Collating Sequence		**Comperand 2 Coercibility and Collating Sequence**		**Collating Sequence Used for This Comparison**
TABLE 18-3 Sequence Usage for Comparisons	**Coercibility**	**Collating Sequence**	**Coercibility**	**Collating Sequence**	
	Coercible	default	Coercible	default	default
	Coercible	default	Implicit	Y	Y
	Coercible	default	No collating sequence		Not permitted: *invalid syntax*
	Coercible	default	Explicit	Y	Y
	Implicit	X	Coercible	default	X
	Implicit	X	Implicit	X	X
	Implicit	X	Implicit	Y ≠ X	Not permitted: *invalid syntax*
	Implicit	X	No collating sequence		Not permitted: *invalid syntax*
	Implicit	X	Explicit	Y	Y
	No collating sequence		Any, except Explicit	Any	Not permitted: *invalid syntax*
	No collating sequence		Explicit	X	X
	Explicit	X	Coercible	default	X
	Explicit	X	Implicit	Y	X
	Explicit	X	No collating sequence		X
	Explicit	X	Explicit	X	X
	Explicit	X	Explicit	Y ≠ X	Not permitted: *invalid syntax*

To use Tables 18-1 through 18-3, you have to know how to determine the coercibility attribute and collation of any specific character string. Once you know these two characteristics of the character string or strings that participate in an operation or comparison, you can determine the outcome of that operation or comparison.

18.2.2 Coercibility Attributes

Individual character strings acquire their coercibility attribute of *explicit, implicit,* or *coercible* as follows:

- If the character string is a `column-reference`, the coercibility attribute is *implicit* (because the referenced column was defined by a column definition that provided, implicitly or explicitly, a collation). The default collation is the collation provided by the column definition.

- If the character string is a value other than a `column-reference` (a parameter, a host variable, or a literal), the coercibility attribute is *coercible* and also has the default collation for its character set.

- In any case, if you provide an explicit `collate-clause` along with the character string, the coercibility attribute is *explicit* and the collation is the one specified in the `collate-clause`.

Here are some examples of character string operations that are affected by character sets. Let's assume that we have the table definition we've been using above.

```
col1 || col3
```

Because the character set for COL3 is LATIN1 and the character set for COL1 is unspecified (and hence is the default), this would be valid if and only if the default character set for CHARACTER columns is LATIN1 or some other character set that has the exact same repertoire as LATIN1 (and, in our example, there is no other such set).

```
t1.col1 = t2.cola
```

This comparison is invalid as stated even though T1.COL1 and T2.COLA have the same character repertoire, because T1.COL1 has the default collation and T2.COLA has the (presumably different) collation FRENCH. An inspection of the Tables 18-1 through 18-3 shows that this in invalid syntax. However, we can remedy that by writing:

```
t1.col1 = t2.cola COLLATE FRENCH
```

or

```
t1.col1 COLLATE FRENCH = t2.cola
```

because either way introduces an *explicit* collation.

18.2.3 ORDER BY

As you recall from Chapter 12, DECLARE CURSOR allows you to specify an ORDER BY clause that tells the DBMS how to sort the rows that the cursor references. When you specify an ORDER BY clause, you identify a column of the retrieved rows (either by column name or by ordinal position of the column in the row). You can also specify whether the DBMS is to do an ascending sort or a descending sort (using the keywords ASC or DESC). All this was discussed in Chapter 12. What we didn't discuss in Chapter 12 was the fact that you can also specify a collation to be used for ordering a particular column.

As with other uses of specifying an explicit collation, you have to use a collation that is appropriate and permitted for the character set of the column where you specify it. For example, you could declare a cursor with this ORDER BY clause:

```
ORDER BY movie_title COLLATE FRENCH
```

to specify that you want the movies sorted by their titles according to French conventions. (Obviously, we're assuming that your database designer was reasonable and used the collation name FRENCH to identify a French collating sequence! If that's true, then it's reasonable to assume that FRENCH was defined to be valid on LATIN-1 characters, which our MOVIE_TITLE could well be.)

18.2.4 GROUP BY

Another place where you can use an explicit collate-clause is in the GROUP BY clause. Recall from Chapter 9 that the purpose of the GROUP BY clause is to break a table into groups in which every row has an equal value in the grouping column or columns. If the grouping columns include one or more character string columns, then the collation of those columns must be well defined. You can always use the default collation, of course, but there may be times when you want to use an alternative collation for a GROUP BY operation. In this case, you simply use:

```
GROUP BY column-name collate-clause
   [ , column-name collate-clause ]...
```

For example, you might say:

```
GROUP BY col1 COLLATE ITALIAN, col2 COLLATE JIS_X0208
```

or to do grouping without regard for case:

```
GROUP BY col3 COLLATE all_upper_case
```

18.3 Translations and Conversions

SQL-92 provides you with the ability to translate character strings from one character set to another. Translations are defined by implementations or by standards, and the set of translations that are available in your implementation are all documented by the product's doc-set. For example, your product may support translation from one encoding to another (such as ASCII to EBCDIC), from a character set with characters that you can't print or display on your hardware into characters that you can (for example, you could translate the German sharp S—β—to two lowercase s characters), from lowercase characters to uppercase equivalents, or even from one alphabet into another (such as Hebrew into Latin characters).

The format of a translation is:

```
TRANSLATE ( source USING conversion )
```

The character set of the translation is defined by the conversion function.

In other cases, you may want to change the form-of-use of a character string for some reason. For example, you may know that internally you have been using a form-of-use with a variable number of bytes per character, but you want to have two bytes per character when you transfer your character data to your host program. A conversion will allow you do specify this operation. The format is:

```
CONVERT ( source USING conversion )
```

As with translations, your product's documentation will tell you which conversions it supports and what those conversions actually do.

18.4 Chapter Summary

We've discussed the internationalization aspects of SQL-92. Unlike previous versions of SQL, and most DBMS products in general, a great deal of caution has gone into allowing for international-class database applications. When you think about the direction in which database applications are headed—distributed, multinational environments that encompass products from vendors in different companies and data in many different character sets—it becomes obvious that built-in internationalization characteristics are needed within the database framework.

SQL-92 features such as multiple character sets and collations help you to achieve international applications in your database environments. Why would these facilities be important to you? Consider our sample application. Assume that our video and music stores become so successful that we begin offering franchises in other countries. In keeping with the spirit of distributed, international computing, we will likely allow individual stores (or at least regional headquarters) to handle the information systems processing tasks, including SQL database management. If we have stores in Japan, the United States, Germany, and a number of other countries, we want each store or region to use appropriate character sets and other local aspects as applicable. By using SQL-92 internationalization facilities, your applications may be easily adapted to whatever countries in which your business operations occur.

CHAPTER 19

· · · · · · · · · · · · · · · · · ·

Information Schema

19.1 Introduction

In each catalog in an SQL-environment, there is a schema named INFORMATION_
SCHEMA. In this chapter, we discuss this schema and its contents, as well as the
associated privileges. We take a brief look at the DEFINITION_SCHEMA, in which
base tables are defined to support the INFORMATION_SCHEMA.

Before we introduce the various schemas, let's briefly review the topic of
metadata.

19.2 Metadata, Repositories, and The INFORMATION_SCHEMA

We discussed the concept of metadata in Chapter 2. As a reminder, metadata is
"data about data." That is, it is a description of the data (and, for that matter, the
metadata itself) contained within a database.

In many information system environments, a dictionary or repository functions as the primary storage mechanism for an organization's metadata. While this
is an implementation-dependent situation, there are two general rules.

- Metadata that applies primarily to the runtime database environment is
  managed through the INFORMATION_SCHEMA
- Metadata that applies to the information system environment as a whole is
  managed through the dictionary or repository

When this type of "dual metadata" environment is present, the INFORMATION_
SCHEMA metadata must be coordinated with that of the overall dictionary/
repository (let's just call it a *repository*, since that is the current politically correct
term) environment.

Why do we mention this? Simply so you realize that your particular SQL implementation may be doing a great deal of behind-the-scenes action to manage this coordination. It is to your benefit to know as much as possible about your particular implementation, and in many organizations there may be multiple SQL-92 DBMS implementations, each with its own different manner of metadata management. In distributed database environments, the metadata management must often be coordinated, or at least known, among implementations. Therefore, you should understand:

- What views are provided within the respective INFORMATION_SCHEMAs, particularly with respect to extensions
- How the metadata of each INFORMATION_SCHEMA interacts with various repositories across the environment

19.3 DEFINITION_SCHEMA and Base Tables

In Chapter 4, we discussed how all SQL views are defined in terms of one or more base tables. The same is true for the tables of the INFORMATION_SCHEMA. The base tables are defined as being in a schema called DEFINITION_SCHEMA. However, these base tables are *not* accessible from any of your SQL statements; the sole purpose for the DEFINITION_SCHEMA is to define a set of hypothetical base tables used in SQL-92 to provide a standard definition of the INFORMATION_SCHEMA views. An implementation can define the INFORMATION_SCHEMA views exactly as specified in SQL-92 and can actually supply the DEFINITION_SCHEMA base tables, or it can define the INFORMATION_SCHEMA views based on other implementation-specific catalog tables or any other source of information.

19.4 Self-Description

The INFORMATION_SCHEMA describes itself. By that we mean that the views of INFORMATION_SCHEMA—such as TABLE_CONSTRAINTS, TABLES, VIEWS, VIEW_COLUMN_USAGE, and the others we discuss in this chapter—have appropriate entries in the base tables of DEFINITION_SCHEMA and, consequently, in the INFORMATION_SCHEMA views.

For example, there is an INFORMATION_SCHEMA view called VIEWS (the VIEWS view . . . . Now stay with us!). In addition, there is a VIEWS base table in DEFINITION_SCHEMA (the VIEWS table . . . . Still following?).

To make it simple, let's see them as defined by their qualified names:

- DEFINITION_SCHEMA.VIEWS   The base table
- INFORMATION_SCHEMA.VIEWS   The view

Self-description means that there will be an entry for INFORMATION_SCHEMA.VIEWS in (1) the DEFINITION_SCHEMA.VIEWS base table (though, as we mentioned above, it may not be a "real" entry since the base tables don't really have to exist); and (2) the INFORMATION_SCHEMA.VIEWS view.

The concept of self-description does *not* apply to the DEFINITION_SCHEMA, however. That is, there won't be an entry in DEFINITION_SCHEMA.VIEWS nor in INFORMATION_SCHEMA.VIEWS for DEFINITION_SCHEMA.VIEWS.

So what does this mean? Simply that your programs or SQL statements may access the numerous views from INFORMATION_SCHEMA but not the tables of DEFINITION_SCHEMA. In nearly every circumstance, this is not a problem because any metadata information you could possibly want is accessible through the INFORMATION_SCHEMA views. Now, let's discuss how privileges apply to the INFORMATION_SCHEMA.

19.5 INFORMATION_SCHEMA and Privileges

The INFORMATION_SCHEMA views all have identical privilege assignments: SELECT is granted to PUBLIC WITH GRANT OPTION. This means (refer to Chapter 13 if you're fuzzy on PUBLIC privileges) that the views may be queried by any user, and that the SELECT privileges can be further granted to user views that may reference the INFORMATION_SCHEMA views.

There are *no* other privileges granted on INFORMATION_SCHEMA; therefore, the views are not updatable. To understand why, let's look at the following situation. Let's say that a particular SQL-92 DBMS implementation controls its metadata, and therefore definitions of all its database objects, through the INFOR-MATION_SCHEMA. Application requests to access a particular user table or column may first be validated against the INFORMATION_SCHEMA to see if the object exists before physical access is actually attempted (for efficiency reasons). This action is similar to an operating system that checks a directory on a disk in order to find out if a requested file exists before actually seeking out the file.

Now let's say that the INFORMATION_SCHEMA tables were updatable; an application or user could come along and delete one or more entries from the INFORMATION_SCHEMA. The physical tables, columns, or whatever might still exist, but an implementation would likely return an error to the next requestor of the lost objects. Maybe all accesses to MOVIE_TITLES would now be invalidated because of lost metadata for the table. For the sake of security and consistency, therefore, the INFORMATION_SCHEMA views aren't updatable.

19.6 INFORMATION_SCHEMA Extensions

SQL-92 implementations are permitted to add viewed tables to the INFORMA-TION_SCHEMA above and beyond the definitions supplied in the standard. If, for example, a particular SQL implementation has object-oriented extensions that require special database contents, the metadata of those objects may be stored in the INFORMATION_SCHEMA.

Correspondingly, additional DEFINITION_SCHEMA base tables are created or simulated as necessary to support the INFORMATION_SCHEMA extensions.

19.7 Identifier Representation

When you create a schema object, such as a table, view, column, character set, or domain, that object is represented by a row in one or more of the DEFINITION_SCHEMA tables and one or more of the INFORMATION_SCHEMA views. In order for you to retrieve information from the INFORMATION_SCHEMA views about one of those objects, you must know how to code a character string literal to represent the name of the object; this, in turn, means that you have to understand how the object is represented in the view.

Consider the TABLES view. It has a column called TABLE_NAME; that column contains the names of all tables in the schema to which you have access (that is, for which you have some privilege). The TABLE_NAME column, of course, has a character string data type. As you see in our samples later in this chapter, the specific data type is CHARACTER VARYING (*L*) CHARACTER SET SQL_TEXT. *L* represents a number that is the maximum length of an identifier for your implementation; in most cases, that number will be something like 18, 31, 32, or 128 (18 is the Entry SQL limit, 31 and 32 are popular implementors' choices, and 128 is required in Intermediate SQL; we recommend that you assume the number is 128 so that your applications will be portable and upwardly compatible with later implementations).

The character set named SQL_TEXT is a special character set that contains every character supported by your implementation. Unfortunately, this means that different implementations will probably support different sets of characters and different definitions of SQL_TEXT. While this will undoubtedly reduce portability of your applications, it also reflects the fact that different vendors have different views of the market's requirements.

Let's assume that SQL_TEXT for some particular DBMS is the character set called Unicode, which is becoming fairly popular among some computer software vendors. Unicode is a character set in which each character is encoded into 16 bits, so potentially it can represent up to 65,536 characters. Therefore, programs written for that DBMS must reserve 2 "bytes" (octets) for each character that they wish to retrieve from the TABLE_NAME column. Since that column is potentially 128 characters in length, your application should set aside 128 2-byte positions (or 256 bytes) for TABLE_NAME retrieval.

More important to this discussion is the question of what the actual characters are (as opposed to their bit encodings). Suppose we execute the following CREATE TABLE statement:

```
CREATE TABLE music_lovers (
   ...
)
```

What are the resulting contents of the TABLE_NAME column of the TABLES view? Actually, the results are

```
MUSIC_LOVERS
```

because SQL-92 has a rule that requires that normal identifiers *always* be treated *in every respect* as though they had been entered in uppercase letters. Therefore, all of the following have the same effect.

```
CREATE TABLE MUSIC_LOVERS (
  ...
)

CREATE TABLE MuSiC_LoVeRs (
  ...
)

CREATE TABLE Music_Lovers (
  ...
)
```

All of these (done independently) would create the following row in TABLES:

CATALOG_NAME	SCHEMA_NAME	TABLE_NAME	TABLE_TYPE
whatever	whatever	MUSIC_LOVERS	BASE TABLE

If you tried to execute two or more of these statements (without an intervening DROP TABLE, of course), the second and subsequent ones would give you an error, because a table with that name already exists.

This is done for two reasons: so that you can use your favorite case conventions (uppercase only, lowercase only, mixed-case, *etc.*) when coding your SQL statements, and so you always know how to retrieve data from the INFORMATION_ SCHEMA. Therefore, you can retrieve information about this table only as follows:

```
SELECT table_name, table_type
  FROM information_schema.tables
  WHERE table_name = 'MUSIC_LOVERS'
```

You can *always* use this statement, regardless of which of the previous four alternatives were used for creating the table. This means that you can retrieve information from the INFORMATION_SCHEMA without knowing in intimate detail how the information was created there.

However, you will recall that SQL-92 also provides something called a *delimited identifier*. The initial purpose of this was to allow you to specify identifiers that are otherwise identical to SQL's reserved keywords (like TABLE or USAGE). Specifically, it allows you to protect yourself against future product (or standard) versions that introduce new reserved keywords that you've already used in your applications. However, SQL-92 also makes delimited identifiers case *sensitive,* so that C and

Unix® programmers can obtain behavior that is more comfortable in their environment. That means that you can execute:

```
CREATE TABLE "Music_Lovers" (
   ...
)
```

and get a *different* table than any of the previous examples! In this case, you'd better know that the table was created with a delimited identifier with mixed case, because that's how you'll have to retrieve it:

```
SELECT table_name, table_type
  FROM information_schema.tables
  WHERE table_name = 'Music_Lovers'
```

In this case, the TABLES view will show both of these rows:

CATALOG_NAME	SCHEMA_NAME	TABLE_NAME	TABLE_TYPE
whatever	whatever	MUSIC_LOVERS	BASE TABLE
whatever	whatever	Music_Lovers	BASE TABLE

and you can, of course, retrieve information about either one of them by using the appropriate character string literal in your WHERE clause:

```
SELECT table_name, table_type
  FROM information_schema.tables
  WHERE table_name = 'Music_Lovers'
```

or

```
SELECT table_name, table_type
  FROM information_schema.tables
  WHERE table_name = 'MUSIC_LOVERS'
```

19.8 The DEFINITION_SCHEMA

Although it may seem a bit backward given the emphasis placed on INFORMATION_SCHEMA as compared with DEFINITION_SCHEMA, let's take a look at the DEFINITION_SCHEMA first. The reason is that as we look at the view definitions of the INFORMATION_SCHEMA, the references to the DEFINITION_SCHEMA base tables won't be as hard to follow.

19.8.1 Schema Definition

The DEFINITION_SCHEMA schema is defined through a simple statement.

```
CREATE SCHEMA DEFINITION_SCHEMA
    AUTHORIZATION DEFINITION_SCHEMA
```

19.8.2 The Base Tables

The following base tables are defined for the DEFINITION_SCHEMA. Note that the complete CREATE TABLE definitions may be found in the SQL-92 standard.

1. USERS: There is one row for each authorization identifier referenced in the INFORMATION_SCHEMA of the catalog. These rows represent the aggregate of all authorization identifiers that may grant or receive privileges as well as those that may create a schema or currently own a schema. The means by which rows are inserted into and deleted from the USERS table are implementation-defined.

2. SCHEMATA: This table has one row for each schema in the catalog. Additionally, a foreign key (see Chapter 10) references the USERS table (item 1 above) to provide a constraint between these two objects.

3. DATA_TYPE_DESCRIPTOR: This table contains (1) one row for each domain and (2) one row for each column in each table that is defined as having a data type in lieu of a domain. That is, if you have a very small database with five domains plus a total of fifteen columns across four tables that had data types (example: CHARACTER (20) or INTEGER) rather than domains, this table will have twenty rows.

4. DOMAINS: One row for each domain exists in this table.

5. DOMAIN_CONSTRAINTS: One row for each domain constraint exists in this table.

6. TABLES: This table contains one row for each table, including views. Temporary tables are also included. A quick note: By viewing the primary key definition of this table:

```
CREATE TABLE TABLES
        (
        TABLE_CATALOG...
        TABLE_SCHEMA...
        TABLE_NAME...
        TABLE_TYPE...


        CONSTRAINT TABLES_PK PRIMARY KEY
            ( TABLE_CATALOG, TABLE_SCHEMA, TABLE_NAME) ..
```

you can see how the namespace management occurs in SQL-92.

7. VIEWS: This table contains one row for each row in the TABLES table (see item 6 above) that has a TABLE_TYPE of VIEW. Additionally, the rows describe the respective query expressions and characteristics that define the various views, including whether the view is updatable.

8. COLUMNS: This table contains one for each column. Note that the PRI-MARY KEY definition is the same as that of TABLES, with one additional column: COLUMN_NAME.

```
PRIMARY KEY (TABLE_CATALOG, TABLE_SCHEMA, TABLE_NAME,
   COLUMN_NAME)
```

We mention this as a reminder that your seemingly simple column references, such as SELECT TITLE, MOVIE_TYPE, and OUR_COST, are in actuality qualified within the database according to the catalog, schema, and table. Another point worth noting, for your general information: There is a column within the COLUMNS table called ORDINAL_POSITION, which is the ordinal position of the column within the table. Therefore, DDL changes that add one or more columns to a table or delete one or more columns from a table likely require adjustments to the ORDINAL_POSITION values for the columns in the table.

9. VIEW_TABLE_USAGE: This table has one row for each table referenced in the query expression of a view. A CHECK constraint ensures that the referenced tables actually exist within the TABLES table, and a FOREIGN KEY constraint maintains the linkage to the VIEWS table.

10. VIEW_COLUMN_USAGE: This table is similar to VIEW_TABLE_USAGE, except that one row exists for each column referenced by a view. A similar CHECK constraint to that discussed in item 9 ensures that the column name really exists.

11. TABLE_CONSTRAINTS: This table contains one row for each table constraint associated with a table. Constraints are defined, using a CHECK constraint on the column CONSTRAINT_TYPE, as being one of the following: UNIQUE, PRIMARY KEY, FOREIGN KEY, and CHECK. Deferrability of the constraint is also specified.

12. KEY_COLUMN_USAGE: This table contains one or more rows for each row in the TABLE_CONSTRAINTS table (see item 11) that has a CON-STRAINT_TYPE of UNIQUE, PRIMARY KEY, or FOREIGN KEY (that is, all except for CHECK constraints).

13. REFERENTIAL_CONSTRAINTS: This table contains one row for each row of the TABLE_CONSTRAINTS table that has been inserted by a referential constraint definition. A variety of update rules—CASCADE, SET NULL, SET DEFAULT, and NO ACTION, all of which we discussed in Chapter 10—may be specified for each constraint.

14. CHECK_CONSTRAINTS: As contrasted with KEY_COLUMN_USAGE, this table has one row for each domain check constraint, table check constraint, or assertion.

15. CHECK_TABLE_USAGE: This table has one row for each table referenced by the search condition of a domain CHECK constraint, table CHECK constraint, or assertion (and, therefore, has a FOREIGN KEY constraint of its own on the CHECK_CONSTRAINTS table discussed in item 14).

16. CHECK_COLUMN_USAGE: This table contains one row for each column referenced by the search condition of a domain check constraint, table check constraint, or assertion. It is the same as CHECK_TABLE_USAGE, except for columns instead of tables.

Authors' interjection: By now, you should be getting an idea of the type of metadata that SQL maintains and manages. We've found that by looking at the DEFINITION_SCHEMA base table definitions, as well as the views of INFORMATION_SCHEMA, you can actually learn a great deal about how SQL works with respect to the various language features. Even if you will have little to do with metadata when you develop your applications, you can still learn a lot by looking at the various constraints and search conditions, as well as at the column values and even the table names, of the metadata tables. Now, back to the rest of the base tables.

17. ASSERTIONS: This table contains one row for each assertion, including whether the assertion is deferrable or not.

18. TABLE_PRIVILEGES: One row exists for each table privilege descriptor. The various privilege types are specified in a CHECK constraint, as is whether or not the privilege is grantable. Additionally, FOREIGN KEYS exist between the GRANTOR and GRANTEE columns to the USERS table (base table 1).

19. COLUMN_PRIVILEGES: Remember that we said privileges may be granted on columns as well as tables (see Chapter 13). This table contains the privilege descriptors for all column-specific privileges.

20. USAGE_PRIVILEGES: One row exists for each usage privilege descriptor, which applies to domains, character sets, collations, and translations.

21. CHARACTER_SETS: This table contains one row for each character set description.

22. COLLATIONS: By now, you should be able to figure out that . . . this table contains one row for each character collation descriptor.

23. TRANSLATION: Of course, this table contains one row for each character translation descriptor.

24. (last one). SQL_LANGUAGES: One row exists for each binding style per host language. Note the complete table description; you can learn a lot about the history, background, and supported languages just from reading the CHECK constraint.

```
CREATE TABLE SQL_LANGUAGES
  (
  SQL_LANGUAGE_SOURCE                   INFORMATION_SCHEMA.CHARACTER_DATA
    CONSTRAINT SQL_LANGUAGES_SOURCE_NOT_NULL NOT NULL,
  SQL_LANGUAGE_YEAR                    INFORMATION_SCHEMA.CHARACTER_DATA,
  SQL_LANGUAGE_CONFORMANCE             INFORMATION_SCHEMA.CHARACTER_DATA,
  SQL_LANGUAGE_INTEGRITY               INFORMATION_SCHEMA.CHARACTER_DATA,
  SQL_LANGUAGE_IMPLEMENTATION          INFORMATION_SCHEMA.CHARACTER_DATA,
  SQL_LANGUAGE_BINDING_STYLE           INFORMATION_SCHEMA.CHARACTER_DATA,
  SQL_LANGUAGE_PROGRAMMING_LANGUAGE INFORMATION_SCHEMA.CHARACTER_DATA,
```

```
CONSTRAINT SQL_LANGUAGES_STANDARD_VALID_CHECK
  CHECK ( ( SQL_LANGUAGE_SOURCE = 'ISO 9075' AND
            SQL_LANGUAGE_YEAR IS NOT NULL AND
            SQL_LANGUAGE_CONFORMANCE IS NOT NULL AND
            SQL_LANGUAGE_IMPLEMENTATION IS NULL AND
            ( ( SQL_LANGUAGE_YEAR = '1987' AND
                SQL_LANGUAGE_CONFORMANCE IN ( '1', '2' ) AND
                SQL_LANGUAGE_INTEGRITY IS NULL AND
                ( ( SQL_LANGUAGE_BINDING_STYLE = 'DIRECT' AND
                    SQL_LANGUAGE_PROGRAMMING_LANGUAGE IS NULL )
                  OR
                  ( SQL_LANGUAGE_BINDING_STYLE IN ( 'EMBEDDED', 'MODULE' )
                AND
                SQL_LANGUAGE_PROGRAMMING_LANGUAGE IN
                  ( 'COBOL', 'FORTRAN', 'PASCAL', 'PLI' ) ) ) )
        OR
        ( SQL_LANGUAGE_YEAR = '1989' AND
          SQL_LANGUAGE_CONFORMANCE IN ( '1', '2' ) AND
          SQL_LANGUAGE_INTEGRITY IN ( 'NO', 'YES' ) AND
          ( ( SQL_LANGUAGE_BINDING_STYLE = 'DIRECT' AND
              SQL_LANGUAGE_PROGRAMMING_LANGUAGE IS NULL )
            OR
            ( SQL_LANGUAGE_BINDING_STYLE IN ( 'EMBEDDED', 'MODULE' )
              AND
              SQL_LANGUAGE_PROGRAMMING_LANGUAGE IN
                ( 'COBOL', 'FORTRAN', 'PASCAL', 'PLI' ) ) ) )

        OR
        ( SQL_LANGUAGE_YEAR = '1992' AND
          SQL_LANGUAGE_CONFORMANCE IN
              ( 'ENTRY', 'INTERMEDIATE', 'FULL' ) AND
          SQL_LANGUAGE_INTEGRITY IS NULL AND
          ( ( SQL_LANGUAGE_BINDING  = 'DIRECT' AND
              SQL_LANGUAGE_PROGRAMMING_LANGUGE IS NULL )
            OR
            ( SQL_LANGUAGE_BINDING  IN ( 'EMBEDDED', 'MODULE' )
              AND
              SQL_LANGUAGE_PROGRAMMING_LANGUAGE IN
                  ( 'ADA', 'C', 'COBOL',
                    'FORTRAN', 'MUMPS', 'PASCAL', 'PLI' ) ) ) ) ) )

        OR
        ( SQL_LANGUAGE_SOURCE <> 'ISO 9075' )
      )
  )
```

19.8.3 Assertions on the Base Tables

There are three assertions defined on the base tables. These are:

1. UNIQUE_CONSTRAINT_NAME: This ensures that the same combination of a schema name and a constraint name is not used by more than one constraint. By using an assertion, separate checks on the DOMAINS, TABLE_CONSTRAINTS, and ASSERTIONS tables aren't needed.

2. EQUAL_KEY_DEGREES: This assertion ensures that every FOREIGN KEY is of the same degree as the corresponding UNIQUE constraint. Note the use of GROUP BY below:

3. KEY_DEGREE_GREATER_THAN_OR_EQUAL_TO_1 (whew!): This assertion ensures that every UNIQUE constraint has at least one unique column, and that every referential constraint has at least one referencing column.

FIGURE 19-1	**BASE TABLES**	CHECK_TABLE_USAGE
Summary of DEFINITION_ SCHEMA	USERS	CHECK_COLUMN_USAGE
	SCHEMATA	ASSERTIONS
	DATA_TYPE_DESCRIPTOR	TABLE_PRIVILEGES
	DOMAINS	COLUMN_PRIVILEGES
	DOMAIN_CONSTRAINTS	USAGE_PRIVILEGES
	TABLES	CHARACTER_SETS
	VIEWS	COLLATIONS
	COLUMNS	TRANSLATION
	VIEW_TABLE_USAGE	SQL_LANGUAGES
	VIEW_COLUMN_USAGE	
	TABLE_CONSTRAINTS	**ASSERTIONS**
	KEY_COLUMN_USAGE	UNIQUE_CONSTRAINT_NAME
	REFERENTIAL_CONSTRAINTS	EQUAL_KEY_DEGREES
	CHECK_CONSTRAINTS	KEY_DEGREE_GREATER_THAN_OR_EQUAL_TO_1

19.9 The INFORMATION_SCHEMA

Let's take a look now at the INFORMATION_SCHEMA.

19.9.1 Schema Definition

The schema is defined, as was DEFINITION_SCHEMA, by a simple statement.

```
CREATE SCHEMA INFORMATION_SCHEMA
     AUTHORIZATION INFORMATION_SCHEMA
```

Additionally, there is a single base table definition in the INFORMATION_ SCHEMA along with the views we'll see.

```
CREATE TABLE INFORMATION_SCHEMA_CATALOG_NAME
      (CATALOG_NAME   SQL_IDENTIFIER,
       PRIMARY KEY ( CATALOG_NAME ) )
```

This table identifies the name of the catalog in which the particular information schema resides.

19.9.2 Assertion

There is a single assertion for the INFORMATION_SCHEMA, similar to those we discussed for the DEFINITION_SCHEMA:

INFORMATION_SCHEMA_CATALOG_NAME_CARDINALITY

This assertion ensures that there is exactly one row in the INFORMATION_SCHEMA_CATALOG_NAME table.

19.9.3 Domains

There are three domains in the INFORMATION_SCHEMA.

1. SQL_IDENTIFIER: This defines a domain that allows all valid identifiers of CHARACTER SET SQL_TEXT.
2. CHARACTER_DOMAIN: This domain contains specifications for any character data.
3. CARDINAL_NUMBER: This last domain is defined for nonnegative numbers.

19.9.4 Views

There are 23 views defined within the INFORMATION_SCHEMA. Let's take a look at them. Note that most of these views have special code that allows you to see information about objects for which you have some privilege but prevents you from even seeing a row that concerns an object for which you have no privileges.

1. SCHEMATA: This view identifies the schemas that are owned by a given user. It uses columns from DEFINITION_SCHEMA.SCHEMATA and uses a subquery to match the CATALOG_NAME against the INFORMATION_SCHEMA_CATALOG_NAME base table that resides in this schema.
2. DOMAINS: This view identifies the domains defined in the catalog that are accessible to a given user. The view definition uses a complex JOIN definition to match several base tables, including DEFINITION_SCHEMA.DOMAINS.
3. DOMAIN_CONSTRAINTS: This view identifies the domain constraints, of the domains in the catalog, that are accessible to a given user.
4. TABLES: This view identifies the *persistent* tables, defined in the catalog that are accessible to a given user.
5. VIEWS: This view identifies the views in the catalog that are accessible to a given user.

6. COLUMNS: This view identifies the columns of persistent tables that are accessible to a given user. The actual CREATE VIEW statement and the usage of a number of SQL-92 language constructs, including COALESCE, LEFT JOINs, subqueries, and others, is educational. As a general point of interest (?!) this particular view definition is the longest of those in the INFORMATION_SCHEMA.

7. TABLE_PRIVILEGES: The privileges on persistent tables which are available to or granted by a given user are identified in this view.

8. COLUMN_PRIVILEGES: This view identifies the privileges on columns of persistent tables that are defined in the catalog and are available to or granted by a given user.

9. USAGE_PRIVILEGES: This view identifies USAGE privileges on catalog objects that are available to or owned by a given user.

10. TABLE_CONSTRAINTS: This view identifies table constraints that are owned by a given user.

11. REFERENTIAL_CONSTRAINTS: This view identifies referential constraints that are owned by a given user.

12. CHECK_CONSTRAINTS: In keeping with the current trend, this view identifies CHECK constraints that are owned by a given user.

13. KEY_COLUMN_USAGE: This view identifies columns defined in the catalog that are constrained as keys by a given user.

14. ASSERTIONS: This view identifies the catalog's assertions that are owned by a given user.

15. CHARACTER_SETS: This view identifies the catalog's character sets that are accessible to a given user.

16. COLLATIONS: This view identifies character collations for the catalog that are accessible to a given user.

17. TRANSLATIONS: This view identifies character translations for the catalog that are accessible to a given user.

18. VIEW_TABLE_USAGE: This view identifies the tables on which the catalog's views that are owned by a given user are dependent.

19. VIEW_COLUMN_USAGE: This view identifies the columns on which the catalog's views that are owned by a given user are dependent.

20. CONSTRAINT_TABLE_USAGE: This view identifies tables that are used by constraints—referential, unique, and assertions—and owned by a given user.

21. CONSTRAINT_COLUMN_USAGE: Similar to the view #20, columns are identified for the various constraints that are owned by a given user.

22. COLUMN_DOMAIN_USAGE: This view identifies columns for the catalog that are dependent on domains defined in the catalog and owned by a given user.

23. SQL_LANGUAGES: This view identifies the conformance levels, options, and dialects supported by a given SQL implementation. Earlier, we showed you the base table definition for SQL_LANGUAGES. Let's take a look at the view definition defined on top of that base table.

```
CREATE VIEW SQL_LANGUAGES
  AS SELECT
    SQL_LANGUAGE_SOURCE, SQL_LANGUAGE_YEAR, SQL_LANGUAGE_CONFORMANCE,
    SQL_LANGUAGE_INTEGRITY, SQL_LANGUAGE_IMPLEMENTATION,
    SQL_LANGUAGE_BINDING_STYLE, SQL_LANGUAGE_PROGRAMMING_LANGUAGE
      FROM DEFINITION_SCHEMA.SQL_LANGUAGES
```

· ·

FIGURE 19-2 Summary of INFORMATION_ SCHEMA	**VIEWS**	**COLLATIONS**
	SCHEMATA	TRANSLATIONS
	DOMAINS	VIEW_TABLE_USAGE
	DOMAIN_CONSTRAINTS	VIEW_COLUMN_USAGE
	TABLES	CONSTRAINT_TABLE_USAGE
	VIEWS	CONSTRAINT_COLUMN_USAGE
	COLUMNS	COLUMN_DOMAIN_USAGE
	TABLE_PRIVILEGES	SQL_LANGUAGES
	COLUMN_PRIVILEGES	
	USAGE_PRIVILEGES	**DOMAINS**
	TABLE_CONSTRAINTS	SQL_IDENTIFIER
	REFERENTIAL_CONSTRAINTS	CHARACTER_DATA
	CHECK_CONSTRAINTS	CARDINAL_NUMBER
	KEY_COLUMN_USAGE	
	ASSERTIONS	**ASSERTION**
	CHARACTER_SETS	INFORMATION_SCHEMA_CATALOG_ NAME_CARDINALITY

19.10 Chapter Summary

We've spent some time discussing the INFORMATION_SCHEMA for several reasons. First, if you are developing system programs using an SQL DBMS, you will likely find yourself with the need to access metadata. It's important that you understand not only how SQL manages metadata, but also how your own particular environment's dictionary, repository, or other metadata storage mechanism handles metadata.

Second, as we mentioned earlier, the base table and view definitions themselves provide a learning tool about SQL-92. Think of a metadata management environment as a more or less complete subsystem. There are defined functions and missions of that subsystem. By looking at base table definitions and, more importantly, the views created on top of those tables, the "what I have to do" aspect of table creation starts to become somewhat second nature. As you create your own tables, you will find yourself instinctively thinking questions such as, "What constraints do I have to apply to this table or view to make it useful?" and "What accessibility should this view have?"

In the next chapter, we'll discuss some of the anticipated characteristics and features of future versions of SQL. Stay tuned.

A Look to the Future

20.1 Introduction

Now that we've examined the contents of SQL-92 in detail, you must be wondering what the future of SQL is likely to bring. In this chapter, we take a brief look at the progress currently being made to develop the next generation of the language.

The standardization process makes it impossible to predict exactly what the future of the standard will be, but we can make some fairly reasonable guesses based on our participation in the various committees that are involved in this effort. Work has been in progress on the next generation of the SQL standard, which has the working title SQL3, for a couple of years (at publication), so at least some of the probable contents have become apparent. There are broad hopes that SQL3 will be published in the 1995 or 1996 timeframe, thereby keeping up the cycle of about every three years that SQL has enjoyed so far.

20.2 SQL3 Overview

It appears that SQL3 will have two primary foci: enhanced relational capabilities, and support for the object paradigm. Let's look at these separately. Please keep in mind that this discussion reflects the current work on SQL3 at the time of publication, but that significant changes may be made (indeed, are quite likely for some features) before SQL3 becomes a standard.

20.2.1 Enhanced Relational Support

There are many different database features that did not make the cut into SQL-92 but which are in demand by users of relational database systems and are often provided by vendors of relational DBMSs. For example, many DBMSs provide support for *active rules*, often called *triggers*, but SQL-92 lacks a definition for them.

SQL3 does specify this feature, but it simply didn't make it into SQL-92. Why? Many factors contributed, but the main reason is that the standards committees simply guessed wrong: they didn't realize how rapidly the demand for triggers and the implementations of triggers would come along. In addition, several reviewers felt there were remaining problems with triggers that would require significant effort to resolve. However, most vendors have simply gone beyond SQL-92 and used the SQL3 trigger specification as the basis for their implementations. (Of course, that is a calculated gamble. If the SQL3 specification changes significantly, those implementations will be out of conformance and will eventually have to change.)

20.2.2 Triggers

A trigger is a schema object that tells a DBMS what other actions to perform after certain SQL statements have been executed. For example, you may want to have the DBMS insert a row into a log table every time some application updates the MOVIES table so you can keep track of who is making changes to your data.

The format of a trigger definition is:

```
CREATE TRIGGER trigger-name time event
    ON table-name [ referencing ] action
```

Of course, trigger-name is the name given to the trigger. The only place where you need to use this name is in the DROP TRIGGER statement. The time is either BEFORE or AFTER, indicating whether the trigger is fired before or after the specified event occurs. event is either INSERT, DELETE, or UPDATE (optionally UPDATE OF column-name [, column-name]..., to specify that only updates of the specified columns will fire the trigger), indicating that the execution of an INSERT statement, a DELETE statement, or an UPDATE statement will fire the trigger.

The table-name identifies the table that the DBMS must watch for a triggering event. When the statement specified in event is executed for that table, the trigger fires. A trigger can specify referencing only when the event is UPDATE; it is used to specify a correlation name that can identify the values of columns in the row being updated before the update occurs and after the update occurs (regardless of whether the time is BEFORE or AFTER). The format of referencing is:

```
REFERENCING OLD [AS] old-correlation-name
    [ NEW [AS] new-correlation-name ]
```

or

```
REFERENCING NEW [AS] new-correlation-name
    [ OLD [AS] old-correlation-name ]
```

Finally, action specifies the actions that the DBMS is required to take whenever the trigger fires. The format of action is:

```
[ WHEN ( search-condition ) ]
  ( statement [ , statement ]... ) [ granularity ]
```

where search-condition, our old friend, allows the database designer to identify specific conditions that will cause a trigger to fire. For example, you may want the trigger to fire only when one or more rows in MOVIE_TITLES is updated to lower the cost by more than 10% or when a movie is deleted and the total number of movies being tracked falls below 500. statement is an SQL statement; at present, it is limited to the searched DELETE and UPDATE statements and the INSERT statement. However, recent discussions suggest interest in extending it to include almost any SQL statement (though there will probably be some limits based on what makes sense in specific circumstances).

Finally granularity is either FOR EACH ROW or FOR EACH STATEMENT. If granularity is not specified, FOR EACH STATEMENT is the default. If you specify FOR EACH ROW, the trigger's action is executed for every row that is inserted, deleted, or updated by the event; otherwise, the action is executed only once.

The combinations of time and event and their effects are as follows:

- BEFORE INSERT means that the action is performed before the insert is performed (either before the insertion of each row or before any insert, depending on FOR EACH; as this relationship affects all of these combinations, we won't bore you by saying it every time). Any references to values of columns in the row being inserted are obviously to the value *after* insertion.

- AFTER INSERT means that the action is performed after the insert is performed. References to row values have the same meaning here as for BEFORE INSERT.

- BEFORE DELETE means that the action is performed before the deletion is performed. Any references to values of columns in the row being deleted are obviously to the value *before* deletion.

- AFTER DELETE means that the action is performed after the deletion is performed. References to row values have the same meaning here as for BEFORE DELETE.

- BEFORE UPDATE means that the action is performed before the update of the specified columns is performed. If you specify referencing, then the old-correlation-name (if any) can be used in the SQL statements of the action to identify the value of the row being updated *before* the update actually takes place and the new-correlation-name (if any) can be used in the SQL statements of the action to identify the value of the row being updated *after* the update actually takes place.

- AFTER UPDATE means that the action is performed after the update of the specified columns is performed. Referencing has the same effect here as for BEFORE UPDATE.

As with other schema objects, you can drop a trigger.

```
DROP TRIGGER trigger-name
```

To define a trigger on some table, you must have been granted TRIGGER privileges on that table. This prevents others from obtaining information about the data in your table by roundabout means.

20.2.3 Recursive Operations

Another relational-oriented feature of SQL3 is the RECURSIVE UNION operation. This operation provides SQL with the ability to perform "bill of material" operations, something long requested by users. In SQL-92 and earlier versions of SQL, the only way that you could generate a list of parts for some assembly was to use several cursors to scan the parts table; whenever you encountered a part that was made up of other parts, you started another cursor to determine the components of that part. SQL3 contains a special set operator, analogous to UNION or JOIN, that will perform these operations for you. RECURSIVE UNION effectively traverses a tree of rows in the database. To follow this discussion, you should have at least a basic understanding of computer graph theory and tree structures.

The format of RECURSIVE UNION is:

```
( initial RECURSIVE UNION correlation-names
    [ ( columns ) ] iteration
    [ search ] [ cycle ] [ limit ] )
```

Initial is a query expression that determines the starting point for your search. If you are building a parts list for, say, a particular type of automobile, you would provide a query expression to locate the primary row for that automobile type. correlation-names is:

```
correlation-name [ , correlation-name ]...
```

and specifies one or more correlation-names that can be used in the iteration to identify the parents of any row being accumulated into the result. If each accumulated row has only one parent (as in a parts database), then there is only one correlation-name and the RECURSIVE UNION is said to be *linear*. If accumulated rows have more than one parent (for example, if you are constructing human genealogy), there will be one correlation-name for each parent and the RECURSIVE UNION is said to be *nonlinear*.

Columns is:

```
column-name [ , column-name ]...
```

and can be optionally used to name the columns that result from the RECURSIVE UNION. The number of column-names must be exactly equal to the degree of the initial query-expression.

The iteration is another query expression that specifies how child rows of any parent row are to be found. The degree of iteration must also be identical to the degree of initial.

If a search is specified, then it is:

    SEARCH order SET column-name

and order is either PREORDER or DEPTH FIRST BY sort-spec or BREADTH FIRST BY sort-spec (sort-spec is the same as for DECLARE CURSOR). PREORDER basically means "do the accumulation in whatever order is convenient for the implementation"; DEPTH FIRST means "traverse the tree structure depth first"; and BREADTH FIRST means "traverse breadth first," as you would expect. The column identified by column-name must be an integer column and is set to a value that indicates when the accumulated row was found (a sort of sequence number).

The cycle is used to help the DBMS determine whether a row that has already been accumulated into the result is encountered again—a condition that can cause serious problems. This rarely happens with real-life objects (for example, very few of us are our own ancestors, and very few machines that we build have themselves as components). However, databases are often imperfect because they are loaded with faulty data; by flagging such cycles as this, we can avoid getting into infinite loops.

Similarly, limit is used to control how long we want a search to go on. Even if we catch loops by the use of cycle, we may not wish to exhaustively traverse trees all the way to the end. For example, if we're working on a human genealogy, we may be satisfied with 10 generations for our current purposes, so we could specify a limit to control that. If the specified limits are reached, the limit clause controls whether the RECURSIVE UNION simply returns or gives you an error.

20.2.4 New Data Types

Still another relational feature in SQL3 is the addition of two new data types: enumerated and Boolean. The Boolean data type can have only the values True and False (and, like all others, null) and can be used to capture the results of predicates. The format is

    BOOLEAN

For example, in a table definition, you might write:

```
CREATE TABLE MOVIE_TITLES (
  TITLE CHARACTER VARYING (30),
  IN_STOCK BOOLEAN,
  ...
)
```

The enumerated data type is quite like that of C and Pascal. It permits you to define a domain whose values are restricted to a small set of values. For example, you might define a domain named COLORS whose permissible values are BLUE, RED, and YELLOW. Any time you store a value into a column with that domain, you can store only one of those three colors. To define such a domain, you could write:

```
CREATE DOMAIN colors ( blue, red, yellow )
```

Then you can use this in a column definition:

```
...
PAINT_JOB colors,
...
```

Later, when you want to insert a row into that table, you might code:

```
INSERT INTO xyz
    VALUES (..., colors::yellow, ...);
```

You must always use the name of the domain when you write an enumeration literal, and the :: is used to separate the domain name from the specific enumeration name.

In the case of our sample video/music application, you may have:

```
CREATE DOMAIN movie_types (children, comedy,
    adventure, children, musical, historical,
    other)

.....
CREATE TABLE movie_titles
    ( title    CHARACTER VARYING (30),
      type     MOVIE_TYPES,
    ..... )

....
INSERT INTO movie_titles VALUES
    (....,movie_types::musical,....)
```

20.2.5 Other Relational Features

A number of other new features, or enhancements to existing features, are currently expected in SQL3, but they are either less significant than those already discussed or they have not yet been defined. They include:

- Enhancements to assertions (including the ability specify that they be checked only under certain conditions, similar to triggers)
- Enhancements to cursors (including the ability to keep cursors open even when transactions are terminated)
- Stored procedures

20.3 Support for the Object Paradigm

A great deal of work is going on in SQL3 to support object-oriented technology. The work is very intensive and quite dynamic, so we will not go into any details here. However, a list of the concepts for which support either has been provided or is expected includes:

- User-defined abstract data types
- Encapsulation
- Object identity
- Unification of SQL tables and abstract data types
- Subtypes and supertypes
- Inheritance of type attributes and methods
- Parameterized types
- Type generators
- A control language for implementation of methods
- Computational completeness
- Functions and procedures written in SQL
- Functions written in host languages
- Exception handling for SQL functions and procedures
- Persistent SQL modules
- Static and dynamic binding of methods
- "Built-in" data type generators (*e.g.,* for sets, multisets, lists)
- SQL variables, temporary variables

This work is very exciting and promises to dramatically change the face of the database world as we know it today. It combines the best of relational database features (for managing your traditional data) and object-oriented database features (for managing your nontraditional data) into one package that allows you to manage all of your data in one database and one application.

Furthermore, additional standards for multimedia, geographic, and other complex applications are expected to be defined as layers on top of the SQL3 work.

20.4 Chapter Summary

Standards evolve over time. While there is no way to know exactly what features and aspects will wind up in SQL3 several years from now, this chapter will give you a pretty good idea. You can even start developing your applications with these features in mind. For example, your movie and music database might now have a column of MOVIE_TITLES.TYPE as a CHARACTER or CHARACTER VARYING data type. You can, however, use CHECK to limit the permissible values to HORROR, CHILDREN, COMEDY, and so on. In a way, you have simulated an enumerated data type. When your particular DBMS comes out with true enumerated data types, you can easily switch your code from "pseudo-enumerated" to enumerated variables and columns.

Again, remember that certain DBMS products may jump the gun and introduce tentative SQL3 features into their products. While this may give you a head start with these features, keep in mind that syntax, behavior, and other aspects may vary from those eventually adopted into the next iteration of the standard. In these cases, the usual good programming practices—specifically, isolation and modularization of system-specific features, documentation, and the like—will help ease any subsequent transformations that you must make.

PART V

Appendices

Designing SQL-92 Databases

A.1 Introduction

In earlier chapters, we based our SQL-92 examples around a sample database environment for a retail video and music store. Let's take a brief look at some techniques you can use to design your own SQL-92 databases. In this appendix, we discuss techniques to design databases in a graphical, conceptual—that is, a non-implementation-dependent—manner. We also discuss how your conceptual database design can be converted into a usable logical database design upon which you can create SQL-92 relational tables. We also learn about an issue that is very important to relational databases and their subsequent ease-of-use and maintainability: normalization.

Entire textbooks and hundreds, maybe thousands, of technical papers have been written on the subjects that we briefly discuss in this appendix. We make no pretenses about thoroughly covering database design in these pages; rather, we attempt to provide a quick-start guide for those readers unfamiliar with the issues and techniques of designing useful databases.

A.2 Overview of Database Design

A frequently heard complaint common since the early days of relational databases has been, "My $%#@! DBMS product is so slow! It takes ten times longer to perform than my old CODASYL product (or hierarchical system or flat-file environment or . . .)." While it's true that early relational products often suffered in terms of performance—especially when compared against pointer-based products (CODASYL or hierarchical systems, specifically) that supported other database models—it's interesting to note that increases in relational DBMS performance (via enhanced optimization techniques and other product improvements) were often *not* accompanied by corresponding improvements in overall user database performance. The reason? Many relational databases were so poorly designed that no product enhancements could overcome the built-in obstacles to performance.

One of the reasons for such poor design is the ease by which relational database objects can be created and populated. By contrast, hierarchical and CODASYL databases require a great deal of planning to determine not only record structures but access methods across an organizational database. Since most access in those models is handled via pointers and traversing linkages, all access paths have to preplanned, and this has often been accompanied by human-intervention optimization in access techniques. (Example: What are the most efficient ways to access our database to produce reports X, Y, and Z? Okay, make sure the proper linkages are there.)

Nearly anyone, however, can could create tables and columns for relational databases. In fact, it is so easy to do that the typical sequence of events has been:

- Create some tables and columns
- If there is missing information, add columns to a table somewhere or create some new tables
- Create still more tables and columns
- And so on

Following this sequence, it doesn't take long before application developers are faced with a plethora of database objects from which they need to extract data for their particular transactions: a little bit from here, some from there, some more from that table over there that was created yesterday. . . .

The point is that the absence of thorough database design, both *at the beginning of the development process* and *during any and all modifications,* has been and continues to be a major pitfall of relational databases, which of course continues to hinder performance. All the power of SQL-92 and products based on the standard cannot fully overcome design flaws.

A.3 Levels of Database Design

In the purest sense, database design encompasses three distinct levels.

- *Conceptual Database Design:* Often called *data modeling,* this level entails little or no concern for underlying products (or even the implementation model: relational, object-oriented, or some other model).
- *Logical Database Design:* In the particular context of this book, this level entails the creation of SQL tables, columns, schemas, constraints, and other objects transformed from the conceptual objects of the previous stage. However, little or no attention is given to performance enhancement techniques or other system-specific details.

- *Physical Database Design:* This level includes adjustments that make databases running under a specific product (or products) more efficient than they would without undergoing this step. This includes data placement, "denormalization," and other techniques we discuss later.

In real life, there is some overlap among these phases. For example, pure logical design may require you to transform conceptual objects to certain relational objects based on the transformation mapping rules we discuss shortly. Some DBMS products may support certain facilities, such as feature enhancements, that are absent from comparable products. In these cases, some degree of product-specific concern (which is typically reserved for the physical design stage) must be considered; it makes no sense to create logical objects that aren't supported by your implementation, nor to forgo features that your product supports because the "standard" mapping rules don't take those features into account.

Let's now take a further look at these different levels and the further breakdowns in each level.

A.4 Conceptual Database Design

Ideally, all databases—whether relational, network, hierarchical, object-oriented, or of some other structure—should first be designed in a conceptual manner. That is, the issue of collecting and modeling database requirements should precede and should not be confused by issues of tables, columns, and views in the relational database model and their corresponding cousins in other models (records, sets, *etc.*). Conceptual database design is sometimes referred to as *data modeling;* often it is based around one of several graphical techniques.

Before we discuss some of the conceptual database objects you may use to model your databases, there are several things we wish to emphasize.

1. There are many different data modeling, and therefore conceptual database design, techniques. The objects we present are from the *extended entity relationship modeling* (EER) branch of the art. Other data models, such as the *binary-relationship model,* utilize different objects and different modeling rules. In fact, many "religious wars" rage among advocates of the various database design models, with each camp claiming superiority over its competitors in terms of ability to express database requirements.

2. There are no standards within any of the various models. For example, extended entity relationship modeling may vary across different implementations in terms of supported objects (supporting CASE tools, textbooks, technical papers, and so on).

3. Notations vary across various model implementations. For example, there are many different ways to represent relationships (discussed shortly) and their properties (such as cardinality and naming).

4. A *model* is not the same as a *methodology*. We will be discussing models—in our case, extended entity-relationship, in other cases, binary-relationship, IDEF, and MERISE, among others. A methodology, in contrast, is the manner in which a model is used. For example, EER models may be used in top-down methodologies (starting with certain objects and decomposing them) or bottom-up methodologies (working with low-level objects and grouping them into similar categories). Correspondingly, these two (and other) methodologies may utilize not only EER models but any of the others we mentioned above.

A.4.1 Conceptual Objects

Rather than concentrate on defining tables, columns, and the parameters of those columns, practitioners of conceptual database design might specify the following objects:[1]

Entities

These are the primary objects around which your database is organized. In our sample database, entities are *movies, music objects* (CDs, cassettes, *etc.*), *employees,* and *customers.*

There are several variations of entities: *regular* entities (such as those mentioned above) and *weak* entities (see Figure A-1). A weak entity can be based on either existence or identification, depending on the version of entity-relationship modeling being used. That is, in the first case, the existence of a weak entity depends on the existence of another entity. In the second case, the unique identification of a given weak entity is dependent on its relationship with another entity. An example of the first type would be a weak entity entitled *employee salary history,* which we may wish not to retain if we delete an *employee.* An example of the second type might be a *customer credit history* that does not contain some sort of identifying customer name or number; instead, it derives its identification by virtue of its relationship to a particular *customer.*

Attributes

These are the components of entities: those parts that help define the uniqueness and usefulness of a particular entity. For example, the *movie* entity contains the attributes *movie title, our cost, regular rental price, number of VHS units in stock,* and many others as defined below.

A special type of attribute, the multivalued attribute, can be used to indicate, in a conceptual manner, that more than one value of a particular attribute can exist. For example, an *employee* or *customer* can have more than one phone number. There is some debate over whether multivalued attributes should be used in data models

---

1 Note that other database design models feature other types of objects. Also, there are a number of variations of extended entity relationship (EER) models. Database design models tend to be governed by practice (when CASE tools are used) as well as by the objects supported by particular tools.

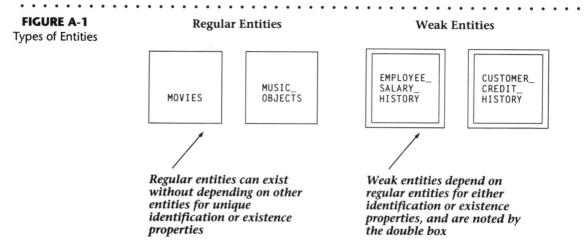

FIGURE A-1
Types of Entities

Regular entities can exist without depending on other entities for unique identification or existence properties

Weak entities depend on regular entities for either identification or existence properties, and are noted by the double box

that will be transformed into relational databases, since the relational model doesn't support multivalued columns. Some experts[2] advocate automatically representing a multivalued attribute as an entity with a corresponding relationship (described next) to the parent entity. The alternative view is that since some pseudorelational products, such as 4GLs built on top of databases, and some alternative database models support multivalued fields, it is more "semantically pure" to represent conceptual objects as multivalued attributes (if applicable) and to execute the appropriate mapping transformation to relational tables with foreign keys if you are using a standard relational database.

Additionally, some attributes may be identified as *key field* attributes in that they help uniquely identify a particular entity instance. For example, the *employee number* may be enough to uniquely identify an employee. *Title,* however, is not enough to uniquely identify a particular movie (remakes may use the same title, as in *A Star is Born*). In that case, multiple attributes (such as combining *title* with some other attribute like *year released*) would be required to function together as key field attributes. Figure A-2 illustrates the different kinds of attributes and how they can be conceptually represented.

Properties of Attributes

Each attribute has various properties, such as its data type, size, mandatory inclusion (*e.g.,* whether NULL values are permitted in a particular instance), and relationships to other attributes. For example, the *movie titles* attribute of the *movies* is of data type *character* (or string), is 30 characters long, and cannot have NULL values (that is, cannot have an empty field in a given instance). There is no standard graphical representation for attribute properties, though CASE tools typically represent and manage them through pop-up windows or dialog boxes (see Figure A-3).

2 Toby J. Teorey, *Database Modeling and Design: The Entity-Relationship Approach*, Morgan Kaufmann Publishers, San Mateo, CA, 1990, pp. 36-37.

FIGURE A-2
Attributes

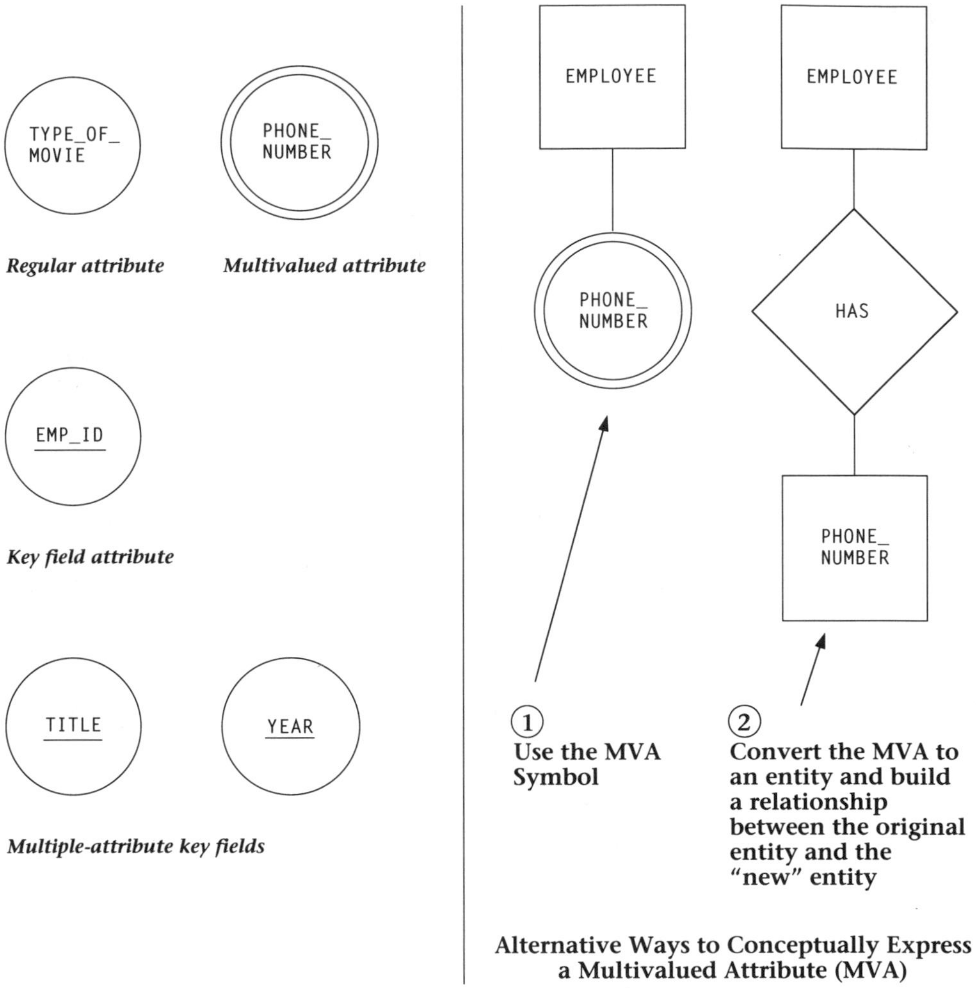
TYPE_OF_ MOVIE
PHONE_ NUMBER
Regular attribute
Multivalued attribute
EMP_ID
Key field attribute
TITLE
YEAR
Multiple-attribute key fields
EMPLOYEE
PHONE_ NUMBER
EMPLOYEE
HAS
PHONE_ NUMBER
1 Use the MVA Symbol
2 Convert the MVA to an entity and build a relationship between the original entity and the "new" entity
Alternative Ways to Conceptually Express a Multivalued Attribute (MVA)

Relationships

Entities and attributes are related to one another. Entity-to-attribute relationships occur by default; that is, *movies* and *movie titles* are automatically related to each other. Relationships between and among entities are represented by the relationship object, which in turn has certain properties such as:

Cardinality: A given instance of an entity has a one-to-one, one-to-many, or many-to-many relationship with other entities (examples are shown later). Some EER models support two types of cardinality: *minimum cardinality* and *maximum cardinality*. Minimum cardinality represents the minimum number of occurrences required in a particular relationship. For example, if any given occurrence of a

. . . .

FIGURE A-3
Sample
Attribute
Property
Specification

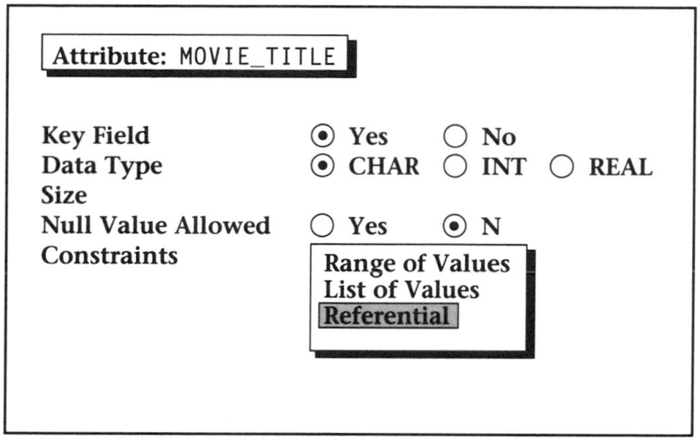

```
┌─────────────────────────────────────────────────────┐
│   ┌────────────────────────────┐                       │
│   │ Attribute: MOVIE_TITLE     │                       │
│   └────────────────────────────┘                       │
│                                                         │
│   Key Field           ⦿ Yes    ○ No                    │
│   Data Type           ⦿ CHAR   ○ INT   ○ REAL          │
│   Size                                                  │
│   Null Value Allowed  ○ Yes    ⦿ N                     │
│   Constraints         ┌─────────────────────┐          │
│                       │ Range of Values     │          │
│                       │ List of Values      │          │
│                       │ Referential         │          │
│                       └─────────────────────┘          │
│                                                         │
└─────────────────────────────────────────────────────┘
```

movie must have at least one *distributor,* you might specify a minimum cardinality of 1 for that particular relationship. Alternatively, a *movie* may not have a *movie star* (such as a documentary or animated feature). In that case, the minimum cardinality would be 0. Some models allow a number other than 0 or 1 to further indicate a minimum number of occurrences. For example, if a *music title* must have at least two candidate *music distributors,* you could specify a minimum cardinality of 2 to express that rule.

n-ary: This concept defines whether relationships exist only between two entities or may exist among more than two entities. There are three different types of relationships (see Figure A-4).

- Binary (not to be confused with the binary relationship model we mentioned earlier), in which two entities participate
- Unary, in which an entity has a "relationship with itself" (Example: a *person* may be a *parent* of another *person*).
- *n*-ary, in which three (or more) entities participate. Be cautioned, however, that many relationships that initially appear to be *n*-ary may be decomposed into two or more binary relationships.

Generalizations (hierarchies)

Extended entity-relationship modeling techniques utilize generalization hierarchies. Hierarchies are a means by which inheritance of common attributes can be conceptually specified, in a manner similar to that of object-oriented databases (see Figure A-5). The components of a hierarchy are sometimes referred to as *supertypes* and *subtypes*. An example would be a *movie* entity, which may have a subtype of *movie sequel.* All movies have certain attributes—title, year released, and so on—but sequels have at least one additional attribute: the number in the series of that particular movie (Example: *The Empire Strikes Back: number-in-series = 2*).

FIGURE A-4
Relationships
and Their
Properties

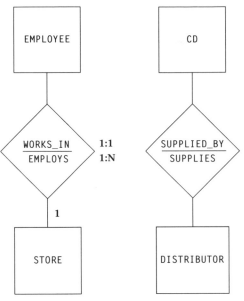

1:1
1:N

1:N RELATIONSHIP
WITH
BIDIRECTIONAL
NAMING,
MINIMUM AND MAXIMUM
CARDINALITIES

2:N
1:N

N:N RELATIONSHIP
WITH BIDIRECTIONAL
NAMING, VALUED
MINIMUM CARDINALITY

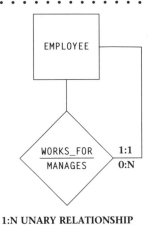

1:1
0:N

1:N UNARY RELATIONSHIP
WITH BIDIRECTIONAL
NAMING AND MINIMUM
CARDINALITY:

READ AS: An employee
works for at least one and at
most one employee; an
employee manages from 0
to n (many) employees.

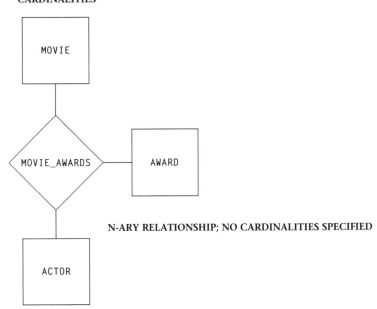

N-ARY RELATIONSHIP; NO CARDINALITIES SPECIFIED

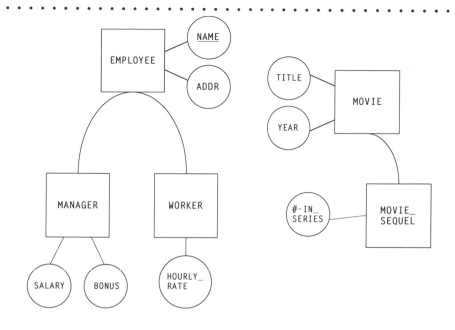

FIGURE A-5
Generalization
Hierarchies

A.4.2 Performing Conceptual Design

We mentioned that there are a number of different methodologies through which conceptual database design can be accomplished. Some are oriented around top-down design, where *superentities* are identified and iteratively decomposed into more refined entities and, eventually, are coupled with attributes and relationships. Other methodologies promote bottom-up design, where low-level entities and all of their attributes are defined and subsequently linked together through defined relationships.

Some methodologies couple conceptual database design with a process-oriented design technique such as data flow diagramming, using both techniques in concert. Other methodologies require their practitioners to complete either the data or the process side of the design before proceeding to the other.

Regardless of which methodology you decide to follow—and different development efforts often require different methodologies—you eventually will come to the process of conceptual database design. Let's look at our video and music store and illustrate how our conceptual database model is derived. Because we're only dealing with a small database in our example, let's utilize a bottom-up methodology, one in which we will first define entities and attributes and subsequently relate them to one another.

The five entities shown in Figure A-6 are defined during an initial pass at superentities. Your next step is to decompose each of the superentities into subentities within that particular category. For example, *movies* can be decomposed to *movies* and *actors. Music* can be decomposed into *albums, singles,* and *artists* (see Figure A-7). At this time, you can start identifying some of the attributes of each of the entities.

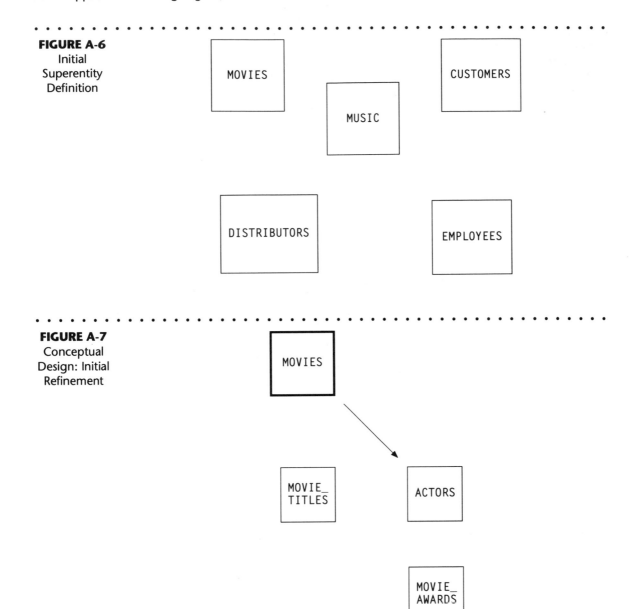

FIGURE A-6
Initial
Superentity
Definition

FIGURE A-7
Conceptual
Design: Initial
Refinement

Next, you can start identifying relationships among the various entities. For example, *movies* and *actors* are related to one another; actors *star* in movies.[3] Similarly, customers *check out* movies (see Figure A-8).

3 Some EER models support bidirectional naming of relationships: actors *star* in movies, and movies *feature* actors. Depending on the "direction" you are addressing in the relationship, you would use the appropriate name. This is purely for readability, since it doesn't make sense to say "movies *star* in actors."

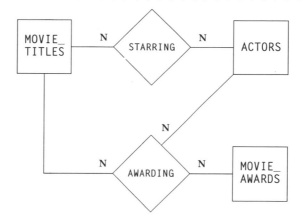

FIGURE A-8
Definition of
Relationships

This process continues until you have defined all of your entities, attributes, attribute properties, and relationships. Keep in mind that this is an iterative process; in real life you can go back to users (those whom you interviewed to gather this information for your model) and run them through your initial and intermediate findings (Hey, Sue, are all of these attributes of customers correct? Do we have to maintain a customer's credit history if they always pay cash?).

At some point, you determine that your conceptual model is complete. It's time then to move on to the logical design phase.

A.5 Logical Database Design

A.5.1 Model-to-Model Design Transformation

Your conceptual model must be transformed into a relational form (one which conforms to SQL-92 rules) in order to be used in your applications. There are several transformation rules to guide you in this process. In general, entities are transformed into tables, with the attributes of those entities transformed into the columns of the table. The different relationships and their properties, such as minimum cardinality (existence dependency), maximum cardinality, and degree (unary, binary, *n*-ary), may cause certain conditions to occur. For instance, foreign keys may become "embedded" as columns in other tables, or "intersection tables" may be created.

Let's look at a couple of examples.[4] A relationship with a many-to-many maximum cardinality would be transformed as illustrated in Figure A-9. In contrast, a relationship with a one-to-many maximum cardinality would be transformed as shown in Figure A-10. The transformation from the conceptual level to the logical level, according to the respective cardinalities, is made in a certain way

---

[4] A complete discussion can be found in Teorey, *Database Modeling and Design: The Entity-Relationship Approach,* Morgan Kaufmann Publishers, San Mateo, CA, 1990, pp. 61-78.

in keeping with the principles of normalization (see section A.5.2)—that is, a transformation of a many-to-many relationship must be done in the way shown to avoid violating 1NF rules.

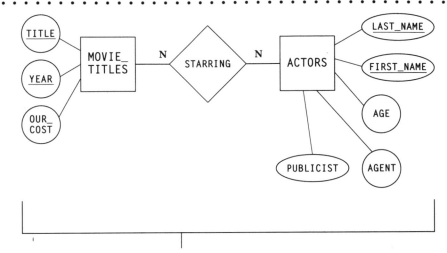

FIGURE A-9
Transformation of Many-to-Many Relationship

```
CREATE TABLE movie_titles (
    title            CHARACTER (30) NOT NULL,
    year_released    DATE NOT NULL,
    our_cost         DECIMAL (7,2),

    CONSTRAINT title_pk PRIMARY KEY
       (title, year_released )   )

CREATE TABLE actors  (
    last_name        CHARACTER (20) NOT NULL,
    first_name       CHARACTER (15) NOT NULL,
    age              SMALLINT,
    agent            CHARACTER (30),
    publicist        CHARACTER (30),

    CONSTRAINT actor_pk PRIMARY KEY
       (last_name, first_name )   )

CREATE TABLE movies_stars (
    title             CHARACTER (30) NOT NULL,
    year_released     DATE NOT NULL,
    actor_last_name   CHARACTER (20) NOT NULL,
    actor_first_name  CHARACTER (15) NOT NULL,

    CONSTRAINT stars_pk PRIMARY KEY
       (title, year_released, actor_last_name,
        actor_first_name ),

    CONSTRAINT stars_fk FOREIGN KEY
       (title, year_released ) REFERENCES
movie_titles

    )
```

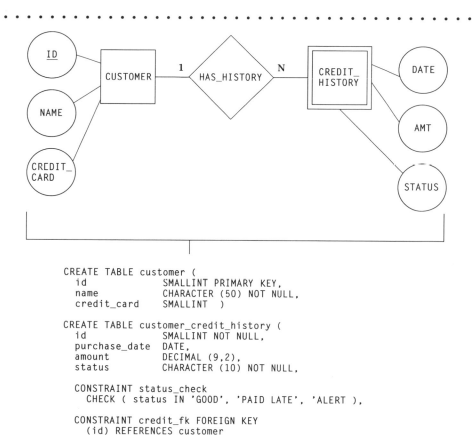

```
CREATE TABLE customer (
   id              SMALLINT PRIMARY KEY,
   name            CHARACTER (50) NOT NULL,
   credit_card     SMALLINT  )

CREATE TABLE customer_credit_history (
   id              SMALLINT NOT NULL,
   purchase_date   DATE,
   amount          DECIMAL (9,2),
   status          CHARACTER (10) NOT NULL,

   CONSTRAINT status_check
     CHECK ( status IN 'GOOD', 'PAID LATE', 'ALERT ),

   CONSTRAINT credit_fk FOREIGN KEY
     (id) REFERENCES customer
```

A.5.2 Normalization

After your conceptual objects have been transformed into tables and columns, it's time to *normalize* your database. Normalization is the process of placing your database into a particular *normal form;* that is, making your database subscribe to certain rules.

There are various normal forms, each with increasing restrictions about what columns should and shouldn't be included in various tables. For purposes of simplifying our discussion, we'll deal only with first, second, and third normal forms. Keep in mind, though, that you can also normalize your database according to the rules of Boyce-Codd, fourth, and fifth normal forms (BCNF, 4NF, and 5NF, respectively).[5]

The formal definitions of normalization take into account functional dependencies, candidate keys, and other technical aspects. In our brief space, we'll defer

---

5 See footnote 4, pp. 96, 112-114.

discussion of these concepts in lieu of a catchy phrase that can help you remember the basic normalization rules:

A column must be dependent on the key, the whole key, and nothing but the key.

Let's look at this statement and how we perform basic normalization. First normal form (1NF) is simple: no repeating groups (*e.g.*, multivalued attributes) are permitted. Let's take an example of movies and stars. You conceivably could have modeled these objects as shown in Figure A-11.

These objects in turn could have been transformed into the following SQL table if you hadn't followed the transformation rules correctly:

```
CREATE TABLE movie_titles
    (title CHARACTER (30) NOT NULL,
    ....
        actor_last_name_1       CHARACTER (30),
        actor_first_name_1      CHARACTER (25),
        actor_last_name_2       CHARACTER (30),
        actor_first_name_2      CHARACTER (25),
        actor_last_name_3       CHARACTER (30),
        actor_first_name_3      CHARACTER (25),
    .....
```

FIGURE A-11
Multivalued
Attribute as a
First Normal
Form Violation

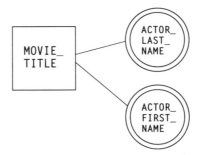

The big question is, for how many actors should you allow space (columns) in each row? Some movies like *The Big Chill* have seven or eight stars, while others have only one (or even none). The simple rule is: for 1NF compliance, no repeating groups are allowed (in the above case, the ACTOR information would be considered a repeating group). Instead, separate tables and columns (as in our example database) are used to remove repeating groups (as in our MOVIES_ STARS).

For second normal form (2NF), we go to our saying above: "the whole key." That is, any column must be dependent on the entire key; no *partial key dependencies* may exist. If a table has only one column that makes up its key, achieving 2NF is easy. If multiple columns make up the key of a table, you must ensure that there are no partial key dependencies. If there are, your table must be divided into two or more tables to remove the partial key dependencies.

Finally, we go back to our saying, "and nothing but the key." To achieve third normal form (3NF), no column may be dependent on any other column that isn't part of the key; that is, no *non-key dependencies* may exist.

For further information on the above normal forms, as well as on BCNF, 4NF, and 5NF, see the references cited, by Teorey.[6]

A.6 Physical Database Design

After you have completed logical database design, there are a number of physical design areas that you can address. These include:

1. Using surrogate identifiers in place of long key values to save storage space. For example, you may choose to add an ACTOR_NUMBER for each actor in place of the ACTOR_LAST_NAME and ACTOR_FIRST_NAME to use as a surrogate key in related tables.
2. Placing data elements (specific row instances) on mass storage in such a way as to maximize access throughput
3. Adding and tuning index structures
4. *Denormalizing* (deliberately violating the normalization rules we discussed earlier) your tables to improve access. As an example, two tables that are frequently joined together may be combined into a single physical table even if 2NF and 3NF rules are violated.

Physical design tends to differ among various DBMS products, even ones utilizing SQL.

A.7 Use of CASE Tools

When possible, you should try to utilize computer aided software engineering (CASE) tools that support data modeling in your database design efforts. Graphical EER tools, for example, may allow you to draw entities, attributes, hierarchies, and relationships, and subsequently generate SQL tables from your conceptual objects that automatically conform to normalization and transformation rules.

When evaluating CASE tools, keep in mind that the richer the overall environment, the more assistance you will receive with your database design. For example, a CASE tool that permits you to specify attribute properties such as ranges and lists of values should transform these properties into the appropriate CHECK clauses at SQL generation time. Correspondingly, all SQL PRIMARY KEY and FOREIGN KEY constraints should be automatically generated based on the cardinalities of your conceptual relationships.

---

6 See footnote 4.

A.8 Appendix Summary

We hope that our short sojourn into discussing database design proves useful for those readers unfamiliar with this area. As we mentioned, much greater detail is available on the design issues we've discussed.[7] Database design is essential to your overall system's success. The degree to which you cover the various levels throughout your system's development life cycle will determine how well you are able to prevent database-related problems.

There are other issues relative to database design that are beyond our scope of discussion—reverse engineering and distributed database design, for example—which you should also investigate to gain a complete perspective on the design process.

---

[7] For references to further reading, see Toby J. Teorey, *Database Modeling and Design: The Entity-Relationship Approach,* Morgan Kaufmann Publishers, San Mateo, CA, 1990.

APPENDIX B

. . . .

A Complete SQL-92 Example

B.1 Introduction

In this appendix we present a (more or less) complete example of an SQL-92-based information system, built around the video/music retail store model that we've used throughout this book. We've tried to include as many SQL-92 statements and features as possible to cover the range of tasks in our application. In a few cases, we've introduced artificial requirements to permit us to use some feature of SQL-92 that we thought worth demonstrating, but for the most part we've tried to avoid such artificiality.

Many real-life systems can be built around the sample queries and other facets included in our example. Most information systems share many of the same characteristics: data must be entered, modified, and removed; queries must be processed against the database; and so on. Even though you may not operate a retail video and music store, the example in this appendix may be used as a reference around which you can design and develop your own customized information systems.

In the example, we first define the metadata—the schema for our store—and then we provide the SQL and 3GL code to implement the application itself. We take advantage of features in all levels of SQL-92 (including Full SQL), which means that you probably won't be able to actually run all of this example until the mid-1990s.

Also, we should warn you that this complete example does not conform exactly to the portions of the example used throughout the book. In the various chapters of the book we "tweaked" the example frequently to better illustrate points that we were making. However, in this appendix, we are more careful to be coherent among the different portions of the example.

B.2 The Schema Definition

A schema definition can be written as a standalone piece of code that depends on the (unspecified) standalone schema processor implicitly required by SQL-86 and SQL-89. Alternatively, it can be written as an SQL statement in a procedure in a module (or, equivalently, as an embedded SQL statement in an embedded SQL program). For illustrative purposes, we have chosen the former representation, although most implementations would actually require the latter. It will be a trivial exercise for you to convert from our notation here to the other form.

```
CREATE SCHEMA video_and_music
  AUTHORIZATION m_s_enterprises
  DEFAULT CHARACTER SET "Latin-1"

-- The definition of the schema for the store includes definitions
--   of base tables, views, privileges, referential constraints,
--   integrity constraints, assertions, and domains.

-- Following our own advice, we will (almost always) specify all the
--   default values and characteristics explicitly; this will make the
--   schema definition more nearly self-documenting.

-- First, we define the domains that we'll use in the schemas definition.

CREATE DOMAIN price AS DECIMAL (5,2)
  CONSTRAINT price_not_negative CHECK (VALUE >= 0) NOT DEFERRABLE

CREATE DOMAIN revenue AS DECIMAL (9,2)
  CONSTRAINT revenue_not_negative CHECK (VALUE >= 0) NOT DEFERRABLE

CREATE DOMAIN name AS CHARACTER VARYING (50) COLLATE american_english

-- Next, we create the base tables required for the application.

-- The tables in the example were derived from the design principles
--   discussed in Appendix A.  They reflect the initial stages, prior
--   to modifications to table structures, that we illustrate later in
--   this example.

CREATE TABLE movie_titles (
        title                   name
          CONSTRAINT movie_titles_not_null NOT NULL,
        year_released           DATE,
        our_cost                price,
        regular_rental_price    price,
        current_rental_price    price,
        regular_sale_price      price,
        current_sale_price      price,
        part_of_series          CHARACTER (3),
        movie_type              CHARACTER (10),
        vhs_owned               INTEGER,
        beta_owned              INTEGER,
        vhs_in_stock            INTEGER,
        beta_in_stock           INTEGER,
```

```
        total_vhs_units_rented          INTEGER,
        total_beta_units_rented         INTEGER,
        total_vhs_units_sold            INTEGER,
        total_beta_units_sold           INTEGER,
        total_vhs_rental_revenue        revenue,
        total_beta_rental_revenue       revenue,
        total_vhs_sales_revenue         revenue,
        total_beta_sales_revenue        revenue,
        CONSTRAINT movie_titles_primary_key
          PRIMARY KEY (title, year_released)
)

CREATE TABLE movies_stars (
        movie_title                     name
          CONSTRAINT movies_stars_movie_title_not_null NOT NULL,
        year_released                   DATE,
        actor_last_name                 name
          CONSTRAINT movies_stars_actor_last_name_not_null NOT NULL,
        actor_first_name                name,
        CONSTRAINT movies_stars_unique
          UNIQUE (movie_title, actor_last_name, actor_first_name)
            NOT DEFERRABLE,
        CONSTRAINT movies_stars_fk_movie_titles
          FOREIGN KEY (movie_title, year_released)
            REFERENCES movie_titles (movies, year_released)
              ON DELETE CASCADE
              ON UPDATE CASCADE
)

CREATE TABLE music_titles (
        title                           name
          CONSTRAINT music_titles_not_null NOT NULL,
        artist                          name
          CONSTRAINT artist_not_null NOT NULL,
        artist_more                     name,
        distributor                     name,
        record_label                    name,
        type                            CHARACTER (10),
        greatest_hits_collection        CHARACTER (15),
        category                        CHARACTER (10),
        date_released                   DATE,
        our_cost                        price,
        list_price                      price,
        current_price                   price,
        still_available                 CHARACTER (1),
        cd_in_stock                     INTEGER,
        cassette_in_stock               INTEGER,
        eight_track_in_stock            INTEGER,
        lp_in_stock                     INTEGER
        total_cd_sold                   INTEGER,
        total_cassette_sold             INTEGER,
        total_8_track_sold              INTEGER,
        total_lp_sold                   INTEGER,
        total_cd_returned               INTEGER,
        total_cassette_returned         INTEGER,
```

```
                        total_8_track_returned        INTEGER,
                        total_lp_returned             INTEGER,
                        CONSTRAINT music_titles_unique
                          UNIQUE (music_titles, artist, artist_more)
                )

CREATE TABLE song_titles (
                song            name
                  CONSTRAINT song_titles_song_not_null NOT NULL,
                music_title     name,
                artist          name
                  CONSTRAINT song_titles_artist_not_null NOT NULL,
                artist_more     name,
                single          CHARACTER (1),
                CONSTRAINT song_titles_unique
                  UNIQUE (song, artist, artist_more) NOT DEFERRABLE,
                CONSTRAINT song_titles_fk_music_title
                  FOREIGN KEY (music_title, artist, artist_more)
                    REFERENCES music_titles (title, artist, artist_more)
                        ON DELETE CASCADE
                        ON UPDATE CASCADE
                )

CREATE TABLE customers (
                cust_last_name            name
                  CONSTRAINT customers_cust_last_name_not_null NOT NULL,
                cust_first_name           name
                  CONSTRAINT customers_cust_first_name_not_null NOT NULL,
                cust_address              CHARACTER VARYING (30),
                cust_city                 CHARACTER VARYING (15),
                cust_state                CHARACTER (2),
                cust_zip                  CHARACTER VARYING (9),
                cust_phone                CHARACTER (8),
                cust_credit_card          CHARACTER VARYING (20)
                  CONSTRAINT customers_cust_credit_card_not_null NOT NULL,
                cust_current_charges      DECIMAL (9,2),
                cust_total_charges        DECIMAL (10,2),
                number_of_problems        SMALLINT,
                last_access               TIMESTAMP
                )

CREATE TABLE employees (
                emp_id                    integer
                  CONSTRAINT employees_emp_id_pk PRIMARY KEY,
                emp_last_name             name
                  CONSTRAINT employees_emp_last_name_not_null NOT NULL,
                emp_first_name            name
                  CONSTRAINT employees_emp_first_name_not_null NOT NULL,
                emp_address               CHARACTER VARYING (30),
                emp_city                  CHARACTER VARYING (15),
                emp_state                 CHARACTER (2),
                emp_zip                   CHARACTER VARYING (9),
                emp_phone                 CHARACTER (8),
                emp_start_date            DATE,
                emp_hourly_rate           DECIMAL (7,2)
                )
```

```
-- Third, we create a couple of views that help us manage some aspects
--   of our business.

CREATE VIEW problem_customers (last, first, addr, city, state) AS
  SELECT cust_last_name, cust_first_name, cust_address, cust_city, cust_state
    FROM customers
    WHERE number_of_problems > 0.8 * (SELECT MAX (number_of_problems)
                                        FROM customers)
    GROUP BY cust_zip

CREATE VIEW employee_customers AS
  SELECT emp_id, cust_current_charges
    FROM customers INNER JOIN employees
      ON cust_last_name = emp_last_name AND
         cust_first_name = emp_first_name AND
         cust_address = emp_address AND
         cust_city = emp_city AND
         cust_state = emp_state AND
         cust_zip = emp_zip AND
         cust_phone = emp_phone
    WHERE cust_total_charges > 1000.00 AND
          emp_hourly_rate < 5.00

CREATE VIEW emp_view AS
  SELECT emp_id, emp_last_name, emp_first_name, emp_address,
         emp_city, emp_state, emp_zip, emp_phone, emp_start_date,
         emp_hourly_rate
    FROM employees
    WHERE emp_id = SESSION_USER

-- The next thing we do is define the various privileges that will be
--   required by our employees, managers, auditors, etc., to do their jobs.

GRANT ALL PRIVILEGES ON names TO store_manager WITH GRANT OPTION

GRANT ALL PRIVILEGES ON price TO store_manager WITH GRANT OPTION

GRANT ALL PRIVILEGES ON revenue TO store_manager WITH GRANT OPTION

GRANT ALL PRIVILEGES ON movie_titles TO store_manager WITH GRANT OPTION

GRANT ALL PRIVILEGES ON movies_stars TO store_manager WITH GRANT OPTION

GRANT ALL PRIVILEGES ON music_titles TO store_manager WITH GRANT OPTION

GRANT ALL PRIVILEGES ON song_titles TO store_manager WITH GRANT OPTION

GRANT ALL PRIVILEGES ON customers TO store_manager WITH GRANT OPTION

GRANT ALL PRIVILEGES ON employees TO store_manager WITH GRANT OPTION

GRANT ALL PRIVILEGES ON problem_customers TO store_manager WITH GRANT OPTION

GRANT ALL PRIVILEGES ON employee_customers TO store_manager WITH GRANT OPTION
```

```
GRANT SELECT (title, year_released, regular_rental_price,
             current_rental_price, regular_sale_price,
             current_sale_price, movie_type) ON movie_titles TO PUBLIC

GRANT SELECT ON movie_titles TO movie_clerk

GRANT UPDATE (vhs_owned, beta_owned, vhs_in_stock, beta_in_stock,
             total_vhs_units_rented, total_beta_units_rented,
             total_vhs_units_sold, total_beta_units_sold,
             total_vhs_rental_revenue, total_beta_rental_revenue,
             total_vhs_sales_revenue, total_beta_sales_revenue)
      ON movie_titles TO movie_clerk

GRANT INSERT ON movie_titles TO movie_clerk

GRANT DELETE ON movie_titles TO movie_clerk

GRANT INSERT ON movies_stars TO movie_clerk

GRANT SELECT ON movies_stars TO PUBLIC

GRANT SELECT (title, artist, artist_more, record_label, type,
             greatest_hits_collection, date_released, list_price,
             current_price, still_available) ON music_titles TO PUBLIC

GRANT SELECT ON music_titles TO music_clerk

GRANT UPDATE (cd_in_stock, cassette_in_stock,
             eight_track_in_stock, lp_in_stock,
             total_cd_sold, total_cassette_sold,
             total_8_track_sold, total_lp_sold,
             total_cd_returned, total_cassette_returned,
             total_8_track_returned, total_lp_returned)
      ON music_titles TO music_clerk

GRANT INSERT ON music_titles TO music_clerk

GRANT DELETE ON music_titles TO music_clerk

GRANT SELECT ON song_titles TO PUBLIC

GRANT INSERT ON song_titles TO music_clerk

GRANT REFERENCES ON music_titles TO music_clerk

GRANT DELETE ON song_titles TO music_clerk

GRANT SELECT (cust_last_name, cust_first_name, cust_address, cust_city,
             cust_state, cust_zip, cust_phone, cust_credit_card)
      ON customers TO register_clerk

GRANT UPDATE (cust_current_charges, cust_total_charges,
             number_of_problems, last_access)
      ON customers TO register_clerk

GRANT INSERT ON customers TO register_clerk
```

```
-- This next GRANT looks dangerous, but it isn't because the view definition
--   itself limits the rows that can be seen through the view.

GRANT SELECT ON emp_view TO PUBLIC

-- Finally, we create a couple of assertions that will implement
--   rules placed on us by our bank.

CREATE ASSERTION limit_total_stock_value
  CHECK ( (SELECT SUM (our_cost * (vhs_owned + beta_owned)
           FROM movie_titles)
        +
          SELECT SUM (our_cost * (cd_in_stock + cassette_in_stock +
                                  eight_track_in_stock + lp_in_stock)
           FROM music_titles)
        < 1000000.00 )

CREATE ASSERTION do_not_sell_to_many_problem_customers
  CHECK ( ( SELECT COUNT(*)
              FROM customers
              WHERE cust_total_charges > 150.00 AND
                    cust_total_charges < 1000.00 AND
                    number_of_problems > 5 )
        < 10 )
```

B.3 Application Code

The various functions that we need to perform for our video and music store can be executed in many ways. We have chosen to illustrate a *few* of these either as embedded SQL programs or as SQL modules and the 3GL programs that invoke the procedures in those modules. The remainder are presented as standalone SQL statements, and the binding of these SQL statements to application programs is left as an exercise for you to perform.

There is no attempt to present the application code in any sequence that may conform to the order in which operations are performed during a business day in the store. Instead, we have attempted to group SQL statements according to their function, with related operations grouped together. This is closer to how you would write a real application system.

B.3.1 Data Input

```
MODULE data_input
      NAMES ARE "Latin-1"
      LANGUAGE COBOL
      SCHEMA video_and_music

-- By not specifying AUTHORIZATION, we're requiring that the authID
--   of the user executing the procedures in the module be the one used
--   for privilege checking.
```

```
-- Insert a new movie title into MOVIE_TITLES, and star information into
-- MOVIES_STARS.

-- First, insert into MOVIE_TITLES

        PROCEDURE insert_movie_titles
                ( SQLSTATE,
                :title      CHARACTER (50),
                :year       CHARACTER (10),
                :cost       DECIMAL (5,2),
                :reg_rental DECIMAL (5,2),
                :cur_rental DECIMAL (5,2),
                :reg_sale   DECIMAL (5,2),
                :cur_sale   DECIMAL (5,2),
                :series     CHARACTER (3),
                :ser_ind    INTEGER,
                :type       CHARACTER (10),
                :vhs_owned  INTEGER,
                :beta_owned INTEGER,
                :vhs_stock  INTEGER,
                :beta_stock INTEGER );

        INSERT INTO movie_titles
          VALUES (:title, CAST(:year AS DATE), :cost,
                  :reg_rental, :cur_rental, :reg_sale, :cur_sale,
                  :series INDICATOR :ser_ind, :type,
                  :vhs_owned, :beta_owned, :vhs_stock, :beta_stock,
                  :0, 0, 0, 0, 0.00, 0.00, 0.00, 0.00);

-- Insert corresponding information into MOVIES_STARS.

        PROCEDURE insert_movies_stars
                ( SQLSTATE,
                :title      CHARACTER (50),
                :"date"     CHARACTER (10),
                :first      CHARACTER (50),
                :last       CHARACTER (50),
                :last_ind   INTEGER );

        INSERT INTO movies_stars
          VALUE (:title, CAST(:"date" AS DATE),
                 :first, :last INDICATOR :last_ind);

-- Insert a new customer into the CUSTOMERS table.

        PROCEDURE insert_customers
                ( SQLSTATE,
                :last       CHARACTER (50),
                :first      CHARACTER (50),
                :addr       CHARACTER (30),
                :addr_ind   INTEGER,
                :city       CHARACTER (15),
                :city_ind   INTEGER,
                :state      CHARACTER (2),
                :st_ind     INTEGER,
```

```
              :zip        CHARACTER (9),
              :zip_ind    INTEGER,
              :phone      CHARACTER (8),
              :phone_ind  INTEGER,
              :credit     CHARACTER (20),
              :credit_ind INTEGER );

      INSERT INTO customers
        VALUES (:last, :first, :addr INDICATOR :addr_ind,
                :city INDICATOR :city_ind, :state INDICATOR :st_ind,
                :zip INDICATOR :zip_ind, :phone INDICATOR :phone_ind,
                :credit, 0.00, 0.00, 0, CURRENT_TIMESTAMP);

-- Insert a group of new CD/tape titles from an "input source table" into
-- the MUSIC_TITLES table.

      PROCEDURE insert_new_titles_from_temp_titles
                ( SQLSTATE );

      INSERT INTO music_titles SELECT * FROM temp_titles;

-- We need a procedure to COMMIT a transaction in any module.

      PROCEDURE commit_transaction
                ( SQLSTATE );

      COMMIT;

-- We also need a procedure for GET DIAGNOSTICS.

      PROCEDURE get_diagnostics
                ( SQLSTATE,
                  message       CHARACTER(128) );

      GET DIAGNOSTICS EXCEPTION 1 MESSAGE;
```

Here is a COBOL program to use the procedures in the preceding module.

```
      IDENTIFICATION DIVISION.
      PROGRAM-ID.
        DATA-INPUT.

      ENVIRONMENT DIVISION.
        ...

      DATA DIVISION.

      FILE SECTION.
        ...

      WORKING-STORAGE SECTION.
    * Variables for interfacing with SQL procedures
      01 SQLSTATE    PICTURE X(5).
      01 TITLE       PICTURE X(50).
```

```
01 YEAR          PICTURE X(10).
01 COST          PICTURE S999V99 USAGE DISPLAY LEADING SEPARATE.
01 RENTAL-REG    PICTURE S999V99 USAGE DISPLAY LEADING SEPARATE.
01 RENTAL-CUR    PICTURE S999V99 USAGE DISPLAY LEADING SEPARATE.
01 SALE-REG      PICTURE S999V99 USAGE DISPLAY LEADING SEPARATE.
01 SALE-CUR      PICTURE S999V99 USAGE DISPLAY LEADING SEPARATE.
01 SERIES        PICTURE X(3).
01 SER-IND       PICTURE S9(5) USAGE BINARY.
01 TYPE          PICTURE X(10).
01 VHS-OWNED     PICTURE S9(5) USAGE BINARY.
01 BETA-OWNED    PICTURE S9(5) USAGE BINARY.
01 VHS-STOCK     PICTURE S9(5) USAGE BINARY.
01 BETA-STOCK    PICTURE S9(5) USAGE BINARY.
01 FIRST-NAME    PICTURE X(50).
01 LAST-NAME     PICTURE X(50).
01 LAST-NAME-I   PICTURE S9(5) USAGE BINARY.
01 ADDRESS       PICTURE X(50).
01 ADDRESS-IND   PICTURE S9(5) USAGE BINARY.
01 CITY          PICTURE X(50).
01 CITY-IND      PICTURE S9(5) USAGE BINARY.
01 STATE         PICTURE X(50).
01 STATE-IND     PICTURE S9(5) USAGE BINARY.
01 ZIP-CODE      PICTURE X(50).
01 ZIP-CODE-IND  PICTURE S9(5) USAGE BINARY.
01 PHONE-NUMBER  PICTURE X(50).
01 PHONE-IND     PICTURE S9(5) USAGE BINARY.
01 CREDIT        PICTURE X(50).
01 CREDIT-IND    PICTURE S9(5) USAGE BINARY.

*        Variable definitions

01 MESSAGE       PICTURE X(128).

PROCEDURE DIVISION.
MAIN-ROUTINE.
*
* Here would be some code to get input of some sort to determine
* which function to perform and what data to use for that function.
* Rather than bore you (and fill pages) with code that has little
* or nothing to do with the purpose of this example, we leave
* these details as an exercise for you to do on a slow weekend.
*
* We will assume that one of the following COBOL paragraphs will
* be PERFORMed by the preceding code, though.
*

INSERT-NEW-MOVIE.
  CALL "INSERT_MOVIE_TITLES"
    USING SQLSTATE, TITLE, YEAR, COST, RENTAL-REG, RENTAL-CUR,
          SALE-REG, SALE-CUR, SERIES, SER-IND, TYPE,
          VHS-OWNED, BETA-OWNED, VHS-STOCK, BETA-STOCK.
  IF SQLSTATE IS NOT '00000' THEN
    DISPLAY 'Error INSERTing MOVIE_TITLES; SQLSTATE = ', SQLSTATE.
    CALL "GET_DIAGNOSTICS"
      USING SQLSTATE, MESSAGE.
```

```
        DISPLAY 'Message in Diagnostics Area is: ', MESSAGE.
    END-IF.

    CALL "INSERT_MOVIES_STARS"
      USING SQLSTATE, TITLE, YEAR, FIRST-NAME, LAST-NAME, LAST-NAME-I.
    IF SQLSTATE IS NOT '00000' THEN
      DISPLAY 'Error INSERTing MOVIES_STARS; SQLSTATE = ', SQLSTATE.
      CALL "GET_DIAGNOSTICS"
        USING SQLSTATE, MESSAGE.
      DISPLAY 'Message in Diagnostics Area is: ', MESSAGE.
    END-IF.

    CALL "COMMIT_TRANSACTION"
      USING SQLSTATE.
    IF SQLSTATE IS NOT '00000' THEN
      DISPLAY 'Error INSERTing MOVIE_TITLES; SQLSTATE = ', SQLSTATE.
      CALL "GET_DIAGNOSTICS"
        USING SQLSTATE, MESSAGE.
      DISPLAY 'Message in Diagnostics Area is: ', MESSAGE.
    END-IF.

INSERT-NEW-CUSTOMER.
    CALL "INSERT_MOVIE_CUSTOMERS"
      USING SQLSTATE, LAST_NAME, FIRST_NAME,
            ADDRESS, ADDRESS-IND, CITY, CITY-IND, STATE, STATE-IND
            ZIP-CODE, ZIP-CODE-IND, PHONE-NUMBER, PHONE-IND,
            CREDIT, CREDIT-IND.
    IF SQLSTATE IS NOT '00000' THEN
      DISPLAY 'Error INSERTing CUSTOMERS; SQLSTATE = ', SQLSTATE.
      CALL "GET_DIAGNOSTICS"
        USING SQLSTATE, MESSAGE.
      DISPLAY 'Message in Diagnostics Area is: ', MESSAGE.
    END-IF.

    CALL "COMMIT_TRANSACTION"
      USING SQLSTATE.
    IF SQLSTATE IS NOT '00000' THEN
      DISPLAY 'Error INSERTing MOVIE_TITLES; SQLSTATE = ', SQLSTATE.
      CALL "GET_DIAGNOSTICS"
        USING SQLSTATE, MESSAGE.
      DISPLAY 'Message in Diagnostics Area is: ', MESSAGE.
    END-IF.

INSERT-NEW-TITLES.
    CALL "INSERT_NEW_TITLES_FROM_TEMP_TITLES"
      USING SQLSTATE.
    IF SQLSTATE IS NOT '00000' THEN
      DISPLAY 'Error INSERTing NEW MOVIE_TITLES; SQLSTATE = ',
              SQLSTATE.
      CALL "GET_DIAGNOSTICS"
        USING SQLSTATE, MESSAGE.
      DISPLAY 'Message in Diagnostics Area is: ', MESSAGE.
    END-IF.
```

```
CALL "COMMIT_TRANSACTION"
  USING SQLSTATE.
IF SQLSTATE IS NOT '00000' THEN
  DISPLAY 'Error INSERTing MOVIE_TITLES; SQLSTATE = ', SQLSTATE.
  CALL "GET_DIAGNOSTICS"
    USING SQLSTATE, MESSAGE.
  DISPLAY 'Message in Diagnostics Area is: ', MESSAGE.
END-IF.

EXIT-PARAGRAPH.
  STOP RUN.
```

B.3.2 Data Modification

```
MODULE data_modification
  NAMES ARE "Latin-1"
  LANGUAGE C
  SCHEMA video_and_music
```

-- By not specifying AUTHORIZATION, we're requiring that the authID
-- of the user executing the procedures in the module be the one used
-- for privilege checking.

-- Put a movie title on sale.

```
PROCEDURE movie_on_sale
          ( SQLSTATE,
            :title CHARACTER VARYING (50) );

UPDATE movie_titles
    SET current_sale_price = current_sale_price - 2.00
  WHERE title = :title;
```

-- We need a procedure to COMMIT a transaction in any module.

```
PROCEDURE commit_transaction
          ( SQLSTATE );

COMMIT WORK;
```

-- A customer rents a movie; update the CUSTOMERS and MOVIE_TITLES tables
-- to reflect all current status information regarding the rental.

```
PROCEDURE update_for_movie_rental_1
          ( SQLSTATE,
            :title       CHARACTER VARYING (50) );

SELECT COUNT(*)
  FROM movie_titles
  WHERE title = :title;

PROCEDURE update_for_movie_rental_2
          ( SQLSTATE,
                -- :title isn't necessary, 'cause we don't use it,
```

```
                                        -- but it doesn't do any harm, either
                        :title          CHARACTER VARYING (50),
                        :last           CHARACTER VARYING (50),
                        :first          CHARACTER VARYING (50),
                        :phone          CHARACTER (8),
                        :phone_ind      INTEGER,
                        :cust_cc        CHARACTER VARYING (20),
                        :cust_cc_ind    INTEGER,
                        :cust_cur_chg   REAL,    -- Because C doesn't have DECIMAL
                        :cust_chg_ind   INTEGER,
                        :num_probs      SMALLINT,
                        :num_probs_ind  INTEGER );

            SELECT cust_credit_card,
                   CAST (cust_current_charges AS REAL),
                   number_of_problems
              INTO :cust_cc INDICATOR cust_cc_ind,
                   :cust_cur_chg INDICATOR cust_chg_ind,
                   :num_probs INDICATOR num_probs_ind
              FROM customers
             WHERE last_name = :last AND
                   first_name = :first AND
-- We can test the indicator parameter and the "regular" parameter
-- separately, as this example illustrates. However, it is not
-- recommended, as this bypasses the essential semantics of
-- indicator parameter usage, which is to supply "nullness"
-- information about the regular parameter.
                   ( ( :phone_ind >= 0 AND phone = :phone_no ) OR
                     ( :phone_ind < 0 AND phone IS NULL ) );

        PROCEDURE update_for_movie_rental_3
                    ( SQLSTATE,
                      :title       CHARACTER VARYING (50) );

          UPDATE movie_titles
             SET vhs_in_stock = vhs_in_stock - 1,
                 total_vhs_units_rented = total_vhs_units_rented + 1,
                 total_vhs_revenue = total_vhs_revenue + current_rental_price
           WHERE title = :title;

        PROCEDURE update_for_movie_rental_4
                    ( SQLSTATE,
                      :title          CHARACTER VARYING (50),
                      :last           CHARACTER VARYING (50),
                      :first          CHARACTER VARYING (50),
                      :phone_no       CHARACTER (8),
                      :phone_ind      INTEGER );

          UPDATE customers
             SET cust_current_charges = cust_current_charges +
                                          (SELECT current_rental_price
                                             FROM movie_titles
                                            WHERE title = :title),
```

```
                    cust_total_charges = cust_total_charges +
                                    (SELECT current_rental_price
                                     FROM movie_titles
                                     WHERE title = :title),
                    last_access = CURRENT_TIMESTAMP
            WHERE last_name = :last AND
                  first_name = :first AND
-- This is the preferred way of using indicator parameters and
--   regular parameters; it preserves the essential semantics.
                  ( ( :phone_no INDICATOR :phone_ind IS NOT NULL AND
                      :phone_no INDICATOR :phone_ind = phone ) OR
                    ( :phone_no INDICATOR :phone_ind IS NULL AND
                      phone IS NULL ) );

-- Put all music titles by a specific artist or group on sale (mark down
--   by 10%).

        PROCEDURE artist_music_on_sale
                  ( SQLSTATE,
                    :artist          CHARACTER VARYING (50),
                    :artist_other    CHARACTER VARYING (50),
                    :other_ind       INTEGER );

        UPDATE music_titles
            SET current_price = current_price * 0.9
          WHERE artist = :artist AND
                ( ( :artist_other INDICATOR other_ind IS NOT NULL AND
                    artist_more = :artist_other INDICATOR other_ind ) OR
                  ( artist_more IS NULL AND
                    :artist_other INDICATOR other_ind IS NULL ) );

-- Let's put all movies and music titles on sale (mark down by 10%)
--   for a given artist.

        PROCEDURE artist_music_and_movies_on_sale_1
                  ( SQLSTATE,
                    :artist          CHARACTER VARYING (50),
                    :artist_other    CHARACTER VARYING (50),
                    :other_ind       INTEGER );

        UPDATE movie_titles
            SET current_sale_price = current_sale_price * 0.9
          WHERE ( :artist_other INDICATOR :other_ind IS NOT NULL AND
                  (:artist, :artist_other)
                    IN ( SELECT actor_last_name, actor_first_name
                         FROM movie_titles mt INNER JOIN movies_stars ms
                           ON mt.title = ms.movie_title AND
                              mt.year_released = ms.year_released ) )
                OR
                ( :artist_other INDICATOR :other_ind IS NULL AND
                  :artist IN ( SELECT actor_last_name
                         FROM movie_titles mt INNER JOIN movies_stars ms
                           ON mt.title = ms.movie_title AND
                              mt.year_released = ms.year_released
                         WHERE ms.actor_other IS NULL ) );
```

```
PROCEDURE artist_music_and_movies_on_sale_2
          ( SQLSTATE,
            :artist        CHARACTER VARYING (50),
            :artist_other  CHARACTER VARYING (50),
            :other_ind     INTEGER );

UPDATE music_titles
   SET current_price = current_price * 0.9
   WHERE artist = :artist AND
       ( ( :artist_other INDICATOR :other_ind IS NOT NULL AND
           artist_more = :artist_other INDICATOR :other_ind ) OR
         ( artist_more IS NULL AND
           :artist_other INDICATOR :other_ind IS NULL ) );
```

-- Place an order for ten copies of each R.E.M. music title.

-- Although it's common to declare all your cursors at the beginning
-- of a module, it's not necessary; it's perfectly permissible to
-- declare them immediately before all/any procedures that reference
-- them.

```
DECLARE CURSOR rem_cursor FOR
   SELECT title, distributor, our_cost
     FROM music_titles
     WHERE artist = 'R.E.M.' AND artist_other IS NULL;

PROCEDURE open_rem_cursor
          ( SQLSTATE );

OPEN rem_cursor;

PROCEDURE fetch_rem_cursor
          ( SQLSTATE,
            :title     CHARACTER VARYING (50),
            :dist      CHARACTER VARYING (50),
            :cost      REAL,
               -- Note that there is no reason to keep the
               -- indicator parameters together with the
               -- associated data parameters
            :dist_ind  INTEGER,
            :cost_ind  INTEGER );

FETCH rem_cursor
   INTO :title,
        :dist INDICATOR :dist_ind,
        :cost INDICATOR :cost_ind;

PROCEDURE close_rem_cursor
          ( SQLSTATE );

CLOSE rem_cursor;
```

And here is the sample C program to invoke the procedures in the preceding module:

```
#include ...

#ifndef NULL
#define NULL 0
#endif

int video_music ()

{

        char   movie_name[51];
        char   SQLSTATE[6];
        char   SQLSTATE_OK[6] = "00000";
        char   last_name[51], first_name[51], phone_number[8]
        char   credit_card[21], distributor[51]
        int    phone_indicator, credit_card_ind, number_of_problems
        int    first_ind, distributor_ind, cost_ind
        real   curchg, cost

/* Assume that there is a "main" segment to the program here that acquires
   instructions about what operation to perform and invokes the appropriate
   section of the program; assume also that the relevant data is acquired
   as well. */

func1:
        MOVIE_ON_SALE ( SQLSTATE, movie_name );
        if (SQLSTATE != SQLSTATE_OK)
          { GET_DIAG ( SQLSTATE, message );
            return ( -1 ); }

        COMMIT ( SQLSTATE );
        if (SQLSTATE != SQLSTATE_OK)
          { GET_DIAG ( SQLSTATE, message );
            return ( -1 ); }

func2:
        UPDATE_FOR_MOVIE_RENTAL_1 ( SQLSTATE, movie_name );
        if (SQLSTATE != SQLSTATE_OK)
          { GFT_DIAG ( SQLSTATE, message );
            return ( -1 ); }

        UPDATE_FOR_MOVIE_RENTAL_2
          ( SQLSTATE,
            movie_name,
            last_name,
            first_name,
            phone_number, &phone_indicator,
            credit_card, &credit_card_ind,
            &curchg, &0,
            &number_of_problems, &0 );
```

```
        if (SQLSTATE != SQLSTATE_OK)
          { GET_DIAG ( SQLSTATE, message );
            return ( -1 ); }

        UPDATE_FOR_MOVIE_RENTAL_3 ( SQLSTATE, movie_name );
        if (SQLSTATE != SQLSTATE_OK)
          { GET_DIAG ( SQLSTATE, message );
            return ( -1 ); }

        UPDATE_FOR_MOVIE_RENTAL_4
          ( SQLSTATE,
            last_name,
            first_name,
            phone_number,
            &phone_indicator );
        if (SQLSTATE != SQLSTATE_OK)
          { GET_DIAG ( SQLSTATE, message );
            return ( -1 ); }

        COMMIT ( SQLSTATE );
        if (SQLSTATE != SQLSTATE_OK)
          { GET_DIAG ( SQLSTATE, message );
            return ( -1 ); }

func3:
        ARTIST_MUSIC_ON_SALE
          ( SQLSTATE,
            last_name,
            first_name,
            &first_ind );
        if (SQLSTATE != SQLSTATE_OK)
          { GET_DIAG ( SQLSTATE, message );
            return ( -1 ); }

        COMMIT ( SQLSTATE );
        if (SQLSTATE != SQLSTATE_OK)
          { GET_DIAG ( SQLSTATE, message );
            return ( -1 ); }

func4:
        ARTIST_MUSIC_AND_MOVIES_ON_SALE_1
          ( SQLSTATE,
            last_name,
            first_name,
            &first_ind );
        if (SQLSTATE != SQLSTATE_OK)
          { GET_DIAG ( SQLSTATE, message );
            return ( -1 ); }

        ARTIST_MUSIC_AND_MOVIES_ON_SALE_2
          ( SQLSTATE,
            last_name,
            first_name,
            &first_ind );
```

```
            if (SQLSTATE != SQLSTATE_OK)
              { GET_DIAG ( SQLSTATE, message );
                return ( -1 ); }

            COMMIT ( SQLSTATE );
            if (SQLSTATE != SQLSTATE_OK)
              { GET_DIAG ( SQLSTATE, message );
                return ( -1 ); }

func5:
            OPEN_REM_CURSOR (SQLSTATE);
            if (SQLSTATE != SQLSTATE_OK)
              { GET_DIAG ( SQLSTATE, message );
                return ( -1 ); }

            while (1==1) {

              FETCH_REM_CURSOR
                ( SQLSTATE,
                  movie_name,
                  distributor,
                  cost,
                  &distributor_ind,
                  &cost_ind );
              if (SQLSTATE != SQLSTATE_OK)
                { GET_DIAG ( SQLSTATE, message );
                  return ( -1 ); }

              if (SQLSTATE != NO_DATA)
                {
                 /* Perform the ordering function; presumably, this involves
                    printing order forms, etc. */
                }
              else break;

            }

            CLOSE_REM_CURSOR (SQLSTATE);
            if (SQLSTATE != SQLSTATE_OK)
              { GET_DIAG ( SQLSTATE, message );
                return ( -1 ); }

}
```

B.3.3 Table Structure Modification

1. We decide to streamline inventory by getting rid of all Beta movies and 8-track tapes. The tables must be updated to delete unneeded columns and their data, but some data—such as total revenue per title—must be retained.

```
-- Note that this operation can be performed safely (that is, in the
--   context of a single transaction) only in implementations that permit
--   the mixing of DDL and DML in one transaction.  We will assume that
--   we have such an implementation.  If yours does not, then you will
```

```
--   have to use a series of transactions; one possible scenario would be
--   to use one transaction to add the new columns to MOVIE_TITLES,
--   a second transaction to fill in those new columns with data from
--   other columns (combining as required to preserve the data), and
--   a third transaction to ALTER the MOVIE_TITLES table to delete the
--   unwanted columns.  The same conceptual sequence would be required to
--   fix the MUSIC_TITLES table, too, except that we don't keep overall
--   totals on MUSIC_TITLES and we won't collapse the 8-track information
--   into the column for any other medium.

        ALTER TABLE movie_titles
          ADD COLUMN units_owned INTEGER;

        ALTER TABLE movie_titles
          ADD COLUMN units_in_stock INTEGER;

        ALTER TABLE movie_titles
          ADD COLUMN total_units_rented INTEGER;

        ALTER TABLE movie_titles
          ADD COLUMN total_units_sold INTEGER;

        ALTER TABLE movie_titles
          ADD COLUMN total_rental_revenue INTEGER;

        ALTER TABLE movie_titles
          ADD COLUMN total_sales_revenue INTEGER;

        UPDATE movie_titles
          SET units_owned = vhs_owned,
              units_in_stock = vhs_in_stock,
              total_units_rented =
                total_vhs_units_rented + total_beta_units_rented,
              total_units_sold =
                total_vhs_units_sold + total_beta_units_sold,
              total_rental_revenue =
                total_vhs_rental_revenue + total_beta_rental_revenue,
              total_sales_revenue =
                total_vhs_sales_revenue + total_beta_sales_revenue;

    ALTER TABLE movie_titles DROP COLUMN beta_owned;

    ALTER TABLE movie_titles DROP COLUMN beta_in_stock;

    ALTER TABLE movie_titles DROP COLUMN total_beta_units_rented;

    ALTER TABLE movie_titles DROP COLUMN total_beta_units_owned;

    ALTER TABLE movie_titles DROP COLUMN total_beta_rental_revenue;

    ALTER TABLE movie_titles DROP COLUMN total_beta_sales_revenue;

    ALTER TABLE music_titles DROP COLUMN eight_track_in_stock;

    ALTER TABLE music_titles DROP COLUMN total_8_track_sold;
```

```
ALTER TABLE music_titles DROP COLUMN total_8_track_returned;

COMMIT;
```

2. We decide to add several new suppliers of CDs and tapes, which results in the creation of a new table MUSIC_SUPPLY_COST. This table contains expanded information about suppliers and costs, particularly quantity pricing. In addition to the creation of this new table, the MUSIC_TITLES table must be modified (removing the OUR_COST and DISTRIBUTOR columns).

```
CREATE TABLE music_supply_costs (
   title              name
     CONSTRAINT music_supply_costs_title_not_null NOT NULL,
   artist             name
     CONSTRAINT music_supply_costs_artist_not_null NOT NULL,
   artist_more        name,
   record_label       name,
   distributor        name,
   cost_qty_1         price,
   break_point        INTEGER,
   cost_qty_large     price
);

ALTER TABLE music_titles
  DROP COLUMN our_cost;

ALTER TABLE music_titles
  DROP COLUMN distributor;

COMMIT;
```

3. We now will carry digital audio tape (DATs). Add a new column to handle this.

```
ALTER TABLE music_titles
  ADD COLUMN dat_in_stock INTEGER;

ALTER TABLE music_titles
  ADD COLUMN total_dat_sold INTEGER;

ALTER TABLE music_titles
  ADD COLUMN total_dat_returned INTEGER;

COMMIT;
```

B.3.4 Data Removal

1. We need to delete an employee who has left the company.

```
DELETE FROM employees
  WHERE emp_id = :id;
```

2. We decide to remove some movies from inventory. This requires deletion from multiple tables, with referential integrity control enforced.

```
                    DELETE FROM movie_titles
                      WHERE title = :title AND
                            year_released = :year;
```

3. We decide to automatically remove all customers who have had more than four problem reports.

```
                    DELETE FROM customers
                      WHERE number_of_problems > 4;
```

B.3.5   Data Access and Management

The Customer Assistance Subsystem

1. Produce a comprehensive listing of all movie titles and the stars for that movie.

```
int cust_assist ()

{

    char    title[51], year[11], result[102], star_name[51]

    EXEC SQL DECLARE CURSOR movie_cursor FOR
                SELECT title, CAST (year_released AS CHARACTER(10))
                    FROM movie_titles;

    EXEC SQL DECLARE CURSOR star_cursor FOR
                SELECT TRIM (BOTH ' ' FROM actor_last_name) || ',' ||
                        TRIM (BOTH ' ' FROM actor_first_name)
                    FROM movies_stars
                    WHERE movie_title = :title AND
                            year_released = CAST (:year AS DATE);

    EXEC SQL OPEN movie_cursor;

    if ( SQLSTATE != "00000" )
      { /* Print, display, or otherwise record SQLSTATE value */
        EXEC SQL GET DIAGNOSTICS EXCEPTION 1 MESSAGE;
        /* Print, display, or otherwise record MESSAGE text */
      }

    while (1==1)

      EXEC SQL FETCH NEXT FROM movie_cursor
                INTO :title, :year;

      if ( SQLSTATE != "00000" )
        { /* Print, display, or otherwise record SQLSTATE value */
          EXEC SQL GET DIAGNOSTICS EXCEPTION 1 MESSAGE;
          /* Print, display, or otherwise record MESSAGE text */
        }
```

```
              /* Check SQLSTATE for '02000'; if so, then skip to abc */

              if (SQLSTATE != "02000")

                  { /* Print, display, or otherwise output movie title */

                    EXEC SQL OPEN star_cursor;

                    if ( SQLSTATE != "00000" )
                      { /* Print, display, or otherwise record SQLSTATE value */
                        EXEC SQL GET DIAGNOSTICS EXCEPTION 1 MESSAGE;
                        /* Print, display, or otherwise record MESSAGE text */
                      }

                    while (1==1)

                      { EXEC SQL FETCH NEXT FROM star_cursor
                                    INTO :name;

                        if ( SQLSTATE != "00000" )
                          { /* Print, display, or otherwise record SQLSTATE value */
                            EXEC SQL GET DIAGNOSTICS EXCEPTION 1 MESSAGE;
                            /* Print, display, or otherwise record MESSAGE text */
                          }

                        /* Check SQLSTATE for '02000'; if so, then get out of loop
                           Otherwise, print and then loop to FETCH star_cursor */

                        if ( SQLSTATE == '02000' ) break;

                      }

                    EXEC SQL CLOSE star_cursor;

                    if ( SQLSTATE != "00000" )
                      { /* Print, display, or otherwise record SQLSTATE value */
                        EXEC SQL GET DIAGNOSTICS EXCEPTION 1 MESSAGE;
                        /* Print, display, or otherwise record MESSAGE text */
                      }

              } \* Loop to FETCH movie_cursor */

              EXEC SQL CLOSE movie_cursor;

              if ( SQLSTATE != "00000" )
                { /* Print, display, or otherwise record SQLSTATE value */
                  EXEC SQL GET DIAGNOSTICS EXCEPTION 1 MESSAGE;
                  /* Print, display, or otherwise record MESSAGE text */
                }

          }
```

2. Produce a list of all movies starring Barbra Streisand.

```
SELECT m.title
  FROM movie_titles m, movies_stars s
  WHERE s.actor_first_name = 'Barbra' AND
        s.actor_last_name = 'Streisand';
```

3. Produce a list of all movies starring both Nick Nolte and Eddie Murphy.

```
SELECT m.title
  FROM movie_titles m, movies_stars s
  WHERE (s.actor_first_name, s.actor_last_name )
        IN ( ('Nick', 'Nolte'), ('Eddie', 'Murphy') );
```

4. What movies currently have a special rental price (are on sale)?

```
SELECT m.title
  FROM movie_titles m
  WHERE current_rental_price < regular_rental_price;
```

5. What movies are on sale, either as a rental or by sales price?

```
SELECT m.title
  FROM movie_titles m
  WHERE current_rental_price < regular_rental_price OR
        current_sale_price < regular_sale_price;
```

6. List all soundtrack CD/tape titles for which the movies are in stock.

```
SELECT mus.title
  FROM music_titles mus INNER JOIN movie_titles mov
    ON mus.title = mov.title
  WHERE mov.unit_in_stock > 0 AND
        mus.category = 'Soundtrack' AND
        ( mus.cd_in_stock > 0 OR
          mus.cassette_in_stock > 0 );
```

7. List all music titles where the CD/tape title is the same as that of the singer or group.

```
SELECT title
  FROM music_titles
  WHERE title = artist AND artist_more IS NULL;
```

8. List all CDs/tapes where the group's or artist's name is part of the music title.

```
SELECT title
  FROM music_titles
  WHERE ( title LIKE '%'||artist||'%' OR
          title LIKE '%'||artist_more||'%' ) AND
        cd_in_stock > 0 AND
        cassette_in_stock > 0 );
```

9. List all artists that have greatest hits collections.

```
SELECT artist, artist_more
  FROM music_titles
  WHERE greatest_hits_collection IS NOT NULL;
```

10. Does the store have a soundtrack for the movie *Yentl*?

```
SELECT CASE COUNT(*) WHEN 0 THEN 'No' ELSE 'Yes' END
  FROM music_titles
  WHERE title = 'Yentl' AND
        category = 'Soundtrack';
```

11. Does the store have a Beta tape in stock for a particular movie soundtrack?

```
SELECT CASE COUNT(*) WHEN 0 THEN 'No' ELSE 'Yes' END
  FROM movie_titles
  WHERE title = :title AND
        beta_in_stock > 0;
```

12. List all artists who have both a CD/tape music title and a movie in which they star, currently in stock in the store.

```
SELECT artist, artist_more
  FROM movie_titles movies
    INNER JOIN movies_stars stars
      USING movies.title = stars.title AND
            movies.year_released = stars.year_released
    INNER JOIN music_titles music
      USING stars.actor_last_name = music.artist AND
            ( ( stars.actor_last_name IS NULL AND
                music.artist_more IS NULL ) OR
              stars.actor_last_name = music.artist_more )
  WHERE ( music.cd_in_stock > 0 OR
          music.cassette_in_stock > 0 ) AND
        ( vhs_in_stock > 0 OR
          beta_in_stock > 0 ) )
```

13. List all CD/tape titles on which a given song appears.

```
SELECT title
  FROM music_titles INNER JOIN song_titles
     USING title = music_title
  WHERE song_title = :song AND
        ( cd_in_stock > 0 OR
          cassette_in_stock > 0 );
```

14. List all CD/tape titles, except for greatest hit collections, on which a specific song title exists.

```
SELECT title
  FROM music_titles INNER JOIN song_titles
    USING title = music_title
  WHERE song_title = :song AND
        ( cd_in_stock > 0 OR
          cassette_in_stock > 0 ) AND
        greatest_hits_collection IS NULL;
```

Inventory Management and Sales Reporting Subsystem

1. Produce a list of all tape rentals, showing the number of tapes rented and the rental revenue generated.

```
SELECT total_vhs_units_rented +
       total_beta_units_rented AS tapes_rented,
       total_vhs_rental_revenue +
       total_beta_rental_revenue AS total_revenue
  FROM movie_titles
  WHERE total_vhs_units_rented + total_beta_units_rented > 0;
```

2. Produce a list of rental, sales, and total revenue by tape title.

```
SELECT total_vhs_rental_revenue +
       total_beta_rental_revenue AS total_rental,
       total_vhs_sales_revenue +
       total_beta_sales_revenue AS total_sales,
       total_vhs_rental_revenue +
       total_beta_rental_revenue +
       total_vhs_sales_revenue +
       total_beta_sales_revenue AS total_revenue
  FROM movie_titles
  ORDER BY title;
```

3. Produce a summary listing of revenue generated by tape category (horror, children, *etc.*)

```
SELECT SUM (total_vhs_rental_revenue +
            total_beta_rental_revenue) AS total_rental,
       SUM (total_vhs_sales_revenue +
            total_beta_sales_revenue) AS total_sales,
       SUM (total_vhs_rental_revenue +
            total_beta_rental_revenue +
            total_vhs_sales_revenue +
            total_beta_sales_revenue) AS total_revenue
  FROM movie_titles
  GROUP BY movie_type
```

4. Which actor's movies generates the most total revenue?

```
SELECT DISTINCT actor_last_name || ',' || actor_first_name
  FROM movie_titles mt INNER JOIN movies_stars ms
```

```
                      USING title = movie_title AND
                          ms.year_released = mt.year_released
              WHERE total_vhs_rental_revenue + total_beta_rental_revenue +
                   total_vhs_sales_revenue + total_beta_sales_revenue
                  = SELECT MAX (total_vhs_rental_revenue +
                                total_beta_rental_revenue +
                                total_vhs_sales_revenue +
                                total_beta_sales_revenue)
                      FROM movie_titles
```

5. List the top five titles by the number of returns (looking for manufacturing defects).

```
DECLARE top_returns CURSOR FOR
  SELECT title
    FROM music_titles
    WHERE total_cd_returned + total_cassette_returned +
          total_8_track_returned + total_lp_returned > 0;

OPEN top_returns;

FETCH top_returns
  INTO :title;

FETCH top_returns
  INTO :title;

FETCH top_returns
  INTO :title;

FETCH top_returns
  INTO :title;

FETCH top_returns
  INTO :title;

CLOSE top_returns;

COMMIT;
```

6. List all CD/music titles for which we have multiple distributors.

```
SELECT mt.title
  FROM music_titles mt INNER JOIN music_supply_costs msc
      USING mt.title = msc.title AND
            mt.artist = msc.artist AND
            ( mt.artist_more = msc.artist_more OR
              ( mt.artist_more IS NULL AND
                msc.artist_more IS NULL ) )
  WHERE NOT UNIQUE
          ( SELECT distributor
              FROM music_titles mt1 INNER JOIN
                   music_supply_costs msc1
```

```
                         USING mt1.title = msc1.title AND
                             mt.title = mt1.title AND
                             mt1.artist = msc1.artist AND
                             mt.artist = mt1.artist AND
                             ( ( mt1.artist_more = msc1.artist_more AND
                                 mt.artist_more = mt1.artist_more ) OR
                               ( mt1.artist_more IS NULL AND
                                 msc1.artist_more IS NULL AND
                                 mt.artist_more IS NULL ) ) )
```

7. List the lowest cost distributor for each music title.

```
SELECT distributor
  FROM music_titles mt INNER JOIN music_supply_costs msc
     USING mt.title = msc.title AND
           mt.artist = msc.artist AND
           ( mt.artist_more = msc.artist_more OR
             ( mt.artist_more IS NULL AND
               msc.artist_more IS NULL ) ) AND
  WHERE msc.cost_qty_1 =
           SELECT MIN(cost_qty_1)
             FROM music_titles mt1 INNER JOIN
                  music_supply_costs msc1
               USING mt1.title = msc1.title AND
                     mt.title = mt1.title AND
                     mt1.artist = msc1.artist AND
                     mt.artist = mt1.artist AND
                     ( ( mt1.artist_more = msc1.artist_more AND
                         mt.artist_more = mt1.artist_more ) OR
                       ( mt1.artist_more IS NULL AND
                         msc1.artist_more IS NULL AND
                         mt.artist_more IS NULL ) ) )
```

8. List the distribution company that has the most titles for which it is the lowest cost distributor.

```
SELECT distributor
  FROM music_supply_costs
  WHERE SELECT COUNT(DISTINCT title)
          FROM ...
       >= SELECT MAX(COUNT(DISTINCT title))
            FROM ...
```

9. Which distributor is the least expensive supplier for ten copies of *Bad*?

```
SELECT distributor
  FROM music_titles mt INNER JOIN music_supply_costs msc
     USING mt.title = msc.title AND
           mt.artist = msc.artist AND
           ( mt.artist_more = msc.artist_more OR
             ( mt.artist_more IS NULL AND
               msc.artist_more IS NULL ) ) AND
```

```
WHERE title = 'Bad' AND
      break_point >= 10 AND
      msc.cost_qty_large =
          SELECT MIN(cost_qty_large)
            FROM music_titles mt1 INNER JOIN
                 music_supply_costs msc1
               USING mt1.title = msc1.title AND
                     mt.title = mt1.title AND
                     mt1.artist = msc1.artist AND
                     mt.artist = mt1.artist AND
                     ( ( mt1.artist_more = msc1.artist_more AND
                         mt.artist_more = mt1.artist_more ) OR
                       ( mt1.artist_more IS NULL AND
                         msc1.artist_more IS NULL AND
                         mt.artist_more IS NULL ) ) )
               WHERE break_point >= 10;
```

APPENDIX C

. . . .

The SQL-92 Annexes: Differences, Implementation-Defined and Implementation-Dependent Features, Deprecated Features, and Leveling

C.1 Introduction

The SQL-92 standard contains several Annexes. These are not normative, or enforceable, parts of the standard, but are informative in nature. In fact, four of the six Annexes merely summarize information that is available in other places in the standard; the other two offer material that would be difficult to ascertain in other ways. In this chapter, we will capture the essence of the Annexes, without actually going into the detail that is inevitably present in the standard. We'll discuss the differences between SQL-89 and SQL-92 (including incompatibilities as well as additions), implementation-defined and implementation-dependent features, deprecated features, and a summary of leveling.

C.2 Differences Between SQL-89 and SQL-92

Most SQL programmers, especially those familiar with SQL-89, will want to know all the differences between the new standard and the earlier one. There really are quite a few differences, and we can divide them into two broad categories: incompatible differences and compatible differences.

C.2.1 Incompatible Differences

The incompatible differences are very few in number; the standards process is heavily biased against introducing incompatibilities between versions of a standard, and it is generally done only with great debate and reluctance. Here are all of the incompatibilities between SQL-89 and SQL-92.

1. In SQL-89, there was a rule that said that if you opened an unordered cursor, closed it, and then reopened it in the same transaction, the cursor

would contain the same rows in the same order both times. Because no known implementation actually behaves this way and because unordered cursors are not supposed to have a known order, this requirement has been removed in SQL-92. Therefore, should there be some implementation somewhere with this behavior and some application that depends on it, that application may behave differently under SQL-92 than under SQL-89.

2. In SQL-89, the names of parameters used in procedures in SQL modules were simple identifiers; therefore, these names shared a namespace with column names, and SQL-89 had a rule to disambiguate the use of such names. (Because you could always qualify a column name with a table or correlation name, unqualified ambiguous names were assumed to be parameter names.) In SQL-92, this ambiguity has been removed in favor of the notation used with host variables in embedded SQL programs: parameter names must now be preceded by a colon.

3. In SQL-89, the specification of the semantic of views defined WITH CHECK OPTION was ambiguous; in SQL-92, the definition has been clarified. It is possible that some application programs may have depended on implementation-specific behavior in SQL-89-conformant implementations and may have to be changed for SQL-92-conformant behavior.

4. In SQL-89, users were not required to have SELECT privilege on tables referenced in contexts other than SELECT statements or query expressions. Therefore, in certain unusual circumstances, a user without SELECT privilege on some table could actually learn the contents of the table. SQL-92 has added rules that require SELECT privilege for those circumstances.

5. In SQL-89, a schema could contain two or more UNIQUE or PRIMARY KEY constraints with identical unique column lists. SQL-92 has prohibited defining such multiple constraints with identical unique column lists.

6. In SQL-89, it was possible (though meaningless) to define a view in terms of itself (perhaps through several levels of intermediary views). SQL-92 has added rules to prohibit this sort of specification.

7. In SQL-89, you were permitted to use "outer references" in set functions in subqueries that were contained in the search condition of HAVING clauses, but it did not define the semantics of doing so. SQL-92 has prohibited the construction entirely.

8. In SQL-89, the module that is effectively derived from an embedded SQL program had an authorization identifier that was said to be implementation-defined. That was interpreted to mean that the authID could be determined at compilation time or at runtime. SQL-92 has clarified the situation to require that the authID be determined at runtime.

9. In SQL-89, if a cursor is on or before a row, and that row is deleted, then the cursor is positioned before the row that is immediately after the position of the deleted row. In SQL-92, if the deletion is made through a DELETE statement other than one using that same cursor, the effect of the deletion is implementation-dependent.

10. Finally, SQL-92 has defined a large number of additional reserved keywords:

ABSOLUTE	ACTION	ADD
ALLOCATE	ALTER	ARE
ASSERTION	AT	BETWEEN
BIT	BIT_LENGTH	BOTH
CASCADE	CASCADED	CASE
CAST	CATALOG	CHAR_LENGTH
CHARACTER_LENGTH	COALESCE	COLLATE
COLLATION	COLUMN	CONNECT
CONNECTION	CONSTRAINT	CONSTRAINTS
CONVERT	CORRESPONDING	CROSS
CURRENT_DATE	CURRENT_TIME	CURRENT_TIMESTAMP
CURRENT_USER	DATE	DAY
DEALLOCATE	DEFERRABLE	DEFERRED
DESCRIBE	DESCRIPTOR	DIAGNOSTICS
DISCONNECT	DOMAIN	DROP
ELSE	END-EXEC	EXCEPT
EXCEPTION	EXECUTE	EXTERNAL
EXTRACT	FALSE	FIRST
FULL	GET	GLOBAL
HOUR	IDENTITY	IMMEDIATE
INITIALLY	INNER	INPUT
INSENSITIVE	INTERSECT	INTERVAL
ISOLATION	JOIN	LAST
LEADING	LEFT	LEVEL
LOCAL	LOWER	MATCH
MINUTE	MONTH	NAMES
NATIONAL	NATURAL	NCHAR
NEXT	NO	NULLIF
OCTET_LENGTH	ONLY	OUTER
OUTPUT	OVERLAPS	PAD
PARTIAL	POSITION	PREPARE
PRESERVE	PRIOR	READ
RELATIVE	RESTRICT	REVOKE
RIGHT	ROWS	SCROLL
SECOND	SESSION	SESSION_USER

SIZE	SPACE	SQLSTATE
SUBSTRING	SYSTEM_USER	TEMPORARY
THEN	TIME	TIMESTAMP
TIMEZONE_HOUR	TIMEZONE_MINUTE	TRAILING
TRANSACTION	TRANSLATE	TRANSLATION
TRIM	TRUE	UNKNOWN
UPPER	USAGE	USING
VALUE	VARCHAR	VARYING
WHEN	WRITE	YEAR
ZONE		

Whew! That probably seems like a lot of incompatibilities, but most of them are pretty trivial and address really unusual situations. The lengthy list of new reserved words is clearly the most problematic for most users, but we note that you can now use the delimited identifiers (identifiers in double quotes) to get around that problem. Therefore, if you happened to name one of your columns ZONE, you can modify your programs to now refer to it as "ZONE."

C.2.2 Compatible Differences

Now, let's look at the compatible differences—the new features.

- A better definition of direct invocation of SQL language
- Improved diagnostic capabilities, especially a new status parameter (SQLSTATE), a diagnostics area, and supporting statements
- Support for additional data types (DATE, TIME, TIMESTAMP, INTERVAL, BIT string, variable-length character and bit strings, and NATIONAL CHARACTER strings)
- Support for character sets beyond that required to express SQL language itself and support for additional collations
- Support for additional scalar operations, such as string operations for concatenate and substring, date and time operations, and a form for conditional expressions
- Increased generality and orthogonality in the use of scalar-valued and table-valued query expressions
- Additional set operators (for example, union join, natural join, set difference, and set intersection)
- Capability for domain definitions in the schema
- Support for schema manipulation capabilities (especially DROP and ALTER statements)
- Support for bindings (modules and embedded syntax) in the Ada, C, and MUMPS languages

- Additional privilege capabilities
- Additional referential integrity facilities, including referential actions, subqueries in CHECK constraints, separate assertions, and user-controlled deferral of constraints
- Definition of an information schema
- Support for dynamic execution of SQL language
- Support for certain facilities required for remote database access (especially connection management statements and qualified schema names)
- Support for temporary tables
- Support for transaction consistency levels
- Support for data type conversions (CAST expressions among data types)
- Support for scrolled cursors
- A requirement for a flagging capability to aid in portability of application programs

C.3 Implementation-Defined and Implementation-Dependent

It would have been very nice, indeed, if the SQL standard had completely defined every aspect of every element. However, there are a number of elements that the standard did not define for one reason or another. The precise definition of these aspects of the language will, of course, be determined in one way or another by each implementation.

The standard uses the phrase *implementation-defined* to indicate one of these areas. This is meant to imply that the implementation *must* document the syntax, value, or behavior of the element. For example, the standard leaves the exact precision of the INTEGER data type as implementation-defined, and in order to claim conformance to the standard, the implementation *must* document the precision.

The other phrase the standard uses is *implementation-dependent.* This phrase means that the implementation need not document the syntax, value, or behavior of some element and that application programs certainly must never depend on it. For example, the physical representation of a value of any given data type is implementation-dependent. Implementation-dependent information is typically the sort that may change from version to version of a product, that is unusually difficult to describe, or is of no (logical) use to applications.

SQL-92 identifies no fewer than 149 items that are implementation-defined and 75 that are implementation-dependent. While that may sound like the standard is left wide open for almost anything, many of these items are closely related to others, many are so obvious that they may be overlooked by a more casual specification, and others are descriptive of realistic behaviors in any situation. Let's try to summarize at least the more important of them.

C.3.1 Implementation-Defined

The following lists contain the implementation-defined items of SQL-92.

Data Types

1. The specific character set associated with the subtype of character string represented by the key words NATIONAL CHARACTER is implementation-defined.

2. When trailing digits are removed from a numeric value, the choice of whether to truncate or to round is implementation-defined.

3. When an approximation is obtained by truncation or rounding and there are two or more approximations, which approximation is chosen is implementation-defined.

4. It is implementation-defined which numerical values have approximations obtained by rounding or truncation for a given approximate numeric type.

5. The boundaries within which the normal rules of arithmetic apply are implementation-defined.

6. When converting between numeric data types, if least significant digits are lost, it is implementation-defined whether rounding or truncation occurs.

7. If a precision is omitted, an implementation-defined precision is implicit.

8. The decimal precision of a data type defined as DECIMAL for each value specified by an explicit precision is implementation-defined.

9. The precision of a data type defined as INTEGER is implementation-defined but has the same radix as that for SMALLINT.

10. The precision of a data type defined as SMALLINT is implementation-defined but has the same radix as that for INTEGER.

11. The binary precision of a data type defined as FLOAT for each value specified by an explicit precision is implementation-defined.

12. The precision of a data type defined as REAL is implementation-defined.

13. The precision of a data type defined as DOUBLE PRECISION is implementation-defined but greater than that for REAL.

14. For every data type, the limits of the data type are implementation-defined.

15. The maximum lengths for character string types, variable-length character string types, bit string types, and variable-length bit string types are implementation-defined.

16. If CHARACTER SET is not specified for a character string type, the character set is implementation-defined.

17. The character set named SQL_TEXT is an implementation-defined character set that contains every character in the basic set of characters necessary to represent SQL language and all characters that are in other character sets supported by the implementation.

18. For the exact numeric types DECIMAL and NUMERIC, the maximum values of precision and of scale are implementation-defined.

19. For the approximate numeric type FLOAT, the maximum value of precision is implementation-defined.

20. For the approximate numeric types FLOAT, REAL, and DOUBLE PRECISION, the maximum and minimum values of the exponent are implementation-defined.

21. The maximum number of digits in a fractional seconds precision is implementation-defined but shall not be less than 6.

22. Interval arithmetic that involves leap seconds or discontinuities in calendars will produce implementation-defined results.

Metadata

1. The default schema for preparable statements that are dynamically prepared in your session through the execution of PREPARE statements and EXECUTE IMMEDIATE statements is initially implementation-defined but may be changed by the use of SET SCHEMA statements.

2. The creation and destruction of catalogs is accomplished by implementation-defined means.

3. The set of catalogs that can be referenced in any SQL statement, during any particular transaction, or during the course of a session is implementation-defined.

4. The default catalog for modules whose module authorization clause does not specify an explicit catalog name to qualify schema name and the default catalog name substitution value for execution of preparable statements that are dynamically prepared in your session through the execution of PREPARE statements and EXECUTE IMMEDIATE statements are implementation-defined.

5. A cluster is an implementation-defined collection of catalogs.

6. Whether or not any catalog can appear simultaneously in more than one cluster is implementation-defined.

7. The constituents of an SQL-environment beyond those specified in the standard are implementation-defined.

8. The rules determining whether a module is within the environment are implementation-defined.

9. The mechanisms by which modules are created or destroyed are implementation-defined.

10. The manner in which an association is made between a module and an SQL agent is implementation-defined.

11. Whether a compilation unit may invoke or transfer control to other compilation units, written in the same or a different programming language, is implementation-defined.

12. The names of character sets that are implementation-defined or defined by national or international standards that are supported by your implementation are implementation-defined.

13. The names of collations that are implementation-defined or defined by national or international standards that are supported by your implementation are implementation-defined.

14. The names of translations that are implementation-defined or defined by national or international standards that are supported by your implementation are implementation-defined.

Sessions, Transactions, and Connections

1. It is implementation-defined whether or not the nondynamic or dynamic execution of a data manipulation statement is permitted to occur within the same SQL transaction as the nondynamic or dynamic execution of a schema definition or manipulation statement. If it does occur, the effect on any open cursor, prepared dynamic statement, or deferred constraint is also implementation-defined.

2. If an implementation detects unrecoverable errors and implicitly initiates the execution of a ROLLBACK statement, an error is returned.

3. It is implementation-defined how an implementation uses SQL server name to determine the location, identity, and communication protocol required to access the environment and create a session.

4. When a session is initiated other than through the use of an explicit CONNECT statement, a session associated with an implementation-defined environment is initiated. The default environment is implementation-defined.

5. The mechanism and rules by which an environment determines whether a call to a procedure is the last call within the last active module are implementation-defined.

6. A session uses one or more implementation-defined schemas that contain the instances of any global temporary tables, created local temporary tables, or declared local temporary tables within the session.

7. When a session is initiated other than through the use of an explicit CONNECT statement, there is an implementation-defined default authorization identifier that is used for privilege checking the execution of statements contained in modules not having an explicit module authorization identifier.

8. When a session is initiated, there is an implementation-defined default catalog whose name is used to effectively qualify all unqualified schema names contained in preparable statements that are dynamically prepared in the current session through the execution of PREPARE statements and EXECUTE IMMEDIATE statements or are contained in direct SQL statements when those statements are invoked directly.

9. When a session is initiated, there is an implementation-defined default schema whose name is used to effectively qualify all unqualified names contained in preparable statements that are dynamically prepared in the current session through the execution of PREPARE statements and EXECUTE IMMEDIATE statements or are contained in direct SQL statements when those statements are invoked directly.

10. When a session is initiated, there is an implementation-defined default character set that is used to identify the character set implicit for identifiers and character string literals that are contained in preparable statements when those statements are prepared in the current session by either an EXECUTE IMMEDIATE statement or a PREPARE statement or are contained in direct SQL statements when those statements are invoked directly.

11. When a session is initiated, there is an implementation-defined default time zone displacement that is used as the current default time zone displacement of the SQL session.

12. When an agent is active, it is bound in some implementation-defined manner to a single client.

13. If the module that contains a procedure is associated with an agent that is associated with another module that contains a procedure with the same procedure name, the effect is implementation-defined.

14. The isolation level that is set for a transaction is an implementation-defined isolation level that will not exhibit any of the phenomena that the explicit or implicit level of isolation would not exhibit.

15. If any error has occurred other than one specified in the *General Rules* preventing commitment of the transaction, then any changes to data or schemas that were made by the current transaction are canceled and an error is returned.

16. It is implementation-defined whether or not an SQL implementation may support transactions that affect more than one server. If it does so, then the effects are implementation-defined.

17. If a user name is not specified in a CONNECT statement, an implementation-defined user name for the connection is implicit.

18. The restrictions on whether or not the user name in a CONNECT statement shall be identical to the module authorization identifier for the module that contains the procedure that contains the CONNECT statement are implementation-defined.

19. If DEFAULT is specified, the method by which the default environment is determined is implementation-defined.

20. The method by which SQL server name is used to determine the appropriate environment is implementation-defined.

21. Whether or not the authorization identifier for the session can be set to an authorization identifier other than the authorization identifier of the

session when the session is started is implementation-defined, as are any restrictions pertaining to such changes.

SQL Statements

1. This International Standard permits implementations to provide additional, implementation-defined statements; the classification of such statements is also implementation-defined.

2. If a value V is approximate numeric and a target T is exact numeric, then whether the approximation of V retrieved into T is obtained by rounding or by truncation is implementation-defined.

3. If a value V is approximate numeric and a target T is exact numeric, then whether the approximation of V stored into T is obtained by rounding or by truncation is implementation-defined.

4. If all of the data types in a set of values are exact numeric, then the result data type for the purposes of UNION or other similar requirements is exact numeric with implementation-defined precision.

5. If any data type in a set of values is approximate numeric, then each data type in the set of values shall be numeric and the result data type is approximate numeric with implementation-defined precision.

6. If character set specification is not specified on a CREATE SCHEMA, a character set specification containing an implementation-defined character set specification is implicit.

7. The privileges necessary to execute CREATE SCHEMA are implementation-defined.

8. Whether null values shall be considered greater than or less than all non-null values in determining the order of rows in a table associated with a DECLARE CURSOR is implementation-defined.

9. If WITH MAX is not specified, an implementation-defined default value that is greater than 0 is implicit.

10. The maximum number of SQL descriptor areas and the maximum number of item descriptor areas for a single SQL descriptor area are implementation-defined.

11. Restrictions on changing TYPE, LENGTH, PRECISION, DATETIME_INTERVAL_CODE, DATETIME_INTERVAL_PRECISION, SCALE, CHARACTER_SET_CATALOG, CHARACTER_SET_SCHEMA, and CHARACTER_SET_NAME values resulting from the execution of a DESCRIBE statement before the execution of an EXECUTE statement, a dynamic OPEN statement, or a dynamic FETCH statement are implementation-defined, except as specified in specific rules for the USING clause.

12. The format and syntax rules for a preparable implementation-defined statement are implementation-defined.

13. The method of invoking direct SQL statements, the method of raising conditions as a result of direct SQL statements, the method of accessing diagnostic information, and the method of returning the results are all implementation-defined.

14. The value specification that represents the null value in direct invocation of SQL is implementation-defined.

15. The format, syntax rules, and access rules for direct implementation-defined statements are implementation-defined.

16. Whether a direct implementation-defined statement may be associated with an active transaction is implementation-defined.

17. Whether a direct implementation-defined statement initiates a transaction is implementation-defined.

18. The methods of raising a condition and of accessing diagnostics information are implementation-defined.

19. The method of returning the results from multirow SELECT statements in direct invocation is implementation-defined.

Literals, Names, and Identifiers

1. The end-of-line indicator *(newline)* is implementation-defined.

2. The character set name of the character set used to represent national characters is implementation-defined.

3. If a schema name contained in a schema name clause but not contained in a module does not contain a catalog name, an implementation-defined catalog name is implicit.

4. If a schema name contained in a module authorization clause does not contain a catalog name, an implementation-defined catalog name is implicit.

5. The data type of the simple value specification of an extended statement name shall be character string with an implementation-defined character set.

6. The data type of the simple value specification of an extended cursor name shall be character string with an implementation-defined character set.

7. Those identifiers that are valid authorization identifiers are implementation-defined.

8. Those identifiers that are valid catalog names are implementation-defined.

9. All form-of-use conversion names are implementation-defined.

Value Expressions and Functions

1. Whether the character string of the value specifications CURRENT_USER, SESSION_USER, and SYSTEM_USER is variable-length or fixed-length, and its

maximum length if it is variable-length or its length if it is fixed-length, are implementation-defined.

2. The value specified by SYSTEM_USER is an implementation-defined string that represents the operating system user who executed the module that contains the SQL statement whose execution caused the SYSTEM_USER value specification to be evaluated.

3. In Intermediate SQL, the specific data type of indicator parameters and indicator variables shall be the same implementation-defined data type.

4. The precision of the value derived from application of the COUNT function is implementation-defined.

5. The precision of the value derived from application of the SUM function to a data type of exact numeric is implementation-defined.

6. The precision and scale of the value derived from application of the AVG function to a data type of exact numeric is implementation-defined.

7. The precision of the value derived from application of the SUM function or AVG function to a data type of approximate numeric is implementation-defined.

8. The precision of the POSITION expression is implementation-defined.

9. The precision of the EXTRACT expression is implementation-defined. If datetime field specifies SECOND, the scale is also implementation-defined.

10. The precision of the various LENGTH expressions is implementation-defined.

11. The maximum length of a character translation or form-of-use conversion is implementation-defined.

12. Whether to round or truncate when casting to exact or approximate numeric data types is implementation-defined.

13. When the data type of both operands of the addition, subtraction, multiplication, or division operator is exact numeric, the precision of the result is implementation-defined.

14. When the data type of both operands of the division operator is exact numeric, the scale of the result is implementation-defined.

15. When the data type of either operand of an arithmetic operator is approximate numeric, the precision of the result is implementation-defined.

16. Whether to round or truncate when performing division is implementation-defined.

17. When an interval is produced from the difference of two datetimes, the choice of whether to round or truncate is implementation-defined.

18. The maximum value of an interval leading field precision is implementation-defined but shall not be less than 2.

19. The maximum value of an interval fractional seconds precision is implementation-defined but shall not be less than 6.

Diagnostics

1. The negative (exception) values for the SQLCODE status parameter are implementation-defined.

2. The actual length of variable-length character items in the diagnostics area is implementation-defined but shall not be less than 128.

3. The character string value set for CLASS_ORIGIN and SUBCLASS_ORIGIN for an implementation-defined class code or subclass code is implementation-defined but shall not be 'ISO 9075.'

4. The value of MESSAGE_TEXT is an implementation-defined character string.

5. The character set associated with the class value and subclass value of the SQLSTATE parameter is implementation-defined.

6. The values and meanings for classes and subclasses that begin with one of the digits 5, 6, 7, 8, or 9 or one of the upper case letters *I, J, K, L, M, N, O, P, Q, R, S, T, U, V, W, X, Y,* or *Z* are implementation-defined. The values and meanings for all subclasses that are associated with implementation-defined class values are implementation-defined.

7. The negative values returned in an SQLCODE parameter to indicate exception conditions are implementation-defined.

Information Schema

1. If the containing `ADD TABLE CONSTRAINT` definition does not specify a constraint name definition, the values of CONSTRAINT_CATALOG, CONSTRAINT_SCHEMA, and CONSTRAINT_NAME are implementation-defined.

2. The values of FORM_OF_USE and NUMBER_OF_CHARACTERS, in the row for the character set INFORMATION_SCHEMA.SQL_TEXT, are implementation-defined.

3. The value of PAD_ATTRIBUTE for the collation SQL_TEXT is implementation-defined.

4. The value of SQL_LANGUAGE_IMPLEMENTATION is implementation-defined. If the value of SQL_LANGUAGE_SOURCE is not 'ISO 9075,' the value of all other columns is implementation-defined.

Embedded SQL and Modules

1. Whether a portion of the namespace is reserved by an implementation for the names of procedures, subroutines, program variables, branch labels, modules, or procedures is implementation-defined; if a portion of the namespace is so reserved, the portion reserved is also implementation-defined.

2. If the explicit or implicit schema name does not specify a catalog name, an implementation-defined catalog name is implicit.

3. If a module character set specification is not specified, a module character set specification that specifies the implementation-defined character set that contains every character that is in SQL language character is implicit.

4. Whether or not a given authID can invoke procedures in a module with an explicit module authorization identifier is implementation-defined, as are any restrictions pertaining to such invocation.

5. If the value of any input parameter provided by the SQL agent falls outside the set of allowed values of the data type of the parameter, or if the value of any output parameter resulting from the execution of the procedure falls outside the set of values supported by the SQL agent for that parameter, the effect is implementation-defined.

6. There is an implementation-defined package and character type for use in Ada bindings. The precisions and scales of the Ada types for SQL data types and the exact numeric type of indicator parameters are implementation-defined.

7. The null character that defines the end of a C character string is implementation-defined.

8. The number of bits in a C character is implementation-defined.

9. The precision of an SQLCODE parameter in an embedded COBOL program is an implementation-defined value between 4 and 18, inclusive.

10. The number of bits contained in a COBOL character is implementation-defined.

11. The precision of a COBOL data type corresponding to SQL INTEGER or SMALLINT is implementation-defined.

12. The number of bits contained in a Fortran character is implementation-defined.

13. The number of bits contained in a Pascal character is implementation-defined.

14. The precision of an SQLCODE parameter in an embedded PL/I program is implementation-defined.

15. The precision of a PL/I data type corresponding to SQL INTEGER or SMALLINT is implementation-defined.

16. If an embedded character set declaration is not specified, then an embedded character set declaration containing an implementation-defined character set specification is implicit.

17. If character set specification is not specified when CHAR is specified, an implementation-defined character set specification is implicit.

18. SQLCODE_TYPE describes an exact numeric variable whose precision is the implementation-defined precision defined for the SQLCODE parameter.

19. If character set specification is not specified when a C character variable or C VARCHAR variable is specified, an implementation-defined character set specification is implicit.

20. The COBOL data description clauses, in addition to the PICTURE, SIGN, USAGE, and VALUE clauses, that may appear in a COBOL variable definition are implementation-defined.

21. If character set specification is not specified when a COBOL character type is specified, an implementation-defined character set specification is implicit.

22. The precision of the COBOL type specification that corresponds to SQLCODE is implementation-defined.

23. If character set specification is not specified when CHARACTER is specified in Fortran, then an implementation-defined character set specification is implicit.

24. In a MUMPS character variable, an implementation-defined character set specification is implicit.

25. If character set specification is not specified when PACKED ARRAY OF CHAR is specified in Pascal, an implementation-defined character set specification is implicit.

26. The PL/I data description clauses, in addition to the PL/I type specification and the INITIAL clause, that may appear in a PL/I variable definition are implementation-defined.

27. If character set specification is not specified when CHARACTER is specified in PL/I, an implementation-defined character set specification is implicit.

28. The precision of the PL/I type specification that corresponds to SQLCODE is implementation-defined.

Miscellaneous

1. If an SQL implementation provides user options to process conforming SQL language in a nonconforming manner, it is required that the implementation also provide a flagger option, or some other implementation-defined means, to detect SQL conforming language that may be processed differently under the various user options.

2. The default collating sequence of the character repertoire specified by an implementation-defined character repertoire name or by an implementation-defined universal character form-of-use name is implementation-defined. Whether that collating sequence has the NO PAD attribute or the PAD SPACE attribute is also implementation-defined.

3. The collating sequence resulting from the specification of EXTERNAL in a collation definition is implementation-defined.

4. The method of flagging nonconforming SQL language or of processing conforming SQL language is implementation-defined, as is the list of additional keywords that may be required by the implementation.

C.3.2 Implementation-Dependent

The following lists contain the implementation-dependent features of SQL-92.

Information Schema

1. The actual objects on which the Information Schema views are based are implementation-dependent.
2. The values of DEFAULT_COLLATE_SCHEMA, DEFAULT_COLLATE_CATALOG, and DEFAULT_COLLATE_NAME for default collations specifying the order of characters in a repertoire are implementation-dependent.

Miscellaneous

1. The treatment of language that does not conform to the SQL formats and syntax rules is implementation-dependent.
2. It is implementation-dependent whether expressions are actually evaluated left-to-right when the precedence is not otherwise determined by the formats or by parentheses.
3. If evaluation of the inessential parts of an expression or search condition would cause an exception condition to be raised, it is implementation-dependent whether or not that condition is raised.
4. Because global temporary table contents are distinct within SQL sessions, and created local temporary tables are distinct within modules within SQL sessions, the effective schema name of the schema in which the global temporary table or the created local temporary table is instantiated is an implementation-dependent schema name that may be thought of as having been effectively derived from the schema name of the schema in which the global temporary table or created local temporary table is defined and from the implementation-dependent SQL-session identifier associated with the SQL-session.
5. The effective schema name of the schema in which the created local temporary table is instantiated may be thought of as being further qualified by a unique implementation-dependent name associated with the module in which the created local temporary table is referenced.
6. Whether or not a temporary viewed table is materialized is implementation-dependent.
7. The mapping of authorization identifiers to operating system users is implementation-dependent.
8. When a session is initiated, the current authorization identifier for the session is determined in an implementation-dependent manner, unless the session is initiated using a CONNECT statement.
9. An SQL agent is an implementation-dependent entity that causes the execution of SQL statements.

10. The schema definitions that are implicitly read on behalf of executing an SQL statement are implementation-dependent.

11. The session module contains a module authorization clause that specifies SCHEMA schema-name, where the value of schema-name is implementation-dependent.

12. A unique implementation-dependent session identifier is associated with each session.

13. The module name of the module that is effectively materialized on an SQL server is implementation-dependent.

14. Diagnostic information passed to the diagnostics area in the client is passed in an implementation-dependent manner.

15. If the number of conditions is not specified in a SET TRANSACTION statement, an implementation-dependent value not less than 1 is implicit.

16. If ALL is specified in a DISCONNECT statement, then *L* is a list representing every active connection that has been established by a CONNECT statement by the current SQL agent and that has not yet been disconnected by a DISCONNECT statement, in an implementation-dependent order.

Diagnostics

1. The effect on diagnostic information of incompatibilities between the character repertoires supported by the SQL client and SQL server environments is implementation-dependent.

2. The effect on target specifications and SQL descriptor areas of an SQL statement that terminates with an exception condition, unless explicitly defined by the standard, is implementation-dependent.

3. If more than one condition could have occurred as a result of execution of a statement, then it is implementation-dependent whether diagnostic information pertaining to more than one condition is made available.

4. The actual size of the diagnostics area is implementation-dependent when the SQL agent does not specify the size.

5. The ordering of the information about conditions placed into the diagnostics area is implementation-dependent, except that the first condition in the diagnostics area always corresponds to the condition corresponding to the SQLSTATE or SQLCODE value.

6. The value of ROW_COUNT following the execution of an SQL statement that does not directly result in the execution of a searched DELETE statement, an INSERT statement, or a searched UPDATE statement is implementation-dependent.

7. If the condition number in a GET DIAGNOSTICS statement has a value other than 1, the association between condition number values and specific conditions raised during evaluation of the general rules for that SQL statement is implementation-dependent.

SQL Statements

1. If the DECLARE CURSOR does not include an ORDER BY clause, or includes an ORDER BY clause that does not specify the order of the rows completely, then the rows of the table have an order that is defined only to the extent that the ORDER BY clause specifies an order and is otherwise implementation-dependent.

2. When the ordering of a cursor is not defined by an ORDER BY clause, the relative position of two rows is implementation-dependent.

3. The effect on the position and state of an open cursor when an error occurs during the execution of an SQL statement that identifies the cursor is implementation-dependent.

4. If a cursor is open and a change is made to SQL data from within the same transaction other than through that cursor, then whether or not that change will be visible through that cursor before it is closed is implementation-dependent.

5. The specific character set chosen is implementation-dependent, but shall be the character set of one of the data types in the set of values being evaluated for UNION compatibility.

6. The order of assignment to targets in the fetch target list of values returned by a FETCH statement, other than status parameters, is implementation-dependent.

7. If an error occurs during assignment of a value to a target during the execution of a FETCH statement, the values of targets other than status parameters are implementation-dependent.

8. If the cardinality of the query expression in a single-row SELECT statement is greater than 1, it is implementation-dependent whether or not values are assigned to the targets identified by the select target list.

9. The order of assignment to targets in the select target list of values returned by a single-row SELECT statement, other than status parameters, is implementation-dependent.

10. If an error occurs during assignment of a value to a target during the execution of a single-row SELECT statement, the values of targets other than status parameters are implementation-dependent.

11. If an exception condition is raised in a GET DESCRIPTOR statement, the values of all targets are implementation-dependent.

12. For a select list column described by a DESCRIBE statement, if the column name is implementation-dependent, then NAME is the implementation-dependent name for the column and UNNAMED is set to 1.

13. For a dynamic parameter specification described by a DESCRIBE statement, the values of NAME and UNNAMED are implementation-dependent.

14. Item descriptor area fields not relevant to the data type of the item being described are set to implementation-dependent values.

15. If an exception condition is raised in a SET DESCRIPTOR statement, the values of all elements of the descriptor specified in the SET DESCRIPTOR statement are implementation-dependent.

16. The validity of an extended statement name value or a statement name in a transaction different from the one in which the statement was prepared is implementation-dependent.

17. When a DESCRIBE OUTPUT statement is executed, the values of DATA and INDICATOR, as well as the value of other fields not relevant to the data type of the described item, are implementation-dependent. If the column name is implementation-dependent, then NAME is set to that implementation-dependent name.

18. When a DESCRIBE INPUT statement is used, the values for NAME, DATA, and INDICATOR, as well as the value of other fields not relevant to the data type of the described item, in the SQL dynamic descriptor area structure are implementation-dependent.

19. If an unrecoverable error has occurred, or if the direct invocation of SQL terminated unexpectedly, or if any constraint is not satisfied, a ROLLBACK statement is performed. Otherwise, the choice of ROLLBACK or COMMIT is implementation-dependent. The determination of whether a direct invocation of SQL has terminated unexpectedly is implementation-dependent.

Literals, Other Value Expressions, Functions, Predicates, and Queries

1. The implicit qualifier of a column reference for which there is more than one possible qualifier with most local scope is implementation-dependent.

2. The time of evaluation of the CURRENT_DATE, CURRENT_TIME, and CURRENT_TIMESTAMP functions during the execution of an SQL statement is implementation-dependent.

3. The start datetime used for converting intervals to scalars for subtraction purposes is implementation-dependent.

4. The names of the columns of a row value constructor that specifies a row value constructor list are implementation-dependent.

5. When a column is not named by an AS clause and is not derived from a single column reference, the name of the column is implementation-dependent.

6. If a simple table is not a query specification, the name of each column of the simple table is implementation-dependent.

7. If a non-join query term is not a non-join query primary and the column name of the corresponding columns of both tables participating in the non-join query term are not the same, then the result column has an implementation-dependent column name.

8. If a non-join query expression is not a non-join query term and the column name of the corresponding columns of both tables participating in the

non-join query expression are not the same, then the result column has an implementation-dependent column name.

9. If a collation has the NO PAD attribute, the pad character is an implementation-dependent character different from any character in the character set associated with the collation that collates less than any string under that collation.

10. When the operations MAX, MIN, DISTINCT, references to a grouping column, and the UNION, EXCEPT, and INTERSECT operators refer to character strings, the specific value selected by these operations from a set of such equal values is implementation-dependent.

Data Types and Metadata

1. The constraint name of a constraint that does not specify a constraint name definition is implementation-dependent.

2. The specific value to use for cascading among various values that are not distinct is implementation-dependent.

3. The physical representation of a value of a data type is implementation-dependent.

4. The null value for each data type is implementation-dependent.

Embedded SQL and Modules

1. If the SQL agent that performs a call of a procedure in a module is not a standard program in the language specified in the language clause of the module, the results are implementation-dependent.

2. The procedure name should be a standard-conforming procedure, function, or routine name of the language specified by the subject language clause. Failure to observe this recommendation will have implementation-dependent effects.

3. After the execution of the last procedure, if an unrecoverable error has not occurred, and the SQL agent did not terminate unexpectedly, and there aren't any unsatisfied constraints, then the choice of whether to perform a COMMIT statement or a ROLLBACK statement is implementation-dependent. The determination of whether an SQL agent has terminated unexpectedly is implementation-dependent.

4. If there are two or more status parameters, the order in which values are assigned to these status parameters is implementation-dependent.

5. The module name of the implied module derived from an embedded SQL program is implementation-dependent.

6. The module authorization identifier of the implied module derived from an embedded SQL program is implementation-dependent.

7. In each DECLARE CURSOR in the implied module derived from an embedded SQL program, each embedded variable name has been replaced consistently with a distinct parameter name that is implementation-dependent.

8. The procedure name of each procedure in the implied module derived from an embedded SQL program is implementation-dependent.

9. In each procedure in the implied module derived from an embedded SQL program, each embedded variable name has been replaced consistently with a distinct parameter name that is implementation-dependent.

10. For SQL statements other than OPEN statements, whether one procedure in the implied module derived from an embedded SQL program can correspond to more than one SQL statement in the embedded SQL program is implementation-dependent.

11. In each procedure in the implied module derived from an embedded SQL program, the order of the instances of parameter declaration is implementation-dependent.

C.4 Deprecated Features

There are some features in the SQL-92 standard that, although retained in this version to permit continued use of programs written against the SQL-89 standard, will likely be removed from later versions. These features are *deprecated,* meaning that application programs should not use the feature and existing applications should remove their use of the feature whenever they are updated. Each of these deprecated features has been replaced by some new feature in SQL-92. These are listed below.

1. The SQLCODE status variable (or parameter); this has been replaced by the SQLSTATE variable (and parameter).

2. The use of USAGE COMPUTATIONAL (and any abbreviations of it) in embedded COBOL programs; this has been replaced by USAGE BINARY.

3. The use of an integer in a sort specification of a DECLARE CURSOR to indicate that sorting should be done on a column identified by position instead of by name; this has been rendered unnecessary by the ability to name columns in a select list that are otherwise unnamed (using the AS clause).

4. The writing of procedures in modules with parameter lists that don't use the enclosing parentheses and commas to separate the parameters; this has been replaced by the ability to enclose parameter lists in parentheses and separate the parameters by commas.

C.5 Leveling of SQL-92

In several places in this book, we've referred to the leveling of SQL-92, and in Chapter 1 (section 1.6.3.) we described what the levels are. Briefly: Entry SQL is designed to be very close to SQL-89 with the following differences:

1. Interfaces to three new programming languages (Ada, C, and MUMPS) have been added.
2. Features to replace deprecated SQL-89 features have been added. These are:
   - Commas and parentheses in parameter lists
   - The SQLSTATE status variable (and parameter)
   - The AS clause for naming (or renaming) columns in a select list
3. Features that are incompatible with SQL-89 have been included. These are:
   - Colons are now required preceding parameter names in procedures in modules.
   - The semantics of WITH CHECK OPTION have been clarified.
4. Aids for transitioning from SQL-89 to SQL-92 have also been included. This category includes the ability to delimit identifiers with double quote marks.

Intermediate SQL was designed to be approximately half of the remaining differences between SQL-89 and SQL-92. Precedence was given to features that were already implemented (or being implemented) by several vendors, features that were thought to be relatively easy to implement by most vendors, and features that were felt to have particularly high value to users. They include:

1. Dynamic SQL
2. Schema manipulation statements
3. Enhanced transaction semantics (especially several isolation levels)
4. The CASCADE DELETE referential action for referential integrity constraints
5. Support for multiple modules in one application (for users of module language)
6. Row and table value constructors
7. The UNION JOIN operator
8. The INTERSECT and EXCEPT operators
9. Character string operations and functions, such as SUBSTRING, concatenation, and FOLD
10. Domain support
11. The CASE expression
12. Data type CAST capabilities
13. The GET DIAGNOSTICS statement and the diagnostics area
14. Support for character sets beyond the default for the implementation
15. Datetime and interval data types and operations on these
16. Variable-length character strings
17. A "flagger" to aid in writing portable applications

Full SQL comprises, of course, all the remainder of the language. Notable features in the Full SQL level include:

1. Additional orthogonality features (for example, the ability to use subqueries wherever you can use any value expression and subqueries in CHECK constraints)

2. Deferred constraint checking and the ability for users to name their constraints explicitly

3. Additional options on datetime and interval data types

4. Self-referencing updates and deletes (UPDATE and DELETE statements that reference the table they're modifying in the WHERE or HAVING clauses of the statements)

5. CASCADE UPDATE referential actions and additional options for referential integrity constraints

6. SCROLL cursors

7. Additional internationalization features, such as character translations

8. BIT and BIT VARYING data types

9. Temporary tables

10. Assertions

C.6 Appendix Summary

With the information in this appendix, you should now have a thorough understanding of (1) what is contained in the various levels of SQL-92, (2) how SQL-92 differs from its predecessor standard (SQL-89), and (3) how the various implementation-defined and implementation-dependent aspects of the language are defined. The topics discussed in this appendix are useful in several ways. First, you can evaluate commercial DBMS products that claim SQL-92 compliance and support, based on to the degree to which SQL-92 is supported. Additionally, you can check product features that are implementation-specific against the lists provided here. Since these variables are likely to be among the major differentiators for DBMS products, you can concentrate on these aspects in your product-to-product comparisons. Finally, you can also use the list of deprecated features to avoid future applications-related problems with respect to potentially unsupported SQL facilities.

APPENDIX D

· · · · · · · · · · · · · · · · · ·

Relevant Standards Bodies

D.1 Introduction

If you would like to acquire a copy of the SQL-92 standard, you should do so by contacting the accredited standards body for your country. You can request a copy of the ISO SQL-92 standard by specifying "ISO/IEC 9075:1992." If you live in the United States, you can get the ANSI standard (which is identical to the ISO standard except for such trivial matters as the name of the standard and the list of referenced standards) by specifying "ANSI X3.135-1992."

In this appendix, we provide the names, addresses, telephone numbers, and (where available) fax numbers for the national standards bodies for several countries. If we have omitted your country, we apologize, but it is not feasible to list every country, so we have focused on those countries we believe are most likely to have interested readers.

Some countries have adopted the ISO standard and put their own standard number on it. However, this practice is not widespread and often lags publication of the ISO standard by as much as two or three years, so we won't attempt to provide that information.

The information we provide here was current at the time of publication but is always subject to change.

D.2 List of Standards Bodies

- Australia
  Standards Australia (SAA)
  P.O. Box 458
  North Sydney, New South Wales 2059

Phone: +61.2.963.4111
Fax: +61.2.959.3896

- Canada
  Standards Council of Canada (SCC)
  45 O'Connor Street, Suite 1200
  Ottawa, Ontario K1P 6N7
  Phone: +1.613.238.3222
  Fax: +1.613.995.4564

- People's Republic of China
  China State Bureau of Technical Supervision (CSBTS)
  P.O. Box 820
  Beijing
  Phone: +86.1.89.4905
  Fax: +86.1.831.2689

- Denmark
  Dansk Standardiseringsraad (DS)
  Baunegarrdsvej 73
  DK-2900 Helierup
  Phone: +45.39.77.0101
  Fax: +45.39.77.0202

- France
  Association Française de Normalisation (AFNOR)
  Tour Europe
  Cedex 7
  F-92049 Paris La Défense
  Phone: +33.1.42.91.55.55
  Fax: +33.1.42.91.56.56

- Germany
  Deutsches Institut für Normung (DIN)
  Burggrafenstrasse 6
  Postfach 1107
  D-1000 Berlin 30
  Phone: +49.30.26.01-1
  Fax: +49.30.260.1231

- Hungary
  Magyar Szabványüfyl Hivatal (MSZH)
  1450 Budapest 9
  Pf 24
  Phone: +36.1.118.3011
  Fax: +36.1.118.5125

- Ireland
  National Standards Authority of Ireland (NSAI)
  Glasnevin
  Dublin-9

Phone: +363.1.37.0101
Fax: +363.1.36.9821

- Israel
  Standards Institution of Israel (SII)
  42 Chaim Levanon Street
  Tel Aviv 68877
  Phone: +972.3.54.54.154
  Fax: +972.3.641.9683

- Italy
  Ente Nazionale Italiano di Unificaziono (UNI)
  Via Sattistotti Sassi 11
  I-20133 Milano
  Phone: +39.2.70.02.41
  Fax: +39.2.70.10.61.06

- Japan
  Japanese Industrial Standards Committee (JISC)
  c/o Standards Department
  Agency of Industrial Science and Technology
  Ministry of International Trade and Industry
  1-3-1, Kasumigaseki, Chiyoda-ku
  Tokyo 100
  Phone: +81.3.3501.9295/6
  Fax: +81.3.3680.1418

- Republic of Korea
  Bureau of Standards (KBS)
  Industrial Advancement Administration
  2, Chungang-dong, Kwachon-city
  Kyonggi-do 427-010
  Phone: +82.2.503.7928
  Fax: +82.2.503.7941

- The Netherlands
  Nederlands Normalisatie-instituut (NNI)
  Kalfjeslaan 2
  P.O. Box 5059
  2600 GB Delft
  Phone: +31.15.69.0390
  Fax: +31.15.69.0190

- Norway
  Norges Standardiseringsforbund (NSF)
  Postboks 7020 Homansbyen
  N-0306 Oslo 3
  Phone: +47.2.46.6094
  Fax: +47.2.46.4457

- Russian Federation
  State Committee for Standardization and Metrology (GOST)
  Leninsky Prospekt 9
  Moskva 117049
  Phone: +7.095.236.4044
  Fax: +7.095.236.8209

- Spain
  Asociación Española de Normalización y Certificación (AENOR)
  Calle Fernandez de la Hoz, 52
  E-28010 Madrid
  Phone: +34.1.410.4851
  Fax: +34.1.410.4975

- Sweden
  Standardiseringkommissionen i Svarige (SIS)
  Box 3295
  S-103 55 Stockholm
  Phone: +46.8.613.5200
  Fax: +46.8.11.7035

- Switzerland
  Swiss Association for Standardization (SNV)
  Kirchenweg 4
  Postlach
  CH-8032 Zurich
  Phone: +41.1.384.4747
  Fax: +41.1.384.4774

- United Kingdom
  British Standards Institute (BSI)
  2 Park Street
  GB-London W1A 2BS
  Phone: +44.71.629.9000
  Fax: +44.71.629.0506

- United States of America
  American National Standards Institute (ANSI)
  11 West 42nd Street, 13th floor
  New York, NY 10036
  Phone: +1.212.642.4900
  Fax: +1.212.398.0023

APPENDIX E

● ● ● ● ● ● ● ● ● ● ● ● ● ● ●

Status Codes

E.1 Values of SQLSTATE and SQLCODE

In this appendix, we list the various values of SQLSTATE and SQLCODE. We discussed both of these status code types in Chapter 17, and we talked about exception handling and program structure in Chapter 11.

TABLE E-1
SQLCODE
Values

Value	Condition
0	successful completion
+100	no data
−n	exception

TABLE E-2
SQLSTATE
Values

Condition	Class	Subcondition	Subclass
ambiguous cursor name	3C	(no subclass)	000
cardinality violation	21	(no subclass)	000
connection exception	08	(no subclass)	000
		connection does not exist	003
		connection failure	006
		connection name in use	002
		SQL-client unable to establish SQL-connection	001

TABLE E-2 *(continued)*	Condition	Class	Subcondition	Subclass
			SQL-server rejected establishment of SQL-connection	004
			transaction resolution unknown	007
	cursor operation conflict	09	(no subclass)	000
	data exception	22	(no subclass)	000
			character not in repertoire	021
			datetime field overflow	008
			division by zero	012
			error in assignment	005
			indicator overflow	022
			interval field overflow	015
			invalid character value for cast	018
			invalid datetime format	007
			invalid escape character	019
			invalid escape sequence	025
			invalid fetch sequence	006
			invalid parameter value	023
			invalid time zone displacement value	009
			null value, no indicator parameter	002
			numeric value out of range	003
			string data, length mismatch	026
			string data, right truncation	001
			substring error	011
			trim error	027
			unterminated C string	024
	dependent privilege descriptors still exist	2B	(no subclass)	000
	dynamic SQL error	07	(no subclass)	000
			cursor specification cannot be executed	003
			invalid descriptor count	008
			invalid descriptor index	009

TABLE E-2	Condition	Class	Subcondition	Subclass
(*continued*)			prepared statement not a cursor specification	005
			restricted data type attribute violation	006
			using clause does not match dynamic parameter specifications	001
			using clause does not match target specifications	002
			using clause required for dynamic parameters	004
			using clause required for result fields	007
	feature not supported	0A	(no subclass)	000
			multiple server transactions	001
	integrity constraint violation	23	(no subclass)	000
	invalid authorization specification	28	(no subclass)	000
	invalid catalog name	3D	(no subclass)	000
	invalid character set name	2C	(no subclass)	000
	invalid condition number	35	(no subclass)	000
	invalid cursor name	34	(no subclass)	000
	invalid cursor state	24	(no subclass)	000
	invalid schema name	3F	(no subclass)	000
	invalid SQL descriptor name	33	(no subclass)	000
	invalid SQL statement name	26	(no subclass)	000
	invalid transaction state	25	(no subclass)	000
	invalid transaction termination	2D	(no subclass)	000
	no data	02	(no subclass)	000
	Remote Database Access	HZ	(see ISO/IEC DIS 9579-2 for the definition of protocol subconditions and subclass code values)	
	successful completion	00	(no subclass)	000
	syntax error or access rule violation	42	(no subclass)	000

TABLE E-2
(*continued*)

Condition	Class	Subcondition	Subclass
syntax error or access rule violation in direct SQL statement	2A	(no subclass)	000
syntax error or access rule violation in dynamic SQL statement	37	(no subclass)	000
transaction rollback	40	(no subclass)	000
		integrity constraint violation	002
		serialization failure	001
		statement completion unknown	003
triggered data change violation	27	(no subclass)	000
warning	01	(no subclass)	000
		cursor operation conflict	001
		disconnect error	002
		implicit zero-bit padding	008
		insufficient item descriptor areas	005
		null value eliminated in set function	003
		privilege not granted	007
		privilege not revoked	006
		query expression too long for information schema	00A
		search condition too long for information schema	009
		string data, right truncation	004
with check option violation	44	(no subclass)	000

APPENDIX F

. . . .

The SQL Standardization Process

F.1 Introduction

In this appendix, we present an overview of the ANSI and ISO standardization processes with an emphasis on SQL. While this material isn't essential to use SQL, it will give interested readers some background about how certain facets of the language have been developed. Those who wonder why SQL doesn't have such-and-such a feature or why SQL does things in a particular way will likely understand a bit more about the standardization process from this discussion.

F.2 The Various Standards Bodies

F.2.1 National Standards

ANSI, the American National Standards Institute, is the primary formal standards-making body in the United States. Other countries (at least the developed countries, but also many so-called third-world countries) have their own standards bodies: for example, BSI (the British Standards Institute) in the UK, AFNOR (Association Française de Normalization) in France, and DIN (Deutsches Institut für Normung) in Germany. We will limit our national standards overview to ANSI, since no other national standards body has developed its own SQL standard.

ANSI is really an oversight organization. The actual work of developing standards is the responsibility of ACMOs (accredited standards-making organizations). Responsibility for standards in the area of information processing has been given to an organization called X3 (the letter and number don't have any explicit meaning; it's just an identifier). The day-to-day affairs of X3 are managed by an industry group called CBEMA (Computer and Business Machine Manufacturer's Association), headquartered in Washington, DC.

X3's responsibilities are very broad and extensive, so it further delegates the actual technical work to technical committees (TCs) and to special working groups. One primary special group is called SPARC (Standards Planning and Requirements Committee), whose job it is to determine the need for standards in certain areas and to oversee the development of those standards. SPARC has its own subgroups, one of which is named DBSSG (Database Systems Study Group), which is concerned with broad issues of database standardization (as opposed to specific standards like SQL).

There are many X3 technical committees. One of these is named X3H2, which has the title "Database." X3H2's responsibilities include SQL and other projects not relevant to this book. (For more information about X3H2's other responsibilities, please contact CBEMA.)

When "somebody" believes that the time is ripe to develop a standard for some area of information processing, "they" write a project proposal for submission to ANSI X3 (actually, to ANSI X3 SPARC). This document, called *an SD-3* (for "Standing Document number 3") sets forth the details of the standards development activity proposed for the specific area. This includes information such as the proposed name, the relationship to existing standards or developing standards, the affected industry, the likely participants in the project, and so forth.

If SPARC agrees that an effort should be made to standardize the area in question, it will either assign the project to an existing X3 technical committee (who may have been the "somebody" who wrote the SD-3 in the first place) or recommend the formation of a new technical committee to do the work.

The TC responsible for the project then produces a working draft of the standard (indeed, many SD-3s are accompanied by a proposed working draft, which considerably accelerates the work). At some point, the committee conducts a formal ballot to decide if the working draft is ready for broader review. This decision requires a ballot agreement of at least two-thirds of the committee. If ready, the TC asks X3 to approve the initiation of a public review of the document. The purpose of a public review is to permit the general public, in the United States and elsewhere, to review the document and comment on it. The TC is required to respond to every comment within a relatively short period following a public review (although they are obviously not required to satisfy every request!).

The document may iterate through several cycles of development and public review. At some point, though, the TC members will decide that the document is complete and will make no further changes as a result of public review comments. The document is then forwarded to BSR (the Board of Standard Review) for its review. BSR's review ensures that the ANSI and X3 rules have been followed and that no one has been deprived of due process. Assuming that these requirements have been met, the document is then published as an ANSI standard. X3's standards are published with an identifying number: X3.*n*, where X3 identifies the standard as coming from X3, and *n* identifies the *n*-th standard published by X3. In addition, the year of publication is attached to the number: X3.135-1986 is the number of the first version of the SQL standard, published in 1986.

F.2.2   International Standards

Once upon a time, when the world was a larger and simpler place to do business, national standards were quite sufficient for most people's purposes. In fact, one often found that ANSI developed a standard for some area of information processing technology and other national standards bodies adopted the ANSI standard unchanged. This process occasionally worked the other way, too: ANSI sometimes adopted other countries' standards unchanged.

However, as the world became smaller and more complex, businesses and other users of information processing systems realized that they were faced with using products that had to conform to one standard in one country and a different standard in another country. That fact cost many organizations countless millions of dollars and untold difficulties. These organizations, and others who became aware of the problems, realized that only international standards would address their requirements. The International Organization for Standardization (ISO) was formed specifically to address these concerns.

Note: ISO was not the only such organization. The International Electrotechnical Commission (IEC) exists specifically to address international standards in the electrotechnical area (obvious, isn't it?); CCITT (Comité Consultatif International de Téléphone et Télégraph) exists to standardize communications issues (that's why you can telephone other countries!).

Like ANSI, ISO has far too broad a scope to permit actual work to be done at that level. Instead, ISO also assigns areas of work to technical committees (TCs). In some cases, such as information technology, the scope is still too broad, so subcommittees (SCs) are formed. In a few cases, the work is still too extensive, so working groups (WGs) are given the responsibility.

In ISO, work on information technology was assigned to TC97. This committee was later reorganized, in cooperation with IEC, as JTC1. An area of information technology called Open Systems Interconnect (or OSI) was divided into two groups; the responsibility for "Information Processing, Transfer, and Retrieval for OSI" was given to SC21. In turn, responsibility for database issues was given to WG3 (full title: ISO/IEC JTC1/SC21/WG3, where JTC1 stands for "Joint Technical Committee 1").

F.2.3   Standards Development in ISO

As you might expect, the ISO process is quite different from the ANSI process. In the former, only countries—that is, the standards body from each country—are allowed to vote at ISO meetings, to propose projects, or to raise issues. By contrast, in ANSI, individuals who attend meetings represent their employers or may even represent themselves. Of course, individual humans represent their countries at ISO meetings, but the decisions must have been previously coordinated in the national standards body. The United States is represented in ISO by ANSI, the UK by BSI, France by AFNOR, and so forth.

When some country believes that it's time to standardize some aspect of information technology, it raises an issue as a national position either directly with

ISO/IEC JTC1 or with one of the SCs, such as SC21, who (if approved at that level) forwards the request to JTC1. A JTC1 ballot is initiated to determine if JTC1 member countries believe that such a project should be initiated and if there is likely to be sufficient resources (read "active representation") to develop a standard based on the project. If enough countries agree (at least five countries must commit to participation in the development), then the work is assigned to an existing SC or, in some situations, a new SC is formed and the project assigned to it. The SC then decides whether the work can be done by the SC as a whole or whether it should be assigned to an existing or new WG for development.

As in ANSI, a working draft is developed (and may accompany the project proposal) by the assigned group. At some point, the group believes that the document is ready for wider review, so it distributes the document as a Working Draft (note the capital letters); the document still has no real formal standing at this point. However, the document may be formally registered as a Committee Draft (CD), which implies distribution at least throughout the SC participants. It also implies the initiation of a CD ballot. A successful CD ballot means that the document (after an editing meeting, at which ballot comments are resolved) progresses to become a Draft International Standard, or DIS. That, in turn, implies the initiation of a DIS ballot. If the CD ballot is unsuccessful (as a result of too many substantial changes, regardless of the actual vote), then the assigned group does more work and tries again. (Common wisdom says that a document that fails three CD ballots is probably dead in the water.) Once the document reaches DIS status, a DIS ballot is initiated (sometimes after doing a bit more editorial work, but not changing the document substantially). Again, if that ballot is unsuccessful, there may be more work and additional DIS ballots; indeed, the document may be pushed back to CD status or even WD status. However, a successful DIS ballot means that (after an editing meeting to resolve comments) the document is advanced to International Standard (IS) status and is forwarded to the ISO Central Secretariat (via the SC and TC or JTC responsible for it) for a review of the process used. If it passes this review, then the document is published with an ISO or ISO/IEC number. SQL, for example, was initially published as ISO 9075-1987. (Recently, ISO changed the convention so that a colon was used to separate the standard number from the year of publication, so that the next revision was ISO 9075:1989.)

Usually, this process works very well. SQL, for example, has been published both as an ANSI and an ISO standard. Except for such obvious matters as the standard number and references to other ANSI and ISO standards, the two publications are identical. This represents an ideal model of cooperation between a national standards group and the international process. Other standards have been less fortunate, and national bodies have developed standards that are incompatibly different from the international version.

F.3   History of the SQL Standard

In 1978, ANSI X3 SPARC recommended the formation of a new technical committee called X3H2; the project assigned to this new committee was the development of a data definition language for CODASYL databases (CODASYL = Common Data System Languages; CODASYL developed COBOL and also developed a specification for the network database model). It quickly became apparent to the participants of this TC that developing a DDL alone would not satisfy the requirements of the marketplace, so the scope of work was enlarged to include a data sublanguage for network databases. This language was called Database Language NDL (and it was broadly understood that NDL stood for "Network Database Language").

During development of NDL, it became apparent that the relational data model was increasingly important, so the DBSSG (q.v.) recommended a second project for the development of a relational database standard, and in 1982 that project was also assigned to X3H2. X3H2 decided to base the standard on the SQL database language, since it had been implemented by more than one vendor and appeared to be gaining widespread acceptance. For a couple of years, X3H2 "improved" SQL with many changes based on 20-20 hindsight, and, since a good many of those changes made the draft standard incompatible with SQL, the working name was changed to RDL, for "Relational Database Language." In 1984, the committee reassessed this effort and concluded that the changes it had made to the SQL specification did not in fact improve the language enough to justify the incompatibilities. The committee therefore decided to revert to the original SQL specifications. These specifications were refined somewhat and then published as the initial SQL standard in 1986. Subsequently, almost all of the improvements and generalizations that had been developed for RDL were added to SQL in the SQL92 revision; as it turned out, most of them could be accomplished in an upward compatible manner.

In about 1984, ISO TC97/SC5 (which previously had responsibility for programming languages, graphics, database languages, and various other areas) was reorganized along with TC97/SC16. Some of the projects were assigned to one new subcommittee—TC97/SC22 (programming languages)—while others were assigned to another new SC—TC97/SC21 (related to OSI). The database work went into SC21.

In fact, TC97/SC5 was already reviewing the NDL and RDL work as early as 1982. When SC21 was formed, the actual project assigned was titled "Data Definition Language" and was only later evolved into NDL. As ANSI X3H2 began serious development on RDL and, later, on SQL, TC97/SC21 also picked up that work.

These efforts resulted in the late 1986 publication of ANSI X3.135-1986, "Database Language SQL" in the United States. Because of differences in the process, it was early in 1987 before ISO published ISO 9075-1987, "Database Language SQL." This standard was very close to the IBM implementation, but with sufficient restrictions, escape hatches, and unspecified areas that it served as a sort of least common denominator for several implementations. Unfortunately, it left users with little ability to write meaningful applications that were portable among products from different vendors (indeed, IBM's several implementations were not completely compatible even among themselves).

This standard was defined to have two levels, called (cleverly enough) Level 1 and Level 2. Level 1 was designed to be an intersection of features that were already widely implemented by most SQL vendors, while Level 2 added a few additional features and relaxed some restrictions.

One significant comment in the various public reviews and ISO ballots was that the language was missing a very important feature: referential integrity (see Chapter 10). A compromise was reached that allowed the first version of SQL (often referred to as SQL-86 or, less often, SQL-87 because of the publication date) to go forward; the compromise required the rapid turnaround of a revised standard that included at least basic referential integrity.

Work had begun on that revision even before SQL-86 was published. However, because the TCs (and WGs) were unfamiliar with publishing revised standards and because both ANSI and ISO had undergone some reorganization, delays mounted until the so-called rapid turnaround became three years. It was thus mid-1989 when ISO published ISO 9075:1985, "Database Language SQL With Integrity Enhancement" and late 1989 when ANSI published the corresponding X3.135-1989.

Some U.S. government users were critical of SQL-86 because the specification of how to embed SQL in conventional programming languages was contained in an appendix that was explicitly "informative." These users worried that this fact might mean that portable implementations of embedded SQL wouldn't be supported because they weren't "normative" (required). These concerns caused X3H2 to develop a second standard that made the embedding specifications normative; that standard was published in 1989 as ANSI X3.168-1989, "Database Language Embedded SQL." ISO chose not to publish an analogous standard because of a lack of similar concerns in the international community. Unfortunately, this decision meant that ISO had no definition for embedding SQL into Ada or C until SQL-92 was published, while ANSI did.

SQL-89 retained the two levels of SQL-86. It also made the Integrity Enhancement Feature optional, so that vendors could claim conformance to the standard without having to implement that feature.

F.3.1 SQL2

Because of the delays in publishing SQL-89 (as it became known), work was already in full swing for a second revision of SQL by late 1987. This project, code-named "SQL2" by both X3H2 and ISO/IEC JTC1/SC21, was to define a major revision to the language, making it a more complete language instead of a least common denominator.

Work was completed on that project in late 1991 (though fine-tuning persisted into early 1992), and the document was published in late 1992 by ANSI as X3.135-1992, "Database Language SQL," and by ISO as ISO/IEC 9075:1992, "Database Language SQL." This book focuses on SQL-92, as it is commonly known, because it is a (nearly proper!) superset of SQL-89 and Embedded SQL.

F.4 NIST and the FIPS

In the United States, the federal government is a major user of computer systems, including database systems. Agencies of the U.S. federal government depend on the National Institute of Standards and Technology (NIST, formerly known as the

National Bureau of Standards, or NBS) to advise them on information technology procurements. In many cases, this advice takes the form of a Federal Information Processing Standard (FIPS).

A FIPS may specify a particular way to conform to an existing ANSI standard, or to an existing ISO standard, or it may define a completely independent specification itself. In the case of SQL, in early 1987 NIST wrote a FIPS that specified conformance to ANSI X3.135-1986. This FIPS was published as FIPS PUB 127 (PUB standing for "publication"). It ignored Level 1 of SQL-86 and required conformance to Level 2 of that standard.

In 1989, NIST published a revised FIPS called FIPS PUB 127-1, which specified conformance to Level 2 of X3.135-1989. Like the SQL-89 standard, FIPS PUB 127-1 specifies the Integrity Enhancement Feature as an optional feature. It also specifies the required minimum values for many elements of the language that the standard left as implementation-defined.

NIST published another revision in 1992, called FIPS PUB 127-2. That revision specifies conformance to ANSI X3.135-1992, with the emphasis on the Entry SQL level. It also specifies minimum values for additional implementation-defined elements as well as requiring additional "system tables" to document some aspects of the implementation. NIST has also developed a conformance test suite that allows it to test implementations that claim conformance to SQL-89. FIPS PUB 127-2 permits claims of conformance to the Intermediate SQL and Full SQL levels but does not provide additional requirements or clarification. NIST will probably publish future revisions of the FIPS that add such information. Additional test capabilities continue to be developed.

F.5 Other SQL-Related Organizations

So far, we've talked about the *de jure,* or formal, standards organizations that produce SQL standards. However, there are also several additional bodies that are concerned with SQL. These groups do not publish formal standards, but their work is sometimes referred to as a *de facto* standard because it gets widely implemented.

X/Open Company, Ltd. is a consortium of companies (initially Unix® system vendors) that publishes Portability Guides for many computer-related areas, including operating system interfaces (Unix®), programming languages (C and COBOL), networking, security, and data management. The X/Open Data Management Working Group is responsible for producing the XPG (XPG = X/Open Portability Guide) text for SQL. The fourth generation of these guides (XPG4) was published late in 1992 and includes a definition of SQL closely based on the Entry SQL level of SQL-92, but with several extensions. These extensions are based on commonly implemented vendor extensions (such as CREATE INDEX and DROP INDEX) and several features of Intermediate SQL (such as the diagnostics area, the GET DIAGNOSTICS statement, and parts of dynamic SQL).

X/Open works closely with another consortium, called the SQL Access Group (SAG), in database-related matters (we mentioned SAG in Chapter 15 when discussing connections). SAG was formed to prototype the (then) emerging ISO standard for Remote Database Access (RDA); that work inevitably led to SQL-related questions and issues, so X/Open and SAG joined forces to update X/Open's SQL definition to better conform to the ANSI and ISO SQL-92 standards and to "fill in the blanks" where the ANSI and ISO standards left elements implementation-defined.

As mentioned in the preceding paragraph, ISO has produced a standard called "Remote Database Access," or "RDA" (ISO/IEC 9579-1, *Remote Database Access, Part 1: Generic,* and ISO/IEC 9579-2, *Remote Database Access, Part 2: SQL Specialization*). This standard specifies the formats and protocols for accessing an SQL database system across an OSI (Open Systems Interconnect) network. The 1992 version of RDA supports Entry SQL-92; future work will support Intermediate and Full SQL-92 as well as future versions of the SQL standard.

We should also point out that, although SQL defines language for metadata operations (CREATE, ALTER, and DROP) and a place where the metadata is "reflected" (the information and definition schemas, which we discussed in Chapter 19), you shouldn't look at SQL as the answer to all data dictionary or repository questions. ANSI X3H4 has produced a standard called IRDS that addresses repository issues without using SQL at all. ISO/IEC JTC1/SC21/WG3 has produced a *different* standard, also called IRDS, that addresses repository issues, but with a close relationship to SQL (in fact, it uses SQL language in many places for the definition). At present, these standards are incompatibly different, but both groups are working closely to develop a new standard (IRDS2) that will be the same in both bodies—which has to be good for the vendors and the users of repositories.

F.6 Appendix Summary

As we mentioned at the outset of this appendix, you don't need to know much about the background and history of SQL, nor about the standards process, to use SQL-92. You can, however, amaze your friends and co-workers with your in-depth knowledge about the standards process. Who knows, you may even get elected (or drafted) to participate in a standards development process.

APPENDIX G

. . . .

The Complete SQL-92 Language

And finally, we present the Backus Naur Form (BNF) for the complete SQL-92 language. Please note that in the course of this presentation, we sometimes use the notation: !! See the Syntax Rules. This is relevant only if you have a copy of the SQL-92 standard and can examine the rules for the appropriate syntax element.

```
<SQL terminal character> ::=
      <SQL language character>
   | <SQL embedded language character>

<SQL language character> ::=
      <simple Latin letter>
   | <digit>
   | <SQL special character>

<simple Latin letter> ::=
      <simple Latin upper case letter>
   | <simple Latin lower case letter>

<simple Latin upper case letter> ::=
        A | B | C | D | E | F | G | H | I | J | K | L | M | N | O
    | P | Q | R | S | T | U | V | W | X | Y | Z

<simple Latin lower case letter> ::=
        a | b | c | d | e | f | g | h | i | j | k | l | m | n | o
    | p | q | r | s | t | u | v | w | x | y | z

<digit> ::=
    0 | 1 | 2 | 3 | 4 | 5 | 6 | 7 | 8 | 9

<SQL special character> ::=
      <space>
   | <double quote>
```

```
      | <percent>
      | <ampersand>
      | <quote>
      | <left paren>
      | <right paren>
      | <asterisk>
      | <plus sign>
      | <comma>
      | <minus sign>
      | <period>
      | <solidus>
      | <colon>
      | <semicolon>
      | <less than operator>
      | <equals operator>
      | <greater than operator>
      | <question mark>
      | <underscore>
      | <vertical bar>

<space> ::= !! space character in character set in use

<double quote> ::= "

<percent> ::= %

<ampersand> ::= &

<quote> ::= '

<left paren> ::= (

<right paren> ::= )

<asterisk> ::= *

<plus sign> ::= +

<comma> ::= ,

<minus sign> ::= -

<period> ::= .

<solidus> ::= /

<colon> ::= :

<semicolon> ::= ;

<less than operator> ::= <

<equals operator> ::= =

<greater than operator> ::= >
```

```
<question mark> ::= ?

<underscore> ::= _

<vertical bar> ::= |

<SQL embedded language character> ::=
      <left bracket>
    | <right bracket>

<left bracket> ::= [

<right bracket> ::= ]

<token> ::=
      <nondelimiter token>
    | <delimiter token>

<nondelimiter token> ::=
      <regular identifier>
    | <key word>
    | <unsigned numeric literal>
    | <national character string literal>
    | <bit string literal>
    | <hex string literal>

<regular identifier> ::= <identifier body>

<identifier body> ::=
    <identifier start> [ { <underscore> | <identifier part> }... ]

<identifier start> ::= !! See the Syntax Rules.

<identifier part> ::=
      <identifier start>
    | <digit>

<key word> ::=
      <reserved word>
    | <non-reserved word>

<reserved word> ::=
      ABSOLUTE | ACTION | ADD | ALL
    | ALLOCATE | ALTER | AND
    | ANY | ARE
    | AS | ASC
    | ASSERTION | AT
    | AUTHORIZATION | AVG

    | BEGIN | BETWEEN | BIT | BIT_LENGTH
    | BOTH | BY

    | CASCADE | CASCADED | CASE | CAST
    | CATALOG
    | CHAR | CHARACTER | CHAR_LENGTH
```

```
| CHARACTER_LENGTH | CHECK | CLOSE | COALESCE
| COLLATE | COLLATION
| COLUMN | COMMIT
| CONNECT
| CONNECTION | CONSTRAINT
| CONSTRAINTS | CONTINUE
| CONVERT | CORRESPONDING | COUNT | CREATE | CROSS
| CURRENT
| CURRENT_DATE | CURRENT_TIME
| CURRENT_TIMESTAMP | CURRENT_USER | CURSOR

| DATE | DAY | DEALLOCATE | DEC
| DECIMAL | DECLARE | DEFAULT | DEFERRABLE
| DEFERRED | DELETE | DESC | DESCRIBE | DESCRIPTOR
| DIAGNOSTICS
| DISCONNECT | DISTINCT | DOMAIN | DOUBLE | DROP

| ELSE | END | END-EXEC | ESCAPE
| EXCEPT | EXCEPTION
| EXEC | EXECUTE | EXISTS
| EXTERNAL | EXTRACT

| FALSE | FETCH | FIRST | FLOAT | FOR
| FOREIGN | FOUND | FROM | FULL

| GET | GLOBAL | GO | GOTO
| GRANT | GROUP

| HAVING | HOUR

| IDENTITY | IMMEDIATE | IN | INDICATOR
| INITIALLY | INNER | INPUT
| INSENSITIVE | INSERT | INT | INTEGER | INTERSECT
| INTERVAL | INTO | IS
| ISOLATION

| JOIN

| KEY

| LANGUAGE | LAST | LEADING | LEFT
| LEVEL | LIKE | LOCAL | LOWER

| MATCH | MAX | MIN | MINUTE | MODULE
| MONTH

| NAMES | NATIONAL | NATURAL | NCHAR | NEXT | NO
| NOT | NULL
| NULLIF | NUMERIC

| OCTET_LENGTH | OF
| ON | ONLY | OPEN | OPTION | OR
| ORDER | OUTER
| OUTPUT | OVERLAPS
```

    | PAD | PARTIAL | POSITION | PRECISION | PREPARE
    | PRESERVE | PRIMARY
    | PRIOR | PRIVILEGES | PROCEDURE | PUBLIC

    | READ | REAL | REFERENCES | RELATIVE | RESTRICT
    | REVOKE | RIGHT
    | ROLLBACK | ROWS

    | SCHEMA | SCROLL | SECOND | SECTION
    | SELECT
    | SESSION | SESSION_USER | SET
    | SIZE | SMALLINT | SOME | SPACE | SQL | SQLCODE
    | SQLERROR | SQLSTATE
    | SUBSTRING | SUM | SYSTEM_USER

    | TABLE | TEMPORARY
    | THEN | TIME | TIMESTAMP
    | TIMEZONE_HOUR | TIMEZONE_MINUTE
    | TO | TRAILING | TRANSACTION
    | TRANSLATE | TRANSLATION | TRIM | TRUE

    | UNION | UNIQUE | UNKNOWN | UPDATE | UPPER | USAGE
    | USER | USING

    | VALUE | VALUES | VARCHAR | VARYING | VIEW

    | WHEN | WHENEVER | WHERE | WITH | WORK | WRITE

    | YEAR

    | ZONE

<non-reserved word> ::=
      ADA

    | C | CATALOG_NAME
    | CHARACTER_SET_CATALOG | CHARACTER_SET_NAME
    | CHARACTER_SET_SCHEMA | CLASS_ORIGIN | COBOL | COLLATION_CATALOG
    | COLLATION_NAME | COLLATION_SCHEMA | COLUMN_NAME | COMMAND_FUNCTION
    | COMMITTED
    | CONDITION_NUMBER | CONNECTION_NAME | CONSTRAINT_CATALOG | CONSTRAINT_NAME
    | CONSTRAINT_SCHEMA | CURSOR_NAME

    | DATA | DATETIME_INTERVAL_CODE
    | DATETIME_INTERVAL_PRECISION | DYNAMIC_FUNCTION

    | FORTRAN

    | LENGTH

    | MESSAGE_LENGTH | MESSAGE_OCTET_LENGTH | MESSAGE_TEXT | MORE | MUMPS

    | NAME | NULLABLE | NUMBER

    | PASCAL | PLI

```
      | REPEATABLE | RETURNED_LENGTH | RETURNED_OCTET_LENGTH | RETURNED_SQLSTATE
      | ROW_COUNT

      | SCALE | SCHEMA_NAME | SERIALIZABLE | SERVER_NAME | SUBCLASS_ORIGIN

      | TABLE_NAME | TYPE

      | UNCOMMITTED | UNNAMED

<unsigned numeric literal> ::=
      <exact numeric literal>
    | <approximate numeric literal>

<exact numeric literal> ::=
      <unsigned integer> [ <period> [ <unsigned integer> ] ]
    | <period> <unsigned integer>

<unsigned integer> ::= <digit>...

<approximate numeric literal> ::= <mantissa> E <exponent>

<mantissa> ::= <exact numeric literal>

<exponent> ::= <signed integer>

<signed integer> ::= [ <sign> ] <unsigned integer>

<sign> ::= <plus sign> | <minus sign>

<national character string literal> ::=
     N <quote> [ <character representation>... ] <quote>
       [ { <separator>... <quote> [ <character representation>... ] <quote> }... ]

<character representation> ::=
      <nonquote character>
    | <quote symbol>

<nonquote character> ::= !! See the Syntax Rules.

<quote symbol> ::= <quote><quote>

<separator> ::= { <comment> | <space> | <newline> }...

<comment> ::=
     <comment introducer> [ <comment character>... ] <newline>

<comment introducer> ::= <minus sign><minus sign>[<minus sign>...]

<comment character> ::=
      <nonquote character>
    | <quote>

<newline> ::= !! implementation-defined end-of-line indicator
```

```
<bit string literal> ::=
    B <quote> [ <bit>... ] <quote>
      [ { <separator>... <quote> [ <bit>... ] <quote> }... ]

<bit> ::= 0 | 1

<hex string literal> ::=
     X <quote> [ <hexit>... ] <quote>
      [ { <separator>... <quote> [ <hexit>... ] <quote> }... ]

<hexit> ::= <digit> | A | B | C | D | E | F | a | b | c | d | e | f

<delimiter token> ::=
      <character string literal>
    | <date string>
    | <time string>
    | <timestamp string>
    | <interval string>
    | <delimited identifier>
    | <SQL special character>
    | <not equals operator>
    | <greater than or equals operator>
    | <less than or equals operator>
    | <concatenation operator>
    | <double period>
    | <left bracket>
    | <right bracket>

<character string literal> ::=
    [ <introducer><character set specification> ]
    <quote> [ <character representation>... ] <quote>
      [ { <separator>... <quote> [ <character representation>... ] <quote> }... ]

<introducer> ::= <underscore>

<character set specification> ::=
      <standard character repertoire name>
    | <implementation-defined character repertoire name>
    | <user-defined character repertoire name>
    | <standard universal character form-of-use name>
    | <implementation-defined universal character form-of-use name>

<standard character repertoire name> ::= <character set name>

<character set name> ::= [ <schema name> <period> ] <SQL language identifier>

<schema name> ::=
    [ <catalog name> <period> ] <unqualified schema name>

<catalog name> ::= <identifier>

<identifier> ::=
    [ <introducer><character set specification> ] <actual identifier>
```

```
<actual identifier> ::=
      <regular identifier>
    | <delimited identifier>

<delimited identifier> ::=
    <double quote> <delimited identifier body> <double quote>

<delimited identifier body> ::= <delimited identifier part>...

<delimited identifier part> ::=
      <nondoublequote character>
    | <doublequote symbol>

<nondoublequote character> ::= !! See the Syntax Rules.

<doublequote symbol> ::= <double quote><double quote>

<unqualified schema name> ::= <identifier>

<SQL language identifier> ::=
    <SQL language identifier start>
      [ { <underscore> | <SQL language identifier part> }... ]

<SQL language identifier start> ::= <simple Latin letter>

<SQL language identifier part> ::=
      <simple Latin letter>
    | <digit>

<implementation-defined character repertoire name> ::=
    <character set name>

<user-defined character repertoire name> ::= <character set name>

<standard universal character form-of-use name> ::=
    <character set name>

<implementation-defined universal character form-of-use name> ::=
    <character set name>

<date string> ::=
    <quote> <date value> <quote>

<date value> ::=
    <years value> <minus sign> <months value> <minus sign> <days value>

<years value> ::= <datetime value>

<datetime value> ::= <unsigned integer>

<months value> ::= <datetime value>

<days value> ::= <datetime value>
```

```
<time string> ::=
    <quote> <time value> [ <time zone interval> ] <quote>

<time value> ::=
    <hours value> <colon> <minutes value> <colon> <seconds value>

<hours value> ::= <datetime value>

<minutes value> ::= <datetime value>

<seconds value> ::=
      <seconds integer value> [ <period> [ <seconds fraction> ] ]

<seconds integer value> ::= <unsigned integer>

<seconds fraction> ::= <unsigned integer>

<time zone interval> ::=
    <sign> <hours value> <colon> <minutes value>

<timestamp string> ::=
    <quote> <date value> <space> <time value>
        [ <time zone interval> ] <quote>

<interval string> ::=
    <quote> { <year-month literal> | <day-time literal> } <quote>

<year-month literal> ::=
      <years value>
    | [ <years value> <minus sign> ] <months value>

<day-time literal> ::=
      <day-time interval>
    | <time interval>

<day-time interval> ::=
    <days value>
      [ <space> <hours value> [ <colon> <minutes value> ]
        [ <colon> <seconds value> ] ] ]

<time interval> ::=
      <hours value> [ <colon> <minutes value> [ <colon> <seconds value> ] ]
    | <minutes value> [ <colon> <seconds value> ]
    | <seconds value>

<not equals operator> ::= <>

<greater than or equals operator> ::= >=

<less than or equals operator> ::= <=

<concatenation operator> ::= ||

<double period> ::= ..
```

```
<module> ::=
    <module name clause>
    <language clause>
    <module authorization clause>
    [ <temporary table declaration>... ]
    <module contents>...

<module name clause> ::=
    MODULE [ <module name> ]
      [ <module character set specification> ]

<module name> ::= <identifier>

<module character set specification> ::=
    NAMES ARE <character set specification>

<language clause> ::=
    LANGUAGE <language name>

<language name> ::=
    ADA | C | COBOL | FORTRAN | MUMPS | PASCAL | PLI

<module authorization clause> ::=
      SCHEMA <schema name>
    | AUTHORIZATION <module authorization identifier>
    | SCHEMA <schema name>
          AUTHORIZATION <module authorization identifier>

<module authorization identifier> ::=
    <authorization identifier>

<authorization identifier> ::= <identifier>

<temporary table declaration> ::=
    DECLARE LOCAL TEMPORARY TABLE
        <qualified local table name>
      <table element list>
      [ ON COMMIT { PRESERVE | DELETE } ROWS ]

<qualified local table name> ::=
    MODULE <period> <local table name>

<local table name> ::= <qualified identifier>

<qualified identifier> ::= <identifier>

<table element list> ::=
      <left paren> <table element> [ { <comma> <table element> }... ] <right paren>

<table element> ::=
      <column definition>
    | <table constraint definition>

<column definition> ::=
    <column name> { <data type> | <domain name> }
    [ <default clause> ]
```

```
      [ <column constraint definition>... ]
      [ <collate clause> ]

<column name> ::= <identifier>

<data type> ::=
        <character string type>
            [ CHARACTER SET <character set specification> ]
      | <national character string type>
      | <bit string type>
      | <numeric type>
      | <datetime type>
      | <interval type>

<character string type> ::=
        CHARACTER [ <left paren> <length> <right paren> ]
      | CHAR [ <left paren> <length> <right paren> ]
      | CHARACTER VARYING <left paren> <length> <right paren>
      | CHAR VARYING <left paren> <length> <right paren>
      | VARCHAR <left paren> <length> <right paren>

<length> ::= <unsigned integer>

<national character string type> ::=
        NATIONAL CHARACTER [ <left paren> <length> <right paren> ]
      | NATIONAL CHAR [ <left paren> <length> <right paren> ]
      | NCHAR [ <left paren> <length> <right paren> ]
      | NATIONAL CHARACTER VARYING <left paren> <length> <right paren>
      | NATIONAL CHAR VARYING <left paren> <length> <right paren>
      | NCHAR VARYING <left paren> <length> <right paren>

<bit string type> ::=
        BIT [ <left paren> <length> <right paren> ]
      | BIT VARYING <left paren> <length> <right paren>

<numeric type> ::=
        <exact numeric type>
      | <approximate numeric type>

<exact numeric type> ::=
        NUMERIC [ <left paren> <precision> [ <comma> <scale> ] <right paren> ]
      | DECIMAL [ <left paren> <precision> [ <comma> <scale> ] <right paren> ]
      | DEC [ <left paren> <precision> [ <comma> <scale> ] <right paren> ]
      | INTEGER
      | INT
      | SMALLINT

<precision> ::= <unsigned integer>

<scale> ::= <unsigned integer>

<approximate numeric type> ::=
        FLOAT [ <left paren> <precision> <right paren> ]
      | REAL
      | DOUBLE PRECISION
```

```
<datetime type> ::=
      DATE
    | TIME [ <left paren> <time precision> <right paren> ]
          [ WITH TIME ZONE ]
    | TIMESTAMP [ <left paren> <timestamp precision> <right paren> ]
          [ WITH TIME ZONE ]

<time precision> ::= <time fractional seconds precision>

<time fractional seconds precision> ::= <unsigned integer>

<timestamp precision> ::= <time fractional seconds precision>

<interval type> ::= INTERVAL <interval qualifier>

<interval qualifier> ::=
        <start field> TO <end field>
    | <single datetime field>

<start field> ::=
      <non-second datetime field>
        [ <left paren> <interval leading field precision> <right paren> ]

<non-second datetime field> ::= YEAR | MONTH | DAY | HOUR | MINUTE

<interval leading field precision> ::= <unsigned integer>

<end field> ::=
        <non-second datetime field>
    | SECOND [ <left paren> <interval fractional seconds precision> <right paren> ]

<interval fractional seconds precision> ::= <unsigned integer>

<single datetime field> ::=
        <non-second datetime field>
            [ <left paren> <interval leading field precision> <right paren> ]
    | SECOND [ <left paren> <interval leading field precision>
            [ <comma> <interval fractional seconds precision> ] <right paren> ]

<domain name> ::= <qualified name>

<qualified name> ::=
    [ <schema name> <period> ] <qualified identifier>

<default clause> ::=
        DEFAULT <default option>

<default option> ::=
        <literal>
    | <datetime value function>
    | USER
    | CURRENT_USER
    | SESSION_USER
    | SYSTEM_USER
    | NULL
```

```
<literal> ::=
      <signed numeric literal>
    | <general literal>

<signed numeric literal> ::=
    [ <sign> ] <unsigned numeric literal>

<general literal> ::=
      <character string literal>
    | <national character string literal>
    | <bit string literal>
    | <hex string literal>
    | <datetime literal>
    | <interval literal>

<datetime literal> ::=
      <date literal>
    | <time literal>
    | <timestamp literal>

<date literal> ::=
    DATE <date string>

<time literal> ::=
    TIME <time string>

<timestamp literal> ::=
    TIMESTAMP <timestamp string>

<interval literal> ::=
    INTERVAL [ <sign> ] <interval string> <interval qualifier>

<datetime value function> ::=
      <current date value function>
    | <current time value function>
    | <current timestamp value function>

<current date value function> ::= CURRENT_DATE

<current time value function> ::=
      CURRENT_TIME [ <left paren> <time precision> <right paren> ]

<current timestamp value function> ::=
      CURRENT_TIMESTAMP [ <left paren> <timestamp precision> <right paren> ]

<column constraint definition> ::=
    [ <constraint name definition> ]
    <column constraint>
      [ <constraint attributes> ]

<constraint name definition> ::= CONSTRAINT <constraint name>

<constraint name> ::= <qualified name>
```

```
<column constraint> ::=
      NOT NULL
    | <unique specification>
    | <references specification>
    | <check constraint definition>

<unique specification> ::=
    UNIQUE | PRIMARY KEY

<references specification> ::=
    REFERENCES <referenced table and columns>
      [ MATCH <match type> ]
      [ <referential triggered action> ]

<referenced table and columns> ::=
      <table name> [ <left paren> <reference column list> <right paren> ]

<table name> ::=
      <qualified name>
    | <qualified local table name>

<reference column list> ::= <column name list>

<column name list> ::=
    <column name> [ { <comma> <column name> }... ]

<match type> ::=
      FULL
    | PARTIAL

<referential triggered action> ::=
      <update rule> [ <delete rule> ]
    | <delete rule> [ <update rule> ]

<update rule> ::= ON UPDATE <referential action>

<referential action> ::=
      CASCADE
    | SET NULL
    | SET DEFAULT
    | NO ACTION

<delete rule> ::= ON DELETE <referential action>

<check constraint definition> ::=
    CHECK
        <left paren> <search condition> <right paren>

<search condition> ::=
      <boolean term>
    | <search condition> OR <boolean term>

<boolean term> ::=
      <boolean factor>
    | <boolean term> AND <boolean factor>
```

```
<boolean factor> ::=
    [ NOT ] <boolean test>

<boolean test> ::=
    <boolean primary> [ IS [ NOT ] <truth value> ]

<boolean primary> ::=
      <predicate>
    | <left paren> <search condition> <right paren>

<predicate> ::=
      <comparison predicate>
    | <between predicate>
    | <in predicate>
    | <like predicate>
    | <null predicate>
    | <quantified comparison predicate>
    | <exists predicate>
    | <unique predicate>
    | <match predicate>
    | <overlaps predicate>

<comparison predicate> ::=
    <row value constructor> <comp op>
        <row value constructor>

<row value constructor> ::=
      <row value constructor element>
    | <left paren> <row value constructor list> <right paren>
    | <row subquery>

<row value constructor element> ::=
      <value expression>
    | <null specification>
    | <default specification>

<value expression> ::=
      <numeric value expression>
    | <string value expression>
    | <datetime value expression>
    | <interval value expression>

<numeric value expression> ::=
      <term>
    | <numeric value expression> <plus sign> <term>
    | <numeric value expression> <minus sign> <term>

<term> ::=
      <factor>
    | <term> <asterisk> <factor>
    | <term> <solidus> <factor>

<factor> ::=
    [ <sign> ] <numeric primary>
```

```
<numeric primary> ::=
      <value expression primary>
    | <numeric value function>

<value expression primary> ::=
      <unsigned value specification>
    | <column reference>
    | <set function specification>
    | <scalar subquery>
    | <case expression>
    | <left paren> <value expression> <right paren>
    | <cast specification>

<unsigned value specification> ::=
      <unsigned literal>
    | <general value specification>

<unsigned literal> ::=
      <unsigned numeric literal>
    | <general literal>

<general value specification> ::=
      <parameter specification>
    | <dynamic parameter specification>
    | <variable specification>
    | USER
    | CURRENT_USER
    | SESSION_USER
    | SYSTEM_USER
    | VALUE

<parameter specification> ::=
    <parameter name> [ <indicator parameter> ]

<parameter name> ::= <colon> <identifier>

<indicator parameter> ::=
    [ INDICATOR ] <parameter name>

<dynamic parameter specification> ::= <question mark>

<variable specification> ::=
    <embedded variable name> [ <indicator variable> ]

<embedded variable name> ::=
    <colon><host identifier>

<host identifier> ::=
      <Ada host identifier>
    | <C host identifier>
    | <COBOL host identifier>
    | <Fortran host identifier>
    | <MUMPS host identifier>
    | <Pascal host identifier>
    | <PL/I host identifier>
```

```
<Ada host identifier> ::= !! See the Syntax Rules.

<C host identifier> ::= !! See the Syntax Rules.

<COBOL host identifier> ::= !! See the Syntax Rules.

<Fortran host identifier> ::= !! See the Syntax Rules.

<MUMPS host identifier> ::= !! See the Syntax Rules.

<Pascal host identifier> ::= !! See the Syntax Rules.

<PL/I host identifier> ::= !! See the Syntax Rules.

<indicator variable> ::=
    [ INDICATOR ] <embedded variable name>

<column reference> ::= [ <qualifier> <period> ] <column name>

<qualifier> ::=
      <table name>
    | <correlation name>

<correlation name> ::= <identifier>

<set function specification> ::=
      COUNT <left paren> <asterisk> <right paren>
    | <general set function>

<general set function> ::=
      <set function type>
          <left paren> [ <set quantifier> ] <value expression> <right paren>

<set function type> ::= AVG | MAX | MIN | SUM | COUNT

<set quantifier> ::= DISTINCT | ALL

<scalar subquery> ::= <subquery>

<subquery> ::= <left paren> <query expression> <right paren>

<query expression> ::=
      <non-join query expression>
    | <joined table>

<non-join query expression> ::=
      <non-join query term>
    | <query expression> UNION [ ALL ]
        [ <corresponding spec> ] <query term>
    | <query expression> EXCEPT [ ALL ]
        [ <corresponding spec> ] <query term>

<non-join query term> ::=
      <non-join query primary>
    | <query term> INTERSECT [ ALL ]
        [ <corresponding spec> ] <query primary>
```

```
<non-join query primary> ::=
      <simple table>
    | <left paren> <non-join query expression> <right paren>

<simple table> ::=
      <query specification>
    | <table value constructor>
    | <explicit table>

<query specification> ::=
    SELECT [ <set quantifier> ] <select list> <table expression>

<select list> ::=
      <asterisk>
    | <select sublist> [ { <comma> <select sublist> }... ]

<select sublist> ::=
      <derived column>
    | <qualifier> <period> <asterisk>

<derived column> ::= <value expression> [ <as clause> ]

<as clause> ::= [ AS ] <column name>

<table expression> ::=
    <from clause>
    [ <where clause> ]
    [ <group by clause> ]
    [ <having clause> ]

<from clause> ::= FROM <table reference>
    [ { <comma> <table reference> }... ]

<table reference> ::=
      <table name> [ [ AS ] <correlation name>
          [ <left paren> <derived column list> <right paren> ] ]
    | <derived table> [ AS ] <correlation name>
          [ <left paren> <derived column list> <right paren> ]
    | <joined table>

<derived column list> ::= <column name list>

<derived table> ::= <table subquery>

<table subquery> ::= <subquery>

<joined table> ::=
      <cross join>
    | <qualified join>
    | <left paren> <joined table> <right paren>

<cross join> ::=
    <table reference> CROSS JOIN <table reference>
```

```
<qualified join> ::=
    <table reference> [ NATURAL ] [ <join type> ] JOIN
        <table reference> [ <join specification> ]

<join type> ::=
        INNER
    | <outer join type> [ OUTER ]
    | UNION

<outer join type> ::=
        LEFT
    | RIGHT
    | FULL

<join specification> ::=
        <join condition>
    | <named columns join>

<join condition> ::= ON <search condition>

<named columns join> ::=
    USING <left paren> <join column list> <right paren>

<join column list> ::= <column name list>

<where clause> ::= WHERE <search condition>

<group by clause> ::=
    GROUP BY <grouping column reference list>

<grouping column reference list> ::=
    <grouping column reference>
        [ { <comma> <grouping column reference> }... ]

<grouping column reference> ::=
    <column reference> [ <collate clause> ]

<collate clause> ::= COLLATE <collation name>

<collation name> ::= <qualified name>

<having clause> ::= HAVING <search condition>

<table value constructor> ::=
    VALUES <table value constructor list>

<table value constructor list> ::=
    <row value constructor> [ { <comma> <row value constructor> }... ]

<explicit table> ::= TABLE <table name>

<query term> ::=
        <non-join query term>
    | <joined table>
```

```
<corresponding spec> ::=
    CORRESPONDING [ BY <left paren> <corresponding column list> <right paren> ]

<corresponding column list> ::= <column name list>

<query primary> ::=
      <non-join query primary>
    | <joined table>

<case expression> ::=
      <case abbreviation>
    | <case specification>

<case abbreviation> ::=
      NULLIF <left paren> <value expression> <comma>
          <value expression> <right paren>
    | COALESCE <left paren> <value expression>
          { <comma> <value expression> }... <right paren>

<case specification> ::=
      <simple case>
    | <searched case>

<simple case> ::=
    CASE <case operand>
      <simple when clause>...
    [ <else clause> ]
    END

<case operand> ::= <value expression>

<simple when clause> ::= WHEN <when operand> THEN <result>

<when operand> ::= <value expression>

<result> ::= <result expression> | NULL

<result expression> ::= <value expression>

<else clause> ::= ELSE <result>

<searched case> ::=
    CASE
      <searched when clause>...
    [ <else clause> ]
    END

<searched when clause> ::= WHEN <search condition> THEN <result>

<cast specification> ::=
    CAST <left paren> <cast operand> AS
        <cast target> <right paren>

<cast operand> ::=
      <value expression>
    | NULL
```

```
<cast target> ::=
     <domain name>
   | <data type>

<numeric value function> ::=
     <position expression>
   | <extract expression>
   | <length expression>

<position expression> ::=
    POSITION <left paren> <character value expression>
       IN <character value expression> <right paren>

<character value expression> ::=
     <concatenation>
   | <character factor>

<concatenation> ::=
    <character value expression> <concatenation operator>
       <character factor>

<character factor> ::=
    <character primary> [ <collate clause> ]

<character primary> ::=
     <value expression primary>
   | <string value function>

<string value function> ::=
     <character value function>
   | <bit value function>

<character value function> ::=
     <character substring function>
   | <fold>
   | <form-of-use conversion>
   | <character translation>
   | <trim function>

<character substring function> ::=
    SUBSTRING <left paren> <character value expression> FROM <start position>
              [ FOR <string length> ] <right paren>

<start position> ::= <numeric value expression>

<string length> ::= <numeric value expression>

<fold> ::= { UPPER | LOWER }
     <left paren> <character value expression> <right paren>

<form-of-use conversion> ::=
    CONVERT <left paren> <character value expression>
       USING <form-of-use conversion name> <right paren>

<form-of-use conversion name> ::= <qualified name>
```

```
<character translation> ::=
    TRANSLATE <left paren> <character value expression>
        USING <translation name> <right paren>

<translation name> ::= <qualified name>

<trim function> ::=
    TRIM <left paren> <trim operands> <right paren>

<trim operands> ::=
    [ [ <trim specification> ] [ <trim character> ] FROM ] <trim source>

<trim specification> ::=
      LEADING
    | TRAILING
    | BOTH

<trim character> ::= <character value expression>

<trim source> ::= <character value expression>

<bit value function> ::=
    <bit substring function>

<bit substring function> ::=
    SUBSTRING <left paren> <bit value expression> FROM <start position>
        [ FOR <string length> ] <right paren>

<bit value expression> ::=
      <bit concatenation>
    | <bit factor>

<bit concatenation> ::=
    <bit value expression> <concatenation operator> <bit factor>

<bit factor> ::= <bit primary>

<bit primary> ::=
      <value expression primary>
    | <string value function>

<extract expression> ::=
    EXTRACT <left paren> <extract field>
        FROM <extract source> <right paren>

<extract field> ::=
      <datetime field>
    | <time zone field>

<datetime field> ::=
      <non-second datetime field>
    | SECOND

<time zone field> ::=
      TIMEZONE_HOUR
    | TIMEZONE_MINUTE
```

```
<extract source> ::=
      <datetime value expression>
    | <interval value expression>

<datetime value expression> ::=
      <datetime term>
    | <interval value expression> <plus sign> <datetime term>
    | <datetime value expression> <plus sign> <interval term>
    | <datetime value expression> <minus sign> <interval term>

<interval term> ::=
      <interval factor>
    | <interval term 2> <asterisk> <factor>
    | <interval term 2> <solidus> <factor>
    | <term> <asterisk> <interval factor>

<interval factor> ::=
    [ <sign> ] <interval primary>

<interval primary> ::=
      <value expression primary> [ <interval qualifier> ]

<interval term 2> ::= <interval term>

<interval value expression> ::=
      <interval term>
    | <interval value expression 1> <plus sign> <interval term 1>
    | <interval value expression 1> <minus sign> <interval term 1>
    | <left paren> <datetime value expression> <minus sign>
          <datetime term> <right paren> <interval qualifier>

<interval value expression 1> ::= <interval value expression>

<interval term 1> ::= <interval term>

<datetime term> ::=
      <datetime factor>

<datetime factor> ::=
      <datetime primary> [ <time zone> ]

<datetime primary> ::=
      <value expression primary>
    | <datetime value function>

<time zone> ::=
    AT <time zone specifier>

<time zone specifier> ::=
      LOCAL
    | TIME ZONE <interval value expression>

<length expression> ::=
      <char length expression>
    | <octet length expression>
    | <bit length expression>
```

```
<char length expression> ::=
    { CHAR_LENGTH | CHARACTER_LENGTH }
        <left paren> <string value expression> <right paren>

<string value expression> ::=
        <character value expression>
    | <bit value expression>

<octet length expression> ::=
    OCTET_LENGTH <left paren> <string value expression> <right paren>

<bit length expression> ::=
    BIT_LENGTH <left paren> <string value expression> <right paren>

<null specification> ::=
    NULL

<default specification> ::=
    DEFAULT

<row value constructor list> ::=
    <row value constructor element>
        [ { <comma> <row value constructor element> }... ]

<row subquery> ::= <subquery>

<comp op> ::=
        <equals operator>
    | <not equals operator>
    | <less than operator>
    | <greater than operator>
    | <less than or equals operator>
    | <greater than or equals operator>

<between predicate> ::=
    <row value constructor> [ NOT ] BETWEEN
        <row value constructor> AND <row value constructor>

<in predicate> ::=
    <row value constructor>
        [ NOT ] IN <in predicate value>

<in predicate value> ::=
        <table subquery>
    | <left paren> <in value list> <right paren>

<in value list> ::=
    <value expression> { <comma> <value expression> }...

<like predicate> ::=
    <match value> [ NOT ] LIKE <pattern>
        [ ESCAPE <escape character> ]

<match value> ::= <character value expression>
```

```
<pattern> ::= <character value expression>

<escape character> ::= <character value expression>

<null predicate> ::= <row value constructor>
    IS [ NOT ] NULL

<quantified comparison predicate> ::=
    <row value constructor> <comp op> <quantifier> <table subquery>

<quantifier> ::= <all> | <some>

<all> ::= ALL

<some> ::= SOME | ANY

<exists predicate> ::= EXISTS <table subquery>

<unique predicate> ::= UNIQUE <table subquery>

<match predicate> ::=
    <row value constructor> MATCH [ UNIQUE ]
        [ PARTIAL | FULL ] <table subquery>

<overlaps predicate> ::=
    <row value constructor 1> OVERLAPS <row value constructor 2>

<row value constructor 1> ::= <row value constructor>

<row value constructor 2> ::= <row value constructor>

<truth value> ::=
      TRUE
    | FALSE
    | UNKNOWN

<constraint attributes> ::=
      <constraint check time> [ [ NOT ] DEFERRABLE ]
    | [ NOT ] DEFERRABLE [ <constraint check time> ]

<constraint check time> ::=
      INITIALLY DEFERRED
    | INITIALLY IMMEDIATE

<table constraint definition> ::=
    [ <constraint name definition> ]
    <table constraint> [ <constraint attributes> ]

<table constraint> ::=
      <unique constraint definition>
    | <referential constraint definition>
    | <check constraint definition>

<unique constraint definition> ::=
    <unique specification> <left paren> <unique column list> <right paren>
```

```
<unique column list> ::= <column name list>

<referential constraint definition> ::=
    FOREIGN KEY
        <left paren> <referencing columns> <right paren>
      <references specification>

<referencing columns> ::=
    <reference column list>

<module contents> ::=
        <declare cursor>
    | <dynamic declare cursor>
    | <procedure>

<declare cursor> ::=
    DECLARE <cursor name> [ INSENSITIVE ] [ SCROLL ] CURSOR
      FOR <cursor specification>

<cursor name> ::= <identifier>

<cursor specification> ::=
    <query expression> [ <order by clause> ]
      [ <updatability clause> ]

<order by clause> ::=
    ORDER BY <sort specification list>

<sort specification list> ::=
    <sort specification> [ { <comma> <sort specification> }... ]

<sort specification> ::=
    <sort key> [ <collate clause> ] [ <ordering specification> ]

<sort key> ::=
        <column name>
    | <unsigned integer>

<ordering specification> ::= ASC | DESC

<updatability clause> ::=
    FOR { READ ONLY | UPDATE [ OF <column name list> ] }

<dynamic declare cursor> ::=
    DECLARE <cursor name> [ INSENSITIVE ] [ SCROLL ] CURSOR
        FOR <statement name>

<statement name> ::= <identifier>

<procedure> ::=
    PROCEDURE <procedure name>
        <parameter declaration list> <semicolon>
      <SQL procedure statement> <semicolon>

<procedure name> ::= <identifier>
```

```
<parameter declaration list> ::=
      <left paren> <parameter declaration>
          [ { <comma> <parameter declaration> }... ] <right paren>
    | <parameter declaration>...

<parameter declaration> ::=
      <parameter name> <data type>
    | <status parameter>

<status parameter> ::=
    SQLCODE | SQLSTATE

<SQL procedure statement> ::=
      <SQL schema statement>
    | <SQL data statement>
    | <SQL transaction statement>
    | <SQL connection statement>
    | <SQL session statement>
    | <SQL dynamic statement>
    | <SQL diagnostics statement>

<SQL schema statement> ::=
      <SQL schema definition statement>
    | <SQL schema manipulation statement>

<SQL schema definition statement> ::=
      <schema definition>
    | <table definition>
    | <view definition>
    | <grant statement>
    | <domain definition>
    | <character set definition>
    | <collation definition>
    | <translation definition>
    | <assertion definition>

<schema definition> ::=
    CREATE SCHEMA <schema name clause>
      [ <schema character set specification> ]
      [ <schema element>... ]

<schema name clause> ::=
      <schema name>
    | AUTHORIZATION <schema authorization identifier>
    | <schema name> AUTHORIZATION <schema authorization identifier>

<schema authorization identifier> ::= <authorization identifier>

<schema character set specification> ::=
DEFAULT CHARACTER SET <character set specification>

<schema element> ::=
      <domain definition>
    | <table definition>
    | <view definition>
```

```
    | <grant statement>
    | <assertion definition>
    | <character set definition>
    | <collation definition>
    | <translation definition>

<domain definition> ::=
    CREATE DOMAIN <domain name> [ AS ] <data type>
      [ <default clause> ]
      [ <domain constraint>... ]
      [ <collate clause> ]

<domain constraint> ::=
    [ <constraint name definition> ]
    <check constraint definition> [ <constraint attributes> ]

<table definition> ::=
    CREATE [ { GLOBAL | LOCAL } TEMPORARY ] TABLE <table name>
      <table element list>
      [ ON COMMIT { DELETE | PRESERVE } ROWS ]

<view definition> ::=
    CREATE VIEW <table name> [ <left paren> <view column list> <right paren> ]
      AS <query expression>
      [ WITH [ <levels clause> ] CHECK OPTION ]

<view column list> ::= <column name list>

<levels clause> ::= CASCADED | LOCAL

<grant statement> ::=
    GRANT <privileges> ON <object name>
      TO <grantee> [ { <comma> <grantee> }... ]
        [ WITH GRANT OPTION ]

<privileges> ::=
        ALL PRIVILEGES
      | <action list>

<action list> ::= <action> [ { <comma> <action> }... ]

<action> ::=
        SELECT
      | DELETE
      | INSERT [ <left paren> <privilege column list> <right paren> ]
      | UPDATE [ <left paren> <privilege column list> <right paren> ]
      | REFERENCES [ <left paren> <privilege column list> <right paren> ]
      | USAGE

<privilege column list> ::= <column name list>

<object name> ::=
        [ TABLE ] <table name>
      | DOMAIN <domain name>
      | COLLATION <collation name>
```

```
        | CHARACTER SET <character set name>
        | TRANSLATION <translation name>

<grantee> ::=
        PUBLIC
      | <authorization identifier>

<assertion definition> ::=
        CREATE ASSERTION <constraint name> <assertion check>
          [ <constraint attributes> ]

<assertion check> ::=
        CHECK <left paren> <search condition> <right paren>

<character set definition> ::=
        CREATE CHARACTER SET <character set name>
          [ AS ] <character set source>
          [ <collate clause> | <limited collation definition> ]

<character set source> ::=
        GET <existing character set name>

<existing character set name> ::=
        <standard character repertoire name>
      | <implementation-defined character repertoire name>
      | <schema character set name>

<schema character set name> ::= <character set name>

<limited collation definition> ::=
        COLLATION FROM <collation source>

<collation source> ::=
        <collating sequence definition>
      | <translation collation>

<collating sequence definition> ::=
        <external collation>
      | <schema collation name>
      | DESC <left paren> <collation name> <right paren>
      | DEFAULT

<external collation> ::=
        EXTERNAL <left paren> <quote> <external collation name> <quote> <right paren>

<external collation name> ::=
        <standard collation name>
      | <implementation-defined collation name>

<standard collation name> ::= <collation name>

<implementation-defined collation name> ::= <collation name>

<schema collation name> ::= <collation name>
```

```
<translation collation> ::=
    TRANSLATION <translation name>
        [ THEN COLLATION <collation name> ]

<collation definition> ::=
    CREATE COLLATION <collation name> FOR
        <character set specification>
      FROM <collation source>
        [ <pad attribute> ]

<pad attribute> ::=
      NO PAD
    | PAD SPACE

<translation definition> ::=
    CREATE TRANSLATION <translation name>
      FOR <source character set specification>
      TO <target character set specification>
      FROM <translation source>

<source character set specification> ::= <character set specification>

<target character set specification> ::= <character set specification>

<translation source> ::= <translation specification>

<translation specification> ::=
        <external translation>
      | IDENTITY
      | <schema translation name>

<external translation> ::=
    EXTERNAL <left paren> <quote> <external translation name> <quote> <right paren>

<external translation name> ::=
        <standard translation name>
      | <implementation-defined translation name>

<standard translation name> ::= <translation name>

<implementation-defined translation name> ::= <translation name>

<schema translation name> ::= <translation name>

<SQL schema manipulation statement> ::=
        <drop schema statement>
      | <alter table statement>
      | <drop table statement>
      | <drop view statement>
      | <revoke statement>
      | <alter domain statement>
      | <drop domain statement>
      | <drop character set statement>
      | <drop collation statement>
      | <drop translation statement>
      | <drop assertion statement>
```

```
<drop schema statement> ::=
    DROP SCHEMA <schema name> <drop behavior>

<drop behavior> ::= CASCADE | RESTRICT

<alter table statement> ::=
    ALTER TABLE <table name> <alter table action>

<alter table action> ::=
      <add column definition>
    | <alter column definition>
    | <drop column definition>
    | <add table constraint definition>
    | <drop table constraint definition>

<add column definition> ::=
    ADD [ COLUMN ] <column definition>

<alter column definition> ::=
    ALTER [ COLUMN ] <column name> <alter column action>

<alter column action> ::=
      <set column default clause>
    | <drop column default clause>

<set column default clause> ::=
    SET <default clause>

<drop column default clause> ::=
    DROP DEFAULT

<drop column definition> ::=
    DROP [ COLUMN ] <column name> <drop behavior>

<add table constraint definition> ::=
    ADD <table constraint definition>

<drop table constraint definition> ::=
    DROP CONSTRAINT <constraint name> <drop behavior>

<drop table statement> ::=
    DROP TABLE <table name> <drop behavior>

<drop view statement> ::=
    DROP VIEW <table name> <drop behavior>

<revoke statement> ::=
    REVOKE [ GRANT OPTION FOR ]
        <privileges>
        ON <object name>
      FROM <grantee> [ { <comma> <grantee> }... ] <drop behavior>

<alter domain statement> ::=
    ALTER DOMAIN <domain name> <alter domain action>
```

```
<alter domain action> ::=
      <set domain default clause>
    | <drop domain default clause>
    | <add domain constraint definition>
    | <drop domain constraint definition>

<set domain default clause> ::= SET <default clause>

<drop domain default clause> ::= DROP DEFAULT

<add domain constraint definition> ::=
    ADD <domain constraint>

<drop domain constraint definition> ::=
    DROP CONSTRAINT <constraint name>

<drop domain statement> ::=
    DROP DOMAIN <domain name> <drop behavior>

<drop character set statement> ::=
    DROP CHARACTER SET <character set name>

<drop collation statement> ::=
    DROP COLLATION <collation name>

<drop translation statement> ::=
    DROP TRANSLATION <translation name>

<drop assertion statement> ::=
    DROP ASSERTION <constraint name>

<SQL data statement> ::=
      <open statement>
    | <fetch statement>
    | <close statement>
    | <select statement: single row>
    | <SQL data change statement>

<open statement> ::=
    OPEN <cursor name>

<fetch statement> ::=
    FETCH [ [ <fetch orientation> ] FROM ]
      <cursor name> INTO <fetch target list>

<fetch orientation> ::=
      NEXT
    | PRIOR
    | FIRST
    | LAST
    | { ABSOLUTE | RELATIVE } <simple value specification>

<simple value specification> ::=
      <parameter name>
    | <embedded variable name>
    | <literal>
```

```
<fetch target list> ::=
    <target specification> [ { <comma> <target specification> }... ]

<target specification> ::=
      <parameter specification>
    | <variable specification>

<close statement> ::=
    CLOSE <cursor name>

<select statement: single row> ::=
    SELECT [ <set quantifier> ] <select list>
      INTO <select target list>
        <table expression>

<select target list> ::=
    <target specification> [ { <comma> <target specification> }... ]

<SQL data change statement> ::=
      <delete statement: positioned>
    | <delete statement: searched>
    | <insert statement>
    | <update statement: positioned>
    | <update statement: searched>

<delete statement: positioned> ::=
    DELETE FROM <table name>
      WHERE CURRENT OF <cursor name>

<delete statement: searched> ::=
    DELETE FROM <table name>
      [ WHERE <search condition> ]

<insert statement> ::=
    INSERT INTO <table name>
      <insert columns and source>

<insert columns and source> ::=
      [ <left paren> <insert column list> <right paren> ]
            <query expression>
    | DEFAULT VALUES

<insert column list> ::= <column name list>

<update statement: positioned> ::=
    UPDATE <table name>
      SET <set clause list>
        WHERE CURRENT OF <cursor name>

<set clause list> ::=
    <set clause> [ { <comma> <set clause> }... ]

<set clause> ::=
    <object column> <equals operator> <update source>
```

```
<object column> ::= <column name>

<update source> ::=
      <value expression>
    | <null specification>
    | DEFAULT

<update statement: searched> ::=
    UPDATE <table name>
      SET <set clause list>
      [ WHERE <search condition> ]

<SQL transaction statement> ::=
      <set transaction statement>
    | <set constraints mode statement>
    | <commit statement>
    | <rollback statement>

<set transaction statement> ::=
    SET TRANSACTION <transaction mode>
        [ { <comma> <transaction mode> }... ]

<transaction mode> ::=
      <isolation level>
    | <transaction access mode>
    | <diagnostics size>

<isolation level> ::=
    ISOLATION LEVEL <level of isolation>

<level of isolation> ::=
      READ UNCOMMITTED
    | READ COMMITTED
    | REPEATABLE READ
    | SERIALIZABLE

<transaction access mode> ::=
      READ ONLY
    | READ WRITE

<diagnostics size> ::=
    DIAGNOSTICS SIZE <number of conditions>

<number of conditions> ::= <simple value specification>

<set constraints mode statement> ::=
    SET CONSTRAINTS <constraint name list>
        { DEFERRED | IMMEDIATE }

<constraint name list> ::=
      ALL
    | <constraint name> [ { <comma> <constraint name> }... ]

<commit statement> ::=
    COMMIT [ WORK ]
```

```
<rollback statement> ::=
    ROLLBACK [ WORK ]

<SQL connection statement> ::=
      <connect statement>
    | <set connection statement>
    | <disconnect statement>

<connect statement> ::=
    CONNECT TO <connection target>

<connection target> ::=
      <SQL-server name>
        [ AS <connection name> ]
        [ USER <user name> ]
    | DEFAULT

<SQL-server name> ::= <simple value specification>

<connection name> ::= <simple value specification>

<user name> ::= <simple value specification>

<set connection statement> ::=
    SET CONNECTION <connection object>

<connection object> ::=
      DEFAULT
    | <connection name>

<disconnect statement> ::=
    DISCONNECT <disconnect object>

<disconnect object> ::=
      <connection object>
    | ALL
    | CURRENT

<SQL session statement> ::=
      <set catalog statement>
    | <set schema statement>
    | <set names statement>
    | <set session authorization identifier statement>
    | <set local time zone statement>

<set catalog statement> ::=
    SET CATALOG <value specification>

<value specification> ::=
      <literal>
    | <general value specification>

<set schema statement> ::=
    SET SCHEMA <value specification>
```

```
<set names statement> ::=
    SET NAMES <vue specification>

<set session authorization identifier statement> ::=
    SET SESSION AUTHORIZATION <value specification>

<set local time zone statement> ::=
    SET TIME ZONE <set time zone value>

<set time zone value> ::=
      <interval value expression>
    | LOCAL

<SQL dynamic statement> ::=
      <system descriptor statement>
    | <prepare statement>
    | <deallocate prepared statement>
    | <describe statement>
    | <execute statement>
    | <execute immediate statement>
    | <SQL dynamic data statement>

<system descriptor statement> ::=
      <allocate descriptor statement>
    | <deallocate descriptor statement>
    | <set descriptor statement>
    | <get descriptor statement>

<allocate descriptor statement> ::=
    ALLOCATE DESCRIPTOR <descriptor name>
       [ WITH MAX <occurrences> ]

<descriptor name> ::=
    [ <scope option> ] <simple value specification>

<scope option> ::=
      GLOBAL
    | LOCAL

<occurrences> ::= <simple value specification>

<deallocate descriptor statement> ::=
    DEALLOCATE DESCRIPTOR <descriptor name>

<set descriptor statement> ::=
    SET DESCRIPTOR <descriptor name>
       <set descriptor information>

<set descriptor information> ::=
      <set count>
    | VALUE <item number>
       <set item information> [ { <comma> <set item information> }... ]

<set count> ::=
    COUNT <equals operator> <simple value specification 1>
```

```
<simple value specification 1> ::= <simple value specification>

<item number> ::= <simple value specification>

<set item information> ::=
    <descriptor item name> <equals operator> <simple value specification 2>

<descriptor item name> ::=
      TYPE
    | LENGTH
    | OCTET_LENGTH
    | RETURNED_LENGTH
    | RETURNED_OCTET_LENGTH
    | PRECISION
    | SCALE
    | DATETIME_INTERVAL_CODE
    | DATETIME_INTERVAL_PRECISION
    | NULLABLE
    | INDICATOR
    | DATA
    | NAME
    | UNNAMED
    | COLLATION_CATALOG
    | COLLATION_SCHEMA
    | COLLATION_NAME
    | CHARACTER_SET_CATALOG
    | CHARACTER_SET_SCHEMA
    | CHARACTER_SET_NAME

<simple value specification 2> ::= <simple value specification>

<item number> ::= <simple value specification>

<get descriptor statement> ::=
    GET DESCRIPTOR <descriptor name> <get descriptor information>

<get descriptor information> ::=
      <get count>
    | VALUE <item number>
       <get item information> [ { <comma> <get item information> }... ]

<get count> ::=
    <simple target specification 1> <equals operator> COUNT

<simple target specification 1> ::= <simple target specification>

<simple target specification> ::=
      <parameter name>
    | <embedded variable name>

<get item information> ::=
    <simple target specification 2> <equals operator> <descriptor item name>>

<simple target specification 2> ::= <simple target specification>
```

```
<prepare statement> ::=
    PREPARE <SQL statement name> FROM <SQL statement variable>

<SQL statement name> ::=
      <statement name>
    | <extended statement name>

<extended statement name> ::=
    [ <scope option> ] <simple value specification>

<SQL statement variable> ::= <simple value specification>

<deallocate prepared statement> ::=
    DEALLOCATE PREPARE <SQL statement name>

<describe statement> ::=
      <describe input statement>
    | <describe output statement>

<describe input statement> ::=
    DESCRIBE INPUT <SQL statement name> <using descriptor>

<using descriptor> ::=
    { USING | INTO } SQL DESCRIPTOR <descriptor name>

<describe output statement> ::=
    DESCRIBE [ OUTPUT ] <SQL statement name> <using descriptor>

<execute statement> ::=
    EXECUTE <SQL statement name>
      [ <result using clause> ]
      [ <parameter using clause> ]

<result using clause> ::= <using clause>

<using clause> ::=
      <using arguments>
    | <using descriptor>

<using arguments> ::=
    { USING | INTO } <argument> [ { <comma> <argument> }... ]

<argument> ::= <target specification>

<parameter using clause> ::= <using clause>

<execute immediate statement> ::=
    EXECUTE IMMEDIATE <SQL statement variable>

<SQL dynamic data statement> ::=
      <allocate cursor statement>
    | <dynamic open statement>
    | <dynamic fetch statement>
    | <dynamic close statement>
    | <dynamic delete statement: positioned>
    | <dynamic update statement: positioned>
```

```
<allocate cursor statement> ::=
    ALLOCATE <extended cursor name> [ INSENSITIVE ]
        [ SCROLL ] CURSOR
      FOR <extended statement name>

<extended cursor name> ::=
    [ <scope option> ] <simple value specification>

<dynamic open statement> ::=
    OPEN <dynamic cursor name> [ <using clause> ]

<dynamic cursor name> ::=
        <cursor name>
    | <extended cursor name>

<dynamic fetch statement> ::=
    FETCH [ [ <fetch orientation> ] FROM ] <dynamic cursor name>
        <using clause>

<dynamic close statement> ::=
    CLOSE <dynamic cursor name>

<dynamic delete statement: positioned> ::=
    DELETE FROM <table name>
      WHERE CURRENT OF
          <dynamic cursor name>

<dynamic update statement: positioned> ::=
    UPDATE <table name>
      SET <set clause>
          [ { <comma> <set clause> }... ]
        WHERE CURRENT OF
            <dynamic cursor name>

<SQL diagnostics statement> ::=
    <get diagnostics statement>

<get diagnostics statement> ::=
    GET DIAGNOSTICS <sql diagnostics information>

<sql diagnostics information> ::=
        <statement information>
    | <condition information>

<statement information> ::=
    <statement information item> [ { <comma> <statement information item> }... ]

<statement information item> ::=
    <simple target specification> <equals operator> <statement information item name>

<statement information item name> ::=
        NUMBER
    | MORE
    | COMMAND_FUNCTION
    | DYNAMIC_FUNCTION
    | ROW_COUNT
```

```
<condition information> ::=
    EXCEPTION <condition number>
        <condition information item> [ { <comma> <condition information item> }... ]

<condition number> ::= <simple value specification>

<condition information item> ::=
    <simple target specification> <equals operator> <condition information item name>

<condition information item name> ::=
      CONDITION_NUMBER
    | RETURNED_SQLSTATE
    | CLASS_ORIGIN
    | SUBCLASS_ORIGIN
    | SERVER_NAME
    | CONNECTION_NAME
    | CONSTRAINT_CATALOG
    | CONSTRAINT_SCHEMA
    | CONSTRAINT_NAME
    | CATALOG_NAME
    | SCHEMA_NAME
    | TABLE_NAME
    | COLUMN_NAME
    | CURSOR_NAME
    | MESSAGE_TEXT
    | MESSAGE_LENGTH
    | MESSAGE_OCTET_LENGTH

<embedded SQL host program> ::=
      <embedded SQL Ada program>
    | <embedded SQL C program>
    | <embedded SQL COBOL program>
    | <embedded SQL Fortran program>
    | <embedded SQL MUMPS program>
    | <embedded SQL Pascal program>
    | <embedded SQL PL/I program>

<embedded SQL Ada program> ::= !! See the Syntax Rules.

<embedded SQL C program> ::= !! See the Syntax Rules.

<embedded SQL COBOL program> ::= !! See the Syntax Rules.

<embedded SQL Fortran program> ::= !! See the Syntax Rules.

<embedded SQL MUMPS program> ::= !! See the Syntax Rules.

<embedded SQL Pascal program> ::= !! See the Syntax Rules.

<embedded SQL PL/I program> ::= !! See the Syntax Rules.

<embedded SQL declare section> ::=
      <embedded SQL begin declare>
        [ <embedded character set declaration> ]
        [ <host variable definition>... ]
```

```
        <embedded SQL end declare>
      | <embedded SQL MUMPS declare>

<embedded SQL begin declare> ::=
      <SQL prefix> BEGIN DECLARE SECTION [ <SQL terminator> ]

<SQL prefix> ::=
        EXEC SQL
      | <ampersand>SQL<left paren>

<SQL terminator> ::=
        END-EXEC
      | <semicolon>
      | <right paren>

<embedded character set declaration> ::=
      SQL NAMES ARE <character set specification>

<host variable definition> ::=
        <Ada variable definition>
      | <C variable definition>
      | <COBOL variable definition>
      | <Fortran variable definition>
      | <MUMPS variable definition>
      | <Pascal variable definition>
      | <PL/I variable definition>

<Ada variable definition> ::=
      <Ada host identifier> [ { <comma> <Ada host identifier> }... ] :
      <Ada type specification> [ <Ada initial value> ]

<Ada type specification> ::=
        <Ada qualified type specification>
      | <Ada unqualified type specification>

<Ada qualified type specification> ::=
        SQL_STANDARD.CHAR [ CHARACTER SET
          [ IS ] <character set specification> ]
            <left paren> 1 <double period> <length> <right paren>
      | SQL_STANDARD.BIT
            <left paren> 1 <double period> <length> <right paren>
      | SQL_STANDARD.SMALLINT
      | SQL_STANDARD.INT
      | SQL_STANDARD.REAL
      | SQL_STANDARD.DOUBLE_PRECISION
      | SQL_STANDARD.SQLCODE_TYPE
      | SQL_STANDARD.SQLSTATE_TYPE
      | SQL_STANDARD.INDICATOR_TYPE

<Ada unqualified type specification> ::=
        CHAR <left paren> 1 <double period> <length> <right paren>
      | BIT <left paren> 1 <double period> <length> <right paren>
      | SMALLINT
      | INT
      | REAL
```

```
        | DOUBLE_PRECISION
        | SQLCODE_TYPE
        | SQLSTATE_TYPE
        | INDICATOR_TYPE

<Ada initial value> ::=
    <Ada assignment operator> <character representation>...

<Ada assignment operator> ::= <colon><equals operator>

<C variable definition> ::=
        [ <C storage class> ]
        [ <C class modifier> ]
        <C variable specification>
    <semicolon>

<C storage class> ::=
        auto
      | extern
      | static

<C class modifier> ::= const | volatile

<C variable specification> ::=
        <C numeric variable>
      | <C character variable>
      | <C derived variable>

<C numeric variable> ::=
    { long | short | float | double }
    <C host identifier> [ <C initial value> ]
            [ { <comma> <C host identifier> [ <C initial value> ] }... ]

<C initial value> ::=
    <equals operator> <character representation>...

<C character variable> ::=
    char [ CHARACTER SET
            [ IS ] <character set specification> ]
      <C host identifier>
        <C array specification> [ <C initial value> ]
        [ { <comma> <C host identifier>
          <C array specification>
                [ <C initial value> ] }... ]

<C array specification> ::=
    <left bracket> <length> <right bracket>

<C derived variable> ::=
        <C VARCHAR variable>
      | <C bit variable>

<C VARCHAR variable> ::=
    VARCHAR [ CHARACTER SET [ IS ] <character set specification> ]
        <C host identifier> <C array specification> [ <C initial value> ]
            [ { <comma> <C host identifier> <C array specification> [ <C initial value> ] }... ]
```

```
<C bit variable> ::=
    BIT <C host identifier> <C array specification> [ <C initial value> ]
      [ { <comma> <C host identifier> <C array specification> [ <C initial value> ] }... ]

<COBOL variable definition> ::=
    {01|77} <COBOL host identifier> <COBOL type specification>
      [ <character representation>... ] <period>

<COBOL type specification> ::=
      <COBOL character type>
    | <COBOL bit type>
    | <COBOL numeric type>
    | <COBOL integer type>

<COBOL character type> ::=
    [ CHARACTER SET [ IS ]
        <character set specification> ]
    { PIC | PICTURE } [ IS ] { X [ <left paren> <length> <right paren> ] }...

<COBOL bit type> ::=
    { PIC | PICTURE } [ IS ]
        { B [ <left paren> <length> <right paren> ] }...

<COBOL numeric type> ::=
    { PIC | PICTURE } [ IS ]
     S <COBOL nines specification>
    [ USAGE [ IS ] ] DISPLAY SIGN LEADING SEPARATE

<COBOL nines specification> ::=
      <COBOL nines> [ V [ <COBOL nines> ] ]
    | V <COBOL nines>

<COBOL nines> ::= { 9 [ <left paren> <length> <right paren> ] }...

<COBOL integer type> ::=
      <COBOL computational integer>
    | <COBOL binary integer>

<COBOL computational integer> ::=
    { PIC | PICTURE } [ IS ] S<COBOL nines>
      [ USAGE [ IS ] ] { COMP | COMPUTATIONAL }

<COBOL binary integer> ::=
    { PIC | PICTURE } [ IS ] S<COBOL nines>
      [ USAGE [ IS ] ] BINARY

<Fortran variable definition> ::=
    <Fortran type specification>
    <Fortran host identifier> [ { <comma> <Fortran host identifier> }... ]

<Fortran type specification> ::=
      CHARACTER [ <asterisk> <length> ]
          [ CHARACTER SET [ IS ] <character set specification> ]
    | BIT [ <asterisk> <length> ]
    | INTEGER
```

```
        | REAL
        | DOUBLE PRECISION

<MUMPS variable definition> ::=
    { <MUMPS numeric variable> | <MUMPS character variable> }
        <semicolon>

<MUMPS numeric variable> ::=
    <MUMPS type specification>
        <MUMPS host identifier> [ { <comma> <MUMPS host identifier> }... ]

<MUMPS type specification> ::=
        INT
    | DEC [ <left paren> <precision> [ <comma> <scale> ] <right paren> ]
    | REAL

<MUMPS character variable> ::=
    VARCHAR <MUMPS host identifier> <MUMPS length specification>
    [ { <comma> <MUMPS host identifier> <MUMPS length specification> }... ]

<MUMPS length specification> ::=
    <left paren> <length> <right paren>

<Pascal variable definition> ::=
    <Pascal host identifier> [ { <comma> <Pascal host identifier> }... ] <colon>
        <Pascal type specification> <semicolon>

<Pascal type specification> ::=
        PACKED ARRAY
            <left bracket> 1 <double period> <length> <right bracket> OF CHAR
            [ CHARACTER SET [ IS ] <character set specification> ]
    | PACKED ARRAY
            <left bracket> 1 <double period> <length> <right bracket> OF BIT
    | INTEGER
    | REAL
    | CHAR [ CHARACTER SET [ IS ] <character set specification> ]
    | BIT

<PL/I variable definition> ::=
    {DCL | DECLARE}
        {    <PL/I host identifier>
          | <left paren> <PL/I host identifier>
                [ { <comma> <PL/I host identifier> }... ] <right paren> }
    <PL/I type specification>
    [ <character representation>... ] <semicolon>

<PL/I type specification> ::=
        { CHAR | CHARACTER } [ VARYING ] <left paren> <length> <right paren>
            [ CHARACTER SET [ IS ] <character set specification> ]
    | BIT [ VARYING ] <left paren> <length> <right paren>
    | <PL/I type fixed decimal> <left paren> <precision>
            [ <comma> <scale> ] <right paren>
    | <PL/I type fixed binary> [ <left paren> <precision> <right paren> ]
    | <PL/I type float binary> <left paren> <precision> <right paren>
```

```
<PL/I type fixed decimal> ::=
      { DEC | DECIMAL } FIXED
    | FIXED { DEC | DECIMAL }

<PL/I type fixed binary> ::=
      { BIN | BINARY } FIXED
    | FIXED { BIN | BINARY }

<PL/I type float binary> ::=
      { BIN | BINARY } FLOAT
    | FLOAT { BIN | BINARY }

<embedded SQL end declare> ::=
    <SQL prefix> END DECLARE SECTION
        [ <SQL terminator> ]

<embedded SQL MUMPS declare> ::=
    <SQL prefix>
      BEGIN DECLARE SECTION
        [ <embedded character set declaration> ]
        [ <host variable definition>... ]
      END DECLARE SECTION
    <SQL terminator>

<embedded SQL statement> ::=
    <SQL prefix>
      <statement or declaration>
    [ <SQL terminator> ]

<statement or declaration> ::=
      <declare cursor>
    | <dynamic declare cursor>
    | <temporary table declaration>
    | <embedded exception declaration>
    | <SQL procedure statement>

<embedded exception declaration> ::=
    WHENEVER <condition> <condition action>

<condition> ::=
    SQLERROR | NOT FOUND

<condition action> ::=
    CONTINUE | <go to>

<go to> ::=
    { GOTO | GO TO } <goto target>

<goto target> ::=
      <host label identifier>
    | <unsigned integer>
    | <host PL/I label variable>

<host label identifier> ::= !!See the Syntax Rules.
```

```
<host PL/I label variable> ::= !!See the Syntax Rules.

<preparable statement> ::=
      <preparable SQL data statement>
    | <preparable SQL schema statement>
    | <preparable SQL transaction statement>
    | <preparable SQL session statement>
    | <preparable implementation-defined statement>

<preparable SQL data statement> ::=
      <delete statement: searched>
    | <dynamic single row select statement>
    | <insert statement>
    | <dynamic select statement>
    | <update statement: searched>
    | <preparable dynamic delete statement: positioned>
    | <preparable dynamic update statement: positioned>

<dynamic single row select statement> ::= <query specification>

<dynamic select statement> ::= <cursor specification>

<preparable dynamic delete statement: positioned> ::=
   DELETE [ FROM <table name> ]
      WHERE CURRENT OF <cursor name>

<preparable dynamic update statement: positioned> ::=
   UPDATE [ <table name> ]
      SET <set clause list>
      WHERE CURRENT OF <cursor name>

<preparable SQL schema statement> ::=
      <SQL schema statement>

<preparable SQL transaction statement> ::=
      <SQL transaction statement>

<preparable SQL session statement> ::=
      <SQL session statement>

<preparable implementation-defined statement> ::=
      !! See the Syntax Rules.

<direct SQL statement> ::=
      <directly executable statement> <semicolon>

<directly executable statement> ::=
      <direct SQL data statement>
    | <SQL schema statement>
    | <SQL transaction statement>
    | <SQL connection statement>
    | <SQL session statement>
    | <direct implementation-defined statement>
```

```
<direct SQL data statement> ::=
      <delete statement: searched>
    | <direct select statement: multiple rows>
    | <insert statement>
    | <update statement: searched>
    | <temporary table declaration>

<direct select statement: multiple rows> ::=
    <query expression> [ <order by clause> ]

<direct implementation-defined statement> ::=
    !! See the Syntax Rules

<SQL object identifier> ::=
    <SQL provenance> <SQL variant>

<SQL provenance> ::= <arc1> <arc2> <arc3>

<arc1> ::= iso | 1 | iso <left paren> 1 <right paren>

<arc2> ::= standard | 0 | standard <left paren> 0 <right paren>

<arc3> ::= 9075

<SQL variant> ::= <SQL edition> <SQL conformance>

<SQL edition> ::= <1987> | <1989> | <1992>

<1987> ::= 0 | edition1987 <left paren> 0 <right paren>

<1989> ::= <1989 base> <1989 package>

<1989 base> ::= 1 | edition1989 <left paren> 1 <right paren>

<1989 package> ::= <integrity no> | <integrity yes>

<integrity no> ::= 0 | IntegrityNo <left paren> 0 <right paren>

<integrity yes> ::= 1 | IntegrityYes <left paren> 1 <right paren>

<1992> ::= 2 | edition1992 <left paren> 2 <right paren>

<SQL conformance> ::= <low> | <intermediate> | <high>

<low> ::= 0 | Low <left paren> 0 <right paren>

<intermediate> ::= 1 | Intermediate <left paren> 1 <right paren>

<high> ::= 2 | High <left paren> 2 <right paren>
```

INDEX

· · · · · · · · · · · · · · · · ·